10-2-2011

Best wishes for
success with Bailey

LJ.

HANDBOOK OF ENGAGED SCHOLARSHIP

Transformations in Higher Education: The Scholarship of Engagement

HANDBOOK OF ENGAGED SCHOLARSHIP

CONTEMPORARY LANDSCAPES, FUTURE DIRECTIONS

VOLUME TWO

Community-Campus Partnerships

EDITED BY

Hiram E. Fitzgerald, Cathy Burack, and Sarena D. Seifer

Michigan State University Press • *East Lansing*

♾ The paper used in this publication meets the minimum requirements
of ANSI/NISO Z39.48-1992 (R 1997) (Permanence of Paper).

The Handbook of Engaged Scholarship is a joint project of Michigan State University's National Center for the Study of University
Engagement and the Higher Education Network for Community Engagement (HENCE).

Michigan State University Press
East Lansing, Michigan 48823-5245

Printed and bound in the United States of America.

16 15 14 13 12 11 10   1 2 3 4 5 6 7 8 9 10

LIBRARY OF CONGRESS CATALOGING-IN-PUBLICATION DATA

Handbook of engaged scholarship: contemporary landscapes, future directions / edited by Hiram E. Fitzgerald, Cathy Burack, and
Sarena Seifer.
    v. cm.—(Transformations in Higher Education: The Scholarship of Engagement)
    Includes bibliographical references and index.
    ISBN 978-0-87013-974-1 (v. 1 : cloth : alk. paper)—ISBN 978-0-87013-975-8 (v. 2 : cloth : alk. paper) 1. Community and college—
United States—Handbooks, manuals, etc. 2. Service learning—United States—Handbooks, manuals, etc. 3. Education, Higher—Aims
and objectives—United States. I. Fitzgerald, Hiram E. II. Burack, Cathy. III. Seifer, Sarena D.
    LC238.H36 2010
    378.1'03—dc22
    2010003500

Cover design by Adina Huda
Book design by Aptara

Michigan State University Press is a member of the Green Press Initiative and is committed to developing
and encouraging ecologically responsible publishing practices. For more information about the Green Press
Initiative and the use of recycled paper in book publishing, please visit www.greenpressinitiative.org.

Visit Michigan State University Press on the World Wide Web at: www.msupress.msu.edu

Transformations in Higher Education: The Engaged Scholar

Higher education is being challenged to connect with communities to develop solutions to major social and economic problems affecting contemporary society. Pressures to build strong university-community collaborations pose difficult problems for the academy because they demand interdisciplinary cooperation, rejection of provincial disciplinary turfism, changes in the faculty reward system, a re-focusing of unit and institution missions and the breaking down of firmly established and isolated silos. Partially in response to societal challenges to higher education, education-oriented social critics and reformists began to articulate a new vision for American higher education. Public support of higher education was being bound to public expectations that "their" colleges and universities would become more directly engaged in the transformation of society across the broad disciplinary domains that define higher education.

The Kellogg Commission's challenge for higher education to engage with communities was a significant catalyst for action. It built upon the work of individuals such as Boyer and Lynton and organizations such as the American Association for Higher Education's Forum on Faculty Roles and Rewards and Campus Compact and other activist events of the 1990s. These events funneled into a nexus around which both engaged scholarship and the scholarship of engagement could evolve and become distinctively defined scholarly approaches to campus-community partnerships. Engaged scholars study the processes, relationships, and impacts of outreach and engaged work on engaged faculty, the Institution, disciplines, the academy as a whole, and the community partners with whom they work. Indeed, engaged scholars recognize that community based scholarship requires community involvement based on principles that reflect mutual respect, recognition that community knowledge is valid, and that sustainability must be an integral part of the partnership agenda.

Higher education has responded strongly to its critics. During the past decade, numerous conferences, journals (peer-reviewed and on-line open source), books, and visionary reports have been published. Countless evidence-based models for partnerships have been disseminated, and new individual and institutional membership associations have been formed. Clearly, a disciplinary aura around engaged scholarship and the scholarship of engagement is forming.

When leaders at Michigan State University's National Collaborative for the Study of University Engagement conceived of the idea for a Handbook of Engaged Scholarship, they approached the Higher Education Network for the Study of University Engagement to solicit its support for the project. The response was quick and positive. Across the two volumes, we have attempted to capture the rich diversity of institutions and partnerships that characterize the contemporary landscape and the aspirational future of engaged scholarship.

We are indebted to all of the authors and editors who have contributed their time and energy to create this seminal handbook. Each chapter was edited by one of the three volume editors, and chapters in each sub-section were also independently edited by the individuals who provide overviews for the section. When leaders from the National Collaborative for the Study of University Engagement proposed the *Transformations in Higher Education: Engaged Scholarship* book series to Gabriel Dotto, Director of the Michigan State University Press, he enthusiastically endorsed the project with little more than a page of descriptive information in support of the concept. We thank him for his enthusiastic support throughout the process of crafting the *Handbook of Engaged Scholarship* as the anchor volume in the series. We are equally indebted to Kristine M. Blakeslee, Project Editor at the MSU Press, whose difficult task was to guide over sixty authors through the production cycle. Lisa Devereaux worked diligently to assure that all chapters were in a common format for submission to the publisher, and Julie Crowgey tracked chapters through the final revision cycle. To each we owe special thanks. It is our hope that publication of the *Handbook* will be a catalyst for moving higher education closer to alignment with the call to action issued by the Kellogg Foundation task force, which challenged higher education to renew its covenant with society through engaged scholarship.

Hiram E. Fitzgerald
Cathy Burack
Sarena D. Seifer

Contents

Foreword

James C. Votruba

Over the past twenty years there has developed within American higher education a rich conversation concerning how colleges and universities can better utilize their vast knowledge resources to support public progress. Beyond the production of graduates, what is the value-added that we bring to such public goals as strengthening economic competitiveness, improving P–12 education, enhancing health care, and a host of other challenges that confront our nation and its communities? What form should this public engagement take? Who should be involved? How can this involvement contribute to our mission to educate students and produce cutting-edge research? The contributors to this handbook represent some of the most thoughtful and influential leaders in this national conversation. Together, their work represents the most comprehensive set of perspectives yet assembled on behalf of higher education's public engagement mission.

American higher education has a long and rich tradition of involvement in advancing public priorities. Over the past 150 years, our colleges and universities have brought science to agriculture, produced the workforce for economic expansion, provided the most direct pathway for intergenerational mobility, contributed to national defense, and produced cutting-edge research that has improved nearly every dimension of our lives. Our faculty members as well as our institutions themselves have often served as voices of reason and conscience related to highly charged matters of public concern. In short, American higher education has been both a catalyst and a launching pad for much of America's breathtaking economic and social progress.

Twenty years ago, I was part of an effort at Michigan State University to develop a deeper understanding of the scholarship of engagement and to determine what role such scholarship should play in the life of the university. Many of the contributors to this handbook were part of that effort, which helped launch similar efforts on campuses across the nation. Although often different in mission, size, focus, and funding, what these institutions shared in common was an interest in better defining the role of higher education in fostering citizenship and helping to address some of the difficult challenges confronting the public. In this sense, the focus was on higher education's public role, which is also the focus of this handbook.

We've come a long way in understanding the role of public engagement in the life of our colleges and universities. Still, we have a long way to go before the scholarship of engagement is fully embraced as a core campus mission.

Several years ago, I chaired a national task force on public engagement sponsored by the American Association of State Colleges and Universities. We surveyed more than four hundred universities to help us better understand the nature and extent of their public engagement involvement and how this work fits in the overall institutional mission. Two outcomes are particularly notable for our purposes here. First, we found that there was a vast array of public engagement activity being conducted by faculty across the full spectrum of the university, from arts and sciences to the professions. Second, we discovered that this work tends to be fragile and very person-dependent. That is, it tends to flourish when there is a president, provost, dean, or chair who champions the engagement mission and supports faculty involvement. However, when the leader departs, the engagement mission often flounders.

Contrast this fragility with the institutionalization of research and scholarship in the major research-intensive universities. In these institutions, presidents and provosts, deans and chairs may come and go, but the importance of the research mission is so deeply embedded in the fabric of the institution that it continues uninterrupted. The next great challenge for advocates of the public engagement mission is to achieve this same level of institutionalization: to so deeply eimbed the scholarship of engagement in the fabric of the campus at every level that it becomes a thoroughly integrated part of the institution's core academic mission.

What would such an institution look like? Public engagement would be grounded in a strong intellectual foundation that relates it to the other mission dimensions. The voice of the public would be institutionalized at every level. Key institutional leaders would be selected and evaluated based, at least in part, on their capacity to lead the public engagement function. Faculty and unit-level incentives and rewards would encourage and support the scholarship of engagement. Faculty selection, orientation, and development would highlight the importance of the public engagement mission. The curriculum would include public engagement as a way to both support community progress and enhance student learning. Institutional awards and recognitions would reflect the importance of excellence across the full breadth of the mission, including engagement. The planning and budgeting process would reflect the centrality of public engagement as a core institutional mission. And the university would take seriously its public intellectual role and have the courage to be a safe place for difficult public conversations.

The chapters that follow touch on many of these dimensions. They provide a rich overview of how the scholarship of engagement has emerged as an important higher education movement; how this work expresses itself in a variety of institutions and disciplines; the variety of forms that the scholarship of engagement can take; and how public engagement can result in enhanced student learning and a deeper public appreciation of the role that higher education can play in their lives and the lives of their communities.

I've followed the public engagement movement for well over twenty years, both as an observer and as a participant. As our nation and its communities struggle to cope with a broad range of complex and formidable challenges, it's time to take the public engagement movement to a new level of development and maturation. Let me suggest several areas that deserve special focus as we work to advance higher education's public engagement mission.

First, we need public policy that supports the scholarship of engagement. On most university campuses, the scholarship of engagement is a cost center, not a revenue center. I would argue that the reason research is so deeply embedded in the research-intensive universities is because there is a massive amount of federal funding that supports both the individual investigator and the institution itself. Until we have federal and state policy that supports the scholarship of engagement, this work is not likely to become institutionalized.

There are some encouraging signs that the federal agencies are broadening their funding focus to include what is being described in this handbook as engaged scholarship. For example, the National Institutes of Health (NIH) is placing greater emphasis on translational science as well as efforts directed at underserved and vulnerable populations. The National Science Foundation is requiring social significance as part of its review criteria. The point is that community-based research and scholarly activity are open to all research methodologies, including qualitative ones and mixed methods, and NIH and other agencies are funding such efforts. There are early signs that the new Obama administration values the role that engaged scholarship can play in advancing public progress. If this is the case, the higher education community must move quickly and strategically to make the case that engaged scholarship is an important element in advancing important public priorities.

There are also encouraging signs at the state policy level. For example, Kentucky recently became the first state to create a funding stream to support university public engagement work. Access to these funds requires both campus and community input and clearly defined and measurable public outcomes. In the first few years of the program, the focus has been on strengthening community economic competitiveness, improving P–12 education, enhancing the nonprofit sector, and improving health care access and delivery. We need more states to develop similar policies.

It is doubtful that public engagement will become a broadly accepted core campus mission until there is significant federal and state policy that supports it. Absent public policy support, the scholarship of engagement is less likely to attract sustained attention from large numbers of faculty members or from the institutions themselves. However, if significant support is forthcoming from both the federal and state levels, we can expect institutions to quickly adapt as they and their faculty members turn their attention to these new funding sources.

Second, we need to do a far better job of assessing our engagement work. We've made progress in this regard but, until we have reached agreement regarding what constitutes excellence in this domain, it will remain difficult to measure and reward. For example, should we focus on assessing activities or outcomes? What role does self-assessment play? How about peer assessment? Absent appropriate and generally accepted standards for evaluating the scholarship of engagement, faculty members are less likely to embrace it because of the risk that it will not be recognized and rewarded.

Third, we must do a better job of aligning our colleges and universities in a way that supports the institutionalization of this work. In their 1994 book *Built to Last*, Jim Collins and Jerry Porras studied the defining qualities of companies that achieved very high levels of success over a long period of time. What they found was that these high-performing companies had every organizational element aligned to support intended outcomes. If higher education is going to produce outstanding public engagement, every element of the institution must be aligned to support that outcome. To what extent are campus leadership, faculty incentives and rewards, planning and budgeting, annual evaluations, awards and recognitions, and public policy aligned to support the scholarship of engagement? Absent such alignment, involvement will more likely be based on *individual* faculty commitment rather than *institutional* commitment.

Fourth, it's time to focus on the development of professional standards related to the public engagement mission. Such standards exist for research and teaching. Public engagement needs generally accepted standards that can be used to guide the development, administration, and evaluation of public engagement initiatives. What should be the standards that a faculty member uses to define her or his involvement in a particular initiative? What standards should be applied when a campus is deciding whether to make an institution-wide commitment to a particular engagement focus? Well-defined and generally accepted standards for public engagement can provide guidance at both the individual and institutional level and can help avoid some of the major pitfalls that can develop as a result of pursuing this work.

Fifth, it's time for us to become far more intentional in the preparation of campus- and system-level leaders who are expected to lead on behalf of the public engagement mission. Department chairs, deans, vice presidents, and presidents generally assume their leadership positions with little or no involvement in the scholarship of engagement, yet we expect them to lead in this domain. Several months ago, I hosted a group of twenty-three university presidents for two days of discussion on their role in leading the engaged university. These leaders want their institutions to be deeply committed to public engagement. What they were looking for was insight on how to advance the scholarship of engagement as a core campus priority. As with any movement, leadership matters, and it will be indispensable as we move public engagement to the next level.

Sixth, the scholarship of engagement is more easily focused and carried out if it is conducted in response to a well-defined public agenda. A decade ago, Kentucky defined a public agenda for higher education that connected with a larger set of state goals. The agenda is focused on five questions. Are more Kentuckians ready for postsecondary education? Is Kentucky postsecondary education affordable for its citizens? Do more Kentuckians have certificates and degrees? Are college graduates prepared for life and work in Kentucky? Are Kentucky's people, communities, and economy benefiting? Each year, Kentucky's colleges and universities are asked to demonstrate their contributions to these overarching public priorities.

On a more local level, I recently co-chaired a regional planning process called Vision 2015. It involved hundreds of citizens from throughout the northern Kentucky region coming together to establish goals for regional progress and strategies for achieving them. Having these goals in hand, it became far easier to focus higher education's human and financial resources in a way that supported their achievement.

Universities can provide important leadership in helping to define and pursue state and regional priorities. We can conduct applied research to help better understand the nature of a problem. We can identify "best practice" from other locations and help test those practices in local settings. We can engage in outcomes assessment intended to measure the impact of problem interventions. We can help formulate public policy approaches that attempt to reduce or eliminate problems that influence public progress. And we can add the knowledge and experience of our faculty to help inform citizens who are attempting to frame goals for their state and communities.

Finally, the next level of public engagement will include a more cautious representation of higher education's capacity to impact matters of public concern. Too often, with our hearts in the right place, we overpromise related to problems that are far beyond our capacity or expertise to resolve. In doing so, we can create false hope among the public that often results in resentment because the college or university fails to deliver. In the most fundamental sense, we are learning institutions. We promote learning through the generation, transmission, and application of knowledge. In our public engagement work, our goal should be to promote learning so that the public can act from an informed position. In this sense, colleges and universities don't solve social problems, although we have an indispensable role to play in helping to understand a problem as well as frame a strategy for its resolution. It is when we promise to go beyond the promotion of learning that we embark on a slippery slope that can result in frustration and disappointment for both the campus and community.

The scholarship of engagement generates great benefit not only for the larger society but also for our colleges and universities themselves. By involving students in addressing complex "real-world" challenges, we can deepen their educational experience and better prepare them to assume the responsibilities of citizenship in a democratic society. By involving our faculty members, we can strengthen and enhance the link between their research and scholarship and the challenges that confront the larger society that we look to for support.

By having a robust public engagement mission, colleges and universities can help ensure that they will never lose touch with the public whom we serve. Back in the early 1980s, I was in a meeting with the recently retired chairman and CEO of the General Motors Corporation. He was asked what caused the American auto industry to fall so far, so fast during the 1970s. His response is never too far out of my mind. He said that it wasn't the unions. It wasn't plant obsolescence. It wasn't the time that it took to get design into production. Fundamentally, it was hubris. It was a belief that American auto manufacturers had always built the best vehicles and always would build the best vehicles—that the problem was a marketing problem, not a product problem. In fact, the industry had lost touch with their market, and their own arrogance created a filter that didn't allow them to see what was so clear to everyone else.

American higher education, like financial institutions and automobile manufacturers, is a mature industry. We are described as the best higher education in the world and we embrace this mantle with great pride and enthusiasm. The danger in all mature industries is that hubris can take hold and we can lose touch with the public whom we serve. The scholarship of engagement can help ensure that our colleges and universities will always remain deeply rooted in the larger world on which we depend.

The chapters that follow provide penetrating and often original insight into the scholarship of engagement. Although engagement with the larger society dates back to the beginning of the last century, it is only recently that the conversation has expanded to include all academic disciplines and professional fields. In the most fundamental sense, the scholarship of engagement challenges American higher education to move to a new level of civic involvement. It calls on us to be far more intentional in our approach to advancing public progress. And it requires us to think more deeply not just about public engagement but about every dimension of our academic mission and purpose. This handbook is a useful guide along this path.

PART 1

Types of Engaged Scholarship

Edited by Craig D. Weidemann

Types of Engaged Scholarship

Craig D. Weidemann

True engagement is based on reciprocity, though the manner of collaborating may be very different. In this section, we consider the essential elements of teaching, research, and service as they relate to engagement across a spectrum of community engagement platforms.

Thomas G. Coon calls to our attention one of the earliest models of university engagement, the Cooperative Extension Service (CES), in "Expertise, the Cooperative Extension Service, and Engaged Scholarship." Initially, Extension focused on one-way delivery of information; however, after nearly a century, it has become more focused on co-determining the information that needs to be addressed. As Professor Coon notes, this new model reflects recognition that the stakeholders served by CES are well educated and have access to information apart from that provided by the university.

Hiram E. Fitzgerald, Angela Allen, and Peggy Roberts discuss "Campus-Community Partnerships: Perspectives on Engaged Research," with a focus on principles and practices that support both the development and maintenance of urban regional university-community partnerships framed within the context of scholarship-focused engagement. They focus on an initiative in Jackson, Michigan, that illustrates the critical academic foundation in university-community partnerships with sound pragmatic advice regarding how to manage such collaborations.

In "From 'Preflection' to Reflection: Building Quality Practices in Academic Service-Learning," Nicole C. Springer and Karen McKnight Casey examine the surging popularity of service-learning, seeing it as creating an environment that not only "focuses on the creation of novel information but also collaborates with community members and agencies to help inform the practices of both the university and the community at large." Their practical

3

guide to structuring student service-learning offers a "best practices" approach to student-community engagement.

In "Engaged Scholarship and Transformative Regional Engagement," Nancy E. Franklin and Timothy V. Franklin extend the concept of engaged scholarship to include the human capital of the entire university—faculty, staff, and students—and postulate that by investing in regional partnerships characterized by reciprocity and mutual respect, universities can strategically impact the economic welfare of communities while advancing their research, teaching, and service missions.

Finally, Mike Offerman and I offer a look at "The New Landscape of Engaged Scholarship: How Does Online Education Play a Role?" We contend that the online landscape opens new opportunities for formerly location-bound students and faculty to work in virtual communities, engage in scholarship based in social networking, co-create course content, and involve external as well as university-based experts in curricular choices and assessment.

Throughout, these chapters suggest that engagement opportunities abound, whether through the application of new teaching models that encourage collaborative creation of content, through the application of research to address community-based concerns, or through opportunities for students to work and learn reciprocally with communities. The engaged landscape is ever-expanding, daily offering new opportunities for mutually beneficial programs.

Campus-Community Partnerships: Perspectives on Engaged Research

Hiram E. Fitzgerald, Angela Allen, and Peggy Roberts

Partnerships do not simply deal with our responsibilities to the community or with new challenges of making knowledge relevant. They make us confront questions about the nature of expertise, about disciplinary allegiances, about reward systems, about local applications versus national prominence, and about the uneasy relationship that urban universities maintain with their surrounding communities.—Linda Silka

Higher education is under increasing pressure to develop solutions to major social and economic problems affecting society. Critics contend that higher education has drifted too far from its core mission and moved too far from its historical commitment to help meet the broad and diverse needs of society (Boyer, 1996; Coye, 1997). Research universities, in particular, are cited as devaluing applied research and overemphasizing basic or pure research as the gold standard for faculty promotion and reward. Both critics (Boyer, 1994; Glassick, Huber, & Maeroff, 1997; Kezar, Chambers, & Burkhardt, 2005) and commissions (Kellogg Commission, 1999) have offered alternate visions for higher education, visions that broaden the definitions of scholarship-based teaching, research, and service and encourage university-community partnerships designed to resolve a wide range of societal problems.

In 1990, Ernest Boyer published his challenge to higher education to recast its mission to reflect what he termed the scholarship of discovery, teaching, integration, and application.

Boyer (1994) later challenged higher education to become immersed in solution-focused engagement in order to help solve societal problems that threaten the stability and viability of democratic society, including infant mortality, child poverty, homelessness, substandard housing, failing schools, youth crime and violence, and adolescent pregnancy. Today, Boyer likely would add a host of economic and regional development issues to this problem list.

Boyer's challenge is as apt today as it was two decades ago (Driscoll & Lynton, 1999). Children and youth in particular, seem to be involved in the risks and lowered life choices associated with America's societal problems. For example, estimating annual statistics from the Children's Defense Fund's (CDF, 2008) one day in the life of American children and youth indicates that 2,920 children and youth are killed by firearms, 904,835 are abused or neglected (1,460 of whom are killed), 2,190 commit suicide, 1,648,800 are arrested (of whom 73,365 are arrested for a violence crime), 223,200 are corporally punished in school, 426,060 drop out, and 3,328,740 are suspended. These are not the kinds of statistics that support efforts to build a new creative, knowledge economy or efforts to renew America's commitment to a civic and democratic society.

In this chapter, we focus on efforts to transform the life-course pathways for many children and families through campus-community partnerships. Although statistics such as those compiled by the Children's Defense Fund are inclusive across ethnicity, gender, and place of residence, we focus primarily on efforts to impact outcomes for individuals residing in metropolitan regions. We review principles and practices that support both the development and maintenance of urban regional university-community partnerships. As a part of this review, we provide examples of community change models of regional transformational change framed within a scholarship-focused engagement context (Franklin, 2008; Goodman & Wandersman, 2004).

University-Community Interface

During the past century, transitions from rural to urban life have accelerated at such an unprecedented rate worldwide that 83 percent of all humans now reside in urban areas. Further, 85 percent of all jobs created today are created in urban areas. Yet, the quality of individual and family life in the inner core of most urban areas increases in direct relation to the distance one lives away from the urban core. Urbanization has led to increased specialization, exacerbated division of labor, and increased size, density, and heterogeneity of the population. It contributes directly to weakening relationships among individuals through social isolation and to decreasing the social networks that traditionally provided neighborhood and community support systems to families. For individuals remaining in urban core residential areas, neighborhoods all too often are characterized by concentrated poverty, racial separation and isolation, low levels of academic achievement among children, low levels of quality-of-life indicators, a poor economic base for industry, weak neighboring and social ties, low informal social control, and a sense of powerlessness and isolation. This lack of self-sufficiency and self-determination among those who live in urban core residential areas undermines the human and social capital that is essential to restoration of neighborhood, community, and the preservation of democratic values (Boyte, 2004; Harkavy, 2005).

Transformative Urban Regeneration

How has community been restored in the context of urbanization? Efforts to transform urban communities must face the reality that communities are complex, dynamic systems.

Urban community efforts call to question approaches to "fix" residential areas by focusing narrowly on single program initiatives (e.g., preschool literacy programs, construction of a casino, cleaning up a neighborhood park). Moreover, debate persists as to whether or not these efforts demonstrate the broad-based impact necessary to fuel a transformational process that will take years to complete. Many causal dynamics about specific community problems themselves are not well understood, such as substance abuse, failing schools, or neighborhood violence, and it is difficult to decide which interventions will be most effective. Community psychologist Pennie Foster-Fishman and her colleagues refer to this as the first of three "key lessons": the need to create a community "that is ready and able to mobilize is time consuming, requires ongoing attention at multiple levels, and demands a flexible, responsive approach" (Foster-Fishman et al., 2006, p. 150).

Community Ownership

Prevention science has made considerable progress in identifying the efficacy of content-specific, evidence-based programs. Model programs exist for a wide range of specific outcomes. However, the strength of a well-controlled efficacy prevention program is also its weakness. Efficacy-based trials often do not replicate when tested for effectiveness in broad community disseminations. The reason for the disjunction between efficacy and effectiveness is due to the fact that efficacy trials are designed to demonstrate the effectiveness of a specific intervention targeting a specific program: for example, a well-designed literacy curriculum to enhance skills of preschool children. They are not built on systemic, community change models designed to promote community self-determination and sustainability, such as a parent education program to promote literacy in the home, connections between preschool and kindergarten for seamless curricular transitions, or neighborhood reading clubs. Thus, the community is not a part of the change process; nor is the public involved in the identification of the problem, design of proposed solutions, or dissemination of the results of the efficacy trial. In short, the community is not invited to participate actively in the programs that are designed to provide solutions to "their" problems. In part, exclusion of the community from attempts to resolve community-based problems stems from the failure of the university to view itself as situated in the community. When the university views itself as being *in* community, it is easier to foster an understanding that it must work *with* community to solve problems of mutual concern. Rigorous use of community-based participatory research approaches in conjunction with equally rigorous research/evaluation designs can generate effectiveness trials that can generalize across contexts. Caution must prevail, however, because community-based participatory research approaches have a built-in local context component that may continue to constrain generalization. What works in a neighborhood in one urban area might not work in a neighborhood in another urban area because neither neighborhoods nor cities are identical systems (Silka, 1999).

In many urban communities, change must start with programs that motivate and involve residents to be empowered and to take control of change processes in their immediate environments: their home, block, or neighborhood (Goodman & Wandersman, 1994). Residents who live in neighborhoods characterized by poor social relationships or low individual and collective sense of community and efficacy must change if there is any hope to sustain community change. Therefore, the first step in community change is to focus on neighborhoods within communities (or subcommunities) to identify positive natural leaders within the neighborhood, and to identify resources or practices that will enhance their ability to motivate residents to focus on changing neighborhood problems (Foster-Fishman, Berkowitz, Lounsbury, Jacobson, & Allen, 2001). This first step helps foster collective efficacy, neighborhood networks, a sense of community connectedness, and a sense of self-determination and power to effect positive change.

Networks and Social Capital

Efforts to create environments that will stimulate community change and expand an individual and collective sense of community are based on the ability to develop social networks, sustained relationships among individuals, and individuals with place (e.g., neighborhood, institutions, communities) (Stoecker et al., 2003). Networks that are strong enable leaders to develop interconnections, to build neighborhoods into subcommunities, and subcommunities into communities. Network density refers to the interconnections between other networks to which a particular network is linked. For example, human service agencies that are connected into networks are more likely to share client information, resources, and joint projects than are agencies that are isolated from networks (Foster-Fishman, Allen, & Fahrbach, 2001). Building relationships among networks that themselves have relationships with other networks expands the sense of community for residents who are part of relationship networks. The implication, of course, is that communities are social constructions more than they are geographic, place-bound regions.

Networking means sharing information, cooperation, coordination, coalition building, and collaboration. Networking means building social capital (Putnam, 1995). Effective networks are open systems that allow for multidirectional flow of information. When networks become rigidly defined, boundaries for information flow and access induce chaos and system disintegration and disorganization, stifling innovation and change. Without organized networks built on sustained relationships, all of the components of networking are difficult to accomplish. When systems are open and relationships flourish, networks can enhance individual self-sufficiency and community self-determination. Networking implies ownership and ownership requires active, strong, and sustained community involvement. Foster-Fishman et al. refer to this as their second key lesson: "Community ownership requires ongoing communication and is strengthened when programming efforts are run by the community" (2006, p. 151).

Planning, Flexibility, and Systems

The third aspect of relational community building refers to institutional aspects of community where control is primarily external to the community. Examples of this are business enterprises, such as automobile plants located in a community or government services that may change ways that are independent of any direct community control. Decisions from systems external to the neighborhood or subcommunity affect resource availability (such as local employment, social support services for families and children, and parks and recreational facilities). This in turn affects resident perceptions of community life and sense of efficacy and control. As communities change, the impact of changes within neighborhoods and subcommunities will depend on the extent to which neighborhoods are marked by cohesion or conflict and strong network leadership, and the extent to which vested interests within neighborhoods affect building network density (interconnections among networks). This leads to a third key lesson: "the role of social planning processes within the context of a comprehensive community building initiative is complicated!" (Foster-Fishman et al., 2006, p. 151).

Thus, transforming communities requires transformation of neighborhoods, which requires transformation in residents by creating a sense of shared meaning, organized participation, formal and informal neighboring, and a belief in collective efficacy (the ability to actually achieve change). All of these are foundational to creating a sense of well-being, individually and collectively. These changes in attitudes and behaviors are achieved by participation in block, neighborhood, and building associations, faith-based community service or advocacy committees and coalitions, school-based associations, and other grass-roots community organizations. It involves approaches that focus on the core components of social networks that include involvement in communities at the personal, relationship, social, educational, and economic levels. It involves building self-determination, self-confidence, personal skills, relationships among neighbors and between neighborhoods and institutions, and a sense of power over personal life and neighborhood life, as well as access to and control of resources. It requires dialogue and opportunities to generate through intersubjectivity a sense of shared meaning, cohesiveness, and purpose. As noted by John W. Gardner (2006), founder of Common Cause, and former U.S. Secretary of Health, Education, and Welfare, "the surest cure for the sense of powerlessness that afflicts so many citizens today is for them to take action on the problems of their own communities, restoring belief in their capacity to make a difference."

Comprehensive community-building initiatives enable citizens, neighborhoods, and communities to restore their belief that change is possible. Such programs require commitments from funding agencies, universities, and other societal institutions to partner with citizens over significant time periods in order to enable communities to effect changes that enhance the quality of life and well-being for all members of the community.

Principles and Practices of Scholarship-Focused Community Partnerships

At Michigan State University, scholarship-focused engagement is a conceptual framework for facilitating and guiding university *in* community partnerships, in order to generate university *with* community solutions. This approach is grounded in Michigan State University's definition of engaged scholarship, which supports engagement as a core value of the university, historically from its land-grant mission, and contemporaneously in its efforts to expand the land-grant concept (Bonnen, 1998) into the global arena. Whether local, statewide, national, or international, the mission of the university embeds community transformational change within its scholarship mission.

Outreach (engagement) is a form of scholarship that cuts across teaching, research, and service. It involves generating, transmitting, applying, and preserving knowledge for the direct benefit of external audiences in ways that are consistent with university and unit missions (Provost's Committee on University Outreach, 1993).

This definition aligns with definitions of community engagement that subsequently emerged from actions of the Committee on Institutional Cooperation's Committee on Engagement, the National Association of State Universities and Land Grant Colleges' Council on Engagement and Outreach, and the Carnegie Foundation for the Advancement of Teaching. Although these definitions have slight variations, they have in common that engagement involves partnerships (private or public), provides mutual benefit, is scholarship focused, enriches knowledge, supports democratic values and civic responsibility, and, by focusing on societal concerns, contributes to the public good (Calhoun, 2006; Kezar et al., 2005; Pasque, Smerek, Swyer, Bowman, & Mallory, 2005).

At Michigan State University, there are four key concepts that circumscribe the institution's approach to community partnership development:

1. Community Embeddedness: working in long-standing partnerships that are embedded in communities to identify the needs of families, businesses, neighborhoods, and community organizations.
2. Stressing Asset-Based Solutions: focusing on asset-based solutions that build on the strengths and advantages of community partners.
3. Building Community Capacity: building capacity within families, businesses, and communities to address their challenges and build on the opportunities they face.
4. Partnering with Collaborative Networks: partnering with or building networks among communities and organizations that lead to regional collaborations and innovations that are sustainable.

Community engagement demands an interdisciplinary approach to the development of solution-focused, university-community research/evaluation partnerships (Fitzgerald, 2000; Fitzgerald, Abrams, Church, Votruba, & Imig, 1996), and to direct the expertise of the academy and the community toward resolution of the diverse problems of society. Although there are diverse activities that are subsumed within engaged research, engaged teaching/learning, and engaged service (see table 1), currently, community partnerships and programs focus on community collaborations that stress knowledge generation through applied research and evaluation, and dissemination practices designed to transfer knowledge directly to the community. In this chapter, we focus on the first of these domains, campus-community partnerships that are solution focused, community driven, and faculty embraced.

Characteristics of Community Engagement

The strength of scholarship-focused engagement is that it brings people with experience in many walks of life together to collectively generate questions and seek solutions. Reaching a common ground and a sense of shared meaning is facilitated by adherence to a common theoretical framework (Fisher et al., 1993; Fitzgerald et al., 1996; Ford & Lerner, 1992), methodological orientation (Levine & Fitzgerald, 1992), emphasis on ecological validity (Bronfenbrenner & Ceci, 1994), commitment to community capacity building (Groark & McCall, 1993,

Table 1. Types of Engaged Scholarship, Teaching, and Service

Engaged Research/Discovery/Creative Works
- Applied research
- Community-based (participatory) research
- Contractual research
- Demonstration projects
- Exhibitions/performances
- Needs assessments/program evaluations
- Knowledge transfer and research
- Technical assistance
- Publications/presentations

Engaged Teaching and Learning
- Service-learning
- Academic-service learning
- Study abroad programs/Spring break
- Distance education and off-campus instruction
- Continuing education
- Contract courses or programs designed for specific audiences
- Conferences, seminars, and workshops
- Educational programs for alumni
- Participatory curriculum development

Engaged Service
- Clinical services
- Consulting
- Policy analysis
- Service to community-based institutions
- Knowledge transfer and workshops
- Expert testimony
- Technical assistance
- Contributions to managed systems
- Leading professional societies and associations
- Commercialization of discoveries
- New business ventures

1996; Kretzmann & McKnight, 1993), and dedication to shared responsibility for all aspects of partnership activity (Fitzgerald et al., 1996; Votruba, 1992). From this framework embedded in applied developmental science, system theory, ecological models, community-based participatory research, and action research methodologies, successful university-community partnerships have (at least) five key characteristics: they are systems based, attend to issues of diversity, recognize the importance of context, focus on assets and strengths, and are fully collaborative.

Systems Perspectives and Models

The first characteristic of successful partnerships is that they focus on the processes regulating system development, organization, and change; that is, individuals, groups, and agencies are conceptualized as interrelated systems. Systems theory provides a perspective for modeling the emergent properties of organization and for investigating inter- and intrasystem dynamics. From a systems perspective, individuals are embedded in families,

11

Outcomes—Assets Impact Model for Systems Change

Relationship among Actions at the Various Levels

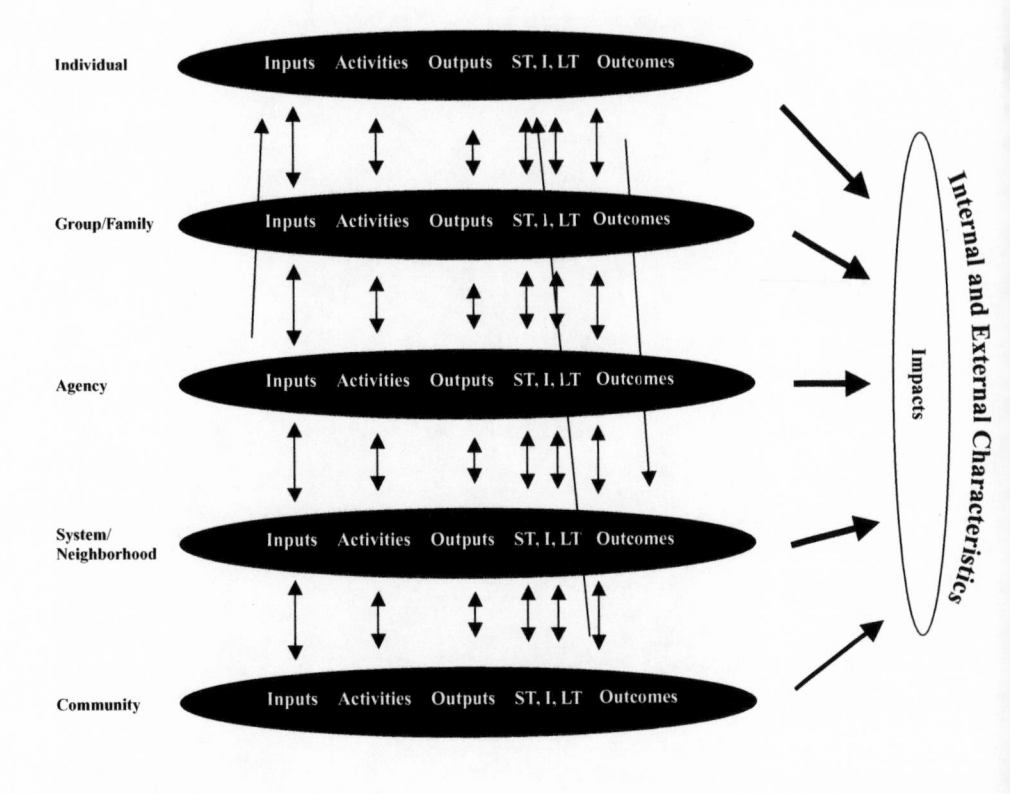

Robert Brown and Celeste Sturdevant Reed
© Outreach Partnerships **Check Points Training** Michigan State University

FIGURE 2.1 Systems Logic Model for Use in Creating Capable Communities Framework for Transformative Change

families are embedded in neighborhoods, and neighborhoods are embedded in communities, states, and nations. The key concept is that ultimately, individuals, families, neighborhoods, communities, cities, and nations are intertwined, they share systemic relationships, and, therefore, solutions are best modeled within the context of systems dynamics.

Figure 1 illustrates the a framework that is useful for guiding partnership development focused on community change. For example, the model was used by Robert Brown as he worked with the Jackson Community Action Agency (JCAA) to answer a deceptively simple question that the agency posed as it launched a strategic planning process related to its role in the Jackson, Michigan community: "When we talk about self-determination, what do we mean?" (JCAA, 1999). Over a six-month period, Brown facilitated meetings of various community groups to develop a common language about self-sufficiency to enhance the JCAA's ability to effectively evaluate their programs. The project evolved, however, to include a broader segment of the city itself. The end product was a set of checklists for assessing

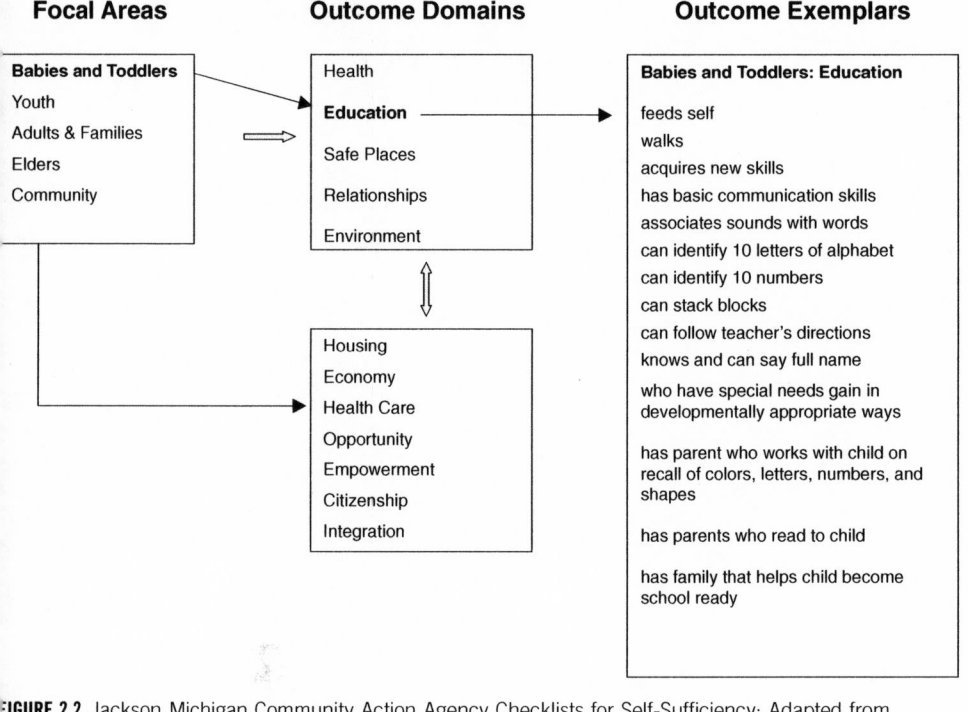

| Focal Areas | Outcome Domains | Outcome Exemplars |

FIGURE 2.2 Jackson Michigan Community Action Agency Checklists for Self-Sufficiency: Adapted from Exemplars from Building a Self-determine Community

self-sufficiency at five levels across five key domains: health, education, safe places, relationships, and environment. An additional five domains were added to the community level (see figure 2). The checklists provided a common perspective for diverse segments of the city to generate innovative programs that fit within the systemic framework that was both multilevel and anchored in five core content areas related to the health and well-being of all of Jackson's citizens.

Context

Context exists at all levels—biological, physical/ecological, social-cultural, political, economic—and invites systemic approaches to research, program design, and implementation. Poverty, family size, birth order, single parenthood, supplemental child care, parental psychopathology, unemployment, and workplace stress all help to set the context within which individuals, families, and social groups behave, develop, and interconnect. Because the political context is an inescapable component of all community-based programs (at the state, county, or local community levels), involving policy staff in the design, implementation, and utilization of community change initiatives can enhance the likelihood that policies and practices can be effective stimulants for change.

Asset Focus

The fourth component emphasizes assets so that the capacity to act is strengthened at the most basic level possible, whether that level is the individual person, the local school, human

13

Scholarship-Based Approach to
Campus-Community Partnerships

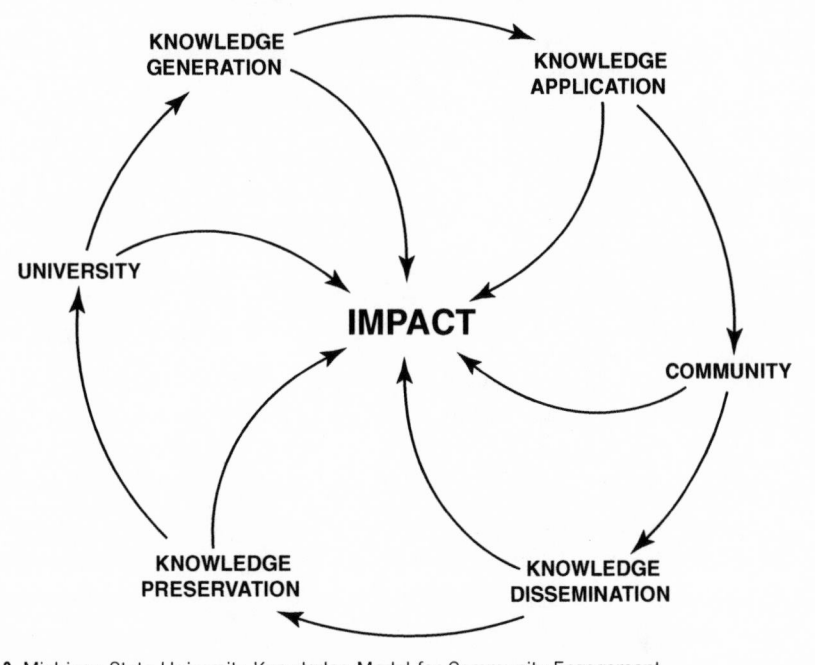

FIGURE 2.3 Michigan State University Knowledge Model for Community Engagement

service agency, neighborhood, or community. Universities exist to generate, apply, preserve, and disseminate knowledge (see figure 3), and they do so across the spectrum of disciplines, centers, and institutes that make up the modern university. In all instances, university programs are tied to anticipated outcomes. Capacity building requires the community to be implicitly involved in the development of community programs so that there is an explicit match between the expected outcomes at both the university and community levels. Thus, engaged scholarship emphasizes partnership capacity-building in an ongoing fashion and binds capacity building to outcomes.

Collaborative Partnership

The fifth component stresses the principle that models for community intervention tested in a community setting must involve full collaboration with community partners, where the community participates in the design and evaluation of community programs. Application of knowledge generates new questions, which in turn demands new knowledge generation (e.g., new approaches, new strategies, new program designs) in a seemingly never-ending cycle. If effectively done, this dynamic process ultimately results in the generation of principles or "best practices" that may be context or program specific, or may generalize to new situations or new contexts depending on a range of methodological considerations such as sample characteristics, sample size, and evaluation methods employed.

Standards of Practice for University-Community Partnerships

Regardless of the exact nature of the partnership or the particular community group with whom the partnership is formed, community engagement works most efficaciously when partners adhere to a set of practices that have been empirically derived from successful partnerships (Strand, Marullo, Cutforth, Stoecker, & Donohue, 2003). Engaged scholarship's emphasis on equality of commitment is designed to benefit community and university simultaneously, with each partner aware of the other's needs from the outset and with each agreeing to respect those needs throughout the duration of the partnership (Rosean, Foster-Fishman, & Fear, 2009). Although the standards of practice are continually evolving, six practices have proven to be effective for regulating campus-community partnerships: (1) shared mission statement, (2) shared outcome-oriented work plan, (3) shared program policy rounds, (4) shared resource investment and development, (5) shared learning and scholarship, and (6) shared commitment to cross-site linkages (Fitzgerald, 1997).

Shared Mission Statement

Members of a partnership develop a mission statement that defines their work and outlines one or more major partnership activities. This statement has two essential components: (1) a commitment to program implementation, and (2) a commitment to a plan for sustainability. Long-term commitment is essential for university-community collaborations for several reasons. First, community needs are multifaceted, involve diverse stakeholders, and rarely are responsive to quick-fix solutions. The process of establishing trust and credibility can be time consuming and delicate. It is not uncommon for trust building to consume all of the first-year interactions between partners. As discussion leads to refinement of the mission statement and new constituents are brought into the strategic planning process, the primary system redefines itself, as do the goals and objectives of the partnership. Of course, this has profound implications for faculty, especially those who have not yet earned tenure. If community collaborations are conceptualized in years rather than months or days, scholarship generation will follow the same metric, and this, of course, has implications for evaluation of faculty performance. Evaluation of faculty performance at most research universities is based on finished products, not promised outcomes. Moreover, finished products too often are narrowly defined as peer-reviewed disciplinary journal articles, although sometimes authored or edited books, book chapters, research grants received, and public performances also count. University-community collaborations require a broader definition of product, particularly products that are useful and accessible for members of the community, who ultimately will be more impressed with a useful technical manual or set of policy recommendations than they will with a disciplinary publication.

Sustainability is the second key component of the mission statement. As noted previously, universities exist to generate, apply, disseminate, and preserve knowledge; they do not exist to provide services that are more appropriately the responsibility of government and/or the private business sector. A university-community partnership can focus on evaluation of the impact of an adolescent pregnancy intervention program, but funding of the program itself is not a university responsibility. In short, the engaged scholarship model

15

brings science to the community in an effort to help generate solutions to community-defined problems, and to provide community partners with the evidence needed to sustain program funding.

Shared Outcome-Oriented Work Plan

Team members working on each identified activity develop a concrete plan for achieving team objectives from their mission statement. This plan clarifies how the team interprets the mission statement and guides its ongoing activities. Collaborative development of the work plan provides opportunities for faculty and their community colleagues to confront their respective agendas directly, and to produce a final approach that achieves mutual benefit. For example, because the faculty member wants an outcome that provides an opportunity to generate scholarship, he or she may stress the importance of a particular evaluation design. The national evaluation of Early Head Start, for example, required random assignment of infants (Raikes & Love, 2002) to an Early Head Start program or to an alternate community child care program. The requirement for random assignment caused great consternation to community partners. Resolution of the issue was achieved through dialogue, community-based participatory research practices, cost-benefit analyses, and a desire to have outcome information guide quality improvement efforts in the Early Head Start system (Mann, 2002). Shared efforts to develop an outcome-oriented work plan and sound feedback practices enhance the likelihood that members of the partnership are equally invested in program goals and work plan objectives.

Shared Program Policy Rounds

Periodically, a diverse audience meets to discuss lessons learned from the partnership's activities and to consider work plan and program modifications, policy agendas, future directions for collaboration, and the potential for linkages with others involved in similar activities. Change can involve any or all components of a system, and change at any level affects the overall system and in turn the work plan. One way to incorporate change into one's work plan is to periodically evaluate the work plan itself. At least annually, members of the broader community, including local and statewide representatives of government, could be invited to participate in a session that typically is organized first to present progress made to date and second to have open discussion about future directions. Progress reports include discussion of failures as well as successes, and recommendations for revisions to the work plan if necessary. Discussions about program failures and successes not only inform the collaborative partners, but also inform policy makers about factors that positively and negatively impact program outcomes. Because program policy rounds involve policy makers in the discussion of work plan objectives, they can develop a deeper understanding of the overall project and the meaning of the project's eventual outcomes.

Shared Resource Development

Long-term commitment, sustainability, and focus on knowledge generation, application, and dissemination are among the issues that force partners to address sustainable funding early in the planning process. All members of a partnership should contribute responsibly and work together to seek both short-term and long-term funding for program activities. If the partnership focuses on evaluation, both the university and the community are expected to include fund raising as part of the planning process. Occasionally, seed grants are required in order to obtain pilot data for larger funding requests. Such grants can be viewed as venture capital and require some type of "match" from each partner so that no partner views the other as a prime source of funding for program evaluation. This is especially important with respect to sustainability.

Shared Learning and Scholarship

Throughout all phases of the partnership, shared scholarship is essential. Shared learning and scholarship through university-community partnerships has proven more effective over time, where the historical misperceptions of university faculty by community members and vice versa have lessened as both partners have learned that mutual respect and trust are the foundation to their efforts. As one of our community partners quipped, "the intricate university ballet must meet the down-and-dirty community boogie on the same dance floor, and new steps and a common language must be learned by both partners" (Williams, 1997, p. 47). From the university's perspective, a core issue in all partnerships is that they should be anchored in scholarship, regardless of whether the partnership involves research, teaching, or service aspects of the university's mission (Fear, Rosaen, Foster-Fishman & Bawden, 2000). Although the definition of scholarship that we use is much broader than that typically used in the academy for promotion and tenure decisions, it is consistent with the "effective communication" standard of scholarship espoused by *Scholarship Assessed* (Glassick et al., 1997). Five scholarly product domains have been identified with a variety of outcomes possible within each domain:

1. Stakeholder Needs (research applicable to community settings, policies and funds focused on community needs, evaluation research),
2. Capacity Building (teaching curricula, training manuals, evaluation reports),
3. Knowledge Generation (literature reviews, research tools, publications),
4. Information Dissemination (briefs, reports, presentations, publications), and
5. Resource Generation (concept papers, presentations to potential funders, grant proposals).

Engaged scholarship involves community stakeholders at the beginning and throughout the process of knowledge generation and dissemination. Where possible, products also should build community capacity to foster independence and self-sufficiency (McCall, 1995a, 1995b; McCall, Groark, Strauss, & Johnson, 1998). Nevertheless, traditional scholarship is essential for faculty-staff involvement. This blending of traditional and nontraditional forms of scholarship challenges the academy's traditional reward structure. The question of how academic disciplines value community-engaged scholarship is being debated throughout higher education, and the nature of the debate varies across disciplines and type of institution. Various institutions of higher education, including colleges, universities, and professional associations, have developed guidelines for community-engaged scholarship that are being tested around the country (Ellison & Eatman, 2008; Gelmon, Holland, Driscoll,

17

Table 2. Four Dimensions of Quality Outreach and Engagement as Identified in *Points of Distinction: A Guidebook for Planning and Evaluating Quality Outreach*

SIGNIFICANCE: To what extent does the engagement initiative address issues that are important to the public, specific stakeholders, and the scholarly community?
    Importance of issue/opportunity to be addressed
    Goals/objectives of consequence
CONTEXT: To what extent is the engagement effort consistent with the mission of the university and unit, the needs of the stakeholders, and the available and appropriate expertise, methodology, and resources?
    Consistency with university values and stakeholder interests
    Appropriateness of expertise
    Degree of collaboration
    Appropriateness of methodological approach
    Sufficiency and creative use of resources
SCHOLARSHIP: To what extent is the engagement activity shaped by knowledge that is current, cross-disciplinary, and appropriate to the issues? To what extent does the work promote the generation, application, dissemination, and preservation of knowledge?
    Knowledge resources
    Knowledge application
    Knowledge generation
    Knowledge utilization
IMPACT: To what extent does the outreach effort benefit and affect the issue, community, or individuals, and the university?
    Impact on issues, institutions, and individuals
    Sustainability and capacity building
    University-community relations
    Benefit to the university

Spring, & Kerrigan, 2001). What follows is Michigan State University's *Points of Distinction* guidelines (Michigan State University Board of Trustees, 1996) for evaluating quality community engaged scholarship (table 2).

Shared Commitment to Cross-Site Linkages

The generation of new knowledge and the development of innovative responses to community concerns stimulates efforts to test innovations in other contexts. Such efforts, of course, involve issues of replication and generalization. From a systems perspective, however, it also involves assessing the extent to which context influences program outcomes. A teen health clinic located in an urban area may have different outcomes than a clinic located in the suburbs, or in a rural area, and by linking the two clinics one can evaluate outcomes relative to a set of theoretically driven criteria, such as population density, family composition, social support systems, and community resources. All contextually based ecological models hypothesize variation across settings and by linking programs from city to city, or from urban to rural settings, one enhances the possibilities of generating comparative studies in order to assess the impact of shared and nonshared variables on program outcome. Not only do such studies help to isolate crucial person-environment transactions, but they assist the formulation of public policy by providing evidence that interventions need to be tailor-made to fit the identifying characteristics of the target area.

18

On one hand, it is easy to describe a set of standards or descriptive guidelines for university-community partnerships. On the other hand, it is more difficult to manage the partnerships through the development process. It is particularly helpful to have an overlaying organizational structure for each partnership, although these usually must be soft structures with oversight functions rather than rigid, intrusive managerial systems.

Partnership Management

An administrative management team is created for each partnership in order to facilitate and guide partnership activities and goals. The team usually consists of one to two individuals from each side of the partnership. This team meets periodically to review program activities, schedules program policy rounds, works to minimize intersystem conflicts, and generally plays a soft oversight role for the partnership. The management team does not engage in micromanagement of the partnership, which is predicated on campus faculty-community "faculty" shared responsibility for partnership success.

Experiences with our partners have generated what one of our partners has described as a "working recipe for success," the components of which are (1) an early victory, (2) reconciliation of differences in community and university cultures, (3) reciprocal, long-term commitment, (4) coherent, common community-building agenda, (5) candor and confidentiality, (6) patient clarification and reclarification of mutual expectations and benefits, (7) creative solutions to other challenges, (8) rewards, incentives, and support for both staff and faculty, and (9) shared responsibility for long-term funding. Working from their jointly developed mission statement, partners should develop a work plan that more or less guarantees early success. Examples of such early outputs include completing a literature review, conducting a needs assessment, or bringing other community stakeholders into the partnership discussion and planning process. Early victories assist in trust building, goal setting, and confidence building, all essential objectives for building team concepts between university and community cultures, each of which must reconcile historical forces that have isolated their respective cultures from one another. Early success also *helps* to reinforce the reciprocal, long-term commitment to program development, evaluation, and change. Early successes build a foundation for trust and reciprocity, facilitate an atmosphere of candor and confidentiality with community partners, and provide the essential substrate for successful project co-management and coordination as well as sustainability.

University *in* Community for University *with* Community Transformations

Traditionally, university-community research or teaching/learning collaborations were formed by an individual faculty member or group of faculty, who approached a community entity requesting access to a particular target population that would enable the faculty member to test a disciplinary driven theory or practice. During the second half of the twentieth century, countless studies of children's academic achievement, social behavior, aggression, and friendship development as well as studies of family function, the impact of poverty, teen parenting, and the like were published in mainstream scientific journals. Theory abounded, facts flew, disciplines and journals grew, but little concrete change occurred in communities. In fact, evidence suggests that the health and well-being of children and families continued to decline for significant segments of the population. During the end of the twentieth century, the community engagement movement emerged from its roots in feminist theory, action research, and issues related to empowerment and social justice, to transform the nature of faculty-community collaboration to faculty-community engaged partnerships, with all of the structural features described in this chapter thus far. But the nature of how faculty members connect to communities continued to follow the individual faculty to individual community partner model. As higher educational institutions introduced outreach and engagement support services to their academic missions, new models for approaching communities began to emerge, largely driven by growing awareness and acceptance of the systemic interconnectedness of community problems. Higher education engagement support services began to develop broker models, models of community engagement that provided community "linkers" to help ease faculty access to community partners based as much on community needs as faculty interests. In Michigan, changes in state government policies provided the opportunity to develop a collaborative model driven by community organizational processes that presented opportunities for deep and far-reaching community-university engagement.

In the 1990s, the state of Michigan mandated establishment of multipurpose collaborative bodies, minimally at the county level or in cross-county cooperatives, consisting of diverse organizations and agencies existing within community. The multipurpose bodies were to address issues that influenced the quality of health and well-being of children, families, and special segments of society within the defined catchment area of the collaborative body. Stress was placed on community-wide efforts to organize vested interest groups (coalitions), to develop strategies to implement preventive-interventions and direct services, to share information about existing programs and policies that affect program delivery, to report progress made in enhancing the quality of citizen health and well-being, to coordinate resources and cross-agency referrals, and to build relationship and action networks within the defined multipurpose collaborative's boundaries. One of these multicollaborative bodies, the Power of We Consortium, has developed a deep and far-reaching relationship with its local higher education system, including Michigan State University.

Networks for Regional Transformation

The Power of We Consortium in Ingham County, Michigan, is changing the way individuals and organizations come together to mobilize community assets to solve complex social problems. Originally created as a state-mandated community collaborative in the mid-1990s, the Power of We Consortium has evolved into a unique, sustainable entity devoted to creating a healthier community through collaboration. Often referred to as a "network of networks," the Consortium focuses its efforts on brokering relationships, information, and resources to tackle intractable community issues too complex for any single organization to address.

The efficacy of the Power of We Consortium begins with its diverse membership, convening cross-sector leaders of community and faith-based organizations, municipalities,

Power of We Consortium Structure

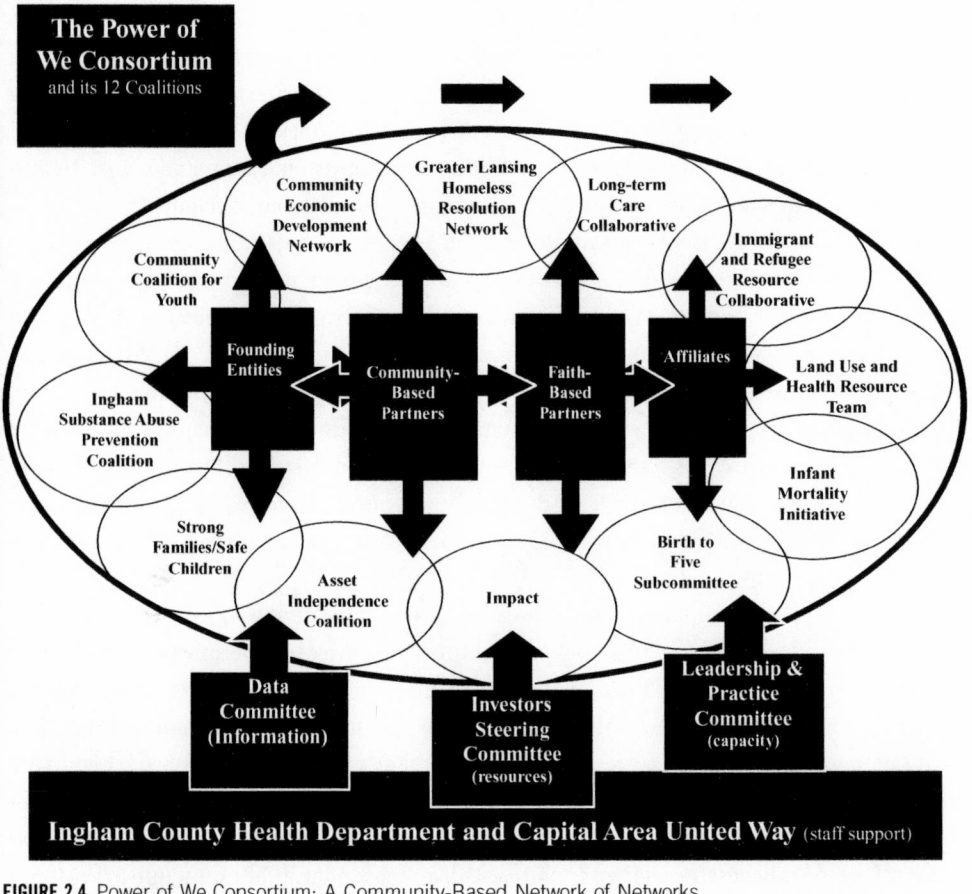

FIGURE 2.4 Power of We Consortium: A Community-Based Network of Networks.

learning institutions, human service organizations, and community funders. Monthly meetings of the full membership allow regular opportunity for networking, learning about emerging community issues, dialogue, and action. In addition, the monthly meetings provide for informal connections between community leaders to network and address interests specific to their individual entities, further strengthening collaborative relationships within the Power of We Consortium.

The goals of the Consortium are substantial, seeking to (1) advance intellectual and social development; (2) build a dynamic, diverse, and vibrant economy; (3) promote physical and mental health; (4) keep homes and communities safe by strengthening families and neighborhoods; (5) steward natural resources; and (6) strengthen the sense of community cohesion by actively engaging residents in the change process.

Twelve community coalitions working under the support of the Consortium, each a network of agencies and individuals, focus on key issue areas such as infant mortality, at-risk youth, substance abuse, early childhood development, refugees and immigrants, long-term

21

care, asset independence, land use and health, homelessness, and community and economic development (figure 4). The Consortium serves as the vehicle for these coalitions to move emerging issues and opportunities into the community vision.

Over the past decade, the Power of We Consortium has benefited from the support of the W. K. Kellogg Foundation. The Ingham County Community Voices initiative was first funded in 1999 by the W. K. Kellogg Foundation as part of its Community Voices Initiative designed to increase access to health care for vulnerable populations. The Ingham County Health Department (the home of the Initiative), though instrumental in the development and operation of the Power of We Consortium, strategically positioned itself in the background of the effort, in order to facilitate shared ownership and to create a collaborative community improvement process among multiple partners. Community partners were, and continue to be, engaged throughout the process in community summits, dialogues, development and implementation of action plans, outreach to vulnerable populations, and ongoing evaluation of the initiative. This process has led participants to identify common goals and look beyond their previously perceived borders for new relationships and partnerships (Public Sector Consultants, 2008). Although funding for the Community Voices Initiative has ended, its product, the Power of We Consortium, continues to grow in scope, building on the Community Voices foundation.

Through a process of participatory research, five community practices were identified that reveal the method by which this community's initiatives move through the change process. These five practices include (1) engaging and mobilizing community members, (2) facilitating dialogue and creating connections, (3) identifying and supporting civic leadership, (4) using all the assets of the community for change, and (5) sharing and using data and information to support and monitor progress. Coalitions and agencies of the Power of We Consortium are utilizing these practices as they set their agendas and establish work plans. Successful change initiatives have been plentiful and include: providing access to health care for more than 60 percent of the formerly uninsured in Ingham County; building and sustaining a neighborhood-based system of community centers and community development initiatives that support grassroots change; engaging and mobilizing residents in support of early childhood and youth development, reducing poverty, preventing substance abuse, and ending homelessness; and assisting community and faith-based organizations to build their own organizational capacity in order to better serve vulnerable populations.

The work of the Power of We Consortium is supported by three primary committees: the Community Data Committee, the Investors Steering Committee, and the Leadership and Practice Committee. The Community Data Committee is charged with developing and monitoring indicators of well-being, to produce periodic reports to the community, and to promote data democratization. Its Community Indicator Project, a publication of thirty-three indicators of well-being, measure the area's intellectual and social development, economy, health, safety, environment, and community life (social capital) (see table 3). Collectively, the indicators provide residents and stakeholders with a picture of the overall health of the community. Year-to-year measures provide valuable information regarding change and trends.

Table 3. The Power of We Indicators of Community Health and Well-Being

Intellectual and Social Development
        School readiness indicators
        High school graduate rates
        Education beyond high school
        Teen pregnancy
        Juvenile delinquency and crime
Economy
        Greater Lansing business index
        Knowledge economy
        Per capita income
        Poverty
        Unemployment
        Use of job improvement resources
        Home ownership
        Homelessness
Health
        Infant mortality
        Childhood immunizations
        Substance abuse
        Health care coverage
        Life expectancy
Safety
        Child abuse and neglect
        Domestic violence
        Unintentional injury deaths
        Violent crime
        Neighborhood safety
Environment
        Indoor air quality
        Outdoor air quality
        Surface water quality
        Groundwater quality
        Land use
Community Life
        Social capital

The Investors Steering Committee was created with a charge to coordinate and leverage community investments (with external resources) in order to expand application of the five community practices. The committee was also asked to assist the Consortium in responding to the following challenge: How can community organizations, groups, and neighborhoods be prompted to see the resources of public institutions as community assets, and how can public institutions be prompted to see community assets as a resource for achieving their goals?

The Leadership and Practice Committee is charged with identifying the capacity-building needs of faith-based and community organizations and coordinating efforts to meet them. Specifically, the committee facilitates peer-to-peer learning and networking; the dissemination of information about capacity-building resources and opportunities; the matching of community and faith-based organization capacity building needs with the

23

expertise and resources of public and private institutions; and the leveraging of local and external funding in support of capacity-building initiatives. The Leadership and Practice Committee serves as a "virtual" nonprofit resource center, in order to maximize community and faith-based organizational access to capacity-building opportunities without the cost and administrative burden associated with maintaining an organization charged with those responsibilities. Within this context, successful university-community partnerships require the university to become embedded in the community so that it can effectively work with community partners and networks to achieve shared goals.

Framing Embeddedness via the Birth to Work Framework

A community-based research network primed to embrace project-level collaborations with diverse university partners, impressive as it may be, presents unique challenges both to the community network and to the university. A key question is how one manages specific project activities within the overall complexity of the community network in ways that enable the network to achieve its goals. A second question concerns tracking of specific projects so that projects do not contaminate expected outcomes because they involve activities with the same schools, grades, children, or families. In short, how does one manage the systemic interconnections within the university, within the community network, and across the countless possible project specific interconnections between university and community?

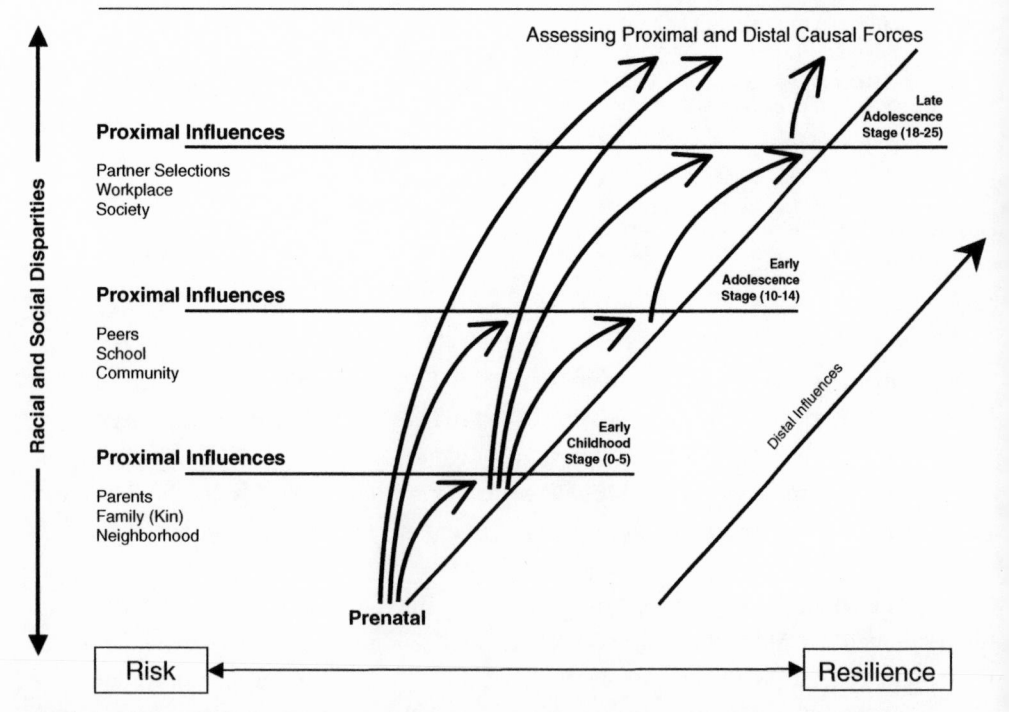

Transitional States, Relationship Impacts

FIGURE 2.5 Birth to Work Framework: Connecting Specific Program Impacts to Community Indicators of Health and Well-Being

Deliberative discussions around the dynamics of structuring effective network-university collaborations lead to development of a model, partially derived from the Jackson Community Action Agency self-determination project. We took the six core domains of interest to the Power of We Consortium—Intellectual and Social Development, Economy, Health, Safety, Environment, and Community Life—and mapped them onto three major life-course developmental transitional periods: birth to 5, 9 to14 years, and 18 to 25 years, on the premise that if development proceeded well during each of these transitional age periods, the child was "equipped" to be successful in the interim prior to the next transitional period. So, if risk exposure was low and resilience exposure was high across the six core areas during the birth to 5 years period, the child would be prepared to be successful during the elementary years. If similar circumstances held during the middle school years, the child would be prepared for success in high school, and so forth. At each transitional period, different sources of proximal influence affect the organizational processes during development, whereas cumulative risk or resilience ought to demonstrate some degree of continuity of outcome. We developed the birth-to-work developmental model as an organizing framework to locate specific project activities within the Power of We Consortium (figure 5). This research network structure and developmental framework will enable the Michigan State University–Power of We Consortium to track specific programs and assess the extent to which they impacted Power of We Consortium core content priorities. In this way, we have two complex systems, one emphasizing network relationships and community capacity building and the other emphasizing evidence-based projects, blended together in an effort to achieve transformational changes throughout a metropolitan region. Repeated monitoring of each of the system outputs, social network analyses in the former case, and project-specific outcomes in the latter, is best done by an overarching structure responsible for monitoring regional change. That structure is provided by the administrative linkages between the university and the Power of We Consortium. Constant monitoring is essential to prevent these dynamic systems from slipping into chaos.

Summary

In this chapter, we have discussed a variety of issues related to engaged research, particularly from the perspective of a research university. This approach embraces the emergent interdisciplinary field of community-engaged scholarship. With its emphasis on outcomes and evidence-based practice, this approach is explicitly anchored in scholarship-focused, community-driven applied research (Provost's Committee on University Outreach, 1993; Votruba, 1992): what Boyer (1990) referred to as the scholarship of application, and what we have defined as the knowledge model of engagement. We believe that scholarship-focused engagement at Michigan State University has emerged as a novel approach to university-community partnerships for three key reasons: (1) it demands shared responsibility for all aspects of partnership activities, (2) it is grounded in a scholarship model of knowledge generation, application, dissemination, and preservation, and (3) it operates as an organization, intent on brokering connections between individual faculty or interdisciplinary faculty teams of faculty and community partners and community partnership networks. One of our

25

explicit objectives is to help advance the university's mission, which "is committed to emphasizing the applications of information; and contributing to the understanding and the solution of significant societal problems."

References

Bonnen, J. T. (1998). The land-grant idea and the evolving outreach university. In R. Lerner & L. A. K. Simon (Eds.), *University-community collaborations for the 21st century: Outreach scholarship for youth and families.* New York: Garland.

Boyer, E. L. (1990). *Scholarship reconsidered.* Princeton, NJ: Carnegie Foundation for the Advancement of Teaching.

Boyer, E. L. (1994, March). Creating the new American college. *Chronicles of Higher Education, 41,* 48A.

Boyer, E. L. (1996). The scholarship of engagement. *Journal of Public Service and Outreach, 1,* 11–20.

Boyte, H. (2004). *Going public: Academics and public life.* Dayton, OH: Charles F. Kettering Foundation.

Bronfenbrenner, U. & Ceci, S. J. (1994). Nature-nurture reconceptualized in developmental perspective: A bioecological model. *Psychological Review, 101,* 568–586.

Calhoun, C. (2006). The university and the public good. *Thesis Eleven, 84,* 7–43.

Coye, D. (1997, May/June). Ernest Boyer and the new American college. *Change,* 21–29.

Driscoll, A., & Lynton, E. A. (1999). Making outreach visible: A guide to documenting professional service and outreach. Washington, DC. American Association for Higher Education.

Ellison, J. & Eatman, T. K. (2008). *Scholarship in public: Knowledge creation and tenure policy in the engaged university. A resource on promotion and tenure in the arts, humanities, and design.* Imagining America: Artists and Scholars in Public Life Tenure Team Initiative on Public Scholarship. New York: Syracuse University.

Fear, F. A., Rosaen, C. L., Foster-Fishman, P., & Bawden, R. (2000). Outreach as scholarly expression: A faculty perspective. *Journal of Higher Education Outreach and Engagement, 6,* 21–34.

Fisher, C. B., Murray, J. P., Dill, J. R., Hagen, J. W., Hogan, M. J., Lerner, R. M., et al. (1993). The national conference on graduate education in the applications of developmental science across the life span. *Journal of Applied Developmental Psychology, 14,* 1–10.

Fitzgerald, H. E. (1997). *Standards of practice for university-community partnerships.* East Lansing: Michigan State University Outreach and Engagement.

Fitzgerald, H. E. (2000). Interdisciplinary graduate education in applied developmental science: Systems, science and the scholarship of practice. Plenary paper presented at the 11 biennial meeting of the Developmental Psychobiology Group Retreat on "Recent research in developmental psychobiology and implications for practice." Estes Park, Colorado.

Fitzgerald, H. E., Abrams, L. A., Church, R. L., Votruba, J. C., & Imig, G. L. (1996). Applied developmental science at Michigan State University: Connecting university and community via programs for children, youth, and families. *Journal for Research on Adolescence, 6,* 55–69.

Ford, D. H., & Lerner, R. M. (1992). *Developmental systems theory.* Newbury Park, CA: Sage.

Foster-Fishman, P. G., Salem, D. A., Allen, N. A., & Fahrbach, K. (2001). Facilitating interorganizational collaboration: The contributions of interorganizational alliances. *American Journal of Community Psychology, 29,* 875–905.

Foster-Fishman, P. G., Berkowitz, S., Lounsbury, D., Jacobson, S., & Allen, N. A. (2001). Building collaborative capacity in community based coalitions. *American Journal of Community Psychology, 29,* 241–262.

Foster-Fishman, P. G., Fitzgerald, K., Brandell, C., Nowell, B., Chavis, D., & Van Egeren, L. (2006). Mobilizing residents for action: The role of small wins and strategic supports. *American Journal of Community Psychology, 38,* 143–152.

Franklin, N. (2008). *The land grant mission 2.0: Distributed regional engagement.* Unpublished doctoral dissertation, University of Pennsylvania, Philadelphia.

Gardner, J. W. (2006). *There is more than a ray of hope for America's future: Rebuilding America's sense of community.* Available at www.worldtrans.org/qual/Tramericancommunity.html.

Gelmon, S. B., Holland, B. A., Driscoll, A., Spring, A., & Kerrigan, S. (2001). *Assessing service-learning and civic engagement: Principles and techniques.* Providence, RI: Campus Compact.

Glassick, C. E., Huber, M. T., & Maeroff, G. I. (1997). *Scholarship assessed: Evaluation of the professoriate.* San Francisco: Jossey-Bass.

Goodman, R. M., & Wandersman, A. (1994). FORECAST: A formative approach to evaluating community coalitions and community based initiatives. *Journal of Community Psychology, 22,* 6–25.

Groark, C. J., & McCall, R. B. (1993). Diversity: Building mutually beneficial collaborations between researchers and community service professionals. *Newsletter of the Society for Research in Child Development,* pp. 6, 14.

Groark, C. J., & McCall, R. B. (1996). Building successful university-community human service agency collaborations. In C. B. Fisher, J. P. Murray, & I. E. Sigel (Eds.), *Applied developmental science: Graduate training for diverse disciplines and educational settings.* Norwood, NJ: Ablex.

Harkavy, I. (2005). Higher education collaboratives for community engagement and improvement: Faculty and researchers perspectives. In P. A. Pasque, R. E. Smerek, B. Dwyer, N. Bowman, & B. L. Mallory (2005). *Higher education collaboratives for community engagement and improvement* (pp. 22–27). Ann Arbor, MI: National Forum on Higher Education for the Public Good.

Jackson Community Action Agency (JCAA). (1999). *Building a self-determined community: checklists for self sufficiency.* Jackson, MI: Jackson Community Action Agency and Jackson Community Foundation.

Kellogg Commission on the Future of State and Land-Grant Institutions. (1999). *Returning to our roots: The engaged institution.* Washington, DC: National Association of State Universities and Land-Grant Colleges. Available at http://www.nasulgc.org/publications/Kellogg/engage.pdf.

Kezar, A. J., Chambers, A. C., & Burkhardt, J. C. (Eds.), 2005. *Higher education for the public good: Emerging voices from a national movement.* San Francisco: Jossey-Bass.

Kretzmann, J. P., & McKnight, J. L. (1993). *Building communities from the inside out: A path toward finding and mobilizing a community's assets.* Evanston, IL: Northwestern University, Center for Urban Affairs and Policy Research.

Levine, R. L., & Fitzgerald, H. E. (1992). Living systems, dynamical systems, and cybernetics: Historical overview and introduction to systems dynamics. In R. L. Levine & H. E. Fitzgerald (Eds.), *Analysis of dynamic psychological systems: Vol. 1. Basic processes.* New York: Plenum.

Mann, T. L. (2000). The role of training and technical assistance in supporting the delivery of high quality services in Early Head Start. *Infant Mental Health Journal, 23,* 36–47.

McCall, R. B. (1995a). Promoting interdisciplinary and faculty-service professional relations. *American Psychologist, 45,* 1219–1324.

McCall, R. B. (1995b). Birds of a feather: Administrative choices and issues in creating a specialized applied, multidisciplinary, developmental unit. In C. B. Fisher, J. P. Murray, and I. E. Sigel (Eds.), *Applied developmental science: Graduate training for diverse disciplines and educational settings.* Norwood, NJ: Ablex.

McCall, R. B., Groark, C. J., Strauss, M. S., & Johnson, C. N. (1998). Challenges of university-community outreach to traditional research universities: The University of Pittsburgh Office of Child Development Experience. In R. M. Lerner & L. A. K. Simon (Eds.). *Outreach universities for America's youth and families: Building university-community collaborations for the 21st century.* New York: Garland.

Michigan State University Board of Trustees. (1996). *Points of distinction: A guidebook for planning and evaluating quality outreach.* East Lansing, MI: Author.

Pasque, P. A., Smerek, R. E., Dwyer, B., Bowman, N., & Mallory, B. L. (2005). *Higher education collaboratives for community engagement and improvement.* Ann Arbor, MI: National Forum on Higher Education for the Public Good.

Provost's Committee on University Outreach. (1993, October). *University outreach at Michigan State University: Extending knowledge to serve society.* East Lansing: Michigan State University.

Public Sector Consultants. (2008, November). *Ingham County voices—Final evaluation report.* Lansing, MI.

Putnam, R. D. (1995). Bowling alone: America's declining social capital. *Journal of Democracy, 6,* 65–77.

Raikes, H. H., & Love, J. M. (2002). Early Head Start: A dynamic new program for infants and toddlers and their families. *Infant Mental Health Journal, 23,* 1–13.

Rosaen, C. L., Foster-Fishman, P. G., & Fear, F. A. (2009). The citizen scholar: Joining voices and values in the engagement interface. *Metropolitan Universities,* 10–29.

Silka, L. (1999). Paradoxes of partnerships: Reflections on university-community collaborations. *Research in Politics and Society, 7,* 335–359.

Strand, K., Marullo, S., Cutforth, N., Stoecker, R., & Donohue, P. (2003). Principles of best practice for community-based research. *Michigan Journal of Community Service Learning, 9,* 5–15.

Stoecker, R., Ambler, S. H., Cutforth, N., Donohue, P., Dougherty, D., Marullo, S., et al. (2003). Community-based research networks: Development and lessons learned in an emerging field. *Michigan Journal of Community Service Learning, 9,* 45–56.

Votruba, J. C. (1992). Promoting the extension of knowledge in service to society. *Metropolitan Universities, 3,* 72–80.

Williams, H. S. (1997, April). Evaluating and developing urban community-based interventions. In F. L. Parker, J. Hagen, C. Clark & R. Robinson (Eds.). *Making a difference for children, families, and communities* (pp. 45–48). Proceedings of Head Start's Third National Research Conference. Washington, DC: Administration for Children, Youth, and Families.

From "Preflection" to Reflection: Building Quality Practices in Academic Service-Learning

Nicole C. Springer and Karen McKnight Casey

Service-learning is taking the academic world by storm. Evidence of national and international interest in service-learning and civic engagement abounds in the numbers and types of scholastic publications, dedicated conferences, seminars, colloquia, and awards, as well as web-based and other online resources such as clearing houses and electronic mailing lists. Campus Compact, the premier organization for service learning and civic engagement in higher education, celebrated its twentieth anniversary in October 2006. This was a milestone anniversary that spoke to the appreciation of its work. Campus Compact has encouraged campuses across the United States to build cultures of civic engagement and has developed and promoted tools to help (Casey & Springer, 2006). The Compact assists more than 950 member colleges and universities with the engagement endeavors that are an intrinsic part of the purpose of higher education (Butin, 2006). Launched at the Campus Compact anniversary event, the Corporation for National and Community Service implemented the "President's Higher Education Community Service Honor Roll," designed to recognize "colleges and universities nationwide that support innovative and effective community service and service-learning programs. The Honor Roll's Presidential Award, given each year to only a handful of institutions, is the highest federal recognition a college or university can receive for its commitment to volunteering, service learning, and civic engagement" (Learn and Serve America, n.d.).

In 2008, Michigan State University (MSU) was one of six institutions to receive this Presidential Award and one of only three to win in category of general service to community. MSU received this recognition, in part, for the dramatic, but steady increase in service-learning and student civic engagement since 2000. As shown in figure 1, the percent of undergraduate students engaged in service with community has grown from 15 percent to 40 percent in eight years.

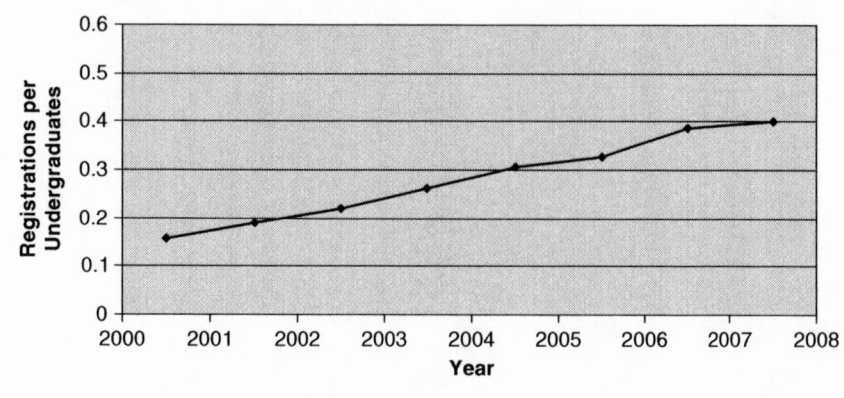

FIGURE 3.1   Service-Learning Registrations per Undergraduates

Projected growth puts the number of students involved at approximately twenty thousand by the 2011–2012 academic year and continuing to grow throughout that year. This is more than half of the current undergraduate population of 36,337 and still more than half of the projected 2011 population of 38,819 students (Michigan State University, n.d.). Figure 2 demonstrates the trend of growth service-learning registrations and the projected numbers for the 2011–2012 academic year.

Michigan State University, as a very high research university, is not alone in its commitment to student civic engagement. In 2006, Tufts University, with support from Campus Compact, and others launched a network of peer institutions for the purpose of examining and empowering engaged service on the institutional level. This network, which includes MSU and was named The Research University Civic Engagement Network (TRUCEN) in 2008, expanded membership in 2007 and again in 2009, further exemplifying the growth in interest in service-learning and other forms of student civic and community engagement (Campus Compact, n.d.). The emergence of the International

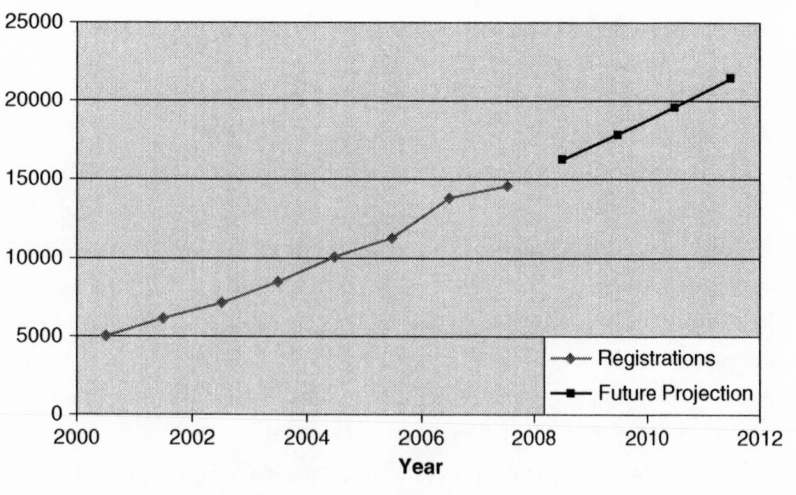

FIGURE 3.2   Total Service-Learning Registrations with Projections

Association for Research on Service-Learning and Community Engagement (IARSLCE) (IARSLCE, n.d.) in 2005 as an entity designed to perpetuate the international service-learning research conference and corresponding book series, begun in 2001 with funding from the Kellogg Foundation and others, addresses the service-learning research agenda for a wide range of institutional types and sizes and further speaks to the rise and proliferation of service-learning on a variety of levels.

In 2003, the Higher Learning Commission of the North Central Association of Colleges and Schools, a regional accreditation body, revamped its criteria for accrediting colleges and universities in its region, specifically addressing civic and community engagement and service in Criterion Five, while also acknowledging the role of service-learning pedagogy to promote effectiveness within other criteria. The sixth edition of the *CAS Professional Standards for Higher Education* featured standards for service learning (Council for the Advancement of Standards in Higher Education, 2006). In February 2006, the Carnegie Foundation for the Advancement of Teaching, a hundred-year-old, congressionally chartered, nationally recognized, independent policy and research institution "whose charge is to do and perform all things necessary to encourage, uphold, and dignify the profession of the teacher and the cause of higher education," invited colleges and universities to apply to participate in the new Community Engagement Elective Classification. This proliferation of evidence, products, and resources documents both interest and a trend toward institutionalization of service-learning pedagogy and practice. This chapter examines that trend as it pertains to higher education.

The increase in civic engagement and the call for service-learning is not something that is merely seen in documents and resources. Institutions are driving this call for this specific form of experiential service and it is reflected in their mission statements. In fact, Kathleen Weigert, associate director for academic affairs and research at the University of Notre Dame, published an article in *New Directions for Teaching and Learning* in which she presented readers with a broad statement about how universities address the three major components of higher education (1998). She stated that these institutions focus their attention toward teaching, research, and service. The weight of each of these items varies according to the ultimate focus of the universities. Tulane University, a private, mid-sized, research-intensive institution, defines its purpose as creating, communicating, and conserving knowledge in order to "enrich the capacity of individuals, organizations, and communities to think, to learn, and to act and lead with integrity and wisdom" (n.d.). This is done by creating an environment that not only focuses on the creation of novel information but also collaborates with community members and agencies to help inform the practices of both the university and the community at large. This focus on the broader community provides many opportunities to participate in the scholarly engagement of service-learning. Concordia College, a small, religiously affiliated liberal arts school in Moorhead, MN, has this for its mission: "The purpose of Concordia College is to influence the affairs of the world by sending into society thoughtful and informed men and women dedicated to the Christian life" (n.d.). Concordia looks to its roots in the Lutheran tradition to inform its approach to teaching, research, and service. Students are prepared for a life of service to others, and in the process they are introduced to community-based research. The combination of these two activities makes for a ripe opportunity to engage in academic service-learning. Michigan State University provides an example of a large, very highly research-intensive institution that has civic engagement at its roots. MSU is the pioneer land-grant institution, which brings with it an inherent sense of community engagement. Its mission is to "advance knowledge and transform lives" by preparing students to fully contribute as global citizens, conduct research to increase human comprehension and "make a positive difference" in both local and global arenas, and finally to future outreach, engagement, and economic development for the public good (Office of President LouAnna K. Simon, n.d.). These are three of the many institutions across the United States that address engagement in their mission statements and show evidence of creating opportunities to engage in the daily practice of scholarship.

Evidence of Quality Service-Learning

As more and more universities are addressing their explicit and sometimes implicit call for civic engagement, the need to have quality service-learning becomes even more imperative. It is not enough to simply incorporate service-learning into a course as either a requirement or an option without looking to best practices designed to produce the desired learning outcomes. Quality academic service-learning is able to achieve the goals of course requirements while students engage in community service. This is done by following the PARE model as laid out by the University of Maryland in the 1999 edition of their *Faculty Handbook for Service-Learning* (Resource Center, 2002). The PARE model deals with the content areas of preparation, action, reflection, and evaluation. It is imperative that these four aspects of service-learning be implemented properly to create the best possible experience.

Preparation

All students who engage with the community need to be equipped with the tools to have a successful experience. In order for this to happen, the preparation piece of the equation needs to start well before the students are in the classroom. The logistics piece starts with coordination of a service site. Some universities have specific units on their campuses that deal with the collaboration with community agencies. Michigan State University, for example, has the Center for Service-Learning and Civic Engagement (CSLCE), which is responsible for keeping a elsewhere of more than 360 agencies in the community surrounding the university. These agencies have all requested service-learning students to engage with them in a variety of ways. Some agencies need students to provide a direct service such as tutoring, whereas others are looking for assistance related to infrastructure support and/or capacity building, for example, creating websites or brochures. Each position that is created at the CSLCE comes as a direct result of communication and collaboration with community partners with careful attention paid to each partner's needs. This commitment to listening to the voice of the community has yielded more than 873 unique positions. Each position may have several openings within it. For example, a local elementary school may have need for people to be academic mentors (the position) and then ask for sixty students to fill this position. These types of requests and numerous others with one or more openings make it possible for the CLSE to accommodate more than 14,500 student service-learning applications per academic school year.

Other institutions that may not have the same kind of support base and faculty find that they must do the "leg work" to find community partners. It is important that faculty and staff understand that the service-learning opportunity they are designing for implementation into their specific course objectives should include input from the community agency with whom they wish to work. In fact, as with the community partners of the CSLCE, other institutions should treat the personnel at their partner agencies as co-creators of the service-learning experience and should not try to impose their personal agenda/curriculum onto the agency. In some cases, the idea that a particular faculty member has for incorporation of service-learning in their class may not meet the needs of the agency. The opposite can also be true in that an agency's request may not match the needs of particular faculty or staff member. In these situations, it is useful to have a network of interested parties to communicate the needs of community agencies within a university. This can occur within departments, colleges, or even university-wide. The network approach within these entities is important when thinking about how service-learning can and should be mutually beneficial. The community agency is receiving assistance with programs and/or projects, the students are able to look at the world in a more relational way, and the university is gaining knowledge that cannot be captured in textbooks from the community. All of this creates a cyclical effect with each piece enhancing the next.

Once the foundation has been laid for creating these partnerships and co-creating service-learning experiences, faculty members must then take time to closely examine how they would like to include service-learning into their curricula. Some may choose to have every student participate in the same project with one organization; others may have students participate in similar activities at a variety of locations; and still others may have students go and participate in different activities as long as they address the goals and objectives of the course. These are all time-tested approaches to including service-learning into a course curriculum. Each option has its advantages and disadvantages when it comes to the early preparation part of implementation. Faculty members who would like to focus on a specific issue may choose to have students participate in a project with one organization. This is beneficial if an organization is in need of assistance with a large-scale project. Students would then be able to experience teamwork and collaboration in a structured manner. This would also allow for very specific reflection questions. This method of service-learning works well for classes with lower enrollment numbers. Students get hands-on experiences while working on a project that is small in scope. The second type of service-learning project placement is one that works best in larger classrooms or across sections of a specific course. At MSU, the 200-level teacher education course focuses on diversity, power, and opportunity in social institutions (Office of the Registrar, n.d.). This course has a required service-learning component where each MSU student must serve in an educational setting and work with a student who is different from them in at least one significant way. The college students enrolled in this course all serve in similar settings that address a similar issue but are located at different agencies. Some students serve in a school during the school day, some participate in before- or after-school programs, and still others are in community agencies that offer educational programming. These students all bring their experiences back into the classroom and talk about their time in these different institutions. This makes for a wide range of discussion topics and the ability to compare experiences. The final method is to have students serve in a variety of agency types as long as the major concept of the course is addressed. This is different from the aforementioned method because it is not limiting in agency type. This works very well in courses that are extremely large, cover a variety of sections, or are part of a core curriculum for the student body. This may require considerably more groundwork in advance of during the course, and faculty at universities that do not have a centralized service-learning department may find that this is not the option for them. The important part of this preparation piece is to make sure that it remains something that is manageable for all involved.

The final step is to prepare the students for their actual service experience. This is done by providing students with an orientation that explain the essential expectations and also an overview of the community with whom they will be working. As part of this preparation process, students should also be made aware of their position as a service-learning student. One way to do this is by having students participate in a preflection. A preflection is a reflection activity that students do before their service experience. This has proven to be very useful in bringing to light some of the preconceptions that students may have about either the people they are working with or the subject area they are studying for which they are participating in service-learning. Being able to do this allows students to think about how these biases may affect their experience, find ways to think about the situation that does not reinforce their current beliefs, or allow them to look for ways that these stereotypes or behaviors affect others around them (Eyler, 2002). The key that is important is that all preparation activities have a primary focus on collaboration. Faculty must embrace the approach of working with communities and not working to help them. This steers students away from viewing their service-learning as coming from a place of sympathy and allows them to see their relationship as one of collaboration and mutual benefit.

Michigan State University has developed a web-based modular curriculum that can be incorporated into any course curriculum to assist with the preparation piece. This curriculum is called the *Tools of Engagement (ToE)* and is designed to ready students for community engagement. It addresses five fundamental parts of the engagement process and looks at a variety of ways that students (and others) can become involved with the community or enhance their current interactions. First available for faculty use in 2007, *ToE* has already proven to be a useful tool for students who are enrolled in service-learning courses. The authors of the curriculum were very intentional in its design and created this curriculum either to be used on its own or to be integrated into a class syllabus.

The modules are presented in depth later in this chapter as an example of best practice, but an overview of the different core areas is presented here. One very important aspect of the modules is that their base comes from the core belief that outreach and engagement at MSU is scholarly, community based, collaborative, responsive, capacity building for the public good. These are the pillars of the *ToE* Modules. The first module, "The Engaged Scholar," gives the history of the MSU land-grant mission as it relates to civic engagement. Through written and video media, students see how civic engagement is the root of their institution. Community-based engagement requires students to understand the dynamics that are in play both inside and outside of the university. Module 2 introduces and elaborates on the varying layers of power and privilege. The information from module 2 feeds into the next module on collaborative negotiation. Considerable research has been done in this field, and much of it comes from a business background. Students who work with the *ToE* curriculum will learn to negotiate in such a way that they can be instrumental in forming successful, reciprocal partnerships. These partnerships, of course, do not work in a vacuum, and the curriculum continues on with a fourth module on the principles of engagement that gives tools for making groups work. The curriculum ends with a final module on capacity building. This allows students to become acquainted with using an asset-based approach to working with community partners and with assessing the needs that these agencies may have.

Action

Academic service-learning is a unique form of experiential learning technique, eimbedded in the principles of outreach for the public good, which brings course information to life. The experience piece is the method by which faculty achieves the action piece of this equation. Students can be involved in action in three distinct ways. The first is through direct action. In this method, students go out into the community and have some form of personal contact with the community with whom they are working (Ayers & Lavin, 2003). One example of this comes from the department of teacher education at MSU. Students who have enrolled in one of the prerequisite classes for acceptance into the College of Education must complete a minimum of twenty hours of service learning. The class is a comparative study of schools and other social institutions. It is a foundational course that is based in civic engagement and community interaction. This is different from the more traditional courses that are practical and focus on delivery of curricula. The course material focuses on social construction and maintenance of diversity and inequality and the political, social, and economic consequences for individuals and groups (Brown et al., 2008). Students enrolled in this course perform direct action activities by going into local schools or agencies and provide needed tutoring services. During this time they are asked to observe the students who are at their site (both the ones they work with and others who are at the site) and also the organization itself. Students in this course are all doing the same type of service at different agencies, so they have the ability to make comparisons within each section. The course material helps to inform their observations, and their observations can be brought back to the class and used as part of their learning and reflective processes.

A second way students can participate is through infrastructure capacity-building support to agencies/organizations rather than through direct service to clients. In this type of service, students do not necessarily have to have direct interaction with recipients of service, agency clientele who eventually will benefit from their work. Instead, they are involved in efforts that support the work of the agency and help to build capacity and sustainability. Students may choose to work on creating promotional materials for and subsequently implementing clothing and/or food drives, crafting, planning, and putting into action fund-raisers or special and/or promotional events, or participating in the design and execution of newsletters, promotional materials, social networking, and/or websites. In the case of generally graduate-level courses, students may consult regarding and/or co-author documents related to organizational policies. A few examples of courses at MSU that engage in such practice include the first year/freshman writing course, Writing, Rhetoric and American Culture (WRA) 135: Public Life in America: The Service Learning Writing Project (Cooper, 2006); the junior-level professional writing course, WRA 331: Writing in the Public Interest; and the sophomore to senior (depending on major or specialization) course Journalism 205: Writing for the Media (certain sections only of the latter). Certain graduate-level courses, such as Psychology 864: Personnel Selections (with specific faculty), examine issues surrounding both paid and volunteer personnel and assist agencies and organizations with capacity building.

The final type of action that students can participate in is advocacy. A variety of MSU courses incorporate advocacy, and utilization is often faculty/instructor dependent. For example, one course section of WRA 135 partnered with the local America's Promise/Community of Promise to assist local high school students to poll their peers regarding perceived, age-related community social issues. The MSU first-year writing students engaged with the AmeriCorps youth group leader and a select group of interested high school students to design surveys and administer them to fellow high school students during lunch hours. MSU students then worked with youth group members to compile and report the results, as well as to isolate actionable items. One prevailing issue identified was safety and security concerns at the downtown transit authority/ public bus station. MSU students coached the high school students in the use of PowerPoint in creating presentation materials and in presentation and public-speaking skills. Youth group members presented their research findings and advocated to the city council and to transit authority board. As a result, security patrols at the bus station were increased, especially during the prime late afternoon and early evening travel times for adolescents. Additional examples of classes engaged in advocacy include deliberative dialogue forums on topics such as "Who Is College For?"—college access, letter-writing campaigns to legislatures and special interest groups, and proposed university student-community group plays and performances on food security and sustainability issues.

Reflection

According to Janet Eyler, "reflection is the hyphen in service-learning; it is the process that helps students connect what they observe and experience in the community with their academic study" (2001). This piece of the service-learning pedagogy and experience is crucial to separating service-learning from purely service. In the process of reflection, students are asked to think about all the things that they have experienced up to this point. The amount of reflection that is done by a student is at the discretion of the faculty member teaching the class in which it is implemented. The research does show, however, that the more time a student has to reflect on her experiences, the greater connection between her experiences and the learning objectives of the class (Shumer, 1997). It is even more important that one be very intentional in choosing the method of reflection.

Just as there are options for completing one's service, there are also options for participating in reflection. Depending on the needs of a class, students can reflect alone, with classmates, with the community partner, or some combination of these options. Each type of reflection brings with it a different layer to the reflective process. All of these reflection types can also be done before the service, during service, and after the service.

Individual, self-directed reflection is an effective way to have students critically think and speak openly about their service-learning experience. There has been some debate over which terminology to use when referring to the experience and how it relates to the reflective process. In some circles, the term "project" connotes something that is short term and not on par with other academic pursuits. It is more often associated with student group activities as opposed to academic service-learning and student civic engagement. They authors of this chapter have chosen to speak about service-learning as an experience. It is important to have students reflect on more than the project in which they may be involved. They need to take it to the next level and talk about their own learning, the prevailing issues leading to the community request or need for the services they have provided, and the meaning to the community partner and/or the clientele.

Many faculty members have found that students are more likely to be honest about their biases and viewpoints when they believe that the information shared is something that will remain within a small group of people. This small group can consist of just the professor or the faculty member and another outside reviewer. This is consistent with the research done on self-disclosure. In a recent publication of *The Qualitative Report,* Vernon and Emily Harper have reported on their investigation of the use of blogs, which are online journals, as reflection tools (Harper & Harper, 2006). They write that students felt that this venue gave them a place to critically think about their experiences and also convey their opinions in a location where they felt safe to make comments that might disagree with their professor. Although most faculty members still utilize a paper method of journaling, this type of information can be extrapolated to that method as well. Quality reflection is facilitated by using these methods for both inquiry and assessment. First, students need to be given direction by way of cues or prompts. This helps to make the journal responses truly reflective and not merely descriptive. Not only does this help lead to authenticity of the thoughts and writing, but it also minimizes what the students could perceive as negative feedback. Students will also need to receive individualized feedback as a part of their reflective exercise. This helps students feel that their voices are being heard and that what they say has value. Reviewers can take this time to respond to the students in order to address any concerns that the service-learning student may have or any clear biases that may need to be addressed before, during, or after the reflection.

Students who engage in individual reflection before the service can do so by writing a goal statement or a letter to themselves. In this assignment, students will have the chance to really think about the community they are entering and how that relates to them and their lives. It is important that students feel free to be open and honest about any biases, stereotypical thinking, or concerns that they have before the project starts. These are the issues that need to be addressed in a timely fashion so as to not allow for a perpetuation of assumptive thinking. As the service-learning experience continues, faculty may choose to have their students continue to participate in reflective activities. In fact, it is the preferred method of this process. Individual reflection can be done throughout the project by having students keep a journal of their experiences and their reactions to them. It is important to remember that service-learning is not about putting in a specific amount of hours, but it is about relating how the experiences during those hours have affected the student and the community constituent in some way. For the student, this can be shown by improvements in problem solving and/or trouble shooting skills or in the way she/he now assesses situations. The community partner could display positive changes in the way they provide service to their clients or implement innovative programming as a result of their connection to service-learning. Students should also be allowed to discuss how their previous thoughts or biases about a certain community or behavior have either changed or remained the same. These writings should also have students speak to more than the direct impact they felt; they should also include critical analysis of how social structures or conditions have contributed to the particular community need they are addressing. Some students may need some prompting when it comes to reflections, and staff should be prepared to offer guidance throughout the semester. At the end of the service opportunity, it is important that students have a way of giving a capstone of what they have learned and how they can relate that back to the course requirements and even their individual lives. This is most often done with an end-of-semester project or paper, but it can take other forms of visual representation as well.

Faculty members who choose to have their students reflect in a group can arrange these interactions in a variety of ways. The most common way is through a group discussion with classmates. This can be done in a large group (the whole class), or students can divide up into multiple groups and reflect in smaller venues. It is very important to have a facilitator in each group. This person would be able to give appropriate feedback to students as much as the reviewer of a reflection paper would do. This is the method of checks and balances during the expression of the student voice. One of the challenges of using this method is that in a large classroom it works best to split into small groups, but it is then difficult to have a facilitator in every group. When this is the case, constructs can be established in the preflection that then are utilized during the reflection process. For example, during the preflection, members of the community organization could come in and speak with the groups. It is during this process that students can use some of the information from their preparation to talk to their community partners about a needs assessment. This can be done in a way that looks at what the community partner brings to the community and how they feel they can better serve their constituents. In conjunction with the presentation, student scribes are assigned to take detailed notes. These scribes become discussion leaders/facilitators in the group reflection process, brining the community voice back into play in the absence of the actual agency/organization partner. Students would have the opportunity to really see how their work will effect change for that organization. However this type of group reflection is set up, it is important that students receive feedback during their discussion time. As seen in individual reflection, course instructors who choose a group reflection model will need to have their students continue the reflection during the engagement experience. This can be done either with or without the community partner involvement. Students may participate in reflection circles that are held outside of class either with the professor as the facilitator or finding a facilitator from an outside source. Michigan State University holds reflection circles that are run by a local, university-affiliated community group, graduate students in higher education/student services administration, and staff members from their Center for Service-Learning and Civic Engagement. This allows for a broader set of experiences to be involved in the reflection process. If the community partner is involved in the continuing reflection of the service-learning student cohort, it may prove to be beneficial if they either offer an on-site debriefing at the end of each day, or perhaps assign special times during the week when their students can talk about what they experienced and look to make their connections to their course requirements. It is important that the community partners be involved in the co-creation of this service-learning opportunity so they can be more insightful when making the connections to the class in which service-learning students are enrolled. Students will be able to reap the full rewards of their service-learning experience by doing a group presentation at the end. Students can give a presentation to their class, or they can include their community partners by giving the presentation to them. In both cases, students need to receive feedback on their reflection.

Research in the field of academic service-learning shows that all assignments rooted in the service must be assessed and evaluated accordingly (Weigert, 1998). Reflective assignments cannot occur in a vacuum. One major goal of service learning is to challenge the students' base assumptions about social issues. Reflective assignments allow students to explore their biases, and the evaluation of the assignments allows there to be a chance to think about social issues in a new way. Without this kind of feedback, people have a tendency to continue to view things in their traditional way without challenging why this is their thought process (Eyler, 2002).

Evaluation

Evaluation of the service-learning experience is twofold. First, there needs to be an evaluation of the assignments. Faculty members should look for evidence of learning and whether the student was able to achieve the goals set out at the beginning of the course. The rubric that will be used should be decided on an individual basis, because it needs to be molded to the course into which the service-learning experience is integrated. Evaluation does not stop at assignments, but goes further into what can be considered program satisfaction. Questions of satisfaction and efficacy need to be asked of the agency, people who benefit from the agency's services, and the participants. Two major factors influence this need for deeper evaluation. Shumer tells us that students will actually learn more and be able to make better connections to the course objectives if they feel that their service has value to the organization with which they worked (1997). Being able to ask the agencies some very important questions about how they felt about the service-learning project lets the agency have a voice and also lets the students know that the work they did was beneficial to others. These are all beneficial to the multidirectional flow of information.

As mentioned previously, the purpose of evaluation is not purely for the students. It is crucial in maintaining a strong working relationship with the community partner. Interaction with these community agencies and organizations include assessments in a variety of forms. Through the use of phone conversations, emails, and site visits, the community agency is able to analyze the usefulness of the service-learning students and see how they have impacted the agency's ability to better serve their constituents. This information is vital to organizations that seek to grow and to focus their attention on best practices.

At an institution like MSU with a Center for Service-Learning and Civic Engagement, the assessment process also includes reporting to that office. The CSLCE puts out an anonymous survey at the end of each semester to ask for student input on their service experience. These students are asked questions that touch on their motivation to participate in service-learning, their achievement of broader service-learning goals, and self-analysis of their efficacy and attentiveness during their service experience, and include the chance for the student to give a written response to what they liked best and least about the experience and recommendations for future placements. Students also have a chance to relay their assessment of their service-learning experience through follow-up emails and coordinator meetings.

Best Practices

One of the major challenges of following the PARE method of administering a successful service-learning is having a streamlined process for faculty to follow. Michigan State University Outreach and Engagement and the CSLCE created the *ToE* mentioned earlier in this chapter to address what service-learning means to higher education and how to address it in a meaningful way. *ToE* give faculty members a way to introduce the basic premises behind service-learning and civic engagement in such a way that it will truly enhance the service-learning experience for the students and the community partners with whom they work. It is important to note that although *ToE* was tailored to MSU students and even more broadly to students attending a land-grant institution, much of what is in the modules can be tailored to fit different institutional types.

The modules are set up to provide content, examples, application, and reflection. This online curriculum is set up with a split-screen design. On the left side, students are introduced to concepts in a more traditional teaching style that is content driven. The right side of the screen provides students with the examples and application aspects of the curriculum. These more personal pieces involve quotes from students and examples from the field. At the end of every module, and even sometimes within the module, readers are presented with reflection questions that are designed to bring the module together in a meaningful way.

Module 1: The Engaged Scholar—MSU's Land-Grant Mission

The first module is designed to introduce students to the concept of an engaged scholar. The model of outreach and engagement at MSU focuses on a scholarly approach that builds a reciprocal and mutually beneficial relationship between the university and the community in which it is housed. This model has its foundations in the co-creation and application of knowledge, a combination that builds the capacity of both that community and the university.

This module challenges students to accept the responsibility of engaging with community partners, and it describes a process (as elaborated by the other modules) of how they may become engaged. It also presents examples of student community engagement projects. When students have mastered this module, they should be able to understand what it means to be a part of an engaged institution, how that directly relates to the lives of students and their experiences at the institution, and how the mission connotes a responsibility of the faculty and students to engage with the community. As noted at the beginning of this chapter, the mission statement of virtually every institution of higher education articulates commitment to community, public service, outreach, and/or engagement for the public good. The basic premise of dedication to service in some form transcends institutional types. Therefore, although the current version of Module 1 draws heavily on MSU land-grant roots, such an introductory module could be revised and adapted to address the needs of any college/university and its mission.

Since its inception as a land-grant college focused on agriculture, MSU has continued to focus on its values of quality, inclusiveness, and connectivity. This has been done by reframing how these values are viewed in light of the more modern challenges. This concept of a land-grant university and what it means in the twenty-first century requires an engaged institution both in Michigan and around the world (Beekman, 2005).

Although these goals and values are explicitly spelled out as part of the land-grant mission, other schools have similar values and goals. This module can be useful for these students at these schools as well. It is important that students be able to see that engagement is a scholarly activity. This type of preparation helps students go from the feeling that service-learning is something extra they have to do to seeing it as part of their college curriculum.

As this module continues, students are asked to explore the world outside their own university. The concept of community is a broad one, and students need to think about how other people who are not directly associated with their university bubble exist in this world. In this section of Module 1, students are given a list of disparities that are a part of everyday life in America. Disadvantaged groups in society have been demarcated by race, gender, and class. This has created inequalities in income and also fewer opportunities. As highlighted in Module 1, reducing these social disparities and inequalities are at the heart of MSU's mission as a land-grant institution. At the end of this section, students are asked to reflect on what they have read and think about social disparities and how they might have a personal responsibility as students of this land-grant university to work toward equity.

As mentioned earlier, it is important that students feel that they have ownership in their service-learning. The end of Module 1 gives students five steps they can take to becoming an engaged student scholar. After this module, the student will have learned the importance of service as a way to not only give back to the community but also see it as an integral part of his/her student experience. This mindset works well whether students are part of a land-grant institution or not. The goal is to get students who are in their first year of higher education to start to think about how they can use service to make their coursework come alive, and then continue to stay engaged as community citizen-scholars and contributing citizens as they continue throughout their academic, professional, and personal lives.

Module 2: Community-Based Engagement—Power and Privilege

Once students are comfortable with or at least introduced to the importance of service-learning within their academic careers, the *ToE* modules take their last piece of information about disparities and take it to the next level with Module 2. Students are now learning about power and privilege and how they relate to community-based engagement. This is important for a variety of reasons. First, students should understand that people differ in their levels of power and privilege. The module goes beyond the boundaries of race and gender and talks about power and privilege as it relates to culture, language, and even education levels. This module further explains that privilege, although sometimes assumed to be a natural part of society, is in fact merely a presumption that impacts how people interact. However, being sensitive to these differences allows people to communicate better and work more effectively with each other.

This module follows the same format as Module 1 and gives a brief explanation of its integration with the other modules that precede and follow it. In the introduction, the author identifies five core issues that are essential in identifying while working with community. These five issues are identity, personality, group dynamics, privilege, and the basic concept of community. The example given in the introduction brings in a story about the intersection of many of these five issues. The story is of two women, one White and one Black, who are talking about the commonality of sisterhood. Students have the opportunity to look at this story and see that we all view ourselves (and society views us) in different ways. So, whereas the White woman saw herself as a woman, the other woman saw herself as a Black woman. These constants are being pointed out so that people can embrace them and know how to work within the dynamics they create.

It is also important to have students think about privilege in a way that does not hinge on identifiable markers. Students very often do not perceive themselves as having power simply by virtue of being a university student. With their status as students, they frequently feel that others in the university structure, such as faculty, advisors, administrators, and even resident advisors, have more power than they. Yet, in the context of working with community, especially in settings of marginalization, college/university students are seen as having "power" because they have "made it" to the university. This section helps to show that some issues of power are explicit while others are implicit.

The first main section of content is grounded in the work of Beverly Tatum and her approach to understanding race and identity. Students are presented with what she defines as the five major concepts that shape identity: individual characteristics, family dynamics, historical factors, social contexts, and political contexts. First-year students and others who are just beginning to engage with the community need to be aware of these different aspects and be able to identify what role they play in people's lives. The impact of these identity shapers may shift and vary depending on the context of the situation in which a person may find himself. There is more than just how an individual self-identifies; there are also social cues from those around them. All of this is further explained through an example of identity conflicts. Students should understand that simply understanding what makes up one's identity is not the full picture. When working in partnerships (whether with a community partner or with an assigned group), there is the chance that conflicts will arise. This conflict may be within a person because we have many intersecting identities, and that may manifest itself in an outward manner if there is not an effort to hear all voices. The example in this section talks about a meeting of a lesbian, gay, bisexual, and transgender organization. A student who also identifies as a person of color may feel as if her racial identity is seen as secondary or is being ignored all together. This also can be applied to chosen identities such as a sport or group affiliation. This section ends with a chance for the students to reflect about how they perceive themselves and also how other people's perceptions of them have had an impact on their own identity.

In addition to identity, the author of this module felt that it is important to talk about personality types and how that relates to engagement in the context of power and privilege. This does not seem like a likely comparison, but when one thinks about the way in which people function in society, personality has a big part in that interaction. Students are invited to take a personality test to see what their true personality is without it being told to them by someone else. Most people do not have this insight, but allowing people to look at how their personality is viewed by others helps them think about their personalities from a more scientific approach. It allows them to think about how others see them as opposed to how they see themselves and how that may help foster opportunities or create challenges when working with others.

Learning about group dynamics is another critical part of being able to form successful partnerships. This section of the module talks about the concepts of dominant and target groups. Students are invited to think about what it might mean to be a part of either group and how that factors into their lives. In an attempt to see how power and privilege are interrelated, this module draws on the work of Peggy McIntosh and her essay "Unpacking the Invisible Knapsack." In her writing, McIntosh speaks primarily of White privilege, but it can also be broadened to the other seven categories of otherness that Tatum addresses. This is about more than the oppression of groups that are based on identifiable markers. This module goes on to talk about how the division of dominant and target group can be based on something as "simple" as participation in a sport and the adoption of the identity of athlete. There will be some cases where this is considered an advantage and others where students may find themselves as part of the target group. Understanding this type of fluidity helps students to be able to see the need to be attentive to where they are fitting into a community at any moment.

All of this information can be a bit daunting for students, and sometimes they are unsure about how to work through this information. It can be especially poignant if there is a great divide between the demographic of the school and the community in which they are located or with whom they work. One of the ways this curriculum tries to deal with this is by providing an end to the module that discusses how to use one's feelings about one's own privilege. In the final example, the students are not presented with a story that deals specifically with an inequity based on identifiable markers, but instead read a story about how people are affected by time. What does it mean to be a member of a dominant society that is deeply concerned about time and whose members surround themselves with time-telling devices, and then to go into a community that is more lenient about such things and believes in a more organic approach to time? Can the person from the dominant society simply impose his or her beliefs on these other people, or is there perhaps a different way that this type of dynamic based on privilege should be handled?

Module 3: Collaborative Negotiation

Knowing about the way people and groups interact paves the way to being able to form a collaborative unit. In a society that is driven in large part by businesses and corporations, there is a chance that students or other people just beginning their journey of civic engagement will have been introduced to negotiation as a process in which someone wins and someone loses. The skills it takes to negotiate within a collaborative framework are slightly different and point students to an understanding of reciprocal relationships. The authors of this curriculum believe that there needs to be a different type of negotiating framework that allows for mutual benefit. Students need to learn to use this problem-solving process in such a way that they will understand why it is at the heart of good engagement. This module is strategically situated to bridge the connection of self-knowledge and group knowledge and is based on the practices presented in the Harvard Negotiation Project and the book *Getting to YES* (Fisher, Ury, & Patton, 1991). These steps include separation of people from problems, focusing on interests rather than positions, and working together to create opinions that are pleasing to all parties involved. By following the steps and the information included in managing these steps, students will also learn how to work with people who might have more power and privilege, refuse to play by the rules, or even resort to using "dirty tricks."

This module is unique in that the same scenario is used throughout the module to illustrate the three steps of successful negotiation as presented in the concept portion of this module. The scenario is one taken from an actual occurrence, but the names and some of the situations have been changed. Students have the opportunity to work with the story and reflect on the situations throughout the module. This allows them to feel they are a part of the process, rather than simply reading about it. As students read through the module, they are also presented with reflection questions in three separate areas. This is to help them think about each step in the negotiation process and how they can or cannot relate to it.

The major points from this module help students also integrate their knowledge from the modules before. The first step in negotiation is to separate people and issues. In the content part of this module, students are asked to use their perception in negotiation and try to really gain an understanding of a situation, or at least the viewpoint of the other party, before making conclusions. It addresses the common communication blunder in which people start to position themselves in such a way that the issue they are concerned with becomes who they are. Those who have differing viewpoints are therefore not challenging or questioning an issue/position, but are attacking the person himself. Emotions play a large role in this, along with perception and communication. This also includes both recognizing emotions and finding a way to navigate within these confines. Emotions are important, but they need to be acknowledged and to be explicit. Students can think about what they learned in their personality test and how that would apply to negotiation. The central question here is why it would be important to learn about oneself before working with others.

Module 4: Principles of Engagement—How to Make Groups Work

Negotiation is one of the earliest steps in creating a working group. The question then becomes how to make these groups work. By the time students have made it to the collegiate level, they have been in a variety of groups. Churches, social organizations, and group project participation are all examples of groups, and they can either perform effectively or not. After the completion of this fourth module, students will be able to actively improve their interactions with community partners by using the principles for good partnerships and will also learn about the pieces of the puzzle that create an effective partnership. This is done by looking to the Community-Campus Partnership for Health (CCPH) and using the set of principles they have created to produce and fortify the partnerships between community agencies and higher education institutions. This organization has come up with nine principles of good partnerships and was chosen as the exemplar for the content area of this module. Following the setup for the other modules, students are presented with examples to help illuminate the reading. Sometimes students need to start from an area that is more closely related to their lives. Faculty and staff at Michigan State University who have used the modules have found it useful to have students think about how these principles fit into their personal lives and their own relationships.

One example of how this is presented is in the first principle covered in the module. The CCPH principle states that effective partnerships are ones that are based on mutual trust, respect, genuineness, and commitment. Students learn about this principle and are then given an example of building trust. This information includes how to communicate so that value and worth are given to all ideas that are presented. This doesn't mean that everyone has to agree in the end, but it helps if the information is presented in such a way that people can all feel as if their voice was heard. Sometimes students need to start from an area that is more closely related to their lives.

This module solidly illuminates how some of the previous modules have been useful in getting to this stage of collaboration and will be instrumental in maintaining a successful group. The second principle presented in this module speaks to the balance of power and the sharing of resources. Not only are students provided a link to Module 2 in the reading, they are also given a brief example of why it is crucial to understand the dynamics of power and privilege. The portrayal of power and privilege in this module continues to ask students to think about what it means to have power. The example in this module talks about how students, faculty, and community members all have power that is very fluid as they move throughout this collaborative process. This example also serves to illustrate to students that their perceptions of engagement with community need to move beyond that of helping to that of serving/working with in the true context of engaging.

Module 5: Capacity Building

When used in succession, this final module can be used to tie everything together and give students one final tool for engaging with communities. Module 5 is about capacity building and is based on an asset-based approach. This module goes on to develop the information in Module 4, but also allows for reflection on the other modules. After students finish this module, they should be able to define capacity in its various forms and also the major tenets of capacity building, appreciate the differences in capacity building and problem-focused approaches to the work they will be doing in communities, be able to ascertain the five levels of capacity using the seven types of community assets, and understand that the nature of capacity building is sensitive to context, continuous, and may involve the movement of people, places, and ideas.

This module also presents another dimension of academic service-learning. Many of the examples from this module come from MSU's Community Engagement in Rural Ireland (CERI). In this study-abroad program, which is offered every summer, students work with local host families, community mentors, and native experts to get a firmer understanding of how engagement works in an international setting in collaboration with the Tochar Valley Rural Community Network, Co. Mayo, Ireland. These examples include reflections from both students and the faculty member who accompanies them on their six-week course. This piece illuminates the broad range and reach of service-learning and how versatile the *ToE* curriculum can be.

Capacity building is a topic that is very challenging to cover in one module, so this module is rich in text and references. The author was well aware of the level of critical thinking that is needed to really understand this topic. In fact, a student could take an entire class on this alone. The rich context is paired well with the accompanying examples. These examples go beyond scenarios and have pragmatic application tips that faculty can use to help further their utilization of the modules. These tips will also be useful for the students, providing a more in-depth look at where their engagement and their service can take them.

Conclusion of Modules

A student participating in the *ToE* curriculum or a faculty member who has chosen to investigate the different modules will both see that the modules build on each other in such a way that readers are constantly asked to review and reflect on the curriculum as a whole. This is one of the distinct advantages of using this type of curriculum: it not only prepares students to engage in service learning but it also allows them a space to have thoughtful reflections before, during, and after the action.

Modules 1 and 2 are quite useful for preflection activities. Module 1 gives the basis for service-learning and its importance to students in their academic and personal lives. For students from any type of higher education institution, the mission and act of service is addressed, and that is the foundation for the connection between the student and service. The essence is to make sure that the learning is scholarly and reflects the goals and objectives of the class. This is what helps the students make the connection between their service and their learning. After progressing to Module 2 and learning about themselves and what makes them unique, students are well equipped to work in groups and learn how the power dynamic, regardless of the form in which it comes, is an essential part of how their service-learning project will work. They will see that incorporating service into the learning experience is inherent in the mission of their college/university of choice, and that they are asked to follow in that vein. Beyond this call for service to reach out to different communities, it is essential to use this preparation time to focus on the understanding that this is work with and service with the community, and not a "helping" scenario. Power and privilege are not a reason to pity those who may have less or different privilege at any given point; students must realize the interplay and fluidity of these concepts.

Modules 3 and 4 are best used during the service-learning experience. Students will most likely have met their community agency partner by this time and will have had the opportunity to really think about their role in the service. This is important because Module 3 couples the information in the first two modules by presenting a way for students to be involved in the creation of the service project along with the community partner. Again, this continuity points to the desire students have to create ownership of the service-learning experience. Module 4 goes on to help guide the service-learners on the path of effective partnerships. It is important that these modules and the information within them be studied in conjunction with the students' service and engagement so the learning is even deeper. Students are using their service-learning opportunities to inform their course texts, as well as using the curriculum to inform their service-learning.

Conclusion

The web-based *ToE* modules exemplify a technology-rich, non-discipline-specific approach to handling the core service-learning components of preparation/preflection and reflection. More importantly, their development and implementation underscore the need for institutions embracing service-learning and their faculty to adhere to the basic principles and premises of quality service-learning as the pedagogy and practice proliferate. Service-learning and student civic engagement have moved from the "margins to the mainstream" (Pikerel & Peters, as cited in Langseth and Plater, p. 33), but such institutionalization need not and should not lead to complacency and diminished standards. Quite the opposite: if service-learning is to live up to its promise and provide a high-quality and desirable mechanism for institutions, faculty, and students to engage with community in the context of teaching and learning, then foundational work, while needing to adapt to circumstances of the twenty-first century, must continue to be embraced and implemented.

References

Ayers, J., & Lavin, J. (2003). *Preparation, action, reflection.* Retrieved December 22, 2008, from http://www.marylandpublicschools.org/MSDE/programs/servicelearning/PARDIA.htm.

Beekman, B. (2005, Fall). What it means to be a land-grant university. *MSU Alumni Magazine,* pp. 21–24.

Brown, R. E., Casey, K. M., Doberneck, D., Springer, N. C., Thornton, D. W., & Georgis, G. (2008). *Tools of engagement: Collaborating with community partners.* East Lansing: Michigan State University, University Outreach and Engagement. Retrieved August 5, 2008, from http://outreach.msu.edu/ tools/.

Butin, D. W. (2006). The limits of service-learning in higher education. *Review of Higher Education, 29*(4), 473–498.

Campus Compact. (n.d.). *Civic engagement at research universities.* Retrieved May 4, 2009, from http:// www.compact.org/initiatives/civic-engagement-at-research-universities/.

Carnegie foundation for the Advancement of Teaching. (2006). *The Carnegie classification of institutions of higher education.* Retrieved May 2, 2006, from http://carnegiefoundation.org/classifications/ index.asp?key=1213.

Casey, K. M., & Springer, N. C. (2006). Ancillary to integral: Momentum to institutionalize service-learning and civic engagement. In K. M. Casey, G. Davidson, S. Billig, & N. C. Springer (Eds.), *Advancing knowledge in service-learning: Research to transform the field* (pp. 207–222). Greenwich, CT: Information Age.

Concordia College. (n.d.). *Mission statement.* Retrieved December 22, 2008, from http://www.cord.edu/ About/mission1.php.

Cooper, D. D. (2006, Fall). Public Life in America (WRA 135): The Service-Learning writing project. *The Engaged Scholar Magazine, 1.*

Council for the Advancement of Standards in Higher Education. (2006). CAS *professional standards for higher education* (6th ed.). Washington, DC: Author.

Eyler, J. (2001, Summer). Creating your reflection map. *New Directions for Higher Education, 114,* 35–43.

Eyler, J. (2002). Reflection: Linking service and learning—linking students and communities. *Journal of Social Issues, 58*(3), 517–534.

Fisher, R., Ury, W., & Patton, B. (1991). *Getting to yes: Negotiating agreement without giving in* (2nd ed.). New York: Penguin.

Harper, V. D., & Harper, E. J. (2006). Understanding student self-disclosure typology through blogging. *The Qualitative Report, 11*(2), 251–261.

Higher Learning Commission: A Commission of the North Central Association of Colleges and Schools. (2003). *Institutional accreditation: An overview.* Retrieved May 3, 2006, from http:// ncahigherlearningcommission.org/download/20030verview.pdf.

International Association for Research on Service-Learning and Community Engagement (IARSLCE). (n.d.). *About us.* Retrieved May 4, 2009, from http://www.researchslce.org/Files/aboutus.html.

Langseth, M., & Plater, M. (Eds.). (2004). *Public work and the academy: An academic administrator's guide to civic engagement and service-learning.* Bolton, MA: Anker.

Learn and Serve America. (n.d.). *President's higher education community service honor roll.* Retrieved January 15, 2009, from http://www.learnandserve.gov/about/programs/higher_ed_honorroll.asp.

Michigan State University. (n.d.). *MSU Facts.* Retrieved May 4, 2009, from http://www.msu.edu/ thisismsu/facts.html.

Office of President LouAnna K. Simon. (n.d.). *MSU mission statement.* Retrieved December 22, 2008, from http://president.msu.edu/mission.php.

Office of the Registrar. (n.d.). *Course Description: TE 250.* Retrieved December 22, 2008, from http://www.reg.msu.edu/Courses/Request.asp.

Resource Center. (2002). *Using the PARE model in service-learning.* Tools and training for volunteer and service programs. Retrieved December 22, 2008, from http://www.nationalserviceresources.org/practices/17486.

Shumer, R. (1997). What research tells us about designing service learning programs. *NASSP Bulletin, 81*(18), 18–24. DOI: 10.1177/019263659708159104.

Tulane University. (n.d.). *University mission statement,* Retrieved August 2008 from http://www2.tulane.edu/administration_mission.cfm.

Weigert, K. M. (1998, Spring). Academic service learning: Its meaning and relevance. *New Directions in Teaching and Learning, 73,* 3–10.

Additional Reading

Holland, B. A. (2001, November). *Measuring the role of civic engagement in campus missions: Key concepts and challenges.* Speech presented at the ASHE Symposium on "Broadening the Carnegie Classification's Attention to Mission: Incorporating Public Service," Richmond, VA.

Eyler, J., & Giles, D. (1999). *Where's the learning in service-learning?* Jossey-Bass Higher and Adult Education Series. San Francisco: Jossey-Bass.

Fear, F. A., & Miller, P. P. (2006). *Coming to critical engagement: An autoethnographic exploration.* Lanham, MD: University Press of America.

The New Landscape of Engaged Scholarship: How Does Online Education Play a Role?

Craig D. Weidemann and Michael J. Offerman

Engaged scholarship has focused on teaching, research, and service within the concrete landscape of the university and its students, constituencies, and communities. The online landscape opens new opportunities for formerly location-bound students and faculty to work in virtual communities, engage in scholarship based in social networking, co-create course content, and involve external as well as university-based experts in curricular choices and assessment. Key issues surround the context and assessment of curricula and engagement at public, fully online, and other universities.

The Distance Education Student: A New Breed

When Ernest Boyer (1990) posited that "the 1990s will be the decade of undergraduate education" (p. xiii), he could not have foreseen the sea change in education soon to be brought about by technology. Within the decade of the '90s, the World Wide Web, email, cell phones, and other technologies fundamentally changed the way students received knowledge, shared knowledge, and used knowledge. That change has continued thanks to the advent of Web 2.0 and its many applications already in place. Technology, including wikis, Flickr, Twitter, blogs, and dozens of interactive social networks, has the potential of becoming omnipresent within a very short time, foretelling a major new avenue of engagement, especially in the teaching process, and a new way for students to participate in the creation of knowledge and content. The concrete landscape of engagement—universities, students, and communities—has been joined by the virtual landscape of networked online education.

Distance education, which in the early 1990s was primarily conducted through correspondence, had accommodated older technologies of radio and television delivery without

51

substantive change, relying primarily on the lecture/reading format. Certain technologies such as Pic-Tel, which allowed two-way audio and video communication, were available; however, they required both teacher and students to be location-bound. Most learning designers and faculty members did not take full advantage of even the simple communication tools that they had available. List serves, for example, provided fine learner-to-learner, and learner-to-group opportunities for text-based communication. Coupled with a simple website and an FTP client, there could be plenty of group work. That said, faculty members were missing a lot in terms of multimedia, version control, and other niceties such as synchronized voice and simple syndication.

Initially, educators hailed the Internet as a repository for even more readings—a veritable library at the student's fingertips. Even though email and print-structured correspondence courses posted online allowed students and teachers to communicate directly, the process was ponderous and time-consuming. There was little opportunity for student-to-student interaction and the collaboration and engagement that results from such interaction. Early online courses, in part because instructors had not yet learned to make the most of their asynchronous or nonconcurrent nature, did not lend themselves well to active learning and collaborative models (Egan, Sebastian, & Welch, 1991).

Education at a distance, since its inception in the 1890s with the advent of rural free delivery, was considered of particular value to students who were location-bound. Online education still serves that audience, though the appeal of online education has spread to on-campus students; to many highly mobile learners who connect via wireless networks at a distance, including adult students in both in rural and urban environments; and to active-duty military stationed around the world. In this chapter, we explore new opportunities for formerly location-bound students and faculty to work in virtual communities, engage in scholarship based on social networking, co-create course content, and involve external as well as university-based experts in curricular choices and assessment.

The Current State of Online Education

The 2006 National Survey of Student Engagement (NSSE) polled almost four thousand students from 367 different colleges and universities who identified themselves as distance education learners in that they were taking all their courses online during the current academic term. NSSE found that distance education students differed substantially from their on-campus counterparts. Distance education students are older, with the median age of first-year learners being 25 and that of seniors being 32 versus 18 and 22 years, respectively, for on-campus students. Fully 70 percent were caring for dependents and half worked at a job for more than 30 hours a week. The survey showed that "distance education students generally chose this format for reasons of convenience and being able to work at their own pace." Moreover, 63 percent of distance education students were the first in their families to attend college, compared with 42 percent of other students (p. 15). "While distance education students are comparable to other students in terms of academic activities, they were much less likely to participate in active and collaborative learning activities. Even so, distance education students report greater educational gains and are more satisfied overall with their college experience. These mixed results illustrate that the educational and personal needs of such students may differ from those of other students" (p. 15). These findings are supported by other studies including Hvorecký (2004), who focuses on the potential of e-learning in third-world countries and cites several barriers to achieving goals because of economic and organizational issues.

It should be noted that the NSSE data apply to students who indicated that they took all their courses online. The most recent report from the Alfred P. Sloan Foundation—*Online Nation* (Allen & Seaman, 2007)—notes that the number of students taking at least one online course grew to 3.48 million in 2006, more than double the number reported four years earlier (p. 7).

The New Landscape of Web 2.0

The NSSE study, published in 2006, was just beginning to see the possibilities of education enhanced or enabled by Web 2.0. In a presentation to the American Center for the Study of Distance Education, Miller (2008) predicted "a changing relationship between our institutions and our students" (p. 2). At the beginning of the Internet revolution, he postulated "the rise of the 'empowered student' or 'community of scholars' as a result of students having better direct access to large databases, video and textual materials" (p. 2).

In and of themselves, Web 2.0 applications represent a shift in access to and use of Technology-Mediated Distance Education (TMDE). As Ozdemir and Abrevaya (2007) indicated in a review of TMDE across higher education institutions for the years 1997–1998 and 2000–2001, decisions to adopt one- or two-way video or audio, synchronous or asynchronous Internet or CD-ROM technology were the purview of the institutions (p. 8). Today, however, distance education students, perhaps more than the institutions they attend, have access to dynamic social networks through blogs, wikis, Facebook, YouTube, social bookmarking, and other Web 2.0 applications. The result, as Miller (2008) describes it, is "a demand for a new, more collaborative, more inquiry-oriented approach to learning—on campus and off—that reflects how people use technology at work and at home" (p. 2). Through interactive technology and engaged teaching, distance education students are becoming empowered to collaborate in their courses and add to academe's knowledge base. And across the spectrum of distance education, "instruction is becoming more learner-centered, non-linear, and self-directed" (Howell, Williams, & Lindsay, 2003, p. 7).

Diffusion and Acceptance

So, within twenty years, the landscape for education has changed radically. The cumbersome 28K dial-up has given way to broadband; slow downloads and a curriculum still lodged in the print world have yielded to a robust community of online teachers and learners using multiple technologies to advance the curriculum; and the concept of engaged scholarship is finding a foothold in the online landscape.

That is not to say that all concerns have been met or all challenges overcome. Entrance into the online environment requires certain characteristics that not all students have.

These learners must be already well educated. In order to take these "excellent" courses from leading universities, students typically need prerequisite credentials, usually of a fairly high order.

They must be proficient in reading and writing English, at a high academic level. They must have ready access to powerful computing hardware and software, and a high-speed and reliable Internet connection. They must be computer literate. The more at ease they are with a wide variety of sophisticated computer applications, the more benefit they will derive from Web-based courses (Spronk, 2002, p. 4).

It is, for example, a mistaken assumption that all young people are adept at using the Internet. Hargittai (2008), speaking at the Supernova Conference, found that 43 percent of a group of students attending the University of Illinois at Chicago were not able to complete a search task primarily because of their misunderstanding of Internet terminology and inability to navigate links (paragraph 1). Hargittai looks across age, ethnicity, and gender, finding "that there is great deal of variance in abilities to locate content online. Merely offering people a network-connected machine will not ensure that they can use the medium to meet their needs because they may not be able to maximally take advantage of all that the Web has to offer" (conclusion).

Trends and Drivers

"Online education," according to Paulsen (2003, as cited in Zondiros, 2008), is "characterized by the use of a computer network to present or distribute some educational content and the provision of two-way communication via a computer network so that students may benefit from communication with fellow students, teachers and other staff" (p. 3). "Juler (1990, as cited in Zondiros) puts it in the right context: 'Distance education means creating educational communities in which teachers, students and others are linked in discourse wherever they may be through networks appropriate to their circumstances'" (p. 2).

Li (2008), speaking at the Supernova conference organized by Wharton Legal Studies, commented that how people actually interact with the web and utilize online collaborative tools has not been studied well. "Yet much of today's Internet revolves around individual users, the content they create, the communities they form, and the transactions they choose" (paragraph 4). Li proposes a "social technology ladder." On the lowest rung of the latter are those she terms "inactives," comprising 44 percent of all U.S. adults who were online in 2007. The next 25 percent consists of the "joiners," who visit social networking sites like MySpace. A further 15 percent collect and aggregate information, post ratings and reviews, or contribute to blogs and online forums. According to Li, "Only 18 percent of all online Americans actually create content, publishing an article or a blog at least once a month, maintaining a webpage or uploading content to sites like YouTube" (paragraph 7). Furthermore, as Loechner (2008) states, "According to a recent ThirdAge/JWT Boom study, people over age 40 participate heavily in word-of-mouth and value personal recommendations and expert opinions, but they have not embraced social networking or blogs despite being heavy users of other online services" (paragraph 1). "Boomers want to connect and interact with others in their communities around shared interests and common issues, but they use more traditional web communications tools, such as email, to keep in touch" (Loechner, paragraph 2). However, Li predicts, "In 5–10 years, social networks will be everywhere" (paragraph 9).

Engagement Informs Pedagogy and Scholarship at Research 1 Universities

The definition of engagement in any institution of higher education will inevitably inform the way that institution perceives the value of teaching and scholarship in the online environment. Definitions proposed in the 1990s focused on integration of teaching research and service and encouraged faculty, staff, and students to address pressing societal changes faced by communities. This form of outreach was, in every practical way, unidirectional.

In 2000, Penn State joined a number of major research universities to lead a national effort to advance engaged scholarship. To advance this agenda, a faculty-led group, the UniSCOPE Learning Community, published a report challenging the university community to "implement a model of scholarship for the 21st century that equitably recognizes the full range of teaching, research, and service scholarship" (Hyman et al., 2000, p. 42).

One specific contribution of UniSCOPE has been to recognize the importance of outreach and engaged scholarship as dimensions of the scholarship of teaching, research and creative accomplishment, and service. The term *outreach* suggests a unidirectional flow of information, technology transfer, and technical assistance from university to community. The notion of *engaged scholarship* reflects, most importantly, a reciprocal, mutually beneficial, two-way exchange between university and community, where the knowledge, expertise, and experience of each both inform and are informed by the other. Both outreach and engagement can reflect legitimate and credible scholarship. Engagement offers the promise of achieving a sustainable connection between university and community and enriching university teaching, research, and service (Pennsylvania State University Faculty Senate Report, 2008, p. 2).

So, within that academic community, the definition of engagement appears to be migrating toward an understanding that engagement is scholarship of teaching, research, creative accomplishment, and service that involves citizens and the university working in partnership to create and apply knowledge that addresses pressing societal issues and strengthen civic responsibility and democracy through mutually beneficial relationships.

The UniSCOPE report with its emphasis on counting engagement toward tenure was a response from a Research I institution to Boyer's (1990) comments on applied scholarship: "Today, almost all colleges and universities say faculty should engage in teaching, research, *and* service, but when it comes to tenure and promotion, the latter often is forgotten" (p. 36).

However, whatever the platform, on campus or online, assessment of the value of the engaged scholarship at most Research I Institutions has been the purview of the faculty. Boyer (1998) commented, "The work of the professoriate—regardless of the form it takes— must be carefully assessed. Excellence is the yardstick by which all scholarship must be measured. ... Faculty who engage in research, in teaching, in service, or in integrative work must demonstrate to the satisfaction of their peers that high performance standards have been met" (p. 28). The concept that online engaged scholarship and teaching may be informed by the community of learners—in fact, that there may be co-production of knowledge—might be disruptive for traditional pedagogy. Within the Penn State UniSCOPE report, as well as in policies at a growing number of other public institutions, is the concept that "mechanisms for documenting and disseminating outreach and engaged scholarship" should be developed (Pennsylvania State University Faculty Senate, 2008, p. 3).

Engagement and Online Institutions

Engagement within a wholly online institution is both similar to and different from that found in other types of universities. As in other universities, engaged scholarship in the online university must be informed by the community of learners and by the broader community or communities of interest. How that engagement occurs is affected, in part, by the audience served. Online universities primarily serve adult students who demand program curricula that result in clear learning outcomes that will have positive impact on their careers. Within an engaged online university, faculty work consists not only of curriculum development, teaching, and learning outcomes assessment, but also engagement with interested communities, including employers and professional organizations.

The definition of community for an online institution, more than a traditional residential campus academic community, is altered in that there really is not a geographical community but rather one or more communities of interest that come together around the discipline, profession, or area of practice. These communities include the faculty, students, alumni, professional associations, individual practitioners, and employers of people prepared in this profession. Capella University, for example, seeks to engage the entirety of the community and believes that the community can be engaged in the co-creation of curriculum, content, and even assessment. Further, the university asserts that alumni, employers, and the professions have a role to play in informing the faculty of what program outcomes are necessary and desired as well as other aspects of the curriculum. Students have a role to play in making learning activities, courses, and programs relevant, rigorous, and meaningful. And these community members can help co-create in ways that ensure high-quality learning outcomes. Faculty performance reviews should consider how effectively faculty engage not only with the student community but also with the broader communities of interest. Although it is clear that co-creation of content and collaboration around communities of interest does occur in traditional settings, the technologies available in the online environment offer mechanisms for engaging specific communities across the virtual landscape. It is impossible to predict the future of online learning, but Web 2.0, digitally borne content, and open educational resources (OER) are already moving the discussion toward open distribution and reuse, sharing, and remixing of derivative works, thus allowing for community/university co-developed pedagogy on lesson, course, and program levels (Hargittai & Walejko, 2008).

Curricular Design with Industry Credentialing Bodies

Where this has taken Capella, among other online institutions, is to a strong commitment to transparency, resulting in a very engaged process of curriculum development with key external communities. The concept of transparency requires that the university be open about how it makes decisions, what those decisions are and mean, and how the results of the decisions are evaluated. For example, with curriculum, faculty start by engaging practitioners and employers from a profession to help identify outcomes for someone who wants to earn a bachelor's degree, master's degree, or doctorate in that professional practice area. The program is then designed and redesigned to focus on those outcomes and to create clarity for students about what activities they will engage in. These activities ultimately demonstrate that outcomes have been achieved and provide coherence to each program offered.

That concept is not unknown at research institutions, such as Penn State, where content for professional degrees and credit certificate programs is informed by industry professionals, though course development, learning objects, and assessment are the purview of the faculty.

In many instances, transparency offers value inside and outside the institution. For example, being transparent about program-level learning outcomes, planned learning activities, curriculum maps, and rubrics is very important to both faculty and students. Transparency about the aggregate results of assessments of learning outcomes achievement, program performance, and alumni feedback is important to employers and practitioners. Best practices, then, would anticipate that an institution, offering a professional program, whether online or on campus, would ensure that it delivers on its promise of value and specific curricular elements for the specified industry sector.

Engaging Students in Program Assessment and Improvement

"As a flexible educational application, distance education is linked to absolute freedom of choice when it comes to the means employed in communicating and conveying information" (Lionarakis, 2008, p. 3). A teacher may present information in ways designed to reach students with different learning styles. No longer committed to being the "sage on the stage," the teacher can use video case histories to engage visual learners, provide vocal feedback to encourage those who need auditory cues, even employ external devices to allow tactile learners to manipulate data. Students, too, create context for their coursework, often drawing from external sources, creating personal commentary, and building alternative discussion tracks that may persist past the ending of the course.

The combination of transparency and openness to hearing from students about how a program is working provides an opportunity for them to become actively engaged in program improvement. This assessment may be done formally, using student surveys and evaluations, or informally, and it may be made unique through the advancement of new online social networking pedagogies. Alumni may also be surveyed to assess the impact of degree completion on their career and professional lives. And employers of graduates may be asked about the impact they realized from employee degree completion. Online institutions, in addition to professional and adult-serving institutions, see transparency as what is expected in terms of program outcomes and whether these outcomes are being achieved. Reporting the aggregate results creates a powerful way to engage in continuous quality improvement based on the involvement and engagement of the communities being served. This process includes both the profession and the student body and, by extension, the broader community at large.

This process can produce a vibrant set of discussions among faculty about what constitutes a program, a curriculum, a rubric, an assessment, and so on. These discussions deal with the fundamentals of the professoriate and serve to energize the faculty as a whole. In turn, students become engaged in offering reactions and reality checks on what is being done. Online learning allows the construction of relationships and communities where engaged scholarship can take place.

The Scholarship of Online Engagement

It appears, then, that whatever the type of institution of higher education, public, private, campus-based, or online, there is interest in and a possibility for engaged scholarship with virtual communities. As noted, access to online communities of learners is governed in some ways by demographics: younger students, those in the military, and those accessing courses from other countries are more apt to use Web 2.0 technologies than older students, who are lower on the social technology ladder.

With those restrictions in mind, the scholarship of online engagement may be focused on delivery and effectiveness of instruction, curricular issues, retention of knowledge and measurement practices, technical needs of differing segments, and use of extracurricular resources or authorities, including student input. Moreover, scholarship may be informed by data generated in online delivery. Data collected online or through social networks may be converted into actionable information in ways not possible in other delivery modes. The very fact that learning is occurring online means that the demonstration of learning outcomes occurs in a digital format and is captured data. The resulting data can be managed to allow for rapid understanding and any necessary corrective action to improve quality of instruction, support, or other aspects of the learning experience. Information can be used openly and transparently, engaging the learner and the broader community in unprecedented ways. Not only might it be possible for digital artifacts to be created, making analysis and transparency easier than with nondigital artifacts, but online learning might also change the nature of learning and the artifacts that are created. If a learner is engaging in a pedagogy designed around reflective learning (didactic, individual, or socially networked), the digital nature of the reflective artifacts (process and content) may change the nature of learning.

Critical Issues Related to Engaged Scholarship

To develop mutually beneficial, reciprocal relationships and engaged scholarship that address public problems and benefit broadly defined communities in an online environment calls for attention to critical issues that may not be of concern in other areas. Engaged scholarship is "shaped by multiple perspectives and deals with difficult, involving questions that require long-term effort during which results may be, known over time as particular pieces of the puzzle are solved" (Holland, 2005, p. 3).

Among the issues that face engagement within the online community are access, educational technologies, faculty and institutional support, online pedagogy, and accountability or transparency.

Access

As we've seen, the question of access to online learning opportunities is multifaceted and clearly not limited only to the critical issue of affordability. Affordability must be addressed through new models of financial aid, innovative scholarships, and new public policy and programs to support online students, especially adults studying part-time. However, there are other many other key issues that impact the access to effective online learning, including the abilities and needs of diverse communities. Access to broadband or wireless technologies has an obvious impact; however, more subtle issues, such as opportunity and mastery of Web 2.0 technologies, age, location, and ethnicity, may also play roles in restricting or limiting participation in social networks (Hargittai, n.d.). Access includes the creation of an open, welcoming, engaging community that is open to diverse backgrounds and perspectives. Increasingly, we are learning to utilize new technologies to create such environments more effectively (Diverse Issues in Higher Education, 2008).

Educational Technologies

Within the landscape of online education, new educational technologies are providing not only platforms for communication but also ways of adapting teaching to meet the needs of learners. A Penn State World Campus student, for instance, may find materials on Facebook, discover virtual student services on Second Life, or contribute to an online chat room or blog. The discussions generated may be used to prepare a case, contribute to a portfolio, or provide feedback.

There is controversy among faculty regarding the openness of the online environment. Many faculty members are strong supporters of the national open courseware initiative, led by MIT and other institutions. In fact, more than 70 percent of MIT faculty have made their course syllabi available online through the university's Open Courseware project. However, there are an equal number of faculty members who are wary of allowing open access to their intellectual property. Thierstein (2008), for example, addresses the role of the faculty in the OER world, specifically the question of intellectual property in the online environment. "Because of its open nature, does the OER community demand that the university faculty member give up their intellectual property and place their creations into the open space?" (paragraph 5). Questions of a similar nature may be posted on a blog that serves as a collection point for individual reflection. Although not tied to university policy-making entities, the discussion within the online community may inform the deliberations of governing bodies in the future. Miller (2008) comments "As the Web moves from a publishing environment to a collaboration environment ... we enter what some are calling a 'conversation economy'" (p. 2).

Faculty and Institutional Support

Faculty and institutional support for engagement has been growing as the application of engagement criteria to tenure review (UniScope, 2000) indicates. The Sloan Consortium's *Online Nation* (Allen & Seaman, 2007) disclosed that 59.1 percent of academic leaders now see online learning as "critical to the long-term strategy" of their institutions (p. 16). However, there is still widespread lack of understanding of online teaching and the research that may be conducted in the online environment. Although in some cases a faculty member's entire teaching load may be online, universities may not have equitable reward systems for such teaching. Time pressures apply to all faculty; however, managing online learner expectations may result in 24/7 office hours. Also, unique nuances of teaching online must be

59

considered in the promotion and tenure process. For example, early reports indicate that, on average, student evaluations of online instructors are lower than they are for face-to-face instruction. This is an area for research and must be studied further. That may put the faculty member at a disadvantage in a tenure-track institution where research and publication provide additional academic pressures. However, as Miller (2008) points out, "New kinds of academic communities are emerging that may redefine the relationship between faculty members and their institutions in the long run. Projects like the CIC's CourseShare, the Great Plains IDEA, and the Worldwide University Network's shared programs ... bring faculty from multiple institutions into an inter-institutional community where they can expand the impact of their specialized research" (p. 8).

Pedagogy in the Online Environment

Miller (2008) was quoted earlier in this chapter as describing a demand for a new, more collaborative, more inquiry-oriented approach to learning that is driven by technology (p. 3). There are opportunities to rethink pedagogy in online learning. Restricting online learning by merely asking if it is equivalent to face-to-face learning may limit learning innovation and may set the bar too low. What may need to emerge and may, in fact, be emerging is a separate online pedagogy that is very different from what is done in either face-to-face or blended learning situations. This new pedagogy may be built, in part, on the collaborative and social networking aspects of technology that offer exciting new ways to think about, to link teaching and engagement to, and to conceptualize scholarship as different in the campus-based mode and the online mode. In doing so, it is understood that different roles will be required, different outcomes anticipated, and different expectations and assessments acknowledged.

Accountability/Transparency

As we learn more about the advantages online delivery offers for engagement, we can hope that transparency and collaboration are emphasized. Working as an engaged and informed society should be held as a strong value and a bond by both the institution and the community.

In addition to the faculty who provide the foundation of knowledge, online curricula, in the transparent world, should be informed by at least two critical audiences: the profession which students are preparing to practice, and the students and alumni in the programs. The new technologies of Web 2.0 allow faculty members to engage these groups, to listen to their concerns and contributions, to involve them in decision making, and to communicate clearly to them the factors that are used to construct and evaluate courses and curricula. At the heart of the issue is the determination of how much emphasis should be placed on comments from outside academe. Miller (2008) puts this succinctly:

> Today's world demands that people have the skill to work collaboratively across boundaries and to participate in communities that are not defined by geography and time. This, in turn, calls for a new pedagogy that redefines what we mean by a "learning community." For most public colleges and universities—which need to be responsive to workforce and community needs—the new environment demands a curriculum that not only ensures that students gain discipline-based core knowledge but that also emphasizes active and collaborative learning, inquiry-based approaches that help students create useable knowledge out of information and apply that to solving problems. (p. 9)

In the process of becoming more transparent and engaged with students, programs, and support services at universities delivering distance education have shifted, sometimes rather substantially, in recognition of the makeup and needs of the student body. Surveys, focus groups, and listening sessions with students as well as faculty are used extensively. Faculty and administration hear what is on students' minds and can locate roadblocks in terms of services and/or learning. These sessions are one part of being open, transparent, and engaged with what is actually an engaged national/international community of distant or online learners.

A Dialogue for the Next Decade

Any look into the future of engagement in an online environment must acknowledge the failure of imagination in the past. Who in 1988 or even 1998 could have dreamed of the proliferation of social networks? Who would have imagined the breakthroughs in digital technology that pack an entire world into a handheld "phone"? Even the cost of technology has performed in astounding ways—allowing distribution in rural Africa of basic computers that can be powered by cranking them and can connect via satellite to the Internet.

Can we extrapolate the engaged landscape of 2018 or 2028? Here, then, are five issues that may still be under discussion.

1. **What are the implications of social networking and collaboration technology on the concept of "engaged scholarship in the online environment"?**

To begin to address this question, we may look first to a broadly accepted definition of engagement. Although many institutions work toward an accommodation of engagement within the traditional rubrics of scholarship, the variations evident in the literature may hamper wholehearted acceptance of any single institution's definition of engaged scholarship. Additionally, differing metrics of traditional faculty-determined investigations and measures determined by learners and/or industry-specific credentialing organizations may be mutually exclusive through use of different vocabularies, collection methods, and modes of analysis.

Web 2.0 yields a very different community dynamic than does a geographic community. Reciprocity may be enhanced, though ability to observe in situ might be complicated by the difficulty of data validation online. Social networking leads to concerns about privacy, anonymity, and confidentiality, just as physical networking does; however, protecting confidential information may become even more of an issue, as may intellectual property rights in an "open" network.

2. **What are the implications of the shift from teacher-centered to learner-centered for faculty and students?**

One of the basic tenets of a shift to being learner-centered is that learners become more responsible for their own learning. The teacher is not going to be in charge and guide them through a course or program. With this shift in responsibility comes a shift in perceived authority, with learners, over time, expecting to be engaged in the way learning is planned, developed, delivered, and even assessed. There is a collaboration that occurs between faculty and the learner community. This shift is not without problems and challenges, but it also offers opportunities for engagement of the entire community. It offers a way to realize

Miller's description of a new, more collaborative and inquiry-oriented approach to teaching and learning.

The power of engaged online learning portends amazing discoveries and learning in virtual communities. The opportunity to engage online with students with common interests from the residence hall to the far corners of the world will challenge their interest in traditional face-to-face instruction. However, rather than advancing a dichotomy between face-to-face and online instruction, there will be a merging of online learning with traditional classroom instruction. This blending of both pedagogies will provide a format that will enable learners to find richer and far more participatory learning opportunities. It will also have a tremendous impact on the role of the professoriate.

3. What will the impact of open courseware be?

There has been an explosion of interest in open courseware across the globe. The digital publication of generally well-regarded educational materials allows free and open use. However, in most cases, people using the courseware will not have access to instructors nor will they earn credits or receive certification. The very fact that MIT (a leader in open access to its courses) has 1,800 courses—lectures, notes, exams, and videos—on the MIT OpenCourseWare site (http://ocw.mit.edu) demolishes the notion that universities are of value because they hold knowledge. Students anywhere can sample a class or plunge into a curriculum. Curiosity can be satisfied, ambition excited. Although issues of intellectual property ownership must be addressed, accessible open courseware actually may encourage the knowledge seeker to take the next step and apply for admission to the academy. In much the same way that a library of great books is accessible to everyone, OER opens virtual doors to lectures, readings, and more.

Perhaps the greatest potential is the opportunity for engagement on a global scale. MIT reports (2005–2006) that the site averages a million visitors a month, with translations adding another half a million. Visitors come from virtually every nation, with educators and self-identified learners forming the audience. As more and more universities invite everyone to share courses, the evolution of new courses becomes more probable.

4. What issues of globalization and worldwide competition will be relevant in ten years?

Will China be the place to study in 2018? Will academic institutions internationalize their curricula? The relevance of U.S. and European academic disciplines has been called into question insofar as they relate to the perceived problems of the world's population. If they trend toward "class-and race-based geospatial polarization" (AERA, 2007, paragraph 1), will they be able to remain germane?

The experience of European nations in adopting the Bologna Accord suggests that any move toward shared standards will take time to enact. Cross-border standard setting has not worked smoothly among the states in the United States and takes even more time among nations. Although partnerships are important in connecting communities, both local and international, to global issues and resources through higher education, mechanisms for attaining agreements seem to be unaffected by the urgency of the challenge.

However, access online and through Web 2.0 has already begun to enable multinational and cross-cultural collaborations and new opportunities to create and disseminate knowledge globally.

5. How will ease of use impact lifelong learning?

One of the features of online education is its flexibility in dealing with learner needs and educational ambitions. Adult learners will constitute a continuing "bubble" in the educational system. As the technical world changes, they will need to update skills. Changing careers can be anticipated, as can changes within industries. It is already possible to personalize the online educational experience for many adult learners, taking into account their preferred learning mode (e.g., auditory/visual/kinetic learning). Computer simulations are used to teach surgical procedures, model dealing with hazmat situations, and instruct pilots.

Adult learners will continue to demand quality and accountability from their educational providers. It will be up to those institutions to adapt, measure, and control the technologies of the future in a manner that is transparent and engages the adult learner and the broader community.

Conclusion

The landscape of online learning has changed significantly through Web 2.0 applications, especially social networking, interactivity, and use of multiple platforms. Key issues surround the context and assessment of curricula and engagement at public and other types of universities. Increasingly, both context and content are being proffered by online learners. The extent to which that input is used to modify or inform the online curriculum has rested with faculty and administration; however, more and more individuals and community or credentialing organizations are influencing curriculum and course development. Additionally, students are building inquiry-based skills that allow them to use online communities, in conjunction with faculty, to add to the knowledge of their disciplines.

References

Allen, I. E., & Seaman, J. (2007, October). *Online nation: Five years of growth in online learning*. The Sloan Consortium. Retrieved June 5, 2008, from http://www.sloan-c.org/publications/survey/pdf/online_nation.pdf.

American Educational Research Association (AERA). (2007). *2008 AERA program theme: Research on schools, neighborhoods, and communities: Toward civic responsibility*. Retrieved August 11, 2008, from http://www.aera.net/meetings/Default.aspx?menu_id=342&id=2898.

Boyer, E. L. (1990). *Scholarship reconsidered: Priorities of the professoriate*. Princeton, NJ: Carnegie Foundation for the Advancement of Teaching.

Diverse Issues in Higher Education. (2008, October 9). *Minority students turn to online schools for advanced degrees*. Retrieved October 9, 2008, from http://www.diverseeducation.com/artman/publish/article_6493.shtml.

Egan, M., Sebastian, J., & Welch, M. (1991, March). Effective television teaching: Perceptions of those who count most … distance learners. In Proceedings of the Rural Education Symposium, Nashville, TN (ED342 579). Retrieved June 5, 2008, from www.uidaho.edu/eo/dist9.html.

Hargittai, E. (n.d.). As quoted in *"Not a Site, but a Concept": Tapping the Power of Social Networking*. Retrieved July 9, 2008, from http://Knowledge@Wharton.upenn.edu.

Hargittai, E. (2008). *Second-level digital divide: Differences in people's online skills.* Retrieved October 22, 2008, from http://www.firstmonday.org/issues/issue7_4/hargittai/#author.

Hargittai, E., & Walejko, G. (2008, March). The participation divide: Content creation and sharing in the digital age. *Information, Communication and Society, 11*(2), 239–256.

Holland, B.A. (2005). *Scholarship and mission in the 21st century university: The role of engagement.* Australian Universities Quality Agency Forum Proceedings. Retrieved June 5, 2008, from http://www.auqa.edu.au/.

Howell, S. L., Williams, P. B., & Lindsay, N. K. (2003, Fall). Thirty-two trends affecting distance education: An informed foundation for strategic planning. *Online Journal of Distance Learning Administration, VI* (III). State University of West Georgia, Distance Education Center. Retrieved June 5, 2008, from http://www.westga.edu/~distance/ojdla/fa1163/howel163.html.

Hvorecký, J. (2004). Can e-learning break the digital divide? *European Journal of Open, Distance, and E-Learning (EURODL).* Retrieved October 7, 2008, from www.eurodl.org/materials/contrib/2004/Hvorecky.htm.

Hyman, D., Ayers, J. E., Cash, E. H., Fahnline, D. E., Gold, D. P., Gurgevich, E. A., et al. (2008). *UniSCOPE 2000: A multidimensional model of scholarship for the 21st century.* University Park, PA: The UniSCOPE Community.

Knapp, L. G., Kelly-Reid, J. E., & Grinder, S. A. (2008, October). Postsecondary institutions in the United State: Fall 2007 degrees and other awards conferred: 2006–07, and 12-month enrollment: 2006–07. *First Look.* U.S. Department of Education, IES-National Center for Education Statistics.

Li, C. (2008, July 9). *"Not a site, but a concept": Tapping the power of social networking.* Paper presented at the Supernova Conference. Retrieved July 9, 2008, from http://Knowledge@Wharton.upenn.edu.

Lionarakis, A. (2008). The theory of distance education and its complexity. *European Journal of Open, Distance, and E-Learning (EURODL).* Paper presented at EDEN Annual Conference 2008, Lisbon, Portugal.

Loechner, J. (July 24, 2008). *Boomers are not bloggers.* Research Brief from the Center for Media Research in PRSA Issues and Trends. Retrieved July 24, 2008, from http://www.mediapost.com/blogs/research_brief/?m=200807.

Massachusetts Institute of Technology. (2005–2006). *MIT OpenCourseWare.* MIT Reports to the President, 2005–2006. Available at http://web.mit.edu/annualreports/pres06/02.04.pdf.

Miller, G. E. (2008). *Convergence or transformation: Optional futures for distance education.* Paper presented at National University Telecommunications Network Conference. Park City, UT.

National Survey of Student Engagement (NSSE). (2006). *Engaged learning: Fostering success for all students.* Bloomington, IN: Center for Postsecondary Research School of Education. Retrieved May 5, 2008, from http://nsse.iub.edu/NSSE_2006_Annual_Report/docs/NSSE_2006_Annual_Report.pdf.

Ozdemir, Z. D., & Abrevaya, J. (2007). Adoption of technology-mediated distance education: A longitudinal analysis. *Science Direct.* Retrieved October 15, 2008, from http://www.sciencedirect.com/.

Spronk, B. (2002). *Globalisation, ODL and gender: Not everyone's world is getting smaller.* Unpublished manuscript, International Extension College, Cambridge, UK.

Zondiros, D. (2008). Online distance education and globalization: Its impact on educational access, inequality and exclusion. *European Journal of Open, Distance, and E-learning (EURODL).* Retrieved October 30, 2008, from http://www.eurodl.org/materials/special.2008/Dimitris_Zondiros.htm.

Expertise, the Cooperative Extension Service, and Engaged Scholarship

Thomas G. Coon

One of the earliest models of university engagement in the United States is the Cooperative Extension Service (CES). The CES was created by an act of Congress (Smith-Lever Act, 1914) as a partnership between the U.S. Department of Agriculture (USDA) and state governments through their land-grant universities. Originally termed the agricultural extension service, its intent was to "diffuse among the people of the United States useful and practical information on subjects relating to agriculture and home economics, and to encourage application of the same." The service was quickly embraced by universities across the nation. In fact, many states had already begun to create an agricultural extension system before passage of the federal legislation. For example, the Michigan legislature had adopted legislation two years earlier that authorized county governments to form memoranda of understanding that would allow counties to provide funds to Michigan's land-grant institution, Michigan Agricultural College, in order to provide services of agricultural agents to citizens of the counties. Even earlier, the first agricultural agent in the United States was hired in 1906 to address challenges faced by cotton farmers in Texas brought on by the introduction of boll weevils from Mexico.

The language of the Smith-Lever legislation does not reflect an engagement philosophy; it speaks more from the perspective of a one-way delivery of information, the content of which would be determined by experts from the university and from the federal agency. And for much of the early history of CES, that model prevailed as the norm, reflecting a sense that because farmers and homemakers were less educated than university faculty, they were less informed of what information might be useful to them. However, over nearly a century of practice, Cooperative Extension systems across the nation have become more focused on co-determining the information needs to be addressed, reflecting recognition that the stakeholders served by CES are well educated and have access to information apart from that provided by the university. This is manifested in several ways. For example, the U.S. Department of Agriculture requires that universities with CES programs conduct a statewide assessment of needs every five years and develop a plan that prioritizes those needs and addresses them (e.g., Johnsrud & Rauschkolb, 1989). More locally, most CES systems rely on county extension councils to participate in the needs assessment and prioritization process and to provide informal feedback on program effectiveness and impact. In Michigan State University Extension, the County Extension Director is charged with the responsibility of engaging in regular consultation with both an advisory council of volunteers and the elected County Board of Commissioners.

Among the many changes in CES since its early decades, several key alterations reflect the movement of CES toward a model of engagement as defined by the Kellogg Commission (1999). These include (1) a formalization of the needs assessment process that engages the public in identifying and prioritizing information needs; (2) an expansion of the reach of community relationships to go beyond the county government and to include other governmental entities, corporations, nongovernmental nonprofit organizations, and individual enterprises; and (3) efforts to engage the broader university in the delivery of information and education beyond issues related to agriculture and home economics.

From the outset, the Cooperative Extension system has been implemented through a partnership between the USDA and the individual states. The state side of the partnership varies between states, but in all cases it involves the land-grant university or universities in the state, and the aspects of state authority that are vested in county or parish governments. In Michigan, for example, Michigan State University (MSU, formerly Michigan Agricultural College) is the designated university partner for Cooperative Extension across the state and has formal agreements with the County Boards of Commissioners in all of Michigan's eighty-three counties to provide the services of the Cooperative Extension system. Two American Indian tribal colleges, Bay Mills Community College and Saginaw Chippewa Community College, were incorporated into the system of land-grant colleges and universities in 1994, but because they are not universities of state governments, they are not vested with the same connections to county governments that MSU has been granted.

Throughout the history of MSU Extension, local Extension programming has been developed in partnership with county governments. In eighty-two of Michigan's eighty-three counties, the county government provides an office for MSU Extension and provides support staff and funds for operating costs associated with Extension programs. The County Extension Director is an employee of MSU Extension and in many cases is treated by the county as a department head within the county governmental structure. Funding for the office and hiring of the staff is contributed by the county. The County Extension Director works with county leaders to identify the program priorities for that county and coordinates the work of county support staff and MSU Extension professionals assigned to the county. Extension professionals are funded by a combination of federal, state, and county appropriations, along with funds from grants and contracts from governmental agencies and nongovernment partners.

The needs assessment process has grown from a periodic discussion between county extension officials and county government to a regular process that involves more formalized means of needs assessment, including surveys, structured focus groups, and systematic interviews. This process is implemented not only at the county level, but also at the state level, and among representatives of other governmental units and nongovernment organizations. In its most recent statewide needs assessment, MSU Extension combined efforts with the Michigan Agricultural Experiment Station to carry out a process that involved nearly ten thousand residents statewide (MAES and MSUE, 2006). What was once a fairly informal process has become more systematic, and implemented with tools of survey science and market research.

Although the relationship with county governments still remains strong in CES systems in many states, the relationship is undergoing significant challenges and changes in response to several forces. First, in some communities, for example in urban settings, CES is working more closely with municipal governments [in across the nation] often while maintaining a relationship with county governments. In other cases, CES is working with regional authorities, such as regional planning commissions and economic development authorities or regional public health districts. In addition, CES works closely with community foundations and with nongovernmental organizations, such as county multiagency collaborative human resource commissions. The relationship with county governments is being challenged in many states as revenues for local and state governments have become more restricted and the counties' ability to partner in funding positions and programs becomes more limited. In addition, economic developers are focusing more on regional economies and the need for communities to collaborate across political borders in order to foster growth and transformation in broader regions.

In 2004, the University of Minnesota Extension program implemented a restructuring plan that split community-based educators into two groups, regional extension educators, who are funded entirely by state and federal Extension funds and are based out of one of eighteen regional extension centers; and local extension educators, who are funded entirely by county partners and are based in county extension offices, also provided by the county partners (Morse, 2006). Supervision of both groups of educators was moved from district directors to faculty and specialists whose content expertise matches that of the educator. Other states have taken different approaches, but with the same intent of increasing the level of expertise required of extension educators in more narrowly defined areas of expertise, connecting educators more effectively with campus-based experts, and allowing county governments clear options for investing in the level of Extension that balances the needs of their residents with the revenues available to pay for service.

In Michigan, the move to more specialized educators has been implemented by retaining the housing of educators in county Extension offices, but narrowing the focus of expertise of educators and assigning them responsibility to serve clients in multiple counties. Most educators serve multiple counties, and county partners understand that they have access to educators across a broader region than just their county. Similarly, the move to increase the collaboration between educators and campus-based specialists has been achieved by assigning educators and specialists to issue-based Area of Expertise teams, with the expectation that the teams work collaboratively to identify program needs and develop delivery mechanisms for those teams (Bethel, Kells, Chatfield, Leholm, & Vlasin, 2006; Leholm, Hamm, Suvedi, Gray, & Poston, 2003).

67

The role, nature, and importance of scholarship in Extension has attracted dialogue and discussion in recent years. Boyer's (1990) work on scholarship initiated a dialogue that is ongoing. Norman (2001), Alter (2003), Smith (2004), McDowell (2004), Adams, Harrell, Maddy, & Wiegel (2005), and McGrath (2006) have each made recommendations aimed at increasing the level of scholarship within Extension programs and among Extension professionals, and institutionalizing greater rigor in Extension scholarship through such mechanisms as graduate education, hiring, promotion and tenure policies, and publication criteria. Although a single definition of scholarship in Extension has not been widely accepted, many authors and policies center on the need for Extension work to be creative, based on foundations of scientific inquiry, subject to peer review or validation, and made publicly available for peers to use and apply.

Challenges in the Years Ahead

The challenges facing Cooperative Extension are manifold, and Extension professionals frequently articulate a sense that these challenges are unprecedented. Yet a simple review of the history of Cooperative Extension suggests that this is an organization and a program that has been viewed as vulnerable since its inception. An unpublished report found in the files of the Oceana County Extension office in Michigan serves as a poignant illustration. The report details a threat to county funding of the agricultural extension agent and the home economics extension agent in Oceana County in 1928, just a few years after the first agent began working in the county. Some members of the County Board of Supervisors felt that it was unnecessary for county funds to be used to hire agents from Michigan Agricultural College and called for a vote of the people to determine the future course of the program. The decision to put the question on the ballot was reached less than two months before the August 1928 primary election, and just as the agricultural agent was beginning the busiest time of his work assignment during the crop-growing season. The report, authored by the threatened agent, reflects the sense of urgency he felt, but also the sense of mission he assumed in reaching out to the public through meetings held throughout the county. Stakeholders became engaged in the process immediately and wrote and spoke frequently and throughout the county in favor of continuing the county investment in Cooperative Extension. The election resulted in a majority supporting continuation of county funding for the agents, and even in 2008 Ocean County remains invested in MSU Extension. Similar threats to state funding for Extension have been proposed repeatedly since Michigan's government began facing funding challenges in 2002, yet on each occasion, public support voiced to the Michigan Legislature has prevented severe reduction or elimination of state funding for Extension.

Currently and in the years ahead, Cooperative Extension is facing challenges in several key areas.

Technology

Technology has fundamentally changed the means by which people find access to expertise and has even changed the definition of expertise. Whereas the county extension office used to be viewed as the ultimate source of "how to" information—how to can tomatoes, how to grow broccoli, how to cook on a limited budget, how to balance a checkbook, how to raise a child—

today, consumers can find multiple perspectives on a particular task by making a few clicks on a web browser. Consumers who have access to the Internet can find hundreds of solutions to their questions through sites such as eHow.com, wikiHow.com, or expertvillage.com.

King and Boehlje (2000) sounded an alarm that Extension was at risk of becoming obsolete if it did not adapt to the competitive marketplace of information that the Internet has created. They argued for the creation of a virtual Extension Service that would be nationwide and would adopt some elements of the new culture of web information while maintaining Extension's market identity as a source of reliable, unbiased, and research-based information. The trend toward user-provided content was only beginning in 2000, yet the idea of providing Extension professionals a way to collaborate across state lines to develop expert web-based content was implicit in King and Boehlje's focus on user demand as the driving force for content development rather than expert-driven prioritization of content.

Extension was slow to react to the proposition articulated by King and Boehlje, but by 2004 a process was underway to create such a system. Extension programs across the country agreed to invest funds in the creation of this new web presence for Extension, and soon federal funding was provided to match the university investments. This new presence, called eXtension (www.extension.org), was first available in 2005 and was structured around areas of interest identified by groups of Extension professionals who formed virtual communities of practice. They develop content related to their area of interest (e.g., personal finance, organic agriculture, or disaster preparedness) in the form of frequently asked questions, explanations of news items, and delivery of web-based seminars and instructive web content. Each community of practice remains active in responding to queries for information from users of the site and often follows up on their response with a recommendation to contact the local county Extension office.

It is clear that eXtension.org or any other Extension effort to provide content on the web will be challenged to keep up with commercial information sources. User-provided content has revolutionized the definition of expertise (Tapscott & Williams, 2006), yet provides a basic conflict with the concept of expertise associated with Extension. Peer review and validation is still an element in user-provided content, particularly on sites that allow users to correct or critique other users' content, but the concept of *peer* has been democratized in the wiki environment to the extent that an established and credentialed scientist and a high school senior are treated as peers. eXtension.org is intended to give consumers an alternative that associates the quality of its content with the brand recognition of Cooperative Extension. Perhaps the greatest opportunity for Extension online is to provide mechanisms for Extension professionals to collaborate quickly and efficiently across state boundaries by creating a workspace they can use to share, co-develop, review, and critique educational materials more rapidly than traditional peer-review processes permit.

In addition to the opportunities afforded by Internet connectivity, technological advances have created opportunities to enhance and enrich curricula and learning resources by incorporating video, audio, and interactive media. Whereas the adoption of commercial presentation software changed the structure of program delivery in the 1990s, the adoption of a broader palette of instructional design tools is required of Extension professionals today and into the future.

Perhaps the most important aspect of the challenges technology presents to Extension is the opportunity it provides to further refine the unique role Extension can and should play. First, Extension maintains a face-to-face presence in communities that helps to ensure that programs are responsive to local needs. And second, Extension maintains access to a more advanced level of expertise in the form of faculty at leading research universities. Enhancing knowledge may have been relevant to a rural and agrarian audience with limited access to information in the early twentieth century, but as knowledge has become more accessible, Extension's role has shifted to become associated with more challenging outcomes of education, including changes in behavior and changes in community settings. Margaret Bethel, former Director of MSU Extension, adapted Merizow's (1991) theory of transformative learning (McDowell, 2001) to articulate a vision of Extension's mission as one that should focus on advanced levels of process and content that result in transformational outcomes for audiences (Blewett, Keim, Leser, & Jones, 2008). For example, complex issues of land use change require deliberative dialogue, facilitated by a trained expert, and incorporation of complicated policy and landscape research findings to achieve adoption of policies and land use practices whose ultimate outcomes may not be realized for years or decades in the future. Extension professionals require a sophisticated toolkit that includes social science applications (facilitation, survey science) and an advanced understanding of complex scientific and policy research. Technological advances can assist in the application of these skills, but at the core, they still represent a fundamental and personal engagement by Extension professionals with the audiences they serve.

Audience

In spite of the diversification of Extension programs into urban communities and broad issues associated with economic development, Extension still is frequently viewed as primarily serving rural communities and agricultural needs. Extension programs across the nation have focused increasingly on application of market research and marketing principles in order to change the public perception of what audiences Extension serves and what base of expertise it represents. The greatest challenge is in changing the perceptions of citizens about Extension while Extension has worked to broaden its focus rather than to redirect it. Extension still remains heavily invested in rural America and still engages with the growing and diversifying agrifood sector of our nation's economy. Its move to address needs of urban and suburban communities and enterprises has been built on top of the traditional resume, and with that, Extension is perhaps rightfully perceived as a naïve partner in the urban and business landscape.

Even with these limitations, it is essential for Extension programs to build their resumes and their identity in urban communities, whether by associating more closely with non-land-grant urban universities and community colleges or by forming partnerships with municipal governments instead of or in addition to county governments. Other partners who can help to establish Extension's presence as an agent of change in urban communities are chambers of commerce, economic development corporations, and other community service providers.

Another adjustment needed to serve urban communities is to attend to the most critical issues facing urban settings, including health care, poverty reduction, economic development, urban landscape renewal, and the dynamic interplay of diverse cultures. This involves not only making an effort to hire educators with educational and experiential background in these areas, but also connecting more deliberately with faculty from academic programs that have not been in the mainstream of Extension in the past: urban planning, entrepreneurship and enterprise development, social justice, health sciences, social work, and conflict resolution.

Expanded Partnerships

As Extension programs need to expand the diversity of expertise that they rely on, it will be important for Extension to expand their partnerships with organizations beyond county governments. This is important not only in urban communities, but also in rural settings, where public health departments, township or city governments, private enterprises, and nongovernmental organizations bring unique resources and connections to a relationship with Extension. Indeed, one of the services that Extension can provide is to facilitate collaboration across these different entities in communities, whether urban or rural. The role of the new Extension professional is becoming more and more a role of connecting the breadth of university expertise with family, business, and community needs through whichever community partner is most closely associated with the needs and the community served.

One of the greatest challenges facing American communities and businesses is the rapidly increasing cost of the health care system. Although federal reforms may develop, there is increasing recognition that reducing service is not likely to be accepted as a means of reducing costs. Rather, costs will need to be reduced by creating more efficient and less costly health delivery systems. And part of this will depend on educating health care recipients and helping them to adapt their behaviors so as to reduce the need for expensive health care through application of prevention and risk reduction behaviors and practices. In a recent news release, K. Grumbach, professor and chair of the Department of Family and Community Medicine at the University of California, San Francisco, called for the creation of a Cooperative Extension Service for health care (Arvantes, 2009). In part, these discussions reflect a misperception that the existing Cooperative Extension Service is restricted to working on agricultural issues. However, proposals to expand CES expertise into health care programs identify needs to connect at the level of the consumer of health care and at the level of the health care professional. This represents a great opportunity for CES to adapt its expertise in engagement with needs in an area where its past activity has been limited to education about nutrition and early childhood development. Similarly, for health science faculty and health delivery professionals to work closely with CES programs will help them to adapt a more engaged approach to sharing of expertise, one that looks to the community and the health care user to articulate the services needed and adapts the best understanding of health care policy and practice to address those needs.

Formalized Needs Assessment

Cooperative Extension programs have much to learn in the adoption of more scientific approaches to needs assessment and issue prioritization. For a university of the twenty-first century to be responsive to the "the problems the communities it serves faces," it must use the most sophisticated tools of the social scientist in understanding what those problems

71

are and how community members wish to address them. Extension programs are recognizing the need to address this challenge (e.g., Kalambokidis, 2004), and they must continue to advance the scholarship associated with determining community, family, and enterprise needs, whether through face-to-face mechanisms or through use of interactive media.

Survival

Finally, the nature of the public investment in CES presents perhaps the greatest challenge to Extension now and in the near future. The current economic downturn has generated fundamental shifts in thinking about the role of public institutions and their dependence on public funds for their operations. A general trend to decrease taxes at all levels of government at a time when existing taxes are generating significantly lower revenues has put governments in the position of eliminating all but the most essential services they provide. County, state, and federal partners are seeking ways to reduce the costs of Extension without necessarily doing away with the services. This presents Extension leaders with the challenge to restructure and redesign their system while seeking other sources of funding. And there are opportunities available, ranging from instituting fees for services provided to depending more heavily on competitive grants from governmental agencies as well as nongovernmental organizations and foundations. The need for engagement by university expertise with the communities they serve has grown at the very time that the resources for fostering that engagement have declined. The challenge going forward will be to leverage resources wisely and to pursue new partnerships and funding mechanisms in order to further advance the process of engagement. The case for the engaged university is stronger than ever before. The opportunity for Extension is to adapt the experience of a century of practice to the needs of today without being burdened by the institutional inertia that resists change.

References

Adams, R. A., Harrell, R. M., Maddy, D. J., & Wiegel, D. (2005). A diversified portfolio of scholarship: The making of a successful extension educator. *Journal of Extension* [Online], *43*(4), Article 4COM2. Available at http://www.joe.org/joe/2005august/comm2.php.

Alter, T. (2003). Where is Extension scholarship falling short, and what can we do about it? *Journal of Extension* [Online], *41*(6). Available at http://www.joe.org/joe/2003december/comm2.shtml.

Arvantes, J. (2009). *Family physician calls for cooperative extension service for primary care.* Retrieved May 11, 2009, from http://www.aafp.org/online/en/home/pulbications/news/nows-now/governmentmedicine/20090505grumbach-coop.html.

Bethel, M., Kells, J., Chatfield, J., Leholm, A., & Vlasin, R. (2006). Michigan State University Extension and Ohio State University Extension Self-Directed Teams. In A. Leholm & R. Vlasin (Eds.), *Increasing the odds for high-performance teams* (pp. 200–237). East Lansing: Michigan State University Press.

Blewett, T. J., Keim, A., Leser, J., & Jones, L. (2008). Defining a transformational education model for the engaged university. *Journal of Extension* [Online], *46*(3), Article 3COM1. Available at http://www.joe.org/joe/2008june/comm1.php.

Boyer, E. L. (1990). *Scholarship reconsidered: Priorities of the professoriate.* Princeton, NJ: Carnegie Foundation for the Advancement of Teaching.

Johnsrud, M., & Rauschkolb, R. (1989). Extension in transition: Review and renewal. *Journal of Extension* [On-line], *27*(1), Article 1TP1. Available at http://www.joe.org/joe/1989spring/tp1.php.

Kalambokidis, L. (2004). Identifying the public value in Extension programs. *Journal of Extension* [On-line], *42*(2). Available at http://www.joe.org/joe/2004april/a1.shtml.

Kellogg Commission. (1999). *Returning to our roots: The engaged university.* Washington, DC: Kellogg Commission on the Future of State and Land Grant Universities, National Association of State Universities and Land Grant Colleges. Available at http://www.cpn.org/topics/youth/highered/pdfs/Land_Grant_Engaged_Institution.pdf.

King, D., & Boehlje, M. (2000). Extension: On the brink of extinction or distinction? *Journal of Extension* [On-line], *38*(5), Article 5COM1. Available at http://www.joe.org/joe/2000october/comm1.html.

Leholm, A., Hamm, L., Suvedi, M., Gray, I., & Poston, F. (1999). Area of expertise teams: The Michigan approach to applied research and extension. *Journal of Extension* [On-line], *37*(3), Article 3FEA3. Available at http://www.joe.org/joe/1999june/a3.php.

MAES & MSUE. (2006). *Strengthening Michigan's economy: Roles for the Michigan Agricultural Experiment Station and Michigan State University Extension.* East Lansing: Michigan Agricultural Experiment Station and Michigan State University Extension. Available at http://portal.msue.msu.edu/objects/content_revision/download.cfm/item_id.369340/worspace_id.4/Strengthening%20Michigan's%20Economy:%20Roles%20for%20MAES%2and%2MSUE.pdf/.

McDowell, G. R. (2001). *Land-grant universities and Extension into the 21st century.* Ames: Iowa State University Press.

McDowell, G. R. (2004). Is Extension an idea whose time has come—and gone? *Journal of Extension* [On-line], *42*(6), Article 6COM1. Available at http://www.joe.org/joe/2004december/comm1.php

McGrath, D. M. (2006). The scholarship of application. *Journal of Extension* [On-line], *44*(2), Article 2FEA8. Available at http://wwww.joe.org/joe/2006april/a8.php.

Merizow, J. (1991). *Transformative dimensions of adult learning.* San Francisco: Jossey-Bass.

Morse, G. W. (2006). Minnesota Extension's Regional and County delivery system: myths and reality. *Journal of Extension* [On-line], *44*(4), Article 4COM1. Available at http://www.joe.org/joe/2006august/comm1.php.

Norman, C. L. (2001). The challenge of Extension scholarship. *Journal of Extension* [On-line], *39*(1). Available at http://www.joe.org/joe/2001february/comm1.html.

Smith, K. L. (2004). Scholarship: Shout about it. *Journal of Extension* [On-line], *42*(5). Available at http://www.joe.org/joe/2004october/comm1.html.

Tapscott, D., & Williams, A. D. (2006). *Wikinomics: How mass collaboration changes everything.* New York: Penguin.

Engaged Scholarship and Transformative Regional Engagement

Nancy E. Franklin and Timothy V. Franklin

In 1990, Ernest Boyer called upon the academy to redefine the priorities of faculty in the context of four forms of scholarship: discovery, integration, application, and teaching (Boyer, 1990). In this taxonomy, the scholarship of application was intended to focus faculty members on "scholarly service" through two-way disciplinary-associated interactions with people and problems in the world beyond the campus (p. 23). So, in an important sense, engaged scholarship is concerned with the scholarly service of higher education's core asset—the faculty.

However, in a larger sense, the notion of "engaged scholarship" can be applied to institutions of higher education at large. Many kinds of expertise beyond the faculty exist within universities—whether in the information technology division, the university architect's office, university engagement units, the buildings and grounds operations, or the office of multicultural affairs. Because professionals in these nonacademic parts of higher education institutions often approach their work with the same attention to best practice as faculty scholars, we can extend our concept of engagement to include the scholarly service of university staff in partnership with communities. Another component of engagement can involve students, the third human resource asset of higher education. Students who apply scholarly knowledge from their academic studies to community issues, typically under the guidance of faculty teachers, can be powerful contributors to engaged scholarship.

It is such a broad, holistic notion of university engagement—faculty, staff, student, and institution—that frames this chapter on engaged scholarship and regional economic engagement. In what ways might the academy consider how to bring the totality of its expertise and assets to bear on the tremendous economic and social issues of our day? How might the human capital and innovation engines of universities be focused on the needs of economic regions in partnership with the citizens of those places to benefit communities and advance scholarship? What more can be accomplished for both regions and academe through intentional, institutional engagement? By investing in regional partnerships characterized by reciprocity and mutual respect, universities can strategically impact the economic welfare of communities while advancing their research, teaching, and service missions.

Ironically, at a time when universities may be the most effective contributor to regional economic prosperity (Purcell & Mundy, 2003), public financial contributions to higher education are declining as a percentage of total operating funding and as a proportion of state budgets. Rather than providing incentives for university-regional partnerships that build long-term capacity through human capital development and technological asset deployment (supply-side strategies), the lion's share of state and local economic development funding continues to be directed to such short-term strategies as shell building construction, worker skills training specific to a single employer, and tax mitigation (demand-side strategies). Universities, meanwhile, are too often seen as inwardly focused on specialized faculty interests and campus-centric student education rather than as high-capacity, extendable innovation engines. This institutional focus should not be surprising; student tuition and research funding comprise the largest slices of revenues at large research universities. Thus, a policy disconnect has occurred between regional competitiveness development and university incentives to partner with regions.

This chapter presents the synergies between the competencies needed by regions to effectively compete in a global economy, university strengths that correlate with critical innovation assets, opportunities to increase higher education mission capacity through regional partnerships, and integrated program models for engagement. A model illustrating the virtuous circle of engagement is presented and described. We conclude the chapter with some thoughts about future trends in economic development and a proposal for institutionalizing university engagement in regions.

The Context and Opportunity

The University Engagement Interface

Higher education can trace a long history of involvement with the economic well-being and development of communities—from the creation of the cooperative extension service, to manufacturing extension programs, to technology transfer, to the establishment of research parks. What has characterized these entrenched, widely replicated efforts has been the development of a specialized corps of professional staff that has assumed primary responsibility for interfacing with the public. Increasingly, as de facto public policy has seen a college education shift to being a private good from a public good and because of the ever-ratcheting cost pressures on higher education associated with attracting students, professional outreach staff have come under pressure to generate revenue to support their activities. The result is an engagement interface with limited capacity for public work.

Faculty work, meanwhile, has been very effectively steered by the federal government toward basic research associated with national priorities—originally associated with the Cold War and now encompassing a broader range of purposes (Jones, 2005). Competitively awarded federal grants drive the academy's research financial engine, its faculty reward structure, and the ever-important prestige rankings. The vast majority of research faculty do not consider community issues and challenges to be relevant or important in the context of professional development and recognition. On the student side of the equation, an upwardly spiraling "arms race" has focused attention on more and more campus amenities to attract students (Kirp, 2005; Zemsky, Wegner, & Massy, 2005). The resulting student focus on self, rather than self in relation to society, further disconnects the academy from locally based public needs.

This combination of influences has resulted in the development of programs and services, research agendas, and student experiences that are driven more by internal—even commercial—interests of the university than by external, public needs of citizens and communities. As a result, universities have become niche players, rather than central partners, in locally or regionally based economic and community development.

What is required of higher education to find a more central place at the economic development partnering table? First, universities must become better educated about critical success factors associated with community-based economic growth in the innovation economy. Then, higher education needs to examine the roles it can play to contribute to sustained community vitality while reinforcing its own research, teaching, and service missions. Finally, to gain resources for an expanded role in regional stewardship, universities must advance a clear value proposition of benefit to regional economic and community development. Such a value proposition will be necessary to build public support for credible programs, policies, and accountabilities.

Transformative Regional Engagement

Through a critical examination of the landscape and opportunities, universities can shape their own particular paths to regional economic engagement. One option that holds much promise but requires a new way of thinking about community engagement is investing in multifaceted, long-term partnerships that are centered on the economic transformation of a region. Transformative regional engagement is grounded in an understanding of the virtuous circles associated with regional economic vitality and research university well-being, respectively. The nexus of transformative regional engagement is centered in an understanding of ways to structure university-regional partnerships to transform communities and strengthen universities. In figure 1, the well-being of the university and region, along with the engagement interface join as three virtuous circles. These circles are conceived as the constructive interface between the needs and assets of regions and universities, coalescing through leadership, partnership structures, and policy, and accelerating into a positive vortex when designed and managed so the benefits to both region and university are truly reciprocal.

In the following sections, we unbundle the intertwined virtuous circles to discuss each component circle. First, we address innovation economy needs in a regional context and how addressing those needs leads to a set of spin-out benefits that increase the competitive capacity of a region. Second, we turn to the university circle and explore the needs of a vibrant research university and associated spin-out benefits that create innovation ecosystem value. At the end of the section, we show the synergies made possible by interconnecting the regional and university circles, and the resultant benefits.

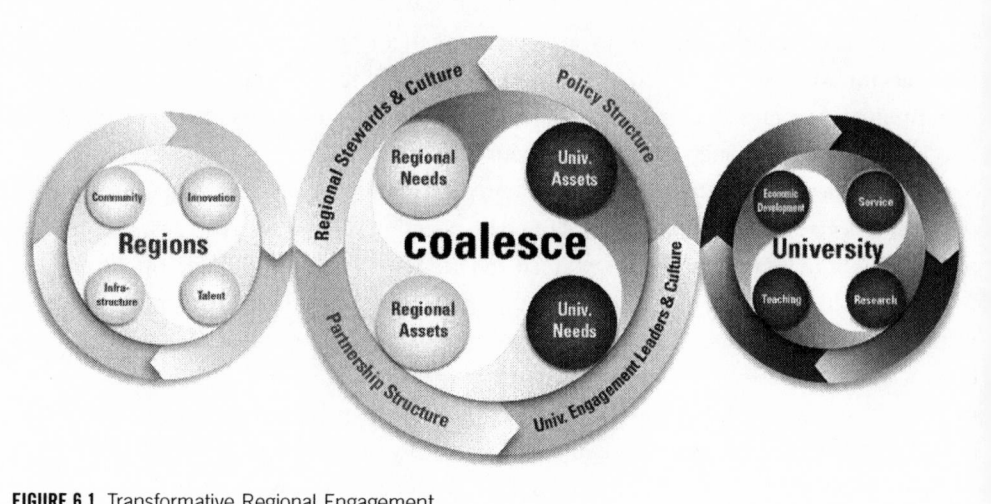

FIGURE 6.1 Transformative Regional Engagement

The Virtuous Circle of Regional Needs Satisfaction

Why Regions Matter

Regions—functional economic geographies—are not only the building blocks of national economies (Porter, Monitor Group, ontheFRONTIER, & Council on Competitiveness, 2001) but are also the minimum geographic unit needed to establish competitive advantage in a global economy. No longer do local governmental jurisdictions, such as towns or counties, constitute sufficient critical mass in terms of concentration of industry or workforce to compete effectively (Drabenstott, 2005). Therefore, rule number one in advancing the economic competitiveness of a place is to identify the regional economic context in which it is situated. Strategies to advance the well-being of a place, therefore, must consider the entirety of the region, not just a single community.

Attaining Regional Competence

Clues to core competencies needed by regions can be deduced from lessons learned in economic development prospecting. According to a survey of U.S. business executives regarding barriers to innovation investment (Council on Competitiveness & New Economy Strategies, 2005), the elements that are most likely to *eliminate* a prospective business location from consideration are:

- Poor communications infrastructure,
- Small science and engineering talent pool,
- Low quality of life, and
- Poor school system.

Therefore, regions seeking to be attractive to businesses in the clusters they are targeting must build high-speed communications infrastructure, develop a high-end technical workforce, create community and cultural amenities, and ensure high-quality schools. In other words, regions need to address critical infrastructure, talent pool, and quality of life.

Moving to Regional Competitive Advantage

Innovation is absolutely critical to twenty-first century economic competitiveness. Healthy regions build from within by identifying regional assets and developing competitive advantage around them through innovation. As the Council on Competitiveness (2008) has noted, "in the face of growing global competition, the only sustainable advantage for U.S. regions is continuous innovation" (p. 1). Further, competitiveness is enhanced by the geographic concentration of companies that are interrelated as competitors and collaborators, as both producers and suppliers to those producers (Porter, 2007). These industry concentrations, referred to as sectors or clusters, in most regions constitute the primary economy; that is, they serve as the vehicle by which the region is able to funnel new wealth into the region, rather than just re–circulating dollars already in the region. Industry sectors that are aligned with regional assets and contribute to continuous innovation are a region's best opportunity to create competitive advantage.

Economic Vitality Essentials

In a regional context, we postulate that there are four dimensions of community capacity that are critical to economic vitality:

- Innovation base,
- Talent pool,
- Critical infrastructure, and
- Community development.

When each of these dimensions is well developed, the region benefits from high-wage employment, high-value workers, ubiquitous transit and utility access, and excellent quality of life. In turn, more human, technological, and financial resources flow to the region, creating an upward economic spiral. (See Figure 2.)

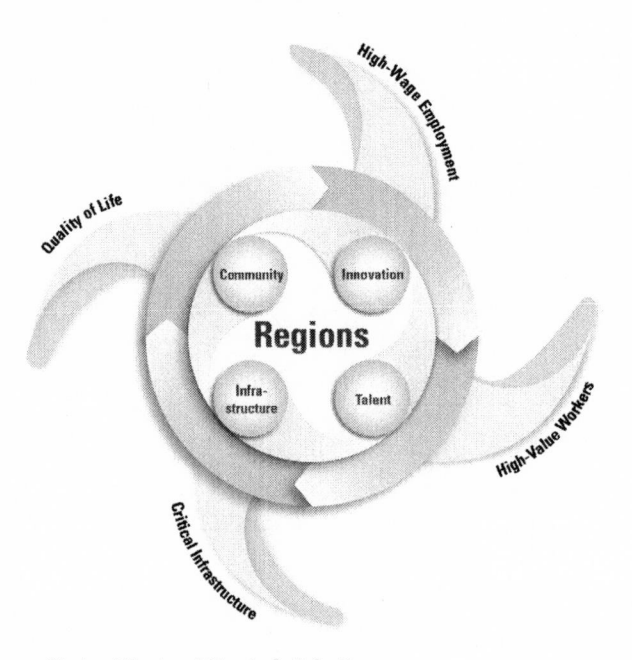

FIGURE 6.2 The Virtuous Circle of Regional Needs Satisfaction

The Virtuous Circle of University Needs Satisfaction

The University Flywheel

The core cultural interest of universities is knowledge creation, knowledge accumulation, and knowledge application. Universities do this through what has traditionally been a tripartite mission: research, teaching, and service. In pursuit of this mission, higher education spins off a number of benefits, including innovation, talent, and expertise. Increasingly, a fourth mission, economic development, is being identified and elevated to equal status with the first three (Council on Competitiveness, 2008). The economic development mission of a university can become the crossroads for meshing the cultural values of regional stakeholders with the internal cultural values of the university. (See figure 3.)

The university flywheel of research, education, and service requires a constant infusion of funding, world-class talent, viable and relevant research projects, state-of-the-art laboratories, and public goodwill. Regional partnerships brokered through a higher education institution's economic development arm can add to the speed of the flywheel.

Enhancing Research and Education

For faculty members, external partnerships provide opportunities to convert relationships and interaction with the "real world" into new research agendas and lessons for the classroom. In addition to informing research agendas on campus, regional partnerships offer fresh avenues for scholarship and open new opportunities for sponsored funding. Many faculty members are able to advance their scholarly interests by focusing on an aspect of community need, engaging with community partners to address the need, then converting the experience to a peer-reviewed publication. Long-standing relationships with community

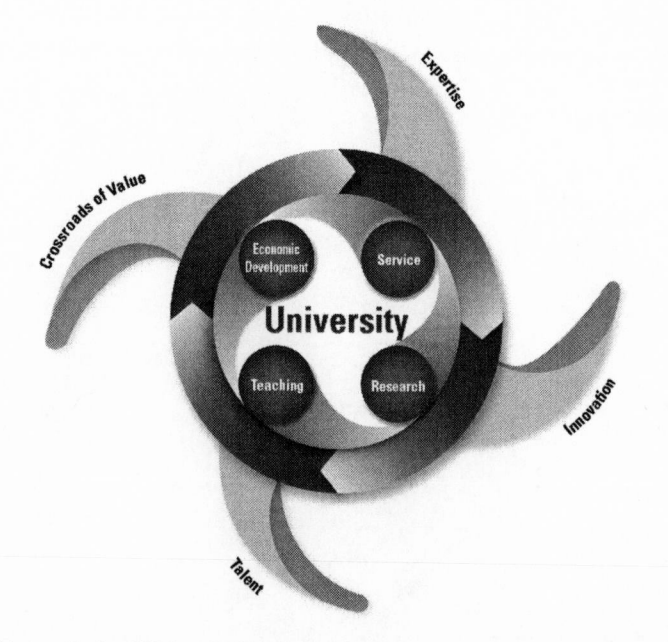

FIGURE 6.3 The Virtuous Circle of University Needs Satisfaction

partners can lead to opportunities to capture sponsored funds and for student learning that extends concepts from the classroom to applied community settings.

Enhancing Public Goodwill

As universities have focused on rankings and the concomitant recruitment of superstar faculty and top-tier students, the public has increasingly asked about the value of these institutions to everyday people. Higher education has an opportunity to demonstrate public value through engagement with high-priority local issues, particularly if those local issues are associated with regions of the state not contiguous with the university's campus. Through engagement of faculty and students with citizens and community challenges, especially if done on the community's terms, universities can build public trust and goodwill. Such public goodwill can spill over to political goodwill and policy decisions about allocation of public funds.

Expanding University Assets

Partnering with regions offers universities opportunities to increase their asset base. Combinations of new sources of funding available to and in regions provide possibilities for regionally located laboratories, classrooms, specialized equipment, faculty lines, and graduate students. Public and private funders may see better funding mission alignment for investments in economically distressed regions than in university campuses. In this manner, universities willing to manage a distributed asset base may be able to grow their physical and human infrastructure capacity despite low or flat direct public funding appropriations.

Coalescing Regional Engagement

University Assets Aligned with Regional Needs

Regional engagement efforts bring together regions and universities in ways that draw upon their respective assets to meet each other's needs. Regions need universities to help them develop local technology-based assets. Universities, in turn, draw on the unique physical, business, financial, and political assets of or connected to regions to advance their scholarship, attract talent, and build their reputations. When university-regional partnerships are focused on addressing an array of interconnected needs, strong leadership from both partners is necessary. These leaders work together to set the course, commit the resources, and keep everyone at the partnering table over the course of several years. In a fundamental sense, these activities, shared agenda setting and coordinated implementation by the partners, form the foundation of reciprocal relationship. The "two-way streets" of regional engagement must be formed around a shared agenda leading to reciprocal needs satisfaction. Critical to the success of a university-regional partnership are the facilitators of engagement: leaders in the regions and at the universities who bring their respective entities to the partnering table, partnership structures that reward cooperation, and policy structures that clarify the constructs of a partnership. When needs and assets of universities and regions are aligned and facilitators of engagement are present, the coalescence can spin out benefits to the region, to the university, and to the state. (See figure 4.)

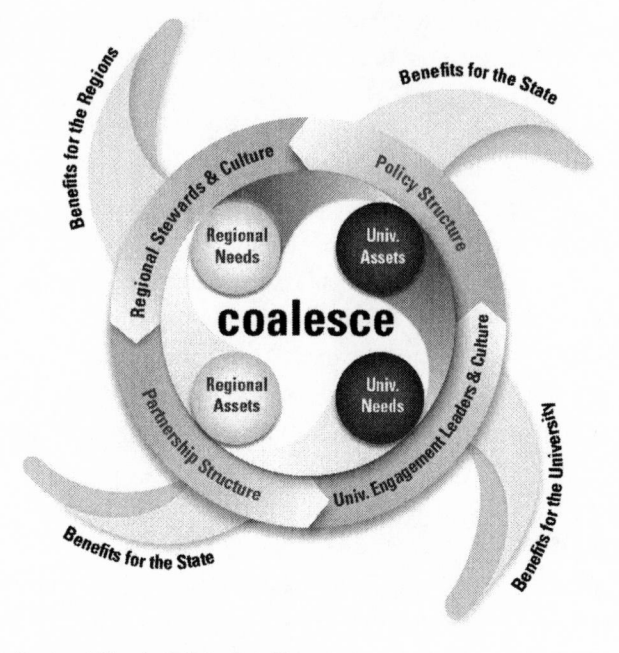

Benefits for the Regions
Benefits for the State
Regional Stewards & Culture
Policy Structure
Regional Needs
Univ. Assets
coalesce
Regional Assets
Univ. Needs
Univ. Engagement Leaders & Culture
Partnership Structure
Univ. Engagement Leaders & Culture
Benefits for the State
Benefits for the University

FIGURE 6.4 University-Regional Needs Satisfaction Alignment

Facilitators of Engagement

Successful university-region engagements bridge the fundamentally different cultures of a region and university to match needs with corresponding partner assets. Thus, university expertise is applied to regional innovation capacity-building needs and regional assets are employed to advance the knowledge creation, application, and accumulation (or scholarship) needs of universities. The connections between needs and assets across partners are facilitated by regional stewards and university engagement leaders (described in the next section), as well as by policy and partnership governance structures. When needs and assets are in alignment in university-regional transformative partnerships, significant benefits accrue to the region, to the university, and to the state.

The mindset of regional players is centered on economic development and operational efficiency. So, the cultural value that a region presents puts a high priority on job creation, cost containment (efficient use of tax dollars), or profit. These priorities are not central to the cultural values associated with higher education organizations. The challenge for fledgling regions is how to partner effectively with research universities to develop innovation infrastructure. This requires an understanding that universities are not government functionalities whose core purpose is the economic development of the region in question. Leadership from both the region and the university must bridge the perspectives of each partner around the economic development mission by avoiding seeing the university as another economic development agency and defining a mutually beneficial role that considers the cultural assumptions of each.

Regional Stewards

University partnerships with regions will be most successful when the "right" kinds of people from the region and from the university are involved in formulating the partnering agenda and engaging appropriate human and physical capital from their respective domains. Henton, Melville, and Walesh (2002) argue that the economic, environmental, and social complexities posed by globalization require a new type of leadership to position regions to compete effectively—specifically, *regional stewards* (p. 11). Regional stewards are defined as self-selected individuals committed to a place who take an integrated approach in addressing issues and building coalitions. Regional stewards are familiar with local needs and priorities. They have access to regionally based physical, human, and financial assets that can be brought to the partnering table. Universities planning regional engagement should seek out the leaders who serve as regional stewards.

University Engagement Leaders

On the university side of the equation, consideration should be given to the kinds of institutional representation that will be able to engage a wide cross-section of university expertise and articulate the value of the partnership to the institution. A university-regional partnership formed to address substantive economic and community development issues will need to draw upon university expertise resident across departments, colleges, and offices. It will need to be grounded in an institutional value proposition that goes beyond benefits to individual faculty members. As universities consider entering into robust regional engagement, they need to ensure that the university leadership in the partnership can work broadly across structural components of the institution and ensure, as Vidal, Nye, Walker, Manjarrez, and Romanik (2002) articulated, that the partnership's goals are consistent with the university's mission and goals.

Building Regional Cooperation and Resource Alignment

As industry clusters nested in regional economies have become the central organizing principle for business vitality, public approaches to economic, workforce, and community development have adopted approaches, referred to as sector strategies, by which public effort is aligned to build from or strengthen a region's best opportunities at establishing distinctive economic niches that are globally competitive (Porter, 2007). Efforts to bring regional cooperation and align resources across jurisdictions and public service entities increase in importance when regions attempt to maximize impacts from limited resources. Regional authorities, regional stewarding institutions, and state and federal policy all have developed to introduce partnership structures that facilitate a regional perspective to program development and public leadership. The U.S. Department of Labor's Workforce Innovations in Regional Economic Development (WIRED) is a notable federal policy effort to coalesce regional cooperation and place greater focus on building competitive economic niches in thirty-nine U.S. regions. In Virginia, higher education centers, regional research-technology-education-and commercialization centers, and regional authorities all have developed to govern and advance regional program and development efforts. Each of these efforts notably attempts to overcome more parochial perspectives created by existing jurisdictional or organizational structures.

Effective Policy Structures

Effective engagement partnerships address policy and governance issues early in the relationship (Franklin, 2008). Identifying and articulating the goals of the partnership in written form assists all parties in clarifying what they expect to accomplish and the associated time parameters. Goals assist various actors in shaping intervention strategies and measuring progress over time. Accountability to key stakeholders in the region, at the university, and associated entities and publics is critical to garnering credibility and maintaining support for the work of the partnership. Partners need to develop clear strategies for obtaining the financial resources needed for the engagement activities, including resource requirements, potential funding sources, and roles of partners in obtaining and managing funds. Governance of the partnership is also a critical consideration. Governance structures assist partners address issues such as how the engagement agenda will be developed, who will assume responsibility for prioritizing shared activities, what strategies will be used to ensure inclusiveness in decision making, and how progress toward goals will be monitored.

The Transformative Regional Engagement Agenda

Innovation Infrastructure and Global Connections

Innovation capacity, talent pool, community development, and critical infrastructure become the "soft" and "hard" framework of a healthy economic region. Far more than simply transferring technology or offering a niche program, universities potentially provide a unique capacity for supplying soft infrastructure, anchoring "creative" climates, and introducing global networks of value to needy regions. This innovation infrastructure has far greater relevance than shell buildings, sewer lines, and low-cost labor to a region's twenty-first-century global competitiveness.

The "innovation infrastructure" considerations become the basis for an engagement agenda focused on regional economic and community development. It is universities' strength in developing innovation capacity through applied research and world-class education that positions higher education as a logical partner for economically distressed regions (Initiative for a Competitive Inner City & CEOs for Cities, 2002). Universities have the expertise to assist communities in addressing a breadth of capacity-building needs, including human capital development, community development, fund raising, brand credibility, and advanced physical infrastructure.

Universities can contribute to the development of a competitive economic base, provide a pipeline of highly educated talent, contribute to building critical leadership and physical infrastructure, and assist in quality-of-life improvements. Single university contributions in any of these areas can be marginally helpful, such as through the engagement of a faculty member or outreach staff member. However, much more significant impacts will occur through the simultaneous engagement of many university experts linked to an integrated partnering plan.

Intentional Technology-Based Economic Development

Universities frequently supply many innovation infrastructure benefits unintentionally in the regions in which they are located. However, increasing effort is being directed to intentional technology-based economic development. Despite their innovation infrastructure building capacity, universities generally have not been particularly focused on applying that

Table 1. Purposes Public Research Universities Serve in Engaging Regions for Their Economic Competitiveness	
Economic Base	Foster a new or strengthened economic/job base
Talent Base	Develop and strengthen the twenty-first-century workforce
Leadership and Policy Base	Provide leadership and connect partners to vital, external resources
Community Base	Lead community development and improve regional quality of life

expertise in regional contexts or on integrating their programs into the larger economic context. However, more and more institutions are making intentional efforts to bring this capacity to bear in regions both near and distant from campus (Franklin, 2008; Moore & Franklin, 2008). As one looks across these pioneering examples, numerous initiatives align university-led programs with the needs of regions. In synthesizing these examples, we pose four contexts for public research university engagement with regions to advance economic competitiveness: foster a new economic base, develop the talent capacity, provide leadership and broker connections to resources, and contribute to key quality-of-life factors. (See table 1)

Strengthening the Economic Base

Universities can foster the development of a higher end economic base and job base in a region through distributed research facilities and faculty whose focus is aligned with existing regional capabilities and opportunities. By connecting regionally housed applied research and development activities to local assets, universities can be a catalyst for strengthening existing industries, attracting businesses located elsewhere to the region, and spurring the development of new companies. Universities can also facilitate the development of a suite of technology-based economic development support systems and services, from business and entrepreneurial support services, to business incubators, to research parks. These business development support services and their associated facilities influence the economic climate by creating distinctiveness and housing intellectual talent hubs. On many dimensions, then, universities can contribute to the development of a new or strengthened economic base in a region. Table 2 provides a summary of higher education's primary abilities to contribute in this regard.

Strengthening the Human Capital Base

Intellectual talent hubs can be stimulated by university-region partnerships that focus on talent attraction as well as talent development. Particularly in the early years of implementing a technology-based economic development strategy, it may be desirable to consciously focus on importing talent by using the university-based research and development activities in the region as an attractor. Scientists, engineers, and technologists can be attracted to a place that is home to state-of-the-art research, development, and communications facilities.

85

Table 2. Economic Base: Fostering a New or Strengthened Economic/Job Base

Institutional Leadership	Leading, managing, and programming durable, in-region education, research and development, commercialization, outreach, and business development activities in partnership with economic development entities.
Research and Development	Producing knowledge, applying it to create technology, and creating regional spillovers supportive to economic growth both close to campus and near distributed in-region research settings.
Talent Attraction and Hosting Permanent Hubs of Intellectual Capital	Reversing brain drain by anchoring/leading intellectual mini-hubs (regional institutions) to provide magnets for talent, diverse ideas, entrepreneurial networks, thriving innovation centers, and regional stickiness for talent and technology spillover.
Creating Contexts, Economic Distinctiveness, and Talent Crossroads	Producing knowledge, applying it to create technology, and creating regional spillovers supportive to economic growth both close to campus and near distributed in-region research settings.
Innovation Infrastructure and Facilities	Creating and leveraging world-class critical infrastructure and facilities (i.e., specialized labs, unique technology, technology accelerators, innovation parks, business incubators/accelerators, network infrastructure, etc.)
Influencing Economic Climate	Influencing regional business climate and creating a cauldron for innovation and serendipity by providing a nexus for business, university, and government.
Asset-Based Economic Development	Identifying new economic clusters that can be developed in a region, based on the region's existing strengths.
Technology-Based Economic Development	Providing intellectual capital-based products and services to knowledge-based companies that support industrial research, technology transfer, commercialization, innovation, and access to networks of entrepreneurs, innovators, and funders.
Business and Entrepreneur Support and Services	Creating and supporting globally competitive businesses through business advice, technical assistance, value networks, and access to capital.

They, in turn, will attract graduate students to conduct research and staff grant (and contract) activities. Such a cluster of university-affiliated intellectual talent in a region will begin to attract other scientific and technological talent through private-sector growth.

In-Region Talent Development
Developing talent is clearly an arena in which universities have much to offer. They can provide access to noncredit and degree-based programs for local citizens. Innovative formats

and delivery methodologies permit the availability of a breadth of offerings even in regions located far from university campuses. Programs that build local science, technology, engineering, and math capacity as well as entrepreneurship skills are particularly critical for developing a higher tech economic base. At the graduate level, nonresearch and professional master's degree programs are desirable. Additionally, university partners can work with educational systems and organizations in the region to create pathways of learning opportunities that connect achievement and course credits across systems in a seamless manner.

Building a region's talent base, therefore, may consist of both talent attraction and talent development strategies. Universities have much to offer regions in partnering to enhance their human capital base. Table 3 offers a summary of many of the most salient talent development strategies that universities are well positioned to support.

Table 3. Talent Base: Developing and Strengthening a Twenty-first-Century Workforce

Access to Degrees	Increasing access to higher education programs
Innovations in Format	Offering customized credit and noncredit distance and continuing education programs designed to improve workforce skills
Innovations in Delivery	Offering multiple delivery formats, involving various instructional technologies, to reach audiences via multiple delivery systems
Professional Master's and Continuing Education	Offering customized master's degrees and continuing education to professionals that strengthen high-skilled workforce areas (i.e., interdisciplinary terminal science degrees to high value-added sectors)
Coordinating Talent Development Pipelines	Convening partnerships with workforce systems, K–12 districts, community colleges, and senior institutions and leading efforts to align seamless pathways to create comprehensive workforce solutions for targeted economic sectors.
Educational Enrichment and Training Programs	Inspiring, developing, and initiating adults, youth, business managers, K–12 teachers, and government personnel through targeted outreach, management training, workforce development, and education programs
STEM Enrichment	Enriching in-region K–12, postsecondary, and informal educational offerings in science, technology, engineering, and math (STEM) fields
Entrepreneur Development	Providing intellectual capital–based products and services to knowledge-based companies that support industrial research, technology transfer, commercialization, innovation, and access to networks of entrepreneurs, innovators, and funders.
Business and Entrepreneur Support and Services	Creating and supporting globally competitive businesses through business advice, technical assistance, value networks, and access to capital.

Fair Broker Leadership and Convening Authority

Universities can play a critical leadership role in regional economic development. Existing organizations in a region tend to have limited parameters in terms of mission responsibility, but universities generally have much broader missions so they can provide leadership across jurisdictional and organization boundaries. Universities can lead and convene partnerships that involve federal, state, regional, foundation, and corporation partners in addition to providing credibility and a sense of progress. University partners can assist a region in defining issues, accessing expertise, and mapping assets and through this effort provide planning and policy capacity to local leaders. Refer to table 4 for a summary of possibilities for universities to provide leadership to regions in conjunction with economic development strategy development and implementation.

Community Base

Community development and associated quality-of-life improvements are another domain in which universities can partner with regions. Universities can assist regions in planning public infrastructure, whether it is parks and trails, telecommunications and bridges, or arts centers and historic building preservation. In addition, higher education can build community capacity by providing locally based leadership and professional development to assist a region in creating a pipeline of leadership talent. University partners can assist regional leaders in creating a strategy for developing a targeted set of social and cultural quality-of-life amenities that will be attractive to young professionals. Arts and entertainment programs can sometimes be extended from campus to enhance quality of life in other regions. Finally,

---

Table 4. Leadership and Policy Base: Providing Leadership and Connecting Partners to Vital, External Resources

Leading and Convening Partnerships	Convening potential federal, state, regional, foundation, and corporate partners and leading collaborations that advance the public good.
Leading Economic and Community Transformation	Developing new models to drive regional economic growth and advocating their implementation to policy makers.
Credibility and Progress	Contributing brand credibility to external audiences for proposed transformation efforts.
Leadership Development	Delivering programs to develop community and regional leaders.
Access to Expertise	Providing access to information, expertise, and outside resources.
Policy and Planning Capacity	Building public policy and planning capacity.
Defining Issues	Mapping regional assets, recommending economic competitiveness strategies, and defining public policy issues and options.

Table 5. Community Base: Leading Community Development and Improving Regional Quality of Life

Direct Economic, Social, and Cultural Impact	Impacting regions directly through institutional spending, employment, culture, programming, and employee demographics.
Convening Community Partners	Convening potential community partners (e.g., K–12, local government, business, nonprofit organizations, and higher education) and leading collaboration to address public needs and advance the public good
Planning for Public Infrastructure	Leading and facilitating community planning around public infrastructure needs (i.e., information technology and network infrastructure, schools, public spaces, etc.).
Quality-of-Life Offerings	Supplying quality news, educational, and entertainment programming through public broadcasting, media services, and live programming.
Building Community Capacity	Developing leaders and building civic capacity.
Sustainability	Community-university planning to ensure sustained development efforts.
Access to Expertise	Providing access to information, expertise, and outside resources.
Quality of Life	Identifying and addressing important factors and convening partners to positively impact a region and, as a consequence, its ability to attract and retain talented workers.

universities bring both technical expertise and brand credibility to a region needing to seek and secure funding. Table 5 offers a summary of the many dimensions on which universities can partner with regions to build the community base and associated quality of life.

Integrated Program Models

If the first step of regional engagement is developing a shared agenda, its manifestation must be a program model that brings the university into a region with deliberate efforts to realize the benefits of the university in that specific region. A virtuous circle of engagement, or reciprocation, is created through integrated program models that have the dual effect of building regional innovation infrastructure assets while feeding the scholarship needs of universities. Beyond addressing the needs of both partners, integrated program models address the transformation needs of the region through multidimensional, multidisciplinary, and, at times, multi-institutional university efforts.

Designing in Transformative Regional Effects

Arbo and Benneworth (2007) have catalogued various university approaches to regional development and suggested that such involvement can be broadly categorized into one of two forms. In "first wave" models, universities perform "straightforward" roles, generally by supplying local leaders with expert information. Alternatively, in "second wave" approaches, universities bring external resources to a region and combine it with other external resources. This, in turn, creates a "local buzz" that has a "transformatory effect" on the regional economy as compared to the very limited impacts of first wave approaches (p. 35). The challenge, then, for higher education is to leverage its expertise in ways that bring new, external funds to a region and match those funds against resources from the region to underwrite the development of distributed academic, innovation, and engagement infrastructure.

A case in point is Virginia Tech's engagement with economically distressed Southside Virginia, which yielded commitments of $80 million of new resources to the region over a six-year period and resulted in the establishment in or relocation to Southside of several high-tech companies and recapitalization of two large Fortune 100 branch manufacturing plants during the same period (Franklin, Sandmann, Franklin, & Settle, 2008). The engagement strategy employed in this partnership was to marry university research expertise with regional industry and natural assets that could be leveraged into a higher tech economic base. Regionally situated university-led applied research coupled with state-of-the-art laboratories and equipment created new regional assets that could generate new intellectual property, develop a supply of talent and technology benefits, and serve as a magnet for private sector research and development looking for a competitive edge.

The research activity led by Virginia Tech was complemented with a tailored set of educational offerings to attract and develop engineering, science, and technology talent relevant to the newer economic enterprises being established in the Southside region. These offerings included science, technology, engineering, and math (STEM) competency-building noncredit learning opportunities in addition to seamless academic pathways connecting certificates and degree programs in K–12 through community college and senior higher education institutions. The third leg of the university engagement–regional transformation stool was the design and deployment of a fiber-optic-based advanced network infrastructure over a seven-hundred-mile geography in south central Virginia.

Each of the three research, education, and technology components of the Virginia Tech–Southside Virginia partnership began by drawing new financial resources to the region because of the university's partnership with the region, which in turn attracted additional funding to the partnership. The establishment of new physical and talent assets in the region began to create an upward spiral of opportunity for the region. The opportunity to partner with the region in creating these new assets meant new financial, physical, and academic assets for Virginia Tech, too. Essentially, money flowed to the Southside region to engage university partners in regionally based research, education, and technology-based activities. Virginia Tech expanded its scholarly footprint through a willingness to locate substantial laboratories, faculty, and graduate students in the region supported by the new funding.

Transformative Impact

In a broad sense, an integrated program model can address the economic base through applied research (innovation) conducted by faculty and students, the talent base through education both by attracting new talent and by developing existing human capital in a region, the infrastructure base through service of university faculty and staff with expertise in infrastructure issues, and the community base of a region through faculty, student, and staff engagement with an array of quality-of-life interventions. These four prongs of a partnership can be addressed in an integrated fashion to have a transformative effect on the region's economy. Such "transformative" engagement is grounded in one or more targeted economic sectors for which technology-based assets are developed. Talent aggregation and development strategies are linked specifically to these sectors and assets. Infrastructure is strengthened and developed to permit ubiquitous connectivity to global markets. Community amenities relevant to the talent attraction and stickiness are cultivated.

Future Trends

In the first section of this chapter, "The Context and Opportunity," we outlined the rationale for regional engagement, particularly in strengthening and transforming the economic and community base of regions. The first subsection, "The University Engagement Interface," outlined the challenges associated with university engagement in economic development. We presented an overview of the critical elements needed by regions to be prosperous in an innovation economy in the second section, "The Virtuous Circle of Regional Needs Satisfaction." In the third section, "The Virtuous Circle of University Needs Satisfaction," a synopsis of university drivers was offered in the context of institutional motivators to address mission and reputation. The fourth section, "Coalescing Regional Engagement," included a discussion of the coalescing of regional and university assets and needs through human and structural facilitators of engagement. The elements of an engagement agenda designed to transform a region's economy were outlined in the fifth section, "The Transformative Regional Engagement Agenda." In the sixth section, "Integrated Program Models," the importance of linking regional engagement agendas to building the scholarship capacity of universities was presented.

In the next sections, we highlight future opportunities by presenting university economic development trends and raising policy issues associated with university-engaged economic development. We challenge the academy to consider a new role in community engagement focused on strategies that are aimed at transforming the economies of regions. Finally, we suggest a framework for distributed regional engagement as a central feature in a robust twenty-first-century land-grant mission.

University Economic Development Trends

As innovation and global competition have assumed elevated twenty-first-century profiles, major universities across the United States are participating more actively in state-led economic development efforts. A number of universities have responded by developing senior economic development positions and becoming more involved in the funding opportunities associated with the economic development policy thrust. As further evidence of the expanding role of economic development in university circles, in 2007 the National Association of State Universities and Land Grant Colleges changed the name of one of its member committees to the Commission on Innovation, Competitiveness, and Economic Prosperity.

Universities have adopted economic development as a fourth mission in part because campuses and programs have a great influence on the local and regional economies in which they are located and in part because economic development is a central topic of public relevance and potential support.

As we consider these higher education trends, four themes emerge that frame the posture of universities toward economic development. First, the local economic impact of the university's presence in a community continues to be a source of interest as university leaders advocate the importance of their institution to the fabric of local and state decision making. Second, interest in economic development becomes a way to renew legislative interest in providing public support to university programs, particularly research. Third, as technology-based economic development (TBED) emerges as a central strategy to support growth in the innovation economy, universities, with bountiful innovation infrastructures, find themselves with an opportunity to play a larger role in technology transfer, entrepreneurship, and capital investments in conjunction with fledgling products and firms. Finally, the concept of understanding and intentionally creating an ecology of innovation in the geographies surrounding university campuses has evolved from the TBED trends as universities appropriately seek to increase their effectiveness in leveraging their innovation infrastructures.

In looking to the future, the gap between current university economic development and the pioneering work occurring in a relative few institutions stands out. Current university efforts fall far short of their potential for a larger measure of public support. So, what is missing in the logic of the current campus dialogue? Although it makes a popular factoid in university presidents' speeches, the local economic impact of campuses is associated with little public value because these figures are considered to be of questionable accuracy or largely the function of expectations associated with public investment in facilities and programs. This criticism poses a broader issue with respect to higher education's credibility and public understanding of the academy's claims about its role and impact in economic development.

Conversations about local campus impacts, TBED, the ecology of the innovation economy, and using economic development as a rationale for expanded public support fail to recognize that the economic benefits of each largely impacts communities within a commuting distance of the target of the public expenditure (Kirchhoff, Armington, Hasan, & Newbert, 2002). In the current dialogue, new firm starts, high-paying jobs, college-educated workforce, innovation infrastructure, talent development, talent stickiness, talent spillovers, venture capital investments, and quality-of-life amenities all get concentrated in geographies targeted for investment. The university conversations align with concepts of a twenty-first-century America composed of mega-regions (Florida, 2008) and of a metro-nation (Brookings Institute, 2007) and appear to argue from an efficiency rationale for public policy in which the rich regions get richer. In simple terms, each of these four arguments fails to provide tangible benefits to enough districts to constitute a simple majority of support in most state legislatures. We submit to a simple truth: University-led economic development strategies have not received broader public support not because they are ineffective but because they are not effective in enough places.

Policies to Support University-Engaged Economic Development

As we look forward, it seems clear that the university role in economic development will continue to operate at the intersection of public policy and private enterprise. Policies will attempt to seed a private economy, support its development and acceleration, and fill absent markets with activities that advance prosperity. Four major themes emerge from the first part of this chapter to inform our perspective about economic development policy into the first half of this century: (1) industrial clusters, (2) regional development strategies, (3) innovation, and (4) talent development and stickiness. These themes suggest shifting priorities for investment as policy shifts from supporting an industrial economy to an innovation economy. The logic of demand-side economic development—creating hard infrastructure, tax policy incentives, shell buildings, etc., to absorb excess industrial demand from other regions—will give way to a supply-side rationale. This rationale calls for strong policy supports to create higher paying jobs, competitive companies, and coherent industrial units by investing in an oversupply of talent and technology aligned with a region's industrial clusters. U.S. research universities lead the world in developing these assets and contributing them to the regions in which their campuses reside.

We add to these four themes geographic economic equity and suggest that it is the basis for a broad new university agenda in economic engagement. As neck-down branch manufacturing declines in favor of knowledge-intensive advanced manufacturing and as agricultural production requires fewer and fewer workers, there is a real question about what economy is appropriate for development in the smaller industrial cities and rural regions of the United States. Whatever economy it is, it will require large measures of innovation and talent built around regional cluster development. Friedman (2008) suggests that Americans need to shift our nation building talents to our own country. The role of place in political and economic policy development is hard to overlook as our innovative and noninnovative regions appear to align closely with the lines of political ideology in the U.S. red and blue cultural divide. What is the cost to our fast-growing economic sectors of the lack of consensus about how to make our slow-growing regions more competitive? As consensus develops around place-based investment to support development in needier geographies, what investments would produce an oversupply of technology and talent in order to bring viability for them in an innovation economy?

A New University Role

Universities can do and are doing good work in many communities, but are they having the conversations that help these communities really move the needle on economic and community issues? When we consider the engagement efforts of universities, we need to ask, "To what extent is university engagement significantly impacting high-priority local issues?" Are universities doing things that affect major community economic indicators such as per capita income? Is it rising? Are new businesses forming in those communities? Are citizens of the communities adequately prepared for high-paying jobs?

We submit that universities will need to organize themselves to impact regional prosperity if they want full credit for their engagement work. Universities will have to consider how and where to invest institutional efforts in partnering. They will need to be more strategic about organizing internal people and assets for engagement. Greater clarity about anticipated institutional benefits from regional partnering will have to be articulated and kept at the center of the university's engagement agenda. An understanding of integrated program models that can be driven by the university in response to regional needs and opportunities will need to be developed.

Universities will want to be very deliberate in choosing regional partners. Becoming familiar with the core strengths and challenges of regions through analysis of publicly available demographic, economic, educational, and health data is a suggested first step. With that analysis in hand, engagement leaders at a university should consider such criteria as:

- Evidence of regional stewards who will be prepared to assume significant local responsibility for partnering
- Evidence of regional assets that can serve as a basis for building a new economic foundation
- Match between the opportunities to develop specific economic sectors in a region and capacity of the university to address these sectors
- Supportive local, state, and federal elected leaders associated with a region who will embrace a university partnership, publicly articulate the value, and work to direct public funding to the partnership

Once a regional partner is selected, the university will need to establish relationships in the region that provide an in-depth understanding of the issues, the people, the interests, and the resources associated with the region. It will be possible to develop a shared partnering agenda that builds from public need and regional assets. Together, partners can craft an integrated program model that outlines the primary pillars of higher education's role in the region's development and the innovation infrastructure assets that are to be developed in the region. Once clarity about partnering goals is outlined, regional and university players can craft a funding strategy and policies for partnership governance and accountability. The great challenge before higher education institutions committed to public engagement is to formulate regional partnering strategies that can begin to alter fundamental local dynamics by developing innovation infrastructure assets.

Institutionalizing Engagement

The United States has established and maintained global economic leadership through its ability and willingness to embrace new challenges and conceptualize new institutional structures in response. The Russian launching of Sputnik in 1957 led to a mobilization of U.S. resolve to invest much more significantly in university-based scientific research and education. University leaders saw this expansion as consistent with the missions of their institutions. In the previous century, U.S. economic competitiveness was strengthened through the establishment of a land-grant system of higher education focused specifically on agriculture and mechanical arts—the nation's primary economic drivers during that era.

We suggest that the economic challenges associated with globalization, innovation, and digitalization should similarly spur new thinking about public investments to reconsider how America's higher education strengths can be brought to bear more effectively in broad-based economic capacity building. We propose that a new system of regional stewarding institutions be established, partnering research universities with economic regions in ways that advance the well-being of regions and serve the mission of universities. We submit that investments of this kind would begin with distributed innovation infrastructure designed to distribute technology and talent and aligned with regional assets and existing or prospective industrial clusters.

None of this vision will happen without resources. If consensus for this regional development engagement model develops, reliable sources of funding will be required. We suggest that policy makers turn to the example of funding for Cooperative Extension to design a funding structure for distributed regional stewarding institutions. In this cooperative model, federal, state, and local monies would be combined to develop facilities, provide base funding for faculty and staff, and initiate program activities.

Conclusion

Fundamental messages about partnering are woven into a different kind of engagement tapestry in the model that has been presented in this chapter than in the more conventional thinking about university engagement. First, this model plays to the predominant existing faculty reward structures, which put a premium on securing external sponsored funding for research. Second, this model creates new assets for the university, including research spaces and equipment, and new faculty lines. These new assets allow the university to expand its research footprint, often in places where the cost of space is lower than on campus and the space options more plentiful. Third, this model assumes that engagement activities will be facilitated by new money. Fourth, in this model, resources flow into the region of interest rather than directly to the university. In turn, the regional partnership engages with the university for research activities, educational programs, and technology infrastructure deployment consultation. Fifth, this model assumes that research universities will consider regional partnering opportunities beyond their backyards, in places with no higher education presence up to several hours distant from the partnering university's campus.

A difficult message for universities to hear is that the political will to appropriate more money for higher education is low. No matter how much universities commit to engaging with communities, if the partnership strategies are built on the presumption of directing funding to the universities' campuses for discretionary use, they will be viewed with skepticism if not dismissed outright. Politicians and, to some degree, the public at large will see such proposals as thinly veiled attempts to pad higher education's asset base and faculty resumes. If they see promises of value to the communities, they will likely assume that benefits will be short-lived—only as long as it takes the faculty members involved to publish a journal article.

On the other hand, there is considerable pressure on states to assist ailing regions through redistributive economic policy. Such redistribution not only is a political necessity to keep constituents in poorer communities happy (enough to vote to keep those politicians in office) but also offers a means to increase the overall health of a state. To this point, most states have funds designated for economic development. Historically, such funds have been used for incentives such as shell buildings, targeted worker training, and tax abatements to lure businesses into the state. In an innovation-based economy, these historic economic development approaches are being replaced with strategies that build innovation infrastructure—research, talent, and high-speed networking. What better way to develop innovation capacity than to leverage research universities?

So, it's really the money that's in the economic development space and the expertise in the higher education space that create tremendous win-win-win opportunities: for the state, for the region, and for the university. Each of these three entities has an important and unique role to play.

What we have advanced in this chapter is a model of economic engagement that expands the university's role to meet a true public need in a manner aligned with the university's mission, capabilities, and current public policy. Implementation requires public consensus, university will, shared agenda setting, and significant investments in innovation infrastructure and integrated programs. The result is the promise of more prosperous regions, states, and nation.

References

Arbo, P., & Benneworth, P. (2007). *Understanding the regional contribution of higher education institutions: A literature review*. Organisation for Economic Co-operation and Development Education Working Paper No. 9. Retrieved April 16, 2007, from http://www.oecd.org/dataoecd/55/7/37006775.pdf.

Boyer, E. (1990). *Scholarship reconsidered: Priorities of the professoriate*. Carnegie Foundation for the Advancement of Teaching. San Francisco: Jossey-Bass.

Brookings Institute. (2007). *MetroNation: How U.S. metropolitan areas fuel American prosperity*. Available at http://www.brookings.edu/reports/2007/1106_metronation_berube.aspx.

Council on Competitiveness. (2008). *Cooperate: A practitioner's guide for effective alignment of regional development and higher education*. Available at http://www.compete.org/publications/detail/412/cooperate/.

Council on Competitiveness & New Economy Strategies. (2005). *2005 National Innovation Survey*. Available at http://www.new-econ.com/pdf/2005_National_Innovation_Survey.pdf.

Drabenstott, M. (2005). A *review of the federal role in regional economic development*. Available at http://www.kansascityfed.org/RegionalAffairs/Regionalstudies/FederalReview_RegDev_605.pdf.

Florida, R. (2008). *Who's your city: How the creative economy is making where to live the most important decision of your life*. New York: Basic Books.

Franklin, N. (2008). *The land-grant mission 2.0: Distributed regional engagement*. (Doctoral Dissertation University of Pennsylvania, 2008). Available at: http://gateway.proquest.com/openurl?url ver=Z 39.88–2004&res_dat=xri:pqdiss&rft_val_fmt=info:ofi/fmt:kev:mtx:dissertation&rft_dat=xri:pqdiss:3310496

Franklin, T., Sandmann, L., Franklin, N., & Settle, T. (2008). Answering the question of how: Out-of-region university engagement with an economically distressed rural region. *Journal of Higher Education Outreach & Engagement, 12*(3), 205–220.

Friedman, T. (2008). *Hot, flat, and crowded: Why we need a green revolution—and how it can renew America.* New York: Farrar, Straus and Giroux.

Henton, D., Melville, J., & Walesh, K. (2002). Collaboration and innovation: The state of American regions. *Industry and Higher Education, 16*(1), 9–17.

Initiative for a Competitive Inner City & CEOs for Cities (2002). *Leveraging colleges and universities for urban economic revitalization: An action agenda.* Available at http://www.ceosforcities.org./files/colleges_1.pdf.

Jones, D. (2005). *Shaping state policy to encourage stewardship of place.* Boulder, CO: National Center for Higher Education Management Systems.

Kellogg Commission on the Future of State and Land-Grant Universities. (1999). Returning *to our roots: The engaged institution.* Retrieved from the National Association of State Universities and Land-Grant Colleges Web site, http://www.nasulgc.org/Kellogg/kellogg.htm

Kirchhoff, B., Armington, C., Hasan, I., & Newbert, S. (2002). *The influence of R&D expenditures on new firm formation and economic growth.* Available at http://www.sba.gov/advo/research/rs222tot.pdf

Kirp, D. (2005). This little student went to market. In R. Hersh & J. Merrow (Eds.), *Declining by degrees* (pp. 113–129). New York: Palgrave Macmillan.

Moore, L., & Franklin, T. (2008, October). *University Roundtable on Transformative Regional Engagement: Intentional partnerships, leadership, programming, and policy.* Unpublished proceedings of the University Roundtable on Transformative Regional Engagement, The Pennsylvania State University, University Park, PA.

Porter, M. (2007). *Colleges and universities and regional economic development: A strategic perspective.* Forum for the Future of Higher Education. Available at http://net.educause.edu/forum/ff07.asp?bhcp=1.

Porter, M., Monitor Group, ontheFRONTIER, & Council on Competitiveness (2001). *Clusters of innovation: Regional foundations of U.S. competitiveness.* Washington, DC: Council on Competitiveness.

Purcell, W. D., & Mundy, K. P. (2003). *Research-based guidelines in developing successful university based research and higher education programs in science and technology.* Blacksburg state?: Virginia Tech.

Vidal, A., Nye, N., Walker, C., Manjarrez, C., & Romanik, C. (2002). *Lessons from the community outreach partnership center program.* Available at http://www.oup.org/files/pubs/lessons_learned.pdf.

Zemsky, R., Wegner, G., & Massey, W. (2005). *Remaking the American university: Market-smart and mission-centered.* New Brunswick, NJ: Rutgers University Press.

PART 2

Measuring, Assessing, and Accrediting Engaged Scholarship

Edited by Cathy Burack

Measuring, Assessing, and Accrediting Engaged Scholarship

Cathy Burack

There are two informal tests one can use to determine the extent to which an idea or initiative has gained traction. One is to note if there is still support and momentum after the primary champions of the idea cease to assume that role (e.g., the president who leaves the institution, the committee that is dissolved). The other test is the presence of systems that measure, assess, and accredit. In this section, you will see that this is indeed the case with regard to engaged scholarship.

In some ways this section represents a story of higher education's reclamation of its role as a public good. What is notable is that most of the story occurs within the past thirty years and involves a reconceptualization of how institutions define themselves relative to the community, and how disciplines conceive their purpose and the work of faculty. Remarkably, this history includes the entire higher education landscape: four- and two-year institutions, liberal arts and research, undergraduate and graduate. Thus, the ideas of measuring and assessing start as a way to begin to chronicle the burgeoning numbers of outreach and engagement activities, and become transformative as they require that we include faculty work, student learning, community impact, and institutional structures as necessary components of the analysis of the impact and outcomes of engaged scholarship.

Crystal Lunsford, Burton Bargerstock, and Philip Greasley provide an overview of the measurement of institutional and faculty engagement and note how the public's need for accountability by colleges and universities and internal needs of higher education to gain insight into the quality of the work both served as impetus for measuring engagement. Those forces have contributed to the creation of accreditation criteria such as those included in the Higher Learning Commission of the North Central Association of Colleges and Schools, and the Carnegie Foundation for the Advancement of Teaching's elective classification of

101

Community Engaged Institution. There have been statewide efforts, and efforts by institutional type. Lunsford, Bargerstock, and Greasley identify ten key themes that emerge across the measurement efforts they examined, and faculty engagement figures prominently. They also address how the effort to document, especially faculty work, is transformative in and of itself, and that it requires a common language around engagement and shared notions of what constitutes quality scholarship and teaching.

This section includes two chapters written from the perspective of psychology and sociology. The disciplines (and their related academic departments), in most colleges and universities, are the core structural supports for engaged faculty. These chapters will hold obvious import for psychologists and sociologists. However, their special contributions are as examples of how disciplines can both respond to and advocate for engagement as a necessary focus.

Paul Nelson and Jill Reich offer psychology as a case study of a changing field. They note that "the APA is the largest and most diverse organization of psychologists, the current mission of which is 'to advance the creation, communication and application of psychological knowledge to benefit society and improve people's lives'" and note that this is in contrast to its focus less than one hundred years ago on the individual apart from society. They examine the role that service-learning can play in deepening students' learning and their acquisition of "socially responsive knowledge." Nelson and Reich also make a strong argument that the expertise of faculty must change, and that includes the ways in which we prepare future faculty if the mission of psychology is to be sustained.

Michael Burawoy discusses the role of public sociology as a force for social change, and does so within an international context. He uses Boyer's work on scholarship to draw distinctions between types of sociology and their attendant bodies of knowledge: professional (discovery), policy (application), public (teaching), and critical (integration). Through the role of public sociology, Burawoy argues that "Our discipline can turn from a field-in-itself, with a fragmented division of labor, to a field-for-itself—a symbiotic division of labor that becomes a social movement for an expanded public sphere rooted in a self-organizing civil society." Burawoy's, and Nelson's and Reich's views of the work of faculty within these disciplines requires that institutions and departments have ways to evaluate and reward engaged scholarship.

Dwight Giles, Lorilee Sandmann, and John Saltmarsh provide an overview of a peer-focused framework for documenting an institution's commitment to engagement, the Carnegie Foundation for the Advancement of Teaching's Community Engaged Institution classification. They examined a subset of the first group of colleges and universities that were successful in receiving that distinction to better understand the extent to which engagement was deeply embedded in institutions, and where there were still challenges. They looked at literature on institutional change in higher education and argue that institutions that are successful in meeting the criteria of Carnegie are in fact in a transformational process. Not surprisingly, part of that process is the revision of promotion and tenure policies. The process of change around assessing faculty work fell along a continuum. They noted that the "policy revision processes reveals a continuum. On one end of the continuum is new presidential leadership that pronounces a new vision for the campus and initiates a process of reexamining the academic culture around engagement, but has not yet effected a change in policies…On the other end of the continuum is evidence of campuses with full revised promotion and tenure guidelines incorporating specific criteria for community-engaged scholarship."

One of the significant challenges that emerged from the applications of the 2006 Carnegie Community Engaged Institutions was reciprocity in campus-community partnerships. Randy Stoecker, Mary Beckman, and Bo Hee Min pick up this theme in addressing the issue of assessing community impact. Reasons for the lack of focus on community impact include a dominant focus on student outcomes, inadequate time to fully document the long-term impact of community-based projects, and a lack of familiarity by university-based researchers with community development. Like Burawoy, Stoeker, Beckman, and Min argue that assessing community impact requires a shift in perspective and "puts the emphasis on the social change goals of the community, and the analysis of the causal relationship between those outcome goals and the entire strategy being employed, including any higher education civic engagement activities that are part of that strategic mix." This in turn leads to an argument for a shift in how service projects are constructed in order to really serve the community and the community's agenda; it requires a "community-university infrastructure committed to community development." This transformation in higher education was also discussed by Giles, Sandmann, and Saltmarsh, as they noted that "evidence from the applications indicates that shifting an institutional commitment to community engagement is an enormously complex and difficult undertaking that fundamentally challenges the dominant operating system of higher education."

These chapters give us an overview of what exists with regard to beginning to capture the extent of faculty engagement and higher education–community partnerships. What they also do is raise important questions about how we frame engaged work within disciplinary contexts, how graduate schools teach future faculty, and the roles colleges and universities play as members of communities. To these questions we will need to constantly add a second set that asks us to reflect on the quality of the work, the structures that support it, and the difference it makes.

Measuring Institutional Engagement and Faculty-Based Engaged Scholarship

Crystal G. Lunsford, Burton A. Bargerstock, and Philip A. Greasley

Overview of Chapter

American colleges and universities have historically contributed to the public good in ways that extend beyond traditional undergraduate and graduate education and the production of knowledge (Veysey, 1965). Whether by way of continuing education programs, cooperative extension, international development, service-learning, or faculty service to public bodies, higher education has long promoted service for the public good. Over the past two decades, the conceptualization of such activities has evolved from one of public service to scholarly engagement, the latter emphasizing the importance of reciprocal and mutually beneficial relationships between university participants and the broader society (Kellogg Commission on the Future of State and Land-Grant Universities, 1999). In contrast to service, engagement presupposes the importance of greater involvement by the public in the design and implementation of collaborative activities and also demands that faculty draw on their scholarly expertise for the benefit of the public as well as themselves.

In this chapter, we describe a number of efforts designed to document and measure engagement between higher education and the public. Following a discussion of why it is important to measure engagement, we offer an overview of current documentation and measurement initiatives at the institutional and individual faculty levels. Because this chapter focuses on efforts that account for faculty-based engaged scholarship or which were specifically designed to understand faculty work, we do not incorporate measurement activities aimed primarily at the study of student engagement. We take the position that faculty are fundamental to the engagement mission of higher education institutions and that to understand engagement it is important to focus on faculty work (Church, 2001; Ward, 2003).

As a means to identify and discuss the complexities and challenges of understanding how universities contribute to the public, the chapter provides a case study account of the efforts by Michigan State University (MSU) to document and understand faculty engagement as a means of representing how it contributes to the public. This chapter concludes with a discussion of the limitations of existing measurement efforts and suggests ways in which research and inquiry should be broadened to improve what is known about university engagement.

Why Measure Engagement?

Efforts to measure and document most phenomena depend on shared meanings and definitions. There are challenges to understanding faculty engagement because faculty vary in how they think about and participate in outreach and engagement activities (Holland, 2001; Neumann & Terosky, 2007). Holland (2001) identifies how the "values" embedded in engagement—collaboration, cooperation, shared power, and knowledge exchange—are difficult to operationalize, thus making measuring engagement challenging. She further points out that the variation among institutional definitions of engagement creates additional challenges for conducting research across institutions and for use in institutional comparisons and national benchmarking efforts.

Even though the documentation and measurement of engagement are challenging, colleges and universities are becoming increasingly interested in being able to determine whether they are fulfilling their engagement missions and how to represent their accomplishments. Both external and internal forces are influencing these efforts. First and foremost, the public is a force driving higher education institutions to justify their contributions to alleviating societal problems and contributing to social progress. Ward (2003) draws on the existing literature to describe how "the public has lost faith in higher education" (p. 7). She claims that higher education's failure to inform the public about its contributions, coupled with rising tuition costs, has alienated and created a divide between the general public and higher education. Current national and state economic conditions and their likely unfavorable effects on appropriations for public higher education (Inside Higher Education, 2009) suggest an even greater need to convince the public about the contributions universities make. Because public colleges and universities are competing for fewer resources, they are being called upon to provide evidence to legislatures and government officials of all the ways in which investment in higher education produces positive results for the public.

Second, in this era of accountability, external entities and organizations are requiring higher education institutions to document how their activities reach beyond the university to engage external individuals and groups for the benefit of society. The Higher Learning Commission of the North Central Association of Colleges and Schools (NCA-HLC), a regional institutional accreditor, and the Carnegie Foundation for the Advancement of Teaching have each developed criteria specific to engagement. The NCA-HLC, for example, asks colleges and universities to explain how they identify and serve the needs of the public (Higher Learning Commission, 2003). The Carnegie Foundation developed an elective classification system, described later, that requires participating institutions to describe their involvement with and commitment to community engagement (Carnegie Foundation for the Advancement of Teaching [Carnegie], 2007). Both efforts position university and community relations as collaborative rather than hierarchical and emphasize the needs and concerns of the community, while simultaneously contributing to faculty productivity and student learning.

The documentation and measurement of engagement can also provide a forum for higher education institutions to reflect on engagement, including how they support and facilitate campus engagement. For instance, the Committee on Institutional Cooperation's (CIC) Engagement Committee (Committee on Institutional Cooperation [CIC], 2005) has identified several potential benefits to institutions for understanding campus engagement, beyond merely garnering public and legislative support. First, the CIC identifies measurement as a means for institutions to determine if they are fulfilling the goals and objectives they have established for engagement. Second, data about engagement can provide evidence for holding individual departments and units accountable for contributing to institutional engagement efforts. According to the CIC, measuring engagement can also guide decision making about organizational support and how universities and colleges are contributing to economic and scientific advancement. Finally, institutional efforts can lead to the development of national rubrics for making comparisons among universities on the basis of their engagement efforts. As leaders and stakeholders benchmark institutional performance, against both past performance and that of peer institutions, engagement may receive greater attention.

Efforts to document and measure engagement can also influence the quality of the engagement activities undertaken by campus members. By researching engagement, faculty can gain more insight about their work with and on behalf of the public in ways that can enhance rather than undermine their work (Neumann & Terosky, 2007). As identified throughout the chapters in this book, Boyer's work (1990, 1996) has been fundamental to efforts to redefine scholarship as activity that extends beyond inquiry to account for teaching and engagement-related work (O'Meara & Rice, 2005; Rice, 2002). Even so, there is limited insight about how faculty relate engagement to their scholarship. Understanding how faculty conceptualize engagement in relation to their professional responsibilities—research, teaching, and service—can yield greater benefits for faculty involved in this type of work. Increased information about effective practices and processes for conducting various forms of engaged scholarship and the impacts of such work, particularly related to teaching and research, can be used by faculty to design interventions that are scholarship-based. Data can also influence how college and university leaders develop and implement policies to facilitate faculty involvement in engaged scholarship, including redefining promotion and tenure policies in ways that value faculty work that involves and targets the public.

Current Efforts to Document and Measure Engagement

In this section, we examine approaches to documenting and measuring engagement, first at the institutional level and then as a function of faculty work. Although we do not claim this review to be exhaustive, we attempt to represent the range of indicators and measures currently used to understand engagement as an institutional function and faculty involvement in engagement-related work.

Engagement as an Institutional Function

The existing literature documents a relationship between institutional characteristics and the level of engagement existing between universities and external constituents and communities (Brukardt, Holland, Percy, & Zimpher, 2004; Holland, 1999). It conveys how polices and practices supportive of and conducive to engagement are important institutional structures without which faculty and students are less likely to become involved with the public. Policies that reward faculty for their academic work, including those that address promotion and tenure, are typically identified as hindering faculty involvement in engagement, because at most institutions engagement is not valued by reward systems (O'Meara, 2002).

We describe four different documentation and measurement efforts designed to examine engagement at the institutional level. The foci of the efforts are diverse—national, statewide, and regional, and institutional type—and are presented accordingly. After providing an initial overview of each institutional-level documentation and measurement effort, we identify ten themes that span them and provide examples of the types of indicators and measures supportive of each theme.

Overall, we found that one of the fundamental purposes of existing institutional documentation and measurement efforts has been to identify exemplary instances of engagement. Whether *exemplary* relates to specific institutional types or more specifically to types of policies and practices differs by initiative, but these efforts are primarily aimed at collecting descriptive information about engagement rather than empirically testing and investigating these data. Documentation efforts primarily require a university representative to respond to a series of questions that generally do not require data collected systematically by the university or external organizations. The types of responses required by most documentation efforts are estimates about institutional work or narrative descriptions and explanations about engagement projects. Efforts not specific to documentation-reported findings primarily highlight exemplary approaches to engagement, rather than illuminating the relationships between institutional characteristics and engagement.

National Framework for Classifying Engagement

Developed in response to what Driscoll terms "a concern about the inadequacy of the [Carnegie Foundation's traditional] classification for representing institutional similarities and differences and its insensitivity to the evolution of higher education" (Driscoll, 2008, p. 39), the Carnegie Foundation's community engagement classification documents how higher education institutions are involved with the general public. Through its first two review cycles, this elective classification system has designated 195 institutions as community engaged (Carnegie, 2009). Unlike most national institutional data collection efforts that conduct secondary analyses of existing data, the community engagement classification primarily asks for self-reported types of institutional information. It requires participating institutions to respond to a number of yes/no questions about their outreach and community engagement and to provide evidence and examples to support responses. Driscoll also identifies the instrument as a tool for facilitating institutional understanding of engagement and advancing engagement on individual colleges and universities.

The documentation framework is divided into two parts. The first is designed to determine whether an institution's identity and culture and its commitments are supportive of engagement. Institutions that are identified as having met the requirements of these foundational indicators proceed to the second part of the framework. Through self-study, institutions document their accomplishments in the framework's categories of engagement: "curricular engagement," or teaching and learning activities involving the public, and "outreach and partnerships," such as university-community relationships and the types of university resources provided to the public. By fulfilling the requirements of the framework, institutions can receive classification in one or both of these categories.

Statewide Effort to Characterize Engagement and Its Impact

A statewide documentation and measurement effort commissioned by Minnesota state legislators was undertaken by the Minnesota Higher Education Services Office and Minnesota Campus Compact to determine (1) the outcomes of state-supported engagement and (2) indicators of engagement, and (3) to document engagement at higher education institutions in Minnesota (Bowley, 2003). In contrast to most of the other institutional measurement and documentation initiatives, this study included multiple types of institutions—higher education and community-based organizations. Forty-five colleges and universities in Minnesota were represented in the study, as well as forty community-based organizations. Multiple strategies were used for data collection, including interviews, observations, and document analysis. University people including administrators, faculty, and students were interviewed, and interviews were also conducted with community partners.

The study was designed to collect information across six indicators of civic engagement: (1) culture—campus culture nurtures and encourages civic engagement; (2) leadership—civic leadership is developed and supported at all levels; (3) power and policy—campus supports participatory decision making, and campus policies support engagement; (4) accessibility—campus resources are available and open to "outsiders"; (5) enabling mechanisms—campus structures, systems, and resource allocation support engagement; and (6) breadth and depth of programs—campus supports high-quality forms of engagement.

Findings of the study were reported at the state level, and "highlights" from select institutions were reported by institution. The strongest and weakest indicators of civic engagement in the state of Minnesota were among the findings publicly reported. Many of the significant conclusions or the key findings about university engagement revealed a relationship between institutional type and engagement focus. Several institutional characteristics (e.g., mission, resources, and support structures) were predictive of level of civic engagement at participating institutions.

Institutional Types

Besides national and state efforts, there have also been measurement activities developed to examine engagement by type of institution. Land-grant institutions have traditionally played a significant role in serving the needs of the public (Kellogg Commission, 1999). Community colleges, liberal arts colleges, institutions serving predominately racial minority populations, and urban institutions are also recognized for their engagement

109

accomplishments. More recently, a consortium of research-intensive universities began collaborating to shape and influence how engagement is conceptualized and enacted at peer research universities, because these types of institutions have not typically been associated with this form of work (Gibson, 2006; Stanton, 2007).

The measurement of engagement by institutional type focuses on engagement at particular types of institutions—state and land-grant institutions, community colleges, or minority-serving institutions—rather than examining differences across institutional types. For example, these efforts did not test whether engagement was more common at particular types of institutions. Instead, they primarily sought to identify the existing data collection efforts undertaken by state and land-grant institutions to inform the development of benchmarks, and to highlight exemplary institutional practices and policies at community colleges and institutions predominantly serving racial minorities.

State and Land-Grant Institutions

In 2005, the National Association of State Universities and Land-Grant Colleges (NASULGC) Council on Extension, Continuing Education, and Public Service (CECEPS) conducted a survey of member institutions to identify the types of existing data collected by institutions about engagement (Council on Extension, Continuing Education, and Public Service [CECEPS], 2005). The survey was undertaken as a preliminary step meant to inform the Council's efforts to develop a set of national benchmarks for engagement. Forty-nine NASULGC institutions participated in the study.

In developing the survey, the CECEPS Committee on Measuring University Engagement began working from a framework that organized metrics according to institutional inputs, institutional outputs or actions, and impacts or effects (CECEPS, 2005). CS Participating institutions were asked to indicate whether they measured a number of input, output, and impact variables and at what level the data were collected: institution, unit, or subset of units.

The survey also asked institutions about what methods they employed to assess impacts, several questions about their motivations for collecting these data and how they were organized to do so, what national data collection efforts they participated in, where they looked for best practices, and whether they had undertaken changes in promotion and tenure to accommodate faculty engagement.

Informed by the results of the survey, a review of the CIC's recent work on benchmarks (CIC, 2005), and ongoing discussion, the Committee on Measuring University Engagement began to identify metrics for measuring engagement and outreach activities (CECEPS, 2007a, 2007b). This work is currently ongoing, but to date, the committee has identified six "engagement dimensions" which serve as broad categories for organizing thirty specific metrics. The dimensions include the following: (1) institutional commitment to engagement; (2) faculty and staff are involved in engagement and outreach activities; (3) students are involved in engagement and outreach activities; (4) institution is reciprocally engaged with diverse individuals and groups; (5) impacts and outcomes of engagement and outreach activities are assessed; and (6) resource/revenue opportunities are generated through engagement and outreach activities (CECEPS, 2007a, 2007b).

Community Colleges and Racial Minority–Serving Institutions

Campus Compact documented the engagement policies and practices of community colleges and institutions predominately serving racial minorities—historically Black colleges, Hispanic-serving institutions, and tribal colleges (Zlotkowski et al., 2004, 2005). In the first year of this effort (2002–2003), community colleges were recruited to develop a list of exemplary approaches to share with similar institutions. This effort was also designed to determine how the characteristics of community colleges related to engagement. Data were collected from twenty community colleges. The following year the characteristics and practices of racial minority–serving institutions were investigated to determine how such institutions supported engagement. The findings convey differences among the institutional characteristics of historically Black colleges and universities, Hispanic institutions, and tribal colleges, and illuminate how such characteristics relate to the role engagement plays at each institution.

For both studies, participating institutions were asked to respond to a survey to document their exemplary practices. The criteria listed on the documentation instrument to define *exemplary* represented a range of characteristics from innovative, sustained, transforming, institutionalized, to accepted, widespread, publicized/acknowledged/recognized, and significant. The survey asked an institutional representative to indicate whether their institution had an exemplary approach to multiple criteria representing thirteen indicators of engagement: mission and purpose; academic and administrative leadership; disciplines, departments, and interdisciplinary work; pedagogy and epistemology; faculty development; faculty roles and rewards; enabling mechanisms; internal resource allocation; community voice; external resource allocation; integrated and complementary engagement activities; forums for fostering public dialogue; and student voice. Respondents were then asked to describe their institution's approach and to include supportive details explaining how the approach was exemplary. Follow-up telephone interviews were conducted, and site visits were made to some of the participating institutions.

Criteria Supportive of Institutional Indicators

In addition to the findings highlighted from the four institutional documentation and measurement efforts, we delineate the indicators and measures used across these efforts in this section. These indicators are suggestive of ten key themes. Not all themes are represented in each documentation and initiative effort, but they collectively represent the range of information included across the existing efforts.

Institutional Commitment

One of the key indicators of engagement found within each of the four documentation and measurement initiatives is institutional commitment. Institutional commitment most often refers to how institutional practices and policies support engagement. Overall, the types of indicators used to identify this form of commitment are general and broad. Most measures do not capture level or quality of commitment. As illustrated by the following list, the types of information collected by these efforts garner evidence about the types of resources colleges and universities allocate to engagement. The following indicators were drawn from the

111

Carnegie community engagement classification system and the survey developed by Campus Compact:

- Campus and/or office designated to support engagement
- Money allocated for engagement (internal and external)
- Money generation to support engagement (e.g., fundraising)
- Adequate professional staff and/or coordination to support engagement
- Data collection about impact and the impact on various stakeholders
- Engagement included in strategic planning
- Engagement connected to other institutional priorities
- Provisions made to accommodate engagement (e.g., resources, flexible scheduling)
- Resources used to strengthen community-based and civic engagement activities

Institutional Culture

Institutional culture is another key indicator found across the existing documentation and measurement initiatives. Existing indicators and measures identify university policy and the practices of campus members as evidence of whether the culture of the institution is supportive of engagement. The Carnegie community engagement classification asks institutions to document whether engagement is represented in the mission statement, university leadership, public recognition/awards, and materials advertising the institution. The survey designed by Campus Compact to identify "exemplary practices" also accounts for institutional policies and practices conducive to engagement. In contrast to the Carnegie documentation framework, the Campus Compact survey asks institutions to exemplify a set of criteria suggestive of institutional culture. In relation to mission and purpose, for example, the instrument asks whether the institution's mission statement expresses commitment to the public, if it is used by the institution to promote its work, and whether people on campus "demonstrate familiarity with and ownership of the institution's mission." Institutions that exhibit a culture that is open to reflecting on their efforts and strengthening that effort is the final criterion listed on the Campus Compact survey.

The indicators used in the Minnesota study to determine the impact of engagement include subindicators that define culture primarily in terms of whether campus practices "nurture" and "encourage" civic engagement. The seven indicators include the following: (1) engagement is valued in pedagogy and research; a culture of relevance exists; (2) local knowledge is valued in epistemology/knowledge generation; (3) scholarship of engagement is valued for faculty; (4) faculty, staff, and students are encouraged to be active in the community (voting, volunteerism, activism, etc.); (5) controversy is handled as teachable moment; (6) partnership relationships are built on respect, responsiveness, mutual accountability, and assets; and (7) civic engagement is connected to other institutional priorities.

Faculty Engagement

In some documentation efforts, the investigation of whether faculty engagement and the results of that work are valued by institutions is documented and measured as institutional culture. In this chapter, we identify some of the indicators and measures of faculty engagement that are also indicative of institutional culture under both themes because they are not mutually exclusive. One could make the argument that most institutional indicators of engagement are either directly or indirectly suggestive of an institutional culture conducive to engagement, or that they convey an institutional commitment to engagement.

Most of the institutional-level indicators of faculty engagement highlight the importance of institutional policies and practices necessary for creating an environment that encourages faculty involvement in engagement. In each of the four documentation instruments, institutions are asked to indicate whether their promotion and tenure policies account for engagement, whether engagement is included in hiring policies, and whether faculty data and reporting forms allow for reporting engagement and service. Faculty development is another indicator of engagement. The Minnesota study, for example, included three subindicators of faculty development not included in the other documentation initiatives. Faculty development, in this study, accounted for developing the teaching and instructional abilities of faculty to prepare them to become involved in service-learning and other community-based education. The indicators of faculty development also emphasize the importance of institutional policies, including "access to curriculum development grants" and "reductions in teaching loads," for facilitating and improving faculty involvement in engaged teaching.

Another type of institutional indicator related to faculty engagement included in the measurement and documentation instruments is the value institutions place on academic or scholarly based outcomes of faculty engagement (e.g., engaged scholarship and scholarship of engagement). Although not necessarily only relevant to faculty, the Carnegie community engagement classification asks institutions to document whether scholarship has been produced as a result of the outreach and engagement activities reported.

Engagement as Teaching and Learning

The types of indicators and measures of engaged teaching and learning emphasize institutional support for service-learning and other forms of experiential and community-based learning. The Carnegie community engagement documentation framework requires institutions to indicate whether they have developed an institutional definition for service-learning. Additional questions included in the framework relate to institutional practices, including whether service-learning is a common and widespread campus activity. Institutions are asked to record the number and proportion of courses with a service-learning requirement, departments represented by these courses, and faculty and students involved in service-learning. Similarly, the Carnegie documentation asks participating institutions to indicate whether curricular engagement is an institution-wide initiative and if it accounts for various forms of community engagement (e.g., research, leadership, internships, study abroad) and cuts across diverse types of courses.

Other measurement and documentation initiatives focus more specifically on the extent to which service-learning and other forms of experiential learning are valued by the institution. The instruments designed by Campus Compact to identify "exemplary practices" ask if faculty and administrators believe that experiential learning is a "credible method for crafting meaning and understanding." Other key institutional indicators and measures of engaged teaching and learning included on the survey related more specifically to student learning, including the following: (1) students learn about the cultural and historical perspectives on the meaning of community-based engagement throughout their academic experiences, and (2) community-based work provides an opportunity for students to generate knowledge, develop critical thinking skills, and grapple with the ambiguity of social problems.

In contrast, the 2005 survey administered to land-grant institutions and state universities by CECEPS defined engaged teaching more broadly. This documentation effort asked respondents about instructional activities targeting nontraditional students or that were taught at alternative locations rather than only focusing on experiential forms of teaching and learning. Institutions were also asked to indicate if they collected information about the number of students served by distance and off-campus instruction, noncredit instruction, and programs designed for nontraditional students. CECEPS' later work on its six engagement dimensions focused less on the characteristics of the students (as nontraditional) and included metrics more specifically related to service-learning (CECEPS, 2007b). The dimension on institutional commitment includes a metric on the amount of awards/grants recognizing and supporting engagement activities and curricular innovations. The dimension on faculty and staff involvement in engagement and outreach activities includes the following metrics: proportion of faculty and staff who teach credit courses that contain community-based or service-learning components, and proportion of faculty and staff who participate in clinical, field-based, or professional training programs. The dimension on student involvement includes metrics on the proportions of students enrolled in credit courses that contain a community-based or service-learning component; participating in study abroad; and participating in clinical, field-based, or professional training programs. Last, the dimension on the assessment of impacts includes a metric on evaluating the outcomes and impacts of continuing education and extension activities.

Institution-wide and Institutionalized

As evidenced by several indicators and measures already identified and described, determining whether engagement is an activity that spans the institution is a measure used to understand engagement as a function of institutions. Attempts to understand if engagement is an institution-wide activity focus on determining the breadth of engagement. Questions ask whether engagement spans departments and disciplines and if, in the case of the Campus Compact survey, initiatives span disciplines. Institutionalized forms of engagement are identified by the Campus Compact survey as the responsibility of academic units rather than the work of individual faculty and students. As included on the survey, "academic units (i.e., departments and programs) rather than individual faculty members have assumed ownership of partnering activities." In the case of CECEPS, more than half of the thirty metrics organized within its six engagement dimensions are proportions. Proportions of units (e.g., colleges, departments), faculty and staff, administrators, students, or institutional funds, either bearing particular characteristics or behaving in particular ways, are sought across four of the six dimensions. The selection of proportional as opposed to simple numeric aggregate metrics reflects a design decision by the CECEPS Committee on Measuring University Engagement to identify the relative magnitude or degree of engagement present within institutions, another means of ascertaining the breadth of engagement.

Resources for the Community, Community Involvement, and Community Impact

The measurement and documentation efforts account differently for the community and its role in the engagement process. Differences also exist in the extent the voices and perspectives of community partners are valued by these efforts. In terms of resource allocation, the Carnegie framework emphasizes the types of resources provided to the community by colleges and universities. Resources refer to "outreach programs" such learning centers, tutoring, and noncredit courses and "institutional resources" (e.g., cultural offerings, athletic offerings, library services, technology). The Campus Compact survey requires institutions to account for "exemplary practices" that connect institutional policies to the surrounding communities as an indicator of resource allocation. One example is "purchasing and hiring policies that intentionally favor local residents and businesses." The Minnesota campus engagement study included similar indicators of resource allocation, including whether colleges and universities serve as a forum for the community to "dialogue on important issues" and their involvement in community development.

Both the Minnesota study and the instrument developed by Campus Compact include indicators specific to how community influences university affairs and governance. In the case of the Minnesota study, "power and policy" included subindicators of community involvement:

- Decision-making on campus includes all campus stakeholder voices
- Campus is open to community voice in decisions that affect them
- Endowment policy (how the endowment is invested) considers local, regional, or global impact
- Purchasing/procurement considers public impact—including local or regional community impact
- Facilities management considers environmental and social outcomes and opportunities

The survey designed by Campus Compact includes seven indicators of community voice. Community voice consists of how colleges and universities value community and community involvement, and how these relate to the process of campus engagement.

The 2005 CECEPS survey asked institutions two types of questions about their documentation of community involvement. One type of question related to the provision of services to the community, including clinical services and instructional activities, which were referred to as the allocation of resources. Institutions were also asked to identify if and how they assess the effect of engagement on (1) communities and regions and (2) learners, service clients, and their stakeholders. In 2007, CECEPS went further in acknowledging community involvement, by identifying the reciprocal engagement of institutions with communities as one of its six engagement dimensions. Metrics for this dimension include such things as systematic efforts to assess community needs, the existence of mechanisms for the public to use to request assistance from institutions, institutional assessment of community partners' satisfaction with engagement activities, and the proportions of faculty, staff, and administrators serving on external boards and panels or otherwise engaged with government officials.

Across the four documentation and measurement initiatives, little attention has been devoted to understanding and determining how the university impacts communities and

115

other external constituents. The Minnesota study is the only effort that collects data from nonuniversity people. Based on the information collected through the 2005 CECEPS survey, none of the institutions surveyed measured the outcomes of outreach and engagement from the "perspective of the communities engaged with the university" at the level of the institution. Findings also illustrate that very few institutions measure how knowledge transfer impacts the institution. Nonetheless, the CECEPS Committee on Measuring University Engagement recognized the importance of determining impacts by including impact assessment as one of its six engagement dimensions, going as far as to include a metric on whether assessment tools and plans are collaboratively developed with external partners.

Partnerships

Another category included in the existing documentation and measurement activities is the partnerships existing between colleges and university and external constituents. The Carnegie engagement classification requires institutions to identify up to fifteen partnerships. Institutions are asked to include the purpose, length, number and types of people involved, and grant funding. For each project a description of the impact on community and institution is also requested. The latter begins to address whether engagement is reciprocal and mutually beneficial. The documentation instrument also includes a question about whether the institution promotes these types of partnerships.

The Campus Compact survey accounts for and is suggestive of the role and support of partnerships as subindicators of three of its indicators of engagement—budget and resource allocation, community involvement, and coordination of community-based activities.

Impact on Institution

Across these data collection initiatives, there is not a lot of attention given to determining how engagement impacts colleges and universities. The 2005 CECEPS survey asked institutions to identify whether they document and measure the revenues they receive from outreach and engagement services, as measures of institutional output from outreach and engagement. This survey also accounted for secondary impacts on institutions such as whether institutions measure the number and type of recognition programs related to outreach and engagement (e.g., scholarships, cash awards) and the proportion of faculty involved in engaged research and teaching.

Summary of Institutional Documentation and Measurement

Overall, national, statewide, and institution-type efforts have been primarily based on the documentation of the engagement of colleges and universities. Such efforts can serve to inform the institutionalization of engagement particularly as it relates to self-understanding and assessment. However, the existing initiatives offer limited insight about if and how these indicators and measures matter, and the extent to which they facilitate the development and quality of engagement. Classification and documentation are important, but there is a need to understand the relationship between the indicators of engagement and the processes and practices of engagement.

The breadth of the indicators and measures support documentation efforts, but are not the kind of well-defined measures that could inform more systematic research studies. Furthermore, most institutional indicators rely primarily on soft data from a single source. Both the validity and value of these initiatives would be improved if self-reported findings were triangulated with data from multiple sources. Evidence provided by the 2005 CECEPS study reveals that not a lot of institutions systemically collect engagement-related data at the institutional level. At most institutions where data is collected, it is collected by projects that, in some cases, may be aggregated at the unit level.

Another limitation is the emphasis these initiatives place on the identification of exemplary practice. The appeal of focusing on exemplars is understandable. Narrative accounts of exemplary faculty engagement can be useful for making institutional stakeholders aware and supportive of good work and can provide practical examples to faculty who might be persuaded to become more engaged were they better able to see how it could work within their own institution. That said, the emphasis on identifying exemplars to represent institutional practice can be unrepresentative of the full range of engagement activities that may occur on college and university campuses. This is particularly the case given the amount of soft data requested by the data collection instruments. To measure and document the complete spectrum of its engaged activities, an institution would need to routinely collect data broadly across its colleges and departments, at a fairly discrete unit of analysis, inclusive of modest and even mundane engagement efforts. This is an unlikely outcome of data collection regimens that overemphasize identifying exemplars. Finally, because much of the documentation of exemplars does not include the perspectives and voices of the external individuals and groups involved and targeted by engagement, it may therefore also misconstrue how multiple stakeholders interpret and conceive engagement activities and initiatives.

Engagement as a Faculty Endeavor

Besides documenting and measuring engagement at the institutional level, engagement-related work has also been examined as a function of faculty. We found variation among the terms used to identify and define faculty work that targets and includes external audiences— public service, community service, and engagement. These terms generally reflect differences in the collaborative nature of the work. They also suggest differences in the degree to which the work is grounded in scholarship and produces scholarly artifacts. Because engagement has the potential to cut across the research, teaching, and service obligations of faculty, the kinds of activities that can count as engagement are diverse.

The UCLA Higher Education Research Institute (HERI) survey of faculty, which is administered annually, is a national data collection effort that includes questions about public service. Among a broad range of questions, the survey asks faculty about their personal commitment or attitudes and beliefs toward service, the value students and the institution in which they work place on service-related activities, and faculty beliefs about service as a function of colleges and universities. Faculty are, for example, asked about their involvement in public service and whether they engage in specific public-service activities, such as professional consulting. Respondents are also asked if their scholarship is used "to address local community needs." The institutional priorities accounted for by the survey include the allocation of resources to faculty for "community-based teaching or research" and resources to help faculty "create and sustain partnerships with surrounding communities." Questions about the service-related roles colleges and universities should undertake ask faculty to express their beliefs about whether colleges should encourage students to become involved in community service and whether colleges should collaborate with communities to "address local needs."

A limitation of the utility of this national data for understanding engagement is that the most seemingly relevant HERI survey questions are framed as questions about service. Respondents are asked about both public and community forms of service, rather than engagement or engaged scholarship. Because faculty service is a category of activity that has been traditionally treated as distinct from research and teaching, the survey seems to assume and may imply to respondents that involvement with the public is not a cross-cutting function. Any study of engaged scholarship broad enough to account for engagement in all of its possible forms, including engaged research and teaching, cannot, therefore, equate service with engagement because it may not accurately capture faculty's level of involvement with the public.

Most studies included in this chapter about faculty are not specific to engagement but focus on service instead. The studies on faculty service are research-based rather than documentation and classification efforts. In most studies, emphasis is placed on how the characteristics of faculty inform commitment to and involvement with engagement-related work. We also found empirical evidence about faculty motivation and the factors that influence faculty to become involved with the public. Unfortunately, very few studies were found that provide measures related to faculty members' perceptions of engagement-related work, how engagement relates to the professional responsibilities of faculty, and the processes of faculty engagement.

Level of Faculty Involvement

Faculty involvement includes the time faculty devote to engagement-related work and the characteristics of engaged faculty. Time devoted to outreach and engagement is typically determined by self-reported estimates provided by faculty about the effort they devote to public service activities (Church, 2001). In comparison to research and teaching, findings in the literature suggest that faculty devote less overall time to service than to research and teaching (Antonio, Astin, & Cress, 2000; Fairweather, 1996). Because much of the existing literature that measures percent of time focuses on service, these estimates are unlikely to represent the full extent of time most faculty devote to engagement. We did not find any similar types of studies that examined the time faculty devote to activity with the public that cuts across research, teaching, and service. That said, a review of studies specifically about faculty service can provide some limited insight about faculty involvement in engagement, even if one cannot equate findings specifically about service with engagement.

Studies have examined the relationship between the characteristics of faculty and their involvement in both service and service-learning. Race and gender are the two demographic categories most often examined. Research findings reveal that racial minorities and women are more likely to participate in public service-oriented work than faculty as a whole (Abes, Jackson, & Jones, 2002; Antonio et al., 2000; Hammond, 1994). Another characteristic measured by existing studies is faculty rank (Antonio et al., 2000). As part of their analysis of HERI data, Antonio, Astin, and Cress found that lower-ranked faculty are more committed to community service than tenured faculty. Antonio et al. also describe differences among faculty commitment and involvement in service and institutional type. A faculty member's primary discipline is another factor influencing commitment to engagement and his or her level of involvement in this work (Abes et al., 2002, Antonio et al., 2000).

Faculty Motivation

Empirical findings in the literature suggest that the attitudes, beliefs, and values faculty hold influence their involvement in engagement-related activities. Findings from these studies, both qualitative and quantitative, suggest that faculty involvement in engagement and service-learning are a result of how faculty think about the goals and objectives of their work in relation to higher education and external communities.

Based on an analysis of faculty essays submitted for a national engagement award, O'Meara (2008) found seven reasons faculty become involved in service-learning and engagement. The intersecting categories of motivations identified by O'Meara include (1) to facilitate student learning and growth; (2) to achieve disciplinary goals; (3) personal commitments to specific social issues, places, and people; (4) personal/professional identity; (5) pursuits of rigorous scholarship and learning; (6) a desire for collaboration, relationships, partners, and public-making; and (7) institutional type and mission, appointment type, and/or an enabling reward system and culture for community engagement (p. 14). In this study, O'Meara found differences among the prominence of the seven categories. An interest in facilitating student learning and growth was the most common response (94 percent) and motivation to pursue rigorous scholarship and teaching the least common (44 percent).

The findings from studies about faculty involvement in service-learning were similar. Abes, Jackson, and Jones (2002) investigated why faculty in colleges and universities located in the state of Ohio became involved in serving-learning. The three most common responses provided by faculty to explain their use of service-learning were student learning outcomes and the personal development of students, a commitment to community, and their beliefs about the importance of university-community partnerships. By drawing on a model explaining the diffusion and adoption of innovations, McKay and Rozee (2009) found that faculty integrate community service-learning in their courses as a result of their beliefs about faculty, students, and the community. In this study, faculty indicated that they believe there is a relationship between teaching and the community. Faculty also shared the belief that community-based serving-learning will increase students' opportunities to learn content and acknowledged that they do not hold traditional views about student learning and community-university relationships.

Academic Impacts and Outcomes

The impact of engagement-related work on faculty members themselves has begun to be characterized in terms of academic impact. Public scholarship can either be a form of

119

engagement or an outcome of faculty engagement. The literature suggests that not all faculty create scholarship targeting the public. Boyte (2004) discusses how faculty with a commitment toward social change and activism develop public scholarship at a greater rate than other faculty. There are also findings to suggest that the production of public scholarship is primarily the work of racial minorities and women (O'Meara, 2002).

Calleson, Jordan, and Seifer (2005) identify how faculty can balance the needs of community and also address the promotion and tenure requirements faced by faculty. They identify three types of products—peer-reviewed articles documenting the process of community engagement; applied products, such as changes in policy and the development of training manuals; and products addressing community needs.

Although not specific to engagement, a study designed by Braxton, Luckey, and Helland (2002) examined faculty production of the four forms of scholarship defined by Boyer—application, discovery, integration, and teaching. In this study, scholarship of application was operationalized into three categories: service to the lay public, unpublished scholarly outcomes, and publications. Table 1 illustrates the indicators for each of the three measures of application scholarship used in the study conducted by Braxton, Luckey, and Helland.

Braxton, Luckey, and Helland compared the production of the application scholarship across institutional types, discipline, and faculty characteristics. The authors found differences among scholarship of application and institutional type, discipline, gender, and professional age. They found no differences between scholarship of application and the tenure and race/ethnicity of faculty.

Table 1. Forms of Scholarship of Application

Service to the Lay Public	Unpublished Scholarly Outcomes	Publications
Introduction of some result of scholarship in consultation	Development of an innovative technology	An article that outlines a new research problem identified through the application of the knowledge and skill of one's academic discipline to a practical problem
Provision of expert witness or testimony	Seminars conducted for laypersons on current disciplinary topics	An article that describes new knowledge obtained through the application of the knowledge and skill of one's academic discipline to a practical problem
Engagement in consulting off campus	Development of a new process for dealing with a problem of practice	An article that applies new disciplinary knowledge to a practical problem
	Study conducted for a local organization	An article that proposes an approach to the bridging of theory and practice
	Study conducted for a local nonacademic professional association	An article reporting findings of research designed to solve a practical problem
	Study conducted for a local government agency	
	Study conducted to help solve a community problem	
	Study conducted to help solve a county or state problem	

Summary of Faculty Measures

Existing empirical evidence about engagement-related work focuses primarily on faculty service or does not account for a definition of activity that identifies faculty engagement as cross-cutting. Differences in the definitions and the characterization of faculty work as service rather than engagement mean that there is a lack of empirical evidence about faculty engagement. The measures identified in this section provide an initial place to begin to investigate and document whether and how faculty participate in engagement, and the extent to which findings specific to service can be equated with faculty involvement in engagement. Based on the existing studies, initial attempts to understand faculty involvement and commitment to engagement should account for demographic characteristics of faculty, their discipline, and the type of institution in which faculty work, among others. It is also important for future research to test whether engagement facilitates the production of scholarship and how engaged faculty identify these relationships.

A Case Study of Efforts to Document and Report Faculty Engagement

In order to better explore how institutions might go about collecting data on engagement, a brief case study is presented about how MSU has attempted to represent institutional engagement through faculty work. Although MSU has been involved in several initiatives to examine faculty engagement with external audiences, in what follows we focus on the development and use of the Outreach and Engagement Measurement Instrument (OEMI), a faculty-based, institution-wide data collection instrument. The OEMI collects faculty-level data that inform institutional planning and also represent the institutions involvement with the public. The OEMI collects information at the faculty level through an annual online survey that is then aggregated to illuminate the time and focus of faculty efforts and the characteristics of their work.

Institutional Context

Michigan State University is a large, public research institution. The university serves more than forty-six thousand graduate and undergraduate students and employs more than four thousand faculty and academic professionals. One of the first American land-grant institutions, MSU is well known in the state of Michigan, nationally, and internationally for its commitment to the public. MSU is also a leading research institution and one of the sixty-two members of the Association of American Universities.

Engaging with the public is a core value of MSU. The institutional culture, policies, and practices of the university are supportive of engagement. Outreach and engagement are explicitly referenced in the university's mission statement and are also embedded in its strategic planning documents (Michigan State University, 2005, 2008). The university's commitment to meeting the needs of the public is also evidenced by the actions and rhetoric of the current president. President Lou Anna K. Simon speaks publicly about MSU's commitment to engagement to academic audiences and the community and has also published on the subject (Kenny, Simon, Kiley-Brabeck, & Lerner, 2001). University funds support the University Outreach and Engagement Office (UOE), which is headed by an associate provost,

121

thus closely linking its work with the academic administration of the university. More recently, MSU has supported the creation of the National Center for the Study of University Engagement (NCSUE).

Measuring Outreach and Engagement at MSU

MSU's development of an instrument to document and measure engagement is a result of several initiatives and reforms led by MSU leaders, faculty, and UOE to increase the value of outreach and engagement (Lunsford, Church, & Zimmerman, 2006). Such initiatives began in the early 1990s with the formation of a faculty committee sanctioned by the provost to study and define university outreach. Its report broadened the traditional definition of scholarship to accommodate engagement and also created an institutional definition of outreach and engagement that cuts across research, teaching, and service (Michigan State University, 1993). In response to the committee's recommendations, other faculty committees and work groups were formed to develop guidelines for evaluating outreach and engagement (Michigan State University, 1996), to revise MSU's promotion and tenure documentation to account for engagement (Michigan State University, 2001), and to work with UOE to develop a mechanism for collecting institution-wide measurement data on faculty outreach and engagement. Thus, the OEMI was designed as an institutional tool primarily to support the work of university administration. Church, Zimmerman, Bargerstock, and Kenney (2003) describe the OEMI as not only a way for MSU to understand whether it is fulfilling its engagement mission but as a tool to facilitate "management" and "planning." Church et al. year? also describe the OEMI as mechanism for helping MSU convince stakeholders about its contribution to the public or by "telling [MSU's] engagement story."

The OEMI Measures

The OEMI documents the engagement of faculty and academic staff. Its development team believed that documenting faculty engagement, rather than that of students or academic units, would more accurately capture the institution's relationship to the public because of the integral relationship between engagement and the professional responsibilities of faculty (Church et al., 2003). Because outreach and engagement was defined as a form of scholarship at MSU, it was believed that data should be collected at the level of faculty work. Measuring faculty engagement would also fill a void because existing institutional data collection systems captured aspects of faculty research and teaching, but very little of the information MSU collected could sort engaged research, engaged teaching, or engaged service out from the broader functional categories of work.

The OEMI seeks to capture both the breadth and depth of faculty involvement in outreach and engagement by collecting data about faculty effort and individual projects. The first part of the OEMI consists of several questions about faculty effort. The amount of time faculty devote to outreach and engagement is measured by a self-reported percentage. At the time the OEMI was developed, this measure was believed to be the single best indicator of institutional commitment (Church et al., 2003). To determine if faculty engagement meets state, national, and international needs, the survey captures the range, target, and focus of outreach and engagement. From a list of more than a dozen areas of societal concerns (i.e., business and industrial development, pre-K–12 education, etc.), faculty are asked to select one or two different areas they addressed through their outreach and engagement. The areas were developed and piloted with a group of faculty to ensure that they captured the variation among the potential targets of faculty effort. The diversity of faculty activities is measured by form—research, technical assistance, noncredit/credit instruction, service-learning, and public instruction. Such forms account for engagement as a function that relates to the professional responsibilities of faculty—research, teaching, and service. To measure whether activities reached a range of people and places, the survey asks faculty whether their work had a diversity and urban focus and whether it targeted specific geographic locations (e.g.. counties and cities in Michigan and international countries). Additional questions on the survey account for whether faculty engagement contributed to MSU's five strategic priorities and whether the work generated revenue for the university and partners.

The second part of the OEMI collects data about specific projects and activities. This portion of the survey includes both open- and closed-ended questions, and respondents are invited to report on as many projects as they like. Project information is aggregated to represent the engagement of faculty. Respondents are asked to describe the project, including its purpose and objectives. University involvement in projects is measured by the inclusion of departments, graduate students, and undergraduates involved in the work. To determine if individuals and organizations external to the university are involved in the work, faculty are asked to identify partners and the role of partners. Faculty are also asked whether and how projects are evaluated. The questions about project-level outcomes account for both community and academic impact. Faculty are asked to describe the impact of the project on the targeted audience and any intellectual property or academic and community-based products developed through the project. Measurements of academic impact include faculty descriptions of how the project impacted their scholarship and the development of scholarship of engagement artifacts.

Characteristics about the individual faculty who respond to the OEMI are drawn from the university's central human resource database. These data include faculty demographic characteristics (gender, and ethnicity), rank, department and college, and salary. Such data allows UOE to study such questions as whether engagement is dominated by faculty with specific faculty characteristics. Data can also represent the breadth of engagement across departments and colleges and the amount of salary devoted to this form of work. For example, by joining OEMI data with the salary data collected from human resources, the UOE can report the amount of salary devoted to areas of concern, such as education or health and health care. When aggregated at the institutional level, this measure serves as an indicator of MSU's investment toward addressing specific concerns of society through faculty expertise.

The OEMI has been annually administered online to faculty and academic staff since 2004. Each year approximately one-quarter of eligible faculty and academic staff respond to the survey, accounting for a total of 2,054 unique (nonduplicative) respondents in the first four reporting years (2004–2007). The information collected is provided to individual academic units and university administration. Reports of project-level activity are searched to

123

inform the offices of the president, university development, and others about work undertaken by MSU faculty targeting specific geographic locations and areas of concern. Besides institutional purposes, data collected from OEMI are also currently being analyzed for research purposes.

Dissemination and Partnerships

During its early development, MSU formed a collaborative partnership with the University of Kentucky (UK). Through the partnership, UOE adapted the OEMI for use at UK in order to further refine the Instrument, and also to study its potential utility as a tool for other institutions and for collecting cross-institutional data.

Like MSU, UK has a rich tradition and strong commitment to engaged scholarship. As Kentucky's land-grant (shared with Kentucky State University) and flagship research institution, UK is committed to using its intellectual resources to serve and advance the commonwealth. Commitment to engaged scholarship complements UK's aspiration to become a national top twenty public research institution and is reflected in a number of institutional initiatives. Under the leadership of UK President Lee T. Todd, Jr., measurement and documentation of engaged scholarship are viewed as essential to good stewardship and institutional effectiveness, and to ensuring that the "higher purpose" issues of Kentucky remain integral to institutional metrics. In the words of President Todd, "An institution such as UK may achieve a high level of performance on select indicators, but if it does not serve the needs of the Commonwealth of Kentucky, it will have failed" (University of Kentucky, 2005).

In cooperation with the UK office of the associate provost for university engagement, UOE adapted its OEMI for UK, where it is called the Engagement Measurement Instrument (EMI). During the first year of the partnership, attention was paid to making only modest customizations to the instrument in order to accommodate differences in institutional context. Questions referencing UK's strategic plan were substituted for those about MSU's plan, for example. After the first year of data collection, UK wanted to experiment with a version of the instrument that was briefer and less complex for users and that prioritized collecting discrete project-level data. The first-year pilot convinced UK leaders of the value of project-level data for meeting the data needs of the institution, so UOE worked with UK to redesign the EMI. The redesigned EMI captures the same types of information as the OEMI but does so primarily at the project level.

UK asks engaged faculty and professional staff to complete the EMI annually and reports that each successive year has elicited greater compliance, more engagement activity, higher levels of sophistication, increasingly effective approaches, and greater community and academic outcomes and impacts. Administrators at UK utilize the EMI data to increase the visibility and promote the centrality of engaged teaching, research, and service at the university and in the community. In doing so, they hope to facilitate rising levels of engagement expertise, expectation, and commitment, and to create new models and mentors for engaged scholarship.

In addition to UK, MSU has entered into partnerships with other universities and organizations to advance the development of the OEMI. The OEMI has been implemented and pilot tested institution-wide at the University Tennessee System and Kansas State University. A limited pilot of a continuing education division was also conducted at the University of Connecticut. More recently, UOE entered into a partnership with the American Association of Colleges of Pharmacy to conduct a study of the utility of the OEMI for collecting data across multiple institutions at a disciplinary level.

Complexities, Challenges, and Limitations

Any research effort comes with challenges and limitations. Collecting data on engaged scholarship also adds considerable complexity. A number of challenges stem from using the OEMI to represent institutional commitment and effort. First, at MSU, for instance, the survey garners a response rate of around 25 percent with uneven representation by MSU's colleges. Among the factors believed to limit the response rate are the survey's length (on average it takes at least twenty to thirty minutes to complete) and concerns from faculty about overreporting (funders or the university also ask for reports on some of their projects). Second, measurement at the individual faculty level does not capture the full range of projects and activities that are institutionalized within the management of special facilities (e.g., performing arts center, planetarium, gardens), except to the extent that faculty undertake these activities. It also does not account for public programs that are primarily operationalized by members of the university's large nonacademic professional staff and student engagement. Whereas individual faculty are asked to report their service-learning effort and projects through the OEMI, enrollment data on student engagement connected with courses and instruction is collected through the university's registration system augmented by data on placement attributes collected and documented by MSU's Center for Service-Learning and Civic Engagement.

Because the OEMI seeks to capture a range of engagement activities from a diverse set of respondents involved in a range of activities, methodological issues exist. The potential for double counting in situations where more than one respondent reports on the same project or activity has required some secondary cross-referencing of OEMI reports with other university data sets. Because the instrument was meant to be used with faculty across all disciplines and departments to report widely varying kinds of work, its design may also raise questions of validity. To what extent are disciplinarily diverse respondents interpreting and responding to questions in the same way? Despite common introductory text, instructions, and key term definitions, do ways of thinking about scholarly service, public involvement, outreach, and engagement vary so significantly that respondents report on different types of phenomena? There is some evidence, for example, to suggest that not all activity reported on the OEMI aligns with the university's institutional definition of engagement. Such differences suggest that it is important to understand how discipline shapes faculty work. Relatedly, although the local contexts of OEMI partner institutions have provided useful insights that have informed ongoing refinements of the instrument, they have also raised interesting complexities in thinking about commensurate measures across institutions. A question to consider is to what extent does institutional context mediate understandings of engaged scholarship, however similarly two institutions conceptualize outreach and engagement?

Discussion

The challenges and complexities facing MSU and its partner institutions highlight many of the broad issues that complicate the work of researchers and others involved in understanding university engagement. Yet, all the existing efforts to document and measure engagement provide an important foundation for future measurement initiatives and studies. Attempts to understand the relationship between engagement and the public must build on the current work that has been undertaken by a range of stakeholders—the Carnegie Foundation, higher education organizations, universities, and individual researchers. But future attempts must also begin to address the limitations highlighted in this chapter.

To conclude this chapter, we identify five critical issues that should guide future efforts to measure and document engagement. First, there is a need to design research studies that determine the institutional characteristics that facilitate and hinder campus engagement. It is also important that such studies investigate the importance of individual factors to help inform institutional attempts to promote engagement. It appears that the development of existing documentation and measurement instruments is based on assumptions about institutional characteristics, rather than grounded in empirical findings about the relationship between institutional policies and practices and engagement. Little is known, for example, about the relationship between altering promotion and tenure processes and the prevalence of engagement related activity and faculty involvement in engagement. Determining which institutional characteristics are most conducive to institutional attempts to promote engagement may yield greater and more beneficial results.

There is also a need to improve research quality. Existing measures and indicators of engagement at both institutional and faculty levels are too broad. Because most of the initiatives, particularly those focused on institutions, document engagement, it is not surprising that the types of indicators elicit broad rather than specific forms of data. Development of well-defined measures that can be systematically tested and analyzed would be an important contribution to the field. Such measures should consist of both soft and hard data. Self-reported information needs to be balanced with multiple kinds of data. It is also important that multiple sources of data be collected so that data triangulation can ensure more valid findings. By developing specific measures and establishing strategies for data collection, institutions can better fulfill their obligations to stakeholders, accreditation agencies, and other external organizations.

Most current documentation and measurement initiatives do not account for impact. This is true for efforts at institutional and faculty levels. By *impact*, we refer to the cumulative effect of faculty engagement on the target of their work, whether that is communities, industry, or the general public. Determining the impact of engagement beyond evaluation of individual projects would present a much more accurate representation of how universities shape and influence societal progress and social change. This is not simple, and the nature of engagement complicates any attempt to understand impact. At the faculty level, studies need to be designed to determine how engagement impacts faculty. Understanding how engagement impacts the production of scholarly artifacts is important, but it is also important to investigate a range of potential impacts, including how engagement fulfills the personal interests and commitments of faculty and whether it affects their work satisfaction.

At a more basic level, faculty engagement has been conflated with studies examining faculty service. Equating engagement with service obscures or fails to account for engaged research and teaching. Either future research efforts need to account for the range of faculty engagement, or studies should be designed to test a specific form of engagement. It is important, however, that future studies test whether there are differences in faculty service and engagement, particularly the factors that influence and shape faculty involvement with and commitment to the public. Because little is actually known about whether engagement characterizes the actual practices of faculty, it may be important to begin to investigate how faculty think about their work with the public and how such work relates to creation of scholarship.

Finally, there is a critical need for research that examines how discipline shapes faculty engagement. Findings in the literature about faculty work, in particular how disciplines shape research and teaching, convey the saliency of discipline (Becher & Trowler, 2001; Biglan, 1973a, 1973b; Clark, 1987). Despite an overwhelming amount of evidence suggesting that discipline impacts faculty work, little is known about how discipline shapes faculty engagement. More concisely, future research is needed that investigates the intersection between engagement, discipline, and institutional characteristics.

In conclusion, our recommendations build on existing efforts and convey the key issues that would push researchers and others to begin to capture the complexities of understanding university engagement and the work of engaged faculty. Our times demand that these efforts be undertaken.

References

Abes, E., Jackson, G., & Jones, S. (2002). Factors that motivate and deter faculty use of service learning. *Michigan Journal of Community Service Learning, 9*(1), 5–17.

Antonio, A., Astin, H., & Cress, C. (2000). Community service in higher education: A look at the nation's faculty. *Review of Higher Education, 23*(4), 373–397.

Becher, T., & Trowler, P. (2001). *Academic tribes and territories.* Buckingham: Open University Press.

Biglan, A. E. (1973a). The characteristics of subject matter in different academic areas. *Journal of Applied Psychology, 57,* 195–203.

Biglan, A. E. (1973b). Relationships between subject matter characteristics and the structure and output of departments. *Journal of Applied Psychology, 57,* 204–213.

Bowley, E. (2003). *The Minnesota campus civic engagement Study: Defining civic engagement in a new century.* Minnesota Higher Education Services Office and Minnesota Campus Compact.

Boyer, E. L. (1990). *Scholarship reconsidered: Priorities for the professoriate.* Princeton, NJ: Carnegie Foundation for the Advancement of Teaching.

Boyer, E. L. (1996). The scholarship of engagement. *Journal of Public Service and Outreach, 1*(1), 11–20.

Boyte, H. C. (2004). *Going public: Academics and public life.* Dayton, OH: Kettering Foundation.

Braxton, J. M., Luckey, W., & Helland, P. (2002). *Institutionalizing a broader view of scholarship through Boyer's four domains.* ASHE-ERIC Higher Education Report, Vol. 29, No. 2. San Francisco: Jossey-Bass.

Brukardt, M. J., Holland, B., Percy, S. L., & Zimpher, N. (2004). *Calling the question: Is higher education ready to commit to community engagement? A Wingspread statement 2004* [Electronic version]. Retrieved April 30, 2009, from http://www.uwm.edu/MilwaukeeIdea/elements/wingspread.pdf.

Calleson, D. C., Jordan, C., & Seifer, S. D. (2005). Community-engaged scholarship: Is faculty work in communities a true academic enterprise? *Journal of the Association of American Medical Colleges, 80*(4), 317–321.

Carnegie Foundation for the Advancement of Teaching. (2007). *Elective classification: Community engagement, 2008 documentation framework.* Stanford, CA: Carnegie Foundation for the Advancement of Teaching. Retrieved January 4, 2009, from http://www.carnegiefoundation.org/dynamic/downloads/file_1_614.pdf.

Carnegie Foundation for the Advancement of Teaching. (2009). *Community engagement elective classification.* Stanford, CA: Carnegie Foundation for the Advancement of Teaching. Retrieved January 4, 2009, from http://www.carnegiefoundation.org/classifications/index.asp?key=1213.

Church, R. L. (2001, November). *Counting public service: Can we make meaningful comparisons within and amongst institutions?* Paper presented at the Association for the Study of Higher Education Symposium on Broadening the Carnegie Classification's Attention to Mission: Incorporating Public Service, Ann Arbor, MI.

Church, R. L., Zimmerman, D. L., Bargerstock, B. A., & Kenney, P. A. (2003). Measuring scholarly outreach at Michigan State University: Definition, challenges, tools. *Journal of Higher Education Outreach and Engagement, 8*(1), 141–153.

Clark, B. R. (1987). *The academic life: Small worlds, different worlds.* Princeton, NJ: Princeton University Press.

Committee on Institutional Cooperation (CIC). (2005). *Engaged scholarship: A resource guide.* Champaign, IL: Author.

Council on Extension, Continuing Education, and Public Service. (2005). *CECEPS report—Benchmarking of outreach/engagement survey.* Washington, DC: National Association of State Universities and Land-Grant Colleges. Retrieved January 3, 2009, from http://schoe.coe.uga.edu/benchmarking/Benchmarkingsurveyfina14.pdf.

Council on Extension, Continuing Education, and Public Service. (2007a, June). *Report from CECEPS committee on measuring university engagement.* Washington, DC: National Association of State Universities and Land-Grant Colleges.

Council on Extension, Continuing Education, and Public Service. (2007b, November). *An update from the CECEPS committee on measuring university engagement.* Washington, DC: National Association of State Universities and Land-Grant Colleges.

Driscoll, A. (2008). Carnegie's community-engagement classification: Intentions and insights. *Change: The Magazine of Higher Learning, 40*(1), 38–41.

Fairweather, J. S. (1996). *Faculty work and public trust: Restoring the value of teaching and public service in American academic life.* Boston: Allyn & Bacon.

Gibson, C. M. (2006). *New times demand new scholarship: Research universities and civic engagement—A leadership agenda.* Boston: Tufts University and Campus Compact.

Hammond, C. (1994). Integrating service and academic study: Faculty motivation and satisfaction in Michigan higher education. *Michigan Journal of Community Service Learning, 1*(1), 21–28.

Higher Learning Commission. (2003). The criteria for accreditation. In *The handbook of accreditation* (3rd ed., pp. 3.1–1 to 3.4–4). Chicago: Higher Learning Commission.

Holland, B. A. (1999). Factors and strategies that influence faculty involvement in public service. *Journal of Public Service and Outreach, 4*(1), 37–44.

Holland, B. (2001). *Measuring the role of civic engagement in campus missions: Key concepts and challenges.* Paper presented at the annual meeting of the Association for the Study of Higher Education, Richmond, VA.

Inside Higher Education. (2009, January 9). The states pull back. *Inside Higher Education.* Retrieved January 10, 2009, from http://www.insidehighereducation.com/news/2009/01/09/approps.

Kellogg Commission on the Future of State and Land-Grant Universities. (1999). *Returning to our roots: The engaged institution.* Washington, DC: National Association of State Universities and Land-Grant Colleges.

Kenny, M. E., Simon, L. A. K., Kiley-Brabeck, K., & Lerner, R. M. (Eds.). (2001). *Learning to serve: Promoting civil society through service learning.* Kluwer International Series in Outreach Scholarship, Vol. 7. New York: Springer.

Lunsford, C., Church, R., & Zimmerman, D. (2006). Assessing Michigan State University's efforts to embed engagement across the institution: Findings and challenges. *Journal of Higher Education Outreach and Engagement, 11*(1), 89–104.

McKay, V. C., & Rozee, P. D. (2004). Characteristics of faculty who adopt community service-learning pedagogy. *Michigan Journal of Community Service Learning, 10*(2), 21–33.

Michigan State University. (1993). *University outreach at Michigan State University: Extending knowledge to serve society—A report by the provost's committee on university outreach.* East Lansing: Michigan State University.

Michigan State University. (1996). *Points of distinction: A guidebook for planning and evaluating quality outreach.* East Lansing: Michigan State University.

Michigan State University. (2001). *Form D instructions: Recommendation for reappointment, promotion, or tenure action.* East Lansing: Michigan State University. Retrieved January 3, 2009, from http://www.hr.msu.edu/HRsite/forms/FacultyForms/FormInfoRrptPages.htm.

Michigan State University. (2005). *Boldness by design: Strategic positioning of Michigan State University.* East Lansing: Michigan State University. Retrieved January 3, 2009, from http://boldnessbydesign.msu.edu.

Michigan State University. (2008). *MSU mission statement.* East Lansing: Michigan State University. Retrieved January 3, 2009, from http://president.msu.edu/mission.php.

Neumann, A., & Terosky, A. L. (2007). To give and to receive: Recently tenured professors' experiences of service in major research universities. *Journal of Higher Education, 78*(3), 282–310.

O'Meara, K. (2002). *Scholarship unbound: Assessing service as scholarship for promotion and* tenure. New York: Rutledge Falmer.

O'Meara, K. (2008). Motivation for faculty community engagement: Learning from exemplars. *Journal of Higher Education Outreach and Engagement, 12*(1), 7–29.

O'Meara, K., & Rice, E. (2005). *Faculty priorities reconsidered: Rewarding multiple forms of scholarship.* San Francisco: Jossey-Bass.

Rice, E. R. (2002). Beyond scholarship reconsidered: Toward an enlarged vision of the scholarly work of faculty members. In K. J. Zahorsky (Ed.), *New directions for teaching and learning* (Vol. 90, pp. 7–18). San Francisco: Jossey-Bass.

Stanton, T. K. (2007). *New times demand new scholarship II—Research universities and civic engagement: Opportunities and challenges.* Los Angeles: University of California, Los Angeles.

University of Kentucky. (2005). *Top 20 business plan.* Lexington: University of Kentucky. Retrieved January 9, 2009, from http://www.uky.edu/OPBPA/business_plan.htm.

Veysey, L. (1965). *The emergence of the American university.* Chicago: University of Chicago Press.

Ward, K. (2003). *Faculty service roles and the scholarship of engagement.* ASHE-ERIC Higher Education Report, Vol. 29, No. 5. San Francisco: Jossey-Bass.

Zlotkowski, E., Duffy, D. K., Franco, R., Gelmon, S. B., Norvell, K., Meeropol, J., et al. (2004). *The community's college: Indicators of engagement at two-year institutions.* Providence, RI: Campus Compact.

Zlotkowski, E., Jones, R. J., Lenk, M. M., Meeropol, J., Gelmon, S., & Norvell, K. (2005). *One with the community: Indicators of engagement at minority-serving institutions.* Providence, RI: Campus Compact.

Engaged Scholarship: Perspectives from Psychology

Jill N. Reich and Paul D. Nelson

Psychology as a Discipline

As the science of mind and behavior, having evolved from such disparate disciplines as philosophy, physiology, and physics (James, 1890), psychology has had a predominant focus on the individual or certain characteristics of the individual as its primary unit of analysis. When this focus includes relationships with others, of course, the units of analysis can range from dyads, through small groups, to larger organization or community contexts. In whatever context psychologists have worked, the discipline's predominant methodological paradigms have been described as experimental and correlational (Cronbach, 1957) and its predominant cultures as scientific and humanistic (Kimble, 1984). These epistemological differences among the orientations of psychologists have been evident in more than intellectual approaches to the study of mind and behavior; they also have had consequences for the organization of academic departments of psychology in universities (Capshew, 1999).

Another historical schism among psychologists has been between those whose predominant goal is to advance theory and knowledge in the discipline and those whose predominant goal is to apply this theory and knowledge to problems in society. The history of the American Psychological Association (APA) itself is marked by perceived disenfranchisement by one or another of these groups, initially in the late 1930s by those who formed a separate society for applied psychologists and, following reunification and fifty years, by those who formed a separate society primarily to advance the science of psychology. Yet, as it has been historically and remains today, the APA is the largest and most diverse organization of psychologists, the current mission of which is to advance the creation, communication, and application of psychological knowledge to benefit society and improve people's lives (American Psychological Association, 2008).

This mission statement is significant in the context of the present chapter and the volume of which it is a part. It speaks to the very nature of engaged scholarship, quite in contrast to the purpose of the APA a century ago to advance psychology as a science (Davis, 1907) without reference to the societal or personal context for which it may be important. In fairness to the founding generations of American psychologists in the first half of the last century, however, there were those among the early leaders whose thinking reflected the importance of the social context in understanding human thought and behavior, a context that cannot always be reduced to the controls of a laboratory experiment (Allport, 1940; Dewey, 1900). Moreover, in writing about psychology in the public interest from a psychologist historian perspective, Morawski (2002, p. 500) offers, with support of some case histories, the following commentary:

> Conventional or purely intellectual histories of psychology obscure some fundamental issues of the past: the role of psychology and the psychologist in society, the confrontation with ethical problems, and the relation of psychology to the humanities and other sciences, and the dissemination of psychological knowledge to the public. ... Furthermore, because more comprehensive and critical studies require scrutiny not merely of dusty texts and journals but also of personal papers, institutional records, unpublished manuscripts, and forgotten publications, they attend to the "human" context in which psychological knowledge is created.

In offering this perspective, Morawski does not only provide a vital context for understanding the history of psychology and the work of psychologists. She also advances a fundamental principle of engaged scholarship, that is, the importance of the human context in which knowledge is created, communicated, and applied.

Her commentary reinforces for psychology Boyer's (1996) concept of engaged scholarship as a connection of the academy and its disciplines with the social, civic, and ethical problems of society.

During the past century, other than for the two world wars in which psychologists were engaged in myriad professional roles in support of national defense, there are perhaps three periods during which psychology's engagement with society and social issues not only was prominent, but led to institutional change within the culture and organization of psychologists, and more specifically resulting in academic departments of psychology becoming engaged in social, civic, and ethical problems of society. These periods of time, thirty years apart, were the 1930s, 1960s, and 1990s.

The 1930s and Following Years

In the context of societal problems posed by the Great Depression and the threat to democratic institutions posed by the rise of fascism during pre–World War II years, a small group of psychologists founded the Society for the Study of Psychology and Contemporary Social Issues (Finison, 1986), later to be renamed the Society for the Psychological Study of Social Issues (SPSSI). The group established the *Journal of Social Issues,* a popular journal for publication of social science research. Sufficient was the SPSSI membership that it became one of the first ten interest divisions of the APA when that organization reorganized in 1945, reuniting once again the applied and academic psychologists and expanding its mission to that of advancing psychology as a science and a profession.

Moreover, on the collective basis of their experiences of national service during the war years, those responsible for spearheading the reorganization "agreed with (Gordon) Allport that the promotion of human welfare was a desirable goal, and placed it alongside the more prosaic purposes of advancing psychology as a science and profession in the new APA constitution" (Capshew & Hilgard, 1992, p.171) Such a mission statement certainly reflected the influence of SPSSI psychologists, those concerned with societal issues about which psychology as a scientific discipline and profession could make contributions to public policy.

Among the founding members of SPSSI was the distinguished psychologist Kurt Lewin, whose field theory served as a basis for the advancement of social psychological research and theory for a new generation of psychologists from the 1930s through the 1950s. Lewin's theory recognized the importance of understanding human behavior as the interaction of the person and the environment which he conceptualized as "lifespace." The collective research of Lewin and his colleagues, including graduate students, was characterized by the combination of both laboratory (e.g., studies of group dynamics) and community-based experiments (e.g., action research on effecting change in organizations or the community). Marrow (1969, p. 230) described three characteristics of Lewin's career as (1) his interdependent, collaborative style of work with colleagues and students; (2) his integration of theory and practical action; and (3) his successful combination of scientific with personal and civic concerns. These qualities and Lewin's commitment to experiential learning in the community, as well as in the laboratory, were for his students and university colleagues a prototype of service learning in psychology.

Following a decade of research at the University of Iowa Child Welfare Research Center, Lewin moved to an appointment at MIT, where he established the Research Center for Group Dynamics with the following model in mind.

> Lewin delineated the combination of experiment and application he termed "action research." The combination was ideal, he declared, for scientists whose chief concern was geared towards action, towards changing the world while simultaneously contributing to the advancement of scientific knowledge. ... Before he could start coupling theory with experiment, however, Lewin had to secure an academic location for the proposed center. He wanted it at a large university, preferably in a city troubled by the variety of vexing industrial, community, racial, and leadership problems he wished to study. The center would, of course, have to have the autonomy the project required, but its relations with the university's departments of social science, especially of psychology, sociology, and anthropology, would require close cooperation.. (Marrow, 1969, p. 164)

Thus, what we refer to today as the concept of engaged scholarship and civic engagement of the university was very much what Lewin had in mind as he contemplated the future directions for the collaborative involvement of social scientists and their students in action research.

The 1960s and Following Years

By the 1960s our society, as it had been for different reasons in the 1930s, was wracked with the turmoil of civic unrest related to such issues as civil rights, an unpopular war, and poverty in the midst of increasing wealth. By this time, as well, yet in contrast to the 1930s, psychology had attained greater public recognition as a mental health profession. It was during this period that another movement was begun by a small group of psychologists, many of whom had a community action research model in mind, focused on prevention of social and mental health problems in society, a public health model quite different from the medical treatment model by which individual and group psychotherapy had become a predominant practice among clinically trained psychologists. Watzlawick, Weakland, and Fisch (1974) differentiated between first-order and second-order change in community psychology, the first related to changing the individual and the second to changing the systems environment in which the individual is engaged. It was to the latter that community psychologists began to give greater attention.

The institutionalization of this movement was effected with the establishment of an APA division in 1966, referred to presently as the Society for Community Research and Action: Division of Community Psychology, having a broader focus than mental health, for example, a focus on social policy issues. As SPSSI had done upon its establishment, this new division also started a journal, the *American Journal of Community Psychology*, in which the scholarship of psychologists and other social scientists focused on such issues could be published. Likewise established was an international publication, the *Journal of Community and Applied Social Psychology*. Sarason, Levine, Goldenberg, Cherlin, and Bennett (1966) described the opportunities for psychology's civic engagement in numerous community contexts; but two decades later Sarason (1984) also wrote of missed opportunities for public policy. Between those two publications, in another overview of the field, Rappaport (1977) wrote about the integration of values, research, and action in community psychology.

A similar movement during this period, more among social psychologists than among those who were clinically trained, was that toward the development of an environmental psychology. Roger Barker, who had worked with Lewin at the University of Iowa, had moved to the University of Kansas in the 1940s where he helped establish the Midwest Psychological Field Station. Barker's focus was on the ecology of human behavior, one in which he emphasized the importance of behavior settings, such as schools (Barker & Gump, 1964). Barker's work and that of other social psychology scholars led to a broader formulation in the 1960s and 1970s of environmental psychology (Ittelson, Proshansky, Rivlin, & Winkel, 1974), resulting in the establishment of yet another APA division, that of Population and Environmental Psychology, a field of interest that is especially conducive to multidisciplinary research and action in regard to human-made and natural environments, as well as related research on issues of population and human reproduction. For published work in this area, there is an international *Journal of Environmental Psychology* and the APA division publication *Population and Environmental Psychology Bulletin*.

Historically, psychologists have differed in their opinions about the extent to which the APA as a professional membership organization should be active in public policy matters, the traditional laboratory science community being typically more reluctant than its social activist colleagues on such matters—unless, of course, there is a substantial body of psychological knowledge related to the policy issue, for the basis of which there is scientific evidence. As a means to engage more actively and systematically in promoting human welfare through public policy, therefore, the APA in 1971 established a new governance board, the Board of Social and Ethical Responsibility (subsequently renamed as the Board for Advancement of Psychology in the Public Interest). As there were already APA governance boards for science, practice, and education, the creation of this new board afforded opportunity within the APA governance for policy-related discourse and initiatives on social and ethical issues of society from a psychological perspective. Smith (1992) summarized the early history and types of issues addressed by this new board, the work of which continues.

It was during the 1970s also that the APA, in collaboration with the American Association for the Advancement of Science (AAAS), established a Congressional Fellows Program, the purpose of which is to provide psychologists (and other scientists) a public policy learning experience in a congressional staff office. Psychology is one of several scientific disciplines that continue to participate in this program, a program open to those pursuing academic, research, practice, or public policy careers. For many years, as well, the APA has sponsored an SPSSI Fellows Program, affording psychologists an opportunity to learn about public policy formulation from the disciplinary association's perspective. It is not uncommon for applicants in either of these programs to have a master's degree in public policy as well as a doctoral degree in psychology, and many bring to bear on their policy experience backgrounds of research and scholarly interest in areas of psychological inquiry into community and societal issues, such as child development, poverty, gender equity, racial prejudice, social class, and health behaviors.

The 1990s to the Present

These developments notwithstanding, by the 1990s, the proportion of psychologists engaged in research and practice related to community and other societal issues remained relatively small. The majority of applied psychologists were in clinical and counseling fields with rather traditional types of independent or institutional-based practice, though many contributed pro bono or in contractual consulting roles to the community and its social agencies, for example, in disaster relief. In addition, psychology had become highly specialized in both research and practice, much more so than had been the case in the mid-twentieth century. As the discipline looked ahead to a new century, with a glance through the rear-view mirror at its history, it seemed appropriate to host a national conference on the future of graduate education in the field, inasmuch as that is the level of education from which the next generation of scholars will come.

Bickman and Ellis (1990) edited an array of papers presented at the conference, many of the questions being focused on the theme of centrifugal and centripetal forces operative in the discipline and its environment. It is interesting to note that most of the issues addressed at the conference were related to systemic tensions in the discipline between science and practice, with related curriculum issues. Attention was given also to a few of the issues to be highlighted a few years later by a joint committee of the National Academy of Sciences, the

135

National Academy of Engineering, and the Institute of Medicine in that body's call for reshaping the graduate education of scientists and engineers (Committee on Science, Engineering, and Public Policy, 1995), such as overspecialization and the implications of such for nonacademic careers and general public utility. Nonetheless, very little explicit attention was given to preparing psychologists for careers in public policy or as engaged scholars in the community.

Others in psychology, however, had been writing during this period about psychology's role in public policy matters and about possible new roles for psychologists (DeLeon, 1988; Lorion, Iscoe, DeLeon, & VandenBos, 1996; Sarason, 1988; Schneider, 1990). The salience of public policy for these psychologists was heightened by sensitivity to the changing socioeconomic and demographic context of our society and the implications of such for psychology. Our rural and urban communities were becoming increasingly diverse in ethnic, racial, and related cultural backgrounds; concerns over the quality of public education for diverse communities of our nation were being raised; issues of gender, disability, and sexual orientation discrimination were increasingly subject to public debate; and the implications of growing economic disparities between socioeconomic groups of our nation were of increasing concern to psychologists, especially in regard to health care and other quality-of-life issues. Sufficient was the interest in these issues among psychologists that the APA established several new member divisions related to them, paralleled by policy-oriented task force initiatives of several APA presidents.

It was during this period as well that public awareness was heightened about our interdependence on others in a global economy, accelerated through advances in communication and information technology. In this context, the APA established a new division focused on International Psychology and another one on Peace Psychology for the study of peace, conflict, and violence from psychological perspectives. Thus, whereas Lewin and his colleagues years earlier engaged in action research on conflict resolution in groups, organizations, and the local community, psychologists of the current era became engaged in action research on conflict resolution in the meta-community of international or global regions. Although their research interests and scholarship on such matters began decades earlier, certainly among the recognized leaders among psychologists of the international research on conflict resolution were Morton Deutsch (1985), one of Lewin's doctoral students at MIT, and Herbert Kelman (1965). In 1986, Deutsch established the International Center for Cooperation and Conflict Resolution at Columbia University, and, during the 1990s, Kelman directed the Program on International Conflict Analysis and Resolution at Harvard University's Weatherhead Center for International Affairs. As Lewin had conceived for his own center at MIT fifty years earlier, each of these centers draws on collaborative work among scholars of multiple disciplines for its work.

As these centers exemplify by their location and participant scholars, the academy of higher education is unequivocally the institution in society having the richest mix of scholarly disciplines. They likewise illustrate the engaged academy, with the focus of research and locus of learning external to the academy itself. Their work demonstrates the contribution of the discipline of psychology to a relevant base of knowledge occurring largely at the level of scholarly activity and graduate education. But, was that enough?

A Wake-Up Call for Psychology

It was during this period that Irwin Altman (1996) published a landmark article in the *American Psychologist* on higher education and psychology in the millennium. Altman had been among the leaders of the environmental psychology movement in the 1960s and a keynote speaker on centrifugal and centripetal forces at the 1989 Graduate Education Conference noted previously. In the context of the higher education call for engaged scholarship from the academy, and the discipline of psychology's history of engagement in the community, Altman proposed a model of education that would link the academic curriculum to community needs. Three pillars of the model are foundational knowledge, professional knowledge, and socially responsive knowledge.

The first is characterized by the core content and methods of the discipline combined with the cross-disciplinary knowledge of a liberal education, typically at the undergraduate level. The second, achieved in psychology through graduate education, is knowing how the discipline is practiced or applied as a profession. The goal for the third and newly proposed body of socially responsive knowledge, Altman (374–375), is "first to educate students in the problems of society; second, have them experience and understand first-hand social issues in their community; and third, give students the experience and skills to act on social problems."

Socially responsive knowledge calls on the foundational and professional bodies of knowledge begun in the 1930s and traced earlier. Now, Altman calls for the curriculum in psychology to include socially responsive knowledge among its learning goals, and offers in his article examples from the University of Utah where he served on the faculty and in the administration. With regret, he found little evidence that much weight was given to the construct of socially responsive knowledge as a major learning goal at a national conference on undergraduate education a few years earlier (McGovern, 1991), although the report did include suggestions about the inclusion of service-learning and community service in the curriculum.

A Twist in the Road: From Psychology to the Academy

Just as the discipline of psychology was beginning to be challenged in ways that might have linked our long history of engaged scholarship to goals for undergraduate learning of socially responsive knowledge, the academy became embroiled in defining the roles of the faculty and psychology was distracted from its disciplinary route. Debate ensued about what constitutes teaching, research, and service and what is the appropriate balance of these responsibilities in the life of the faculty. For all disciplines in higher education, the 1990s were characterized by significant concern among state and federal government regulatory agencies about issues of public accountability in our colleges and universities. Accordingly, concerns about fragmentation of and failure to complete undergraduate education, overspecialization in graduate education, silo-like disciplinary departments (and sometimes disciplinary subgroups within large departments), inadequate attention to teaching (especially in large universities), and the changing roles of faculty have been predominant themes in higher education circles over the past two decades. At the same time, colleges and universities were being challenged to prepare a

137

more diverse and often less well-prepared body of students for a changing world, one for which the best preparation is "learning how to learn." In this context, the desired outcomes for a liberal as well as professional education focused on critical thinking, analytic problem solving, communication, and technical skills as well as a broad foundational body of knowledge.

At this time the Carnegie Foundation for the Advancement of Teaching, first through the leadership of Ernest Boyer (1990, 1996) and subsequently under the leadership of Lee Shulman (2004), rallied higher education leaders to new perspectives on teaching and scholarship, including the scholarship of teaching itself and the scholarship of engagement in the community. Ernest Lynton (1995) was one of the foremost leaders in higher education during the 1980s and 1990s, advocating for a socially responsible form of scholarship through professional service, a scholar-practitioner model of faculty work linking academic knowledge with needs of society through professional service. Psychology, with other disciplines in the sciences and humanities, was an active participant in the national initiatives related to these emphases, through collaborative work with the (former) American Association of Higher Education (AAHE) and its affiliate organization Campus Compact, the Association of American Colleges and Universities (AAC&U), the Council of Graduate Schools (CGS), and the American Council on Education (ACE).

Among academic disciplines, most of the work related to these initiatives was accomplished through the national disciplinary societies in partnership with the higher education organizations, augmented by the work of colleagues whose scholarship within the various disciplines was aligned already with the thematic issues central to the partnerships—for example, in psychology, Halpern et al. (1998), Halpern and Reich (1999), and Peterson and Trierweiler (1999). Although in psychology, especially at the undergraduate level, there had been a substantial history of commitment to the scholarship of teaching, including a journal devoted to the area, parallel commitment to service-learning pedagogy and the goal of civic engagement among psychology faculty was certainly not otherwise widespread.

More recent curriculum guidelines for undergraduate majors in psychology (American Psychological Association, 2007) still place most emphasis on what Altman described as foundational knowledge, defined within the context of the discipline and the broader context of a liberal education. The challenge to link the learning of socially responsive knowledge to the discipline's long history of engaged scholarship remained unrealized.

The exception to this is the goal of *Sociocultural and International Awareness,* learning outcomes or objectives for which are stated as follows:

- Interact effectively and sensitively with people of diverse abilities, backgrounds, and cultural perspectives.
- Examine the sociocultural and international contexts that influence individual differences.
- Explain how individual differences influence beliefs, values, and interactions with others and vice versa.

138

- Understand how privilege, power, and oppression may affect prejudice, discrimination, and inequity.
- Recognize prejudicial attitudes and discriminatory behaviors that might exist in themselves and in others.
- Predict how interaction among diverse people can challenge conventional understanding of psychological processes and behavior.

Although these learning outcomes might be achieved through more than one model of pedagogy, the service-learning model, implemented in a local or international community context, is certainly implicated as among the more promising. Psychology as a discipline has experience and published scholarship in each context, as well as in models of service learning.

Service Learning and Engaged Scholarship in Psychology

To be achieved, these learning objectives require understanding of academic disciplinary knowledge as well as local community knowledge, bridging what Walshok (1995) referred to as academic and civic knowledge. They require learning from the social context in which behavior is being observed or problems are being addressed collaboratively by representatives of the community and the academy. This is what service learning is about. It is not simply a matter of defining problems in the community from the academy's perspective or applying to these problems what one knows from the discipline, as might be the case in an "expert" model of service. Rather, it is a transactional collaborative effort in both defining and addressing problems between representatives of the academy and the community based on knowledge of the academy and the community, what Rice (2005) referred to as "cosmopolitan" and "local" knowledge. Nor is service learning simply achieved through volunteer service without a reflective, critical-thinking, curriculum-based requirement. Furco (1996) aptly places service learning between volunteer work and vocational internship, the latter being an application of academic knowledge to problems in the community as diagnosed also by academic knowledge.

In collaboration with Campus Compact, psychology has been a participant in national initiatives to advance models and practices of service learning, despite the fact that the goals of such pedagogy had not become a standard part of the undergraduate curriculum as noted by Altman. Foremost among the publications of such work for psychologists is that edited by Bringle and Duffy (1998). In most instances where service learning models have been employed, as Altman surmised, it has been more the result of individual faculty interest and commitment than that of a systemic curriculum emphasis at the undergraduate level. Drawing upon these committed faculty for leadership, however, the APA has tried to interest and engage more psychology faculty in such endeavors. One effort of this nature was its co-sponsorship with the Upper Midwest Campus Compact Consortium of a workshop in 2004 on service learning in psychology. Another APA initiative was the development of a psychology website on civic engagement and service learning (http://www.apa.org/ed/slce/home.html). The APA Board of Educational Affairs also sponsors annual awards for innovations in undergraduate and graduate education, for each of which examples of engaged scholarship through service learning and other models of teaching and learning would be eligible.

In an edited volume of essays on the teaching of psychology to honor master teachers of the discipline, Wilbert McKeachie and Charles Brewer, Mathie (2002) addresses the scholarship of teaching, learning, and service. She distinguishes the benefits for teaching and learning through faculty roles of professional service and citizenship, that is, engagement in the nonacademic community, from those of institutional service within the academy and disciplinary service within professional organizations of the discipline. To the extent that faculty, at either undergraduate or graduate levels of education, are engaged in professional service in the community, and to the extent that they involve their students in an active service learning manner with them, Mathie states:

> The connections instructors build through their professional service also facilitate the development of service learning opportunities for students. Students not only learn new skills in these experiences, but they also begin to see themselves as change agents in society; become more aware of the complex nature of society and the problems that exist in communities; gain first-hand experience at identifying, experiencing, and solving societal problems; and learn to work collaboratively. (p. 169)

As she also notes, these learning outcomes are what Altman referred to as socially responsive knowledge. Inasmuch as the majority of psychologists these days have developed competencies in applied areas of the discipline, and thus could be engaged in a variety of collaborative activities with the nonacademic community, there is ample opportunity for engagement of their students in the development of socially responsive knowledge. Although the implementation of service learning in psychology has more often than not been through the undergraduate curriculum, its potential is also applicable to the graduate, professional level of education, a few examples of which are provided by Meyers (2008), Schulenberg et al. (2008), and Thomas and Landau (2002). This follows in the tradition of Lewin and other community action research leaders of the past century who worked closely with graduate students in developing their ideas. As Marrow (1969, p. 232) noted: "Lewin left his mark on a whole generation of social scientists." It has been through their work as well that new fields of research for psychologists have been discovered.

Carol Geary Schneider (2000), president of the Association of American Colleges and Universities, speaks to this emergence in colleges and universities of new fields of study, quite often broader than individual disciplines and also defined in societal contexts. "The civic potential of these new fields," she contends (p. 111), "extends beyond their subject matter. Befitting their bridging role between the realms of scholarship and action, curricula in virtually all these new fields and programs routinely foster forms of learning that are engaged, action-oriented, and hands-on." Schneider goes on to mention their most popular pedagogical strategies, namely, collaborative inquiry, experiential learning, service learning, project-based learning, and integrative learning. In writing about the college and university as citizen, Thomas (2000) describes several models of civic engagement implemented on academic campuses.

Mechanisms for Change: Quality Assessment and Accreditation

Preparing students for responsible citizenship and future leadership in society is a goal included in most college and university mission statements (Harkavy, 2002). Yet, the rich diversity of colleges and universities celebrated in our nation leads to different academic models for the achievement of these goals. In his edited volume on higher education and civic responsibility, Ehrlich (2000) invited scholars to write about the perspectives that faculty might have in different categories of higher education institutions, from those of community colleges to those of research universities. Respectful of the diversity of purpose, values, and culture across higher education institutions in our nation, quality assessment and enhancement standards employed in the accreditation of these institutions must be sufficiently general, while also setting common benchmarks of achievement. Over the past quarter of a century, this has been accomplished in accreditation by a major movement to assess learning outcomes in the context of an institution's (or degree program's) goals and mission context. This requires the institution (or program) to be explicit about its goals and priorities, and equally attentive to the assessment of learning achieved in relation to these ends.

In the case of psychology as a discipline, the accreditation of degree programs that is recognized by the U.S. Secretary of Education and the Council on Higher Education Accreditation is only at the doctoral education and postdoctoral levels in particular applied areas of psychology for which licensure to practice is required (American Psychological Association, 2008). The standards noted in the guidelines and principles for accreditation of these programs are clearly consonant with the national practice in accreditation of learning outcomes assessment related to program goals and institutional mission context. For other graduate and undergraduate programs in psychology, however, as with most other liberal arts and science disciplines, their quality is not separately assessed by the disciplinary society but rather as part of the educational system of their college or university, the totality of which is accredited through one of the nationally recognized regional accrediting bodies.

Still, in the context of their institution's accreditation, psychology departments at both undergraduate and graduate education levels have the benefit of defining their goals in the context of their institution's mission but also in the context of reflective action in their discipline, as noted in the previously cited national conferences on undergraduate and graduate education. The goals for learning gleaned from such conferences are especially well articulated in guidelines for undergraduate education of majors in psychology, goals that are specific to the discipline while also relevant to the goals of a liberal education. In addition, psychology scholars of undergraduate education also have developed guidelines for the assessment of learning objectives within the various goal domains (Halonen et al., 2003); and, in conjunction with the recent guidelines for undergraduate majors in psychology, an online cyberguide has been developed for use in planning strategies for assessing learning outcomes expected of discipline majors (http://www.apa.org/ed/guidehomepage.html).

The assessment of learning outcomes is complex enough; when it comes to the learning outcomes derived from service learning and other experiential, collaborative, integrative, project-based pedagogical strategies, even more innovative assessment methodologies will be required (Bringle, Phillips, & Hudson, 2003). Inasmuch as measurement and assessment of individual learning outcomes is a fundamental competency expected of psychologists, the discipline should be up to this challenge in developing models of general applicability to other disciplines as well.

A Look to the Future

Many scholars have written about the challenges posed within the culture of the academy itself for faculty to become engaged scholars and, in turn, devote significantly more time to teaching and engaging their students in the community with them. For psychologists at least, this problem has been exacerbated because the argument for change has been more structural than knowledge based. That is, the force for change has often pointed to education's social responsibilities and civic roles. These are positive forces, to be sure, but a more basic reason for bringing socially responsive knowledge and service learning pedagogy into our curriculum is that in many situations they simply are a more successful way to reach our students.

Although seldom acknowledged, the reasons for the success of this pedagogy can be found in the foundational knowledge of psychology. From the laboratory to the classroom and beyond, research into how we learn repeatedly focuses on the kinds of student understanding and application of knowledge often found in service-learning experiences. It is now well known that learning occurs best when what is being learned is relevant and meaningful to the learner (Lambert & McCombs, 1998). Moreover, meaningfulness is particularly salient to success when learning requires moving to more complex forms of reasoning, content knowledge, and problem solving. Another aspect of effective learning, its durability, likewise is informed by a vast literature in psychology. The National Research Council's report *How People Learn* (Bransford, Brown, & Cocking, 1999, p. 19) identifies several factors involved in the durability of learning, including that:

- Skills and knowledge must be extended beyond the narrow contexts in which they are initially learned;
- The learner develops a sense of when what has been learned can be used—the conditions of application;
- The learner knows and understands underlying principles that can be applied to problems in new contexts; knowledge learned at the level of rote memory rarely transfers.

Although these factors are often more available in a service-learning experience than in the standard classroom, they still require careful attention, course structure, and teacher expertise. For example, the most efficacious experiences include multiple and varied opportunities throughout the placement for student reflection that links their experience to the course material. Discussions among students and with experts from the community as well as the teacher are necessary for the student to identify key concepts and to connect them with their experiences. Students should be challenged to view their experiences from different theoretical perspectives, comparing the varied implications for action, practicing their skills, and testing the outcomes.

As well, research presented by the National Research Council's report points to reasons why this effort begins with individual faculty who are themselves experts with their communities. We have learned that expert teachers are those who know the content and structure of their disciplines and how these interact to produce effective learning. These are the teachers who develop cognitive roadmaps to guide the assignments they give students, the assessments they use to gauge students' progress, and the questions they ask in the give and take of classroom life. Extended to service learning, the expert teacher not only must have content and pedagogical expertise but also must have this kind of expertise about the environment in which the service-learning experience is housed.

Thus, to sustain this work in ways that can extend to a curricular and institutional level requires more than administrative decrees or even faculty legislation. The very expertise of faculty must change. And, although faculty development initiatives are possible and even desirable, a more strategic approach considers how we prepare our future faculty.

In an edited volume by Kerry Ann O'Meara and Eugene Rice (2005), many distinguished scholars address issues related to the reconsideration of faculty priorities in the academy of the future. Among these priorities is the preparation of future faculty (Gaff, 2005), the theme of a national initiative for the past two decades on doctoral degree–granting campuses. Psychology was among the many science and humanities disciplines that participated in this initiative, and remains active in the advancement of its goals today (http://www.apa.org/ed/pff.html).

Clearly, faculty roles and reward systems need to be revisited if we are to have greater civic engagement on our campuses; but equally important is preparing the future faculty of our colleges and universities for different roles as scholars. The APA (Nelson, 2004, 2006) created website resources for possible use by graduate departments of psychology to facilitate a broader understanding of scholarship among today's graduate students, the future stewards and faculty of the discipline. The meaning of engaged scholarship and self-study perspectives on ways in which to prepare graduate students for future leadership roles of civic engagement are addressed.

Moreover, in the most recent national conference on undergraduate education (Munsey, 2008), emphasis was given to the enhancement of teaching, consistent with the scholarship of teaching themes of the past decade, including a more systematic assessment of teaching methods and learning outcomes. Emphasis was likewise placed on the importance of students becoming "psychologically literate" so that as citizens in their communities, they could be better-informed leaders on civic issues related to psychological phenomena. And, there was discussion of ways in which to improve the definition of undergraduate education goals, including the learning goals that will serve students well in their own lives and in contributing to society at large. Although there were other conference topics related to the future of undergraduate education in psychology, these three emphases at least afford venues through which to include socially responsive knowledge among the learning objectives in psychology. For faculty, whose students already are more diverse in background than ever before, socially responsive knowledge might well include a better understanding of how and what their students are learning in relation to the goals of their department and academic institution, as well as for their personal development and career interests. For the students, the socially responsive knowledge translates into how and what they are learning that will prepare them to be effective citizens and leaders in their community in whatever career they pursue.

Psychology, being one of the largest undergraduate and graduate major enrollments among the assemblage of liberal arts and science disciplines, has another opportunity related to its very diverse nature and historical roots. As a discipline, it has relationship roots with most other disciplines of the science and humanities fields, and as such affords potential for collaboration with those disciplines in preparing students, undergraduate and graduate, to think in interdisciplinary terms and, in so doing, to learn how to collaborate with colleagues of other related disciplines. One of the most effective ways for this to be achieved is through models of pedagogy related to civic engagement. For psychologists, as exemplified through the history of their involvement in establishing university centers for multidisciplinary problem-oriented action research, this is not a new idea. Yet, it is a lesson from the discipline's history that seems all too often neglected when future directions for the discipline are contemplated.

From the perspectives of those leading the call for re-envisioning the undergraduate liberal education (e.g., Schneider, 2003) to those envisioning the future of doctoral education (e.g., Golde & Walker, 2006), breadth as well as depth of learning is deemed essential if the graduates of our colleges and universities at these levels of education are to be effective citizens and engaged scholars in local, national, and global communities of the future. Depth of learning in the disciplines is necessary, but not sufficient. It is enriched by breadth of learning across disciplines, especially as such learning includes what Altman referred to as socially responsive knowledge.

It is precisely this multidisciplinary, problem-oriented approach to scholarship and education that affords such a rich learning experience for students and faculty alike, whether it be at the undergraduate or graduate level of education. It is the ideal model for service learning and engaged scholarship. Moreover, it is a model grounded in our discipline, supported by our research, and one that enhances the learning of our students.

References

Allport, G. W. (1940). The psychologist's frame of reference. *Psychological Bulletin, 37*, 1–28.

Altman, I. (1996). Higher education and psychology in the millennium. *American Psychologist, 51*, 371–378.

American Psychological Association. (2007). *APA guidelines for the undergraduate psychology major.* Washington, DC: Author.

American Psychological Association. (2008). *Guidelines and principles for accreditation of programs in professional psychology.* Washington, DC: Commission on Accreditation, American Psychological Association.

Barker, R. G., & Gump, P. V. (1964). *Big school, small school.* Stanford, CA: Stanford University Press.

Bickman, L., & Ellis, H. (Eds.). (1990). *Preparing psychologists for the 21st century: Proceeding of the National Conference on Graduate Education in Psychology.* Hillsdale, NJ: Erlbaum.

Boyer, E. L. (1990). *Scholarship reconsidered: Priorities of the professoriate.* Princeton, NJ: Carnegie Foundation for the Advancement of Teaching.

Boyer, E. L. (1996, Spring). The scholarship of engagement. *Journal of Public Service and Outreach, 1.*

Bransford, J. D., Brown, A. L., & Cocking, R. R. (Eds.). (1999). *How people learn.* Washington, DC: National Academies Press.

Bringle, R. G., & Duffy, D. K. (Eds.). (1998). *With service in mind: Concepts and models for service-learning in psychology.* Washington, DC: American Association of Higher Education in cooperation with the American Psychological Association.

Bringle, R. G., Phillips, M. A., & Hudson, M. (2003). *The measure of service learning: Research scales to assess student experiences.* Washington, DC: American Psychological Association.

Capshew, J. H. (1999). *Psychologists on the march: Science, practice, and professional identity in America, 1929–1969.* Cambridge, UK: Cambridge University Press.

Capshew, J. H., & Hilgard, E. R. (1992). The power of service: World War II and professional reform in the American Psychological Association. In R. B. Evans, V. S. Sexton, & T. C. Cadwallader, *The American Psychological Association: A historical perspective* (pp. 149–176). Washington, DC: American Psychological Association.

Committee on Science, Engineering, and Public Policy. (1995). *Reshaping the graduate education of scientists and engineers.* Washington, DC: National Academy of Science, National Academy of Engineering, and Institute of Medicine.

Cronbach L. J. (1957). The two disciplines of psychology. *American Psychologist, 12,* 671–684.

Davis, W. H. (1907). Report of the Secretary for 1906. *Psychological Bulletin, 4,* 201–205.

DeLeon, P. H. (1988). Public policy and public service. *American Psychologist, 43,* 309–315.

Deutsch, M. (1985). *The resolution of conflict: Constructive and destructive processes.* New Haven, CT: Yale University Press.

Dewey, J. (1900). Psychology and social practice. *Psychological Review, 7,* 105–124.

Ehrlich, T. (Ed.). (2000). *Civic responsibility and higher education.* Phoenix: Oryx Press.

Finison, L. J. (1986). The psychological insurgency, 1936–1945. *Journal of Social Issues, 42,* 21–34.

Furco, A. (1996). Service-learning: A balanced approach to experiential education. In Corporation for National Service (Ed.), *Expanding boundaries: Serving and learning* (pp. 2–6). Columbia, MD: Cooperative Education Association.

Gaff, J. G. (2005). Preparing future faculty and multiple forms of scholarship. In K. A. O'Meara & R. E. Rice (Eds.), *Faculty priorities reconsidered: Rewarding multiple forms of scholarship* (pp. 66–71). San Francisco: Wiley.

Golde, C. M., & Walker, G. E. (Eds.). (2006). *Envisioning the future of doctoral education: Preparing stewards of the discipline.* San Francisco: Jossey-Bass.

Halonen, J. S., Bosack, T., Clay, S., McCarthy, M., Dunn, D. S., Hill, G. W. IV, et al. (2003). A rubric for learning, teaching, and assessing scientific inquiry in psychology. *Teaching of Psychology, 30,* 196–208.

Halpern, D. F., & Reich, J. (1999). Scholarship in psychology: Conversations about change and constancy. *American Psychologist, 54,* 347–349.

Halpern, D.F., Smothergill, D.W., Allen, M., Baker, S., Baum, C., Best, D., et al. (1998). Scholarship in psychology: A paradigm for the twenty-first century. *American Psychologist, 53,* 1292–1297.

145

Harkavy, I. (2002, Fall). Honoring community, honoring place. *Campus Compact Reader,* 1–9.

Ittelson, W. H., Proshansky, H., Rivlin, L., & Winkel, G. (1974). *An introduction to environmental psychology.* New York: Holt, Rinehart & Winston.

James, W. (1890). *Principles of psychology.* New York: Holt.

Kelman, H. C. (Ed.). (1965). *International behavior: A social-psychological analysis.* New York: Holt, Rinehart & Winston.

Kimble, G. A. (1984). Psychology's two cultures. *American Psychologist, 39,* 833–839.

Lambert, N. M., & McCombs, B. L. (Eds.). (1998). *How students learn.* Washington, DC: American Psychological Association.

Lorion, R. P., Iscoe, I., DeLeon, P. H., & VandenBos, G. R. (Eds.). (1996). *Psychology and public service.* Washington, DC: American Psychological Association.

Lynton, E. A. (1995). *Making the case for professional service.* Washington, DC: American Association of Higher Education.

Marrow, A. (1969). *The practical theorist: The life and work of Kurt Lewin.* New York: Basic Books.

Mathie, V. A. (2002). Integrating teaching and service to enhance learning. In S. F. Davis & W. Buskist (Eds.), *The teaching of psychology: Essays in honor of Wilbert J. McKeachie and Charles L. Brewer* (pp. 163–177). Mahwah, NJ: Erlbaum.

McGovern, T. V. (Ed.). (1991). *Handbook for enhancing undergraduate education in psychology.* Washington, DC: American Psychological Association.

Meyers, L. (2008, March). Big-picture psychologists. *Monitor on Psychology,* 36–37.

Morawski, J. G. (2002). Assessing psychology's moral heritage through our neglected utopias. In W. E. Pickren & D. A. Dewsbury (Eds.), *Evolving perspectives on the history of psychology* (pp. 499–525). Washington, DC: American Psychological Association.

Munsey, C. (2008, September). Charting the future of undergraduate psychology. *Monitor on Psychology,* 54–57.

Nelson, P. D. (2004). *Civic engagement and scholarship: Implications for graduate education in psychology.* Washington, DC: American Psychological Association. Available at http://www.apa.org/ed/slce/engage_nelson.pdf.

Nelson, P. D. (2006). *Scholarship in doctoral education: A conceptual framework for self-study in graduate departments of psychology.* Washington, DC: American Psychological Association. Available at http://www.apa.org/ed/graduate/concept_layout.pdf.

O'Meara, K. A., & Rice, R. E. (Eds.). (2005). *Faculty priorities reconsidered: Rewarding multiple forms of scholarship.* San Francisco: Wiley.

Peterson, R. L., & Trierweiler, S. J. (1999). Scholarship in psychology: Advantages of an expanded vision. *American Psychologist, 54,* 350–355.

Rappaport, J. (1977). *Community psychology: Values, research, and action.* New York: Holt Rinehart & Winston.

Rice, R. E. (2005). "Scholarship reconsidered": History and context. In K. A. O'Meara & R. E. Rice (Eds.), *Faculty priorities reconsidered: Rewarding multiple forms of scholarship* (pp. 17–31). San Francisco: Wiley.

Sarason, S. B. (1984). Community psychology and public policy: Missed opportunity. *American Journal of Community Psychology, 12,* 199–207.

Sarason, S. B. (1988). *The making of an American psychologist.* San Francisco: Jossey-Bass.

Sarason, S. B., Levine, M., Goldenberg, I. I., Cherlin, D., & Bennett, E. (1966). *Psychology in community settings: Clinical, vocational, educational, and social aspects.* New York: Wiley.

Schneider, C. G. (2000). Educational missions and civic responsibility: Towards the engaged academy. In T. Ehrlich (Ed.), *Civic responsibility and higher education* (pp. 98–123). Phoenix: Oryx Press.

Schneider, C. G. (2003). *Practicing liberal education: Formative themes in the re-invention of liberal learning.* Washington, DC: Association of American Colleges and Universities.

Schneider, S. F. (1990). Psychology at a crossroads. *American Psychologist, 45,* 521–529.

Schulenberg, S. E., Dellinger, K. A., Koestler, A. J., Kinnell, A. M. K., Swanson, D. A., Boening, M. V., et al. (2008). Psychologists and Hurricane Katrina: Natural disaster response through training, public education, and research. *Training and Education in Professional Psychology, 2,* 83–88.

Shulman, L. S. (2004). *The wisdom of practice: Essays on teaching, learning, and learning to teach.* San Francisco: Jossey-Bass.

Smith, M. B. (1992). The American Psychological Association and social responsibility. In R. B. Evans, V. S. Sexton, & T. C. Cadwallader (Eds.), *The American Psychological Association: A historical perspective* (pp. 327–346). Washington, DC: American Psychological Association.

Thomas, K. M., & Landau, H. (2002). OD students as engaged learners and practitioners: The roles of service-learning. *Organizational Development Journal, 20,* 88–99.

Thomas, N. L. (2000). The college and university as citizen. In T. Ehrlich (Ed.), *Civic responsibility and higher education* (pp. 63–97). Phoenix: Oryx Press.

Walshok, M. L. (1995). *Knowledge without boundaries: What America's research universities can do for the economy, the workplace, and the community.* San Francisco: Jossey-Bass.

Watzlawick, P., Weakland, J., & Fisch, R. (1974). *Change: Principles of problem formation and problem resolution.* New York: Norton.

Public Sociology in the Age of Obama

Michael Burawoy

This is my first visit to Japan, so it is with great trepidation that I address you on the subject of public sociology. As an ethnographer, I am acutely aware of the dangers of bringing to you an idea formulated in a very different national context. Transmitting the notion of sociology is difficult enough, subject as it is to varying national traditions, but when to this is added the multiple meanings of "public," we face apparently insurmountable problems. From Koichi Hasegawa's *Constructing Civil Society in Japan*, I know that the Japanese term for "public" is shot through with ambiguity, having connotations of "officialdom" not found in the English word. Each country poses its own translation problems. For example, in Russia the term "public" is so tainted, in part because of its association with the communist regime, that translators of "public" sociology have tried to find an alternative word, but without much success. "Public sociology" can get truly lost in translation!

These tasks of interpretation and translation are made all the more difficult because of the intense debates, both in the United States and beyond, around the meaning and place, the pitfalls and pathologies of public sociology. Finally, the circulation of an idea is especially dangerous when the originating context is a hegemonic world power, and even more so when the idea is accompanied by claims to universalism. Your suspicion is, indeed, warranted.

Still, I'm persuaded to talk to you about public sociology because I do believe that as sociologists, despite national traditions and global inequalities, we do share a common interest, and even mission, to combat the market fundamentalism that has spread throughout the world—a project that is now showing signs of fissure and exhaustion. Indeed, we

149

might say that Japan is ahead of the game here—its economic crisis of the 1990s was a forerunner to the economic crisis that now besets the United States and, thus, the rest of the world. The three chickens of market fundamentalism—deregulation of the financial sphere, privatization of nature, and the repression of labor—have come home to roost, portending global depression. But, just as the Great Depression of the 1930s gave rise to fascism and Stalinism as well as Social Democracy and the New Deal, so the anticipated depression will present its own dangers as well as possibilities. We are approaching a fork in the road when sociologists can join what Max Weber called the switch men and switch women of history.

The election of Barack Obama as the first African American President of the United States—a historic event in its own right—coincides with a deepening economic crisis. In all likelihood it signals the beginning of a U.S. countermovement against market fundamentalism—a countermovement forced upon the new administration as it was upon the tail-end of the old. What is not clear is the political color of such a countermovement, its connection to the grassroots, and whether it can be confined to the national level, that is, whether an effective countermovement has to be global. Will the grassroots movement the Obama election campaign unleashed continue, and if so, will it be sufficiently powerful to force him into a progressive New Deal–like response to the coming crisis? Will his race and his rhetoric ignite struggles for social justice in the United States, and even abroad? Will he be captive of the hope and the imagination he has inspired? There is real uncertainty about what lies ahead.

Whatever directions the Obama regime will take to counter the impending crisis—and the directions are in any case sure to be contradictory—sociologists have their own interest in channeling the countermovements toward a stronger and more democratic civil society and a more robust and inclusive public sphere. This is so, not simply because it is the progressive thing to do, but because the vitality of sociology is rooted in civil society, because the standpoint of sociology is civil society. Thus, in this era of indeterminacy, public sociology—sociology's public engagement—will have both the opportunity and the obligation to defend sociology's basis for existence, and, thereby, a certain shared universal interest. Not just sociology, but humanity as a whole has an interest in creating and then preserving a vibrant civil society.

So, my address today has five parts. I begin by describing the genesis of the idea of public sociology to help you better assess its meaning and significance. I then move from the particular account to a general formulation of the four types of knowledge comprising our discipline's—and any other discipline's—division of labor. All four types are necessary for a flourishing discipline. From the general I turn back to the particular, pointing to different national articulations of this division of sociological labor and the conflicts they engender. Antagonisms notwithstanding, sociologists do share a distinctive project rooted in the defense and expansion of civil society, which brings me to my final point. With their roots in civil society, sociologists have a stake in responses to market fundamentalism and the economic crises it has wrought. Inspired by these momentous times, public sociologists can now emerge from their academic shells to take their place in shaping the direction of society.

A Vision of Public Sociology

My vision of public sociology was born in South Africa. I returned there in 1990 after the academic boycott had been lifted. It was my first visit since 1968, invited to address the Association of Sociologists of Southern Africa (ASSA). For the previous decade I had been doing field research in industrial workplaces of socialist Hungary, so I was in South Africa to talk about the demise of state socialism as experienced by its working class. There was much interest in this topic because South Africa's liberation struggle—centered as it was on its working class and supported by long-standing connections to the Soviet Union—had deeply imbibed the ideas of socialism. More to the point, the writing was on the wall for the end of the apartheid regime, the last colonial order in Africa. If the class and community struggles provided the dynamite that would bring down the old regime, what would happen to their protagonists in the new South Africa?

Listening to the panels at the ASSA conference in 1990, I was stunned and exhilarated by the immersion of sociologists in the trenches of civil society, the ardent debates that emanated from those trenches, and the originality of their theories of race, state, and social movements. How different from what I had become accustomed in the United States—a hyperprofessionalized sociology that fetishized its separation from society, a self-referential community that organized and policed the exchange of papers and ideas, remote from the world they studied, a community that inducted its graduate students as though they were entering a secret society. Here, then, lay the origin of my distinction between a professional and a public sociology.

I left Hungary's transition to capitalism, and through the 1990s I turned to research in Russia. There, I would follow the tragic decline, or what I called economic "involution," of the Soviet order that created enormous disparities of wealth and living conditions. But before the decline set in, there were moments of hope and possibility. During the twilight of perestroika and the opening years of post-Soviet Russia, I witnessed another vital public sociology that came out of nowhere borne on the waves of an effervescent civil society. The last gasp of the Soviet era gave birth to the golden years of sociology, but the ensuing, calamitous transition to a market economy turned sociologists into opinion pollsters and market researchers, pursuing the crudest form of client-driven policy work. Of course, with a few notable exceptions, Soviet sociology had never had much professional autonomy. It had always been the ideological tool of the party-state, so its relapse into such an instrumental role was not surprising. If South African sociology showed the dark side of U.S. professional sociology, the sorry state of Russian sociology brought out the virtues of a strong professional sociology. Without the strong backbone of professional sociology, there can be no sociology worthy of the name, neither policy sociology nor public sociology. Not for nothing do Russian sociologists say today that public sociology, before anything else, is the public defense of an autonomous professional sociology.

Yes, we need a professional sociology, but we also have to keep an eye on it. It needs to be subject to continual critique—the community of professional sociologists cannot be relied on to supply an auto-critique. So we need to cultivate a band of critical sociologists who will make it their business to interrogate the foundations of professional sociology and its research programs. In the United States, we think of such people as Robert Lynd (1939), Pitirim Sorokin (1956), C. Wright Mills (1959), Alvin Gouldner (1970), or Dorothy Smith (1987) as exemplars of critical sociology. In unearthing the value foundations of professional sociology and holding them up for examination, discussion, and debate, critical sociology not only redirects professional sociology but also sustains and animates public sociology.

Dividing Sociological Labor

We have then four types of sociology—professional, policy, critical, and public—each with its own distinctive practice and purpose, its own notion of truth and politics. I derived this scheme from my experiences in different countries, but its universality follows from two fundamental questions that, as professional sociologists, we all too conveniently repress. The first is: knowledge for whom? Are we talking to ourselves or to audiences beyond the academy? The second question is: knowledge for what? Here I invoke a distinction to be found at the core of the writings of Max Weber and the Frankfurt School of critical theory, namely, the distinction between instrumental knowledge concerned with determining the appropriate means for given ends, and reflexive knowledge concerned with the discussion of ends themselves.

Thus, policy sociology is defined as the solving of "problems" defined by clients. The client may be a nongovernmental organization (NGO), a politician, a trade union, or any entity that has predefined goals and the resources to obtain the services of a sociologist. Professional sociology, on the other hand, pursues "puzzles," defined by research programs. Puzzles are only such within a given framework—Japanese economic development was only a puzzle in the context of an evolutionary modernization theory. Social change was only a puzzle within the framework of structural functionalism that took social stability and value consensus for granted. Student rebellion was a puzzle within political sociology only because anything outside electoral and party politics, that is, social movements, was viewed as irrational. Restriction of output was a puzzle in industrial sociology only because it was assumed that workers and managers had a common interest. National variations in social mobility remained a puzzle within stratification theory so long as the structure of occupations was assumed to be invariant. That is how science develops: by taking as given a range of assumptions that define a paradigm, and then wrestling with its internal contradictions and external anomalies.

A successful researcher can no more question those assumptions—the negative heuristic, as Imre Lakatos (1978) calls them—than a serious chess player can question the rules of the game. Sociologists, embedded in their research programs, cannot pursue their puzzles and at the same time question the assumptions upon which those puzzles are founded. For that, you need people who specialize in the interrogation of assumptions: critical sociologists. Here lies Sorokin's (1956) critique of the obsession with quantification or Gouldner's (1970) critique of structural functionalism. If critical sociology involves a dialogue with other sociologists about the foundations of professional sociology, public sociology is the dialogue about the foundations of society with publics beyond the academy.

Table 1. The Division of Sociological Labor		
	Academic Audience	**Extra-academic Audience**
Instrumental Knowledge	Professional	Policy
Reflexive Knowledge	Critical	Public

There are parallels between the division of sociological labor depicted in table 1 and the scheme developed by Ernest Boyer (1990) and elaborated by others, including many authors in the current handbook. The purpose of these interventions has been to restore the importance of teaching and engagement within the framework of the research university. Accordingly, Boyer expanded the meaning of "scholarship" from discovery and application, to teaching and integration. The four types of scholarship broadly correspond to what I have called professional, policy, public, and critical knowledges, but with the following qualifications. First, professional knowledge includes much more than "discovery" and implies the broader academic context within which research takes place. Second, in contrast to the broad notion of "application," policy knowledge implies a specific relation of scholar to a client or patron, very different from public knowledge, which involves a dialogical relation between scholar and public. Third, "integrative" scholarship, involving the bringing together of different scholarships (disciplines), is only one way that critical knowledge challenges narrow professional knowledge. Finally, teaching is not a separate form of scholarship but lies in the public domain of all four knowledges: professional, policy, public, and critical knowledges all have their distinctive forms of teaching. Broadly speaking, the approached adopted here, based on the division of knowledge production, pays more attention to the national and global context of the disciplinary field and its internal relations of power. The division of sociological labor leads us, for example, to examine the autonomy of academic knowledge with respect to extra-academic forces, and the relations of domination between instrumental and reflexive knowledge. Simply put, the scheme presented here is more sociologically elaborated than Boyer's.

To better explain how I understand public sociology, let me distinguish between traditional and organic public sociology. Traditional public sociology includes the celebrities of our discipline. Examples from my own department at Berkeley would have to include Robert Bellah, a major interpreter of Japan, but also the lead author of the widely read *Habits of the Heart* (Bellah, Madsen, Sullivan, Swidler, & Tipton, 1985), an account of American individualism in a lineage that stretches back to Alexis de Tocqueville and David Riesman—both traditional public sociologists in their own right. Then, we would also have to include Robert Blauner (1972), whose radical exposé of racism, *Racial Oppression in America,* was very widely read in the 1970s. Or, more recently, Arlie Hochschild's (1989, 1997) *The Second Shift* and *Time Bind* were defining texts in the debates about work and family. All these books bring a sociological perspective to public issue, or, in the immortal words of C. Wright Mills (1959), they turn private troubles into public issues. They do so by the specifically sociological exercise of showing the interconnection of microexperience and macrostructure.

153

The publics addressed by traditional public sociology are broad, thin, passive, and mainstream. They have an amorphous presence. Indeed, for Mills, paradoxically, they barely exist in his mass society, just as for Pierre Bourdieu (2000), another traditional public sociologist, people are impervious to the sociological message. Habituated to subjugation, they cannot comprehend the conditions of their existence, and so one wonders: to whom is Bourdieu talking? Anthony Giddens (1984), himself a traditional public sociologist, takes the obverse position that people rapidly absorb the sociological message, so that what is sociology today will be folk wisdom tomorrow! All these commentators share the view that sociological education emanates from above.

Very different is the organic public sociology, which presumes that subjugated populations possess, to use Antonio Gramsci's (1971) language, a kernel of good sense contained in their common sense. Sociological education is an unmediated dialogue between sociologist and a putative or actual public, deploying sociology to elaborate the kernel of insight into social structure that we all possess. Apart from Gramsci, we have such distinguished educators as Paulo Freire (1970) and feminists such as Dorothy Smith (2005) who believe in working from the experience of the oppressed. Here we can also include Alain Touraine's (1988) action sociology that deepens the insights of social movement militants through discussions and interventions orchestrated by sociologists. Here the public is thick rather than thin, local rather than broad, active rather than passive, oppositional rather than mainstream.

The organic public sociologist who works in the trenches of civil society is invisible, very different from the traditional public sociologist whose effectiveness depends upon his or her visibility. The challenge for the organic public sociologist is to negotiate three sets of power relations: first, within the academic community, which often spurns such engagement; second, between him- or herself and the community of engagement; and third, the power relations within the community. The challenge for the traditional public sociologist is primarily to cope with the mediators of his or her message. Not surprisingly, Bourdieu (1998) and Mills (1956) both railed against the power and the distortions of the mass media upon which they relied to disseminate their public commentaries.

There is often a deep animosity between the two types of public sociologist: the traditional public sociologist regards close encounters with publics as contaminating, whereas the organic public sociologists regards knowledge incubated in the academy as serving the powers that be. The mutual hostility has its foundations within the academic hierarchy as well as having ideological roots, but I will argue that each benefits from the presence of the other—the traditional public sociologist gives overarching direction and legitimacy to and receives energy and insight from the intense engagements of the organic public sociologist.

Nation and Global Configurations of the Sociological Field

So far we have moved from the particular to the general, from the specific experiences of sociology in different countries to the fundamental questions that define the matrix of disciplinary knowledge. Now, we must move back to the particular. Our fourfold scheme depicts a division of sociological labor within which sociologists specialize in one or more types of knowledge, and through which they travel as their careers unfold. The division of labor also represents a configuration of domination among the four types of knowledge that varies over time and by country. Thus, U.S. sociology is today heavily weighted in favor of professional sociology, but this was not always the case—U.S. sociology began as a public sociology in the nineteenth century and developed a strong policy moment in the first half of the twentieth century. Nor should we overgeneralize about contemporary U.S. sociology. The configuration of the field looks very different in a community college with its overriding emphasis on teaching than it does in the public universities of the state system, which in turn exhibit a different configuration from the top research departments.

Let us go further afield and take two contrasting national contexts. In Russia, policy sociology is ascendant, but without the backing of a strong professional sociology, whereas in Scandinavia, policy sociology is also strong, but here it is supported by (and beholden to) equally strong professional and public moments. In South Africa, Brazil, and India, the public moment is stronger, although here, too, there is increasing pressure for sociologists to enter the policy realm—pressures from the state and from university administrations—intensified, at least in South Africa, by the demobilization of civil society. In France, the public moment is notoriously strong, accompanied as much by a critical sociology as by a professional sociology. Time and again I have heard French sociologists lament the weakness of their professional sociology, as against "hypercritical" sociology on the one side and the "experts" on the other. Nor should we forget that in many poor countries, sociology barely exists, so to even talk of a division of labor makes no sense. To map the different national fields of sociology would be a major undertaking!

We can also begin to identify the contours of a global division of sociological labor in which national fields come to be organized in some sort of recognizable hierarchy. Thus, we can observe a process of "internationalization" reflected in increasing pressures from states to rank their higher education on an international scale, rating their universities, departments, and individual scholars. The criteria revolve around international accreditation, publications in international journals, and references from international scholars, where "international" generally means North America or Europe. This formal professionalization pushes academics into studying their own countries through the lens of alien paradigms, and it makes them accountable to foreign scholars rather than national and local audiences. It encourages writing in English and "sociologese" for international academic audiences rather than in languages accessible to national or local publics. Extreme cases of such internationalization can be found in such countries as Israel and Taiwan, reflecting their geopolitical position in the world. Yet, even here we find reactions to the dominant trend, bifurcating the field into a cosmopolitan professional wing oriented to the international community and a local public sociology oriented to local communities. Japan is a particularly interesting case, about which I know all too little, where sociology cultivated its own tradition of national folklore at the same time as it was heavily influenced from outside, by German sociology before World War II and by U.S. sociology after World War II. Yet, as it has become a leading global power, it has also developed a resolute independence from international pressures, based on its prestigious universities and academic traditions.

U.S. and European hegemonies generate responses that range from an embrace of internationalization and connection to northern metropolises to rejecting all that is western,

155

promoting indigenous sociologies, and thereby risking isolationism. Steering a middle road are emergent regional dialogues such as that pioneered by the Japanese Sociological Society with South Korea and China, or the powerful communities of collaboration built across Latin America, represented in ALAS (Latin American Sociological Association). In "semiperipheral" countries such as India, Brazil, and South Africa, subaltern sociologies challenge the hegemony of the north by affirming the critical and public moments of sociology against formal professionalism. Such tendencies do not deny the importance of professionalism, but rather make it responsive to local issues, turning it, as Weber might say, from a formal to a substantive professionalization.

The hegemony of European theory and U.S. research programs, the latter backed up by enormous material resources, is palpable the world over. But we should be careful not to essentialize U.S. sociology, because it, too, is divided. This is nowhere more apparent than in the "public sociology wars" waged in a wide range of venues and published in such journals as *Social Forces*, *Social Problems*, *The American Sociologist*, *Contemporary Sociology*, and *Critical Sociology*, as well as in a series of edited volumes. The battle lines, predictably enough, fall along those of the division of labor, so that professional sociologists are likely to condemn public sociology as bad science, as divisive, as discrediting the discipline, or as a cover for politicization. It is said that sociology is not yet mature enough to go public or, if there is to be a public sociology, then it should be under the control of the professionals. Critical public sociologies fire back with attacks on the irrelevance, myopia, and chauvinism of professional sociology, seeing the professional claim to value neutrality as an ideology that conceals a political project of its own. The Sturm und Drang of the public sociology wars is a battle for the (re)articulation of the field's division of labor.

In pointing to the world hegemony of U.S. sociology, therefore, one should talk of two hegemonies, both contested. On the one hand, there is an external global hegemony that depends upon the absorption and radiation of people, resources, methods, and ideas from the United States. Alternative sociologies emanating from Europe but also from the South (Alatas, 2006; Connell, 2007) have sought to challenge U.S. global hegemony. On the other hand, this U.S. external hegemony depends upon an internal national hegemony of professional sociology. As I have suggested, this second hegemony of professional sociology is also contested—the very existence of public sociology wars is testimony to that contestation. Because the U.S. field is far from unified, it should be possible to build cross-national alliances between subaltern perspectives within the United States, such as feminism, critical race studies, liberation sociology, Marxism, and participatory action research, on the one side and subaltern perspectives in other countries on the other. Indeed, the most effective way to dislodge U.S. global hegemony may come from alliances that connect critical public projects within the belly of the beast to similar subaltern projects in other countries.

Sociology's Unity-in-Division

During the past five years, debate, discussion, and symposia about public sociology have spread to countries as far apart as France, Denmark, China, Germany, England, Portugal, Italy, Hungary, Canada, Russia, New Zealand, Australia, South Africa, Iran, Hong Kong, and

156

Brazil. The topic proves to be more or less contentious wherever it insinuates itself. The schisms and conflicts, however, vary dramatically from place to place, reflecting the very different fields that they divide. If there is so much division, can we say there exists a common collective project?

First, although the conflicts are deep, they nonetheless work within a shared understanding of the parameters of our field. The protagonists define themselves in relation to others within the field, in terms of the categories of public, professional, critical, and policy. Indeed, one might say that the antagonisms effectively constitute and then reproduce the contours of the shared division of labor. It is through conflict that the field of sociology is produced and defined, not through any forced or artificial consensus. That is a mark of its vitality.

I would go even further to claim that a thriving sociology requires all four types of knowledge, and that underlying their antagonism is a fundamental interdependence, the foundation of a symbiotic division of labor. Professional sociology derives its energy from infusions of public sociology, advances under pressure from critical sociology, and is often sustained by policy sociology. Equally, public sociology could not exist if there were not a professional sociology that informs it and upholds its autonomy vis-à-vis the publics it engages. It depends on critical sociology for the infusion of values that help it steer a steady course. Critical sociology depends on its antagonist, professional sociology, if only because without the latter it would have nothing to criticize! Antagonists are all locked into a common division of labor, and to the extent that professional sociology becomes irrelevant, critical sociology becomes dogmatic, policy sociology becomes servile, or public sociology becomes populist—that is, to the extent any given type loses touch with and loses respect for the others—so all suffer, and our discipline loses its vitality.

This putative unity-in-division, this antagonistic interdependence is grounded in the standpoint sociologists share, namely, the standpoint of civil society—by which I mean the organizations, associations, and movements that are neither part of the state nor part of the economy. Without civil society, not only public sociology but sociology *tout court* disappears-as occurred in Hitler's Germany, Pinochet's Chile, and Mao's China. Nor is this surprising. Sociology grew up in Europe and the United States, together with the growth of civil society at the end of the nineteenth century. To say we study the world from the standpoint of civil society is not to say we only study civil society. Far from it. Rather, we study the economy from the standpoint of the social—the social conditions of existence of the market, the way production generates labor movements, and so forth. We study the state from the standpoint of its social supports (family, education, political parties, etc.) or its social consequences (atomization, repression, social movements, etc.).

We are different, therefore, from economists, who study the world from the standpoint of the market and its expansion, and from political scientists, who study the world from the standpoint of the state and the consolidation of its power—although in both cases there have always been dissenting voices, because they, like sociology, are fields of domination. The significance of public sociology, therefore, lies not only in the vibrancy it transmits to professional sociology, but through its dialogues with publics promoting the very civil society that is the sine qua non of the discipline itself. Just as the success of economics lies in its capacity to constitute the object we call the economy, and the success of political science is

157

to do the same for the state, the success of sociology lies with the constitution and defense of civil society, all the more important in the present conjuncture.

It has been said that the idea of public sociology romanticizes civil society while demonizing state and market. Far from it. I am only too well aware that civil society is riven with conflicts, dominations, and exclusions. Race, gender, and class divide its terrain. These divisions are one reason why sociology is itself so riven and pluralistic with its numerous subfields. More analytically, we might say that civil society is Janus faced: while organizing consent to the domination of state and capital, it also provides the best, but still far from perfect, terrain for countering the excesses of state and capital—excesses that originate and deepen so many social inequalities, excesses that have become ever more excessive in the recent period.

Sociology and Third-Wave Marketization

Since the middle 1970s we have been living through what I call third-wave marketization. In the United States this entailed the reversal of social and civil rights as well as redistributive policies won since the New Deal—from the decline of state regulation of the economy, to the hemorrhaging of the welfare state, to the assault on labor unions and basic civic rights. In the global south, it entailed the reversal of socialist and state-led projects of development and their replacement by structural adjustment programs of privatization and deregulation. In the communist world, we witnessed the crumbling of Soviet regimes followed by different forms of shock therapy to bring about the most rapid transition to the market. If in China the communist regime did not collapse, it certainly injected the economy with strong doses of marketization. Asian holdouts for state-led economic expansion suffered major setbacks in the aftermath of the financial crises that swept through the region in 1997–1998. This wholesale attack on the social sent sociology itself into a defensive retreat—with some notable exceptions—after its vibrant expansion in the 1960s and 1970s.

This third wave of marketization—the first wave took place in the nineteenth century, and the second wave began in the twentieth century after World War I—like its predecessors, is sowing the seeds of its own demise by generating crises of increasing proportions. We only have to look at the deregulated U.S. banking system, which had gorged itself on bad loans, a house of cards that would come crashing down with the bursting of the real estate bubble. Despite the unprecedented bailout, economists predict that this is but the beginning of a deflationary period, a crisis of overproduction that will lead to shrinking economies all over the world. Certainly credit is getting tighter, job losses are reaching historic proportions, and, failing another huge bailout, the U.S. auto industry has entered its final crisis. The prognosis is bleak.

We can turn to history to see what might happen. So destructive were the consequences of second-wave marketization that began with the end of World War I—widespread destitution and unemployment, as well as fascism and Stalinism, not to mention the World War II—that Karl Polanyi, writing his canonical *The Great Transformation* in 1944, considered that lessons had been learned. There could never be another wave of market fundamentalism. He was wrong, but his theory of fictitious commodities can nevertheless be used to frame the crisis we now face. For Polanyi, human existence depends on three basic elements—land, labor and money—which, if subject to unregulated commodification, threaten human existence. In commodifying land, and we may extend this to air and water, we threaten human sustenance; in commodifying labor, we threaten its productive capacity; and in commodifying money, we threaten economic enterprise. When faced with the commodification of these three elements, Polanyi argues, society either reacts or is destroyed. But the medicine is not always pleasant—too often, it takes the form of repressive regimes that rule over their people with an iron fist.

Sociologists must come out of their shells—the shells into which they retreated as market euphoria raged around them. They must battle for a countermovement that centers society rather than installs a despotic state or appeals to a market utopia. There is no shortage of examples to inspire us. Sociologists have already been deeply involved in struggles over the privatization of land, as in India over Special Economic Zones, as in South Africa over water privatization or the destruction of squatter settlements, as in Brazil over rural land expropriations. Koichi Hasegawa (2004) has written of citizen intervention in various Japanese environmental movements against nuclear power, dams, and reforestation. Sociologists can collaborate with activists on the ground—an organic public sociology—or represent environmental issues in the public sphere as traditional public sociologists. There has to be a place for both.

Similarly, third-wave marketization has dealt devastating reversals to labor organizing across the world, but we also have stirring examples of sociologists giving voice to new ideas about social movement unionism in South Africa, United States, Brazil, and elsewhere. In Spain, sociologists have participated in the Mondragon cooperative as another vehicle to protect labor from unregulated markets. Finally, we can regard the financial meltdown as a specific case of the unregulated commodification of money, leading states across the world to bail out the very banks whose unrestrained pursuit of profit brought about the crisis. This has not been a terrain for public sociologists, although it could have been. After all, the different terms of the bailout have different implications for society. In this realm as in others, Latin America, once again, has proven to be the heartland of shining examples—such as local participatory budgeting to bring municipal finances under popular control—that should inspire traditional and organic public sociologists in other places.

In short, we are living at a crossroads of history, when the old market fundamentalism is dying and the new countermovements have yet to take form. We are moving into uncharted waters when sociologists, armed with an understanding of state and economy from the standpoint of civil society, can help guide the countermovement into safe waters. Our discipline can turn from a field in itself, with a fragmented division of labor, to a field for itself—a symbiotic division of labor that becomes a social movement for an expanded public sphere rooted in a self-organizing civil society. Or our discipline can retreat into irrelevance, fiddling with matches while Rome burns.

References

Alatas, S. F. (2006). *Alternative discourses in Asian social science*. New Delhi: Sage.

Bellah, R., Madsen, R., Sullivan, W. M., Swidler, A., & Tipton, T. (1985). *Habits of the heart: Individualism and commitment in American life*. Berkeley: University of California Press.

Blauner, R. (1972). *Racial oppression in America.* New York: Harper Row.

Bourdieu, P. (1998). *On television.* New York: New Press.

Bourdieu, P. (2000). *Pascalian meditations.* Stanford, CA: Stanford University Press.

Boyer, E. L. (1990). *Scholarship reconsidered: Priorities of the professoriate.* New York: Carnegie Foundation for the Advancement of Teaching.

Connell, R. (2007). *Southern theory.* Australia: Allen and Unwin.

Freire, P. (1970). *Pedagogy of the oppressed.* New York: Continuum.

Giddens, A. (1984). *The constitution of society.* Berkeley: University of California Press.

Gouldner, A. (1970). *The coming crisis of western sociology.* New York: Basic Books.

Gramsci, A. (1971). *Selections from the Prison Notebooks.* New York: International Publishers.

Hasegawa, K. (2004). *Constructing civil society in Japan.* Melbourne, Australia: Trans Pacific Press.

Hochschild, A. (1997). *Time bind: When work becomes home and home becomes work.* New York: Metropolitan Books.

Hochschild, A., with Machung, A. (1989). *The second shift: Working parents and the revolution at home.* New York: Viking.

Lakatos, I. (1978). *The methodology of scientific research programmes.* Cambridge, UK: Cambridge University Press.

Lynd, R. (1939). *Knowledge for what? The place of social sciences in American culture.* Princeton, NJ: Princeton University Press.

Mills, C. W. (1956). *The power elite.* New York: Oxford University Press.

Mills, C. W. (1959). *The sociological imagination.* New York: Oxford University Press.

Polanyi, K. (1944). *The great transformation.* Boston: Beacon Press.

Smith, D. (1987). *The everyday world as problematic.* Boston: Northeastern University Press.

Smith, D. (2005). *Institutional ethnography: A sociology for the people.* Lanham, MD: Roman and Littlefield.

Sorokin, P. (1956). *Fads and foibles in modern sociology and related sciences.* Chicago: Henry Regnery.

Touraine, A. (1988). *Return of the actor.* Minneapolis: University of Minnesota.

Engagement and the Carnegie Classification System

Dwight E. Giles, Jr., Lorilee R. Sandmann, and John Saltmarsh

This chapter focuses on assessing and rewarding engaged scholarship using the 2006 Carnegie voluntary community engagement classification process. This process has been analyzed by those who developed and implemented it (Driscoll, 2008) and by scholars of engagement in higher education (Sandmann, Thornton, & Jaeger, 2009; Saltmarsh, Giles, Ward, & Buglione, 2009). Here, we present some of this scholarship and our analyses of the question of assessment and the promotion of institutional change in the area of engaged scholarship. Of particular importance in understanding how the Carnegie classified institutions are practicing engagement is how and if they are rewarding engaged faculty scholarship along with curricular engagement and partnerships.

Carnegie Classification Revisited

Since its inception in 1905, the Carnegie Foundation for the Advancement of Teaching (CFAT) has served the nation as an independent policy and research center to encourage, uphold, and dignify the profession of the teacher and the cause of higher education in the United States. In particular, since the 1970s, Carnegie has been the developer and custodian of the most prominent higher education classification system in American higher education. Originally conceived as a system to describe, characterize, and categorize colleges and universities to meet the analytic needs of those engaged in research on higher education, it has evolved into a "sort of general–purpose classification employed by a wide range of users for a variety of application" (McCormick & Zhao, 2005, p. 54). It is used by institutional personnel from trustees to faculty; state legislatures, state boards, and state systems; and accreditors, foundations, and other funders, as well as by news magazines and others. In

161

contrast to its original purpose of highlighting the institutional diversity in U.S. higher education, it has had a "homogenizing influence . . . as many institutions have sought to 'move up' the classification system for inclusion among 'research-type' universities" (p. 52).

To acknowledge the changes and complexities in higher education and to overcome the limitations of any single classification, the Carnegie Foundation made significant changes to its classification system in 2005. Among its changes was, in addition to the all-inclusive classification, work on a set of "elective" classifications in which institutions can voluntarily participate and document aspect of activities that are not reflected in national data. The first such elective classification features community engagement.

It should be noted that in addition to the difference in the voluntary nature of an elective classification and its use of institution-supplied documentation, there are basic philosophical differences. The purpose of the all-inclusive, general classification is that of description so meaningful similarities and differences among institutes can be identified; the classifications do not imply quality differences. However, the community-engagement classification is based on a framework that represents a set of practices that, when implemented, actually encourage community engagement. This documentation framework serves to establish expectations and patterns for institutionalizing it.

Carnegie Community-Engagement Classification

Drawing on the benchmarking work of the Big Ten Committee on Institutional Cooperation and the National Association of State Universities and Land-Grant Colleges Council on Extension, Continuing Education, and Public Service, and Campus Compact, a pilot effort led to a framework for documenting the various ways institutions are engaged with their communities for mutual benefit. An equally important outcome was a definition of community engagement, which is, as of this writing, the most widely used standard definition of engagement. The Carnegie elective classification uses community engagement as a term that "describes the collaboration between institutions of higher education and their larger communities (local, regional/state, national, global) for the mutually beneficial exchange of knowledge and resources in a context of partnership and reciprocity" (CFAT, 2008). This alone is a major contribution as the discourse and definitions of engaged scholarship have been both emergent and divergent. (Giles, 2008; Sandmann, 2008.)

The Guiding Framework

The Carnegie community engagement framework was deliberately designed to support multiple definitions, diverse approaches, and institutionally unique examples and data. The framework is used as a basis for documentation and assessment. The "Framework" for the Carnegie Foundation classification for community engagement assesses institutionalization of community engagement. Key elements of practice indicating institutionalization reflected in the framework include (1) vision and leadership, (2) curricular engagement, (3) infrastructure to support community engagement and faculty professional development (which includes developing the capacity for establishing reciprocal community partnerships), (4) multiple means of assessment, and (5) policies that define the incentives that shape faculty scholarly work. The framework reflects an understanding of institutionalization that implies that when it occurs in an educational institution, it is required that it is embedded in core academic work—that it is reflected in the curriculum, in all the faculty roles (teaching, research, and service), and in student learning outcomes.

The "Foundational Indicators" that make up the first section of the framework (focusing on institutional identity, culture, and commitment) reflect this conception of institutionalization and are the key indicators of institutionalization. The first two of these foundational indicators include items such as mission statement, systematic campus-wide assessment mechanisms, and the institutional policies for promotion and tenure reward of community engagement. Only institutions that satisfy the required items in this section proceed to the next section of the framework, "Categories of Community Engagement."

There are three categories: Curricular Engagement, Outreach and Partnerships, and both. Curricular Engagement applies to institutions where teaching, learning, and scholarship engage faculty, students, and community in collaborations with the intention of addressing community-identified needs, deepening students' civic and academic learning, enhancing community well-being, and enriching the scholarship of the institution. Outreach and Partnerships applies to institutions that provided compelling evidence of one or both of two approaches to community engagement: Outreach, which features the application and provision of institutional resources for community use, and Partnerships, which focuses on collaborative interactions with community and related scholarship for the mutually beneficial exchange, exploration, and application of knowledge, information, and resources (research, capacity building, economic development, etc.). In a third categorization, institutions that show substantial commitment to both areas could be awarded classifications in both categories. One optional area for documentation was rewarding community-engaged scholarship. One of the key changes in the framework from 2006 to 2008 is that the questions that were optional in 2006—including the question on institutional reward policies—were required in 2008. In 2006, only thirty-three of the seventy-six, or 43 percent, of campuses that received the classification chose to answer the question on promotion and tenure policies that reward community engagement. In 2008, all the campuses had to address the question, and if current policies did not reward community engagement, the follow-up question was: "If no, is there work in progress to revise promotion and tenure guidelines to reward the scholarship of community engagement?" Further details of the framework as well as links to college and university documentation examples can be found at http://www.carnegiefoundation.org/classifications/index.asp?key=12.

Characteristics of Community-Classified Institutions

The community-engagement classification was first made available in 2006 for voluntary participation by postsecondary institutions who wish to recognize, publicize, and share best practices about community engagement as important elements of their strategically planned and managed missions. Institutions' applications for classification were reviewed by the coordinator of the effort, Dr. Amy Driscoll, Consulting Scholar with the Carnegie Foundation, along with a national advisory panel of leaders and scholars of engagement.

In that first round, seventy-six institutions of higher education—both public and private—submitted successful applications to CFAT documenting their experience in and commitment to community engagement. Sixty-two institutions were awarded the classification in both Curricular Engagement and Outreach and Partnerships. Five institutions were awarded only the Curricular Engagement classification. Nine institutions were awarded only the Outreach and Partnerships classification. These institutions are geographically distributed around the United States, with particular clustering in the Northeast, Midwest, and California.

Carnegie opened the classification to new participants in a second round in 2008 and received a larger and more diverse pool of 147 applications from thirty-four states and Puerto Rico. In terms of representing Carnegie's basic classification, 38 are classified as doctorate-granting universities, 52 are master's colleges and universities, 17 are baccalaureate colleges, 9 are community colleges, and 3 institutions have a specialized focus, arts, medicine, and technology. Among the total applications, 112 institutions were awarded the classification in both curricular engagement and outreach and partnerships. Two institutions were awarded only the curricular engagement classification, and 6 institutions were awarded only the outreach and partnerships classification for a total of 120 campuses. In comparing the first and second rounds of classification, the number of actual applications to CFAT and the number of those institutions classified increased by over 60%.

Classification as an Interpretation of the Status of Engagement

Because of its voluntary nature, the elective classification does not represent a comprehensive national assessment. Carnegie cautions that "an institution's absence from the Community Engagement classification should not be interpreted as reflecting a judgment about the institution's commitment to its community" (2007). However, this first wave of Carnegie community-engaged classified institutions can reveal much about the general state of engagement across types of higher education institutions and functions, and about particular best practices. Of the seventy-six successful institutions, representing all types of classified institutions, fifty-six formally agreed to make their applications available for research analysis (Sandmann et al., 2009). An examination of these materials found impressive examples of institutionalization and innovative activities. Taken as a whole, the submitted information reveals nationwide areas of engagement strength, such as service-learning, as well as widespread areas of weakness, such as support for engagement in tenure and reward policies. Five of the best practices include:

- Leadership matters, particularly executive leadership, including leadership by key faculty members. Also, successful institutions are those with some infrastructure (positional or structural) to support engagement activities.
- Purposeful advancement strategies are critical to providing the necessary resources for engagement activities to be sustained as well as develop. Funders will inevitably require institutions and campus partners to effectively evaluate community-engaged practices.
- Campuses are moving toward more comprehensive, longitudinal assessment plans. These plans would include authentic forms of evidence such as student products that capture student learning in a community-engaged course.

- Constructing policies that reward community engagement across the faculty roles and including and valuing community partners in the peer-review process are both important.
- Community-campus partnerships include those that have a clear focus and direction that coincides with the culture and mission of the community partner and campus. (See Sandmann et al., 2009.)

In addition to best practice, analysis of the 2006 institutions and their applications provided a number of additional insights into areas needing attention. Authentic involvement of community partners in outreach and engagement efforts was weak. Institutions found it difficult to discuss reciprocity in their community relationships and to understand how that central component of engaged scholarship might be documented for purposes of faculty rewards.

- Language is a problem, with Carnegie classified institutions varying widely in their consideration of the terms "community engagement," "curricular engagement," and "outreach and partnerships." This can be an impediment to institutions across the country in communicating engagement ideals, efforts, and achievements to stakeholders, both internal and external.
- The applications were highly marketing-oriented. This orientation may actually signal the institutionalization of community engagement, or this public relations focus may imply a lack of attention to sustained social change by institutions in their engagement efforts and outcomes of strengthened civic awareness and responsibility of students, and with enhanced community and campus capacity to work in partnership to address critical social issues. (See Driscoll, 2008; Sandmann et al., 2009.)

Institutionalization of Community Engagement

When any innovative practice becomes embedded in an institutional culture, there are key areas of work that are implemented simultaneously. When the innovative practice becomes part of the institutional culture, it is considered to be institutionalized. A guiding definition of institutionalization used by Braxton, Luckey, and Helland (2002, p. 5) comes from Clark: "institutionalization, most broadly conceived, is the process whereby specific cultural elements or cultural objects are adopted by actors in a social system" (Clark, 1971, p. 75). As Furco (2002) has illustrated, institutionalized practices have distinct characteristics that distinguish them from more marginal and transient campus practices.

The "Foundational Indicators" that make up the first section of the framework (focusing on institutional identity, culture, and commitment) also reflect an understanding that community engagement is an element of transformative institutional change and that institutional transformation is characterized by changes in institutional culture. Campuses that receive the Carnegie Community Engagement classification demonstrate that they have implemented changes in the core work of the institution. In their 1998 study of transformational change in higher education, Eckel, Hill, and Green defined transformational change as change that "(1) alters the culture of the institution by changing select underlying

165

assumptions and institutional behaviors, processes, and products; (2) is deep and pervasive, affecting the whole institution; (3) is intentional; and (4) occurs over time" (p. 3).

Changes that "alter the culture of the institution" are those that require "major shifts in an institution's culture—the common set of beliefs and values that creates a shared inter-pretation and understanding of events and actions" (Eckel et al., p. 3). Attention to deep and pervasive change focuses on "institution-wide patterns of perceiving, thinking, and feeling; shared understandings; collective assumptions; and common interpretive frameworks"; these "are the ingredients of this 'invisible glue' called institutional culture" (p. 3). It is pre-cisely these elements of institutional culture that constitute the foundational indicators of the Community Engagement Framework.

Eckel et. al. (1998) conclude that the efforts being made in higher education around "connecting institutions to their communities" offer the potential for transformational change. Transformational change occurs when shifts in the institution's culture have devel-oped to the point where they are both pervasive across the institution and deeply embedded in practices throughout the institution (see figure 11.1).

The analysis of the Carnegie Foundation's "Framework" for the Community Engagement Classification in light of the work of Eckel et al. (1998) suggests that campuses that achieve the classification would be located in the third or fourth quadrant of the transformational change model, having undergone shifts in institutional culture that have led to far-reaching change or have transformed the campus such that community engagement is both deep and pervasive.

Campuses in the third quadrant should have achieved far-reaching change associated with community engagement: "it is pervasive but does not affect the organization very deeply" (Eckel et al., 1998, p. 5). A campus in the third quadrant would have most of the elements

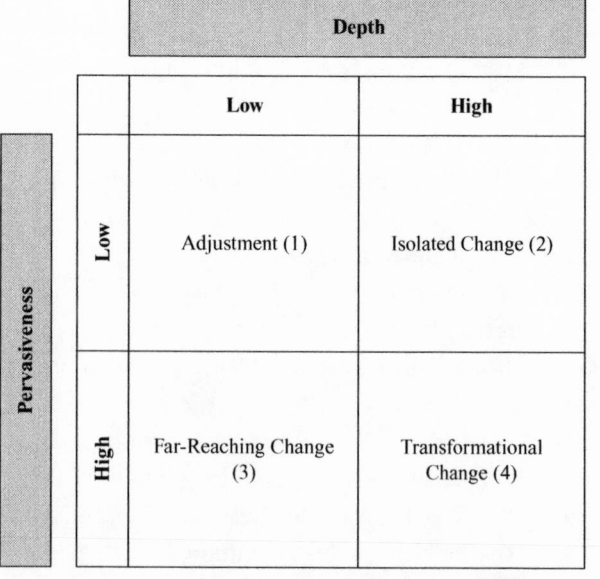

Adapted from Eckel, Hill, & Green (1998).

FIGURE 11.1 Transformational Change

of institutionalization: (1) vision and leadership, (2) curricular engagement, (3) infrastructure to support community engagement and faculty professional development (which includes developing the capacity for establishing reciprocal community partnerships), (4) multiple means of assessment, and (5) policies that define the incentives that shape faculty scholarly work.

Campuses in quadrant 4 should have all the elements of community engagement that are found in quadrant 3, but there is an additional dimension of institutionalization and transformational change associated with changes in institutional culture, particularly what Eckel et al. call "the innermost core of a culture . . . our underlying assumptions; these deeply ingrained beliefs" that "are rarely questioned and are usually taken for granted" (p. 3). Transformational change, they write, "involves altering the underlying assumptions so that they are congruent with the desired changes" (p. 4). Transformation aimed at community engagement would bring about changes in espoused values and the organization's "artifacts," such as reward structures and promotion and tenure criteria (Eckel et al., 1998, pp. 3–4). A campus located in the fourth quadrant would exhibit all of the elements of engagement found in quadrant 3, but would also have an added dimension of institutional reward policies that recognize, reward, and evaluate community-engaged scholarly work.

For example, in response to the question "Do the institutional policies for promotion and tenure reward the scholarship of community engagement?" one campus responded that "Perhaps most basic is recognition through the promotion and tenure process of faculty commitment to community engagement. It is considered both a valid pedagogical technique and a viable foundation for faculty scholarship." The application also referenced the faculty handbook, where teaching is emphasized in promotion criteria and where community engagement is rewarded as dimension "in teaching, service and scholarship."

In short, the Carnegie Framework suggests that classification for community engagement is associated with movement toward the fourth quadrant of the model—toward transformational change and deep and pervasive change that signifies institutionalization.

Rewarding Community-Engaged Scholarship

Higher education leaders seeking to reshape institutional identity and establish community engagement as a core institutional value have the challenge of how to embed the values of community engagement in the institutional reward policies that define the faculty roles of teaching, scholarship, and service (Driscoll & Lynton, 1999; Ellison & Eatman, 2008; Lynton, 1995; O'Meara, 2000, 2002, 2003; Ward, 2003, 2005). Further, because the research university culture dominates the construction of faculty roles in higher education, for community engagement to reshape faculty culture it must be recognized explicitly in the criteria for scholarly work; it cannot be relegated to either the faculty's teaching or service roles exclusively, but also must be included as part of the faculty's scholarship/research role (Weerts & Sandmann, 2008). Although the extent to which community-engaged scholarship is part of the research agenda of any given faculty member is shaped by "the type of institution, as well as the individual goals of the faculty member" (Ward, 2005, p. 224), campuses that want to create a culture supporting community-engaged faculty work, Ward explains, "must define in their promotion and tenure guidelines and faculty handbooks what this work looks like, and how it will be evaluated and rewarded" (p. 229). "No matter how clear the mission statement or presidential proclamation to connect the campus with the community," observes Ward, if community engagement is "unrewarded or seen by faculty as distracting from the pursuit of those kinds of things that count on a dossier, either those public service efforts will be set aside, or the faculty member will be. Either way community approaches to scholarship will not be strengthened" (p. 228).

Faculty scholarly work and its reward provide the context for the questions related to institutional reward policies that appear in the "Optional Questions" section of "Foundational Indicators" of the 2006 Carnegie Community Engagement Framework. The questions on institutional reward policies include a primary question and two subquestions:

Question: "Do the institutional policies for promotion and tenure reward the scholarship of community engagement?"

Sub-Question A: "If yes, how does the institution categorize the community engagement scholarship? (Service, Scholarship of Application, other)"

Sub-Question B: "If no, is there work in progress to revise the promotion and tenure guidelines to reward the scholarship of community engagement?"

The questions are aimed at three aspects of rewarding community-engaged scholarship: (1) what exists in current policy, (2) which of the faculty roles are rewarded for community engagement, and (3) if changes in the promotion and tenure guidelines to reward community-engaged scholarship have not been implemented, is there a process underway to revise the current guidelines?

What It Means to Reward Community-Engaged Scholarship

An analysis of the thirty-three applications that answered this optional question indicates the emergence of significant revision of institutional polices that reward faculty for community-engaged scholarship (Saltmarsh et al., 2009). There are a number of dimensions to this emerging change. First, it is change that takes place over time; thus there is a transitional quality to what is happening on campuses as they go through a process of defining, implementing, and adjusting to the implications of change. These are campuses where institutional reward policies are in a process of transition to reward community-engaged scholarship. There are many more campuses involved in the difficult, often long process of revising their promotion and tenure guidelines than there are campuses that have revised and adopted new policies. For those that have revised their promotion and tenure guidelines to reward community-engaged scholarship, the policies exhibit a quality of establishing conceptual clarity around community engagement, address engagement across the faculty roles, and are grounded in reciprocity.

Policies Are in a Process of Transition

Nearly half of the campuses studied reported they were in the process of revising their promotion and tenure policies. It was not uncommon to have a campus explain in its application that "at the institutional level, we are currently moving to revise Faculty Handbook tenure and promotion guidelines to reflect the importance of community engagement as a scholarly activity" and that "all departments have been asked to review tenure and promotion guidelines to ensure that engagement of students with community is part of the expectations for faculty." The range of policy revision processes reveals a continuum. On one end of the continuum is new presidential leadership that pronounces a new vision for the campus and initiates a process of re-examining the academic culture around engagement, but has not yet effected a change in policies. Along the continuum, campuses indicate an ongoing process with faculty committees involved in making recommendations to change criteria for promotion and tenure, and in some cases evidence reveals that some if not all of the proposed changes have been adopted in revised policies. On the other end of the continuum is evidence of campuses with fully revised promotion and tenure guidelines incorporating specific criteria for community-engaged scholarship. The following examples illustrate actual changes in campus promotion and tenure guidelines, not aspirations for policy revisions.

Most prominent in the revision process is the adoption of guidelines that broaden scholarly activity in Boyer's four realms: the scholarship of discovery, the scholarship of integration, the scholarship of teaching, and the scholarship of application. As the adoption of Boyer represents a transitional movement toward rewarding community-engaged scholarship, community engagement is less specifically written into policies than it is implied in their interpretation. For example, one campus explained its use of Boyer's categories of scholarship in this way:

> The Scholarship category is broadly defined as "Scholarship and Related Professional Activities," and Boyer's four types of scholarship (discovery, integration, application, and teaching) are made explicit. Given these broad definitions, faculty scholarship related to community engagement is rewarded in promotion and tenure decision . . . The point is that our scholarship criteria are broadly defined and community engagement activities are regularly key components of scholarship in successful P&T application . . . Community engagement scholarship fits logically as scholarship of integration, application or teaching.

As the foregoing example indicates, community-engaged scholarship "logically," but without explanation, could be evaluated under integration, application, or teaching. In some cases the campus application noted that "we don't fit the community engagement scholarship into one of Boyer's other categories; we recognize that engagement can cross-cut them all."

More common was to have community-engaged scholarship specifically subsumed under the scholarship of application:

> The Faculty Handbook uses the term "scholarship of application" in its standards for promotion and tenure. Summarizing Boyer, the handbook states, "This involves applying disciplinary expertise to the exploration or solution of individual, social, or institutional problems; it involves activities that are tied directly to one's special field of knowledge and it demands the same level of rigor and accountability as is traditionally associated with research activities."

Occasionally, "application" referred specifically to community-related interactions, such as in "scholarship encompass[es] . . . the application of knowledge in responsible ways to consequential problems of contemporary society, the larger community, so that one's scholarly specialty informs and is informed by interactions with that community." More often "application" was used as a broad category into which community engagement activity most logically fit: "Application involves asking how state-of-the-art knowledge can be responsibly applied to significant problems. Application primarily concerns assessing the efficacy of knowledge or creative activities within a particular context, refining its implications, assessing its generalizability, and using it to implement changes."

Most of the campuses employing Boyer's categories do so in ways that include a broader view of scholarly activity but maintain a traditional approach to evaluation through academic peer-reviewed publications as in the following example: "Scholarship of Application: This involves applying disciplinary expertise to the exploration or solution of individual, social, or institutional problems; it involves activities that are tied directly to one's special field of knowledge and it demands the same level of rigor and accountability as is traditionally associated with research activities." This formulation suggests that community-engaged scholarship must adhere to the criteria of traditional scholarship as judged by publication in disciplinary, peer-reviewed journals.

Conceptual Clarity

Campuses that have revised their promotion and tenure guidelines to explicitly reward the scholarship of community engagement tend to be clear and consistent in the use of terminology that reinforces engaged faculty work, but there is wide variation in the language used to convey engagement activity. In our analysis we found faculty engagement most frequently labeled as service followed by service learning, and when we combined these two, they accounted for almost half of the frequencies of terms used. The next most frequently mentioned terms are community engagement, which may or may not implicitly include scholarship, and outreach/engagement (extension). Only one-quarter of the terms used mentioning the word "scholarship" in some context that indicates that community engaged campuses have linked engagement and scholarship in some consistent and clearly defined way. In addition to indicating an emerging phenomenon, the data also suggest that perhaps it is less prevalent than expected from the Carnegie model and process. In short, very few campuses used clear and consistent terminology that would place them in the fourth quadrant of transformational change of the model we used. Regardless of the unique institutional culture that shapes the framework of engagement on a campus, clear policy formulation rewarding the scholarship of community engagement corresponds with concrete definition of scholarly engagement.

Engagement across the Faculty Roles

Our analysis confirms what Amy Driscoll observes of the 2006 applicants, that "most institutions continue to place community engagement and its scholarship in the traditional category of service and require other forms of scholarship for promotion and tenure" (2008, p. 41). Yet, the applications also reveal that there are examples of scholarly engagement across the faculty roles, especially when there is conceptual clarity and when scholarly engagement is clearly defined and delineated as scholarly work. One campus's policies state that "the University's strong commitment to public engagement may be reflected in any or all of these categories [teaching, research, and service]. Public engagement is defined as discipline-related collaborations between faculty members and communities, agencies, organizations, businesses, governments, or the general public that contribute significantly to the external constituency by sharing the University's intellectual and cultural assets." The way community engagement is defined determines its place in the work of faculty.

Ward notes that "the scholarship of engagement . . . is by definition integrated, and most promotion and tenure guidelines are compartmentalized" (p. 229). For one campus, the promotion and tenure guidelines state that "one should recognize that research, teaching, and community outreach often overlap. For example, a service-learning project may reflect both teaching and community outreach. Some research projects may involve both research and community outreach. Pedagogical research may involve both research and teaching." At another campus, "a faculty member's community engagement activities may be defined and recognized by X College's faculty committee . . . in any of the three categories of expected and assessed performance for tenure-track and tenured faculty: 1) research/scholarship, 2) teaching, and/or 3) service. The Committee . . . is likely to recognize a faculty member's community engagement work as scholarship when it is part of his/her record of research and publication, as teaching when it involves [theory-practice]courses or community engagement or is part of a partnership or community project that enhances the College's service profile." These examples convey not only the seamlessness and integration across faculty roles but also a clear articulation of how community engagement can be rewarded across all areas of faculty work.

Reciprocity

One of the significant challenges that emerged from the 2006 applications was in the area of establishing reciprocal campus-community relationships. As Driscoll reports, "most institutions could only describe in vague generalities how they had achieved genuine reciprocity with their communities" (2008, p. 41). This observation is consistent with our analysis. The discourse around community engagement that is done "to" or "in" the community is contrasted with applications that expressed collaborative, multidirectional relationships that define reciprocity.

One application indicates awareness of the distinction between engagement "in" the community and engagement "with" the community by "distinguishing between (a) community engagement, which is defined solely by the location of the activity (e.g., teaching, research, and service in the community), and (b) civic engagement, which is defined as teaching, research, and service that is both in and *with* the community." For another campus, reciprocity is found in policy documents that codify "accomplishments in extension and engagement represent an ongoing two-way interchange of knowledge, information, understanding, and services between the university and the state, nation, and world."

Campuses that adopted Boyer's categories tended to frame community engagement as "application to" a community, instead of engagement "with." Where reciprocity was clearly apparent was when there was a distinction made between the scholarship of application and the scholarship of engagement as well as a distinction made between partnership and reciprocity. As one campus application stated,

> *Engaged scholarship* now subsumes the scholarship of application. It adds to existing knowledge in the process of applying intellectual expertise to collaborative problem-solving with urban, regional, state, national and/or global communities and results in a written work shared with others in the discipline or field of study. Engaged scholarship conceptualizes "community groups" as all those outside of academe and requires shared authority at all stages of the research process from defining the research problem, choosing theoretical and methodological approaches, conducting the research, developing the final product(s), to participating in peer evaluation.

This conceptualization of reciprocity implies that community-engaged scholarship is assessed differently than traditional scholarship. It redefines what constitutes a "publication" and redefines who is a "peer" in the peer-review process. Although not as comprehensive, other applications express some elements of reciprocity; one application includes criteria for publications that specifies "reports, including technical reports, reports prepared for a community partner or to be submitted by a community partner." In another, evidence of high-quality scholarship can be demonstrated through "letters from external colleagues, external agencies, or organizations attesting to the quality and value of the work." In both cases, reciprocity as an underlying value of engagement is potentially changing the institutional culture of the campus.

The Future of Engaged Scholarship

For administrators and faculty who seek to create a supportive academic culture in which community-engaged scholarship can thrive, the evidence from the 2006 Carnegie Community Engagement Classification applications can provide useful guidance. Evidence from the applications indicates that shifting an institutional commitment to community engagement is an enormously complex and difficult undertaking that fundamentally challenges the dominant operating system of higher education. The shift has implications that are broader than faculty research and scholarship; it has implications for how knowledge is constructed and legitimated, how knowledge is organized in the curriculum, how the curriculum is delivered through instruction (pedagogy), how knowledge is created and shared, and the kind of institutional culture that supports a change in all these educational dimensions. Because of this complexity, shifting institutional identity so that community engagement is both deep and pervasive across the institution is a long and difficult process. It requires long-term commitment, intentionality, and clear understanding of purpose and outcomes.

Evidence from the 2006 applications suggests that campuses intent on encouraging community-engaged scholarship through institutional reward policies should focus attention in three areas: (1) clearly define the parameters of community-engaged scholarship as a precursor to creating clear and specific criteria for the kinds of evidence faculty need to provide to demonstrate community-engaged scholarship; (2) construct policies that reward community engagement across the faculty roles so that research activity will be integrated with teaching and service as seamlessly connected scholarly activity; and (3) operationalize the norms of reciprocity in criteria for evaluating community-engaged scholarship, recon-ceptualizing what is considered as a "publication" and who constitutes a "peer" in the peer-review process. Campuses that incorporate these three dimensions in their institutional reward policies have made a significant transition in transforming the institutional culture to reward community-engaged scholarship. This kind of institutional transformation sup-ports engaged faculty work that contributes not only to the production of new knowledge, but to providing a way for American colleges and universities to more effectively fulfill their academic and civic missions.

The Framework Revisited

In addition to its role in edifying engaged institutions, the community-engaged classification framework has quickly become an evaluation tool for many campuses. But more evaluation, assessment, and impact of their engaged efforts is needed. In the 2006 classified institutions, there was little evidence at the program or institutional level of outcomes, and no longitu-dinal perspectives were offered. What is fairly unknown about the engagement efforts described by classified institutions is who is benefiting the most and the least, whether these engaged efforts are the most efficient way to address community issues and concerns, and whether these efforts are leading to sustained community change.

To provide for predictability and reliability, the Carnegie framework was only minimally revised in the 2008 classification round and will not be changed for the next round as well. Although the framework for this elective classification in community engagement was designed to respect and honor the diversity of institutions of higher education as well as their approaches to community engagement, it may need to progress to fully recognize the diversity of approaches to engagement. For example, it may be important to note institu-tions that adopt a geographic focus in their engagement efforts, such as a local community or a region. Furthermore the current framework implies that all recognized engaged institu-tions are of the same quality. Self-reported data for other Carnegie classification types are based on clear, objective measures, whereas the elective classification in engagement offers institutions the opportunity to distinguish between what they chose to report and what they chose not to include. This self-selection process allows for diversity and uniqueness to be highlighted but also lacks objectivity and consistent quality measures.

The Carnegie Foundation's recent development of an elective classification in commu-nity engagement has given this topic precedence among concerns of the higher education community. According to the National Campus Compact, "this Carnegie classification reaffirms institutional commitment to deepen the practice of service and to further strengthen bonds between campus and community" (Campus Compact, 2008).

Five Challenges for the Next Decade in Measuring, Assessing, and Accrediting Engaged Scholarship

To the extent that our data are representative of how few institutions have yet to implement polices to reward engaged scholarship, then most campuses have significant progress to make. About only 8 percent of the seventy-six campuses whose applications and promotion tenure guidelines we reviewed could be considered in the fourth quadrant of the model of transformational change that we have described here. Our ongoing research will involve campus interviews to determine what is happening "on the ground." Also, it will be instructive to watch the other 10 to 12 percent who could be considered in the third quadrant of change and determine how and if they move to deep and pervasive changes in institutional reward cultures. Additionally, we need to study the 2008 applicants to see if the now-required question on faculty rewards has yielded a different characterization of how engaged scholarship is rewarded. To this end of advancing engaged scholarship, addressing the following five challenges is crucial:

1. If a voluntary classification approach is maintained, then better methods of data verification are needed, especially for self-report data. For example, many of the claims made in applications about changes in promotion and tenure guidelines were not borne out in analysis of these guidelines, at least during the time period we considered (Giles, Saltmarsh, Ward, & Buglione, 2008).
2. So far, the evidence seems to be lacking that classification leads to transformational institutional change, especially around core culture issues such as rewarding engaged faculty work.
3. If institutionalization is to take place around engaged scholarship, there needs to be a way to do follow-up assessment once the classification is granted. As Eckel et al. (1998) note, this type of change occurs over time, so a one-time classification seems inadequate to assess and foster change.
4. Although it can be argued that the voluntary Carnegie classification will stimulate more change over time, preliminary data do not give evidence of this; that raises the question of a needed discussion if we need to consider accreditation in addition to a voluntary classification. Such a discussion might consider the accreditation Criterion 5: Engagement and Service of the Higher Learning Commission of the North Central Association of Schools and Colleges.
5. Benchmarking and analysis of campuses that have successfully undergone transformational change in terms of reward engaged scholarship in a framework of reciprocity need to be undertaken and the results widely known so that they can serve as exemplar campuses.

All of this points to an intriguing and crucial question in the study and promotion of change in higher education: To what extent do external forces such as classification and accreditation promote transformational and lasting change in the heart of academic culture?

References

Boyer, E. (1990). *Scholarship Reconsidered: Priorities of the Professorate.* Princeton, NJ: The Carnegie Foundation for the Advancement of Teaching.

Boyer, E. (1996, Spring). The scholarship of engagement. *Journal of Public Service & Outreach, 1*(1), 11–20.

Braxton, J. M., Luckey, W., & Helland, P. (2002). *Institutionalizing a broader view of scholarship through Boyer's four domains.* ASHE-ERIC Higher Education Report, Vol. 29, No. 2.

Campus Compact. (2008). Civic engagement initiatives. Providence, RI: Brown University. Retrieved June 1, 2008, from http://www.compact.org/initiatives/civic_engagement/.

Carnegie Foundation for the Advancement of Teaching (CFAT). (2007). *Elective classification: community engagement—2008 documentation framework (Revised 10/23/2007).* Stanford, CA: Author. Retrieved June 1, 2008, from http://www.carnegiefoundation.org/dynamic/downloads/file_1_614.pdf.

Carnegie Foundation for the Advancement of Teaching (CFAT). (2008). Community engagement. Stanford, CA: Author. Retrieved June 1, 2008, from http://www.carnegiefoundation.org/classifications/index.asp?key=1213.

Clark, T. N. (1971). Institutionalization of innovations in higher education: Four models. In J. V. Baldridge (Ed.), *Academic governance: Research on institutional politics and decision making* (pp. 75–96). Berkeley, CA: McCutchan.

Driscoll, A. (2008, January/February). Carnegie's community-engagement classification: Intentions and insights. *Change,* 38–41.

Driscoll, A., & Lynton, E. (1999). *Making outreach visible: A guide to documenting professional service and outreach.* Washington, DC: American Association for Higher Education.

Eckel, P., Hill, B., & Green, M. (1998). *On change: En route to transformation.* Washington, DC: American Council on Education.

Ellison, J., & Eatman, T. K. (2008). *Scholarship in public: Knowledge creation and tenure policy in the engaged university: A resource on promotion and tenure in the arts, humanities, and design.* Imagining America: Artists and Scholars in Public Life Tenure Team Initiative on Public Scholarship. Retrieved February 22, 2010, from http://www.imaginingamerica.org/TTI/TTI_FINAL.pdf.

Furco, A. (2002). Institutionalizing service-learning in higher education [Supplemental Issue I: Civic Engagement and Higher Education]. *Journal of Public Affairs, 6,* 39–67.

Giles, D. E., Jr. (2008). Understanding an emerging field of scholarship: Toward a research agenda for engaged public scholarship. *Journal of Higher Education Outreach and Engagement, 12*(2), 97–108.

Giles, D. E., Jr., Saltmarsh, J., Ward, E., & Buglione, S. (2008, November). *An analysis of faculty reward policies for engaged scholarship at Carnegie classified community engaged institutions.* Paper presented at the Association for the Study of Higher Education Conference, Jacksonville, FL.

Lynton, E. (1995). *Making the case for professional service.* Washington, DC: American Association for Higher Education.

McCormick, A., & Zhao, C. M. (2005, September/October). Rethinking and reframing the Carnegie classification. *Change,* 51–57.

O'Meara, K. A. (2000). Service-learning, scholarship, and the reward system. In J.S. Greenberg (Ed.), *Service-learning in health education* (pp. 138–149). Reston, VA: American Association for Health Education.

O'Meara, K. A. (2002, Summer). Uncovering the values in faculty evaluation of service as scholarship. *Review of Higher Education,* 57–80.

O'Meara, K. A. (2003). Reframing incentives and rewards for community service-learning and academic outreach. *Journal of Higher Education Outreach and Engagement, 8*(2), 201–220.

O'Meara, K. A., & Rice, R. E. (Eds.). (2005). *Faculty priorities reconsidered: Encouraging multiple forms of scholarship.* San Francisco: Jossey-Bass.

Saltmarsh, J., Giles, D. E., Jr., Ward, E., & Buglione, S. M. (2009). Rewarding community-engaged scholarship. In L. R. Sandmann, C. H. Thornton, & A. J. Jaeger (eds.). *Institutionalizing community engagement in higher education: The first wave of Carnegie classified institutions.* New Directions for Higher Education. Indianapolis, In: Wiley Publishing.

Sandmann, L. R. (2008). Conceptualization of the scholarship of engagement in higher education: A strategic review, 1996–2006. *Journal of Higher Education Outreach and Engagement, 12*(1), 91–104.

Sandmann, L. R., Thornton, C. H., & Jaeger, A. J. (Eds.). (2009). *Institutionalizing community engagement in higher education: The first wave of Carnegie classified institutions.* New Directions for Higher Education, No. 147. San Francisco: Jossey-Bass/Wiley.

Ward, K. (2003). *Faculty service roles and the scholarship of engagement.* ASHE-ERIC Higher Education Report, Vol. 29, No. 5.

Ward, K. (2005). Rethinking faculty roles and rewards for the public good. In A. J. Kezar, T. C. Chambers, J. C. Burkhardt, & Associates (eds.), *Higher education and the public good: Emerging voices form a national movement.* San Francisco: Jossey-Bass.

Weerts, D. J., & Sandmann, L. R. (2008). Building a two-way street: Challenges and opportunities for community engagement at research universities. *Review of Higher Education, 32*(1), 73–106.

Evaluating the Community Impact of Higher Education Civic Engagement

Randy Stoecker, Mary Beckman, and Bo Hee Min

For at least the past two decades, institutions of higher learning have been promoting the concept of civic engagement. That has meant supporting faculty and students to become more involved in local community issues through such activities as service-learning and community-based research. There is very little evidence, however, that institutions are systematically documenting the outcomes of their contributions and, consequently, little evidence that it matters. Such work can indeed make a contribution, but the evidence of effectiveness is scant.

In this chapter, we explore why colleges and universities have not devoted more resources to understanding the community impacts of civic engagement strategies such as service-learning and community-based research, and identify the difficulties with current civic engagement assessment practices. We then propose a model for the design and assessment of community impacts. Such a model, if used, would assist higher education civic engagement practitioners in understanding how they are affecting communities, and in more effectively applying resources toward community improvement.

Community Engagement's Recent Origins

Institutionsof higher learning increasingly espouse a commitment to improving their local surroundings. Land-grant institutions have a long history of such work, rooted in agricultural development (Peters, 2005). In an era of deindustrialization, urban social challenges have likewise become fields for engagement by university constituents. Many faith-based colleges and universities also have long emphasized a mission of inspiring in students a commitment to fostering human dignity and developing structures that support the common good (Ehrlich, 2000; Parks Daloz, Keen, Keen, & Daloz Parks, 1996).

177

Ernest Boyer's call for a broader framing of faculty members' research agendas, and, subsequently, the Carnegie Foundation's support for the scholarship of teaching and learning have expanded higher education institutional motivations for community engagement. Following the 1990 publication of Ernest Boyer's *Scholarship Reconsidered*, and the formation of the American Association of Higher Education's subgroup on faculty roles, a surge in consideration of what has come to be known as engaged scholarship emerged across the country. This movement continues to use Boyer's framework to argue for a broader understanding of scholarship, one that would reward work that integrated across disciplines, reflected on teaching for the purpose of improving theory and practice, and sought foremost to apply what was learned, in addition to the more standard mode of scholarship that Boyer referred to as discovery scholarship. The Carnegie Foundation for the Advancement of Teaching began what has become its annual conference on the Scholarship of Teaching and Learning, which has grown into an international movement. In addition, regular conferences, various programs, and grants provide incentives to faculty members interested in this kind of work.

Forms of Higher Education Civic Engagement

Such influences have produced a variety of forms of civic engagement. Most institutions support various forms of community service—basically, a campus-based form of volunteerism. Such volunteer community service is done without the reward of formal academic credit, but is nonetheless required by some institutions.

More and more colleges and universities have incorporated service-learning into their curricula. Service-learning attempts to integrate student community service with abstract concepts taught in courses. Through service-learning courses, students are supposed to contribute some kind of service to an off-campus community or organization. Service-learning should involve some kind of reflection on the relationship between course readings, assignments, discussions, and the students' experience of service (Eyler & Giles, 1999). Generally, service-learning is done for academic credit, either as one component of a regular course or in a course focused in its entirety on the service-learning project.

The most recent evolution in the field of service-learning, according to some, is community-based research, in which research constitutes the service. Historically, most forms of participatory and action-oriented forms of research were conducted by faculty members engaging in scholarship from their particular disciplines. More recently, community-based research (CBR) emerged as a progression or development of the field of service-learning, where students are integrally involved in carrying out the research itself as part of their coursework. Regardless of whether students are involved or not, CBR generally includes three key standards. First, the question for investigation arises from a community or nonprofit organization that has a need for the information. Second, the research is conducted collaboratively with expertise from off campus, in particular from the organizations or communities that have the need to know. And third, the outcome of the research is intended to be part of or contribute to some form of community or organizational improvement (Strand, Marullo, Cutforth, Stoecker, & Donohue, 2003). Three federal Corporation for National and

Community Service grants, beginning in the mid-1990s, focused on building community-based research networks across the United States. These initiatives emerged largely from service-learning or community-based learning practitioners who were interested in expanding their work into the research domain (Stoecker et al., 2003).

Results Fall Short of Promise

Clearly, the latest evolution in service-learning, including CBR, and community engagement more generally, articulates a concern with the impact of students and faculty on the communities with which they are engaged. And although superficial satisfaction studies cite the relative satisfaction of community organization staff with service-learning (Bailis & Ganger, 2006), there is increasing evidence that the conclusions of positive impact are reaching beyond the actual practice. Two recent in-depth studies of service-learning have revived earlier concerns that the practice is designed more to benefit students than communities. Community organization staff who supervise service learners often find that they may put more hours into training, supervising, and evaluating service learners than they get back in high-quality service. In addition, many of the students are poorly prepared to enter a non-profit setting and have little to no experience working with culturally different community members (Sandy, 2007; Sandy & Holland, 2006; Stoecker & Tryon, 2009). Another large study on community-based research shows much less emphasis on community participation and empowerment than was previously believed (Stoecker, 2008).

And although the literature is rife with stories of doing service-learning or community-based research, the literature stops when the civic engagement stops. There is a distressing lack of research studying actual outcomes. Service-learning has done a noteworthy job of studying its effects on student learning, but very little research has been devoted to discovering the result of such student work within off-campus environs. There is a striking absence of articles that mentioned anything about community impacts or reactions to service-learning (Bailis & Ganger, 2006; Cruz & Giles, 2000; Stoecker & Tryon, 2009).

For this chapter, the existing literature on community-based research and its related areas was also carefully assessed to try to obtain a sense of how community impacts were documented. After reviewing both disciplinary-based journals and cross-disciplinary journals such as *Action Research*, conducting a keyword web search to identify relevant documents on community organization websites, and following the links on community-based research-related websites such as Community-Campus Partnerships for Health, we identified fifty-three articles that at least mentioned community outcomes. Fewer than half of those articles did anything more than mention outcomes. Among the articles including any discussion of outcomes, none has a section assigned to outcomes, and most of them only have brief mentions of outcomes spread over several paragraphs. As with the service-learning literature, the focus is primarily on outputs.

So there is some consensus that higher education institutions should have a positive impact on their neighboring communities, but the absence of emphasis on such impacts, as opposed to simply documenting community-engagement activities, is striking. What we see from many institutions are lists of civic engagement activities that include such things

179

as free labor to area businesses, classroom presentations, and even field trips (see, for example, University of Wisconsin–Platteville, 2007). The application for the new Carnegie Foundation community engagement classification for higher education institutions allows applicants to make assertions about community involvement and impact with little demand for evidence to support claims (University of Wisconsin–Madison 2008).

Why the Lack of Focus on Community Impact?

Pressure is mounting for institutions of higher learning to show that their civic engagement mission-speak is accompanied by effective action. Recently, congressional representatives have raised questions about the uses of the endowments in large, private universities. Such queries have included concern about whether these entities are "giving back" adequately in their own backyards (Lewin, 2008a, 2008b). Interest in the value that higher education institutions are adding to the cities and states in which they reside is taking on greater importance on political fronts. And, indeed, if there is general agreement that colleges and universities should behave as responsible civic participants, why has there been so little effort to document this?

One reason is that civic engagement in higher education has been focused on student development rather than community development (see, for example, Billig & Waterman, 2003; Mooney & Edwards, 2001; Root, Callahan, & Billig, 2005). The growing literature on student outcomes from service-learning shows the continuing bias of institutional civic engagement programs toward serving their own goals, rather than those of the community. Community impact simply is not as important to document, from an institutional perspective, because the achievement, or lack of achievement, of community change does not directly impact the institution's resource base in the same way that student outcomes do.

Another explanation for the lack of outcomes research is the relative point in time for the actual preparation of the articles. True outcomes—in the sense of documentable community or policy changes—become noticeable usually some time after the civic engagement activity phase and often require a continuing commitment by the institution, sometimes over a period of years. But most articles appear to have been written soon after the civic engagement project ended. Consequently, there was not enough time to observe outcomes when the articles were prepared, and the authors have more to say about what they have done than what their projects have actually produced. Public health seems more likely to address outcomes a certain period of time after the project closure. An article on the community-based participatory research of the Detroit Urban Research Center focuses on the evaluation of the center's first research projects conducted several years earlier (Lantz, Viruell-Fuentes, Israel, Softley, & Guzman, 2001). Metzler et al. (2003) discuss the ongoing evaluation activities by a team of community partners and evaluators on community-based participatory research from 1995 to 1999 at three urban research centers. Community-based research has been employed in health for a somewhat longer time compared to some of the other disciplines, and the model appears to be more developed. Public health projects may also have more systematic and comprehensive evaluation processes as a requirement of project funders (Israel et al., 2005; Lantz et al., 2001). But there is evidence of interest in community

180

impact evaluation beyond public health. The University of Notre Dame Center for Social Concerns is piloting a project to evaluate community-based research projects it has funded over the past five years, in part to see if there have been extensions of the projects or lasting effects over time. In several cases, they are seeing the value of assessing a project several years after its inception (Penney & Long, 2008).

A third reason for the lack of focus on outcomes is the general lack of familiarity with the community development literature on the part of those engaged in community-based learning and research. It is rare for those students and faculty working with nonprofit organizations to have broad familiarity with the literature on nonprofit organizational development, or for those engaged in tutoring programs to know the literature on youth development. Stanton, Giles, and Cruz (1999) provide one of the few examples of linking service-learning and community development, but even they do not develop the theoretical connections between the two. The concepts and theories of community development are largely missing from discussions of service-learning and even community-based learning. How many understand the distinctions developed by Boothroyd and Davis (1993) between forms of community economic development that emphasize empowering the community to guide local economic development, growing the local economy and expecting the community to adapt, or developing the community infrastructure to support certain forms of economic activity that may or may not fit the community? How many have considered the literature on conflict (Staples, 2004) and consensus approaches to community change (Eichler, 2007)? With a few exceptions (Collette, 2004; Sen, 2003; Sohng, 1995), even articles on community-based research focus much more on the research process than on its role in the community development process. In the worst cases, the community is considered a "laboratory" to test academic theories and allow students to make mistakes, and thus a negative community outcome is acceptable if it facilitates student learning and furthers academic knowledge. But it is impossible to understand what positive and negative impacts one is having without understanding how communities develop and change. Even basic community development texts such as Fettig (2007) are virtually unknown in the higher education civic engagement world.

Fourth, the theories that have historically informed civic engagement have not emphasized community change. Charity models, rather than social change models, have predominated in most higher education civic engagement. Although charity indeed addresses a problem, it may not address the root of the problem. Social change models, in contrast, generally seek institutional or policy changes (Brown, 2001; Marullo & Edwards, 2000).

It is worth elaborating this point. John Dewey is the most cited historical influence for service-learning, and his model lends itself much more to the charity approach because it focuses primarily on efforts to change things that are within the control of individuals, such as individual behavior change. In addition, Dewey was a proponent of gradual reform and was less interested in eliminating unfair inequalities than in moderating their negative impacts (Cummings, 2000; Deans, 2000; Saltmarsh, 1996). This perspective fits well with service-learning, which is primarily characterized by more privileged students working with less privileged community members. Such structural privilege allows its beneficiaries to see their achievements as a result of their hard work, rather than as the result of a structural

181

advantage. Of course, that also means that those beneficiaries may be more likely to see those with less as having some kind of personal failing that must be fixed. Consequently, the focus is typically on fixing the individuals rather than changing the system.

Those who have emphasized the contrasting social change approach often have found it risky business in higher education, sometimes resulting in projects and jobs being threatened. Al Gedicks (1996) describes his involvement with anti-mining activists in Wisconsin, and attempts by allies of the mining industry to censor his civic engagement activities with community groups working on the mining issue. Tony Robinson (2000a, b) cites the challenges within higher education institutions from faculty who believe that academics should be strictly neutral in all things political, and from students who often oppose progressive political perspectives, to implementing social change service-learning. Moely and Miron (2005) show the overwhelming preference of students for charity rather than social justice models of service-learning.

Paulo Freire (1970) provides the educational philosophy and strategy to support social change civic engagement, often called popular education. His approach calls for a profound collaboration among those experiencing the dilemma or challenge at hand, one which might easily result in the creation of new institutions. His main work involved improving literacy in Brazil, but his method was not to improve literacy for literacy's sake, but to support social change. He also did not focus on higher education institutions, but on building people's capacity to self-educate. His work is rarely cited in the service-learning literature, however (see, for example, Rhoads, 1997; Robinson, 2000a; Brown, 2001), and it is no wonder, because it does not provide an obvious entry point for those attempting civic engagement from a charity perspective, requiring instead that outsiders engage with community members' social change goals.

If one is emphasizing service to individuals rather than action for change, then one's documentation attempts will be necessarily limited and even assumed. If the focus has been tutoring for the past semester, then the tutor must have helped the tutees because now they can read better. But if the focus is social change, an outcome that must matter is if there have been changes in the policies or institutions that prevented those who were tutored from getting a decent education to begin with.

There are, then, significant challenges to carefully studying the community impacts of higher education civic engagement. And even those institutions that attempt to study impact, if their civic engagement is informed by theories of teaching and learning and research methodology rather than by community development, will of necessity produce inward-looking and partial analyses. The possibility exists that such civic engagement provides little of actual value to the community and may even do harm by neglecting to address that which perpetuates root problems.

Furthermore, studying outcomes is simply extraordinarily difficult. Good evaluation is lacking not only in higher education civic engagement projects but in most community development projects as well, and it is because of the intensity of the resources needed to do it well, and the scarcity of resources to support it. Even in the best community development projects, many of the desired changes are likely to be modest and far down the road. Studying such outcomes requires long-term, labor-intensive commitment. In addition, because the community is not a laboratory, it is often impossible to control the context. Did the crime rate decline because the program worked or because the economy improved? Other outcomes can only be known by building long-term trusting relationships. Finding out whether the teen education program has really reduced risky drug use and sexual activity requires building relationships with the people in the program to get honest information. That is time-intensive and expensive work.

If institutions of higher education truly want to contribute to social improvement in their locales, and if they want to fulfill missions for contributing to the common good or being good citizens, then, despite the difficulties, they must investigate the effects of their civic engagement efforts. Strategic choices about resource allocation are impossible without such information. Without the knowledge that comes from such assessment, universities and colleges can not make legitimate, fact-based claims about their role as citizens.

The Missing Pieces: A Model for Producing and Evaluating Results

What will it take to move universities and colleges to seriously evaluate their community engagement efforts? Our analysis of the reasons institutions are not evaluating the impact of civic engagement provides an agenda for reversing the situation.

Specifically, what we see in the literature and our own experience suggests, from this analysis, three concrete tasks. First, because many projects of social improvement that involve higher education faculty and students are not designed to clearly identify community outcome goals, we need to rethink how such projects are formed and planned. Second, because even those projects that do identify goals may not report on and analyze the attainment of such goals, we need to develop an evaluation model that can be integrated into the project itself. Third, because a training and resource infrastructure does not exist to accomplish the first two tasks, that infrastructure has to be put into place.

Before we jump to evaluating the results of higher education community engagement, then, we need to focus attention on actually producing results.

Project Design

One of the shifts we are seeing in higher education community engagement is focused on the development of projects, rather than simply sending students out to complete volunteer hours. Project-based service-learning is now coming to be a model unto itself (Chamberlain, 2003; Coyle, Jamieson, & Oakes, 2005; Draper, 2004). The idea is that the higher education and community organization partners will sit down and design a project for students to complete. Doing so provides greater assurance that the community engagement will efficiently produce something of value to the organization and its community. Ideally, such projects will be driven by community residents and organizations, but that is not always the case in practice (Bradford, 2005; Joint Education Project, n.d.).

But it is not enough to want to do a project. The partners need to be skilled in designing a project that will produce results. In contrast to the typical focus of higher education civic engagement on student outcomes, good project design actually begins with community outcomes. And that is easier said than done, as most faculty have had no training in producing actual changes in communities. Many community groups, operating on shoestring resources, are also not used to thinking strategically about the relationship between what they do and what they want.

Bringing community development frameworks into the civic engagement process is perhaps the most important step we can take in reshaping higher education civic engagement from being a training ground for students to being a true partnership in improving local communities. We can begin with the Principles of Good Practice of the Community Development Society (2008):

- Promote active and representative participation toward enabling all community members to meaningfully influence the decisions that affect their lives.
- Engage community members in learning about and understanding community issues, and the economic, social, environmental, political, psychological, and other impacts associated with alternative courses of action.
- Incorporate the diverse interests and cultures of the community in the community development process; and disengage from support of any effort that is likely to adversely affect the disadvantaged members of a community.
- Work actively to enhance the leadership capacity of community members, leaders, and groups within the community.
- Be open to using the full range of action strategies to work toward the long-term sustainability and well-being of the community.

We can see immediately from these principles that the focus is on engaging and empowering community members, and that the purpose is to influence their context. So, as we design civic engagement projects, we must do so through a community-driven process. Second, these principles show that our focus should be on building the knowledge capacity and the leadership capacity of the community. Consequently, services and programs brought in from the outside that do not accomplish these things are in violation of the principles. As an example, a tutoring program designed by a university professor, and run by college students, that does not involve community members in its design process, and does not build their leadership skills, does not achieve the principles.

Beyond these principles, there is much to know about on-the-ground community development work. The first and most important practical knowledge to have is strategic planning. Knowing both the process and techniques of planning projects and programs is extremely important both in maximizing impact and being able to evaluate that impact. Some promote the use of logic models as a way of organizing the planning process (Kellogg, 2004) The typical logic model process, however, emphasizes filling in boxes on a chart—a box for goals, a box for tasks, a box for resources—rather than thinking through the theoretical and strategic processes needed to produce community change. Groups focus on filling in the blanks rather than developing a dynamic strategy. The University of Wisconsin Extension (2008) has recently tried to promote a more dynamic logic model process that considers the relationship between inputs, outputs, and outcomes, as they interact with external factors and the project leaders' theories. A more comprehensive model is provided by Bryson (2004). In this model, which can take months to complete, the groups have to engage in values clarification, mission development, organizational assessment, and a variety of other tasks on the way to a strategic plan. Such a process is often more appropriate for large organizations; it can be deathly overkill for community projects that depend on volunteers who are unable to commit the time and resources needed to complete such an arduous process and who can often achieve the same results with a much shorter and more focused strategic planning model. Darling and Bittel (1991) developed a strategic planning model specifically for community development projects. This model focuses more carefully on strategies than the typical logical model process and is much more efficient than the full-powered Bryson model. In addition, it emphasizes community participation more than either of the other models.

The process of carrying out a project also requires many skills not normally considered part of the skill set of the average academic. Recruiting and managing volunteers, organizing productive meetings, building grass-roots organizations, and engaging in community action strategies are not easy things to learn and are even harder to do. The lengthy intellectual deliberations that are part and parcel of middle-class academic decision-making are not acceptable in many community settings where actions speak louder than words (Stout, 2008). Such action skills are the lifeblood of community organizing practice (Staples, 2004) and are often best learned in experiential training. A service-learning or community-based research project without these other activities is simply an exercise, and its likelihood of leading to any important community outcomes is slim.

A successful project, then, will begin with an accurate diagnosis of a community condition. If community members are concerned about crime, they need to be clear on what crimes, when, by whom, and under what conditions they are concerned about it. If their preferred intervention is a youth midnight basketball program, for example, and youth crime is at its worst after school, there is a mismatch between the problem and the solution. One option for a community engagement project, in fact, can be a community-based research project understanding crime in the community so that community members can better choose an intervention. Choosing an intervention—the prescription stage—also requires the community to engage in careful information gathering to improve the chances for success. The best practice in one community may not be the best practice in another community. Here again there are opportunities for higher education civic engagement resources to provide the labor and technical assistance for community-led issue campaigns. The actual implementation may also involve higher education students in various ways. And then, of course, having gone through a careful design process, the possibilities for a useful evaluation are much greater (Stoecker, 2005).

Project Evaluation

For an evaluation to be useful, it needs to collect data that project coordinators can use to improve the project (Patton, 1997). The best way to get that is for the design of a project to include explicit measurable or documentable goals. The community that wants to reduce crime needs to have a clear goal—reducing violent crimes between 3 P.M. and 6 P.M. by 10 percent in one year, for example. The plan ought to lay out the evidence that participants would expect to show goal achievement so that it will be clear whether or not the desired outcomes

185

are attained. It should also develop an analysis for determining if, in fact, the result is due to the research or related programs or projects, as opposed to confounding circumstances.

It is important here to distinguish between different kinds of goals. For too long, funders and community organizations have been willing to accept the achievement of outputs, rather than outcomes, as a measure of project success. The difference is important. In trying to reduce crime, for example, the community decides to start an after-school youth recreation program. Its goal for the program is to get one hundred youth participating. That is an output goal, not an outcome goal (Chinman, Imm, & Wandersman, 2004). The outcome goal is to reduce the crime rate. So, it is not enough to simply say that they got their hundred kids at the community center if they are interested in the outcome goal. They also need to be able to say that crime declined by 10 percent. It is possible that the crime pattern simply got delayed from 3–6 P.M. to 6–9 P.M.. Furthermore, if the research shows that the crime rate does in fact decline by 10 percent, the next step is to show that this was due to the fact that they got a hundred kids to the center, and not because of other factors. In another example, if the project is to create a database of individuals who have sought shelter at the local center for homeless people, the creation of the database would not be sufficient, according to the scheme suggested here. The project ought also to have considered how the creation of such a database would further the reduction in homelessness, or some related, larger concern that impacts the local community.

Evaluating both the outcome goal and its relationship to the community development strategy invokes the distinction made by the evaluation profession between summative and formative evaluation (Patton, 1997). Summative evaluation has been framed as focusing on the outcomes of a program—the "sum" of the effects. Formative evaluation has historically been framed as evaluating a program process—it supposedly focuses on the program "form" (Scriven, 1967). Such distinctions can do more harm than good. Payne (2000), for example, asserts that only formative evaluation is relevant to service-learning. But if the service-learning is part of a crime reduction program, the program coordinator who wants to know if crime has, "in sum," been reduced, and also whether the program has caused that reduction, must do both summative and formative evaluation. In other words, the coordinator must study both the program's form—its strategies and practices—and its outcomes—changes in the target goals—and, most importantly, the relationship between the two.

A crucial aspect of such an evaluation process is that it be as participatory as the project design process. Indeed, a good evaluation design process will be part of the project design process, involving not just researchers and community workers but also community residents, beginning with choosing the issue through developing the overall design and even the evaluation design. This, too, requires the integration of formative and summative evaluation models, because the process must integrate "in-house" evaluation with broader community participation. Ultimately, the evaluation is not separate from the community development process, but is in fact an integral part of it. The main purpose of evaluation is not to find out whether a program worked, but to help it work. The way it does this is by engaging as many people as possible in understanding the program and collectively monitoring its progress so they can use what they are learning as the program develops to maximize its effectiveness.

But this rarely happens. A mistake caused by the artificial distinction between formative and summative evaluation is that much evaluation research focused on outcomes is not done until the project is completed. Formative evaluation requires ongoing data collection throughout the life of a program or project. But if the only interest is the summative evaluation, there is no need to collect data until the end of the program or project. At that point the evaluation is useless. The evaluation should include check-in points within a reasonable timeline so project participants can learn whether their program is being implemented the way they expected and whether it is showing any signs of the outcomes expected. Thus, adjustments can be made periodically using the evaluation research, and ensuring a successful project outcome. And evaluation should not stop when the project stops. Many outcomes will not show up until months or even years after the cessation of the actual program, so good evaluation will continue to see if long-run outcomes actually occur and whether short-run outcomes sustain themselves.

Frameworks for Evaluation of Higher Education Civic Engagement

So, how do we adapt these evaluation principles specifically for higher education civic engagement projects? This involves a shift in perspective. We have been talking about evaluating the overall community development process, which puts the emphasis on the social change goals of the community, and the analysis of the causal relationship between those outcome goals and the entire strategy being employed, including any higher education civic engagement activities that are part of that strategic mix. But what if higher education institutions want to focus on evaluating the effectiveness of their overall civic engagement program?

It is important to recognize that the main outcome goal for the evaluation must still be the extent to which the community met its outcome goal. But in this case the most analytic energy is expended on the question of what role the higher education civic engagement contribution played in that outcome goal. It is quite possible, for example, that the outcome goal was achieved even though the research provided by the professor was irrelevant, or the students actually required more time in training and supervision than they actually provided in service. It is also possible that certain kinds of higher education civic engagement interacted with the other community development strategies in ways that either supported or undermined goal achievement, so we can never ignore an analysis of the other strategies. But we can, for at least part of the evaluation process, analyze in detail higher education's role in the process. In this section, then, we train the lens on that part of the evaluation process that focuses on the influence of higher education civic engagement on community outcomes.

There are only a few models developed to measure the community impact of higher education civic engagement. The most basic model (Bailis & Ganger, 2006) focuses mostly on service-learning outputs from a charity perspective and shows the dangers of not conducting civic engagement as part of a change-oriented community development process. In this model, the outcomes are divided into individual and institutional impacts. At the individual level, the impacts are impacts on service-learning participants, on the "recipients of

187

direct service" and on the individuals with whom those recipients interact. At the institutional level, the focus is on the services and activities of the community agency and its relationships with other agencies. For the most part, these indicators are outputs, not outcomes. Broader community development goals related to social issues such as safety, or economic equity, or other forms of social justice are absent from the model.

A second model proposed by Marullo, Cooke, Willis, Rollins, and Waldref (2003) focuses specifically on community-based research. The authors create a three-dimensional model of evaluation. The first dimension focuses on the level of change: individual changes, program changes, and social system changes. The second dimension specifies four types of social change goals: enhancing capacity, increasing efficiency, empowering constituencies, and altering policies or structures. The third dimension is focused on process or effects outcomes.

The model points to useful indicators to take into account in evaluating higher education community engagement, but it has some conceptual difficulties. The first problem is that the level of change and type of change may not be as distinct as the authors believe. One would think that, because they are on different axes, each type of social change goal would apply to each level. But this is not consistently the case. Although the social change goals of enhancing capacity and increasing efficiency (on one axis) could occur at the individual level (on the other axis), they are likely to occur primarily at the level of the program, and not at all likely to occur at the social system level. On the other hand, altering policies or structures does not fit conceptually at the individual level. Policies and structures are characteristics of collectivities, not individuals, and thus do not logically apply at that level.

In addition, the specification of social change goals does not take into account the important distinction between outputs and outcomes so crucial in community development. Enhancing capacity, increasing efficiency, and empowering constituencies, all referred to in this model as possible outcomes, are, in the community development approach, usually outputs. If these are acceptable as outcomes, then any future contribution they might make to larger structural or policy outcome changes is not captured by the model.

Let's take the earlier example of the creation of a database for a center for homeless individuals. This would be an outcome in the Marullo et al. model, perhaps identified as increasing efficiency of outreach to those who are not housed. In community development thinking, however, this would not be an agreeable endpoint; the design of the project overall would have to show how the attainment of this output would lead to the outcome of reducing homelessness.

As we have seen, from a community development perspective, process and effects (or formative and summative evaluation) are part of a single holistic evaluation model that is concerned with the relation between the community development strategy and its effects. The reason to analyze the process—the implementation of the strategy itself—is to understand its relationship to effects. If, for example, crime—the community development outcome—does not decrease after you put your youth program—the output—into place, is that because of a shortcoming in the youth program or because contextual conditions, such as the health of the regional economy, have changed? By studying the strategy—formative evaluation—you can determine whether you implemented it the way you planned. By studying the outcome—summative evaluation—you can determine whether there has been some change. But only by studying both together, in their social context, do you know whether the causal relationship between the program implementation and the crime rate holds. If the researchers do not locate their outputs in this kind of a larger cause-effect model, they may see abundant evidence of outputs, such as a hundred children attending youth programs, but have no way to say if this is actually related to any reduction in crime.

Another model is being developed by Harrison (2008), specifically for participatory science projects—projects where community members engage in the actual design and implementation of research around issues of concern to them such as pesticide drift. This model specifies six possible outcomes: including more community members in scientific decision-making; addressing neglected research questions; enhancing community member policy influence; boosting civic engagement; producing better science; and connecting science to moral debates. It has some sense of the levels of impact, though it is not as explicit about those levels as the Marullo et al. model. The focus is more on the reactions of the participants than on the ways that such projects begin, are organized in a community, and are part of a broader strategy to influence pesticide drift policy. So we don't get a full sense of the causal variables that may interact to influence the outcomes. The importance of this model, however, is that it focuses on the twin goals of producing both specific policy changes on a specific issue, and changes in the overall social relations of knowledge production—the power relations involved in producing knowledge that empower some and exclude others from the knowledge process (Stoecker, in press). The outcomes of enhancing community member policy influence and boosting civic engagement are focused on impacting policy issues. The outcomes of addressing neglected research questions, including more community members in scientific decision making, producing better science, and connecting science to moral debates are all focused on changing the social relations of knowledge production by including lay participants in the knowledge production process to transform the process itself. This could be part of the capacity emphasis in the Marullo et al. model, because being able to produce and publicly voice knowledge (for individuals and organizations) is an important part of the social change process.

A third model, developed by more than two dozen international participants at a meeting in Paris in 2007 (PAR Outcomes Project, 2007), provides a third perspective. The model focuses on the community-based research process, but we believe that service-learning should also contribute to the changes specified in this model. The model also depicts an ideal-type process. Such full outcomes are rarely achieved, but perhaps by specifying a model that sets such outcomes as goals, we can increase their achievement. As in Marullo et al., this model specifies different levels of change. Changes can occur in individuals, as they gain and use access to power and resources provided by the higher education community engagement process. Changes can also occur in organizations as they develop capacity or increase their organizational effectiveness in specific programming areas and enhance their capacity to develop and use knowledge. As in the Harrison model, such capacity development is at least partly the development of a capacity to do research and influence what research is done. Such changes at the organization partner level, we should note, following the implications of Harrison, can also occur within higher education institutions as they change how they do research and distribute research and other knowledge resources.

189

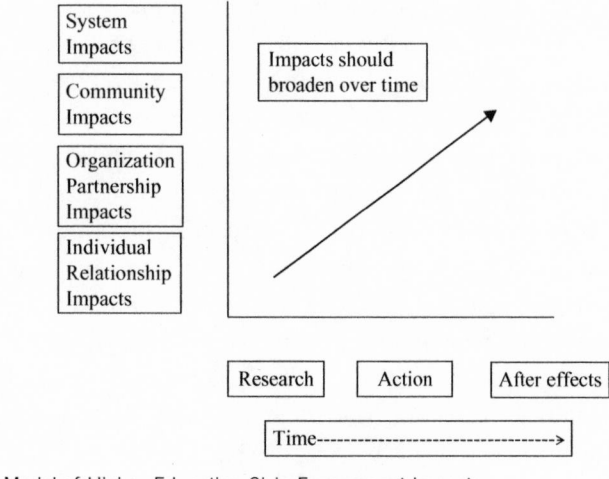

FIGURE 12.1   A Model of Higher Education Civic Engagement Impacts

For the most part, however, these effects at the individual and organizational level are output effects that may or may not lead to broader social change outcomes occurring at the community and societal level. So, if the impacts stop at the organizational level, the ideals of the model will not be achieved. The impacts identified in the existing community-based research literature relate more to the individual or organizational level than to community or system impact. Individual impact and organizational changes are local and directly influenced by community-based research projects and therefore more easily identifiable than broader impacts, particularly during or immediately following a project. Evaluation of community-based research outcomes at higher levels may not be possible until later. But we also fear that such projects are designed without considering higher level outcomes. Because, remember, it is the community outcomes that are central to the community development process. So all evaluation has to begin, at least in terms of the research design, with a method that can document community-level outcomes and their relationship to program strategies (including civic engagement strategies).

The lack of focus on community and social system outcomes is understandable from the point of view of the higher education institution, whose main concern is with its narrow contributions to civic engagement that focus only on knowledge and information, rather than on social change. But they are incomplete in relation to this model. On the X-axis are the steps in the higher education community engagement process. Again, we start with a community-based research process, believing that all good community engagement projects are informed by research to maximize their effectiveness. And those research processes should be engaging the community. Then, however, there must be some form of action. And that is where the difficulty lies, because the action component of the process is seriously neglected, not just among higher education institutions doing civic engagement (Stoecker, in press), but even among social action organizations that erroneously expect the research process to naturally lead to action (Harrison, 2008). This action phase is the implementation phase, where community development and community organizing practices come prominently into play. So, if there are no experts who can organize the action, the chances of higher level impacts are slim indeed.

And, finally, there are societal effects as other communities hear about successful projects and adapt them for their own uses; policy makers devise new policies after hearing about the outcomes of efforts in other places; and so on. Perhaps the most important example of such societal effects, though one regrettably involving little higher education support, is the development of the movement that produced the federal Community Reinvestment Act, or CRA. The CRA prevented banks from blatantly discriminating against poor and racial minority neighborhoods. Begun out of the concerns of a few neighborhoods in different parts of the country who began documenting their inability to get home loans, the research process built into a nationwide mobilization that dramatically changed federal banking regulation (Squires, 2003). Time is the crucial variable in moving from individual impacts to societal-wide impacts such as the CRA. Research and action can be coterminous, but they are more likely to follow a historical progression. Likewise, the first effects we are likely to see will be at the individual and community organization level.

All of this means that our commitment to evaluating the success of our efforts must be as long-term and community-driven as our commitment to the community change process itself. We cannot only care about whether our civic engagement strategies are producing outputs; we must also care about the outcomes. And that means studying the entire community change process, not just that part of the process that concerns the institution's short-term self-interest. It also means engaging community stakeholders—from the grassroots residents to community organization partners—in designing the evaluating process just as we are supposed to engage them in the design of the original civic engagement process. Of course, doing such a resource-intensive evaluation process, in such close relationship with community, requires an infrastructure that does not yet exist in higher education.

A New Civic Engagement Infrastructure

The implications of such a model for designing, documenting, and evaluating higher education civic engagement efforts are profound. Although there have been attempts to develop infrastructural models for higher education civic engagement (Pigza & Troppe, 2003; Strand et al., 2003), they have not considered just how much those models must shift from the norm if we are truly going to truly value and produce community impact. We can now easily see that civic engagement, if it is to matter in the largest sense, cannot be a twenty-hour volunteer experience for an untrained undergraduate. Civic engagement must be the engagement of the entire institution, and not on the institution's terms but on the terms of the community of which the academic institution is a part. For the kind of change being described here, those twenty-hour service-learning placements must be welded on top of a community-university infrastructure committed to community development. As of now, however, neither the infrastructure nor the will to build it is readily apparent.

The will is important. For we cannot build the infrastructure the same way we have done most things in higher education. We in fact must engage in the same community-based research process that we use for community projects. For building higher education infrastructure to support community development is, in fact, a community project, not a university or college project; it is the project of a collective of which the university is a member. Higher education institutions must first accept the potential riskiness of authentic study. Just as any researcher worth his or her salt knows that results may not serve his or her interests or affirm initial hypotheses, so, too, universities and colleges must accept that the choices they face as a result of their studies might present them with moral dilemmas. The implications of doing this are serious—they might require ending some civic engagement practices, restricting others, and starting entirely new approaches. It might be necessary to put in place an institutional review process to control who goes out into the community in the name of the institution. It might require mandatory training for faculty and students just as for traditional research. All of these things are possible results of a serious community outcomes evaluation process.

It would therefore be wrong of us to specify what the model higher education civic engagement program would look like. In a declined rustbelt city, neighborhood decay and local economic weakness may require the higher education infrastructure to develop civic engagement programs that take those conditions into account. In expanding high-tech cities, housing inflation that produces homelessness may lead to a very different kind of higher education civic engagement infrastructure. Racial/ethnic diversity will further impact what such infrastructure would look like. In places where the diversity of the community better matches the diversity of the institution, training programs for faculty and students will look different than in places where they do not at all match.

We can, however, say that there will be substantial training, personnel, and resource allocation shifts. Building civic engagement on the backs of temporary AmeriCorps*VISTA volunteers and even more temporary grants is no substitute for hard budget lines. Acting in accordance with basic community development principles will require new faculty, new staff, and new courses. It will also require new mechanisms of accountability and new training programs for faculty and students. And it will require a reallocation of resources between community and higher education partners in community development activities.

Consequently, serious evaluation is the starting point, not the ending point. Higher education institutions need to commit to documenting, in partnership with community members, their current efforts and their past efforts and engage in a community-wide planning process to put those research results into civic engagement programs that emphasize community development, not only institutional and student development.

References

Bailis, L., & Ganger, T. (2006). *A framework for further research: The community impacts of service-learning.* National Youth Leadership Council. Retrieved September 30, 2008, from http://www.nylc.org/rc_downloadfile.cfm?emoid=14:644&property=download&mode=download.

Billig, S. H., & Waterman, A. S. (2003). *Studying service learning: Innovations in education research methodology.* Mahwah, NJ: Erlbaum.

Boothroyd, P., & Davis, H. C. (1993). Community economic development: Three approaches. *Journal of Planning Education and Research, 12,* 230–240.

Boyer, E. L. (1990). *Scholarship reconsidered: Priorities of the professoriate*. New York: Carnegie Foundation for the Advancement of Teaching.

Bradford, M. (2005). Motivating students through project-based service learning. *THE Journal (Technological Horizons in Education), 32*(6). Retrieved August 3, 2008, from http://thejournal.com/articles/17124.

Brown, D. M. (2001). *Putting it together: A method for developing service-learning and community partnerships based in critical pedagogy*. Corporation for National Service. Retrieved August 3, 2008, from http://www.nationalserviceresources.org/filemanager/download/720/brown.pdf.

Bryson, J. M. (2004). *Strategic planning for public and nonprofit organizations: A guide to strengthening and sustaining organizational achievement* (3rd ed.). San Francisco: Jossey-Bass.

Chamberlain, C. (2003, January 23). Teaching teamwork: Project-based service-learning course LINCs students with nonprofits. *Inside Illinois*. Retrieved August 3, 2008, from http://www.news.uiuc.edu/II/03/0123/linc.html.

Chinman, M., Imm, P., & Wandersman, A. (2004). Getting to outcomes: Promoting accountability through methods and tools for planning, implementation, and evaluation. Rand Corporation. Retrieved September 20, 2008, from http://www.rand.org/pubs/technical_reports/2004/RAND_TR101.pdf.

Collette, W. (2004). Research for organizing. In L. Staples (Ed.), *Roots to power: A manual for grassroots organizing* (2nd ed.). New York: Greenwood.

Community Development Society (2008). *Principles of good practice*. Retrieved September 30, 2008, from http://www.comm-dev.org/.

Coyle, E. J., Jamieson, L. H., & Oakes, W. C. (2005). EPICS: Engineering projects in community service. *International Journal of Engineering Education, 21*(1), 139–150. Retrieved August 3, 2008, from http://epics.ecn.purdue.edu/about/papers/IJEE-0205.pdf.

Cruz, N., & Giles, D. (2000). Where's the community in service-learning research? [Special issue]. *Michigan Journal of Community Service Learning, 7*, 28–34.

Cummings, C. K. (2000). John Dewey and the rebuilding of urban community: Engaging undergraduates as neighborhood organizers. *Michigan Journal of Community Service Learning, 7*, 97–108.

Darling, D. L., & Bittel, S. G. (1991). *Strategic planning for community development*. Cooperative Extensive Service, Manhattan, KS. Retrieved September 30, 2008, from http://www.oznet.ksu.edu/library/agec2/L830.pdf.

Deans, T. (2000). *Writing partnerships: Service-learning in composition*. Urbana, IL: National Council of Teachers of English.

Draper, A. J. (2004). Integrating project-based service-learning into an advanced environmental chemistry course. *Journal of Chemical Education, 81*(2), 221–224.

Ehrlich, T. (2000). *Civic responsibility and higher education*. Phoenix, AZ: Oryx Press.

Eichler, M. (2007). *Consensus organizing: Building communities of mutual self interest*. Thousand Oaks, CA: Sage.

Eyler, J., & Giles, Jr., D. E. (1999). *Where's the learning in service-learning?* San Francisco: Jossey-Bass.

Fettig, L. S. (2007). *The ABCs of development: It's about building capacity*. Bloomington, IN: AuthorHouse.

Freire, P. (1970). *Pedagogy of the oppressed*. New York: Continuum.

Gedicks, A. (1996). Activist sociology: Personal reflections. *Sociological Imagination, 33*(1). Retrieved August 3, 2008, from http://comm-org.wisc.edu/si/sihome.htm.

Harrison, J. (2008, September 4). *Identifying "success" in a participatory science project: Implications for environmental justice.* Paper Presented at Holtz Center for Science and Technology Studies, University of Wisconsin.

Israel, B. A., Parker, E. A., Rowe, Z., Salvatore, A., Minkler, M., López, J., et al. (2005). Community-based participatory research: Lessons learned from the centers for Children's environmental health and disease prevention research. *Environmental Health Perspectives, 113*(10), 1463.

Joint Education Project. (n.d.). *Service learning.* Retrieved August 3, 2008, from http://www.usc.edu/dept/LAS/jep/sl/define_model.htm.

Kellogg Foundation. (2004). *Logic model development guide.* Retrieved September 30, 2008, from http://www.wkkf.org/Pubs/Tools/Evaluation/Pub3669.pdf.

Lantz, P. M., Viruell-Fuentes, E., Israel, B. A., Softley, D., & Guzman, R. (2001). Can communities and academia work together on public health research? Evaluation results from a community-based participatory research partnership in Detroit. *Journal of Urban Health, 78*(3), 495–507.

Lewin, T. (2008a. July 21). With no frills or tuition, a college draws notice. *New York Times.* Retrieved September 30, 2008, from http://www.nytimes.com/2008/07/21/education/21endowments.html?scp=1&sq=With%20no%20frills%20or%20tuition,%20a%20college%20draws%20notice.%20&st=cse

Lewin, T. (2008b, September 9). College presidents defend rising tuition, but lawmakers sound skeptical. *New York Times.* Retrieved September 30, 2008, from http://www.nytimes.com/2008/09/09/education/09college.html?_r=1&scp=1&sq=College%20Presidents%20Defend%20Rising%20Tuition,%20but%20%20Lawmakers%20Sound%20Skeptical.&st=cse&oref=slogin.

Marullo, S., & Edwards, B. (2000). From charity to justice: The potential of university-community collaboration for social change. *American Behavioral Scientist, 43*(5), 895–912.

Marullo, S., Cooke, D., Willis, J., Rollins, A., & Waldref, V. (2003). Community-based research assessments: Some principles and practices. *Michigan Journal of Community Service Learning, 9,* 57–68.

Metzler, M. M., Higgins, D. L., Beeker, C. G., Freudenberg, N., Lantz, P. M., Senturia, K. D., et al. (2003). Addressing urban health in Detroit, New York City, and Seattle through community-based participatory research partnerships. *American Journal of Public Health, 93*(5), 803–811.

Moely, B. E., & Miron, D. (2005). College students' preferred approaches to community service. In S. Root, J. Callahan, & S. H. Billig (Eds.), *Improving service-learning practice: Research on models to enhance impacts* (pp. 61–78). Greenwich, CT: Information Age.

Mooney, L. A., & Edwards, B. (2001). Experiential learning in sociology: Service learning and other community-based learning initiatives. *Teaching Sociology, 29*(2), 181–194.

PAR Outcomes Project. (2007). *The 31 August 2007 planning meeting.* Retrieved September 30, 2008, from http://comm-org.wisc.edu/wcbr/page.php?2.

Parks Daloz, L. A., Keen, C. H., Keen, J. P., & Daloz Parks, S. (1996). *Common fire: Lives of commitment in a complex world.* Boston: Beacon Press.

Patton, M. Q. (1997). *Utilization-focused evaluation: The new century text.* Thousand Oaks, CA: Sage.

Payne, D. A. (2000). *Evaluating service-learning activities and programs.* Lanham, MD: Scarecrow Education.

Penney, N., & Long, J. (2008). *Walking the walk: A pilot study to assess the community impact of 12 community-based research projects.* Center for Social Concerns, University of Notre Dame.

Peters, S. (2005). Introduction and Overview. In S. J. Peters, N. R. Jordan, M. Adamek, & T. R. Alter (Eds.), *Engaging campus and community: The practice of public scholarship in the state and land-grant university system* (pp. 1–36). Dayton, OH: Charles F. Kettering Foundation.

Pigza, J. M., & Troppe, M. L. (2003). Developing an infrastructure for service-learning and community engagement. In B. Jacoby & Associates (Eds.), *Building partnerships for service-learning* (pp. 106–130). San Francisco: Jossey-Bass.

Rhoads, R. A. (1997). *Community service and higher learning: Explorations of the caring self.* Albany, NY: SUNY Press.

Robinson, T. (2000a). Service-learning as justice advocacy: Can political scientists do politics? *Political Science and Politics, 33,* 605–612.

Robinson, T. (2000b). Dare the school build a new social order? *Michigan Journal of Community Service Learning, 7,* 142–157.

Root, S., Callahan, J., & Billig, S. H. (Eds.). (2005). *Improving service-learning practice: Research on models to enhance impacts.* Greenwich, CT: Information Age.

Saltmarsh, J. (1996). Education for critical citizenship: John Dewey's contribution to the pedagogy of community service-learning. *Michigan Journal of Community Service Learning, 3,* 13–21.

Sandy, M. (2007). *Community voices: A California Campus Compact study on partnerships.* California Campus Compact. Retrieved September 30, 2008, from http://www.cacampuscompact.org/cacc_publications/index.html.

Sandy, M., & B. Holland. (2006). Different worlds and common ground: Community partner perspectives on campus-community partnerships. *Michigan Journal of Community Service Learning, 13*(1), 30–43.

Scriven, M. (1967). The methodology of evaluation. In R. W. Tyler, R. M. Gagné, & M. Scriven (Eds.), *Perspectives of Curriculum Evaluation* (pp. 39–83). Chicago: Rand McNally.

Sen, R. (2003). *Stir it up.* San Francisco: Jossey-Bass.

Sohng, S. (1995). *Participatory research and community organizing.* Working paper presented at the New Social Movement and Community Organizing Conference. Retrieved August 3, 2008, from http://www.cdra.org.za/articles/Participatory%20Research%20And%20Community%200rganizing%20by%20Sung%20Sil%20Lee%20Sohng.doc.

Squires, G. D. (2003). *Organizing access to capital: Advocacy and the democratization of financial institutions.* Philadelphia: Temple University Press.

Stanton, T. K., Giles, D. E., Jr., & Cruz, J. I. (1999). *Service-learning: A movement's pioneers reflect on its origins, practice, and future.* San Francisco: Jossey-Bass.

Staples, L. (2004). *Roots to power: A manual for grassroots organizing* (2nd ed.). New York: Praeger.

Stoecker, R., Ambler, S. H., Cutforth, N., Donohue, P., Dougherty, D., & Marullo, S. (2003). Community-based research networks: Development and lessons learned in an emerging field. *Michigan Journal of Community Service Learning, 9,* 44–56.

Stoecker, R. (2005). *Research methods for community change: A project-based approach.* Thousand Oaks, CA: Sage.

Stoecker, R. (2008). Challenging institutional barriers to community-based research. *Action Research, 6,* 49–67.

Stoecker, R., & Tryon, E. (Eds). (2009). *Unheard voices: Community perspectives on service-learning.* Philadelphia: Temple University Press.

Stout, L. (2008). *Reaching across the walls*. Class Matters. Retrieved September 30, 2008, from http://www.classmatters.org/2004_11/stout_interview.php.

Strand, K., Cutforth, N., Stoecker, R., Marullo, S., & Donohue, P. (2003). *Community-based research in higher education: Principles and practices*. San Francisco: Jossey-Bass.

University of Wisconsin Extension. (2008) *Logic model*. Retrieved September 30, 2008, from http://www.uwex.edu/ces/pdande/evaluation/evallogicmodel.html.

University of Wisconsin–Madison. (2008). *The Carnegie elective classification for community engagement: UW-Madison's 2008 Documentation Reporting Form*. Retrieved September 30, 2008, from http://www.apa.wisc.edu/communityengagement.

University of Wisconsin–Platteville. (2007). *2006–2007 UWP service learning*. Retrieved September 30, 2008, from http://www.uwplatt.edu/cup/learning/platteville/files/06%27–07%27_Service_Learning.pdf.

PART 3

Community-Campus Partnership Development

Edited by Sarena D. Seifer

Community-Campus Partnership Development

Sarena D. Seifer

How do we combine the knowledge and wisdom in communities and in academic institutions to solve the major health, social, and economic challenges facing our society? How do we ensure that community-driven social change is central to service-learning and community-based participatory research? Collectively, the chapters in this section seek to answer these questions by holding partners accountable for achieving meaningful and sustainable outcomes at both community and institutional levels.

The section begins with a chapter that is authored by a group of experienced community partners who believe deeply in the value of community-campus partnerships but have equally deep concerns about what they see as a predominant model that tips the balance of power and resources toward institutions. By providing essential perspectives in a community-campus partnership "movement" that has largely reflected the voices of academic partners, they articulate a compelling framework for authentic partnerships that stands in stark contrast to community-campus relationships that are university-owned and managed.

The remaining chapters explore the methods for achieving such partnerships, from pursuing asset-based community development, to strategically leveraging the economic potential of universities, to undertaking community-based participatory and action-oriented models of research. It is clear from the evidence and views presented here that communities can and should be hubs for discovering new knowledge, generating and testing theories, translating research into action, and sharing innovations. In other words, intellectual spaces exist outside of higher educational and research institutions, and these should be embraced and supported.

If building community capacity, creating and mobilizing knowledge, and achieving social justice are the ultimate goals of community-campus partnerships, achieving them may only be possible when communities are at the center of learning, discovery, and engagement. Having certain ingredients present simultaneously can certainly help to accomplish this: compelling community needs, high degrees of organizational capacity, willing and able academic partners with relevant expertise, and leadership and funding that supports community in decision making roles. The chapters in this section challenge us to critically examine our partnership practices and continuously improve upon them.

Achieving the Promise of Community–Higher Education Partnerships: Community Partners Get Organized

Community Partner Summit Group

"We are here because we are passionate about these partnerships, but they are not working."

—*Ira SenGupta, Cross Cultural Health Care Program, Seattle, WA*

"We have identified what authentic partnerships are—what's working and not working is our way of defining what is and isn't authentic. We have come to some consensus about that."

—*E. Yvonne Lewis, Faith Access to Community Economic Development, Flint, MI*

Partnerships between communities and higher educational institutions as a strategy for social change are gaining recognition and momentum. Despite being formed with the best of intentions, however, authentic partnerships are very difficult to achieve. Although academic partners have extensively documented their experiences and lessons learned, the voices of community partners are largely missing. We believe that if true partnerships are to be achieved, community partners must harness their own experiences, lessons learned, and collective wisdom into a national, organized effort to address this issue.

Twenty-three experienced community partners from across the country convened for the Community Partner Summit held April 24–26, 2006, at the Wingspread Conference Center in Racine, WI. The Summit was sponsored by Community-Campus Partnerships for Health, funded by the W. K. Kellogg Foundation, the Johnson Foundation, and Atlantic Philanthropies and supported by the Community-Based Public Health Caucus of the American Public Health Association, the National Community-Based Organization Network, and the National Community Committee of the CDC Prevention Research Centers Program. The overall purpose of the Summit was to advance authentic community–higher education partnerships by mobilizing a network of experienced community partners. The intended outcomes of the Summit were to:

- Develop and gain clarity on the current state of community–higher education partnerships
- Uncover community perspectives on the key insights and ingredients of effective, authentic community–higher education partnerships
- Build the case for the importance of community–higher education partnerships
- Develop a set of actionable recommendations for maximizing the potential of community–higher education partnerships
- Develop ongoing mechanisms for increasing the number and effectiveness of community–higher education partnerships and ensuring that communities are involved in dialogues and decisions about these partnerships

This chapter summarizes the dialogue that occurred at the Summit, our review of the literature on community–higher education partnerships, and the collaborative work we have undertaken since the Summit. In articulating community partner perspectives on community–higher education partnerships, we hope this chapter serves to motivate readers to critically reflect on their partnerships and deepen them. We encourage readers to use this chapter as a tool to facilitate dialogue and action within and across partnerships.

The Current Reality of Community–Higher Education Partnerships

"Where is the respect for working in the community outside of this room? Outside of this room, there is an assumption that we're doing this work because we couldn't 'do' a PhD. But it's a choice. It's about what we value."

—*E. Yvonne Lewis, Faith Access to Community Economic Development, Flint, MI*

"Many communities start doing community-based research with academics because the funding is there. But oftentimes, before any common ground is established through someone who can serve as a bridge or translator, the study moves forward and the community is left with a different understanding of what was supposed to happen."

—*Vince Crisostomo, GUAM HIV/AIDS Network Project and Pacific Island Jurisdictions AIDS Action Group, Arlington, VA*

In order to understand the current reality of community–higher education partnerships, we began by reviewing and discussing the state of these kinds of partnerships on a national level and then assessing how they are being realized on a local level. We have summarized and categorized these into ten overarching observations from community partners about the current state of community–higher education partnerships:

1. **There is a "community engagement buzz" in higher education and funding circles, including a plethora of policy statements and organizations working in this arena.**

Higher educational institutions and funding agencies are getting on board with the idea of higher education community engagement. The number, range, and scope of these "community engagement" and "community-university partnership" initiatives and the funding for them are diverse and growing (Minkler, Blackwell, Thompson, & Tamir, 2003). Examples of funding agencies with specific community–higher education partnership initiatives are the National Institutes of Health, the Centers for Disease Control and Prevention, the Health Resources and Services Administration, the U.S. Department of Housing and Urban Development, the W. K. Kellogg Foundation, and the Robert Wood Johnson Foundation. Some are beginning to understand what it takes to develop and sustain authentic partnerships. Yet, a greater understanding is needed regarding the time, input, and resources required to create and sustain authentic partnerships, as well as ways to properly structure requests for proposals and review processes.

2. **The predominant model of community–higher education partnerships is not a partnership; much of this is due to the fact that the playing field is not level.**

Equal partnerships have yet to be realized on a broad scale, because of inequitable distributions of power and resources among the partners involved. Instead, these partnerships are often driven by the priorities and requirements of funding agencies and higher educational institutions. Funding tends to be invested in building campus infrastructure, not community infrastructure (Seifer, Shore, & Holmes, 2003). We need to level the playing field by employing a variety of strategies that cut to the core of these issues. As a result, there will be greater community participation in the partnership and increased relevancy and validity to the programs and research being conducted by the partnership.

3. **The benefits of partnering with higher educational institutions are not readily apparent to many community members.**

Partnerships with higher educational institutions are not on the radar screen of many community members, because of daily social, professional, and financial responsibilities on the job and at home. It is completely reasonable, then, that the average community member is not aware of the benefits of these partnerships. Even if they do see the benefits, the chance that they have the time it takes to meaningfully participate in these partnerships is low. However, we can respect community members' daily responsibilities and raise awareness, about the benefits of these partnerships by pairing the two together. For example, partnerships can develop values, structures, and activities that reflect community members' needs, priorities, and responsibilities. Compensating community members for their participation; providing them with child care, transportation and interpretation services; and hiring them in staff roles with the partnership are all strategies for meaningful community engagement. For those community members who are aware of the benefits of these partnerships, many will have a "healthy suspicion" of "outside" institutions. Such sentiments often stem from the history of the dominant culture's exploitation of marginalized communities—a history that needs to be explicitly acknowledged and addressed before moving forward in partnership. At the same time, community members who are experienced in community–higher education partnerships need to share with their peers the benefits of these partnerships and seek their input and advice on how we might be

203

able to structure and implement partnerships in ways that meet and respect each partner's priorities and realities.

4. Community–higher education partnerships benefit a variety of stakeholder groups.

We recognize that community–higher education partnerships can bring tangible benefits to all involved. These include, but are not limited to, the following. For community: building of community capacity and community wealth. For example, building an educational pipeline in which local youth gain the knowledge and tools to return to the community to build infrastructure, creating jobs for community members (Ybarra & Postma, 2003). For students: transformational learning, developing and clarifying one's values in relation to broader social justice issues and sense of self, practical skills for the workplace (Richards, 1996). For faculty: transformational learning, fulfillment of personal values and beliefs, external funding, new areas of scholarship (Gelmon, Holland, Seifer, & Shinnamon, 1998). For colleges and universities: transformational learning, student recruitment and retention, increased alumni giving, improved public relations, research participant recruitment, institutional accreditation (Gelmon et al., 1998).

5. The relationship between community and campus partners is largely based on individuals and funding and is not institutionalized.

It is challenging to create change when there is so little institutional memory and no strong relationship between campus and community groups over time. In order to sustain partnerships beyond the specific people at an institution with whom we have relationships, institutions must recognize that there is inherent value of these partnerships to the institution; partnerships need to be sustained for any significant change to take place in the community; and partnerships need to be institutionalized—in other words, the commitment to the partnership will survive despite changes in funding, faculty positions, or campus leadership.

We cannot achieve these goals and realize the full promise of community–higher education partnerships unless the entire institution invests in partnerships as a key strategy and ongoing priority. There is a problem when partnerships develop and continue only because of the availability of resources. A partnership cannot achieve greater social change unless there is a strategy to sustain funding over time.

6. Many of us working in this arena are not "community members," but rather translators and bridge-builders between community members and academic institutions—roles that are often critical to the success of community–higher education partnerships.

Many of us are serving in bridge-building roles between the community and the academy, in some cases as employees of an academic institution. These individuals are often critical to the success of a partnership. The existence of these bridge-builders does not mean that campus-based faculty members can "check out" and delegate community relationship-building to others. Although this may be a convenient approach, communities find this to be an indicator of the level of true interest that the faculty member has in working collaboratively with the community. Without personally getting to know the community members, the faculty member's work is in name only. Community groups can sometimes lose their community ties and legitimacy by partnering with higher educational institutions over time—an even greater risk for community members who serve in bridge-building roles as college or university employees. In either role, we need to be vigilant about keeping ourselves grounded, accessible, and accountable to our communities, while continuing to develop relationships with academic partners.

7. **Academic institutions, funding agencies, and policy makers often assume that community groups need the academy to have legitimate conversations and that academic knowledge has a greater value than knowledge from the community.**

There is often a presumption that university knowledge is more credible than community knowledge. Many researchers do not want to be challenged on their research methods and disregard our points of view. On the other hand, we want the university to be open to input on how their research methods can be tailored to be more sensitive to and appropriate for our communities. We need to convey to our academic partners that community knowledge is credible and invaluable to achieving a successful community–higher education partnership and generating knowledge for a purpose. At the same time, some of us have been mistakenly identified as "Dr." as if it's expected that we have or need advanced degrees to be credible or to be heard.

8. **Building community capacity through strong community-based organizations (CBOs) is not a major conversation or an explicit goal of many community–higher education partnerships.**

Community capacity building and social justice are not explicit goals of most community–higher education partnerships (Seifer & Sgambelluri, 2008). In most cases, it is not something that is even considered as a goal. Partnerships more often invest in the development of individual community leaders rather than the CBOs with which they are connected. It is not enough, for example, for institutions to observe that "community leaders and community partners come and go" without doing something to address the underlying reasons. Such a model does not build capacity or sustainability within CBOs. Building capacity in deprived neighborhoods is a particular challenge we face. We can address this dynamic by advocating for support for community capacity building and community infrastructure through these partnerships.

9. **There are significant ongoing challenges to community–higher education partnerships, but we keep at this work because we know there can be benefits, and because we want to protect our communities.**

Many times, funding agencies and academic partners look for immediate progress in partnerships. Building trust takes time, and to expect an immediate return on our investment is unrealistic. The energy invested in establishing a strong foundation for a partnership is well spent. Real change takes place over time through relationships that are built over the long term. We have identified a number of ongoing challenges in our partnerships with higher educational institutions. These reflect our collective observations, and are not necessarily present in every situation:

205

- Persistent community distrust of academic institutions
- Insufficient respect for community knowledge and expertise
- Unethical behaviors
- Unequal power and distribution of funds
- Academics' resistance to change and loss of control
- The academic culture of needs-based and expert approaches—looking at community problems and needs rather than community assets and capacities
- The conflict between scientific rigor and community acceptability/feasibility
- Faculty review, promotion, and tenure policies that do not value and honor community-engaged scholarship
- Recruitment and hiring of campus-based partnership staff without the input of community partners
- Institutional review board policies that do not consider community consent, participation, and benefit
- Funders that require community partnerships but don't include appropriate review criteria or community-based reviewers
- Communities that harm themselves because of intracommunity conflicts
- Communities do not speak with a united voice, making it difficult to identify, understand, and address community priorities

10. **Despite the challenges, there is good news for communities who are new to partnerships with colleges and universities: Communities are realizing their power to change the nature of their relationships with higher educational institutions.**

Formerly, there was no significant community participation in these partnerships—it was in name only. Now, as communities are beginning to learn from each other and becoming more sophisticated over time, they are identifying and sharing best practices for developing authentic partnerships (Freeman, 2003; Leiderman, Furco, Zapf, & Goss, 2002; Mayfield & Lucas, 2000; Sandy & Holland, 2006). Though there is still a long way to go on a national level, capacity within community partner organizations is increasing. As a group, we are getting serious about changing the culture of partnerships and the paradigm of research, leading to more mutually beneficial outcomes. For example:

- Communities are conducting their own research (Freeman, Brugge, Bennett-Bradley, Levy, & Carrasco, 2006; Heaney, Wilson, & Wilson, 2007).
- Communities are forming their own research committees, community advisory boards, and institutional review boards—many with real decision-making power (Brugge & Missaghian, 2006; Quinn, 2004).
- Communities are developing principles for how to effectively interface with those outside the community who are interested in partnering with them (Blumenthal, 2006).

Along with the maturation of these partnerships comes the need for resources that address their unique needs. Numerous "cookbooks" and tools for emerging partnerships are widely available, but fewer resources exist for mature partnerships. If we aim to bring these partnerships to a higher level, then these resources should be developed and widely disseminated.

What's Working, What's Not Working, and Why

"Our experience has been that the university was there for the community, to share knowledge, not to empower per se. We have had a long history of working together."

—*Lola Sablan Santos, Guam Communications Network, Long Beach, CA*

"Researchers need to ask communities early on what kind of support is needed and what kind of support can be given—instead of making assumptions. If the grant is already written, then it's too late."

—*Mrs. E. Hill DeLoney, Flint Odyssey House Health Awareness Center, Flint, MI*

What's working: When community–higher education partnerships are structured in a manner that develops skills among community members and builds infrastructure for partnerships within the community and the academy. *What's not working:* When university researchers involve the community only as subjects, not as participants and planners of the research; when the community lacks the infrastructure to fully engage in the partnership.

Supportive factors include:

- Articulating clear roles and expectations of all partners through written documents (such as memoranda of understanding, policies, contracts, scopes of work) that help to prevent misunderstanding about respective roles and expectations
- Creating policies and work processes for the partnership that honor each partner, such as policies around how decisions will be made, how conflicts will be resolved, and how information will be communicated
- Employing a community-academic liaison familiar with both community and academic contexts, who can play a "translational role" between each partner
- Appropriately compensating community members for their time and expertise
- Building infrastructure and capacity of the community and CBOs through job placement, training, and indirect overhead costs of CBOs associated with the partnership
- Institutionalizing support and the importance of maintaining authentic partnerships within the college or university

Community knowledge and expertise are often not valued in the academy. This devaluation can lead to little or no funds being written into grants to pay community members for their participation in the partnership. Distribution of resources is one of the most important elements of a partnership and should not be overlooked. At the very beginning of a partnership and during the planning phase for any grant proposals, partners need to be transparent about where and how resources will be shared (Yonas et al., 2006). Disparity between academic and community partners' job expectations and salaries is not always accounted for by academics. Community partner compensation for the time and expertise they devote to their work with academic partners is essential; often, they must take time off of work without pay, or make up their work hours on their own time. Although community participants can be given titles and positions that seem to convey that they have power or receive equal funding, this may not be the case. Finally, it goes without saying that the direct and indirect costs of a CBO's participation in a partnership should be built into grant proposals.

If the partnership is to be sustainable and worthwhile, community partners must gain just as many benefits as academic partners do from the partnership. Training community members in research methods builds community capacity and enables them to participate as equal partners in all phases of the research. Community members can gain transferable skills as part of their involvement in the research process, such as how to design and administer survey and focus groups, how to analyze data, how to present research findings, and how to write grants and papers. When a community–higher education partnership loses a valued faculty member or has only a limited number of faculty involved who understand how to develop and sustain authentic partnerships, the community has to educate and train that person's replacement, engage new faculty members, and build and establish the partnership all over again. There needs to be a shift within many universities to value institutionalizing these partnerships and making a commitment to supporting and sustaining faculty involvement in them.

What's working: Partnerships that are developed and implemented in a way that is transparent, equitable, sustainable, and accountable to both community and academic partners. *What's not working:* Unilateral decision making, inequitable distribution of power and resources, and lack of a partner commitment to the community's future.

Partnerships with strong relationships of trust, honesty, transparency, respect, and equity are based on:

- Shared resources, power, and decision making
- Honest communication and joint learning processes
- Shared commitment to meaningful, sustainable community outcomes
- The use of history, context, lessons learned, and best practices to inform the partnership

CBOs and academic institutions must both be accountable to their primary missions, yet also establish a common ground to achieve shared goals. Community advisory boards need to be accountable to multiple opinions in the community, because the community is not monolithic and does not speak with one voice. There is disagreement among community partners regarding whether community leaders and community boards as "community gatekeepers" are working. Although many of us feel that it was important to have advocates in place to protect communities, others raised the question of "who speaks for the community?" and expressed concern over community gatekeepers who become too powerful. There is never just one spokesperson for a given community. Yet, funders and academia often have a more simplistic view of community, and follow a one-spokesperson model.

Higher education partners need to be aware that their actions in the community must be held accountable to members of the community. They need to recognize, for example, that the work that is being done as part of the partnership can, and will, have effects and consequences on the lives of community members, and the work should be done responsibly and ethically. Community engagement is a promise that needs to last and cannot just end when the funding runs out. In most cases, all partners involved in community–higher education partnerships are participating out of some sort of self-interest. This is only natural and to be expected. However, conducting oneself within a partnership that only serves one's self-interest is quite different from conducting oneself in a way that serves all partners of a partnership. Only when everyone's self-interest is out on the table for all to see can partners truly begin the honest dialogue needed to negotiate an equal partnership that creates mutual benefit. Without mutual benefit, the partnership becomes unstable and unsustainable.

When partners treat each other as they would like to be treated, and value each other's expertise and what they bring to the table, a transformation occurs within the partnership that ultimately creates the "glue" that holds the partnership together. It is imperative for partners to educate each other about their history and current realities, and what they need to establish trust and respect within the partnership.

What's working: When there is an ongoing two-way engagement process whereby community partners and academic partners have an understanding of the reality and context of each other's environments. *What's not working:* When partners fail to learn about each other's unique needs and daily reality, and insist on their needs being met without taking into consideration the reality of their partners.

Partners may think they are ready to fully engage in a partnership, but relationship dynamics are not yet clear. There needs to be sufficient attention to relationship building over time before those dynamics between both partners become clear. For true engagement to take place, partners must be willing to continue despite the inevitable conflicts that arise. Before academic partners enter the community, they must learn about their academic institution's history with the community, be aware of the current political landscape, and be intentional about fostering a meaningful, two-way dialogue. Similarly, community partners need to understand the daily realities that academics have to face within their institutions, departments, disciplines, and professions and be willing to strategize ways in which they can work with their academic partners to bring about needed changes in the academy. Frequently, academic partners leave a partnership after the funding that supports their participation dries up. Although there is recognition that academics have multiple projects on their plate and are pressured to work only on funded projects, there needs to be greater awareness among university presidents, provosts, deans, and department chairs about the time and effort their faculty members need to do community-based work.

What's working: When research topics, questions, and methods are developed and structured in ways that are relevant to the community. *What's not working:* When research topics, questions, and methods are not relevant to the community. In order for research to benefit communities, the topics chosen, the questions asked, and the methods employed must be determined in collaboration with the involved community and must resonate within that community.

Community-based participatory research (CBPR) in particular holds great promise as an approach to research capable of ensuring these aims are met. As defined by the Kellogg Health Scholars Program, CBPR is "a collaborative approach to research that equitably involves all partners in the research process and recognizes the unique strengths that each brings. CBPR begins with a research topic of importance to the community and has the aim of combining knowledge with action and achieving social change" (Kellogg Health Scholars Program, n.d.).

What's working: Partnership support from funding agencies that understand how authentic community–higher education partnerships are developed and sustained, and incorporate their understanding into their guidelines and proposal review processes. *What's not working:* Funding agencies that at best don't support and at worst undermine authentic community–higher education partnerships through their guidelines and proposal review processes.

Funding agencies that understand how authentic partnerships are developed and sustained are those that encourage communities to identify research and service priorities themselves and then engage academic partners to help in carrying them out. Such funding agencies structure their guidelines and "requests for proposals" so that academic partners and community partners are able to take the time they need to build trust and come to a shared understanding of the aims of their partnership before submitting a proposal for funding. The California Breast Cancer Research Program is one example of a funding agency that models this approach through its Community Research Collaborative grants program (Plumb, 2007). Currently, most funding agencies do not use comprehensive criteria to assess whether a partnership is authentic or not. These criteria should explicitly ask how the community was involved in developing and writing the proposal, the history of the partnership, and the longevity and depth of the relationship among the partners. A number of us have served on federal peer-review panels in which academic perspectives dominated the discussion and determinations of scientific rigor and research methods were based on traditional approaches to research, not CBPR approaches—and these were panels formed specifically to review community-based participatory research proposals! There was no acknowledgment that implementing a CBPR approach to research could actually increase scientific rigor and strengthen the research methods.

Why Community–Higher Education Partnerships Are So Challenging

"We need to shape ourselves as a counterbalance to existing forces. This is about community reasserting itself in these partnerships."

—*Daniella Levine, Human Services Coalition of Dade County, Miami, FL*

"Community-campus partnerships are one vehicle. We need to connect with other movements and be a collective force for change."

—*Ira SenGupta, Cross Cultural Health Care Program, Seattle, WA*

There is very little access to lessons learned from the community perspective, like those that were shared among Summit participants (Hanssmann & Grignon, 2007). As a result, new partnerships are not informed by history. There is no accessible forum for community partners to share ideas and experiences with each other. Most of the literature on community–higher education partnerships is written from academic perspectives, and conferences can be expensive and dominated by academics. As a result, many of us end up recreating the wheel and not benefiting from the wisdom of those that have come before us. This is also due to a result of a lack of knowledge about history, or resistance to acknowledging and confronting past injustices or "open wounds." Community partners should exercise their power—through asking questions, making demands, saying "no"—even walking away from a partnership that doesn't suit their needs.

Frequently, community partners do not share their concerns with their academic partners. The infrastructure of these partnerships often does not allow the space for this to take place. It is important for community partners to feel comfortable asking questions of academic partners from the beginning of a relationship. If we do not actively do this, we may end up having to accept the consequences of our inaction. For example, during the process of writing a grant, if questions, concerns, or differences arise around who the fiscal agent should be, how the budget will be determined, or exactly how the project will be implemented, community partners need to speak up. If powerful players are able to hijack the agenda, and the other partners are not in a position to challenge it in a timely manner, then the window of opportunity can be lost. Community partners need to ask for, and take care of, their own needs, rather than waiting for someone else to take care of them.

This dynamic is also related to the need for more community capacity and technical assistance, because for community partners to know what questions to ask in the first place, they must have the requisite background. Sometimes, academics point to the funding agency or their grant administrators as the culprit when they themselves may not have even questioned the status quo and whether it could be changed (for example, assuming a budget cannot be renegotiated or a portion of indirect expenses cannot come back to the project). Community partners must exert their rights and push back when necessary, or be comfortable with implementing exit strategies (such as, for example, the popular education model of "amicable parting"). However, if community partners are not already organized and mobilized, this is difficult to do. The partnership process is rarely community-driven, and communities rarely have decision-making power. Whoever holds the purse strings holds the power.

It is rare that community participates as an equal partner. In most cases, there is an imbalance of power from the beginning. Questions about "Who is the community?" and "Whose voice is at the table?" are rarely explored by partnerships to the extent that they should. Even partnerships that have community boards are often structured as advisory and not decision making, and in some cases are populated by administrative directors of community agencies who may not be knowledgeable about the issues the community cares about. Community decision-making power must be built into the structure of community–higher education partnerships. Examples of this would be partnership boards that have a majority of members from the community, community-based principal investigators, and funding that flows from a CBO to the campus partner, with the campus partner as a subcontractor.

Researchers are often most comfortable doing traditional research, not building community capacity or engaging in community advocacy. Similarly, the research that is proposed by academic institutions tends to be narrowly focused. Communities tend to define health more broadly. Faculty members often have an unwavering academic orientation

211

to research and a tendency to funnel everything into a traditional research model, rather than thinking about how research can be translated to practice, whether through interventions or public policy. Most researchers aren't trained to think strategically in this realm; some are averse to taking a stand and advocating for change, because of a fear of not being seen as objective or undermining their prospects for promotion or tenure. There are exceptions, of course—including among the faculty members with whom we are partnering. But these remain systemic challenges within higher education. By defining health more broadly (including physical, mental, spiritual, and economic health) and not just viewing it through the lens of an academic discipline or profession, one will start to see the intersection of all of the factors that interweave themselves and threaten the health of individuals and their communities, such as lack of access to education, healthy food, educational opportunities, capital, and jobs. We as community partners are in a unique and important position to educate our academic partners in this regard. We need to have more direct roles in the classroom, in faculty development programs, and in curriculum development, for example (appropriately structured and compensated, of course).

One of the significant potential benefits of community–higher education partnerships is the building of social capital. Valid measures of social capital are difficult to capture during the timeframe that most community–higher education partnerships work within. The popularity and interest in "evidence-based" approaches makes it difficult for community partners to continue to receive funding for partnership-based programs, when in reality, building social capital is a long-term process that takes years.

For a variety of reasons, service-learning often doesn't lend itself well to community participatory approaches, authentic partnerships, community capacity building, or social change. The academic calendar, the short period of time that students are usually in the community, and the lack of faculty involvement with students in the community all contribute to explaining why this is the case. Colleges and universities need to understand the difference between these two approaches and work with their community partners to transform service-learning into a field that ultimately views community participation, authentic partnerships, capacity building, and social change as core values and practices. There is often a presumption at many colleges and universities that service-learning and community-based participatory research are equivalent, when communities often view them very differently.

Toward Authentic Community–Higher Education Partnerships

"Nobody expects that investment in the stock market will yield an immediate return. Partnerships take time. We need to put more energy into the partnership itself and to better understand each other."

—*Gerry Roll, Hazard Perry County Community Ministries, Inc., Hazard, KY*

We believe that three ingredients are essential for authentic community–higher education partnerships:

1. Authentic partnerships embrace quality processes.

"Without establishing clear structures and processes in a partnership, it is easy for partners to perceive any conflict as personal. With these structures and processes in place at the beginning of a partnership, it's easier to work through these issues, because they have been depersonalized."

—*Eve Wenger, Pocono Healthy Communities Alliance, Stroudsburg, PA*

"We are not just talking about a process that involves partners. There needs to be a process of shared decision making."

—*Ella Greene-Moton, Flint Odyssey House Health Awareness Center, Flint, MI*

"Without equal respect, there can be no shared ownership of the partnership."

—*Lisette Lahoz, Latinos for Healthy Communities, Allentown, PA*

Quality processes include those that are open, honest, and respectful; supportive of a shared vision and agenda; and allow for shared power and decision making, mutual benefit, transparency, declaring of self-interest, having difficult discussions up front, and clarifying the definition of community.

2. Authentic partnerships achieve meaningful outcomes.

"It is unaffordable to live in Boston. Universities make dollars off of dorms. We took the $25 million subsidy and created condos and townhouses, and now 75 families own homes in the neighborhood. Some units were built for student and faculty housing. Both the community and the university benefited."

—*Elmer Freeman, Center for Community Health Education, Research and Service, Boston, MA*

"OK, we can work together on community-based participatory research, but only if you support our kids in the pipeline. Bring them to campus for programs, teach them skills they can use to be more marketable, give them academic credit."

—*Vickie Ybarra, Yakima Valley Farmworkers Clinic, Yakima, WA*

Tangible and relevant outcomes need to be agreed on and articulated by the partnership. These could include, for example, eliminating health disparities, developing affordable housing, closing the achievement gap in K–12 education, developing communities and their local economies, and undoing institutionalized racism.

3. Authentic partnerships are transformative at multiple levels.

"We must consider the larger context of knowledge production. Creation of knowledge is a political act. We need to change how knowledge is produced, used and valued."

—*Douglas Taylor, Southeast Center for Community Research, Atlanta, GA*

"We build social capital when we're doing this work. We don't often talk about that."

—*Loretta Jones, Healthy African American Families II, Los Angeles, CA*

By multiple levels, we mean:

• Societal transformation: Focusing on the big picture, looking towards achieving social justice through changing systems, policies and how we fundamentally understand community, science, knowledge, and evidence

• Institutional and organizational transformation: Challenging and changing institutional and organizational assumptions, systems, policies, and values

• Personal transformation: Engaging in self-reflection, increasing one's political consciousness, developing a vision of a "different kind of society"

To realize our vision of authentic community–higher education partnerships, multiple strategies are necessary—we must "attack from all fronts." During the Summit, we identified "big ideas" that can support and stimulate more authentic community–higher education partnerships. Taken together, these ideas represent an ambitious agenda for policy development, capacity building, and support for community partners. Community involvement and capacity building are needed at every level. We need to share our lessons with our peers, and be open to learning from others, so that we can collectively strengthen each other. It is important to actively develop community members and CBOs to occupy places at the partnership table by increasing their knowledge and familiarity with this work. There are few opportunities within partnerships to develop community partners as civic leaders and change agents. As one Summit participant noted, "Students are learning and being developed in our agencies, but where are the community and agency folks being developed?"

There are specific actions that need to be taken to realize the full potential of authentic community–higher education partnerships. These include:

Facilitating training and technical assistance for community members and organizations that are new to community–higher education partnerships, equipping them with the tools needed for developing and sustaining authentic partnerships. Community conversations and working conferences, for example, can allow participants to walk away with practical tools and templates for building authentic community–higher education partnerships.

Building infrastructure (such as training, mentoring, and funding) to support people of color and those from marginalized communities who do community-based work to become community-based researchers. With such investments, a greater number of academics who conduct their work in a respectful manner will be available to partner with communities. This is a key step toward shifting the traditional research paradigm. The Harlem Community & Academic Partnership Urban Health Internship Program in New York City, for example, is working to solve this problem by training the next generation of community-engaged faculty.

Creating spaces and structures for CBOs to support each other and exert their power; for example, by forming a collective body of community partners on the national level. For example, at the local level in Flint, Michigan, CBOs involved in a community–higher education partnership (the Michigan Prevention Research Center) came together to form their own space through the Community-Based Organization Partners. Rather than have each CBO speak for themselves at the partnership table, they now have a collective voice that is a more powerful counterbalance to the unified voice presented by the academic partners at the table.

Developing principles of participation to clarify terms of engagement and expectations in our partnerships with academic partners. It is important for communities to develop principles of participation to clarify terms of engagement and expectations in their partnerships with academic partners—each partnership needs to discuss and negotiate these for themselves. Having the dialogue between partners to establish these principles is critical. We can also offer a framework on how to address issues that arise consistently, and provide a process and structure for having that dialogue. Such a framework will not stifle dialogue and can also prevent partnerships from having to reinvent the wheel.

Sharing our collective wisdom and knowledge with both academic institutions and funding agencies is a crucial piece of our agenda, if we are to not only transform our current partnerships, but also plant seeds for future authentic community–higher education partnerships. Community-authored and -disseminated publications and presentations are important vehicles of change and play a role in initiating a dialogue with higher educational institutions. These can include op-ed pieces, journal articles, case stories, monographs, conference presentations, videos, popular education, and other media. Pieces prepared with academic partners should include them as co-authors if they so desire. When our academic partners seek to publish articles and make presentations based on our partnership work, we should articulate how we wish to be involved and recognized.

By educating funders about the current reality of community–higher education partnerships, community partners can advocate to change funding priorities, what is funded, and how funds are distributed. In community–higher education partnerships, money ultimately bestows power. If we want to change the power imbalance, we have to work on changing the practices of funders and other groups that provide resources so that community involvement is required at every level of the process. We need to educate them about the current reality of community–higher education partnerships, and how funding programs can be designed to maximize the ability of communities to participate as equal partners. This will require challenging deeply entrenched views and policies that serve to maintain college and university control over teaching and research. The emerging research paradigm gives us an unprecedented opportunity to redefine the rules. For example, the National Institutes of Health (NIH) is increasingly expecting biomedical research to be community-engaged. We can hold NIH accountable and help support this paradigm shift through advocacy and representation on agency advisory committees such as its Council of Public Representatives. In many respects, the ideal situation is for CBOs to be fiscal agents for partnership funding, with any indirect funds going to build their infrastructure and support their sustainability. Academic institutions, as well as experienced community partners, can train CBOs as needed on how to serve as fiscal agents and manage grants.

215

Educational and economic development must be explicitly linked to these partnerships. Consistent with the transformational nature we articulated in our vision of authentic partnerships, these partnerships have significant opportunities for educational and economic development that are often overlooked. Community partners need to negotiate with their academic partners to integrally link these to their partnerships. For example, community–higher education partnerships can:

- Create jobs in the community
- Create low-income and mixed-income housing in the community
- Provide academic credit for the training that is provided to community partners and community participants
- Create opportunities for K–12 students to be exposed to higher education and health careers

Community partners must insinuate themselves into the culture of higher education, and vice versa. Community partners can start to shift academic culture towards valuing and embracing community–higher education partnerships through such campus-based activities as:

- Teaching in the classroom
- Mentoring students and younger/newer community-oriented faculty members and staff
- Serving on admissions committees
- Voicing concerns about promotion and tenure policies, which currently often undermine the ability of faculty to engage in partnerships
- Submitting letters of support for faculty members involved in their partnerships
- Serving on Institutional Review Boards

Similarly, academic partners can better understand the daily realities of community partners through:

- Participating in community events and meetings
- Understanding the multiple issues affecting their lives through listening and observation
- Shadowing a staff member at a CBO
- Serving on boards of directors or organizational committees

Community partners must work together with academic allies to elevate the credibility and recognition for the life/work experience and context of community partners. Although community partners are often asked by academic institutions to give presentations, conduct trainings, supervise students, and provide input and feedback, they are rarely recognized or rewarded for sharing their expertise. For example, they are usually not compensated or granted faculty status. Similarly, funders expect community partner involvement in service-learning and research but rarely consider them to be qualified for principal investigator roles on community-academic partnership grants. Academic partners can use their influence in collaboration with their community partners to change this dynamic by pushing for greater community partner recognition by academic institutions and funding agencies.

Policy-based options for equalizing power must be explored, such as the potential of community benefits laws as a leverage point for change within higher educational institutions. There has been a massive shift around community benefits of hospitals in order to maintain their tax-exempt status (Barnett, 2007). Higher educational institutions could have a similar obligation. Perhaps higher educational institutions could donate a percentage of their revenues/endowment to community organizations and community capacity building, in line with their mission and tax-exempt status. In Boston, for example, communities have had some success in leveraging such resources from teaching hospitals (Council of Boston Teaching Hospitals, 2007). It is critical to effect change at a structural level. For example, if funding priorities changed and CBOs were better funded, they would be on more equal footing with higher educational institutions and the dynamics of those relationships would change and improve. We must capitalize on policy and advocacy opportunities as they arise.

Toward an Organized Network of Community Partners

"We are engaged as a collective—we are committed to change. We need to negotiate, build consensus, and move forward as a unit."

—*Vickie Ybarra, Yakima Valley Farmworkers Clinic, Yakima, WA*

"We need colleagues to be willing to go deep in this work . . . we need to support each other in various ways. We need to know what it is to be a leader and hold ourselves accountable to a leadership role that truly benefits the greater good. To sustain ourselves, we need to be there for a cause, not just a project."

—*Susan Gust, GRASS Routes, Minneapolis, MN*

Many community partners engaged in community–higher education partnerships work in isolation, whether due to geography, the lack of regular community partner convenings by academic partners, or the lack of funds to meet with their peers at workshops and trainings. Both during the Summit and in the months and years since, participants have remarked again and again about how one of the most valuable benefits of the Summit was that it provided them with a support network of community partner peers that they had not realized existed, to share skills and provide a "safe" place for seeking advice on community–higher education partnership matters. Community partners need a collective body to reduce their feelings of isolation and increase their capacity through mentoring, networking, and advocacy.

As a collective of community partners, we aspire to have an effect, to be applicable and influential in the following ways:

• We want to shape conversations, not just add to them
• We want to convey the spirit behind the message, so that those who were not in the room can understand its context and full meaning
• We want to influence policy

- We want to promote networking and collaboration among community partners
- We want to elevate the credibility and recognition for the life and work experiences of community partners and the context and environment in which we do our work
- We want to eliminate the need for community "translators" who help interpret and negotiate between the worlds of community and academy, which would indicate how the current reality of these partnerships has truly been transformed

A number of products have been developed and disseminated since the Summit. These include Summit proceedings, community-authored case stories, a colorful traveling poster with photos and quotes from the Summit, and a slide show for more formal presentations about the Summit (Community Partner Summit). The Summit has also been replicated in Chicago.

We have formed two "authentic partnership" work groups and an electronic discussion group (Community Partner Listserv, 2007) to continue dialogue and action beyond the Summit. The groups have been meeting via conference call since June 2006, with staff support from Community-Campus Partnerships for Health. The Mentoring Work Group has been working to develop and implement peer mentoring and leadership development activities that build the capacity of community partners to engage in authentic community–higher education partnerships and succeed in their community-building work (Palermo & Fortin, 2006). The Policy Work Group has been working to develop and advocate for policies that support authentic community–higher education partnerships. This includes several community partner-authored policy statements submitted to the NIH (Greene-Moton et al., 2007; Palermo, Park, Seifer, Wong, & Ybarra, 2007; Seifer & Greene-Moton, 2007).

The Summit was a transformational experience for many of us. When asked "What word describes how you were feeling when you arrived at the Summit, and what word describes you upon your departure?" responses included: "from curious to engaged," "from skeptical to determined," "from privileged to empowered," "from interested to invigorated," "from alone to powerful," and "from ambivalent to grateful." We have continued sharing and learning together as a collective. We have broadened participation to include other experienced community partners who couldn't come to the Summit. Although we engage our academic partners and others in academia, we want to protect the space we have created for ourselves as community partners.

We have built a strong foundation from our beginnings at the Summit, and invite community partners to join with us to shape our collective agenda for the future. [Community partners who are interested in joining the network should contact us through Community-Campus Partnerships for Health at http://www.ccph.info] Together, we can move from rhetoric to reality in the conduct of community–higher education partnerships and the social justice outcomes they achieve.

Acknowledgements

We wish to thank the organizations that co-sponsored the Community Partner Summit: Community-Campus Partnerships for Health, the W. K. Kellogg Foundation, the Johnson

Foundation and Atlantic Philanthropies, the Community-Based Public Health Caucus of the American Public Health Association, the National Community-Based Organization Network, and the National Community Committee of the CDC Prevention Research Centers Program. We especially thank the CCPH staff and consultants who helped to coordinate the Summit and have continued to support the Work Groups: Sarena D. Seifer, Kristine Wong, Chris Hanssmann, and Monte Roulier.

The members of the Community Partner Summit Group are Beneta D. Burt, Jackson Roadmap to Health Equity, Jackson, MS; John Caranto, Asian Pacific AIDS Intervention Team, Los Angeles, CA; Vince Crisostomo, GUAM HIV/AIDS Network Project Pacific Island Jurisdictions AIDS Action Group, Arlington, VA; Mrs. E. Hill De Loney, Flint Odyssey House, Inc. Health Awareness Center, Flint, MI; Elmer Freeman, Center for Community Health Education Research and Service, Inc., Boston, MA; Ella Greene-Moton, Center for Public Health Genomics and Community-Based Public Health Caucus, Flint, MI; Susan Gust, GRASS Routes, Minneapolis, MN; Loretta Jones, Healthy African American Families, Los Angeles, CA; Lisette M. Lahoz, Latinos for Healthy Communities, Allentown, PA; Daniella S. Levine, Human Services Coalition of Dade County, Inc., Miami, FL; E. Yvonne Lewis, Faith Access to Community Economic Development, Flint, MI; Ed Lucas, Renacer Westside Community Network, Inc., Chicago, IL; Ann-Gel Palermo, Harlem Community & Academic Partnership, New York, NY; Alice Park, Urban Indian Health Institute, Seattle Indian Health Board, Seattle, WA; Gerry Roll, Hazard Perry County Community Ministries, Inc., Hazard, KY; Lola Sablan Santos, Guam Communications Network, Long Beach, CA; Ira SenGupta, Cross Cultural Health Care Program, Seattle, WA; Douglas Taylor, Southeast Community Research Center, Atlanta, GA; Pearlie M. Toliver, Branch Banking and Trust Co., Macon, GA; Lucille Webb, Strengthening the Black Family, Inc., Raleigh, NC; Eve Wenger, Pocono Healthy Communities Alliance, Stroudsburg, PA; Noelle Wiggins, Community Capacitation Center, Multnomah County Health Department, Portland, OR; Vickie Ybarra, Yakima Valley Farmworkers Clinic, Yakima, WA.

References

Barnett, K. (2007). *Beyond the numerical tally quality and stewardship in community benefit: Uniform standards and lessons from the advancing the state of the art in community benefit demonstration.* Berkeley, CA: Public Health Institute.

Blumenthal, D. S. (2006). A community coalition board creates a set of values for community based research. *Prevention of Chronic Disease, 3*(1), A16.

Brugge, D. & Missaghian, M. (2006) Protecting the Navajo People through tribal regulation of research. *Science and Engineering Ethics, 12*(3), 491–507.

Community Partner Listserv (2007). Retrieved April 2, 2009, from http://mailman.mcw.edu/mailman/listinfo/communitypartnerlistserv.

Community Partner Summit Webpage. (n.d.). Retrieved April 2, 2009, from http://depts.washington.edu/ccph/cps-summit.html,

Council of Boston Teaching Hospitals (2007). *Driving greater Boston and New England: The impact of greater Boston's teaching hospitals.* Boston: Council of Boston Teaching Hospitals.

Freeman, E. R., Brugge, D., Bennett-Bradley, W. M., Levy, J. I., & Carrasco, E. R. (2006). Challenges of conducting community-based participatory research in Boston's neighborhoods to reduce disparities in asthma. *Journal of Urban Health, 83*(6), 1099–3460.

Freeman, N. L. (2003). *A meeting of minds: A handbook for community-campus engagement* (pp. 1–18). Seattle, WA: Community-Campus Partnerships for Health Fellows Program. Retrieved April 9, 2009, from http://depts.washington.edu/ccph/pdf_files/Nola_Freeman_Project04.pdf.

Gelmon, S. B., Holland, B. A., Seifer, S. D., & Shinnamon, A. (1998). Community-university partnerships for mutual learning. *Michigan Journal of Community Service Learning, 5,* 142–160.

Greene-Moton, E., Gust, S., Palermo, A., Park, A., Seifer, S. D., Wong, K., et al. (2007, August 24). *Response to National Center for Research Resources.* Retrieved April 9, 2009, from http://depts.washington.edu/ccph/cps.html.

Hanssmann C, Grignon J. (2007). *Community–higher education partnerships: Community perspectives annotated bibliography.* Seattle, WA: Community-Campus Partnerships for Health. Retrieved April 9, 2009, from http://depts.washington.edu/ccph/pdf_files/CP-Bibliography.pdf

Heaney, C. D., Wilson, S., & Wilson, O. R. (2007). The West End Revitalization Association's community-owned and managed research model: Development, implementation, and action. *Progress in Community Health Partnerships: Research, Education, and Action, 1*(4), 351–358.

Kellogg Health Scholars Program. (n.d.). *Definition of community-based participatory research.* Retrieved March 9, 2009, from http://www.sph.umich.edu/chsp/program/index.shtml.

Leiderman, S., Furco, A., Zapf, J., & Goss, M. (2002). *Building partnerships with college campuses: Community perspectives: A monograph.* Consortium for the Advancement of Private Higher Education (CAPHE)'s Engaging Communities and Campuses Grant Program. Washington, DC: Council of Independent Colleges.

Mayfield, L., & Lucas, E. P. J. (2000). Mutual awareness, mutual respect: The community and the university interact. *Cityscape: A Journal of Policy Development and Research, 5*(1).

Minkler, M., Blackwell, A. G., Thompson, M., & Tamir, H. (2003) Community-based participatory research: Implications for public health funding. *American Journal of Public Health, 93*(8), 1210–1213.

Palermo, A. G., & Fortin, P. (2006). *Engaging campuses as authentic partners: Tips and strategies for community leaders.* Paper presented at Ninth Community-Campus Partnerships for Health conference. Retrieved April 9, 2009, from http://depts.washington.edu/ccph/pastpresentations.html#ninthconf.

Palermo, A., Park, A., Seifer, S. D., Wong, K., & Ybarra, V. (2007, September 7). *Response to NOD-07–074 The NIH Peer Review Process.* Retrieved April 9, 2009, from http://depts.washington.edu/ccph/cps.html.

Plumb, M. (2007). *Transforming partnerships: The relationship between collaboration and outcomes in the Community Research Collaboration Awards.* California Breast Cancer Research Program.

Quinn, S. C. (2004). Ethics in public health research: Protecting human subjects: The role of community advisory boards. *American Journal of Public Health, 94*(6), 918–922.

Richards, R. W. (1996). *Building partnerships: Educating health professionals for the communities they serve.* San Francisco: Jossey-Bass.

Sandy, M. & Holland, B. A. (2006). Different worlds and common ground: Community partner perspectives on campus-community partnerships. *Michigan Journal of Community Service Learning, 13*(1), 30–43.

Seifer, S. D., & Greene-Moton, E. (2007). Realizing the promise of community-based participatory research: Community partners get organized!. *Progress in Community Health Partnerships: Research, Education and Action, 1*(4), 291–294.

Seifer S. D., & Sgambelluri, A. (2008). Mobilizing partnerships for social change. *Progress in Community Health Partnerships: Research, Education and Action, 2*(2), 81–82.

Seifer, S. D., Shore, N., & Holmes, S. L. (2003). *Developing and sustaining community-university partnerships for health research: Infrastructure requirements.* Commissioned by the NIH Office of Behavioral and Social Sciences Research. Retrieved March 3, 2009, from http://depts.washington.edu/ccph/pdf_files/p-nih012903.pdf.

Ybarra, V., & Postma, J. (2007). El Proyecto Bienestar: An authentic CBPR partnership in the Yakima Valley. *Partnership Perspectives, 4*(1), 34–43. Retrieved March 3, 2009, from http://depts.washington.edu/ccph/pdf_files/PP-W07-Ybarra.pdf.

Yonas, M. A., Eng, E., Jones, N., Vines, A., Aronson, B., White, B., et al. (2006). The art and science of integrating community-based participatory research principles and the dismantling racism process to design and submit a research application to NIH: Lessons learned. *Journal of Urban Health, 83*(6), 1004–1012.

Standards of Practice in Community Engagement

David J. Maurrasse

The context in which institutions of higher education sit lays the foundation for the evolution of community engagement into a more central component in the strategic thinking and planning of colleges and universities. In other words, the interdependence between institutions of higher education and their localities and regions has become increasingly apparent on and off campuses. As the theory and practice of higher education's community engagement matures, awareness around what it takes to bring about effective mutually beneficial partnerships emerges.

It is difficult to fully generalize across the entire higher education industry, as the variation in types and settings among colleges and universities is fairly vast. However, for the most part, institutions of higher education maintain strong ties to localities, both benefiting from and contributing to their host towns or cities or regions. Engagement is the degree to which the connection between institutions of higher education and their surroundings become activated through a variety of collaborative efforts.

Community Engagement Concept and Forms

Community engagement is a process that brings together groups of stakeholders from a neighborhood, city, or region (including individuals, organizations, businesses, and institutions) to build relationships and practical collaboration with a goal of improving the collective well-being of the area and its stakeholders. A "community" could be based on spatial parameters such as geography (e.g., region, city, or neighborhood), interest in particular issues, or identity-based affiliations (Carnegie Foundation, 2007; Cavaye, 2001; Fawcett, Paine-Andrews, Schultz, & Williams, 1995; Gottlieb, 2006). In higher education, community engagement is often expressed in multistakeholder partnerships aiming to simultaneously further the mission of higher education and benefit communities (Indiana State University, 2008; Maurrasse, 2001). Partners, various types of resources (e.g., human, financial, information), and the exchange of these resources are among the key elements (Carnegie Foundation, 2007).

The community engagement of higher education can take root in numerous forms, tapping into a range of ways in which colleges and universities contribute physical, economic, intellectual, and human capital. Interest in community engagement has become more central, as colleges and universities are enduring anchor institutions in localities. As most forms of capital fluidly move in and out of communities (e.g., factories), institutions of higher education tend to be more reliable, remaining on particular sites for multiple generations, strengthening roots over time, and establishing long-standing vested interests in the conditions of their areas and neighborhoods.

From higher education's perspective, local living standards significantly influence the ability of a college or university to function effectively. Incentives for community engagement vary among different types of institutions of higher education. For an institution that tends to recruit locally, for example, residents' financial standing affects the ability to afford tuition. For an institution that is largely residential, local conditions could affect recruitment of faculty, staff, and students. Given the educational mission of colleges and universities, hands-on learning opportunities are essential to effective pedagogy and training; it is easier to engage in such experiential learning locally than elsewhere. The list of advantages that institutions of higher education can gain from their surroundings is lengthy and varied.

Longevity of Higher Education Institutions

Long-term commitments seen as investments in community partnerships have been cited as essential to the success of any higher education/community partnership (Maurrasse, 2001; Ostrander, 2004; Wiewel & Perry, 2008). The ability to establish the course and direction of policy is one of the benefits of investing in partnerships over the long term (Maurrasse, 2001).

Key areas in which colleges and universities engage communities include economic opportunity and development, real estate and neighborhood development, and education and research (Maurrasse, 2001; Salim, 2008; Wiewel & Perry, 2008). Institutions of higher education also have a role in policy and social and cultural development (Wiewel & Perry, 2008).

As a part of its higher education classification system, Carnegie (2007) classifies universities with community engagement into three categories: Curricular Engagement, Outreach & Partnerships, and Curricular Engagement and Outreach & Partnerships. In Curricular Engagement, needs are identified by students, and learning by students is academic and civic-oriented, improving the community and contributing to the institution's scholarship. It involves students, faculty, and community organizations in efforts to promote student learning. Outreach provides institutional resources for use by the community, and Partnerships centers on the application, exploration, or exchange of those resources. (A university need only do one of the two for the Outreach & Partnerships category.) The third category reflects engagement in both of the other categories.

The substantial progress made over recent years in the spread and quality of higher education/community partnerships demonstrates a gradual evolution in conceptions of the nature and limitations of the role of higher education and the external expectations of colleges and universities. There is a greater recognition of the interdependency between institutions of higher education and their neighborhoods, cities, and regions. Numerous expressions of higher education/community engagement are being conceived and initiated. Common characteristics for successful realizations of these relationships have been identified, including mutuality, impact, sustainability, inclusion, and institutionalization (Marga, 2007), but the greatest challenges are in overall execution and sustainability. Although mutual interest between institutions of higher education and their communities persists, the act of engagement is hardly smooth, easy, or automatic.

The Challenge of Effective Community Engagement

Community engagement poses a number of challenges for institutions of higher education and their stakeholders (faculty, students, staff, etc.).

Shared Goals and Benefits

Finding appropriate areas of converging interests between higher education and community stakeholders can take time. In initiating partnerships, it is important to communicate openly to establish common ground. Partnerships that emerge hastily, bypassing the degree of dialogue that allows partners to express their respective interests, might seem efficient at the outset, but if the goals of partnership are not commonly owned by participants, joint pursuits can fall apart. There are no guarantees in any collaboration; however, partnerships that have enabled shared goals to emerge are more likely to be sustained and to reflect the diverse perspectives and common interests of participants.

Indeed, when goals are shared, the chances of benefits accruing across the board are higher. The examples of higher education/community partnerships that do not provide mutual benefit are numerous. The difficulty in finding common ground between all types of anchor institutions and their neighbors is well known. The rise of community benefit agreements is one expression of efforts to force widespread advantages where common ground has not been forged. It is critical to ensure benefits; however, highly inclusive gains from partnerships can materialize out of collaboration early on, rather than contention after unbalanced actions not representing the spirit of working together. Overall, purposeful efforts to establish common ground early in the development of partnerships can lead to shared goals and benefits.

Clear Strategies and Approaches (Short and Long Term)

On the one hand, ongoing relations and communication are central to the effectiveness of any type of engagement between institutions of higher education and external parties. On the other hand, those relations can be tapped for practical purposes that lead to demonstrable change. If a group of students and faculty are continually meeting with a cluster of local stakeholders, the purpose of those meetings will continually be questioned. It is possible to justify meeting for the sake of meeting for only so long. Indeed, it takes a tremendous

225

amount of time to establish trust and build the kinds of ties that can nurture productive collaborative work, but at what point do meetings without clear strategies and results appear useless or dysfunctional?

In creating the most appropriate forms of engagement, bringing people to the table is one critical endeavor in itself. Additionally, keeping people at the table is equally significant. When participants in multistakeholder partnerships can see the significance of their collaborative efforts, they are more likely to stay engaged. In many attempts at engagement, one can envision numerous milestones, as is laid out adequately in the University of Pennsylvania's *Anchor Institutions Toolkit*. When considering partnerships involving institutions of higher education and multiple other stakeholders, it is important to acknowledge the various levels of results that can be achieved.

In some instances, merely getting a diverse range of parties to speak with each other is a colossal result in itself. It may take years to simply achieve this end. Ultimately, however, the pursuit of collaborative communication is driven by purpose. For what purpose would a local university, community-based nonprofits, government officials, local businesses, and others come to the same table? The answers vary based on the context; but it is important to establish, clarify, and refresh a sense of purpose in attempts at multistakeholder partnerships of this sort.

Moreover, in developing strategies to enrich and strengthen a sense of purpose in partnerships, linearity may be the desire of many partners at the table, but in reality strategies rarely unfold along the original steps that have been designed. For singular organizations, it is often difficult to stick to strategic plans. As a principle, we could benefit from imagining strategic plans as dynamic, continually renewing, and remaining relevant in the face of change. As our environment evolves, tactics and priorities should adapt accordingly.

A great deal of literature, thinking, and analysis has emerged with respect to strategic planning for singular institutions. Very little, however, has been created around appropriate and effective strategic planning methods for partnerships. Marga Incorporated's *Marga Method* (outlined at www.margainc.com) borrows from traditional approaches to strategic planning for singular organizations, and experience in attempts to design strategies in partnership. Marga's approach emphasizes attention to context, mutual interests among partners, knowledge from other case examples, and other elements.

This methodology speaks to the development of "signature projects"—specific short-term action plans with clear and achievable goals. It is one thing for a group of partners to collectively envision a broad purpose for working together and long-range goals and objectives. In the here and now, some partners may need to see immediate results simply to justify their continued participation in the partnership. When a broad strategic plan is developed for a partnership, what would be the most appropriate, productive, and expedient way to launch that partnership? Where would one begin? Is there a particular issue that everyone agrees needs immediate attention, and a very specific way to take on that issue that can be accomplished in a few weeks or months? This is the kind of inquiry that could serve partnerships well at a critical juncture.

The points at which partnerships agree to joint plans and ideals can be quite exhilarating. These could be peak moments after possibly years of wrangling and ultimate trust building.

The ideas of clarifying collective goals and outlining joint strategies can be so unprecedented in some cases that no acts following such milestones could match such a level of enthusiasm. After the establishment of plans comes their execution. Execution or implementation means less exciting tasks and additional investment of time and money. When these practical realities set in, every partner institution at the table must reflect on its level of commitment. It is a lot easier to cultivate that commitment with a short-term project than with a massive effort that would take years to yield results. In fact, signature projects can establish short-term accomplishments that, in themselves, justify the significance of partnerships.

Institutions of higher education, community-based nonprofit organizations, government, local businesses, and other entities all have their own priorities as institutions. They all have their own resource constraints. Although partnerships add value by creating new formations that can produce benefits that could not materialize without collaboration, they cost time and money. Because of these costs, it is imperative that partnerships demonstrate value across the board—for institutions of higher education, and for their partners as well.

Keeping Work Going over Time and Remaining Relevant

Sustainability remains one of the more elusive dimensions of partnerships. First, all partnerships do not have to last forever. In engaging participants, it is important to develop clarity around the longevity of the effort. Because institutions of higher education are inherently place-based, ongoing local external relations are central to ongoing operations. It is important for colleges and universities to establish a healthy balance between continuous relations in an almost ambassadorial fashion, and active strategic partnerships through which particular projects are initiated and specific results are pursued.

In complex organizations with multiple semiautonomous units, numerous projects will continually emerge. These varying efforts, reflective of the independent spirit of the academy on the whole, can bring rich intellectual and practical resources to communities. However, it is difficult to establish any somewhat uniform strategy when several classes, institutes or centers, or research projects engage external stakeholders. Sometimes these varying efforts are in harmony, but they often overlap, and even conflict. In order for this array of resources in higher education to be truly relevant to communities over time, some combining of efforts would be required. The challenges facing neighborhoods, cities, and regions transcend academic disciplines and the class projects.

Sustained resources for higher education/community partnerships are sometimes hard to secure because efforts are not combined. Funding mechanisms (grants, for example) are often time-limited, emphasizing discrete results that only mildly reflect the magnitude of the picture in question. Subsequently, groups of faculty or specific centers or institutes pursue specific grants that are not developed within the broader context of the community and the collective needs of the range of stakeholders with a vested interest in the area and its future. With little time before proposal deadlines, higher education stakeholders round up as many co-signers as they can find in a short period to secure grants. If they are fortunate enough to receive grants, duties are rapidly performed to meet results absent deeper engagement.

If responses to grant requests emerge out of established partnerships, however, relations with co-signers are more genuine, and results can be applied to address the kinds of priority issues that have already been vetted and discussed collectively. This kind of cooperation, in some academic settings, however, would require a cultural shift.

Working with the Unique Schedule and Structure and Culture of Higher Education (and Adapting to Different Ways of Operating among Partners in General)

Engagement across various stakeholder groups is conceptually exciting, and even necessary to contemporary problem solving. Concurrently, such engagement requires all involved to adapt and transcend comfort zones. Not to mention that colleges and universities are themselves highly diverse internally in terms of culture and practice (engineers don't work like historians); academia is a unique operational space. In higher education, activity is structured in terms, turnover of students is built in, and the pursuit of knowledge for its own sake is productive. Government has its own way of operating, emphasizing bureaucracy and transparency. Community organizations may emphasize results for the most disadvantaged members of society first and foremost. Corporations might prioritize the bottom line and move quickly to make money. In higher education, linearity may not be the only path to an end, speed may not be prioritized over thought and reflection, and unilateral decision making may be reserved for crisis situations.

These differing cultures don't simply work well together once they decide to collaborate. Respect for different priorities and working styles is established over time. With this in mind, continuous engagement (ongoing candid communication and exchange) can be a critical asset through which partnerships become more useful in their ability to solve problems. Additionally, partnerships must structurally adapt to difference. If a professor has an ongoing partnership with a community organization through his/her classes, the community must adapt to academic terms with waves of interest and activity, and the professor and students must figure out a way to attend to community needs in between terms.

Communities don't stop in December or May and wait for a new cadre of students. Within blocks of weeks (terms) students have expectations to meet, and come to expect community organizations to adapt with the requisite speed. However, community organizations may have other priorities within the space of a given term. Community organizations may not respond with the same speed or attention during each different wave of student interest.

Faculty engaged in community partnerships face their own barriers around the culture and priorities within higher education, as definitions of "scholarship" remain rigid. Often, depending on the discipline or the type of institution of higher education, incentives for participatory and applied research can be very limited. In some settings, faculty are discouraged from engagement. Overall, the notion of community partnerships, although essential for the functioning of a college or university, does not receive adequate acknowledgement or even respect. The goals of community engagement are often seen as marginal to the broader mission and purpose of an institution of higher education when the opposite is true. This conception has changed dramatically in recent decades, partly due to the increased visibility of efforts such as service learning, and growing external questioning of the relevance of higher education to the "real world."

Tapping the Full Range of What Institutions of Higher Education Have to Offer (Maximizing Partnerships)
Colleges and universities bring intellectual, human, physical, and monetary capital. Rarely are community partnerships tapping this range of resources and opportunity. Because institutions of higher education often don't internally engage as much as they could as a result of the many silos that spring up on any given campus, the full scope of what is possible in higher education/community partnership is not realized. When partnerships begin to transcend the loose relationships with individuals or units, and think first to tackle issues, institutions of higher education will be viewed in totality rather than in pieces.

The way in which most partnerships are manifested and the semiautonomous nature of higher education present barriers to more comprehensive attempts to harness the wide range of resources that colleges and universities can apply to community needs. It is important to avoid top-down approaches to partnerships, but in higher education, the totality of an institution of higher education is often seen from the top down. Presidents and trustees and very senior officials are responsible for engaging their institution across disciplines and units. The majority of higher education stakeholders are held responsible for their activities within their semiautonomous spaces. Subsequently, higher educational leadership can play a critical role in setting the tone around the significance of external engagement and collaboration, and establishing the spaces in which the various community partnership pursuits on a campus can, at the very least, inform each other, if not actively work together.

The Future of Community Engagement

The enhancement of approaches to community engagement into the future will depend on improvements around challenges that have traditionally hindered the effectiveness of collaborative endeavors. First of all, higher education/community partnerships, although critical to the overall well-being of colleges and universities, are often not fully embraced internally. Efforts to institutionalize community engagement have often been unsuccessful. Securing the buy-in of faculty, senior administrators, and trustees can be daunting in the face of steep traditions. Second, resources in higher education tend to be most available for those areas embraced as mission-critical. External resources are often required to keep community engagement afloat. Third, given that effective community engagement requires steady, long-term relations, lack of incentive for ongoing collaboration, outside of individual external grants, creates inconsistent and episodic communication.

Take-Home Messages for the Future

Resources (Aligning with Private Philanthropy, Coping with Fewer Government Dollars for Higher Education)
The Department of Housing and Urban Development's Office of University Partnerships has been an essential player in providing funding for institutions of higher education to apply their resources to needs in their communities. Resources have also been creatively applied toward higher education/community partnerships via the Department of

229

Education, the Corporation for National and Community Service, and other federal agencies. At local levels, funding for higher education has continued to decline, yet the demand in states has been for greater demonstration of concrete local impact among colleges and universities. At times, colleges such as Bucknell University have been able to secure dollars from state funding programs, such as Pennsylvania's Core Communities Initiative, tailored to local revitalization. Sometimes, the prodding of state officials around higher education's role is an acknowledgment that colleges and universities are critical anchor institutions in places that have few other sustainable resources on which they can rely. The Pennsylvania funding effort logically catalyzes the resources of major institutions to strengthen regions that would further falter absent the engagement of local anchors.

With respect to private funding, some institutions of higher education have been able to secure grants for work with community partners, and some community partners have secured grants in which colleges and university stakeholders are incorporated. However, we seldom find funding programs at private foundations that explicitly support the role of institutions of higher education in community engagement. Numerous foundations have supported the engagement of higher education over the years, including the W. K. Kellogg Foundation the Annie E. Casey Foundation, and the Carnegie Corporation. An explicitly articulated, long-term programmatic commitment to supporting higher education/community partnerships is harder to find at major foundations.

Some colleges and universities have been fortunate enough to leverage alumni dollars toward community engagement, from the University of Pennsylvania, to Tufts University, to Emory University. Looking toward the future, this may be an area where additional attention and effort could be required in order to bring greater sustainability to higher education/community partnerships. Resources have been at the crux of the challenges facing the long-term health and effectiveness of multistakeholder partnerships. As noted, these efforts create the need for new resources, outside of the core budgets of the various partnering entities. Subsequently, additional investors must be engaged at the outset of partnerships.

How can foundations, government funding programs, donors, and others become stakeholders themselves in these partnerships? Who stands to gain from partnerships involving higher education/community partnerships? The value proposition of this kind of work must be more clearly articulated in the earlier stages of partnerships and include discussion around why someone should invest in such efforts. Community foundations, for example, appear to be logical partners in these localized partnerships that stress revitalization in common geographic areas of interest. Additionally, private family foundations with local interests, such as me Goldseker in Maryland, have been significant investors in numerous higher education/community partnerships in that state. It appears they were involved in dialogue early in some of these funded efforts.

Overall, the practice of creative thinking around financing should accompany the practice of engagement in partnerships. Funding entities can be partners themselves; but it is much more difficult to seek new supporters when partnerships are in crisis and losing ground as money runs out. Even if a partnership starts with one significant grant, strategies to secure complementary resources should be addressed at the beginning.

Another important consideration is the nature of funding. Given the nonlinear way in which partnerships emerge and communication and trust are established, flexible dollars not tied to rigid, unrealistic outcomes are essential. It is much easier to secure those funds from private and local individuals and institutions with some stake in the health of the area rather than large national foundations. Duke University has been very fortunate in its relationship to the Duke Endowment, which is grounded in long-standing relationships and common interests. Duke University's community engagement through the Duke Durham Neighborhood Partnership has been continually supported over several years with significant and flexible dollars from the Duke Endowment, which has enabled adequate space and time to explore healthy communication and deep collaboration.

Partnerships 'Collaborating among Institutions of Higher Education'

As much of the discussion around "engagement" has focused on partnerships between higher education and external entities from other sectors, the engagement between colleges and universities within particular geographical settings can be essential to cities and regions. As resources for higher education become increasingly scarce, the need for colleges and universities to collaborate will grow.

In the wake of Hurricane Katrina, former U.S. Presidents Clinton and Bush, Sr., created the Bush Clinton Katrina Fund, which included a giving program focused on colleges and universities in Louisiana, Mississippi, and Alabama. Marga Incorporated was contracted to assess the impact of these grants and work with these thirty-three colleges and universities in order to enhance their long-term capacity and opportunity into the future.

As many of these institutions are significantly tuition-dependent, in the face of enrollment declines, the need to share programs and facilities became more apparent. In New Orleans in particular, the colleges and universities collaborated with each other to address critical social problems that were exacerbated by the storm. In order to function after the storm and its resulting devastation, local institutions of higher education had to collaborate in order to function.

In areas such as New Orleans, where numerous colleges and universities are concentrated, the significance of higher education becomes more apparent when those institutions face adversity. Clusters of jobs, curricula, and commercial enterprises flow from institutions of higher education in bundles. The Atlanta University Center, for example, includes a cluster of Historically Black colleges and Universities. The ongoing resources that this group of institutions brings to this area just south of Atlanta's downtown remain evident; however, the active collaboration of these institutions around their shared role in this region is a next level of engagement.

The Annie E. Casey Foundation's Anchor Institutions grant-making program is supporting an effort to develop a shared vision and strategy for these institutions. This activity focuses on the physical and human development opportunities that can be stimulated by collaboration between these colleges and universities along with the Atlanta Housing Authority, and other external public and community-based entities. It is this next level of deliberate attempts to forge active collaboration among institutions of higher education around common geographic interests that is a new frontier in engagement.

231

Leveraging Consistency (Stability of Higher Education as Anchors, Harnessing the Economic Engine Role)

The concept of "anchor" institutions has emerged, referring to local assets that are geographically grounded, maintaining a rooted vested interest in the health and vitality of a host environment. Historically, some cities and towns have relied on their anchor institutions. In some cases, these anchors were factories or maybe hospitals. The flight of capital from various municipalities challenged the concept of the commitment of various institutions to geographic surroundings among particular institutions. Manufacturing firms, for example, changed the entire landscape of cities in the Northeast and Midwest, as they found new ways of operating through technology or less expensive operational environments in other parts of the United States or other countries.

No category of institutions have proved more geographically reliable over time than colleges and universities. Into the future, we will witness greater recognition of the consistency and value of institutions of higher education to local communities. The current economic downturn is expediting this shift in thinking, as the benefits to those cities with institutions of higher education are becoming apparent. Cities without institutions of higher education do not have the advantage of consistent grounded resources.

If local economies are going to be revived, the starting point must be with reliable assets. The public sector, while investing less in higher education, will look to colleges and universities even more in order to provide jobs, training, interns and graduates, knowledge, physical space, and thinking. Some municipalities are accustomed to leveraging higher education in this manner, particularly those that are dominated by one major institution (for example, Ann Arbor and the University of Michigan), but others are not. How to leverage anchor institutions to benefit local areas is a competency in itself that will be required following the increased realization that colleges and universities will answer some of the challenges as local officials ponder strategies to weather adversity and establish new paths.

Institutionalization (Mission Alignment, Leadership Buy-In)

Within institutions of higher education, one of the barriers to successful engagement has been a mix of reactions among stakeholders in higher education. Some wonder about the scholarly value of service learning or participatory research. Others might think engagement is simply not the business of colleges or universities—that institution of higher education should focus only on their internal needs.

As the field of those focused on higher education/community partnerships evolves and expands, awareness around the relevance of engagement to the mission of colleges and universities has increased. In order for the notion and practice of engagement to be successfully incorporated into the core interests of higher education, leadership and faculty must buy in.

Additionally, with the many segments of any college or university, internal coordination and cooperation among the various manifestations of engagement on any campus can lead to a more holistic institutional view and strategy. Nevertheless, institutionalization of engagement has been elusive.

Overall, these times are bringing together a collection of forces that will revamp the role and expectation of institutions of higher education. These historical alterations will make colleges and universities more relevant to society.

References

Carnegie Foundation. (2007). *Community Engagement Elective Classification*. Carnegie Foundation for the Advancement of Teaching. Retrieved December 18, 2008, from http://www.carnegiefoundation. org/classifications/index.asp?.

Cavaye, J. (2001). *Community Engagement Framework Project: Scoping and review paper*. Cavaye Community Development/CEO Committee on Land Resources. Retrieved December 18, 2008, from http://www.dse.vic.gov.au/DSE/wcmn203.nsf/childdocs/0B996EB412EAB883CA2570360014F01A-6BC40C338B25036ECA257036001555F2?open.

Fawcett, S. B., Paine-Andrews, A., Schultz, J. A., & Williams, E. L. (1995) Using empowerment theory in collaborative partnership for community health and development. *American Journal of Community Psychology*. Retrieved December 18, 2008, from http://gucchd.georgetown.edu/files/conference_calls/Definition%200f%20Community%0Engagement.pdf.

Gottlieb, H. (2006). *Introduction to community engagement*. Help 4 Non Profits: Community Driven Institute. Retrieved December 18, 2008, from http://www.help4nonprofits.com/NP_Mktg_Marketing-vsCommunityEngagement_Art.htm.

Indiana State University. (2008). *NCA special emphasis: Community engagement definition*. Indiana State University. Retrieved December 18, 2008, from http://irt2.indstate.edu/nca2010/assets/pdf/se/definitionDoc.pdf.

Marga Incorporated. (2007). *Real partnerships: A report to the Association for Community and Higher Education Partnerships*. New York: Author.

Maurrasse, D. J. (2001). *Beyond the campus: How colleges and universities form partnerships with their communities*. New York: Routledge.

Ostrander, S. A. (2004, March). Democracy, civic participation, and the university: A comparative study of civic engagement on five campuses. *Nonprofit and Volunteer Sector Quarterly, 33*(1), 74–93.

Wiewel, W., & Perry, D. C. (2008). *Global universities and urban development: Case studies and analysis*. Cambridge, MA: Lincoln Institute of Land Policy.

Action Research as Systems Change

Pennie Foster-Fishman and Erin R. Watson

Real change will occur, finally, when individuals define their work in terms of whom it affects, for what purpose, and with what consequences. We will know that our revolution has been successful when what we do actually matters to society at large, when society is so engaged with the university that our priorities are shaped by societal needs, when the work of every individual can be related purposefully and knowingly to the work of others, and when our habits of living are new habits. (Plater, 1999, p. 171)

For those of us interested in using research as a tool for social change, action research is a valuable, if not necessary tool in our methodological tool belt. Action research (AR) involves a collaborative process between the researcher and members of a targeted community (e.g., organization, neighborhood, small city) where both the insiders (community members) and outsiders (researchers) co-generate meaning, mutually design actions, and jointly assess the impact of these interventions. Of course, many other community-based research methods include such a collaborative process (e.g., community-based participatory research, joint insider-outsider research). What sets action research apart from this collective set of democratized research processes is AR's explicit focus on action. Knowledge is generated for the purpose of action. The need for action is what unites the researcher and the community: the need to resolve some presenting problem or underlying condition is what frames the cycle of inquiry and the purpose for the project. To date, AR has been used to address a variety of organizational, interorganizational, and community concerns including improving interorganizational operations (Adler, Shani, & Styhre, 2004; Coghlan & Brannick, 2001), promoting community development (Minkler, 2000), expanding health care services (Bellman, 2003; Bellman, Bywood, & Dale, 2003; Stringer & Genat, 2004), guiding education and curriculum changes (Meyers & Rust, 2003; Mills, 2003; Sagor, 2000), and enhancing local government (Bell, 2008).

Given this context, it should not be surprising that action research fits well with the values and objectives of an engagement agenda. Both the engagement movement and action research insist upon an active collaboration between faculty and partnering communities; both require dialogue as a means for identifying shared goals and shared methodologies for resolving selected problems; both necessitate processes for eliciting and supporting local expertise to bear upon local problems and local solutions (Fear, Rosaen, Bawden, & Foster-Fishman, 2006). Most importantly of all, both the scholarship of engagement and action research are approaches dedicated to the production of practical knowledge—knowledge that aims to contribute to the greater social good and foster human flourishing because it helps make decisions to improve conditions in society (Heron & Reason, 1997).

The purpose of this chapter is to discuss how engaged faculty members can use action research to promote social change. This paper also considers how AR can become even more effective at promoting social change when researchers and community partners adopt a systems orientation. By taking such a systems change approach, AR researchers and community participants are far more likely to develop a more comprehensive understanding of the problem and design actions that are more likely to lead to transformative change. We first describe AR, discuss the diversity of approaches an AR research can adopt, and then discuss how a systems change orientation can be applied in an AR project when transformative change is desired. We use several case studies throughout this chapter to illustrate the different stages of an AR project and the multiple approaches that are available to an AR researcher.

Defining Action Research

Action research is a term that generally refers to an iterative process involving both researchers and community stakeholders that encompasses three core components: problem identification, action, and analysis (Burns, 2007; Stringer, 2007). Often, these components create a cycle of inquiry (see figure 1) that promotes an ongoing analysis of contextual conditions, discrete actions taken to improve these conditions, an assessment of the efficacy of these actions, and a reanalysis of the current conditions and presenting problématique. If the problem has not been sufficiently addressed, more actions and learning are pursued. In the ideal situation, this cycle continues until the targeted problem is resolved. In reality, solutions enacted in today's environment often lead to future problems as contexts change over time (Rappaport, 1981) making the cycle of inquiry, action, and reflection a continually relevant tool for progress.

The roots of action research are commonly attributed to Kurt Lewin and his work during the 1940s. Like most of Lewin's ideas, the essence of action research is practicality. Unlike more traditional forms of research, which aim to test predetermined variables and generalize theories to multiple contexts, the primary goal of AR is for ordinary people to create practical solutions for issues within their local environment. This local emphasis is of particular importance for many communities because it generates customized solutions that often fare better than generalized practices developed by outside "experts" that frequently have little relevance to the everyday problems set within most community settings (Stringer, 2007).

236

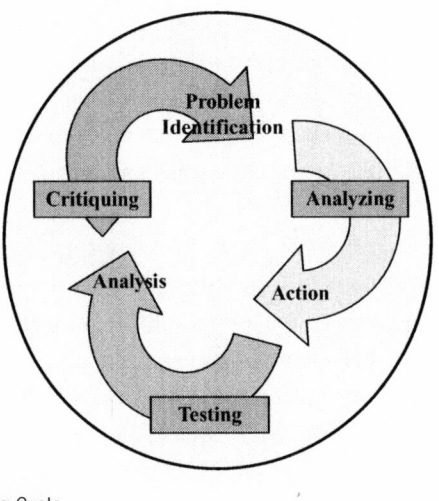

FIGURE 16.1 An Action Learning Cycle

SOURCE: Adapted from Joel Cutcher-Gershenfeld and J. Kevin Ford, Valuable Disconnects in Organizational Learning Systems: Integrating Bold Visions and Harsh Realities (Oxford University Press, 2005).

For example, action research could allow a group of teachers and parents to better understand the issue of teen bullying in their school district and use that understanding to create and implement schoolwide action plans that are customized to the cultural and social norms of the local community. A neighborhood association could use action research to better understand the local barriers to resident involvement and carry out actions to address or mitigate those barriers. A community-based health organization could partner with local residents to investigate the use of safe sex practices in the area and develop interventions to promote healthy behaviors. These examples also illustrate that in addition to being practical, action research is also empowering in that it gives people the capacity to act in ways to improve their lives and gain more control over the future direction of their community. In fact, some argue that such collaborative, problem-solving approaches build the skilled, knowledgeable, and active citizenry base needed to foster the creation of a healthy community (Smock, 2003).

Guiding Values

Different action research scholars have put forth a variety of principles and values meant to serve as a foundation to the action research process. These values are important because they create a common link between the different theoretical and methodological approaches to AR and provide a guide for decision making throughout the full cycle of inquiry. In this paper, we highlight three key values that (1) are common to most AR frameworks (e.g., Greenwood & Levin, 1998; Stringer, 2007); and (2) are congruent with the scholarship of engagement (e.g., Fear et al., 2006). In addition, in our own practice as engaged scholars, we have found these three values particularly useful in ensuring that our projects address local concerns, promote transformative social change, and foster community capacity.

Democratic Inclusion of Stakeholders

Perhaps one of the most important AR values is the democratic inclusion of stakeholders in each of the three core components of the action research cycle (Greenwood & Levin, 1998;

237

Stringer, 2007). Action research assumes that all people, whether they are professional researchers or ordinary citizens, are capable of working together to use information from their surroundings to develop practical interventions to address real-life problems. Democratically including multiple stakeholder perspectives in the AR process not only enhances the quality of the work, but also serves the purpose of building capacity and giving voice.

It is important to highlight that this value strongly suggests that researchers should include stakeholders in the *full* cycle of inquiry (figure 1): problem identification, action design/implementation, and analysis/reflection. Yet, AR projects vary considerably in their design, particularly in the extent to which they involve different stakeholders in each of these three components. In fact, it is often more common for researchers to engage stakeholders in the process of problem identification (e.g., Strack, Magill, & McDonagh, 2004) and intervention design/action (e.g., Gosin, Dustman, Frapeau, & Harthun, 2003; Wilson et al., 2007) than in the analysis process (Foster-Fishman, Law, Lichty, & Aoun, in press). Unfortunately, when AR projects fail to include stakeholders in the full cycle of inquiry, they unnecessarily bound not only the experiences and outcomes for the participants but also the potential impact of the AR project (Foster-Fishman et al., 2005).

Valuing Multiple Perspectives

Another key guiding principle of AR is the valuing of each person's unique lived experience as an integral part of the constructed understanding of the targeted issue (Greenwood & Levin, 1998). Simply put, different individuals hold unique experiences, knowledge sets, and understandings given their situated position within their community context. As a result, each person brings a different lens to the inquiry process. The extent to which the AR process elicits and values these different understandings can significantly determine the feasibility of understanding and solving the targeted issue (Checkland & Scholes, 1990). In other words, the inclusion of multiple perspectives enhances the sophistication and effectiveness of the action research process.

AR processes are more successful at supporting this value when researchers and other participants in the AR process work to create a group climate that accepts the subjective nature of reality and the importance of building a knowledge base that accommodates diversity and conflicting worldviews. When AR projects succeed at having stakeholders explore and address their different perspectives, significant insights into the community landscape and shifts in stakeholders' mindsets can occur (Checkland, 1981; Midgley, 2000).

A Focus on Social Change

The third guiding value is the idea that AR should be used to promote social justice and liberation from oppressive conditions (Greenwood & Levin, 1998; Reason & Bradbury, 2001). Action research projects are most likely to accommodate this goal when they acknowledge the underlying power structures and inequalities within settings (Gaventa & Cornwall, 2001). This requires AR projects to move their action and inquiry processes beyond the boundaries of first-order change. First-order change involves making incremental improvements within existing modes of practice (Bartunek & Moch, 1987) (i.e., doing the same things better). For example, in a community that wants to reduce the school expulsion of children with severe emotional behavioral disorders, an AR project could work to improve the referral processes between local schools and a community mental health center to ensure that these children receive the mental health services and supports they need. Second-order or transformative change, on the other hand, involves a radical shift in how a problem is perceived; ultimately, how things are done is fundamentally altered (Bartunek & Moch, 1987). Using the same example, the schools and local mental health services would work to identify ways to alter the family and classroom environments and peer support system so that the needs of children with severe emotional behavioral disorders are better addressed within their homes and school environment. Overall, AR projects are more likely to succeed at promoting second-order change when they seek to understand root causes and target the requisite systems change (Foster-Fishman, Nowell, & Yang, 2007). This approach to AR is described in more detail hereafter.

Action Research Components

As we have described, the engagement of a diverse set of individuals in the full cycle of inquiry is perhaps the most important process facing an AR researcher. This section describes in more detail each of the three components within the action research cycle and how they might be applied to actual action research projects.

The Problem Identification Phase

Some researchers claim that the problem identification phase is perhaps the most important step in an AR project (e.g., Checkland & Scholes, 1990; Midgley, 2000). Who is involved in problem identification, which perspectives are considered, and ultimately how the problem is defined not only bounds what solutions can be considered but also sets the stage for who and what is valued in the AR process. For these reasons, careful attention to who is included in this process and to the creation of dialogic processes that promote sharing, critique, and reframing is critical.

Overall, the problem identification phase requires two iterative processes: (1) selection of a problem; and (2) gathering and analyzing information about the causes of the problem. It is important to highlight that when the analysis phase promotes deep critique of the current circumstances, the initial problems selected by a group may not remain the focus of an AR project. Often, as participants explore the data they gather, new and sometimes more entrenched systemic problems get identified and prioritized. To ensure that this deep analysis occurs, no perspective should claim a "monopoly" over the problem definition phase, but rather all participants should work together to combine their perspectives and create a fuller picture of the issue at hand (Greenwood & Levin, 1998).

Once the problem is defined, participants begin to gather information about the problem by collecting new data, by reflecting on why this problem has presented itself, or by analyzing past actions taken to address the problem. This information could be gathered using either formal research methodologies or more informal group discussion techniques that are designed to elicit a deep understanding of an issue. For the former, a wide variety of both quantitative and qualitative methods including interviews, focus groups, participant

239

observations, photographs, surveys, questionnaires, archived records and reports, or the research literature can be used. For the latter, a variety of group discussion and reflection techniques exist such as Future Search (Weisbord & Janoff, 1999), soft systems methodologies (Checkland, 1981), and Open Space Technology (Owen, 1999).

However, it is important to remember that the point of this AR stage is less about collecting objective data and more about drawing on people's everyday lived experience with the issue as well as their accompanying assumptions, views, and beliefs about the causes of the problem (Stringer, 2007). This is best facilitated when settings and group processes are created that support and encourage learning and dialogue. For example, as information is gathered or shared, the group enters into a dialogue where everyone's experiences and ideas are used to critique the presented information and refine current understandings. As new questions or insights emerge, additional information is collected or further conversations are pursued. This process continues until a local theory emerges that explains why the problem exists and how it can be solved. These theories then guide the creation of action plans that identify specific strategies that can be leveraged to create the desired change.

An Example AR Project—The Problem Identification Stage in Creek County

The first author was invited to work with a county-wide interagency coordinating council that was developed to improve service delivery to children and families within its county. This council included thirty-five leaders of the key public and private service delivery organizations in Creek County. Although this council was recognized as one of the most effective collaborative bodies in the state, county-wide health indicators remained poor. For example, at the time the AR project was initiated, immunization rates were some of the lowest in the state and teenage pregnancy was on the rise. Initially, the first author was invited to work with the council to conduct an evaluation to understand the effectiveness of its human service delivery improvement efforts.

To ensure that the evaluation project met the needs of the local service delivery system, the first author created an Evaluation Workgroup that included approximately twenty service delivery providers and managers. This group became the context for the AR project, as it was charged with leading the design, implementation, and analysis of the evaluation. To determine the problems and concerns that should be examined in the evaluation, the first author and another faculty member facilitated three retreats with the workgroup members to help identify which outcomes should be prioritized in this evaluation. During these retreats, participants were asked, among other things, to describe the problems they have encountered in meeting the needs of their clients and identify reasons why county health indicators may be on the rise. To guide this discussion, the Technology of Participation's (ToP) Participatory Process (Oyler & Burbidge, 1999) was used. Using an iterative series of individual, small-group, and large-group discussion processes, ToP is designed to ensure that all participants' concerns are considered and that patterns or themes across respondents are identified (see Oyler & Burbidge, 1999, for a description of this process). Through this process, two key concerns emerged: (1) the need for a strengths-based approach to service delivery, and (2) a greater emphasis on service delivery coordination. These two issues replaced the initial focus of the evaluation effort (i.e., understand the impact of the council's service delivery improvement efforts) and became the goal of this AR project from this point forward.

To better understand these problems within the context of this county, the first author met with the workgroup every three to four weeks for approximately six months. During these meetings, participants first worked together to develop a local "theory in use" that described when and under what conditions service providers were able to adopt a strengths-based, coordinated approach to service delivery. Then, to ensure that this emerging framework was informed by recent developments in the academic literature, the first author reviewed the literature on all of the factors identified in this "theory in use." She then presented what she learned to the workgroup, highlighting additional factors or pathways in the framework that the literature would recommend. The workgroup participants then dialogued about the value and appropriateness of these possible additions or changes to their model and worked with the faculty member to create a conceptual model for the project that integrated local theories and ideas from the academy. The final model was presented to the full council for their critique and approval. Council members reported that this model provided them with a more complete understanding of and rationale for the difficulties their county has experienced. This stage of the AR process took approximately eight months.

Designing and Implementing Actions

Using the action plans as a guide, the researcher supports the team of community stakeholders in systematically implementing actions within the setting to address the underlying causes of the problem. Stringer (2007) suggests developing action plans in such a way that participants can easily understand how an action is being carried out (i.e., what outcomes are expected, who is responsible, how long the action should take, and available resources) and visually track when specific actions have been completed. This helps to support participants in implementing their actions, as does providing support, communication, technical assistance, and conflict resolution (Stringer, 2007). As participants carry out their actions in the setting, they are provided with additional opportunities to interact with the problem environment. This often leads to further insights about the sociopolitical causes of the issue as well as other potential strategies for improvement. Sometimes, as the following case illustrates, the initial action phase of an AR project may involve the systematic collection of information to inform local understanding and future action steps.

Example AR Project: Designing and Implementing Actions in Creek County

For the AR project in Creek County described previously, the first action that was targeted was the collection of data from across the service delivery system to better understand the factors influencing the adoption of a more strengths-based, coordinated service delivery model. This action was viewed as the first of many strategies that the council could employ to address the concerns raised by the Evaluation Workgroup. Systematic data collection was also viewed as a necessary step in educating the council members about the problems facing the service delivery system in Creek County and in informing future strategies and actions.

Using the conceptual framework that was developed in the problem identification phase, the workgroup designed the evaluation study. This included working with the faculty members to develop a survey instrument that fit the language and concerns of local service providers, identifying a sampling strategy that would be broad enough in scope to meet the concerns of all council members, and designing a data collection approach that would increase response rates. Workgroup members also helped to collect survey data. Overall, this stage of the AR process took approximately six months.

Analysis. As participants observe and learn from the impact of their actions, they incorporate their insights into the final action research cycle—analysis. In this stage, the researcher facilitates a process where the group observes the consequences of their actions in the setting and analyzes and reflects on the effectiveness of their actions in addressing the problem. As in the initial problem identification stage, it is important to create settings and processes that can facilitate dialogue and the co-construction of different perspectives and experiences during the analysis phase of AR. Sometimes, through this reflection process, participants realize that it is necessary to refine their methods and theories in order to improve their progress in the setting. If this occurs, the group reenters the initial problem identification stage and begins the interactive inquiry and action process over again. Ultimately, AR projects are far more effective when they embrace an ongoing and iterative approach to problem analysis and solution development (Midgely, 2000). This iterative process is illustrated in the following example.

An Example AR Project: The Analysis Process in Creek County:

Following the collection of the survey data, workgroup members worked with the first author to interpret the data and make recommendations based on these findings. Workgroup members interpreted both quantitative and qualitative data. Statistical analyses that were conducted by the faculty member were translated into usable outputs (e.g., regression coefficients were inserted into the conceptual framework) for workgroup members to discuss and analyze. Open-ended survey responses were also thematically analyzed by the workgroup members. The workgroup met every three weeks for approximately four months, analyzing and interpreting the findings. To synthesize these findings and identify key patterns and results, the faculty member facilitated another retreat with the workgroup members. During this retreat, participants critically examined key findings and identified recommendations for additional actions.

Using the insights gained and decisions made at the retreat, workgroup members assisted the faculty member in writing a feedback report that detailed evaluation findings and recommendations for next steps. Workgroup members then presented this report to the full council and, with the council members, developed an action plan for the next AR cycle of inquiry. This cycle included designing and implementing several actions that were created to improve the coordination of service delivery and the adoption and use of strengths-based services. To increase the range of stakeholders engaged in action, different task forces within the council were asked to identify strategies they could implement to support the larger goals of coordinated, strengths-based services. Overall, this analysis phase launched an iterative series of small action research projects within the council, where task forces incorporated the findings into their initial understandings of local problems, designed relevant actions, and then reassessed their impact at a later point.

The Diversity of Action Research

As mentioned earlier, AR processes have been carried out in a variety of contexts and countries since AR was first introduced by Kurt Lewin (e.g., Adler et al., 2004; Baskerville & Wood-Harper, 1996; Bell, 2008; Bellman, 2003; Bellman et al., 2003; Chisholm, 2001; Coghlan & Brannick, 2001; Meyers & Rust, 2003; Mills, 2003; Minkler, 2000; Sagor, 2000;

Stringer & Genat, 2004). For example, Greenwood and Levin (1998) collaborated with residents of a small Norwegian village who were attempting to develop and revitalize their community's decaying infrastructure and neighborhoods. The researchers first met with a small task force within the village to define the problem of preserving their home village. This group then organized a series of village-wide conferences that engaged many community participants in discussions around the issue of planning actions to revitalize the village. These conference discussions resulted in the creation of several additional task forces that took on the actions of constructing or repairing village street lights, a harbor, a school, a community center, individual houses, and roads. Approximately one year after these actions were initiated, the researchers organized several follow-up conferences with all of the members in each of the task forces. These follow-up sessions allowed participants to reflect on their progress toward revitalizing the village, learn from each other's actions, and revise their plans as needed (Greenwood & Levin, 1998). As this example illustrates, the three components of the AR cycle can be effectively adapted to meet the needs of a large and potentially diverse group of people within their unique contexts. The example also shows how the values of AR can be seamlessly woven into the process, such as the democratic prioritizing of issues by the task force, the inclusion of a variety of stakeholder perspectives in the conference sessions, and the organizing of the village toward liberating action.

Since the launch of AR by Kurt Lewin, several different forms of AR have emerged, and each form often involves a unique iteration of core values and approaches to the cycle of inquiry. We next describe two approaches to AR that we have found particularly valuable in our engagement work in the community as we have strived to democratize the knowledge generation process and promote transformative action.

Participatory Action Research

Participatory action research (PAR) is a relatively recent adaptation to AR that draws on the ideas of critical reflection and co-learning to make stakeholder participation more intentional, inclusive, and critical (Minkler, 2000). Although PAR mirrors the same action research cycles as described earlier, it diverges from action research in three important ways. First, PAR intentionally includes—sometimes exclusively—stakeholders who are most affected by the problem (often coming from populations that have been historically disenfranchised, marginalized, or oppressed) yet who are often denied the opportunity to contribute to the process of generating knowledge and conducting action. For example, Wang and her colleagues conducted a PAR project with rural Chinese village women as a way to educate women on their own health needs and to inform Chinese policy makers about the health and community issues faced by rural women (Wang, Burris, & Xiang, 1996). Wilson et al. (2007) had adolescents identify issues of concern within their school and develop and implement actions to address these problems.

Second, PAR aims to promote participant ownership and control over the knowledge generation process (e.g., Minkler & Wallerstein, 2003). Thus, academics using PAR are not, as they often are in AR, co-producers of the knowledge created but instead are relegated to the role of facilitator, assisting stakeholders in discovering their own understandings and designing their own actions (e.g., Minkler & Wallerstein, 2003). In other words, community participants—not the faculty member—control what knowledge is generated and how knowledge is used; as a result, participants gain expanded opportunities for power because they control knowledge production—a process that is often used to determine the definition of problems (and solutions) and to guide future policy change and action (Gaventa & Cornwall, 2001). For example, in a PAR project with low-income youth and adults, participating youth and adults had control over what photos and stories would be included in the citywide Photovoice exhibit (Foster-Fishman, Nowell, Deacon, Nievar, & McCann, 2005; Nowell, Berkowitz, Deacon, & Foster-Fishman, 2006). Although the funder and faculty members were interested in using the exhibit as an opportunity to highlight the issues within the low-income neighborhoods that should become the focus of an emerging community-building effort, participants instead used this opportunity to construct a more hopeful narrative about their lives and their neighborhoods. For example, they primarily selected photos and stories that provided more positive images of their youth and their dreams for a better future. By providing images and stories that countered the prevailing community narrative of despair and hopelessness, the youth and adult participants successfully triggered a larger community discourse about the possibility of change and how residents working together could make change happen.

Third, PAR aims to raise the critical consciousness of stakeholders through the research process. This goal is largely based on Freire's (1970) conviction that helping individuals develop an increased understanding of the societal issues impacting their lives is a fundamental tool in community change. This understanding is more likely to emerge when PAR projects successfully illuminate multiple interpretations of the targeted social problem and help participants discover the underlying structural inequities influencing their lives.

Like AR, PAR has been conducted in an array of settings and for a variety of purposes. For example, Koch, Selim, and Kralik (2002) conducted a PAR project with nurses in a health care organization who had experienced assault or violence on the job with the goal of developing strategies for preventing workplace violence. The research facilitators recruited participants for the project by disseminating flyers throughout the organization inviting nurses who had experienced violence to join the project. After recruitment, a group of nine nurses began meeting regularly with the research facilitator to clarify the issue of workplace violence. The nurses shared with each other their personal experiences of violence on the job and also gathered sixty-eight accounts of violence from other nurses in the organization. This early stage of problem identification not only helped to define the problem of workplace violence in the organization from multiple perspectives, but also served as a consciousness-raising process for the nurses participating in the project. The group next began to critically analyze the various accounts of violence and generated collective knowledge about the causes and solutions to the problem. The group then used this knowledge to create a video on prevention of workplace violence and an accompanying educational pack that was shown to all staff in the organization. After the showing, the group used viewer feedback to reflect on the video's impact and later expanded the project to create a model for best practice that was used throughout the community (Koch et al., 2002).

PAR has become increasingly popular in the past ten years, and examples of participatory action research can be found throughout the literature. For example, PAR has been used with persons with disabilities (Brydon-Miller, 1993), incarcerated women (Fields, González, Hentz, Rhee, & White, 2008), youth (Cahill, 2007; Herr, 1995), community members from multiple sectors (Braithwaite, Cockwill, O'Neill, & Rebane, 2007; Minkler, 2000), psychiatric consumers and staff within self-help organizations (Nelson, Ochocka, Griffin, & Lord, 1998), homeless populations (Whitmore & McKee, 2001), and impoverished women from rural Chinese villages (Wang & Burris, 1997). Some PAR researchers are even beginning to use creative media as a way to engage youth and disenfranchised individuals in the knowledge generation process. For example, photography (Wang & Burris, 1997; Wilson et al., 2007), video (Gutberlet, 2007), internet technologies (Flicker et al., 2008), theater (Bagamoyo College of Arts, Tanzania Theatre Centre, Mabala, & Allen, 2002; Morsillo & Prilleltensky, 2007), and art pieces such as collages (McIntyre, 2000) are increasingly being used as a way to elicit the voice and desires of individuals and groups less accustomed to verbally express-ing themselves.

An Example PAR Project: The Battle Creek Photovoice Project

Photovoice (Wang & Burris, 1994) is an innovative PAR method that integrates documentary photography with empowerment education (Freire, 1970). Participants are given cameras and are asked to capture images that convey meaning about their lives and their concerns (Wang et al., 1996). Then, by sharing their stories and reflecting about the broader meanings of their photos, participants discover shared issues and concerns and often develop a critical awareness of their surrounding context. Typically, these photos and stories are displayed for the broader public and policy makers. Often, the insights that emerge through a Photovoice process can lead to policy change, strategic actions, and an empowered constituency.

The Battle Creek Photovoice Project was launched in summer 2003 as part of the initial plan-ning phase in a comprehensive community building initiative (*Yes we can!*) in the city of Battle Creek, Michigan. The primary goal of *Yes we can!* was to use resident-driven strategies to improve neighborhoods and education and economic outcomes in the city of Battle Creek (see Foster-Fishman et al., 2006, for more details on this initiative). The first author was the leader of the evaluation team for this effort.

Given this resident-driven focus, the evaluation team needed methods that would demon-strate the value of resident engagement while also fostering community awareness of neighbor-hood conditions. The team was also looking for methods that could trigger resident-driven action and policy change. Photovoice was selected because of its ability to support these goals.

Eleven youth and eighteen adults from seven different low-income neighborhoods partici-pated in this PAR project. For five weeks, participants shot a roll of film that focused on the fram-ing questions: (a) "What is your life like?" (b) "What is good about your life?" and (c) "What needs to change?" Each week the film was developed and returned to the photographer, who would select three images and write reflections about each photograph. Participants would share these reflections and their photos in weekly reflective sessions where they met with up to six other participants from their neighborhood. At the end of the five weeks, participants worked to design a public exhibit and a gallery booklet. Thousands of Battle Creek residents including policy

245

makers and community leaders attended this month-long exhibit, and an online Photovoice project was initiated by the local newspaper in response to the positive and compelling impact of this PAR project. Information garnered from this project was used to inform future programmatic efforts in the community-building initiative.

Systemic Action Research

While the bulk of AR that has taken place over the years has targeted issues at the group or organizational level, many believe that the process has the potential to contribute to a larger movement of social change and liberation at a higher level of analysis (Greenwood & Levin, 1998; Reason & Bradbury, 2001). More recently, there has been a call to expand the scope of AR to the level of systems change (Burns, 2007). A "system" can be thought of as a complex web of interrelated networks and processes that operates according to complex patterns and self-organizes in response to changes in the environment. For example, actions aimed at making a discrete change within the system (the creation of a new policy for instance) often create non-linear and unpredictable consequences because all changes to the system must filter through a myriad of interrelated factors and networks (Foster-Fishman et al., 2007). Thus, the key to creating change in a complex system is to understand how the system is structured in order to shift specific connections that have the ability to leverage larger system changes. Kurt Lewin believed that the degree to which one of these shifts could cause large changes to the system relied less on its size than on its strategic placement in the system; some of the most instrumental shifts can be surprisingly small and appear seemingly unrelated to the problem (Lewin, 1952).

Clearly, using AR to promote social change within a complex system encompassing multiple networks of people and institutions is more complicated than using it to promote change within a single organization or group. Because of this complexity, there have been different ideas about how to scale up the practice of AR from the organizational level to the systems level. One of these views was put forth by Foth (2006), who suggested that various AR processes at the organizational level can be linked together through social networks to create a "networked community of practice." Burns (2007) expanded on Foth's view in his theory of systemic action research. This theory is based on the strategy of initiating numerous "parallel and interacting" AR processes at different locations in the system and eventually merging these processes into a unified systems change effort. Although participants within each of these individual AR processes are given the freedom to pursue their own unique direction of inquiry and action, the research facilitator has the task of unifying all processes into one integrated effort aimed at promoting a particular change to the system. Examples of these unified efforts could range from improving a county's service delivery system for children with mental health needs to protecting the well-being of elderly people as they are discharged from health care facilities.

Using the strategy of PAR processes for systems change is important for two reasons, according to Burns (2007). First, each individual can only understand the interconnections within the system through their own personal perspective or vantage point. By initiating parallel inquiry processes with many people at different locations in the system, the research facilitator is able to tap into these multiple perspectives and gain a fuller understanding of the system's patterns and networks. This understanding can highlight connections between the various AR processes (thus aiding in the unification process) and, more broadly speaking, it can help identify leverage points for change within the system. Second, the strategy of parallel action research processes is important because it encourages people to explore creative ways to learn about and address system-level problems without constraining their choices by forcing a need for group consensus. These diverse processes allow for a wider spectrum of inquiry to take place across all participants and also help to maintain participants' motivation by giving them control over the direction of their own action research process.

Examples of systemic AR are less common in the literature. Several systemic action research projects have been carried out in the context of agriculture and rural community development (Luckett, Ngubane, & Memela, 2001; Packham & Sriskandarajah, 2005). Burns (2007) describes some of the systemic AR projects that have been conducted by the SOLAR group. One of these projects engaged patients and staff of a psychiatric care facility in trying to shift policies and procedures in order to improve consumers' experiences of mental health services. The project started by creating two separate groups, one involving consumers and one involving staff of the facility. These two groups held ongoing conversations about the problematic practices and procedures within the facility and ideas for how to shift them. Summaries of each group's conversations were given to the opposite group for comment and became the subject for the next round of group conversation. This process allowed both groups to learn and co-generate knowledge together while maintaining enough space to allow consumers and staff to develop trust of each other. Over time, more groups were created that involved individuals from different areas of the system including people from other wards of the hospital, the medical director, and state and federal policy makers. By the end, this project involved more than two hundred people located at different locations throughout the system, each providing their own particular perspective and ideas for shifting policies and procedures to promote change within the system. As this example shows, systemic AR holds great promise for increasing the potential impact of AR toward attaining broader social change by adopting a systems thinking perspective to the process of inquiry and action.

An Example of a Systemic Action Research Project: The Rural System of Care Project

A system of care is a strategy to coordinate and network community-based services, structures, relationships, and processes in order to improve outcomes for children and their families (Hodges, Ferreira, Israel, & Mazza, 2007). The Rural System of Care Project was initiated in winter 2008 in a rural county in Michigan and is currently ongoing. The main goal of the project is to improve outcomes for children with social emotional disturbances and their families. The two authors are consultants for this effort.

The systemic AR process for this project began with the creation of four separate AR teams that were simultaneously engaged in different AR cycles of inquiry. The first team is made up of the directors and leaders within public agencies serving children with mental health needs in the county. The second team is focused at the provider level and involves social workers, probation officers, therapists, early childhood workers, and child protective services staff. The third team has engaged parents whose children have utilized mental health services in the county. The fourth team is being planned as a future activity to involve youth who are currently receiving mental health services.

One advantage of this model is that each team is able to provide unique perspectives on the relevant issues affecting the provision and availability of children's mental health services in the county. As each homogenous group articulates their particular perspective, the researcher shares these insights with the other teams to foster a holistic understanding of the entire system. In addition, each team is able to leverage unique systemic changes with their actions because they are strategically positioned at different levels within the system. For example, the parent team identified a gap in available supports for family members and is developing a peer-to-peer parent support group to meet the need. The provider team identified a need for social workers and therapists to work together in creating service plans for children and shifted their practice to allow for this collaboration. At the policy level, the leaders group identified a problem with the service coordination between agencies and is working to create a shared consent form to improve information sharing within the county. Throughout this process, the researcher is slowly guiding the separate streams of inquiry and action into a unified effort to meet the goals of the system of care.

Action Research as Systems Change

Systemic AR has great promise as a method for promoting large-scale systems change. By engaging diverse groups in parallel inquiry processes, one is more likely to develop a deep understanding of the targeted system and locate the strategic levers needed to shift system operations. A challenge with systemic AR, however, is the feasibility of simultaneously engaging and supporting multiple PAR projects. When neither the resources nor the capacity is present to support such a process, action researchers need other tools for transforming their ordinary AR project into a transformative social change endeavor.

Overall, the potential impact of an AR project is bounded by the frameworks used to guide the inquiry process. When researchers and community participants use AR to improve existing operations—or to do current things better—they are less likely to significantly shift the existing system because the inquiry process is framed as first-order change. First-order change efforts are guided by questions that aim to understand what Sackmann (1992) refers to as "directory knowledge": How is this done? How is this a problem? How can this be done better? In other words, these projects only aim to understand how the current system operates; they typically refrain from examining why the system operates as it does.

AR projects are more likely to lead to transformative systems change when they apply inquiry frameworks that elicit what Sackmann refers to as axiomatic knowledge. Axiomatic knowledge explains why things are done as they are within a targeted system; it reveals underlying patterns and/or root causes. In other words, axiomatic knowledge can evoke second-order change. Questions that help to foster axiomatic knowledge include: Why are things done this way? Why does this problem exist? What local conditions may have helped to create or sustain this concern?

Systems thinking is one framework that can be useful for action researchers who hope to pursue transformative change and reveal, among other things, the axiomatic knowledge within a targeted context. Systems thinking is a conceptual orientation that looks to understand how systems function by examining interrelationships between parts, the root causes of targeted issues, and how systemic parts work to create a functioning whole (Trochim, Cabrera, Millstein, Gallagher, & Leischow, 2006, pg 539). Within this context, systems refer to entities that include multiple parts working together as a whole (Ackoff & Rovin, 2003). For example, systems could include a human services organization, a mental health service delivery system, and an emergency response system. Because all problems emerge from a system(s), the inclusion of systems thinking in an AR project increases the likelihood of identifying the right problem and of developing the insights needed to actually transform current reality. Systems thinking is a diverse discipline with multiple frameworks available for an AR researcher. Next, we describe one framework that was developed by the first author and her colleagues. This framework was specifically designed to help researchers and practitioners embed a systemic approach to their community-based research and action.

A Framework for Transformative Systems Change

Foster-Fishman and her colleagues (Foster-Fishman et al., 2007) proposed a Transformative Systems Change Framework for developing a "systemic awareness of a problem situation" and designing solutions that would effectively mitigate the systemic causes of a targeted problem. This framework is based on the prominent view of systems (e.g., Senge, 1990) as a complex web of interdependent parts: creating change in one part of a system will only resolve the targeted problem if other critical elements, interdependencies, and patterns within the system shift as well. For researchers and practitioners interested in creating transformative change, this framework can foster the development of a sophisticated understanding of the larger system perpetuating a targeted problem. When using this framework within an AR project, participants are challenged to:

- Understand the multiple stakeholder perspectives of the problem situation;

- Understand the critical parts, patterns, and interdependencies within a system that support the status quo and use this understanding to inform problem definition and action design;
- Identify systemic leverage points that promote transformative change and use this information to inform action design and analysis.

To assist AR researchers and practitioners in their use of the Transformative Systems Change Framework, we next describe some key processes and questions identified by Foster-Fishman and her colleagues.

Defining the Problem

Some systems thinkers argue that the act of defining a problem is both the most critical and potentially transformative step in an AR cycle of inquiry (e.g., Midgley, 2000). Problem definition includes both exploring and clarifying the targeted problem and determining who and what is contained within the system given the selected issue. To ensure that this inquiry process leads to a complete understanding of the targeted problem and relevant system, a diverse set of stakeholders should be engaged in the problem definition stage, and dialogic processes should be used to help these stakeholders negotiate their different perspectives and worldviews. When such negotiations lead to a problem definition that has successfully incorporated competing perspectives, stakeholders may actually experience significant shifts in their worldviews (Checkland, 1981). AR researchers interested in adopting a systems orientation to the problem definition process should:

- Expand whom they include in the problem definition process by engaging individuals who represent different ecological layers, distinct community niches, and opposing perspectives. Individuals most affected by the problem are particularly important to include in this process.
- Engage a diverse set of stakeholders in an ongoing dialogic process where stakeholders have opportunities to understand the distinct perspectives within the room and also work to accommodate competing worldviews in the problem definition.

Understand Critical System Parts, Patterns and Interdependencies

In the Transformative Systems Change Framework, system parts refer to the underlying characteristics of the system that direct system behavior and determine root causes of targeted problems. Foster-Fishman and colleagues identified four key categories of systems parts that AR researchers and practitioners should work to understand in their assessment of a targeted problem: System Norms, System Resources, System Regulations, and System Power Operations. Following are some questions that AR researchers and participants can use to identify and understand these critical system characteristics (see Foster-Fishman et al., 2007, for a more thorough discussion of this model and guiding questions). These questions can be used to inform the full cycle of inquiry within an AR project:

- **Identifying System Norms:** What current assumptions explain why things are done as they are? What are the "theories in use" that stakeholders use to explain why the targeted problem exists? What are the values guiding current programs, policies, and practices within the system? Are they congruent or compatible with proposed actions?
- **Identifying System Resources:** *Human Resources*—Do system members have the skills and knowledge sets needed to support the targeted actions? Are there local champions for the change? Do they know how to leverage change within the system? *Social Resources*—To what extent are relationships among stakeholders a contributing factor to the targeted issue? How will relationships need to shift in order for the proposed actions to be successful? Are policies/procedures put into place to guide, support, and encourage collaborative relationships, shared work, and coordination? *Economic Resources & Opportunities*— Whose needs are prioritized in the ways that current resources are allocated and opportunities distributed? Whose needs are ignored? How does the system need to use its resources differently to support the proposed changes?
- **Identifying System Regulations:** What policies, practices, and procedures exacerbate the problem you want to address? Which ones have made it difficult to fully resolve this problem in the past? What current policies, practices, and procedures are incompatible with the

new or planned actions? Which ones might get in the way of the actions succeeding? What policies, practices, and procedures are not in place but are needed to fully support the goals and philosophies of the targeted action steps?

- **Identifying System Power Operations:** What types of decisions are most critical to the functioning of the system, and where does authority over these decisions rest? What types of information and resources are most important to the system and who controls access to these resources? How do the proposed actions challenge the existing power and decision-making structures? What new power bases or decision-making structures will need to be developed to support the actions?

Thinking systemically about the problems targeted in an AR project also requires attention to the interactions that occur across system parts. According to systems thinking, all system parts directly or indirectly interact with each other and the problems that emerge in a system are the by-products of these interactions (Maani & Cavana, 2000). Thus, AR researchers and practitioners need to also understand the character and quality of the interactions within their system (Senge, 1990). The Transformative Systems Change Framework provides several questions AR researchers and practitioners can consider as they work to understand the interdependencies and patterns that exist within their targeted context:

- **Identifying System Interdependencies:** How do the system parts currently reinforce each other or keep each other in check? How will these interdependencies affect the planned actions? Will strengthening an existing interdependency or adding/deleting a link accelerate the desired change? How do current feedback mechanisms support or impede AR project goals? What additional feedback mechanisms could be added to facilitate the desired change?

Identifying Systemic Leverage Points

AR researchers can trigger transformative shifts by identifying levers that will change system parts, interactions, or patterns. Next, we describe several questions that can help AR researchers and practitioners identify strategic levers for change. AR actions can then be designed to shift these levers.

- **Which parts are incompatible with the overall goals of the AR project? Which parts are most likely to trigger system wide change?** Pay particular attention to systems regulations and parts that have multiple cross-level connections because these are well positioned to influence system behavior.
- **Given current resources and interests, which of the parts can actually be altered or strengthened? Will shifts in those parts actually produce the desired changes?**
- **What linkages could be created or altered to align system functioning with the AR project goals?**

Concluding Comments

In conclusion, AR is a highly flexible methodology that engages community partners in a process of praxis that aims to resolve pressing community concerns and build   251 local capacity to critically analyze and solve targeted issues. Whether an AR project is designed within the traditional AR framework, as a PAR effort, or systemic AR, learning is essential to the process. Action emerges from the insights participants experience as they work to understand a problem—how and why it occurs, and what could be done to address it. Then, from their pursuit of action, participants' knowledge base is further expanded as they assess the success and failures of their actions and then reconstruct their understanding of the presenting problem and surrounding context.

For these reasons, one of the most critical components of an action research project is the creation of a group environment that promotes active learning, critique, and reflection (Fear et al., 2006). When conversations across stakeholders manage to challenge existing perspectives and yield new understandings of presenting problems, more transformative actions—and change—will result (Rosaen, Foster-Fishman, & Fear, 2001). Ultimately, this requires an environment that promotes what Wenger and colleagues refer to as situated learning. For such learning to take place, dialogue across participants must flourish so that differences across stakeholders' understandings can be revealed, assessed, and then reassembled into a shared understanding. This requires the creation of a group environment where trust runs high, and conflict and differences are examined, not ignored (e.g., Foster-Fishman, Berkowitz, Lounsbury, Jacobson, & Allen, 2001)—the very dynamics found in successful engagement efforts (e.g., Driscoll & Lynton, 1999; Fear et al., 2006; Nyden, Figert, Shibley, & Burrows, 1997).

Overall, for engaged scholars interested in generating knowledge that leads to action, AR is a valuable inquiry framework. It is a flexible methodology that can accommodate a range of problems, contexts, and stakeholder compositions. What is most important is that researchers enter an AR effort with an explicit focus on the democratization of knowledge generation, the use of knowledge to create action, and the importance of praxis. Clarification of the values that will be used to guide the AR process, whom to include in the inquiry process, and how to integrate learning so local capacity flourishes are critical guidelines for engaged faculty to follow as they embark on an AR effort. With expanded use of this method, we can expect to see more community settings generating local solutions to entrenched community problems.

References

Ackoff, R. L., & Rovin, S. (2003). *Redesigning society.* Stanford, CA: Stanford Business Books.

Adler, N. B., Shani, A. B., & Styhre, A. (Eds.). (2004). *Collaborative research in organizations: Foundations for learning, change, and theoretical development.* Thousand Oaks, CA: Sage.

Bagamoyo College of Arts, Tanzania Theatre Centre, Mabala, R., & Allen, K. B. (2002). Participatory action research on HIV/AIDS through a popular theatre approach in Tanzania. *Evaluation and Program Planning, 25*(4), 333–339.

Bartunek, J. M., & Moch, M. K. (1987). First-order, second-order, and third-order change and organizational development interventions: A cognitive approach. *Journal of Applied Behavioral Science, 23*(4), 483–500.

Baskerville, R. L., & Wood-Harper, A. T. (1996). A critical perspective on action research as a method for information systems research. *Journal of Information Technology, 11,* 235–246.

Bell, S. (2008). Systemic approaches to managing across the gap in the public sector: Results of an action research programme. *Systemic Practice and Action Research, 21,* 227–240.

Bellman, L. (2003). *Nurse led change and development in clinical practice.* London: Whurr.

Bellman, L., Bywood, C., & Dale, S. (2003). Advancing working and learning through critical action research: Creativity and constraints. *Nurse Education in Practice, 3*(4), 186–194.

Braithwaite, R., Cockwill, S., O'Neill, M., & Rebane, D. (2007). Insider participatory action research in disadvantaged post-industrial areas. *Action Research, 5*(1), 61–74.

Brydon-Miller, M. (1993). Breaking down barriers: Accessibility self advocacy in the disabled community. In P. Park, M. Brydon-Miller, B. Hall, & T. Jackson (Eds.), *Voices of change: Participatory research in the United States and Canada* (pp. 125–144). Westport, CT: Bergin & Garvey.

Burns, D. (2007). *Systemic action research.* University of Bristol: Policy Press.

Cahill, C. (2007). Doing research with young people: Participatory research and the rituals of collective work. *Children's Geographies, 5*(3), 297–312.

Checkland, P. (1981). *Systems thinking: Systems practice.* Chichester, UK: Wiley.

Checkland, P., & Scholes, J. (1990). *Soft systems methodology in action.* New York: Wiley.

Chisholm, R. F. (2001). Action research to develop an interorganizational network. In P. Reason and H. Bradbury (Eds.), *Handbook of action research: Participative inquiry and practice* (pp. 324–332). London: Sage.

Coghlan, D., & Brannick, T. (2001). *Doing research in your own organization.* London: Sage.

Driscoll, A., & Lynton, E. (1999). *Making outreach visible.* Washington, DC: American Association for Higher Education.

Fear, R., Rosaen, C., Bawden, R, & Foster-Fishman, P. (2006). *Coming to critical engagement: An autoethnographic exploration of engaged faculty lives.* Lanham, MD: University Press of America.

Fields, J., González, I., Hentz, K., Rhee, M., & White, C. (2008). Learning from and with incarcerated women: Emerging lessons from a participatory action study of sexuality education. *Sexuality Research and Social Policy: Journal of NSRC, 5*(2), 71–84.

Flicker, S., Maley, O., Ridgley, A., Biscope, S., Lombardo, C., & Skinner, H. A. (2008). e-PAR: Using technology and participatory action research to engage youth in health promotion. *Action Research, 6*(3), 285–303.

Foster-Fishman, P. G., Berkowitz, S., Lounsbury, D., Jacobson, S., & Allen, N. A. (2001). Building collaborative capacity in community based coalitions. *American Journal of Community Psychology, 29*(2), 241–262.

Foster-Fishman, P. G., Fitzgerald, K., Brandell, C., Nowell, B., Chavis, D. M., & Van Egeren, L. (2006). Building a community of possibility: The role of small wins and community organizing. *American Journal of Community Psychology, 38,* 143–152.

Foster-Fishman, P. G., Law, K., Lichty, L., & Aoun, C. (In press). Youth ReACT for social change: A method for youth participatory action research. *American Journal of Community Psychology.*

Foster-Fishman, P., Nowell, B., Deacon, Z., Nievar, A., & McCann, P. (2005). Using methods that matter: The power of reflection, dialogue, and voice. *American Journal of Community Psychology, 36*(3/4), 275–291.

Foster-Fishman, P. G., Nowell, B., & Yang, H. (2007). Putting the system back into systems change: A framework for understanding and changing organizational and community systems. *American Journal of Community Psychology, 39*(3/4), 197–216.

Foth, G. (2006). Network action research. *Action Research, 4*(2), 205–226.

Freire, P. (1970). *Pedagogy of the oppressed.* New York: Herder & Herder.

Gaventa, J., & Cornwall, A. (2001). Power and knowledge. In P. Reason & H. Bradbury (Eds.), *Handbook of action research: Participative inquiry and practice* (pp. 70–80). London: Sage.

Gosin, M. N., Dustman, P. A., Drapeau, A. E., & Harthun, M. L. (2003). Participatory action research: Creating an effective prevention curriculum for adolescents in the Southwestern US. *Health Education Research, 18*(3), 363–379.

Greenwood, D. J., & Levin, M. (1998). *Introduction to action research: Social research for social change.* London: Sage.

Gutberlet, J. (2007). Empowering collective recycling initiatives: Video documentation and action research with a recycling co-op in Brazil. *Resources, Conservation and Recycling, 52*(4), 659–670.

Heron, J., & Reason, P. (1997). A participatory inquiry paradigm. *Qualitative Inquiry, 3,* 274–294.

Herr, K. (1995). Action research as empowering practice. *Journal of Progressive Human Services, 6,* 45–58.

Hodges, S., Ferreira, K., Israel, N., & Mazza, J. (2007). *System implementation issue brief no. 1—Lessons from successful systems: System of care definition.* Tampa: University of South Florida, Louis de la Parte Florida Mental Health Institute, Research and Training Center for Children's Mental Health.

Koch, T., Selim, P., & Kralik, D. (2002). Enhancing lives through the development of a community based participatory action research programme. *Journal of Clinical Nursing, 11,* 109–117.

Lewin, K. (1952). *Field theory in social science.* New York: Harper and Brothers.

Luckett, S., Ngubane, S., & Memela, B. (2001). Designing a management system for rural community development organization using a systemic action research process. *Journal of Systemic Practice and Action Research, 14*(4), 517–542.

Maani, K. E., & Cavana, R. Y. (2000). *Systems thinking and modeling: Understanding change and complexity.* Auckland, New Zealand: Pearson Education New Zealand.

McIntyre, A. (2000). Constructing meaning about violence, school, and community: Participatory action research with urban youth. *Urban Review, 32*(2), 123–154.

Meyers, E., & Rust, F. O. (Eds.). (2003). *Taking action with teacher research.* Portsmouth, NH: Heinemann.

Midgley, G. (2000). *Systemic intervention: Philosophy, methodology, and practice.* New York: Kluwer.

Mills, G. (2003). *Action research: A guide for the teacher researcher* (2nd ed.). Upper Saddle River, NJ: Merrill/Prentice Hall.

Minkler, M. (2000). Using participatory action research to build healthy communities. *Public Health Reports, 115*(2–3), 191–197.

Minkler, M., & Wallerstein, N. (2003). *Community-based participatory research for health.* San Francisco: Jossey-Bass.

Morsillo, J., & Prilleltensky, I. (2007). Social action with youth: Interventions, evaluation, and psychopolitical validity. *Journal of Community Psychology, 3*(6), 1–16.

Nelson, G., Ochocka, J., Griffin, K., & Lord, J. (1998). "Nothing about me, without me": Participatory action research with self-help/mutual aid organizations for psychiatric consumer/survivors. *American Journal of Community Psychology, 26,* 881–907.

Nowell, B., Berkowitz, S., Deacon, Z., & Foster-Fishman, P.G. (2006). Revealing the cues within community places: Stories of identity, history, and possibility. *American Journal of Community Psychology, 37*(1/2), 29.

Nyden, P., Figert, A., Shibley, M., & Burrows, D. (1997). University-community collaborative research: Adding chairs to the research table. In P. Nyden, A. Figert, M. Shibley, & D. Burrows (Eds.), *Building community: Social science in action* (pp. 3–13). Thousand Oaks, CA: Pine Forge.

Owen, H. (1999). Open space technology. In P. Holman & T. Devane (Eds.). *The Change Handbook* (pp. 233–243), San Francisco: Berrett-Kohler.

Oyler, M., & Burbidge, J. (1999). Method matters: The Technology of Participation's participatory strategic planning process. In P. Holman & T. Devane (Eds.), *The change handbook* (pp. 59–72). San Francisco: Berrett-Kohler.

Packham, R., & Sriskandarajah, N. (2005). Systemic action research for postgraduate education in agri-cultures and rural development. *Systems Research and Behavioral Science, 22*(2), 119–130.

Plater, W. (1999). Habits of living: Engaging the campus as citizen one scholar at a time. In R. G. Bringle, E. A. Malloy, & R. Games (Eds.), *Colleges and universities as citizens* (pp. 141–172). Needham Heights, MA: Allyn & Bacon.

Rappaport, J. (1981). In praise of paradox: A social policy of empowerment over prevention. *American Journal of Community Psychology, 9*(1), 1–25.

Reason, B., & Bradbury, H. (2001). Introduction: Inquiry and participation in search of a world worthy of human aspiration. In P. Reason and H. Bradbury (Eds.), *Handbook of action research: Participative inquiry and practice* (pp. 324–332). London: Sage.

Rosaen, C. L., Foster-Fishman, P. G., & Fear, F. (2001). The citizen scholar: Joining voices and values in the engagement interface. *Metropolitan Universities, 12*(4), 10–29.

Sackmann, S. A. (1992). Culture and subcultures: An analysis of organization knowledge. *Administrative Science Quarterly, 37*(1), 140–161.

Sagor, R. (2000). *Guiding school improvement with action research.* Alexandria, VA: Association for Supervision and Curriculum Development.

Senge, P. M. (1990). *The fifth discipline.* New York: Doubleday Currency.

Smock, K. (2003). *CCIs: A new generation of urban revitalization strategies.* Retrieved May 20, 2005, from http://comm-org.utoledo.edu/papers97/smockk/cciweb2.htm.

Strack, R.W., Magill, C., & McDonagh, K. (2004). Engaging youth through Photovoice. *Health Promotion Practice, 5*(1), 49–58.

Stringer, E. (2007). *Action research* (3rd ed.). Los Angeles: Sage.

Stringer, E., & Genat, W. J. (2004). *Action research in health.* Upper Saddle River, NJ: Pearson.

Trochim, W. M., Cabrera, D. A., Milstein, B., Gallagher, R. S., & Leischow, S. J. (2006). Practical challenges in systems thinking and modeling in public health. *American Journal of Public Health, 96*(5), 538–546.

Wang, C., & Burris, M. A. (1997). Photovoice: Concept, methodology, and use for participatory needs assessment. *Health Education and Behavior, 24*(3), 369–387.

Wang, C., Burris, M., & Ziang, Y. (1996). Chinese village women as visual anthropologists: A participatory approach to reaching policymakers. *Social Science and Medicine, 42*(10), 1391–1400.

Weisbord, M., & Janoff, S. (1999). Future search: Acting on common ground in organizations and communities. In P. Holman & T. Devane (Eds.), *The change handbook* (pp. 43–58). San Francisco: Berrett-Kohler.

255

Whitmore, E., & McKee, C. (2001). Six street youth who could. … In P. Reason & H. Bradbury (Eds.), *Handbook of action research: Participative inquiry and practice* (pp. 396–402). Thousand Oaks, CA: Sage.

Wilson, N., Dasho, S., Martin, A. C., Wallerstein, N., Wang, C. C., & Minkler, M. (2007). Engaging young adolescents in social action through Photovoice: The Youth Empowerment Strategies (YES!) Project. *Journal of Early Adolescence, 27*(2), 241–261.

Mixed Methods in Collaborative Inquiry

Miles McNall, Diane M. Doberneck, and Laurie Van Egeren

Community-campus partnerships for research provide critical avenues for engaged scholarship. Increasingly in such partnerships, campus faculty and community partners work in a collaborative manner to identify issues of mutual concern or interest, design interventions, assess impacts, disseminate research findings, and decide on appropriate courses of action given the research findings. Moreover, a progressively diverse array of methods has been deployed within these research partnerships in order to gain a better understanding of the issues and concerns under study.

In recent decades, the literature on collaborative approaches to research and mixed methods has grown by leaps and bounds. In this chapter, we begin by discussing what collaborative research (also known as collaborative inquiry) and mixed methods are and how they are related. We argue that the simultaneous growth of mixed methods and collaborative research is anything but coincidental. Rather, we believe that these two areas have co-evolved in response to limits inherent in past approaches to social research and social problem solving. Second, we provide a brief overview of different ways of mixing methods in collaborative research. Finally, we discuss future directions for developing and applying mixed methods in the context of collaborative inquiry.

Collaborative Inquiry

As used in this chapter, collaborative inquiry (CI) is a term that encompasses all forms of participatory research and evaluation. In CI, members of communities, groups, organizations, programs, or other entities that are the focus of or have an interest in the results of particular research or evaluation projects participate in the research endeavor *beyond merely serving as sources of data for university researchers.* CI ranges from projects that involve the participation of a single group of stakeholders (e.g., program managers) in a single stage of a project (e.g., selecting an appropriate research design) to projects that involve multiple stakeholder groups in every stage, from issue identification to the dissemination of results. Although proponents of certain approaches to CI may object to the broad definition used here, we have sought, in defining CI in this way, to be broadly inclusive of the variants of CI while avoiding promoting some approaches over others. Instead, we adopt the stance that, like the selection of methods, the particular CI approach employed in a project should be based not on loyalty to a particular CI approach, but on what is appropriate given the circumstances of the particular project.

Rationale for Collaborative Inquiry

Broadly speaking, the justifications for CI emphasize either pragmatic or emancipatory considerations. Cousins and Whitmore (1998) have identified two major approaches to participatory evaluation. Practical participatory evaluation (P-PE) is geared toward "program, policy, or organizational decision making" (p. 6). P-PE is based on the premise that when stakeholders participate meaningfully in the conduct of an evaluation, they are more likely to perceive it as relevant, feel ownership over the process, and use the results instrumentally. Although stakeholders may well find these experiences empowering, the primary focus of the P-PE approach is utility. Alternatively, transformative participatory evaluation (T-PE) is explicitly aimed at building stakeholder empowerment. T-PE is inspired by the idea that knowledge production should not be the exclusive domain of professional researchers. Rather, people or communities that are the focus of particular research and evaluation projects should participate in the construction, interpretation, and dissemination of knowledge about themselves, their lives, and their communities (Greene, 2006). Furthermore, participation in the co-creation of knowledge with researchers and evaluators holds the promise of increasing stakeholders' consciousness that existing social practices are not natural or necessary, but "the product of one particular set of intentions, conditions and circumstances" and can therefore be transformed through social action (Kemmis & McTaggart, 2000, p. 279).

The distinction between practical and transformative approaches to participatory evaluation is paralleled by similar developments in a collaborative approach to research that has gained increasing prominence in the field of public health: community-based participatory research (CBPR; Minkler & Wallerstein, 2003). CBPR traces its historical development to northern and southern "traditions." Like P-PE, the northern tradition involves collaborative, utilization-focused research with the practical aim of system improvement (Wallerstein & Duran, 2003). The northern tradition "family" includes action research (Greenwood & Levin, 1998; Lewin, 1948; Reason & Bradbury, 2001), action science (Argyris, Putnam, & Smith, 1985), and soft systems methodology (Checkland & Scholes, 1990). Like T-PE, the southern tradition is characterized by "openly emancipatory research, which challenges the colonizing practices of positivist research and political domination by elites" (Wallerstein & Duran, 2003, p. 28). The southern tradition "family" includes the radical pedagogy of Paolo Freire (1970), participatory action research (Kemmis & McTaggart, 2000; McTaggart, 1991; Whyte,

1991), and participatory rural appraisal (Chambers, 1994a, 1994b). In the following discussion, we use CBPR as a case example of why collaborative approaches to inquiry have gained so much interest of late.

Community Based Participatory Research

CBPR has been defined as:

> A collaborative approach to research that equitably involves all partners in the research process and recognizes the unique strengths that each brings. CBPR begins with a research topic of importance to the community and has the aim of combining knowledge with action and achieving social change . . .—Community Health Scholars Program (n.d.)

Over the past decade, CBPR has come into its own. Evidence for this can be found in the publication of Minkler and Wallerstein's (2003) edited volume *Community-Based Participatory Research for Health;* numerous peer-reviewed articles on CBPR in major health journals; the founding in 1997 of the national membership organization, Community-Campus Partnerships for Health (http://www.ccph.info/); and the proliferation of online resources, such as an online CBPR training curriculum (http://www.cbprcurriculum.info/).

CBPR has emerged as a favored route to engaged scholarship for several reasons (The Examining Community-Institutional Partnerships for Prevention Research Group, 2006), including the following:

- Traditional research approaches have failed to resolve complex social problems by ignoring the roles that social, political, and economic systems play in their etiology
- Community members are demanding that research address their locally identified needs
- Researchers increasingly recognize that community involvement can *enhance* the quality of research
- When research is designed and conducted in collaboration with communities, those communities are more likely to use the findings to develop their own solutions to their problems
- Collaborative research promotes trust between researchers and communities

Among the approaches to CI, CBPR has some of the most clearly articulated guiding principles (e.g., Israel et al., 2003). According to these principles, CBPR:

- Recognizes community as a unit of identity
- Builds on strengths and resources within the community
- Facilitates collaborative, equitable partnership in all phases of the research
- Promotes co-learning and capacity building among all partners
- Integrates and achieves a balance between research and action for the mutual benefit of all partners
- Emphasizes local relevance of public health problems and ecological perspectives that recognize and attend to the multiple determinants of health and disease
- Involves systems development through a cyclical and iterative process
- Disseminates findings and knowledge gained to all partners and involves all partners in the dissemination process
- Involves a long-term process and commitment

259

Degree of Participation

One of the key issues that differentiate various approaches to CI is the degree of participation of community members or stakeholders. Some proponents of CI take what might be called a maximalist position. For example, Israel, Schulz, Parker, and Becker (1998) define CBPR as:

> A collaborative approach to research that equitably involves, for example, community members, organizational representatives, and researchers in *all* aspects of the research process [emphasis ours]. (p. 177)

In other words, to qualify as CBPR, research must involve community members in *every* stage of the research process from identifying the problem to disseminating findings.

Cousins and Whitmore (1998) offer a somewhat less restrictive definition of participatory evaluation:

> Participatory evaluation implies that, when doing an evaluation, researchers, facilitators, or professional evaluators collaborate *in some way* with individuals, groups, or communities who have a decided stake in the program, development project, or other entity being evaluated [emphasis ours] (p. 5).

We argue that the maximalist definition offered by Israel, Schulz, Parker, and Becker (1998), although certainly an admirable ideal, may be impractical in certain circumstances. Participation in all aspects of the research process requires regular meetings among partners to consider issues of concern, research questions, designs, methods, data collection, data analysis, data interpretation, reporting, and dissemination. For community members, participation at this level can conflict with employment and/or familial responsibilities, often requiring substantial investments of personal time to the partnership. Unless such burdens are attended to and compensated for adequately, participation may carry substantial costs for community members (Flicker, 2008). In addition, insisting on the full involvement of stakeholders in every aspect of a research/evaluation project may be contrary to their preferences. In some cases, stakeholders, particularly representatives of community-based organizations and agencies, may prefer substantial front-end (e.g., development of questions and methods) and back-end (e.g., interpretation and reporting of findings) participation, but prefer that the researchers carry out the steps in the middle (e.g., data collection and analysis) on their own.

For these reasons, we advocate for an approach to CI that seeks the maximum degree of participation of stakeholders appropriate within the context of a particular project. In some cases, this may involve limited front-end and back-end involvement of a restricted range of stakeholders; in other cases, it may mean full involvement of a wide range of community members in every aspect of the research.

Having reviewed (1) the reasons for the increasing use of collaborative approaches to inquiry in community-campus partnerships for research, (2) the major principles of collaborative inquiry, and (3) degrees of stakeholder participation in collaborative inquiry, we now turn our attention to an approach to research whose rise in popularity has coincided with that of collaborative inquiry: mixed methods research. Then we discuss why the simultaneous emergence of collaborative inquiry and mixed methods research is no mere coincidence.

Mixed Methods Research

Simply put, mixed methods research (MMR) involves collecting and analyzing both quantitative and qualitative data within the same study (Teddlie & Tashakkori, 2003). Although MMR may still be relatively unfamiliar to basic researchers, the number of studies employing mixed methods designs has grown rapidly since the 1980s, especially in the applied social sciences. Since the turn of the millennium, MMR has arrived as a legitimate research design in its own right (Creswell & Plano Clark, 2007), accompanied by the publication of major texts on MMR, including Tashakkori and Teddlie's (2003) encyclopedic *Handbook of Mixed Methods in Social and Behavioral Research*, Creswell and Plano Clark's (2007) *Designing and Conducting Mixed Methods Research*, and Greene's (2007) *Mixed Methods in Social Inquiry*. The explosion of interest in and the increasing legitimacy of MMR raise the questions: Why mixed methods research . . . and why now?

The End of the Paradigm Wars

One reason for the recent surge in interest in MMR is the end of the paradigm wars. From the 1970s through the 1990s, a battle raged over the superiority of the two dominant social science paradigms—post-positivism and constructivism. According to the post-positivist paradigm, an objective reality exists independent of the observer, but is "only imperfectly and probabilistically apprehendable" (Lincoln & Guba, 2000, pp. 165). In contrast, the constructivist paradigm views reality not as unitary but multiplex, local, and constructed. Whereas the aim of post-positivism is prediction and control, the goal of constructivism is the understanding of subjective, lived realities. Although post-positivist research is primarily associated with quantitative methods, in practice it may employ multiple methods, including qualitative methods, for "capturing as much of reality as possible" (Denzin & Lincoln, 2000, p. 9). Constructivism is more exclusively associated with the use of qualitative methods of various kinds in the co-creation of multiple constructed realities. In the view of Tashakkori and Teddlie (1998), the present "post-paradigm-war" period is characterized by a new pragmatism, or "paradigm relativism," in which researchers are freed to employ the philosophical and/or methodological approaches most suited to particular research problems.

Toward a Better Understanding of Complex Phenomena

A second reason for the interest in MMR is that researchers, particularly those conducting applied research in community settings, find that the complexity of the phenomena they encounter demands the use of multiple methods. Greene (2007) explains this connection between applied research and mixed methods:

> I have long surmised that methodological openness to new ideas—qualitative inquiry in the 1970s and mixed methods inquiry more recently—is more characteristic of highly applied domains than domains centered on laboratory research, precisely because the complex and messy demands of inquiry in the real world compel acceptance of multiple strategies and tools for understanding. (p. 32)

The choice of methods, then, is driven less by researchers' allegiance to a particular paradigm or method than by the nature of the phenomena under study. Employing mixed methods reflects a commitment on the part of researchers to seek answers wherever they may be found using whatever methods are likely to ferret them out. As Creswell and Plano Clark (2007) point out, using mixed methods to better understand a complex world takes advantage of the natural tendency of people to draw on multiple sources of information and modes of reasoning to make sense of their worlds:

> Mixed methods research is . . ."practical" because individuals tend to solve problems using both numbers and words, they combine inductive and deductive thinking, and they (e.g., therapists) employ skills in observing people as well as recording behavior. It is natural, then, for individuals to employ mixed methods research as the preferred mode of understanding the world. (p. 10)

Purposes for Mixing Methods

Within the general aim of mixing methods to achieve a better understanding of complex social phenomena, Greene and colleagues (Greene, 2007; Greene & Caracelli, 1997; Greene, Caracelli, & Graham, 1989) have identified five specific purposes for mixing methods. Developed through the systematic analysis of fifty-seven mixed-methods evaluations, these purposes are: triangulation, complementarity, development, initiation, and expansion (Greene et al., 1989).

Triangulation

Mixed methods research conducted for the purpose of triangulation seeks a convergence of findings from different data sources. Because a finding derived from a single method may be an artifact of the particular method used, the use of different methods can help to cancel out the biases inherent in any one method. When the findings from different methods converge on a single result, one can have greater confidence in the accuracy of those results. For example, if a method, such as face-to-face interviewing, has a strong social-desirability bias, one might compare and contrast the findings from interviews with those derived from a method lacking a strong social-desirability bias, such as anonymous, self-administered questionnaires.

Complementarity

When mixing methods for the purpose of complementarity, qualitative and quantitative methods are used to measure overlapping but distinct aspects of a phenomenon to achieve a richer, more complete understanding of the phenomenon. For example, in a study of early marriage among Hmong refugees in St. Paul, Minnesota (Hutchison & McNall, 1994), quantitative survey results indicated that first-generation Hmong refugees were marrying at very early ages. However, data from qualitative interviews clarified that these marriages were traditional Hmong ceremonies and that the resulting marriages had no legal standing. As this example demonstrates, complementary results from different methods can counteract the narrow, misleading, or distorted view of phenomena that may result from the use of a single method.

Development

Mixing methods for the purpose of development involves the sequential use of qualitative and quantitative methods, so the first method used informs the development of the second method. Frequently, when researchers possess insufficient understanding of a phenomenon to develop good quantitative measures, qualitative methods such as focus groups or qualitative interviews are employed as a first step to gain greater familiarity with the phenomenon of interest. For example, responses to open-ended questions in a survey can be subjected to qualitative coding and transformed into response options in later versions of the survey to improve the efficiency of data analysis.

Initiation

Initiation involves the use of mixed methods to discover paradoxes and contradictions, which in turn generate fresh insights into and new perspectives on a phenomenon. Like complementarity, initiation makes use of different methods to explore different aspects of a phenomenon, but with the aim of finding contradictions among the resulting findings. For example, findings from a closed-end survey that allowed participants in a drug-abuse treatment program to select from a predetermined list of reasons why they had elected to attend the program (e.g., quality of program, type of drug being treated) might contradict findings from observations and casual conversations with participants revealing that the predominant reason for attending was that participants found the setting a congenial environment for passing the time.

Expansion

Mixed methods involve expansion when multiple methods are used to extend the scope and range of the study. For example, a study of the impact of school health centers on student health that involved the use of a quantitative health survey could be expanded to focus on the challenges of operating a school health center using qualitative interviews with health center and school staff.

Mixing Methods versus Mixing Paradigms

In addition to mixing *methods* to better understand complex phenomena, there is value in mixing *perspectives and paradigms* within the same study. Bringing researchers who operate from different paradigmatic frameworks to the same table encourages them to collaborate across the sometimes contentious "qualitative/quantitative divide"—and brings multiple worldviews and paradigms to bear on research problems (Creswell & Plano Clark, 2007). Indeed, for Greene (2007) it is the bringing of contrasting ways of understanding the world—"mental models," in her terminology—together in a single research project that represents the true promise of mixed methods research:

> The core meaning of mixing methods in social inquiry is to invite multiple mental models into the same inquiry space for purposes of respectful conversation, dialogue, and learning one from the other, toward a collective generation of better understanding of the phenomenon being studied. (p. 13)

In Greene's (2007) view, such "difference is constitutive and generative" (p. 14). Whereas justifications for mixing methods, such as triangulation, place a high value on the convergence of findings from various data sources around a single conclusion, Greene and colleagues (Caracelli & Greene, 1997; Greene, 2007; Greene & Caracelli, 1997) stress the generative potential of alternative philosophical paradigms operating within the same study.

Mixed Methods and Collaborative Inquiry

What, then, is the relationship between collaborative inquiry and mixed methods? As the definition of CBPR offered earlier states, "CBPR begins with a research topic of importance to the community" (Community Health Scholars Program, n.d.). If community-based research projects begin with community-defined problems rather than researcher-defined issues, then researchers must be prepared to employ whatever methods are appropriate to the research questions that emerge when communities take the lead in defining the issues of interest. As we have argued, mixed method designs frequently emerge from researchers' encounters with the messy complexity of the phenomena they encounter in community settings—and this complexity cannot be adequately captured by the deployment of a single method, such as a quantitative survey. Genuine partnerships between academic researchers and community partners require what Rog (2008) has referred to as *contextually sensitive evaluation practice*. Contextually sensitive evaluation practice matches the methods to the context and the needs of stakeholders. Researchers who are sensitive to contexts and responsive to stakeholder needs will be ready with the appropriate methodological tools no matter where the twists and turns of the partnership lead. Such responsiveness requires that researchers be at least familiar with if not expert in a variety of methodological tools and be able to apply them deftly in addressing whatever research questions emerge.

Having considered the key features of collaborative inquiry and mixed methods research and explored the reasons for their simultaneous emergence within the past three decades as increasingly dominant approaches to applied research, in the following section we provide an overview of the more practical considerations involved in conducting a type of research that blends a collaborative approach to inquiry with the use of mixed-methods designs: collaborative mixed methods research.

Designing Collaborative Mixed Methods Research

Collaborative mixed methods research (CMMR) is similar to "traditional" quantitative or qualitative approaches to research in the attention devoted to rigorous research designs and well-conceived and implemented research procedures. CMMR differs, however, in its special emphasis on collaboration in the development and implementation of the research design and in the mixing of methods. Considerations about each of these areas are presented separately hereafter; nonetheless, in practice, the hallmark of CMMR is the *iterative process* of considering the purpose of the research, research questions, research methods, the collaborative partners, the researchers, and available resources. In other words, the approach to collaborative mixed methods research emerges from what is authentic, meaningful, and appropriate given the specific circumstances of each particular research study. As a result, we offer a series of questions for researchers to consider with their community partners during the design phase of the research, but avoid presenting a straightforward, step-by-step guide to designing CMMR.

Collaboration Considerations

Although the focus of CMMR is very often on research itself, the working relationship between community partners and campus researchers deserves attention, because it forms the basis of the research collaborative. Community-campus collaborations are complex, dynamic relationships that are based on shared interactions and understandings. Baldwin and Austin (1995) concluded that a unique mix of individual attributes and contextual circumstances influenced the dynamics of the collaborative relationship. They identified six dimensions of collaborative community-campus relationships, including degree of jointness, definition of roles and responsibilities, flexibility of roles, similarities of standards and expectations, proximity of partners, and depth of relationships. Each of these dimensions exists along a continuum—allowing for collaborations to take different forms, rely on different agreements, and change dynamically over time. Successful collaborations are not static, but instead are continuously negotiated (Baldwin & Austin, 1995). Based on Baldwin and Austin's findings, community partners and mixed method researchers may want to ask themselves questions such as:

Along a continuum, to what extent do the community partners and researchers view their relationships with one another as:

- From distinctive roles to seamlessly shared responsibilities?
- From explicitly defined roles and responsibilities to no explicitly agreed-upon guidelines?
- From perennial/rigid role assignments to fluid, flexible roles?
- From uniform/identical to different/conflicting similarities in standards and expectations?
- From physically close proximity to too distant for face-to-face interactions?
- From personal as well as professional relationships to solely work-related interactions?

Degrees of collaboration will vary across different stages of the research design and implementation process. For example, as discussed earlier, community partners may be highly involved in identifying significant issues, less involved in gathering and analyzing data, and then highly involved in data interpretation and dissemination. In other situations, especially when cross-cultural differences exist between the community and the researcher, community members may be highly involved in gathering the data to ensure high response rates and data quality. More generally, the depth of participation by community partners and campus researchers may range from mere consultation to deep participation (Cousins & Whitmore, 1998).

Because there is no standard way to approach mixed methods research in community settings, it is imperative for community partners and campus researchers to engage in discussions about expectations, roles, responsibilities, time commitments, and resources. Intentional conversations about a range of possibilities for participation up front (and throughout the research) will go a long way in preventing misunderstandings. We offer these questions to guide conversations about collaborating across stages of the research process:

How involved do community partners and campus researchers want to be in decision making and implementation in the different stages of the research process, including:

- Selecting stakeholders and making decisions about how they should be involved?
- Identifying significant issues?
- Defining the research questions?
- Developing the research design and methodology?
- Gathering data?
- Analyzing data?
- Interpreting data?
- Disseminating the study's findings?

While a high degree of community-campus collaboration is desirable, Cousins and Earl (2005) caution that *greater* involvement, *deeper* levels of participation, and *more* control over the research process by practitioners do not necessarily signify *better* collaboration. For example, if spending time on data collection limits community partners' capacity to spend time interpreting data or disseminating findings, it may be worthwhile to seek additional assistance (Shulha & Wilson, 2003).

In a similar vein, Stanton (2008), summarizing recent deliberations of The Research Universities and Civic Engagement Network (TRUCEN), warned community-engaged campus researchers against valuing high academic impact/high community impact research above other expressions of community-engaged research, such as high academic impact/low community impact and low academic impact/high community impact. The bottom line—from the community and campus perspective, if not from the perspective of advocates of particular CI approaches—is that community-campus collaborators have a wide range of possible ways to work with one another, pursue mutually beneficial research projects, and disseminate collaborative research to academic and community audiences. The optimal CMMR project is the result of candid negotiations between both parties about expected research purpose, process, and products (Stanton, 2008).

When executed well, collaborative inquiry not only strengthens the end results of the research, it also builds the capacity of both community partners and researchers through its process. Evidence has shown that "more in-depth collaborative partnerships—ones that yield insights into both the object of inquiry and the learning processes that give rise to these insights—leave their participants more capable of extending their understandings into new problem contexts" (Shulha & Wilson, 2003, p. 656).

Research Design Considerations

High-quality research relies on thoughtfully constructed research designs and procedures: CMMR is no exception. Like rigorous qualitative and quantitative researchers, mixed methods researchers should purposefully choose designs and procedures that address the goals of the research within the practical constraints of time, expertise, and resources. At the beginning of the shared inquiry, mixed methods researchers and their community partners should consider these questions about research (Greene, 2007; Stanton, 2008):

- What is the purpose of the research? What is the research problem or focus of the inquiry?
- What are the important constructs or variables? How are they defined? Do community partners and researchers differ in how they define important constructs? Can these differences be harnessed to generate new, more nuanced understandings?
- What is/are the most appropriate method(s) to address the problem?
- Do the researchers and community partners have the necessary skills to implement the methods (e.g., quantitative, qualitative, cross-cultural, and language skills)? If not, are resources adequate to expand the team to include the required expertise? Who has the skills and time to manage an expanded research team?
- What is the timeframe for completing the study?
- What funding sources are available to support the research?
- What expectations do audiences have for the types of evidence produced?
- What data do community partners and researchers need to communicate and report research findings to their multiple audiences (Torres, Preskill, & Piontek, 1996)?

Mixing Methods Considerations

Fundamental to mixed methods research is the claim that mixing methods, rather than using a single method, will lead to a better understanding of the phenomena being studied. As Greene (2007) reminds us:

> Methodology is ever the servant of purpose, never the master. And because mixed methods purposes are *about methodology*, it is critical to think about identifying and selecting the reasons for mixing methods (or mixed methods purposes) *in service to* the broader substantive purpose and questions being pursued in the study. [emphasis original] (p. 97)

Different mixed methods purposes—those that lead to "better understandings"—are connected to different paradigms, worldviews, and mental models. Appreciating how these differences affect research designs is beyond the scope of this chapter, but excellent treatments can be found in Creswell and Plano Clark (2007), Greene (2007), and Tashakkori and Teddlie (2003).

   Despite the significant differences in the underlying ontological, epistemological, axiological, rhetorical, and methodological assumptions of different approaches to research, all mixed method research shares common practical considerations related to bringing the qualitative and quantitative data together—namely, timing, weighting, and mixing. At the outset of the study, mixed methods researchers will want to carefully consider how these three aspects of mixing the data will take place in the study.

Timing

Timing refers to the order in which the data are collected and used in the study. *Concurrent timing* means the quantitative and qualitative portions of the research study will take place simultaneously. Researchers will collect, analyze, and interpret the quantitative and qualitative data at approximately the same time. *Sequential timing*, in contrast, means the data will be collected in distinct phases. Researchers may collect, analyze, and interpret the qualitative data first and the quantitative data second. The reverse may be true as well, with quantitative preceding qualitative data collection. Timing is often influenced by weighting and mixing research design decisions as well as available resources.

Weighting

Weighting refers to the relative importance or emphasis given to the quantitative and qualitative data in relation to answering the study's research questions. The data may be weighted equally, with neither the quantitative nor qualitative data being considered more significant. On the other hand, the data may be weighted unequally, with either the quantitative or qualitative data contributing more to the overall study.

Weighting may be influenced by a number of factors. The researcher's worldview, comfort, and expertise may determine whether quantitative or qualitative data are given more priority. The strength of the methodology for addressing the research question may also influence the decision to weight one type of data more than the other. Practical considerations may also influence decisions to give more credence to one type of data over the other. For example, it costs more to weight the data equally, because resources, such as staff time, must be used to conduct both types of data collection at the same time. In addition, costs associated with data collection and analysis may also influence weighting decisions (e.g., qualitative is often more costly than quantitative). Finally, the audience's preference for qualitative or quantitative data may lead to an unequal emphasis on one type of data over another (Creswell & Plano Clark, 2007).

Regardless of whether the weighting is equal or unequal, weighting of the data should be clearly reflected in language used throughout the study and during its dissemination. The title, the purpose, methods, analysis, and interpretation should consistently communicate weighting decisions. For example, wording such as "primary aim" and "secondary aim" or "dominant" and "less dominant" signals to readers unequal weighting in mixing the quantitative and qualitative data (Creswell, 1994; Creswell & Plano Clark, 2007). For example, in a mixed methods study where, following a quantitative survey, a small number of interviews were conducted to help clarify the meaning of the survey findings, the researcher might describe the survey as the primary method of data collection with the interviews providing a secondary source of data.

Mixing

Mixing is the third and most complex procedural decision in mixed methods research. Mixing refers to how the quantitative and qualitative data will be related or connected to each another. Three main approaches to mixing data are merging the data, embedding the data, and connecting the data (Creswell & Plano Clark, 2007).

Merging the data takes place when the researcher intentionally brings the two sets of data together and integrates them. One option is for researchers to analyze the data separately and bring them together in the interpretation phase. Another option is to integrate the two data sets before analysis takes place. In this case, one type of data needs to be transformed into the other type of data to support integration. For example, results from the coding of qualitative data might be transformed into quantitative data and merged with quantitative survey data for analysis.

Embedding data at the design level refers to mixing one type of design within the other type. Mixed methods researchers may choose to embed qualitative data within a largely quantitative design or vice versa. For example, qualitative interviews may be embedded within a study using quantitative surveys. Embedding may take place concurrently or sequentially, depending on the focus of the research design.

Connecting the data takes place when researchers choose to have one set of data lead to another set of data. Mixed methods researchers may collect quantitative data first, connecting its results to the collection of qualitative data. For example, findings from quantitative surveys may be shared in focus groups to clarify the meaning and significance of the results. The opposite is possible as well. Mixed methods researchers may choose to connect findings from qualitative research to subsequent quantitative research activities. For example, focus group data might be used to inform the wording of questions in a quantitative survey. These connections between one type of data and another may be strategically used to influence research at different stages, including research questions, selecting participants, developing the instrument, or expanding analysis.

Data collection and data analysis flow from the mixed methods research design and procedural decisions about timing, weighting, and mixing of the qualitative and quantitative data. Provisions for judging the quality of CMMR should also be made at the study's outset.

Judging the Quality of Collaborative Mixed Methods Research

Selecting standards of quality for collaborative mixed methods research is a challenging issue, with little consensus in the research literature on approaches to assessing quality that honor both qualitative and quantitative methods, recognize the unique findings and interpretations that can result from mixing the two together, and appreciate the role of community partners. Paradigms, worldviews, and mental models strongly influence the concepts, definitions, and languages used to judge the quality of research. Criteria of quality range from the familiar quantitative procedures for establishing internal validity, external validity, reliability, and objectivity, to traditional qualitative procedures for credibility, transferability, dependability, and confirmability (Lincoln & Guba, 1985), to post-structural alternatives, such as ironic, paralogic, rhizomatic, situated, and voluptuous validity (Lather, 1993). Although it is beyond the scope of this chapter to detail all possible approaches to verifying and judging the quality of mixed methods research, we believe there are some commonalities that collaborative mixed methods researchers should consider during the design stages and tend to throughout their study.

According to Greene (2007), if mixed methods research is predominantly guided by one paradigm or tradition, researchers should follow the accepted procedures for establishing and verifying quality. For mixed methods research that incorporates or straddles multiple paradigms, worldviews, mental models, or perspectives, researchers should warrant both the quality of the methods and the quality of the inferences, conclusions, and interpretations. *Design quality* (or the quality of the methods) refers to an evaluation of the methodological rigor of the mixed methods research. *Interpretive rigor* (or the quality of the inferences and conclusions) refers to the standards for the evaluation of the accuracy or authenticity of the conclusions (Teddlie & Tashakkori, 2003).

In addition to design quality and interpretive rigor, collaborative mixed methods researchers are concerned about community partner perspectives in the process of judging the quality of the research. Onwuegbuzie and Johnson (2006) suggest ensuring that both inside (emic) and outside (etic) perspectives are included; accommodating multiple paradigms and worldviews; and adjusting the design in response to the community partner's context.

Whether mixed methods researchers adopt established approaches to assessing quality in CMMR or devise their own approaches, they are obligated to ensure that their scholarship meets standards of excellence, articulate criteria for those standards, involve community partners in the assessment of quality, and communicate how well their research meets the criteria transparently. Ultimately, collaborative mixed methods researchers should be able to articulate how the understanding of the topic of interest that was achieved through the use of collaborative mixed methods research was superior to what would have been attained through the use of other research methods.

Future of Collaborative Mixed Methods Research

We believe that the need for CMMR will continue to grow, as it is "best suited for addressing many of today's complex research questions, which require context and outcomes, meaning and trends, and narrative and numbers" (Creswell & Plano Clark, 2007, p. 184). As the mixed methods research movement continues to gain increasing acceptance and significance in social, behavioral, and health sciences, mixed methods researchers and their collaborative partners will need to address collaborative, methodological, and training issues. Drawing heavily on Cousins and Whitmore (1998), Creswell and Plano Clark (2007), and Greene (2007), in the sections that follow, we highlight some issues that community collaborators and researchers will need to continue to address as the CMMR movement matures.

Collaborative Issues
Questions related to collaboration that CMMR researcher will need to address in every community-campus partnership include:

- Who controls the research process
- How differences in power and influence are managed between campus and community partners and among community partners themselves
- How degrees of jointness, definitions and roles, flexibility, and depth of the collaborative inquiry partnership are negotiated (Baldwin & Austin, 1995)
- How stakeholders or participants are identified, invited into the collaborative inquiry process, and involved in meaningful ways during different stages of the research process

Methodological Issues

Methodological issues that practitioners of CMMR will continue to struggle with include:

- How different paradigms, worldviews, and mental models affect research design decisions in mixed methods research
- Developing strategies for mixing qualitative and quantitative data that go beyond basic comparisons and contrasts of the data to more generative and synergistic understandings of the phenomena under investigation
- Developing criteria to judge the quality of mixed methods research
- How mixed method research designs vary according to discipline, field, community setting, and culture (Creswell & Plano Clark, 2007; Greene, 2007)

Training Issues

In training the next generation of CMMR practitioners, issues that will need to be attended to include:

- How the next generation of researchers will be introduced to mixed methods research, without sacrificing the development of their expertise as qualitative or quantitative researchers
- What the ethical issues specific to CMMR are and how researchers will have opportunities to learn about them
- Effective ways for mixed methods researchers to understand the complex cross-cultural issues related to campus-community research in general and to research that transcends socioeconomic, political, cultural, and identity boundaries
- How mixed methods researchers will learn to contribute to and coordinate complex collaborative research projects and the research teams needed to fulfill the demands for diverse methodological expertise

Finally, community partners and campus-based faculty will need to continue to come to mutually beneficial agreements about collaborations—seeking the optimal blend of collaboration for each research project and partnership. As mixed methods research comes into its own as the third movement in research methods, CMMR advocates will need to continue to communicate its unique value and contribution—including bottom-line benefits to communities and to scholars—in furthering our collective understanding of complex social and behavioral phenomena to funders, community partners, and research colleagues.

References

Argyris, C., Putnam R., & Smith, D. (1985). *Action science: Concepts, methods, and skills for research and intervention.* San Francisco: Jossey-Bass.

Baldwin, R. G., & Austin, A. E. (1995). Toward greater understanding of faculty research collaboration. *Review of Higher Education, 19*(1), 45–70.

Caracelli, V. J., & Greene, J. C. (1997). Crafting mixed-method evaluation design. In J.C. Greene & V.J. Caracelli (Eds.), Advances in mixed-method evaluation: The challenges and benefits of integrating diverse paradigms. *New Directions for Program Evaluation, 74,* 19–32.

Chambers, R. (1994a). The origins and practice of participatory rural appraisal. *World Development, 22*(7), 953–969.

Chambers, R. (1994b). Participatory rural appraisal (PRA): Analysis of experience. *World Development, 22*(9), 1253–1268.

Checkland, P., & Scholes, J. (1990). *Soft systems methodology in action.* New York: Wiley.

Community Health Scholars Program. (n.d.) *Definitions, rationale, and key principles in CBPR.* Retrieved December 2, 2008, from http://depts.washington.edu/ccph/cbpr/u1/u11.php.

Cousins, J. B., & Earl, L. M. (Eds.) (1995). *Participatory evaluation in education: Studies in evaluation use and organizational learning.* London: Falmer.

Cousins, J. B., & Whitmore, E. (1998, Winter). Framing participatory evaluation. *New Directions for Evaluation, 80,* 5–23.

Creswell, J. W. (1994). *Research design: Qualitative and quantitative approaches.* Thousand Oaks, CA: Sage.

Creswell, J. W., & Plano Clark, V. L. (2007). *Designing and conducting mixed methods research.* Thousand Oaks, CA: Sage.

Denzin, N. K., & Lincoln, Y. S. (2000). Introduction: The discipline and practice of qualitative research. In N. K. Denzin & Y. S. Lincoln (Eds.), *Handbook of qualitative research* (pp. 163–188). Thousand Oaks, CA: Sage.

Flicker, S. (2008). Who benefits from community-based participatory research? A case study of the Positive Youth Project. *Health Education and Behavior, 35*(1), 70–86.

Freire, P. (1970). *Pedagogy of the oppressed.* New York: Seabury Press.

Greene, J. C. (2006). Evaluation, democracy, and social change. In I. F. Shaw, J. C. Greene, & M. Mark (Eds.), *Handbook of evaluation: Policies, programs and practices* (pp. 118–140). London: Sage.

Greene, J. C. (2007). *Mixed methods in social inquiry.* San Francisco: Jossey-Bass.

Greene, J. C., & Caracelli, V. J. (1997). Defining and describing the paradigm issue in mixed-method evaluation. In J. C. Greene & V. J. Caracelli (Eds.), Advances in mixed-method evaluation: The challenges and benefits of integrating diverse paradigms. *New Directions for Program Evaluation, 74,* 5–18.

Greene, J. C., Caracelli, V. J., & Graham, W. F. (1989). Toward a conceptual framework for mixed-method evaluation design. *Educational Evaluation and Policy Analysis, 11*(3), 255–274.

Greenwood, D. J., & Levin, M. (1998). *Introduction to action research: Social research for social change.* Thousand Oaks, CA: Sage.

Hutchison, R., & McNall, M. (1994). Early marriage in a Hmong cohort. *Journal of Marriage and the Family, 56,* 579–590.

Israel B. A., Schulz, A. J., Parker, E. A., & Becker, A. B. (1998). Review of community-based research: Assessing partnership approaches to improve public health. *Annual Reviews of Public Health, 19,* 173–202.

Israel, B. A., Schulz, A. J. , Parker, E. A., Becker, A. B., Allen, A., & Guzman, J. R. (2003). Critical issues in developing and following community-based participatory research principles. In M. Minkler & N. Wallerstein (Eds.), *Community-Based Participatory Research for Health* (pp. 56–73). San Francisco: Jossey-Bass.

Kemmis, S., & McTaggart, R. (2000). Participatory action research. In N. K. Denzin & Y. S. Lincoln (Eds.), *Handbook of qualitative research* (pp. 271–330). Thousand Oaks, CA: Sage.

Lather, P. (1993). Fertile obsession: Validity after poststructuralism. *Sociological Quarterly, 34,* 673–693.

Lewin, K. (1948). Action research and minority problems. In G. W. Lewin (Ed.), *Resolving social conflicts.* New York: Harper.

Lincoln, Y. S., & Guba, E. G. (1985). *Naturalistic inquiry.* Beverly Hills, CA: Sage.

Lincoln, Y. S., & Guba, E. G. (2000). Paradigmatic controversies, contradictions, and emerging confluences. In N. K. Denzin & Y. S. Lincoln (Eds.), *Handbook of qualitative research* (pp.163–188). Thousand Oaks, CA: Sage.

McTaggart, R. (1991). Principles of participatory action research. *Adult Education Quarterly, 41*(3), 170.

Minkler, M., & Wallerstein, N. (2003). *Community-based participatory research for health.* San Francisco: Jossey-Bass.

Onwuegbuzie, A. J., & Johnson, R. B. (2006). The validity issues in mixed methods research. *Research in the Schools, 13*(1), 48–63.

Reason, P., & Bradbury, H. (2001). *Handbook of action research.* London: Sage.

Rog, D. (2008). *Fitting design to context: Using a collaborative design sensitivity approach to produce actionable evidence.* Paper presented at the annual meeting of the American Evaluation Association, Denver, CO.

Shulha, L. M., & Wilson, R. J. (2003). Collaborative mixed methods research. In A. Tashakkori & C. Teddlie (Eds.), *Handbook of mixed methods in social and behavioral research* (pp. 639–670). Thousand Oaks, CA: Sage.

Stanton, T. K. (2008). New times demand new scholarship: Opportunities and challenges for civic engagement at research universities. *Education, Citizenship, and Social Justice 3,* 19.

Tashakkori, A., & Teddlie, C. (1998). *Mixed methodology: Combining qualitative and quantitative approaches.* Thousand Oaks, CA: Sage.

Tashakkori, A. & Teddlie, C. (2003). *Handbook of mixed methods in social and behavioral research.* Thousand Oaks, CA: Sage.

Teddlie, C., & Tashakkori, A. (2003). Major issues and controversies in the use of mixed methods in the social and behavioral sciences. In A. Tashakkori & C. Teddlie (Eds.), *Handbook of mixed methods in social and behavioral research* (pp. 3–50). Thousand Oaks, CA: Sage.

The Examining Community-Institutional Partnerships for Prevention Research Group. (2006). *Developing and sustaining community-based participatory research partnerships: A skill-building curriculum.* Available at www.cbprcurriculum.info.

Torres, R. T., Preskill, H. S., & Piontek, M. E. (1996). *Evaluation strategies for communicating and reporting: Enhancing learning in organizations.* Thousand Oaks, CA: Sage.

Wallerstein, N., & Duran, B. (2003). The conceptual, historical and practice roots of community based participatory research and related participatory traditions. In M. Minkler & N. Wallerstein (Eds.), *Community-based participatory research for health* (pp. 27–52). San Francisco: Jossey-Bass.

Whyte, W. F. (1991). *Participatory action research.* Newbury Park, CA: Sage.

From Community-Based Participatory Research to Policy Change

Meredith Minkler and Nicholas Freudenberg

Community-partnered approaches to research have gained currency in many academic disciplines in recent years, both in the United States and internationally. This increased interest has occurred in part in response to growing recognition that the complexity of many of today's health and social problems often make them poorly suited to traditional outside expert-driven research and interventions (Minkler & Wallerstein, 2008). Within the academy, growing interest in community-academic research partnerships also has emerged as part of the movement for a more engaged scholarship.

In this chapter, "community-based participatory research" (CBPR) is used as an umbrella term for a wide variety of approaches to scientific inquiry that have as their centerpiece the three interrelated elements of education and participation, research, and action (Hall, 1992; Minkler & Wallerstein, 2008). Action research (see the chapter by Foster-Fishman and Watson in this volume), participatory action research, mutual inquiry, and feminist participatory research are among the forms of participatory research that fit beneath the broad rubric of CBPR. Although differing somewhat in specific goals and emphases, these approaches tend to share a set of core principles and values consistent with engaged scholarship (Minkler & Wallerstein, 2008). As summarized by Barbara Israel and her colleagues (Israel, Eng, Schulz, & Parker, 2005), among the fundamental characteristics of such research are that it recognizes community as a unit of identity; is participatory and cooperative; involves co-learning, systems development, and local community capacity building; incorporates a co-learning process and an emphasis on empowerment; balances research and action; and emphasizes sustainability and a commitment to engagement over the long haul (pp. 7–9). We add to this list that CBPR embraces "cultural humility" (Tervalon & Garcia, 1998) recognizing that although we cannot be truly competent in another's culture, we can

275

demonstrate an attitude of critical self-reflection, an openness to others' culture, and a commitment to genuine and authentic partnerships. Further, CBPR pays serious attention to issues of research rigor and validity (Minkler & Wallerstein, 2008) but also "broadens the bandwidth of validity" (Bradbury & Reason, 2008) in part by ensuring that the research question comes from, or is important to, the community.

As the foregoing principles suggest, CBPR is defined in part by its belief that action to help foster community and social change is an integral part of the research process, not something done by others after the fact (Cornwall & Jewkes, 1995; Hall, 1992; Minkler & Wallerstein, 2008). Although this action may take many forms, to influence the lives of large numbers of people, action aimed at the policy level often is critical. In this chapter, we consider how the CBPR process can be applied to promote policy change. After briefly describing key terms and conceptual frameworks that can guide policy-oriented CPBR, we demonstrate their application to engaged scholarship, with particular attention to core steps and processes, illustrated by short, "real-world" examples.

We then discuss several key challenges that frequently arise in the course of policy-focused CBPR. These include (1) a tendency among many community and academic partners to shy away from work on the policy level, whether due to beliefs that "you can't fight city hall," or to a mistaken belief that policy making occurs in a domain that is too far removed from the local focus of much community-level work; (2) the deep roots of individualism in American society, translating into pressure to focus on individual level behavioral rather than policy change; (3) fears that universities and/or community-based nonprofits may lose their tax-exempt status or project funding if they engage in policy advocacy; (4) perceived pressures within academe to avoid an advocacy role, lest that weaken the credibility of the science; and (5) the labor- and time-intensive nature of policy work, which is likely to extend well beyond the funded grant period. Finally, the fact that research tends to be a relatively minor player in the constellation of factors impacting on policy may further discourage engaged scholars and their community partners from investing the time and energy necessary for such work.

As this chapter suggests, however, despite these challenges and obstacles, growing numbers of engaged scholars and their CBPR partners have begun working on the policy level, with some impressive results.

Understanding the Policy Making Process

Key Concepts and Models

Nancy Milio (1998, p. 15) has defined public policy as "a guide to government action at any jurisdictional level to alter what would otherwise occur. The intent is to achieve a more acceptable state of affairs and. . . . a more health-promoting society." She goes on to suggest that *organizational policy* typically involves a single agency or type of organization (e.g., the public schools or the health department), whereas *broader policies* tend to operate across multiple organizations and affect large populations. In this chapter, we focus primarily on using CBPR to help effect change in *public* policy. But we also recognize and consider the importance of promoting change in formal or informal private sector policies that can impact well-being (e.g., corporate policies concerning the advertising, pricing, and retail distribution of products such as junk food, tobacco, and firearms). We use the term "policy initiative" in reference to a planned set of activities, with clear goals and objectives, to change informal or formal practices or rules of the organizations and institutions that affect people's lives. By identifying opportunities for promoting or otherwise influencing policy initiatives, as well as existing policies, at the local and higher levels, engaged scholars and their community-based CBPR partners may be able to make new and sustainable contributions.

Many models of policy processes exist with relevance for CBPR (see, for example, Bardach, 2000; Kingdon, 2003; Longest, 2006; Milio, 1998). Such models tend to have in common an emphasis on the various stages of policy development, from initiation through adoption, implementation, evaluation or assessment, and reformulation or repeal (Milio, 1998). They also frequently place a heavy emphasis on the sociopolitical environments in which policy making takes place, recognizing that developing good policy requires a careful examination of the larger context in which the issue is embedded. Finally, models of the policy process typically stress the often circuitous processes involved in policy development. In Milio's words, policy processes "are not linear, and are often punctuated by legal and social challenges, retrenchment or rescissions. They are always embedded in historical and current social contexts. Policy making processes shape content as interested parties attempt to direct the course and pace of policy development to their own needs and priorities" (1998, p. 17).

Before examining conceptual models in more detail, we briefly consider our use of the term "community." Within most of the CBPR literature, community is considered in traditional geographic terms—a place where a defined population lives and shares social and political interactions. However, the term also is used more broadly to include communities of identity, virtual communities, or even networks or coalitions of concerned individuals and organizations that may not be geographically concentrated (Freudenberg, Rogers, Ritas, & Nerney, 2005). Moreover, in practice, policy campaigns often move from neighborhood to municipal to national levels and back, requiring participants to define community in the context of a particular initiative.

Two Conceptual Models of the Policy-Making Process

Among the most influential models for policy development is one developed by political scientist John Kingdon (2003), which posits that in order to get the attention of policy makers, those seeking to bring about change have to address three processes: convincing decision makers that a problem exists; proposing feasible, politically attractive proposals to solve the problem; and negotiating the politics that influence whether a proposal succeeds in the political arena. The first stage, moving a policy issue onto the political agenda, is often the starting point for CBPR projects, and several authors have used Kingdon's model to analyze opportunities for agenda setting on issues such as gun control, food security, and tobacco control (cf. Blackman, 2005; Vásquez et al., 2007; Wallack, Winnett, & Lee, 2005).

Kingdon also notes the importance of a "policy window" that opens when favorable developments occur in at least two of the three processes (problems, proposals, and politics).

Identifying opening policy windows and being able to jump through them are important skills for policy advocates. Thus, monitoring developments in all three processes is an important task for CBPR policy researchers. As new opportunities arise, CBPR participants can be ready to move in any of the three arenas.

A second model of the policy process builds on Kingdon's work and is described by health policy researcher Beauford B. Longest, Jr. (2006). Longest describes the policy process as highly political, reflecting a mix of influences on both public and individual interests and rarely proceeding on the basis of rational or empirical decision making. Core components of his model suggest that it is also

"distinctly cyclical," with a circular flow of interactions and influences between the various stages, and that it involves an open system in which "the process interacts with and is affected by events and circumstances in its external environment" and includes several distinct and interconnected phases:

- *Policy formulation,* encompassing activities involved in setting the policy agenda and later in the actual development of legislation
- *Policy implementation,* involving all those activities connected with rule making to guide the actual implementing and operationalizing of a policy
- *Policy modification,* including the revisiting and possible alteration of all previous decisions and compromises made during the policymaking process

As Longest's model suggests, the formal enactment of legislation serves as a bridge between the policy formulation process and the subsequent implementation phase. The policy modification phase then comes into play as a feedback loop through which minor tweaking of the legislation or a major revisiting of the agenda-setting process may take place. Both the political nature of policy making and the dynamic nature of the external environment in which policy making occurs underscore the likelihood of policy modification—and in extreme cases, even repeal—during this phase of the process.

Key Steps or Phases in the Policy-Making Process with Relevance to CBPR

We turn now to each of the general areas identified in the frameworks just presented, highlighting their relevance for engaged scholars and their CBPR partners.

Defining the Problem and Framing a Policy Goal

The general policy goal for a CBPR project flows, by definition, from the community's identification of the problem and outcomes of the dialogical processes in which it has engaged in order to better explore this issue or problem. As always, reconciling different perspectives on the problem within various community constituencies is an essential task and often a formidable challenge. Although the community's perception of a problem is one major influence on planned action, a wide range of additional factors influence policy outcomes. Ensuring that these other contextual factors are considered in formulating a policy goal is a vital step for engaged scholars as they work with their community partners in setting goals.

Another major influence on defining the problem is the perspective of the engaged scholars themselves. In the dialogical process described by the Brazilian educator and social activist Paulo Freire (1970), whose work provides an intellectual foundation for CBPR (Wallerstein & Bernstein, 1988), the educator/activist/organizer engages in an ongoing and iterative dialogue with community residents in which each partner's perspectives informs defining the problem and devising solutions. By acknowledging their active role, engaged scholars can bring their critical perspectives to the table while still inviting equal participation from others.

A good policy goal requires framing the issue in a way that leads to effective or doable action. Framing the problem in ways that will attract a wide and diverse constituency whose members care enough about the issue to become actively involved is critical at this stage.

Further, because CBPR, like other forms of engaged scholarship, is always concerned about both process and outcome, the chosen policy goals and activities should help a community or community-based organization or coalition to achieve such goals as:

- Building community and organizational capacity by expanding the leadership base and creating more involved community members
- Solving real problems, ideally through policy results that can be concisely stated in twenty-five words or less
- Contributing to a sense of community, bringing more people together and giving them a sense of their own power and leadership
- Laying the foundation for later policy, serving as an incremental step on the path toward the community partners' larger goals and placing this specific policy goal within a longer-term community strategic action plan
- Linking the policy goal to a broad ethical and moral framework that unites key constituencies and motivates action
- Bringing the community closer to its vision of a healthy community and a better world.

Finally, and particularly in this era of budget cuts and economic recession, another important consideration often is whether or not a proposed new policy will save money or, at minimum, pay for itself. CBPR efforts to reduce the plethora of alcohol and tobacco outlets in low-income communities of color might thus craft a policy goal of establishing local permit fees for the selling of these products or conditional use permits for such environmental land uses as billboards (Themba, 1999).

Selecting a Policy Approach

Once a policy goal has been selected, engaged scholars and their community partners must "do their homework" in order to determine who has the power to make the change, whether that be an elected official, a planning commission, or a business. As noted earlier, although the focus of this chapter is primarily on efforts to influence local public policy (e.g., through initiatives and ordinances), efforts to bring about policy changes at higher levels or in relevant private-sector arenas should also be considered, especially in partnership with other CBPR or advocacy groups in other jurisdictions. Next, we offer a range of possible policy-related strategies with which engaged scholars should be familiar.

Mandated Studies (or Memorials)

Although CBPR can uncover valuable information about an unhealthy or unlawful institutional practice, far more extensive study may be necessary to provide the hard data needed to support a policy change. In such instances, engaged scholars and their CBPR partners may identify a policy goal of getting a mandated study or other data collection performed (or protecting what is currently being collected, such as data on racial/ethnic disparities in public school performance). When a Los Angeles coalition's preliminary investigation led it to fight for and get a mandated city study on wage levels, the resulting information was so disconcerting that it laid an important basis for subsequent work toward a living-wage law (Themba, 1999). Similarly, in New Mexico's Youth Link project, a statewide coalition of youth, with help from their academic partner, succeeded in getting a memorial on school suspensions and expulsions and their impact on school dropout rates (Wallerstein, 2002).

Moratoriums

A moratorium, a temporary halt on a potentially problematic practice, or on policy enactment until more data are available, also can be a useful policy strategy. For example, during the conflicts about the local and state laws that would dictate the process for locating polluting facilities, environmental justice activists in West Harlem called for a moratorium on siting new facilities in their neighborhood, both as a way to protect their community and to set a precedent that could guide future action (Shepard, Brechwich Vásquez, & Minkler, 2008). The "breathing time" allowed by a moratorium also can enable engaged scholars and their community partners to help organize neighborhood hearings or town hall meetings and forums with legislators in attendance. Particularly if they are well publicized and offer a blend of the statistics and stories needed to help influence pubic opinion, such venues can in turn play an important role in helping get support for a policy change (Wallack, Woodruff, Dorfman, & Diaz, 1999).

Voluntary Agreements

Voluntary agreements have been defined as "pacts between a community and one or more institutions that outline conditions, expectations, or obligations without the force of law" (Themba, 1999, p. 91). Such agreements may prove useful when there isn't enough support to enact more formal regulations. In some cases, a voluntary agreement can be an interim step toward more meaningful changes in policy, either because the voluntary agreements do not succeed in solving the problem or because some large organizations prefer public policy change to negotiating many agreements with many communities. Ideally, campaigners should develop written memorandums of understanding (MoUs) that clearly spell out the conditions of the agreement and define steps that can be taken to ensure that the terms of the agreement are being honored.

In the Bayview Hunters Point community in San Francisco, California, a CBPR partnership, working closely with a local city supervisor, helped develop a voluntary policy known as the "Good Neighbor Program." Designed to persuade small local grocery stores to stock healthier foods and reduce their alcohol and cigarette advertising, the voluntary program offered free store advertising and economic and other incentives such as low-cost loans and energy-efficient appliances to participating stores, with stakeholders signing formal MoUs outlining conditions of participation. Four stores have become good neighbors and another five are slated to join the program, improving nutritional choices for local residents. The partnership also contributed to a successful effort to pass, albeit without funding, a state assembly bill supporting a demonstration program taking the Good Neighbor Program to scale through a statewide demonstration program (Shepard et al., 2008). In the wake of the recessions an amendment to allow private funding is under consideration.

Electoral Strategies

Electoral Strategies tend to be extremely time-consuming and labor-intensive. Yet, such approaches, including ballot initiatives, referendums, or even support of candidates can have considerable benefits over the longer term. As Steckler and Dawson (1982, p. 289) suggest, "States which offer the possibility of a referendum or initiative enable citizens themselves to become policy makers." The passage by many municipalities of initiatives banning the sale of assault weapons or of ordinances establishing a living wage are examples of the power of such approaches. In some cases, activists unite to defeat referenda that threaten health or social justice. In South Dakota, for example, reproductive rights groups twice defeated state referenda to severely restrict access to abortion services, thus maintaining this service for women in the state and setting an important national precedent (McDonagh, 2006). Electoral campaigns also can have important short-term advantages: they can help raise the profile of an issue; attract volunteers; and pull an issue out of the purview of non-supportive policy makers and place it directly before a more supportive public. Whether helping to craft an initiative or becoming involved in an effort to react to an existing policy through a referendum, CBPR partners can facilitate bringing an issue to public attention.

Legal Actions

Legal actions such as lawsuits and other court actions can also be expensive and time consuming. They can prove risky; failure to identify the right defendants (e.g., the parent company of a major local polluter) can lead to embarrassing and demoralizing defeats. Yet, when carefully researched and well framed, such actions can accomplish significant long- and short-term goals, even if this simply means getting the other party to the table. Short of bringing a lawsuit, moreover, simply filing complaints about bad or illegal practices with the appropriate regulatory agency can be an effective policy approach. In recent years, community and advocacy groups have used legal action against the food, pharmaceutical, and tobacco industries (Freudenberg, 2005; Jacobson & Soliman, 2002) and against local government. In New York City, CBPR community partner West Harlem Environmental Action (WE ACT) and its colleagues joined in the filing of a legal complaint under the Civil Rights Act as one of many strategies used to put pressure on a public agency to act to reduce air pollution from diesel buses. Although the partners were well aware that they were unlikely to win a legal victory, the added visibility and pressure provided by the filing itself proved an important step forward (Shepard et al., 2008). On a more modest scale, engaged scholars can provide expert testimony in court cases brought by others, and community-based organizations can file amicus or "friend of the court" briefs or use cases as educational tools.

In sum, each of the foregoing policy-related approaches—voluntary agreements, mandated studies and moratoriums, electoral strategies, and legal actions—has both advantages and disadvantages that must be carefully weighed by engaged scholars and their partners in collectively selecting the approach—or combination of approaches—with the best chances of success.

Key Considerations and Advocacy Steps for Engaged Scholars and their Partners in Policy-Focused CBPR

Despite their often substantial differences, successful engagement in any of the forms of policy action just described requires careful attention to a set of core considerations and steps in the policy process. Key among these are the following.

Choosing a Good Target

Decisions made by engaged scholars and their community partners about the particular policy approach best suited to a given CBPR effort should be driven in part by a careful analysis of the change target or decision-making body with the power to bring about the changes sought. Themba (1999) identifies several key questions may be helpful in this process.

- Who or what institutions have the power to solve or ameliorate the problem and grant the community's demands?
- What targets offer the most promising avenues for community mobilization?
- Are there key actors who must be approached first as gatekeepers to the people with real power?
- What would motivate key actors to take the actions you want to see (e.g., would a politician who is up for reelection be aided by your cause)?
- Which targets are appointed? Which are elected?
- Are there relevant bodies (such as commissions or subcommittees) that are open to community participation and that one or more of your members might join?
- What are the most strategic sources of power for influencing the targets (e.g., voters, consumers, faith-based organizations, taxpayers, investors, neighborhood organizations)?
- What are the target's self-interests where this issue is concerned?
- Who would have jurisdiction if you redefined the issue (e.g., if you turned a tobacco advertising issue into a question of fair business practices)? Would this increase your likelihood of success?

To help address these and related issues, strategic analysis should be conducted to narrow down potential targets and research each target's self-interests, strengths, and weak points. Such background research may reveal, for example, the existence of a more vulnerable "primary" target with whom the possibility of success is greater than the more obvious target originally considered. In working to fight billboard advertising of alcohol and tobacco, for example, community partners and engaged scholars have found it more effective to target local and in some cases state governments to restrict the placement and content of ads than to pressure the billboard industry itself to give up a sizable portion of its revenue from such advertisements (Themba, 1999). In other cases, however, additional, "secondary targets" may be needed to effect the desired change.

In addition, engaged scholars and their CBPR partners need to consider the relative importance of short-term wins versus consciousness-raising and longer-term political mobilization. Not infrequently, groups need to choose between more achievable but superficial victories and more time-consuming changes in power relationships. Keeping track of a partnership's activities and campaigns, in order to have a record of these different strategic decisions and outcomes, may be helpful over the long term in helping to balance shorter- versus longer-term objectives and outcomes in mapping further collaborative work.

Identifying Potential Allies and Opponents

An important strategy in CBPR aimed at policy-level change involves building a coalition or group of organizations that come together temporarily for a specific reason (Berkowitz & Wolff, 2000; Wandersman, Goodman, & Butterfoss, 2005). Creating a strong coalition can indicate the breadth of concern about an issue, as well as showing the general public, policy makers, and the mass media "that there is a serious problem that must be addressed, and a consensus about what needs to be done" (www.policylink.org/advocatingforchange/ adminpetitions/launch.html). Coalitions oriented at policy change can work at diverse juris- dictional levels, depending on which level of government or private policy-making group has decision-making authority for the changes being sought (Sofaer, 2001). Before deciding whether and how to put a coalition together, engaged scholars and their CBPR partners should consider the kinds of support needed to achieve their policy goal, which groups are most likely to be supportive, and which can influence the target or decision maker. At this stage in the process, community members of the CBPR team can be particularly helpful, sharing their knowledge of key community players and the potential interests of each. Both informal groups (e.g., parents of children with developmental disabilities) and formal com- munity organizations should be considered as potential allies. The self-interests and com- mitments of each potential member, as well as both the resources and the possible risks and liabilities their involvement might entail, need to be considered in building a base of support for the proposed policy action.

Assessing the Power Bases of Potential Opponents

Concurrently with assessing and building their own power base, engaged scholars and their CBPR partners should think strategically about the interests and potential power base of their likely opponents (Ritas, 2003; Ritas, Minkler, Halpin, & Ni, 2008). Community interests in improved air quality and the like may thus translate into policy initiatives whose imple- mentation would hurt a powerful industry or a local employer's bottom line. Because these likely opponents may also have powerful lobbies or make substantial contributions to the campaigns of elected decision makers, the importance of their opposition should not be minimized. Engaged scholars and their partners need to consider such matters as whose interests may be negatively affected by a policy initiative and how, as well as whether, the

283

proposed initiative will cost money or raise fees or taxes. At this stage, too, getting to a policy win requires the CBPR partnership to "do its homework" in order to understand in detail who pays for a proposed policy. Only then can the engaged scholar and his or her community partners be positioned to justify the proposed policy change to the appropriate decision makers.

Opportunities for Engaged Scholar and CBPR Involvement in Developing and Implementing Policy Change

At each stage of the policy process, there are unique opportunities for engaged scholars and their community and other CBPR partners. Here, we use the stages developed by Makani Themba (1999) as a guide for engagement at these diverse stages.

Assessing the Policy Environment and Testing the Waters

A host of contextual factors, including current socioeconomic, demographic, and political realities, and past experience with similar issues (Milio, 1998), are likely to influence how a proposed policy change is likely to be received and its chances for success. Monitoring the policy environment must therefore begin as a key component of the data gathering that will help shape what a potential policy initiative might look like. While assessing the environment, engaged scholars and other CBPR partners may test a number of potential approaches, considering such criteria as likely community support, legality, and the chances of success. One useful tactic may be to inventory other groups that are in motion on the issue, thus assessing the potential for creating a more powerful coalition and identifying possible partners.

Reframing the Issue and Defining the Initiative

Helping community partners refine the issue they have identified so that it can become a well-crafted policy initiative is a critical step in the policy advocacy process. For engaged scholars, the best policy initiatives often come from having community partners articulate their ideal policy and then looking collectively for the best mechanism to help transform that vision into reality.

Ensuring that the policy initiative is crafted in a way that reflects the community's interests and those of other potential allies, as well as showing sensitivity to broader environmental issues, may well require some reframing of the issue at this point (Milio, 1998). A CBPR project focused on preventing youth violence, for example, and targeting a local city council with the goal of limiting handgun availability and increasing youth employment opportunities, may reframe its initial initiative to emphasize the social and economic aspects of youth violence (Wallack et al., 1999). By identifying those parts of the issue likely to be of the most concern to city council members and reframing the issue to reflect these concerns, engaged scholars and their CBPR partners may substantially increase their chances for success.

Thinking nationally and internationally, rather than simply locally, may also be an important part of the reframing process. Engaged scholars and their CBPR partners attempting to mobilize against the tobacco industry, for example, have sometimes studied and publicized its increased targeting of people of color in Third World countries and Eastern European nations. Revealing such practices overseas may have value at home in delegitimizing the image of multinational parent companies that allow or encourage such practices. It can also serve as a starting point for global alliances that can better contest the power of these multinational companies. Similarly, environmental groups often have researched the practices of companies seeking to build a new plant in order to assess their record on environmental issues in other states or countries. Information that is uncovered about questionable or outright unethical practices can be a potent part of legal or educational campaigns.

Strategic Power Analysis

Once an initiative has been identified, conducting a strategic "power analysis" can enable engaged scholars and their CBPR partners to identify the targets, allies, opponents, and other factors that will be important in the campaign. A variety of power mapping exercises and online resources are available to help partners identify potential targets, allies, and opponents, their relative strength, and ways of weakening opposing forces while building their own power base (cf. PolicyLink, 2005; Ritas et al., 2008). Not infrequently, further refining of the initiative will take place as a result of the new information identified through the strategic analysis.

In their campaign to shut down "Brand X" cigarettes, which were being heavily marketed in African American communities, activists first tried to convince the cigarette's creator—a small, family-operated business in predominantly white Charlestown, Massachusetts, near Boston—to discontinue the brand on health grounds. When this failed, they conducted a strategic and power analysis, which revealed that concerted media pressure would likely force the small company to discontinue the brand. Acting on this knowledge, the activists orchestrated a barrage of media coverage, protests, and bad publicity. Just two weeks later, the company, unable to withstand the onslaught, decided to drop the brand altogether. Had the group not had the benefit of this strategic and power analysis to suggest a media and public relations strategy, they may well have failed to achieve this level of success (Themba, 1996).

Although the X Brand action was a clear success story, strategic analysis and related processes can also be helpful when victory may be less likely or incomplete. As Rochefort and Cobb (1993) suggest, the feasibility analysis conducted during this stage of the policy process may well suggest possible compromise positions, which can in turn be explored in advance but held in reserve as backup positions to be used if a compromise appears necessary.

Organizing Support for the Initiative

Informed by the power analysis and strategic planning, organizing for the proposed policy change begins. A variety of strategies may be useful to engaged scholars and their partners at this stage, including town hall meetings, door-to-door canvassing, outreach to additional organizational partners, and media advocacy. Described as the strategic use of mass media by community groups to tell their story and advocate for a relevant community or policy objective (Wallack et al., 1999), media advocacy has increasingly been used by local community groups and CBPR partners to deliver their message and create pressure for change (Dorfman, Wallack, & Woodruff, 2005).

For better or worse, the media are central to setting the public agenda, with news media playing a particularly important role as the public's "official story." Media advocacy is critical to policy advocacy. Important political debates are carried out in fifteen-second sound bites, and a single news story can be the catalyst for new legislation. It is now nearly axiomatic that what story is chosen for coverage and how it is covered largely determines public sentiment—especially among public officials.

In light of the importance of the media's agenda-setting and legitimizing functions, data and research play critical roles in establishing the credibility of community policy initiatives with policy makers and the public at large. CBPR findings have been particularly important to efforts that were unpopular or focused on communities with few resources. For example, when the Community Coalition in South Los Angeles conducted a survey of local youth, the top concern that emerged was the deplorable condition of their schools. Working closely with an engaged scholar at Loyola Marymount University, the coalition and its youth group undertook a modified Photovoice project and additional documentation of hundreds of examples of faulty wiring, leaky roofs, nonfunctional sinks, and in one case, just one working toilet for a high school with three thousand youth. These findings were particularly ironic— and painful—given the recent passage of a $2.4 billion school bond measure, the vast majority of whose funds were allocated for air conditioning, a new stadium, and other improvements in the wealthier San Fernando Valley schools, with the small amount for South LA schools largely earmarked for security guards and window bars. The CBPR partners arranged a "walkaround" in several of the local schools for a prominent columnist for the *Los Angeles Times*, whose scathing piece on this subject, together with the youth's powerful display of more than two hundred pictures at a school board Oversight Committee meeting, helped get a reallocation of $100 million from the bond measure, plus $53 million in additional city funds, for more than 1,800 repairs and other improvements in the South LA schools (Minkler et al., 2008; Saurwein & Haynes, 1999).

In the Belly of the Beast

Once a policy initiative is on the table and political support appears strong, engaged scholars and their CBPR partners need to work with decision makers to ensure that the policy is actually enacted. Often further research and expertise are needed. It is at this stage that CBPR partnerships are at greatest risk, as decision makers will often look to traditional researchers and other "experts" for input and sometimes act to exclude or co-opt community-based groups that they perceive are less "professional." Many movements have been hurt by these classic "divide and conquer" tactics.

To confront this and related potential problems before they arise, many engaged scholars and their community partners have developed MoU and used protocols for CBPR that can help partners foster more effective community-researcher communication and assess their progress (Brown & Vega, 1996; Mercer et al., 2008).

Victory and Defense

Although CBPR partners have contributed to a number of impressive policy victories (Minkler, 2010; Minkler et al., 2008; Morello-Frosch, Pastor, Sadd, Porras, & Prichard, 2005), achieving a policy goal often means that a corporate or other court challenge may soon follow (Themba, 1999). In their roles as advocates, engaged scholars and their community partners must prepare for the possibility of litigation at the beginning of the initiative and be ready to play an active role in any legal action even if the local government (and not their own group) is the defendant. CBPR partners have played an important role in this stage of the policy process by working with communities to craft public testimony with an eye toward building a strong public record as a defense against any future litigation. For example, Baltimore's Citywide Liquor Coalition made sure that its attorney worked closely with the city attorney throughout an initiative process. Their objective was to carefully craft testimony that would be part of a strong public record in preparation for the litigation that would follow passage of the policy they were supporting (Themba, 1999). In sum, and although celebrating a victory is always in order, preparing for challenges to a controversial new policy is also a critical part of the action in which CBPR partners may usefully engage.

Enforcement and Evaluation

Once a policy has been enacted and has withstood legal challenges, a new and equally important stage of the work begins in ensuring that that the new law or rule is in fact enforced. For initiatives with powerful opposition, negotiation continues around issues such as the timeline for implementing the policy, interpretation of particular clauses, and fitting the new policy in with other staffing priorities. Engaged scholars and community-based groups working together have helped agencies identify existing enforcement models and propose new enforcement procedures that meet community needs. In addition, research partners have helped community groups design processes for evaluating new policies with an eye toward strengthening these policies and their enforcement. One example of such a partnership was the work of South Carolina Fair Share with University of South Carolina researchers on enforcement and effectiveness of new child health insurance policies. Research partners were able to develop a participatory evaluation process that provided accessible information on how well the program was working and why. Armed with good data, community groups could take an active part in the implementation process in an informed, ongoing way (Themba, Delgado, Vribe, & Calpotura, 2000).

From Local to National and Global and Back Again

As noted previously, engaged scholars and their policy-focused CBPR partners have tended to concentrate on the local or regional level—a focus consistent with the often community-based nature of their work. Yet, we are also witnessing the emergence of networks to create opportunities for national and global alliances using CBPR. The first Environmental Justice (EJ) Summit in 1989, which included community activists, engaged scholars, and other stakeholders from around the nation, thus helped organize a national EJ movement, which has subsequently brought new attention to race- and class-based inequities in exposures to environmental hazards, and pressed for national and international policy-level change. (Bullard, n.d.). Similarly, the World Social Forum (n.d.) has brought together diverse stakeholders from around the world to discuss strategies and analyze opportunities to weave together local struggles into a more powerful force. Such national and global networks may offer engaged scholars and their CBPR partners on the local level powerful new allies in the years ahead.

Barriers and Challenges in Policy-Focused CBPR for Engaged Scholars and Their Community Partners in the Decade Ahead

Early in this chapter we identified six critical issues that have challenged engaged scholars and their CBPR partners who have attempted to work on the policy level. Although each of these challenges remains a source of concern as we enter a new decade, some promising strategies and developments have emerged to help address them and are discussed now as we revisit each.

You Can't Fight City Hall

Community partners may see policy-level work as off limits or of little relevance to addressing the more immediate issues of concern in their neighborhoods. Coupled with beliefs that "you can't fight city hall" or powerful corporate interests, these perceptions can be a powerful disincentive for pursuing policy-level change. For engaged scholars, such attitudes can pose a dilemma. On the one hand, they may see that policy advocacy holds real promise for achieving the very change the community has hoped to bring about—and doing so in a broader, more sustainable way. On the other hand, a genuine commitment to community ownership and control suggests that the community's desire, not the scholars', should set the agenda. For example, in a Photovoice project using CBPR approaches, Caroline Wang and her colleagues (Wang, Cash, & Powers, 2000) accepted the decision of their homeless community member partners to focus on individual-level wins rather than broader policy-focused objectives.

In other instances, engaged scholars, sometimes with the help of "policy mentors," have worked to help demystify policy for their community partners. As Citrin (2000, p. 84) notes, "community residents do, in fact, engage in activities to address 'policy issues,'" even though they seldom use this terminology and tend to see policy as an abstract concept. Helping them see the connections between the work they already do (e.g., identifying change objectives and targets, looking for opportunity windows, and working with the mass media) and more formal policy-level work may be an important way to begin. Similarly, a range of user-friendly resources and exercises for learning to be a policy advocate (cf. *Advocating for Change*, PolicyLink, 2005; Ritas, 2003; Ritas et al., 2008) may help engaged scholars increase their own on their community partners' interest in and comfort level with working to effect policy change.

Overcoming the American Creed of Individualism

Given the deep roots of individualism in American culture and a determined corporate effort to promote this value, CBPR participants, like other activists and reformers, often have to confront pressures to focus their efforts on studying and changing individuals rather than changing policies. For example, many neighborhood organizations have wanted to confront growing rates of obesity and its adverse health consequences but have often ended up seeking to convince individuals to eat better or move more, rather than challenging the right of the food industry to promote unhealthy food. Engaged scholars may be able to play a useful role by helping community partners critically analyze the creed of individualism and its political roots and to find new ways to balance individual, government, and corporate responsibilities.

But We Could Lose Our Funding! (Or Tax-Exempt Status)

Another barrier to policy-focused work involves the fact that many academic partners and/or their community partners who are based in nonprofit organizations believe that they may not legally engage in policy advocacy without risking the loss of their funding or their tax-exempt status. In Tillery, North Carolina, a CBPR partnership has been a key player in studying and addressing environmental injustice in the location of industrialized hog operations. Their testimony and their effective media advocacy contributed to such victories as a recent moratorium on new hog operations in the state. Yet, when asked to talk about the partnership's role in influencing policy, a leading community partner replied, "We don't do policy—we just educate legislators!" Citing the fact that their research had NIH funding, this partner added that he couldn't work on the policy level without putting their funding in jeopardy (Tajik & Minkler, 2007). In reality, both university-based partners and community-based nonprofits tend to have far more "wiggle room" to advocate for policy change than they tend to believe. Finding out about what is allowed and not allowed, and clarifying with funders the extent to which policy level work is permissible under your particular funder's guidelines, may go a long way to dispelling this often exaggerated fear about advocating for policy change in conjunction with a CBPR project.

Does Policy Advocacy Weaken the Credibility of the Science?

The renewed emphasis on engaged scholarship arose in part from concerns that in their quest to focus solely on the discovery of new knowledge, universities were sometimes losing touch with the real world, and with the need to translate and apply that new knowledge to help address real-world problems (Boyer, 1996). Yet, particularly in science-based disciplines such as medicine and public health, many academics still believe that when the scientist becomes an advocate, particularly on the policy level, the credibility of his or her work goes out the window. The editorial policies of some "top tier" peer-review journals reinforce this view by discouraging authors from discussing much less advocating for policy recommendations in their original research articles. For example, the instructions to authors of the highly ranked journal *Epidemiology* state: "Opinions or recommendations about public health policy should be reserved for editorials, letters, or commentary, not presented as the conclusions of scientific research" (http://edmgr.ovid.com/epid/accounts/ifauth.htm). Such policies may cause a scholar to rethink the wisdom of an approach that emphasizes policy action as part of the research process itself.

Is It Worth the Time—or the Effort?

With its commitment to engagement over the long haul in order to help achieve sustainable change (Israel et al., 2005), CBPR may extend well beyond the funded grant period. For academics under pressure to bring in new grant funding and turn out papers, and for community partners for whom time and money are typically in short supply, the labor- and time-intensive nature of CBPR, particularly when it is focused on policy change, may pose a major barrier. Conflicting timetables, as when the community partner wishes to use the study findings in policy advocacy well in advance of their publication in academic journals, also may be a source of considerable tension (Minkler, 2004). To help deal with such issues before they arise and to continue to engage with them over time, several useful tools are available. Mercer and her colleagues' (2008) "Reliability-tested guidelines for assessing participatory research projects" include Likert-scale type items that can help partnerships evaluate the extent to which they are effectively addressing these and other barriers to participation. Similarly, guidelines for use by ethical review boards in assessing CBPR proposals were developed by Flicker and her colleagues (Flicker, Travers, Guta, McDonald, & Meagher, 2007) and also provide a useful tool for partnership members in dialoguing about such factors as time constraints and differential reward structures.

Does It Really Make a Difference?

Finally, as Rist (1994) has argued, although research may influence policy, it typically is only one of many often competing and contradictory forces that influence the final outcomes—and tends to be a relatively minor player within this broader context. This fact, combined with the difficulty of teasing apart the contributions of a CBPR partnership's work to a given policy outcome, may discourage some CBPR partnerships from even attempting policy level change. In an effort to help overcome such barriers, both the Kellogg Foundation (Minkler, 2010; Minkler et al., 2008) and The California Endowment (TCE) recently have funded efforts to document the impacts of CBPR on healthy public policy, where "health" is defined broadly to encompass a wide range of areas including education and the built environment. A TCE-funded report by Guthrie, Louise, and Foster (2006) entitled "The Challenge of Assessing Policy and Advocacy Activities" also has made an important contribution in helping advocates and grassroots organizations develop a theory of change or "road map" for moving from activities to policy outcomes, including establishing benchmarks and indicators, and creating evaluation designs "that have the capacity to adapt to changes in the policy environment" (p. 9).

Conclusion

For engaged scholars and their community partners, CBPR can be an important tool in efforts to move from data gathering and interpretation to the use of findings in ways that can help influence the lives of large numbers of people. Policy-focused CBPR can identify, make visible, and legitimize issues so that they in turn are placed on the public's agenda. It can also help partnership members bring the attention of the mass media to long-ignored issues—or newly uncovered problems—based on findings that are both newsworthy and grounded in strong science. Indeed, as Ansley and Gaventa (1997) pointed out more than a decade ago, the best initiatives use research as a way of documenting and elucidating problems that are already of concern to communities, in ways that help build confidence in community-based knowledge and ways of knowing.

CBPR can help democratize information through the active involvement of communities in data gathering and by providing community partners equal access to the kinds of data that help drive policy making. It can help these community groups influence the policy process in ways that can benefit the communities of which these groups are a part.

As noted earlier, CBPR partnerships are, of course, only one influence on policy, and often a relatively minor one in the broader constellation of factors that influence policy (Minkler, 2010). The work is also time- and labor-intensive and fraught with challenges, for both engaged scholars and their community partners, among them real or perceived pressures to "stick with the research," narrowly defined, lest the science be devalued or funding put in jeopardy. For engaged scholars and their partners in the United States, the heavy cultural emphasis on individualism and individual responsibility can further mitigate against efforts to focus more broadly on policy-level interventions and solutions to problems that often are framed in narrow, individualistic terms. Yet, as the examples in this chapter illustrate, engaged scholars and their community partners who are intentional about policy outcomes from the beginning can help build CBPR projects that result in lasting, formal policy changes that can extend social justice and improve the health and well-being of people and their environments over the long haul.

Acknowledgments

Portions of this chapter were adapted from "The Role of Community-Based Participatory Research in Policy Advocacy" by M. Themba Nixon, M. Minkler, and N. Freudenberg (2008), which appeared in *Community-Based Participatory Research for Health: From Process to Outcomes* (2nd ed.), edited by M. Minkler and N. Wallerstein and published in San Francisco by Jossey-Bass. Adapted with permission from the authors and the publisher. We gratefully acknowledge Makani Themba Nixon for her contributions to our thinking and her ongoing leadership in community organizing, policy advocacy, and the power of community-based partnerships for helping to promote policy change.

References

Ansley, F., & Gaventa, J. (1997, January/February). Researching for democracy and democratizing research. *Change*, pp. 46–53.

Bardach, E. (2000). *A practical guide for policy analysis: The eightfold path to more effective problem solving*. New York: Chatham House/Seven Bridges.

Berkowitz, B., & Wolff, T. (2000). *The spirit of the coalition*. Washington, DC: American Public Health Association.

Blackman, V. S. (2005). Putting policy theory to work: tobacco control in California. *Policy, Politics, & Nursing Practice, 6*(2), 148–155.

Boyer, E. L. (1996). The scholarship of engagement. *Journal of Public Service and Outreach, 1*(1), 11–20.

Bradbury, H., & Reason, P. (2008). Issues and choice points for improving the quality of action research. In M. Minkler & N. Wallerstein (Eds.), *Community-based participatory research for health: From process to outcomes* (2nd ed.). San Francisco: Jossey-Bass.

Brown, L., & Vega, W. A. (1996). A protocol for community-based research. *American Journal of Preventive Medicine, 12*(4), 4–5.

Bullard, R. (n.d.). *Environmental justice in the 21st century.* Retrieved November 8, 2008, from http://www.ejrc.cau.edu/ejinthe21century.htm.

Citrin, T. (2000). Policy issues in a community-based approach. In T. A. Bruce & S. Uranga McKane (Eds.), *Community-based public health: A partnership model* (pp. 83–90). Washington, DC: American Public Health Association.

Cornwall, A., & Jewkes, R. (1995). What is participatory research? *Social Science and Medicine, 41,* 1667–1676.

Dorfman, L., Wallack, L., & Woodruff, K. (2005). More than a message: Framing public health advocacy to change corporate practices. *Health Education & Behavior, 32*(3), 320–336.

Flicker, S., Travers, R., Guta, A., McDonald, S., & Meagher, A. (2007). Ethical dilemmas in community-based participatory research: Recommendations for institutional review boards. *Journal of Urban Health, 84*(4), 478–493.

Freire, P. (1970). *Pedagogy of the oppressed.* New York: Continuum.

Freudenberg, N. (2005). Public health advocacy to change corporate practices: Implications for health education practice and research. *Health Education & Behavior, 32*(3), 298–319.

Freudenberg, N., Rogers, M., Ritas, C., & Nerney, M. (2005). Policy analysis and advocacy: An approach to community-based participatory research. In B. A. Israel, E. Eng, A. J. Schulz, & E. A. Parker (Eds.), *Methods in community-based participatory research for health* (pp. 349–370). San Francisco: Jossey-Bass.

Guthrie, K., Louise, J., & Foster, C. C. (2006). *The challenge of assessing policy and advocacy activities: Moving from theory to practice.* Los Angeles: The California Endowment.

Hall, B. (1992). From margins to center? The development and purpose of participatory research. *American Sociologist, 23,* 15–28.

Israel, B. A., Eng, E., Schulz, A. J., & Parker, E. A. (2005). Introduction. In B. A. Israel, E. Eng, A. J. Schulz, & E. A. Parker (Eds.), *Methods in community-based participatory research for health* (pp. 3–26). San Francisco: Jossey-Bass.

Jacobson, P. D., & Soliman, S. (2002). Litigation as public health policy: Theory or reality? *Journal of Law, Medicine & Ethics, 30,* 224–238.

Kingdon, J. W. (2003). *Agendas, alternatives, and public policies* (2nd ed). New York: Addison-Wesley Educational Publishers.

Longest, B. B., Jr. (2006). *Health policymaking in the United States* (3rd ed.). Chicago: AUPH/Health Administration Press.

McDonagh, E. (2006). Abortion rights after South Dakota. *Free Inquiry, 26*(4), 34–38.

Mercer, S. L., Green, L. W., Cargo, M., Potter, M., Daniel, M., Olds, R. S., et al. (2008). Reliability-tested guidelines for assessing participatory research projects. In M. Minkler & N. Wallerstein (Eds.), *Community-based participatory research for health: From process to outcomes* (2nd ed.). San Francisco: Jossey-Bass.

Milio, N. (1998). Priorities and strategies for promoting community-based prevention policies. *Journal of Public Health Management and Practice, 4*(3), 14–28.

Minkler, M. (2004). Ethical challenges for the "outside" researcher in community-based participatory research. *Health Education & Behavior, 31*(6), 684–697.

Minkler, M. (2010). Linking science and policy through community-based participatory research to address health disparities. *American Journal of Public Health, 100*(3), Supplement.

Minkler, M., Brechwich Vásquez, V., Chang, C., Miller, J., Rubin, V., Glover Blackwell, A., et al. (2008). *Promoting healthy public policy through community-based participatory research: Ten case studies.* Oakland, CA: PolicyLink.

Minkler, M., & Wallerstein, N. (Eds.). (2008). *Community-based participatory research for health: From process to outcomes* (2nd ed). San Francisco: Jossey-Bass.

Morello-Frosch, M., Pastor, M., Sadd , J. L., Porras, C., & Prichard, M. (2005). Citizens, science and data judo: Leveraging secondary data analysis to build a community-academic collaborative for environmental justice in Southern California. In B. A. Israel, E. Eng, A. J. Schulz, & E. A. Parker (Eds.), *Methods in community-based participatory research for health* (pp. 371–392). San Francisco: Jossey-Bass.

PolicyLink. (2005). *Advocating for change: Administrative petitioning: Making stronger rules.* Retrieved January 15, 2008, from http://www.policylink.org/AdvocatingForChange/AdminPetitions.pdf.

Rist, C. (1994). Influencing the policy process with qualitative research. In N. K. Denzin & Y. S. Lincoln (Eds.), *Handbook of qualitative research* (pp. 545–557). Thousand Oaks, CA: Sage.

Ritas, C. (2003). *Speaking truth, creating power: A guide to policy work for community based participatory research practitioners.* Retrieved January 15, 2008, from http://futurehealth.ucsf.edu/pdf_files/Ritas.pdf.

Ritas, C., Minkler, M., Halpin, H., & Ni, A. (2008). Using CBPR to promote policy change: Exercises and online resources. In M. Minkler & N. Wallerstein (Eds.), *Community-based participatory research for health: From process to outcomes* (2nd ed.). San Francisco: Jossey-Bass.

Rochefort, D., & Cobb, R. (1993). Definition, agenda, access, and policy choice. *Policy Studies Journal, 21*, 56–71.

Saurwein, K., & Haynes, K. A. (1999, October 15). Schools have no trouble identifying the LA school district's most pressing problems. *Los Angeles Times*, p. 2.

Shepard, P., Brechwich Vásquez, V. B., & Minkler, M. (2008). Using CBPR to promote environmental justice policy: A case study from Harlem, New York. In M. Minkler & N. Wallerstein (Eds.), *Community-based participatory research for health: From process to outcomes* (2nd ed.). San Francisco: Jossey-Bass.

Sofaer, S. (2001). *Working together, moving ahead: A manual to support effective community health coalitions.* New York: Baruch College, School of Public Affairs.

Steckler, A., & Dawson, L. (1982). The role of health education in public policy development. *Health Educational Quarterly, 9*, 275–292.

Tajik, M., & Minkler, M. (2006–2007). Environmental justice research and action: A case study in political economy and community-academic collaboration. *International Journal of Community Health Education, 26*(3), 215–232.

Tervalon, M., & Garcia, J. M. (1998). Cultural humility versus cultural competence: A critical distinction in defining physician training outcomes in multicultural education. *Journal of Health Care for the Poor and Underserved, 9*(2), 117–125.

293

Themba, M. N. (1996). *Chalk one up for David: The African American Tobacco–Education Network and the fight to stop X Brand.* Sacramento, CA: African American Tobacco Education Network.

Themba, M. N. (1999). *Making policy, making change: How communities are taking law into their own hands.* San Francisco: Jossey-Bass.

Themba, M. N., Delgado, G., Vribe, J., & Calpotura, F. (2000). *Grassroots innovative policy program.* Oakland, CA: Applied Research Center.

Vásquez, V. B., Lanza, D., Hennessey-Lavery, S., Facente, S., Halpin, H. A., & Minkler, M. (2007). Addressing food security through public policy action in a community-based participatory research partnership. *Health Promotion Practice, 8*(4), 342–349.

Wallack, L., Winett, L., & Lee, A. (2005). Successful public policy change in California: firearms and youth resources. *Journal of Public Health Policy, 26*(2), 206–226.

Wallack, L., Woodruff, K., Dorfman, L., & Diaz, I. (1999). *News for a change: An advocate's guide to working with the media.* Thousand Oaks, CA: Sage.

Wallerstein, N. (2002). Empowerment to reduce health disparities. *Scandinavian Journal of Public Health, 30,* 72–77.

Wallerstein, N., & Bernstein, E. (1988). Empowerment education: Freire's ideas adapted to health education. *Health Educational Quarterly, 15*(4), 379–394.

Wandersman, A., Goodman, R. M., & Butterfoss, F. D. (2005). Understanding coalitions and how they operate: An "open systems" organizational framework. In M. Minkler (Ed.), *Community organizing and community building for health* (2nd ed., pp. 368–385). New Brunswick, NJ: Rutgers University Press.

Wang, C. C., Cash, J. L., & Powers, L. S. (2000). Who knows the streets as well as the homeless? Promoting personal and community action through photovoice. *Health Promotion Practice, 1,* 81–89.

World Social Forum. (n.d.). *Homepage.* Available at http://www.forumsocialmundial.org.br/index.php?cd_language=2.

Collaborative Approaches to Community Change

Penny A. Pasque

Real [community-university] relationships mean, not that we come to do "show and tell" and "dog and pony shows" about "you want to give us some money"; it means sittin' down and saying, "these are what we're wrestling with, this is what we're failing against, this is what we're trying to do differently." ... And, *then* we can begin to talk about what needs to be done together.

These words are from a community partner, Glenn (a pseudonym), as he passionately speaks to a national conference of approximately 150 university presidents, legislators, faculty, administrators, national association representatives, students, and community partners. The focus of this gathering was on community engagement and strengthening higher education for the public good. Glenn reflects on known relationships between community and university partners as "shows" and stresses the importance of establishing strong, collaborative relationships with honest dialogue about barriers *before* discussing strategies for change. (For the purposes of this chapter, "university" is meant to be inclusive of all higher and postsecondary institutions.) Glenn recognizes a less effective approach to community-university partnerships and argues for a more complex framework for collaboration.

The issues mentioned in this quote serve as an exemplar for the changes in perspective that are needed to foster effective community-university collaborative approaches for social change. More specifically, there are elements of power, collaboration, and community change embedded in such relationships. In terms of power, Glenn describes the unequal relationships between community and university partners where community partners are paraded out when needed or are used for objectification or "show." Further, collaborative conversations include open discussions of the barriers communities and universities face, where people own mistakes and failures. Such authentic conversation is inclusive of the

295

history of the organization and is reflective of different strategies for change that have already been attempted. *"Then,"* collaborative strategies for community change may be envisioned and enacted.

In this chapter, I consider the elements of power, collaboration, and social change in order to deeply explore the complexities of collaborative approaches between community and university partners for community change. This type of collaboration becomes critical during this time of crisis (e.g., environmental, educational, economic, health, housing) where these social issues are inextricably linked. A broad impact on local, national, and global communities is needed, and community-university collaborations have the potential to make deep community change that may impact people's daily lives.

First, I briefly share a research study on this topic that informs my perspective. Next, I offer reflections on power, collaboration, and social change as connected to community-university partnerships. In each of these sections, I draw from the words of Glenn (from the contextual research study) and use the actions of my own institution, the University of Oklahoma, as an example for further exploration of engagement and outreach for critical community change.

Contextual Research Study

A study on strengthening the relationships between higher education and society informs this current chapter, and I offer a cursory review of that research to provide context (see Pasque, 2007, 2010). In this study, I explore higher education leaders' perspectives of higher education's relationships to society as found through (1) a macro-analysis of the current literature and (2) a micro-analysis of face-to-face language during a national conference series. In this case, "leaders" include community partners, university presidents, legislators, faculty, administrators, and graduate students, who may not consider themselves to be leaders, but have published or articulated their thoughts in various national contexts.

Through examination of the linguistic complexities of this national written and verbal discourse, I find something that is sadly already supported in the literature and something quite original. The finding that is not new is that some women, people of color, graduate students, and community partners are silenced and/or their perspectives are reframed or discounted in the national dialogue on engagement. This is not okay, and it is not new information (see Chase, 2005; Gilligan, 1982, 1987, 1988; Green & Trent, 2005; Rowley, 2000; Smith, 2004; Stanley, 2006; Tannen, 1993, 1994). What is unique is that the emergent *Advocacy* perspective about higher education's relationships with society is marginalized. In addition, these *Advocacy* perspectives (presented by people with dominant and/or subordinate social identities; i.e., White male full professors, African American male community partners, Latina graduate students) that question the dominant perspectives are reframed or disregarded. In each case, the dilemmas presented by these advocates are not captured in recrafted models or in revised visions for change that hope to strengthen the relationships between higher education and society. Specifically, the dilemmas surfaced by advocates are couched in "broad, if not universal, agreement" in final reporting mechanisms or are marginalized in the national literature.

It is important to elaborate on the *content* of the *Advocacy* perspectives shared in the national (verbal and written) discourse, which have two similarities. (An analysis of the *process* of the discussions and a more detailed analysis of the content may be found elsewhere [Pasque, 2010].) First, the authors state that there is mutual interdependence between the public and private good of higher education; the location where one ends and the other begins is blurred. Specifically, the private good argument is where educating the private individual through higher education will contribute to the public good through an increase in economic growth, thereby defining the public good as local, state, and national economic vitality. The public good argument is to educate students to participate in a diverse society, and this will contribute to the public good in terms of items such as increased civic engagement and appreciation of diversity.

Second, the authors each passionately describe a crisis in higher education where action from leaders is needed to shift the focus of the higher education from a capitalistic, market-driven emphasis to one that better serves the public good (Giroux & Giroux, 2004; Kezar, 2005; Labaree, 1997; Parker, 2003; Pitkin & Shumer, 1982; Rhoades & Slaughter, 2004). Moreover, higher education's role in a democracy needs to acknowledge the public and private realms as well as privilege the interconnections between them. The authors view this interconnection as the crux of a crisis in the academy where change is needed in leaders' perspectives about, and behaviors regarding, the academy. Political capital and change to actualize a true and inclusive democracy are central. Further, the authors believe it is particularly important for leaders within colleges and universities to initiate this change.

Most scholars with the *Advocacy* perspective identify people with an economic neoliberal view—who support the marketization of higher education—as a problem and believe there is a lack of leadership and governance within the academy. The authors fear that if there is not a change in how stakeholders perceive and act on higher education's relationship with society, then higher education will be increasingly perceived as a private good, or a commodity. This will, in turn, reduce the collaborative connections between communities and universities that focus on social change. The authors often identify solutions as increased access to education, multicultural education, civic engagement for a diverse democracy, university engagement and outreach, and a change in leadership.

It is these *Advocacy* perspectives that are marginalized in the discourse and in national conversations (Pasque, 2010). In these instances, silencing is not necessarily connected to volubility (Tannen, 1993); omitting comments from final reporting documents, rejecting critical approaches in national journals, and crafting committees where recommendations are "filed" (as opposed to "considered" and/or "acted upon") are all methods of silencing perspectives.

Marginalizing the perspectives from (1) community partners, people of color, graduate students, and women and (2) *Advocacy* perspectives limits our available strategies for community change. Based on the findings from this study and in the hopes of encouraging a shift in perspectives and action around higher education's relationships with society, I offer a Tricuspid Model of Interconnected Advocacy and Educational Change that requires (1) rethinking the role of power brokers, (2) centering marginalized perspectives, and (3) including voices of all people in society (Pasque, 2010). Principles of power, collaboration, and change are embedded in the Tricuspid model. In addition, I argue that if a more thorough understanding of leaders' perspectives is not offered, then dominant perspectives shared in academic discourse genres may continue to perpetuate the current ideas of higher education's relationship with society—from an economic rationalization perspective—without consideration of alternative perspectives. The perpetuation of the current trajectory and the continued marginalization of *Advocacy* frames for educational change will be detrimental to working toward social justice and educational equity.

There are additional models that specifically address community-university partnerships and reflect the exemplar offered at the beginning of this chapter. Some of these models will be explored further in the following discussion of power, collaboration, and social change.

Complexities of Power

Social change efforts will not succeed if they do not deal directly with issues of power, difference, and diversity in the community-university relationship and within the communities in which they operate (see outreach and engagement discussions on diversity, including Association of American Colleges and Universities [AAC&U], 1995a, 1995b; Ibarra, 2006; O'Connor, 2004; Rowley, 2000). For example, Dewey (1916/1997) states,

> The notion that experience consists of a variety of segregated domains, or interests, each having its own interdependent value, material, and method, each checking every other, and each is kept properly bounded by the others, forming a kind of balance of powers in education. On the practical side, they were found to have their cause in the divisions of society into more or less rigidly marked off classes and groups—in other words, in obstruction to full and flexible social interaction and intercourse ... resulting in various dualisms such as practical and intellectual activity, labor and leisure, individuality and association. (p. 323)

As Kezar and Rhoads (2001) reflect, "Dewey makes the compelling argument that distinctions emerged to serve the interests of power and privilege" (p. 161). These power dynamics of inequity need to be both acknowledged and addressed in community and university relationships for community change.

Inherent in power relationships and "rigidly marked off classes and groups" are target and agent social identities including race, class, gender, sexual orientation, age, religion, and other social identities. From the social identity approach, people with "target" identities are "members of social identity groups that are disenfranchised, exploited, and victimized in a variety of ways by the oppressor and the oppressor's system or institutions" (Hardiman & Jackson, 1997, p. 20). In contemporary U.S. society, this includes people of different abilities, people of color, non-Christians, working class/poor, gay/bisexual, and women/transgender people. Agents include "members of dominant social groups privileged by birth or acquisition, who knowingly or unknowingly exploit and reap unfair advantage over members of target groups" (Hardiman & Jackson, 1997, p. 20). In contemporary U.S. society, this includes people who are able-bodied, white, Christian, middle and upper-middle class, heterosexual men, and those who have assimilated to U.S. culture. Further, identities are fluid; they may change as people move through life, and the sociopolitical environment may also change over time. It is impossible to separate various personal social identities from people's social group memberships (Bell, 1997) because social identities are fundamentally connected to the cultures in which they are embedded (Bakhtin, 1981; Vygotsky, 1978).

Power (asymmetrical relationships) and *solidarity* (symmetrical relationships) are always operating between and among people (Tannen, 1994) from different social identities within community-university relationships. *Institutional power* comes from the operation of laws, policies, procedures, and historical and cultural paradigms. Foucault (1976) argues that whoever holds power regarding what counts as knowledge also has power over policies and systems. For example, power and solidarity may be found between community members and university students in Students for Access to Justice (SATJ). In March 2004, the students in the University of Oklahoma College of Law started SATJ. The mission states that SATJ "promotes a culture of public service commitment by connecting students with meaningful pro bono volunteer opportunities" (SATJ, 2008, paragraph 2). Each spring, this program holds a fair where volunteer students and community members in need of legal information and support are brought together (with support from licensed attorneys). Students in the program have collaborated with organizations such as the American Civil Liberties Union, Legal Aid, the Equal Opportunity Employment Commission, Oklahoma Indigent Defense System, Oklahoma Lawyers for Children, and Oklahoma Indian Legal Services.

As legal decisions and policies take place in a relevant historical, cultural, and sociopolitical context, power around social identities, such as race, gender, class, or religion, of the student and community partner may add to—or detract from—collaboration toward an integrative community-university partner relationship. In addition, the student has the institutional knowledge about the law and understands the complexities of legal policies and procedures. Similarly, the community partner has the expertise about the community agency and/or the people in the local community.

The Interdisciplinary Collaboration Model (ICM) is instructive in this situation (Amey & Brown, 2005). The ICM shows the transitions from Stage One collaboration, where relationships are top-down and individual, to Stage Three where the relationships are "integrative, collaborative, team, [and] weblike" (p. 28). The "dog and pony shows" are more indicative of Stage One of the ICM, where there is a dominant discipline orientation and university partners serve as experts. The SATJ relationship has the opportunity to be transactional such as is found in Stage One of the ICM (i.e., the student gains legal experience, the organization gains knowledge and assistance) or transformational, as in Stage Three (i.e., all parties learn from each other and collaborate to make change from within or throughout the legal system). Further, attention to (1) rethinking the role of power brokers, (2) centering marginalized perspectives, and (3) including voices of all people in the relationship between community members and SATJ students may continue to deepen what is learned and what is gained from this relationship.

Moreover, *solidarity* is where people join together with other people who hold common social identities or roles. To continue with the SATJ example, a person in need of legal advice may connect with a person based on shared identity or experience. Discourse is often used as a way to signal solidarity. Comments such as, "As another single mother, I also believe ..."

299

or "I'm also an African American man and can relate to …" or "I, too, went to a rural high school and have faced …" as a way of showing solidarity and shared identity between the community member and the university student. Relationships of power and solidarity add further complexity to the community-university relationship as we work toward transformational community change.

It is also important to note that power and solidarity may be explored through the concept of *footing* (Goffman, 1981). "A change in footing implies a change in the alignment we take up to ourselves and the others present as expressed in the way we manage the production or reception of an utterance" (p. 128). For example, when a person says "I'm just a community organizer …" or shares their opinion and follows it up with "but, I'm only a student," the person changes their own footing in the conversation to a one-down position. The reverse changes a person's footing to a one-up position. This one-up happens, for example, when a person says, "As a full professor, I …" or "As a lawyer who works in Washington, D.C., I know that …" It is important to be cognizant of these verbal displays of footing, in addition to power and solidarity across social identities, in order to more completely understand the complexities of community-university relationships, because ignoring these issues may be detrimental to working collaboratively for community change and further entrench conceptualizations of power. This may, in turn, silence participants who could be less likely to share their perspectives when one-up footing is pervasive in the discourse.

Smith's (2004) concept of racial battle fatigue may be useful in uncovering more of the dynamics between community and university partners from target and agent identities as connected to issues of power and solidarity. Smith describes racial battle fatigue as "a response to the distressing mental/emotional conditions that result from facing racism daily (e.g., racial slights, recurrent indignities and irritations, unfair treatments, including contentious classrooms, and potential threats or dangers under tough to violent and even life-threatening conditions)" (p. 180). Further, Smith relates various documented psychological and physiological symptoms (tension headaches, backaches, trembling and jumpiness, chronic pain, upset stomach, extreme fatigue, constant anxiety and worrying, etc.) to the combat fatigue experienced by military personnel. Smith does mention that he does not equate the daily experiences of people in the military with daily experiences of faculty of color, but instead suggests a useful metaphor. In addition, the anticipation of a racist event may add to the stressor. Smith furthers that "unfortunately for African American faculty … higher education was and continues to be much more racially exclusive, oppressive, and antagonistic than society at large" (p. 185). Community and university partners need to be aware of such daily experiences of battle fatigue as related to social inequities around race, gender, class, and other social identities in order to eliminate the perpetuation of such fatigue when collaborating toward social change.

In addition to research about discussions across race in higher education, there is scholarship that addresses the relationship between community organizer/university partner (such as Glenn) and university faculty and staff. Bok (1982) mentions how community members' high hopes are often met with failures that "actually heightened local suspicions and frustrations rather than improving relations with the university" (p. 46). Rowley (2000) furthers this perspective and offers a major premise for considering the relationship between universities and Black urban communities. He states, "The *habitus* of higher education inflicts symbolic violence on individual universities (by defining the traditional university mission and values), and universities in turn inflict symbolic violence on society by either contributing to urban social reproduction (restricted access to and limited distribution of dominant cultural capital) or refusing to help alleviate urban problems (placing little value on public service and civic responsibilities of universities)" (p. 56).

Rowley's analysis also may help add insight into Glenn's community partner perspective quoted at the beginning of this chapter. Glenn may be attempting to make this symbolic violence visible through his narrative in this conference. In turn, his persistence and dedication to expressing his advocacy perspective in the company of people whom he perceives as having the "power" to make change may add to his own racial battle fatigue.

Hurtado (2007) emphasizes that "it is time to renew the promise of American higher education in advancing social progress, end America's discomfort with race and social difference, and deal directly with many of the issues of inequality in everyday life" (p. 186). If higher education leaders truly want to find ways to deal directly with issues of social and educational inequality in ways that will make change regarding race, class, and gender, then we must foster discussions about power and inequity, but in such a way that all voices and perspectives are included. Contrary to some people wanting to be "comfortable" in these types of settings (a quote from a participant [Pasque, 2010]), I believe that discussing issues of power across race, class, and gender as connected to social inequity *is* going to be uncomfortable. And, further analysis of the language and enacted issues of power around strengthening the relationships between higher education and society constitutes one step toward collaboration toward social justice and change.

Approaches for Collaboration

A complex framework for collaboration between communities and universities is critical when working toward broad and deep community change. For example, Bringle and Hatcher (2002) point out that community-university partnerships have complex dynamics similar to those of "interpersonal relationships" (p. 504). Based on this theoretical framework of relationships, they offer practical guidelines at an organizational level. From here, Fogel and Cook (2006) utilize this framework to address specific challenges in university-community partnership projects. They identify relationship formation, development, and maintenance as instrumental in addressing challenges. Glenn echoes the importance of collaborative relationships for community-university partnerships as he describes the importance of teams. Teams are strengthened through an intentional power analysis of who is involved. He asks:

> Who is your team? ... The first question I will always ask people is; what is your power analysis? How many *trustees* are engaged in this conversation? How many of your top administrators are on your team, if you have a team at all? What about faculty, particularly tenured faculty, those that head departments, those who set the, to make the decisions about who's going to be tenured or not? How many of those folk are part of this conversation? What about the support staff in your universities?

301

The importance of collaboration in teams across community-university partnerships cannot be stressed enough and has been discussed elsewhere (Bringle & Hatcher, 2002; Galura, Pasque, Schoem, & Howard, 2004; Thomas, 2004; Weerts & Sandmann, 2008; White, 2006). For such partnerships to sincerely exist in an integrative manner, a space is needed for multiple perspectives and voices—from all members of the team—in multiple venues, including in the community, classrooms, end-of-the-year reports, dissemination of information, research, best practices articles, and policy changes. These efforts intentionally shift the focus from "dog and pony show" collaborations to true, equitable collaboration. Such a shift in climate would also require a shift in the social balance and institutional discourse (Miller & Fox, 2004) so that people with advocacy perspectives, who directly address issues of power and privilege through a collaborative approach, are centered.

It is also important to consider whether the network of practices in higher education needs the current siloed structures that perpetuate inequity in order to exist. As Fairclough (2001) mentions, questions need to be asked about "whether those who benefit most from the way social life is now organized have an interest in the problem not being resolved" (p. 236). Jones, Torres, and Arminio (2006) echo this line of questioning when they ask higher education researchers to "address not only what is being said but also what is not, not only what was said and quoted but also what is being protected from public view and why" (p. 31). This raises the question of whether community and higher education leaders—we—benefit from the use of specific collaborations of outreach and engagement. For example, are concepts of community-university partnerships that reflect the "dog and pony show" model easier or more rewarding than advanced levels in the Commitment to Community Engagement or Interdisciplinary Collaboration models? More specifically, in what ways is social reproduction operationalized in this context? Is a market-driven, "private good" frame (where education is seen as increasing the local, state, and federal economies) more palatable and accepted by policy makers and funders than a "social good" frame, which may in turn help support future funding possibilities? Moreover, is it easier to think of the private and public good as polarized and mutually exclusive in order to perpetuate dominant perspectives and practices?

On a related point, Bok (2003) contends that "the incentives of commercial competition do not always produce a beneficial outcome; they merely yield what the market wants" (p. 103). These days, our "market" is changing on a daily basis. State appropriations have decreased (Brandl & Holdsworth, 2003; Cage, 1991; Hansen, 2004) and faculty experience a tremendous amount of pressure to acquire additional external funds. For example, Slaughter and Leslie (1997) state that

> to maintain and expand resources faculty had to compete increasingly for external dollars that were tied to market-related research, which was referred to variously as applied, commercial, strategic, and targeted research, whether these moneys were in the form of research grants and contracts, service contracts, partnerships with industry and government, technology transfer, or the recruitment of more and higher fee-paying students. (p. 8)

Current faculty and administrators are experiencing pressure to alter agendas in order to guarantee financial support. In *Academic Capitalism and the New Economy,* Slaughter and

Rhoades (2004) describe further the theory of academic capitalism and warn people in the field to be more cognizant of these influences. Such a push toward capitalism may reduce collaborations between communities and universities if they are not seen as profitable financially or academically. Numerous scholars have talked about the need for increased reward structures for faculty such as grants, tenure, and promotion that reflect the university's mission and commitment to engagement and outreach (AAC&U, 2002; Boyer, 1990; Buys & Burnsnall, 2007; Checkoway, 2000, 2001, 2004; Colby, Ehrlich, Beaumont, & Stephens, 2003; Grunwald & Peterson, 2003; Holland, 1999; Jongbloed, Enders, & Salerno, 2008). Further, Weerts and Sandman (2008) found that "promotion and tenure policies were the strongest barrier to faculty engagement with the community, especially at the land-grant universities" (p. 91) and is one example of where the public and private are interconnected. An infrastructure that provides rewards and creates an organizational structure that supports engagement and outreach efforts is vital.

The new Carnegie Community Engagement Elective Classification is arguably one process encouraging institutions to intentionally address issues of engagement through collaboration with community partners and is discussed in detail elsewhere in this handbook. The framework for institutions to document their engagement with communities was designed to:

1. Respect the diversity of institutions and their approaches to community engagement;
2. Engage institutions in a process of inquiry, reflection, and self assessment; and
3. Honor institutions' achievements while promoting the ongoing development of their programs. (Driscoll, 2008)

Although many have pushed for this type of accountability and recognition, others have discussed the questions that are included and absent in this new classification, furthering the idea that the classification system may encourage isomorphic tendencies across campuses (Jaeger & Thornton, 2008).

The University of Oklahoma has actively been seeking this classification. As a member of the university's Community Engagement Committee, I had the privilege of gathering with representatives from across the institution as they/we shared information about their community engagement and outreach efforts and struggled over the ways to represent such meaningful work in such small boxes on the application form. Representatives from across campus, including the medical school, education, business, student affairs, law, and women's and gender studies, articulated their established outreach and engagement programs and learned about the various efforts across campus. Although one aspect of this process was mechanical—the process of encouraging all faculty, staff, and student organizations to document their relationships with communities—there was another aspect that was quite collaborative. This process encouraged colleges and departments to talk across often siloed areas of the institution about their efforts with communities. This dialogue has fostered further collaboration between departments and provided an institutionalized venue for recognizing these important efforts. Ongoing action committees that include students, community partners, faculty, and staff have been formed to further the process.

As the University of Oklahoma and other institutions across the country continue to reflect upon and strengthen collaborative approaches to community change, Fine's (1994) concept of "working the hyphen" across researcher-participant relationships is particularly salient for community-university collaboration. I have inserted these parallel terms where relevant in the following quote by Fine. She states:

> By *working the hyphen*, I mean to suggest that researchers [university faculty, staff, and students] probe how we are in relation with the contexts we study and with our informants [community members], understanding that we are all multiple in those relations ... Working the hyphen means creating occasions for researchers and informants [community and university partners] to discuss what is, and is not, "Happening between," within the negotiated relations of whose story is being told, why, to whom, [and] with what interpretation, and whose story is being shadowed, why, for whom, and with what consequence. (p. 72)

In a similar vein, community-university partners can learn to "work the hyphen" in their collaborations in order to uncover what is happening within and between the relationship/s in the current sociopolitical context. Working the hyphen deepens understandings of the complexities of the community story and consequences of action/inaction. Such awareness of positionality can foster stronger collaboration and set the foundation to work in concert with each other toward social justice and change.

Strategies for Social Change

Higher education leaders have been called upon to change the current trajectory that perpetuates educational stratification (Giroux & Giroux, 2004; Rhoades & Slaughter, 2004). This change can be enhanced through strategic relationships between community-university partners as they work toward social change with deep and/or broad impact. Instructive in these efforts for change are Harro's Cycle of Socialization (2000a) and Cycle of Liberation (2000b). Harro (2000a) describes the Cycle of Socialization process as "*pervasive* (coming from all sides and sources), *consistent* (patterned and predictable), *circular* (self-supporting), *self-perpetuating* (intra-dependent), and often *invisible* (unconscious and unmanned)" (p. 15). More specifically, we are born into a preexisting world and socialized with rules, norms, and expectations. These perspectives are reinforced through institutional and cultural messages that result in dissonance, silence, collusion, ignorance, violence, and internalized patterns of power. The Cycle of Socialization offers two options: do nothing and perpetuate the status quo, or make change by raising consciousness, interrupting patterns, educating one's self and others, and taking action.

Harro (2000b) also offers a Cycle of Liberation regarding individual, collaborative, community, and culture change. Change, in this instance, requires a "struggle against discrimination based on race, class, gender, sexual identity, ableism and age—those barriers that keep large portions of the population from having access to economic and social justice, from being able to participate fully in the decisions affecting our lives, from having a full share of both the rights and responsibilities of living in a free society" (p. 450). Such change interrupts dominant paradigms of oppression through the use of transformational and collaborative relationships. This cycle begins on the intrapersonal level, where social inequities create cognitive dissonance when people cannot rectify in their own minds what they see happening versus what they think should be happening to address critical social issues. From here, a person gets "ready" by empowering him/herself to dismantle collusion, privilege, and internalized oppression. At this point, the person reaches out toward others, seeks experiences, names injustices, and uses tools for change. Next is the interpersonal phase in which people build community. In this work with others, we seek people "like us" for support and people "different from us" for building coalitions and questioning assumptions in structures and systems (p. 464). Coalescing is an important stage where people engage in organizing, action planning, fundraising, educating, renaming, learning about being an ally, and moving into action. Creating such systemic change critically transforms institutions and creates a new culture through influencing policy, structures, leadership, and a shared sense of power. This work is maintained as additional systemic changes are initiated.

I argue that such collaborative efforts must also utilize idiosyncratic methods for critical social change, as a single approach for breaking the cycle of oppression is not enough to combat years of ingrained socialization. Al Gore's approach toward addressing global warming exemplifies such a multifaceted strategy. In myriad speeches and his movie, *The Inconvenient Truth,* Gore discusses the layered complexities of global warming and then offers numerous strategies to simultaneously address this problem with a worldwide approach. In a similar vein, multiple methods for community-university collaborations for social change need to offer differentiated and critical change on multiple levels simultaneously. This idiosyncratic approach toward change reflects the New Science perspective. As Wheatley (1999) describes,

> In organizations, which is the more important influence on behavior—the system or the individual? The quantum world answered the question for me with a resounding "Both." There are no either/ors. There is no need to decide between two things, pretending they are separate. What is critical is the relationship created between two or more elements. (pp. 35–36)

Love and Estanek (2004) expand on the New Science perspective and discuss its relevance for student affairs in higher education. The authors argue for a "both/and" perspective where Newtonian science and the New Science of chaos and unpredictability are combined in dialectical thinking. Their conceptual framework for the future of organizational behavior in student affairs also includes transcending paradigms, recognizing connectedness, and embracing paradox.

Community-university partnerships have the potential to engage in such liberation. For example, the University of Oklahoma's K20 Center for Educational and Community Renewal (K20 Center, 2008) states:

> We envision interactive learning communities where citizens identify, analyze, and help solve problems in their local and global communities. Through cutting-edge research and development, local and international networking, school-university-industry partnerships, and interdisciplinary degree programs, we envision empowered citizens working for the creation of a global society rid of poverty, crime, racism, and other forms of inequality. (paragraph 1)

This interdisciplinary research and development center creates action-oriented partnerships among schools, universities, industries, and community and governmental agencies.

For example, their Four-Phase Model for School and Community Renewal has impacted 794 (45 percent) of schools in 520 (96 percent) of districts in Oklahoma. Fourteen hundred K–12 superintendents and principals have participated in this sustained professional development opportunity designed to support learning communities and the integration of digital game-based learning. Among other things, this project has developed digital game-based learning programs to strengthen math and science scores for children in a way that engages young people and increases educational outcomes (Wilson, Whisenhunt, & Eseryel, 2008). This project includes ten community and industry partners and is funded with grants from six foundations/funding sources, including the National Science Foundation and the Bill and Melinda Gates Foundation.

The Levels of Commitment to Community Engagement is a useful model when considering the complexities of the relationships between communities and universities in this context (Holland, 1997/2006). The model explores various elements of the university (such as mission statement, tenure and promotion, curriculum, and fundraising) across four levels of relevance for said institution. For example, when considering the element "leadership" in Level One: Low Relevance, an institution does not mention engagement as a priority; in Level Four: Full Integration, there is a broad leadership commitment to a sustained engagement agenda with ongoing funding support and community input. The various levels and descriptors are particularly useful for universities interested in assessment efforts and may serve as the impetus for deeper collaborative approaches for community change. The K20 Center reflects Holland's (1997/2006) "Level Four: Full Integration" for a number of reasons, including its utilization of multiple leadership collaborations in order to interrupt the cycle of educational inequity and make change for young children, and their futures.

Such leaders who situate themselves to make this type of systemic change have been described as "boundary-crossers" (Thomas, 2004). Boundary crossers are defined as listeners who connect multiple contrasting views and ideas. They focus on long-term goals and relationships, and they follow a dialogic and inclusive process. Boundary crossers are at ease with numerous people, are comfortable in informal or structured conversations, and continually refine perspectives. I extend this definition and include that boundary crossers acknowledge the various historical and contemporary boundaries that propagate power relationships (Foucault, 1976) and sustain cyclical oppression. Further, they operate with an awareness of Bourdieu's (1986) notion of social capital, which connects sources of capital (economic, cultural, and social) in order to create an aggregate of resources linked to a network of relationships. Bourdieu defines such capital as grounded in theories of symbolic power and social reproduction where social capital is a tool of reproduction for the privileged. In addition, boundary crossers in community-university partnerships will work to break the Cycle of Socialization and operate with a Cycle of Liberation strategy for community change.

Conclusion

The "dog and pony shows" of community-university partnerships need to be a thing of the past if we are to work together to interrupt the cycle of socialization and inequity and make critical social change. We need to increase our awareness of the complexities of power, build an infrastructure for strong collaborative teams, and work to make strategic community change that has direct impact on the lives of people in our local, national, and global communities. Such strategies have the potential to make change in communities around critical social issues such as education, health care, housing, the economy, and the environment.

In this chapter, I explored notions of power, collaboration, and change in hopes of offering different ways in which we may "work-the-hyphen" of community-university partnerships to address inequities in society and collaborate on working toward social justice and change. This chapter builds on—and should be viewed as being interconnected with—the other chapters in this handbook so that we may break siloed efforts and work toward collaborative approaches toward community change.

Acknowledgment

The author would like to thank Nicholas Bowman, postdoctoral research associate, Center for Social Concerns, University of Notre Dame, and Mary John O'Hair, vice provost and director, K20 Center for Educational and Community Renewal, University of Oklahoma, for reviewing earlier drafts of this chapter.

References

Amey, M. J., & Brown, D. F. (2005). Interdisciplinary collaboration and academic work: A case study of a university-community partnership. *New Directions for Teaching and Learning, 102,* 23–35.

Association of American Colleges and Universities. (2002). *Greater expectations: A new vision for learning as a nation goes to college.* Washington, DC: Author.

Association of American Colleges and Universities. (1995a). *American pluralism and the college curriculum: Higher education in a diverse democracy.* Washington, DC: Author.

Association of American Colleges and Universities. (1995b). *The drama of diversity and democracy: Higher education and American commitments.* Washington, DC: Author.

Bakhtin, M. M. (1981). *The dialogic imagination.* Austin: University of Texas Press.

Bell, L. A. (1997). Theoretical foundations for social justice education. In M. Adams, L. B. Bell, & P. Griffin (Eds.), *Teaching for diversity and social justice.* New York: Routledge.

Bok, D. (1982). *Beyond the ivory tower: Social responsibilities of the modern university.* Cambridge, MA: Harvard University Press.

Bok, D. (2003). *Universities in the marketplace: The commercialization of higher education.* Princeton, NJ: Princeton University Press.

Bourdieu, P. (1986). The forms of capital. In J. Richardson (Ed.), *Handbook of theory and research for the sociology of education* (pp. 241–258). Westport, CT: Greenwood.

Boyer, E. (1990). *Scholarship reconsidered: Priorities of the professoriate.* Princeton, NJ: Carnegie Foundation for the Advancement of Teaching.

Brandl, J., & Holdsworth, J. M. (2003). On measuring what universities do: A reprise. In D. R. Lewis & J. Hearn (Eds.), *The public research university: Serving the public good in new times.* New York: University Press of America.

Bringle, R. G., & Hatcher, J. A. (2002). Campus-community partnerships: The terms of engagement. *Journal of Social Issues, 58,* 503–516.

Buys, N., & Bursnall, S. (2007). Establishing university-community partnerships: Processes and benefits. *Journal of Higher Education Policy and Management, 29*(1), 73–86.

Cage, M. C. (1991, June 26). Thirty states cut higher education budgets by an average of 3.9% in fiscal 90–91. *Chronicle of Higher Education,* pp. A1–A2.

Chase, S. E. (2005). Narrative inquiry: Multiple lenses, approaches, voices. In N. Denzin & Y. Lincoln (Eds.), *The Sage handbook of qualitative research* (3rd ed., pp. 651–679). Thousand Oaks, CA: Sage.

Checkoway, B. (2000). Public service: Our new mission. *Academe, 86*(4), 24–28.

Checkoway, B. (2001). Renewing the civic mission of the American research university. *Journal of Higher Education, 72*(2), 125–147.

Checkoway, B. (2004). Dilemmas of civic renewal. In M. Langseth & W. M. Plater (Eds.), *Public work and the academy: An academic administrator's guide to civic engagement and service-learning.* Bolton, MA: Anker.

Colby, A., Ehrlich, T., Beaumont, E., & Stephens, J. (2003). *Educating citizens: Preparing America's undergraduates for lives of moral and civic responsibility.* San Francisco: Jossey-Bass.

Dewey, J. (1997). *Democracy and education.* New York: Simon and Schuster. (Original work published 1916)

Driscoll, A. (2008). Carnegie's community engagement classification: Intentions and insights. *Change, 40*(1), 38–41.

Fairclough, N. (2001). The discourse of new labour: Critical discourse analysis. In M. Wetherell, S. Taylor, & S. J. Yates (Eds.), *Discourse as data: A guide for analysis.* Thousand Oaks, CA: Sage.

Fine, M. (1994). Working the hyphens: Reinventing self and other in qualitative research. In N. K. Denzin & Y. S. Lincoln (Eds.), *Handbook of qualitative research* (pp. 70–82). Thousand Oaks, CA: Sage.

Fogel, S. J., & Cook, J. R. (2006). Considerations on the scholarship of engagement as an area of specialization for faculty. *Journal of Social Work Education, 42*(3), 595–606.

Foucault, M. (1976). *The archaeology of knowledge.* New York: Harper & Row.

Galura, J. A., Pasque, P. A., Schoem, D. & Howard, J. (Eds.). (2004). *Engaging the whole of service-learning, diversity, and learning communities.* Ann Arbor, MI: OCSL.

Gilligan, C. (1982). *In a different voice: Psychological theory and women's development.* Cambridge, MA: Harvard University Press.

Gilligan, C. (1987). Moral orientation and moral development. In E. F. Kittay & D. T. Meyers (Eds.), *Woman and moral theory* (pp. 19–33). Totowa, NJ: Rowman & Littlefield.

Gilligan, C. (1988). Two moral orientations: Gender differences and similarities. *Merrill-Palmer Quarterly, 34*(3), 223–237.

Giroux, H. A., & Giroux, S. S. (2004). *Take back higher education: Race, youth, and the crisis of democracy in the post–civil rights era.* New York: Palgrave Macmillan.

Goffman, E. (1981). *Forms of talk.* Philadelphia: University of Pennsylvania Press.

Green, D. O., & Trent, W. (2005). The public good and a racially diverse democracy. In A. J. Kezar, A. C. Chambers, & J. Burkhardt (Eds.), *Higher education for the public good: Emerging voices from a national movement.* San Francisco: Jossey-Bass.

Grunwald, H., & Peterson, M. (2003). Factors that promote faculty involvement in and satisfaction with institutional and classroom student assessment. *Research in Higher Education, 44*(2).

Hansen, H. (2004, March 15). Granholm, Cherry announce commission on higher education and economic growth. Retrieved April 9, 2004, from www.michigan.gov/printerFriendly/0,1687,7-168-88248-,00.html.

Hardiman, R., & Jackson, B. (1997). Conceptual foundations for social justice courses. In M. Adams, L. A. Bell, & P. Griffin (Eds.), *Teaching for diversity and social justice.* New York: Routledge.

Harro, B. (2000a). The cycle of socialization. In M. Adams, C. Castañeda, H. W. Hackman, M. L. Peters, & X. Zúñiga (Eds.), *Readings for diversity and social justice* (pp. 15–20). New York: Routledge.

Harro, B. (2000b). The cycle of liberation. In M. Adams, C. Castañeda, H. W. Hackman, M. L. Peters, & X. Zúñiga (Eds.), *Readings for diversity and social justice* (pp. 463–469). New York: Routledge.

Holland, B. (1999). Factors and strategies that influence faculty involvement in public service. *Journal of Public Service & Outreach, 4*(1), 37–43.

Holland, B. (1997/2006). Levels of commitment to community engagement. *Michigan Journal of Community Service Learning, 4,* 30–41.

Hurtado, S. (2007). Linking diversity with the educational and civic missions of higher education. *Review of Higher Education, 30*(2), 185–196.

Ibarra, R. (2006) Context diversity: Reframing higher education in the 21st century. In B. Holland & J. Meeropol (Eds.), *A more perfect vision: The future of campus engagement.* Providence, RI: Campus Compact. Available at http://www.compact.org/20th/papers.

Jaeger, A., & Thornton, C. (2008, November). *Perspectives on the state and future of engagement in higher education: A critical and committed view.* Paper presented at the annual conference of the Association for the Study of Higher Education, Jacksonville, FL.

Jones, S. R., Torres, V., & Arminio, J. (2006). *Negotiating the complexities of qualitative research in higher education: Fundamental elements and issues.* New York: Routledge.

Jongbloed, B., Enders, J., & Salerno, C. (2008). Higher education and its communities: Interconnections, interdependencies and a research agenda. *Higher Education, 56,* 303–324.

K20 Center. (2008). *Vision and purpose at K20 center.* Retrieved October 11, 2008, from http://k20network.ou.edu/about/vision.

Kezar, A. J. (2005). Challenges for higher education in serving the public good. In A. J. Kezar, A. C. Chambers, & J. Burkhardt, (Eds.), *Higher education for the public good: Emerging voices from a national movement.* San Francisco: Jossey-Bass.

Kezar, A., & Rhoads, R. A. (2001). The dynamic tensions of service learning in higher education. *Journal of Higher Education, 72*(2), 148–171.

Labaree, D. F. (1997). *How to succeed in school without really learning.* New Haven, CT: Yale University Press.

Love, P. G., & Estanek, S. M. (2004). *Rethinking student affairs practice.* San Francisco: Jossey-Bass.

Miller, G., & Fox, K. J. (2004). Building bridges: The possibility of analytic dialogue between ethnography, conversation analysis and Foucault. In D. Silverman (Ed.), *Qualitative research: Theory, method and practice* (2nd ed.). Thousand Oaks, CA: Sage.

O'Connor, J. (2004). Success and challenges of community-based teaching, learning and research: A national perspective. In J. A. Galura, P. A. Pasque, D. Schoem, & J. Howard (Eds.), *Engaging the whole of service-learning, diversity, and learning communities* (p. 14–19). Ann Arbor, MI: OCSL.

Parker, W. (2003). *Teaching democracy: Unity and diversity in public life.* New York: Teachers College Press.

309

Pasque, P. A. (2007). Seeing the educational inequities around us: Visions toward strengthening the relationship between higher education and society. In E. P. St. John (Ed.), *Readings on equal education* (Vol. 22). New York: AMS.

Pasque, P. A. (2010). *American higher education, leadership, and policy: Critical issues & the public good.* New York: Palgrave Macmillan.

Pitkin, H. F., & Shumer, S.M. (1982). On participation. *Democracy, 2,* 43–54.

Rhoades, G., & Slaughter, S. (2004). Academic capitalism in the new economy: Challenges and choices. *American Academic, 1*(1), 37–59.

Rowley, L. L. (2000). The relationship between universities and black urban communities: The class of two cultures. *Urban Review, 32*(1), 45–62.

Slaughter, S., & Leslie, L. (1997). *Academic capitalism: Politics, policies and the entrepreneurial university.* Baltimore: Johns Hopkins University Press.

Slaughter, S., & Rhoades, G. (2004). *Academic capitalism and the new economy: Markets, state and higher education.* Baltimore: Johns Hopkins University Press.

Smith, W. A. (2004). Black faculty coping with racial battle fatigue: The campus racial climate in a post–civil rights era. In D. Cleveland (Ed.), *A long way to go: Conversations about race by African American faculty and graduate students* (Vol. 14, pp. 171–190). New York: Peter Lang.

Stanley, C. A. (2006). Coloring the academic landscape: Faculty of color breaking the silence in predominantly white colleges and universities. *American Educational Research Journal, 43*(4), 701–736.

Students for Access to Justice (SATJ). (2008). *Mission Statement.* Retrieved October 5, 2008, from http://adams.law.ou.edu/satj/.

Tannen, D. (1993). The relativity of linguistic strategies. In D. Tannen (Ed.), *Gender and conversational interaction.* New York: Oxford University Press.

Tannen, D. (1994). *Talking from 9 to 5: Women and men in the workplace: Language, sex and power.* New York: Avon.

Thomas, N. (2004). Boundary-crossers and innovative leadership in higher education. In J. A. Galura, P. A. Pasque, D. Schoem, & J. Howard (Eds.), *Engaging the whole of service-learning, diversity, and learning communities* (pp. 26–30). Ann Arbor, MI: OCSL.

Vygotsky, L. S. (1978). *Mind in society: The development of higher psychological processes.* Cambridge, MA: Harvard University Press.

Weerts, D. J., & Sandmann, L. R. (2008). Building a two-way street: Challenges and opportunities for community engagement at research universities. *Review of Higher Education, 32*(1), 73–106.

Wheatley, M. J. (1999). *Leadership and the new science: Discovering order in a chaotic world* (2nd ed.). San Francisco: Berrett-Koehler.

White, B. P. (2006). Sharing power to achieve true collaboration: The community role in embedding engagement. In B. Holland & J. Meeropol (Eds.), *A more perfect vision: The future of campus engagement.* Providence, RI: Campus Compact. Available at http://www.compact.org/20th/papers.

Wilson, S., Whisenhunt, T. G., & Eseryel, D. (2008). *An instructional design and development model for effective game-based learning environments.* Paper presented at the annual meeting of the Association for Educational Communications and Technology Conference, Orlando, FL.

Documenting Impacts: Engaged Research Centers and Community Change

Philip Nyden and Stephen Percy

In the past two decades, colleges and universities across the nation, particularly those located in urban and metropolitan areas, have witnessed the creation and growth of a new type of research enterprise: the engaged research center (ERC). These new academic enterprises differ from traditional campus research centers with regard to research focus, practice, and outcomes. The purpose of this article is to explore these new research centers and their contributions to both university-community engagement and the quality of life in the communities, regions, and states in which they are located.

The research focus of traditional urban research centers has generally been driven by research agendas defined within the academy, governmental or large philanthropic funders, or policy-making circles. In most cases, this research is driven by testing of hypotheses derived from political, social, or economic theories. In other cases, it is driven by priorities identified by government representatives. The traditional outcome of this research is peer-reviewed academic articles and high-level papers and reports intended to inform policy makers and other elites. Without question, this research has generated many types of knowledge that have informed efforts to improve the quality of life in American communities and metropolitan areas. This is, however, only one approach to conducting research, gathering knowledge, disseminating knowledge, and improving life quality.

An alternative approach—one followed by ERCs—is to initiate a collaborative research endeavor in which the residents, grassroots organizations, community coalitions, and community leaders have a larger and more prominent role. The collaborative research approach is characterized by community partners—working in tandem with university faculty, staff, and students—*mutually* engaging in defining research questions, designing data collection strategies, interpreting research findings, and disseminating research knowledge. This work

311

often, but not exclusively, follows the general approach of *participatory action research*, "a way for professional researchers and community residents to collaborate on investigations into issues—such as housing, healthcare, and environmental conservation—with the goal of achieving positive social change" (Center for Cultural Understanding and Research, 2007). Research created through university community partnerships has also been termed "public scholarship."

Although operating as part of universities, ERCs have permeable boundaries with close and regular linkages with the communities they serve, operating at was has been called the "engagement interface." It is at this interface where "a combination of faculty, staff and students, and community members work collectively to address important, and sometimes urgent, societal problems that arise out of daily community life. The engagement interface is a dynamic, evolving and co-constructed space—a cooperative community of inquiry— where partners work together with an activist orientation to seek transformative ends for both the community and the academic setting" (Peters, Jordan, Adamek, & Alter, 2005). Life in ERCs is indeed dynamic, nonroutine, community-focused, and evolutionary in practice. Such centers function at the intellectual boundaries where members of the university and community can share expertise and knowledge, creating new forms of research activities and richer forms of learning and insight.

ERCs operate differently than traditional urban research institutes. Rather than going to the community *after* a research project has been designed by university-based faculty, ERCs involve community members *before* a research project is developed and ask for their help in shaping the research. As one advocate for university-community partnerships has noted: "The best way to form relationships with clients [community partners] is to do research with them. Data requires very strong partnerships with different constituent groups. You can reach more people through partnerships, and you can pay your partners back with better research" (Mahoney, 2008, p. 14). Not only does this process bring rich community knowledge into play in the research process—community knowledge and experience that a faculty researcher might not even be aware exists—but it provides an additional perspective and knowledge base that strengthens research outcomes. At the heart of rigorous research is a commitment to exploring social problems from multiple perspectives to better understand its multiple facets. This process of triangulation is a proven methodology in academia, but is often lacking in research when it comes to inviting community eyes, ears, and voices to the process of shaping research.

In sum, ERCs, although operating under varied names with diverse missions, tend to share common elements. These include:

- Developing research focused on local communities;
- Engaging in collaborative research where community partners play significant roles in designing research questions and using research findings. In many cases this will also include collecting and analyzing data;
- Conducting research on a wide variety of community issues rather than focusing on specific policy areas;
- Appreciating the importance of interdisciplinary approaches and participation by university and community partners representing multiple disciplines; and

312

- Demonstrating a willingness to combine "university knowledge" with "community knowledge" as well as sharing knowledge and expertise with other centers outside their university that are also engaged in collaborative research.

Community Connections: Adding Chairs to the Research Table

ERCs add chairs to the research enterprise table. The traditional academic research process involves many informal discussions and meetings with colleagues to shape the research question and design. Ideas are shared with colleagues in hallway conversations or informal brown-bag lunches. In essence, colleagues sit down at the research table to develop research projects. Colleagues question each other as a way of clarifying research questions. One colleague may note a research article that a colleague may not have seen, but which may be helpful in shaping your research. Another might suggest angles on how to structure a focus group, survey, or data analysis. Still other colleagues may argue substantive points related to the proposed research as a way of sharpening research goals and arguments.

These research table discussions have been effective in shaping rigorous research over the years. Adding community colleagues, community perspectives, and community critiques to the same process can only strengthen it. Collaborative researchers do not suggest that this process should replace traditional research avenues. Rather, this collaborative process has the potential of adding valuable new perspectives to existing research efforts. Because this research is informed by community perspectives and essentially already vetted for its relevance to broader publics outside of academia, it is also more likely to get the attention of policy makers and the media. It is research with a constituency and research ready for consumption by academic and nonacademic audiences.

Factors Contributing to the Growth of Engaged Research Centers

The growth of ERCs in colleges and universities in the United States has been stimulated by a variety of factors that include:

- Expanding pressure on higher education to become more engaged in and relevant to solving immediate social and economic challenges in urban and metropolitan communities
- Efforts by a number of disciplines to encourage public scholarship
- Initiatives of federal government agencies and major philanthropic organizations to encourage colleges and universities to contribute their research and outreach efforts to strengthen disadvantaged communities
- New conceptions of "basic" research—from such traditional funders of such research like the National Science Foundation and the Centers for Disease Control—that include expectations for translational research (transmitting findings of basic research to inform practice in the field) and application of research to immediate problems facing communities
- The growth of international networks promoting engaged scholarship

Pressure for Increased Engagement

From Ernest Boyer's *Scholarship Reconsidered* (1990) to the 2004 Wingspread Report, *Calling the Question: Is Higher Education Ready to Commit to Community Engagement* (Bruckhardt,

313

Holland, Percy, & Zimpher, 2004), there have been calls for institutions of higher education to become more connected to the communities, regions, and states in which they are located. There has always been pressure on public institutions to justify state funding. Beyond looking at the general benefits of educating new generations of undergraduate and graduate students, at annual state legislative deliberations, elected officials often want to see how university-based research has helped the state's industries or how it has improved the quality of life for local communities. In the early 1990s, after hearing a presentation and descriptions of a number of university-community research projects completed by a new multiuniversity network in Chicago, a vice provost of Temple University commented to the presenter (Nyden), "Boy, I wish I had a list like that last week when I was making my annual presentation to the state legislature in Harrisburg" justifying the proposed university budget for the upcoming year.

The Carnegie Foundation for the Advancement of Teaching university classification system, the revered yardstick of university pecking order, looks at degrees offered, teaching orientation, and research as ways of classifying U.S. universities. Responding to pressures to better measure universities' level of engagement in research and programmatic activities that matter to the broader public, the Carnegie Foundation created a new classification system in 2006. As Amy Driscoll, the coordinator of the new classification process, explains, "The redesign stemmed from a concern about the inadequacy of the classification for representing institutional similarities and differences and its insensitivity to the evolution of higher education" (Driscoll, 2008, p. 39). Although this is an elective system, seventy-six colleges and universities have received classification as "institutions of community engagement." This is a recent and further reflection of the growing recognition by universities that connection to outside communities and organizations is an increasingly important measure of their academic standing. ERCs and informal networks of community-engaged faculty and students figure prominently in the activities of these universities.

Another facet of increased engagement among U.S. colleges and universities has been the near-universal development of service-learning. On the one hand this reflects growing attention by educators to connecting students to practical experiences through class-based projects, internships, and special service initiatives. On the other hand, most faculty see such activities as separate from the research they are expected to do to gain tenure and promotion—particularly those levels of activity expected from them at research-intensive universities. However, one could argue that student involvement in ERCs represents the more advanced level of service-learning. It is the active use of theoretical and methodological skills in addressing issues of importance to local communities. Typically, the more sophisticated engaged research activities are located in ERCs rather than the service-learning offices. Apart from the need for more specialized oversight in ongoing research activities, ERCs have recognized that if they were to describe their activity as "service-learning," it would most likely diminish the status of their work in their universities and in their disciplines.

A New Emphasis on Public Scholarship

Public scholars have long played a role in American society. These individuals have sometimes functioned outside of university settings. Although he was in and out of university settings at various times of his life, W. E. B. DuBois could be a classic example of such a scholar. Similarly, Jane Addams could be seen as a voice outside of academia. In both cases, this public scholarship was a product of exclusion by the traditional academic world. DuBois's activism in addressing racial inequalities in the United States, as well as Addams's orientation in taking research knowledge and creating institutions that directly worked to ameliorate the dire circumstances faced by new immigrants, took place outside university settings. At other times, public scholars have been based inside university settings but venture out of university settings to engage broader publics in the relevant policy and research issues. Cornell West and Henry Louis Gates are contemporary examples of scholars based in the academy, but very active and visible outside the university in highlighting continuing racial inequalities and identifying solutions to such inequalities.

Whereas many of the professional associations representing the more applied fields such as social work, education, business, urban planning, and law have inherently had links to practical issues outside of higher education, other disciplines have shown increased interest in public scholarship. For example, the American Anthropological Association and American Sociological Association (ASA) both have either sections or task forces focusing on public social science. In 2004, ASA President Michael Burawoy set into motion a new emphasis on public scholarship within his field. He describes the new "public sociology" as "a sociology that seeks to bring sociology to publics beyond the academy, promoting dialogue about issues that affect the fate of society" (Burawoy et al., 2004, p. 104). Burawoy further describes one type of public sociology, "organic" public sociology, where sociologists and publics work together to frame and address social problems (Burawoy, 2005, p. 7). This orientation approximates the approach taken by ERCs.

Craig Calhoun, President of the Social Science Research Council, further underscores that the traditional distinction between "pure" research and "public" or "applied" research is a red herring. He states:

> It distracts attention from the fundamental issues of quality and originality and misguides as to how both usefulness and scientific advances are achieved. Sometimes work undertaken mainly out of intellectual curiosity or to solve a theoretical problem may prove practically useful. At least as often, research taking up a practical problem or public issue tests the adequacy of scientific knowledge, challenges commonplace generalizations, and pushes forward the creation of new, fundamental knowledge. (Calhoun, 2004, p. 12)

Federal and Foundation Funding Encourages Engaged Scholarship

Over the past twenty years, both federal and private funder initiatives have used the carrot of funding to encourage engaged scholarship. In the early 1990s, the U.S. Department of Education's Urban Community Service Program provided funding "to encourage urban academic institutions to work with private and civic organizations to devise and implement solutions to pressing and severe problems in their urban communities" (U.S. Department of Education, 1994). Although budget cuts during the Clinton administration ultimately ended this program, more than $30 million in grants were provided during a six-year period.

The Chicago-based Policy Research Action Group (PRAG) was a distinctive network of four universities and multiple community partners funded under the UCS Program. It involved a partnership among Loyola University Chicago, the University of Illinois Chicago, DePaul University, and Chicago State, and more than fifty community partners over fifteen years. Its more than a hundred community-engaged research projects helped to create or support an environment of engagement among universities and colleges in the Chicago metropolitan area. More information on PRAG is available at http://www.luc.edu/curl/prag/. A special issue of PRAG's journal *PRAGmatics* describes the first ten years of the network: http://www.luc.edu/curl/prag/Winter99.pdf. Some of PRAG's projects are also discussed in *Building Community: Social Science in Action* (Nyden, Burrows, Figert, & Shibley, 1997). The success of PRAG was a significant contributing factor to the development of the Center for Urban Research and Learning (CURL) at Loyola University Chicago (described later in this chapter).

The U.S. Department of Housing and Urban Development's Community Outreach Partnership Program (COPC) and Community Development Work Study Program were among the longer-lasting government initiatives intended to stimulate engaged research initiatives and even formal centers within higher education. COPC typically gave two- to three-year grants up to $400,000. Elaborate guidelines ensured that community engagement and shared resources with nonuniversity, community-level organizations were part of these projects. The hope was that this seed money would help anchor new ERCs in multiple universities. Although there was an opportunity to apply for a smaller follow-up grant after the basic grant was expended, COPC rules prohibited any university or college from getting a second grant. Although this program did stimulate significant new initiatives around the country, its built-in permanent "sunset" provision for funding contributed to the end of the program. Higher education institutions had little incentive to lobby for program continuation or expansion once they had received their $400,000 grant. This, combined with limited interest by the Bush administration to continue it, led to end of funding in the early 2000s.

In the late 1990s, the Fannie Mae Foundation created a University-Community Partnership Initiative that also encouraged research and related housing investment in local communities. Although a relatively short-lived program with a smaller number of funded projects than the COPC program, it also contributed to increased interest by universities in engaged research. Essentially described as model programs, the intent was to encourage other higher education institutions to look at research and local community investment strategies. (Ironically, these initiatives intended to create sustained university-community engagement have been discontinued, in part because higher education itself was not able to quickly recognize the value of engagement and push for continued support to continue it.)

Private foundations have had a long track record of supporting university-community engagement. In most cases these are directly linked to substantive priorities such as community development, food security, public health, affordable housing, and youth participatory action research. For example, in 1989, it was initial discussions at the John D. and Catherine T. MacArthur Foundation and initial funding by the Foundation that provided the foundation for Chicago's Policy Research Action Group. Looking for ways of addressing criticisms of the Foundation's strategy of funding community-based efforts in Chicago's neighborhoods rather than big downtown economic development projects, the Foundation was seeking advice. The idea of bringing academic researchers and community leaders together in research efforts was one of the ideas coming out of this meeting.

The Foundation recognized that researchers and community activists represented two major sources of creative thinking and practical solutions. The historical tensions between activists and academics were seen as creative forces to be harnessed rather than as an impediment to developing innovative grassroots-based policy solutions (Nyden & Wiewel, 1992). Along with the Joyce Foundation, the MacArthur Foundation funded a regional community leader and researcher planning process first determined what were the top ten challenges to Chicago communities. Ten "white papers" on these issues and possible solutions were then commissioned in preparation for a regional working conference. Papers commissioned for the conference were later published in *Challenging Uneven Development: An Urban Agenda for the 1990s* (Nyden & Wiewel, 1991). The creative tension between community activists and academic researchers that was apparent during the planning process and working conference led to the development of PRAG.

The Ford Foundation and Kellogg Foundation have supported numerous collaborative university-community research and action projects over the past two decades. Since 1990, the smaller Bonner Foundation has supported primarily student-oriented engagement programs. Although not necessarily funding research activities, the connections to community organizations and increased visibility on a number of campuses have provided credibility and support to faculty on these campuses who do engage in community-based participatory research.

Translational Research in Health Research

Perhaps one of the most significant changes in funding priorities in recent years has taken place within the health research fields. In 2001, the Agency for Healthcare Research and Quality Conference hosted a working conference on "Promoting Community-Based Participatory Research" with the intent of modifying research strategies for some of the projects funded by the major U.S. government health research organizations, such as the National Institutes of Health (NIH), the National Institute of Mental Health, and the Centers for Disease Control. Subsequent to the conference, the research organizations started new funding programs that explicitly called for the use of community-based participatory research (CBPR) strategies. This grew out of a recognition that CBPR can yield research outcomes and data not obtainable through traditional avenues.

At the same time, the agencies created new offices within the agencies to support "translational research"—research that takes existing bench research and gets it into the hands of practitioners. (More information on NIH translational initiatives may be found at National Institutes of Health, 2008.) Some policy makers recognized a research crisis where health knowledge developed in research centers was taking as much as fifteen years before it got into the doctor's office. Given the massive volume of funding in the health field relative to other areas of academic research, these changes have sent a clear message to higher education regarding priorities for community-engaged research. Also, one of the more effective national networks encouraging community-engaged research is in the public health field.

The Community-Campus Partnerships for Health has been working for a number of years with academic researchers and community-based health care agencies and advocates in changing research priorities in this field. (More information is available at http://www.ccph. info/.)

International Networks

With new communications technologies—most notably, the Internet—comparative international research has been reshaped. It no longer takes high-resourced international research institutes to coordinate international research. Community-based researchers who had previously been relegated to things "parochial" in academic circles can now directly communicate with academic and community colleagues in other countries. In fact, new international organizations to facilitate such "local-to-local" research and action connections have emerged in recent decades. In *Blessed Unrest*, environmentalist Paul Hawken points to massive growth in grassroots organizations around the world that are having an impact on local practices and increasingly influencing global policy (Hawken, 2007).

A number of international networks involving university-community research collaborators have emerged in the past thirty years. Most notable is the European-based LivingKnowledge network (more information is available at http://www.scienceshops.org/). Over the past thirty years, a network of "science shops"—university-based centers that work explicitly to invite community input into research and research priorities—has grown and most recently has received support from the European Union. The network now has bi-annual international conferences of scholars and activists and has created mentoring networks to develop new science shops in other European countries and cities. The Australian Universities Community Engagement Alliance (AUCEA) has worked to promote coordinated research projects in that country (more information is available at http://aucea.med.monash.edu. au:8080/traction). In Canada, the biennial Community-University Exposition has served to bring together community-based researchers and community activists to share information and forge new connections. Participatory action research networks in Latin America have regularly held conferences and seminars to maintain links among community-based projects in multiple countries.

U.S. engaged researchers are increasingly participating in these international networks. Two peer-reviewed journals developed in 2008 are now publishing research outcomes from international projects. *Gateways: The International Journal of Community Research and Engagement* is an e-journal jointly published by CURL and the University of Technology Sydney (UTS) Shopfront (more information can be found at http://epress.lib.uts.edu.au/ojs/ index.php/ijcre). UTS Press has included *Gateways* among its new constellation of free journals intended to make knowledge more accessible to broader audiences. In Canada, *Manifestation: Journal of Learning and Community Engaged Partnership* is another e-journal focusing on participatory action research and other community-engaged scholarship (more information on the journal can be found at http://www.manifestationjournal.org/). The increasingly active international collaborative research networks along with even more visible journals are elevating the legitimacy and appeal of engaged scholarship in many U.S. universities.

Different Pathways in Creating Engaged Research Centers

Truth be told, there is no common pathway through which ERCs have been created. In fact, most have unique backgrounds. Most did not start big; instead, they grew as the result of some stimulating factor or factors, struggled, and found their way. They were not, typically, embraced as consistent with the core values of higher education; instead, they were often viewed as square pegs within the otherwise round, disciplinary-based confines of the academy. They may have been valued by university leaders, anxious to demonstrate the connectedness of their institutions to community problem solving, but they have often been misunderstood, even unappreciated, under academic structures that reward large-scale, traditional research efforts that garner extramural support and indirect costs.

Often, in their formative years, ERCs work hard to find their way and to build meaningful relationships with their local communities. They may stumble as they become acquainted with and build informal relationships into more formal networks, initiatives, and organizations at the levels of neighborhood, community, and region. On the one hand, academic participants in these developing ERCs hear how some communities feel overstudied and underappreciated. Despite university oversight of research ethics through Institutional Review Boards, many community residents and leaders describe "hit and run" research practices by faculty and students. Not only do they not have a voice in what research gets done, but when this university-generated research is completed, they typically do not see the outcomes. They feel abused by university researchers who come into their communities to extract information but who never return to share findings or information. To many community members, "research" is something that is conceptualized by people outside their community, is written in academic language that is hard to understand, is published in obscure journals that they do not read, and ends up on library shelves to gather dust.

On the other hand, where research is framed as a more collaborative and cooperative venture, community resistance to research can quickly disappear. In fact, community partners come to be among the biggest boosters of such research. Faculty and students involved in the development of ERCs see the importance of building credibility and trust in the eyes of the community. This does not happen instantly, but only after both university and community have ventured into cooperative research projects. Over the months and years, this credibility becomes a major resource of ERCs.

Many ERCs begin to gain traction when they become involved in a significant project or community-building initiative. University participants learn to listen to community perspectives, and to reflect on what skills and expertise they can contribute to a partnership with community and the relationship building that must necessarily take place for all partners in the collaboration to work effectively toward common objectives. Dedicated work, commitment to collaboration, and staying the course ultimately create valuable social capital: mutual trust and respect. Once trust and respect emerge, the university faculty and students find themselves invited to engage in more projects, short- and long-term. From here, the opportunities for engagement grow, often exponentially, not just for pro bono work, but for collaborative projects that are attractive to government and foundation funding. Growing opportunities to earn revenues from engagement allows centers to grow staff and expertise, expanding capacity to be effective research partners.

Organizational Features of Engaged Research Centers with the Academy

ERCs take many forms and structures within higher education institutions. Given their diversity, it is difficult to enumerate the exact parameters of what constitutes an ERC. However, ERCs generally share the following features within their institutions of higher education.

1. *Interdisciplinary Focus:* ERCs are usually able, through formal structure or, more commonly, through relationship-based practice, to utilize faculty, staff, and student expertise from across the whole campus, reflecting capacity to create interdisciplinary models and teams to explore community-based issues. These centers often grow with roots within the social sciences, but also have strong connections to professional schools and programs that have had long-standing community connections. The breadth of academic and disciplinary knowledge and expertise that can be called together within such centers is a rich and powerful asset that ERCs bring to community engagement. Faculty from varied disciplines can be drawn into the research when such research is related to their individual research interests and expertise.

2. *Free-Standing Position:* Often, ERCs operate as units outside of individual academic departments. The directors of these centers often report to deans or other campus administrators rather than department chairs and faculties; this reporting arrangement gives them more latitude to build partnerships and interdisciplinary connections than would be the case in an academic department that focuses on a single academic discipline. Illustrating this pattern, for example, one of the authors, the Director of the Center for Urban Learning and Research (Philip Nyden), reports to the Graduate Dean/Associate Provost of Research at Loyola University, and the second author, Director of the Center for Urban Initiatives and Research (Stephen Percy), reports to the Dean of the Graduate School at the University of Wisconsin–Milwaukee.

3. *Utilization of Professional Staff:* ERCs often rely on professional staff as core members of the research activity. These individuals, trained in social science skills and research methods (including research design), devote full attention to research, rather than instructional, efforts (although such staff may teach courses for academic units). These center-based staff members are critical to center operation because they not only understand community-based research, they also understand how to navigate within and build partnerships with the community. They also understand the "community timeline" and the need for time-sensitive research as opposed to the academic schedule that guides action within the academy.

4. *Involvement of Graduate Students:* Many ERCs hire graduate students from a variety of graduate programs, both academic and professional, to join their research teams. Graduate students contribute their knowledge of research activity and their discipline and have the opportunity to learn, firsthand, about community-based research including research design, data collection, data analysis, and report writing. This involvement

320

during their career as graduate students may encourage and empower these young scholars to pursue community-based research as part of their academic careers, meaning that ERCs contribute to building cohorts of community-based scholars within higher education institutions.

5. *Growing Connections to Undergraduate Education:* ERCs are increasingly building connections to undergraduate education. The applied research conducted in the centers offers many opportunities for undergraduates to join research teams and explore research questions based within and immediately relevant to the local communities in which they live. Sometimes students join the staff of centers as hourly employees, and other times their involvement is organized as part of classes focused on service or engaged learning.

6. *Business Models Based on Extramural Funding:* It is common for ERCs to find research sponsors who provide financial resources to cover research costs. Local governments, agencies of state government, nonprofit organizations, school districts, local philanthropic foundations, and community collaboratives are all potential sources for supporting research on such community issues as problem identification, program evaluation, surveys to measure citizen preferences for policies and services, and amelioration of community problems. Few universities can afford to cover the costs of community-based research through their own budgets, meaning that ERCs must become entrepreneurial and build financial models that include extramural financial support. Generation of extramural support is appreciated by campus administrators and links ERCs to university research missions.

7. *Engaged Research Generates Visibility and Support:* Meaningful engaged research brings community visibility to colleges and universities and enhances community appreciation for the immediate value that higher education institutions bring to the communities, region, and states in which they are located. For public institutions, this visibility and community appreciation can enhance the efforts of campus leaders to garner expanded public support for their campus. For example, under the banner of the Milwaukee Idea—the commitment of the University of Wisconsin–Milwaukee to focus energy and talent on community engagement—the university garnered a substantial increment in state funding.

Centers Institutionalize Engaged Research

The creation of formal ERCs within a university represents a significant step toward institutionalizing engaged research in the institution. Not only does this increase the visibility of engaged research in the institution, but formal centers serve other functions: advocates for engaged faculty researchers; mentors to undergraduate and graduate students; developers of interdisciplinary projects; convener of university and community participants in engaged research; points of entry for prospective community research partners; keepers of institutional track-record and credibility in completing effective engaged research; and funders (or funding facilitators) of engaged research projects.

Most universities have scores of faculty and graduate students who are doing some form of engaged scholarship. This represents a growing resource base, but often one that is not fully developed. Separated in the different silos of universities—in the different schools, departments, and subdisciplines—not only do these scholars not see each other, but administrators do not always see the extent of the resource. The outside community may see only that part of the university with which they are working on a particular project, and thus outside community organizations are inclined to see the university-community cooperation in which they are involved as the exception rather than the rule in universities. They may still see universities as inaccessible places. However, as ERCs develop and regularly respond to issues emerging in surrounding communities, they serve to coordinate interdisciplinary research efforts within the universities, bringing together multiple departments and schools.

A Support Network for Engaged, Interdisciplinary Research

ERCs help to increase the visibility engaged scholarship and organize such research *across* the university. Issues developed in collaboration with community partners tend to be interdisciplinary issues. Everyday life is not partitioned into silos that parallel the disciplinary divisions in the typical university. Although those distinct disciplinary perspectives may serve well to focus undergraduate and graduate training as well as shape distinctive theoretical and methodological approaches to research, the boundaries can discourage research that is responsive to the multifaceted needs of individuals, families, and communities. In addition to their ability to cross over the university-community boundary, ERCs can help faculty and students cross over these disciplinary boundaries to create a more robust research environment.

Because engaged scholarship and interdisciplinary research are not top priorities in many academic departments and schools, engaged scholars within those schools and departments can become isolated. However, when interdisciplinary ERCs are established on campus, they provide a home for engaged research faculty from multiple disciplines. Centers become focal points of university research activity and can highlight work of faculty and graduate students in ways that they cannot do as individual faculty.

Centers produce a critical mass of faculty who not only can help themselves in their own engaged work, but provide the visibility, capacity, and credibility that facilitates the recruitment of more faculty, graduate students, and undergraduates into engaged research projects. In the experience of CURL, the positive "buzz" that Center faculty and student researchers have produced in their home departments has become a major recruitment tool for new Center researchers. Centers can even become an attraction for prospective faculty and students. For example, as CURL became more visible and better known inside and *outside* the university among community partners and, nationally, among colleagues in various disciplines, graduate student applicants and faculty candidates have identified CURL as an attraction in coming to Loyola University Chicago. In any given year, CURL staff and fellows are asked to talk with a dozen or more prospective faculty and graduate students as part of recruitment efforts.

Centers also provide organized political counterpoint to the "wait-until-you-get-tenure" advice that many engaged scholars receive from colleagues in their own departments. Many engaged researchers talk about chairpersons, colleagues in their departments, or faculty attending professional meetings freely giving the advice not to do nontraditional engaged scholarship while working toward tenure. The traditionalist's advice is to play it safe, not spend time engaging with community partners, but just define research projects that will yield sufficient data to use in peer-reviewed articles or other professional publications.

Doing engaged research as a lone scholar can be daunting as a researcher works to establish complex relationships with community partners, gain credibility, and develop a track record. However, doing such research in cooperation with other faculty, students, and community partners can make such work less daunting. In fact, once a faculty member has gained a foothold in community-engaged research, the doors to new research opportunities typically open up wide. ERCs help to overcome some of the time-consuming aspects of the engaged scholarship start-up process. Because centers already have established relationships and many other supportive faculty, students and junior faculty can gain instant credibility with community partners and an instant track record by building on the past work of the center with which they are now affiliated.

Similarly, centers become effective sources of support when junior faculty are being considered for tenure. As university administrators and other faculty colleagues see the outcomes of the center research—which include both reports produced for community partner consumption and articles for peer-reviewed publications—center faculty directors and other researchers (both inside and outside the university) connected with past research projects can provide strong recommendations for tenure and promotion. Just as ERCs play a role in faculty tenure and promotion, the centers provide tangible resources to community partners as well as to faculty and students.

Centers Help Community Formulate Research Design

Although community partners may have a clear view of what information and new knowledge they need, they may not know how to systematically collect that knowledge in their own communities or organizations. They benefit from expert help that university faculty and staff can provide in creating appropriate research designs and data collection strategies. The diverse nature of community issues provides opportunities for creative approaches to research design and data gathering. For example, the Center for Urban Initiatives and Research (CUIR) at the University of Wisconsin–Milwaukee worked with a funding collaborative to craft a multifaceted research design aimed at positive youth development and crime reduction. The research approaches included community surveys, electronic surveys, in-person interviews, and focus groups. In another project, one conducted for a local philanthropic foundation, CUIR conducted interviews with a wide set of stakeholders including actual and potential donors, community residents, professional advisors engaged in estate planning, local government officials, and executives in nonprofit organizations. In both cases, the university, in collaboration with community partners, designed research projects and data collection instruments to gather knowledge sought by sponsors.

323

Centers Provide Tangible Resources to Community and University

A center's collective track record of working on successful collaborative projects with community partners facilitates further research connections. As one of CURL's partners put it, the center has become their "research arm." In some cases, one project evolves into another project as new issues are identified in the initial research project. In other cases, organizations come back to the center because it is the part of the university with which they are familiar and have had a positive experience.

It would be naïve to think that the sole attraction of an ERC is the researcher camaraderie it provides and or kudos it gives to faculty and students completing successful research projects. Established ERCs also provide direct research support from fellowships to small research grants. The typically streamlined process for getting research stimulation money is very attractive to faculty interested in pursuing engaged research projects. Rather than playing the low-odds game of getting competitive research dollars from foundations or government agencies, university centers serve as a research grant convenience store that can be a first stop in project development and larger outside funding down the road.

In addition to internal resources provided by centers, their ability to bundle the university's engaged research portfolio gives the center a track record with many prospective funders. Unlike an individual faculty member—particularly a junior faculty member just getting started in the research funding process—a center and its past successful work establishes a collective credibility that creates a favorable response from funders looking at subsequent grant applications. Even though past work may have been completed by three or four different researchers in two or three different projects, it is the overall accomplishments of "the center" that is seen by prospective funders. As an ERC matures, this experience and credibility increasingly becomes a valuable asset to the center and university.

Of course, a well-established ERC also has the staff to provide support in writing and submitting grants for funding. Generally, this includes more than just writing the "boilerplate" wording in applications, which is often what professional grant writers in research services offices do. Grant development and writing by a ERC goes beyond this "boilerplate" grant writing that would just involve the generic wording on the university's "commitment to the community" or budget narratives for basic staff positions. A dedicated ERC is often involved in convening "think tank" meetings of faculty and community partners to discuss general research ideas.

Just as the engaged research process is a shared experience, project development inside the center is a shared experience among faculty, students, and staff. CURL staff and experienced advanced graduate research fellows are actively involved in designing and describing methodologies, CS such as community-based participatory research, participatory evaluation research, or collaborative university-community-run focus groups. They are also involved in writing substantive sections of the research grant that address core theoretical issues that might be anchored in disciplinary-based research literature or policy issues relevant to community partners. Also, new research projects often emerge out of existing projects completed by the center. Unlike an individual faculty member, who may have limits in his/her ability to complete a current project and write a new grant, with center help CURL not only can pull together a new grant application, but potentially can recruit new faculty and students from contacts that are constantly being developed throughout the university.

Stimulating New Research

A key function of ERCs is to coordinate research efforts, from hosting "idea meetings" where faculty and community partners discuss research ideas to facilitating project development and completion. CURL offers an example of the multiple ways in which new ideas are generated. Because fifteen or more research projects are going on at any one time, new ideas are generated from these ongoing projects themselves. In other cases, potential issues arising in multiple places may attract staff attention. For example, in three different projects—one on impacts of gentrification on communities of color, another on homelessness, and a third on aging—evidence of increasing inequality among Chicago's over-65 population became apparent. This led to more discussion among staff and ultimately the convening of a group of faculty, colleagues from nonprofit social service agencies, and local and state government officials to discuss shaping a research project that would not only address the details of this growing inequity, but explore effective policy and social service agency approaches that could address this trend.

In addition to meetings that might be convened to address emerging issues, CURL has regular meetings among staff, faculty, and student researchers to discuss ongoing research projects. There are three types of meetings monthly. First, at regular meetings of full-time staff (eight to ten normally), pressing project needs, overall center administrative issues (e.g., timing of newsletters, follow-up on Advisory Board meetings, new staff needs), and quick updates on project status are discussed. These have more of an organizational and bureaucratic focus. Second, at "idea meetings" among all staff, faculty fellows, and graduate fellows, topics of discussion are new ideas that are emerging out of existing projects; ideas that community partners may have mentioned; or ideas that are timely given emerging local, regional, or national policy issues. Typically, these lead to follow-up meetings with existing or prospective community partners. Finally, monthly meetings are held among all research team participants to discuss both the substantive and "nuts-and-bolts" aspects of ongoing projects. The leadership of these meetings is rotated among members of research teams—mostly graduate fellows. Meetings typically focus on particular issues, such as questions about Institutional Review Board comments on multiple participatory evaluation procedures, logistics of working with community partners in collecting survey data, or how to best manage undergraduate participation in CURL research teams.

During the semester, CURL schedules Friday morning seminars where presentations are made by a variety of speakers. These range from faculty talking about ongoing (non-CURL-related) research to community organization leaders or government officials talking about policy matters facing local communities. Still other seminars provide new findings from CURL projects. In addition to providing a broad view of research and policy issues, these seminars function to demystify the research and policy-making process. The give and take in discussions during the seminars, and the fact that all of those attending the seminars are themselves involved in research projects, serves to engage students, faculty, and staff in broad research and policy discussions.

325

A Culture of Participation and Engagement

Through all of the different CURL meetings, a culture of research engagement is created inside the center. Rather than being something that "someone else does," research and policy become something in which all CURL faculty, students, and staff participate. The participatory culture of the center has even spread to administrative support staff not typically viewed as researchers. In multiple projects, the administrative manager, who is a native Spanish speaker, has been involved in doing interviews and focus groups in Spanish with local community members.

This participatory and engaged ethos complements the overall participatory research focus of the center and further strengthens its work. On more than one occasion, graduate fellows have reported that their home departments have questioned whether they want to "go down to the center" when they might be better "socialized" into their discipline and research by staying in the department and accepting a department-based research fellowship. The common response to this by students is that the typical department research assistantship involves working with one faculty member with direct contact 1 or 2 hours a week and mostly independent research work for the remaining 18 or 19 hours of their weekly work obligations.

In contrast, work at CURL is much more interdisciplinary and social. At any given time, graduate research fellows work along side twelve to fifteen other staff, faculty, and undergraduate students. Representing more than ten different disciplines, colleagues at the center provide a very effective resource. Questions about methodologies, experience working in the same community, new research in different fields, and just how to work a computer application are routinely raised and answered efficiently and effectively in this environment. Students have also noted that this creates a less alienating environment than the typical lone-range model into which they are socialized in their home departments. This further prepares them for collaborative research environments where there are multiple team members on projects.

Funding and Developing Centers

ERCs generally do not emerge overnight. Often, they emerge after an initial collaborative project (or projects) receives funding and has shown results. There is not one funding source or one funding strategy to provide the financial support for ERCs. Individual research projects and informal research networks are often the front end of center development. In most cases, this also means initial uncompensated work by faculty and community partners. It also means thinking creatively about how existing university and community resources can be utilized to support initial engaged research efforts. The best way of illustrating this process is to provide brief discussions of the funding and development of CURL and the CUIR.

The Center for Urban Research and Learning

The Center for Urban Research and Learning at Loyola University Chicago was established in 1996. It grew out of a successful experience in Loyola's role in coordinating the Policy

Research Action Group (PRAG), the multiuniversity network of engaged researchers in Chicago described earlier in this chapter. It was the research outcomes and the almost $4 million in funding that PRAG received that got the attention of Loyola administrators in the mid-1990s. In discussions with the McCormick Tribune Foundation, the Foundation and university administrators were exploring ways of better engaging the university with the local community. The growing national interest in university engagement, combined with the experience and track record of PRAG, led the foundation to fund a new ERC at Loyola.

What was particularly distinctive about initial funding was the provision of a $600,000 grant, but also a $900,000 endowment gift to support student and faculty fellowships (later expanded to include community partner fellowships). Based on the experience of Loyola faculty with PRAG, a nontraditional research center was created at Loyola. CURL involves community partners at all levels of the research: from conceptualization and design to data collection, analysis, and report writing. After three years of success in collaborative projects, an additional grant of $750,000 and an additional endowment challenge award of $2.5 million (with the University expected to raise another $2.5 million) was provided by the McCormick Tribune Foundation. By the 2007, the endowment had grown to over $10 million, and with additional annual research funding, CURL had an average annual budget of $1.5 million.

What was significant about the endowment award—even the initial $900,000—was the legal obligation that the university was assuming in maintaining the new center and the fellowship program it was funding. CURL would not be a temporary center created to jump on the latest trend and then disappear a few years later. Rather, it became a permanent part of the university. This gave CURL staff, faculty fellows, student fellows, and community partners ample time to shape a successful center.

Employing close to ten full-time staff members, working with an average of twenty faculty members annually, and involving more than eighty-five undergraduate and graduate students (half of whom receive paid fellowships) in its research teams, CURL has become highly visible in the university. Fellowship programs have been expanded and new positions have been created over the years to meet the demands of engaged research. For example, CURL now funds full-time predoctoral (or postdoctoral) fellowships to provide opportunities and practical experience for advanced, or recently graduated, PhD students. Because graduate students have been the key coordinators of CURL's collaborative research teams (including faculty, graduate students, undergraduates, community partners, and CURL staff), this has helped to expand the center's capacity to successfully complete all phases of research projects—from project development and proposal writing to data analysis and report writing. (More information on CURL can be found on its website: www.luc.edu/curl.)

The Center for Urban Initiatives and Research

The Center for Urban Initiatives and Research at the University of Wisconsin–Milwaukee (UWM) began as the Urban Research Center, founded in 1972 as part of the university's mission as an urban research university. The center's mission evolved over time, moving from an original mission of academic exploration of issues related to urban life to a broader focus on

327

university-community engagement. In 1995, the then chancellor appointed a faculty commission to explore ways in which the university could expand its research connections to the community. The commission recommended that the Urban Research Center be renamed the Center for Urban Initiatives and Research and charged with a leadership role in engaging UWM faculty and staff with the greater Milwaukee community.

The Center's commitment to engagement was strengthened through grants from the U.S. Department of Education (Urban Community Services Program), U.S. Department of Housing and Urban Development (Community Outreach Partnerships Center and Community Development Work Study programs), and the Fannie Mae Foundation (University Partnership Program). In all cases, CUIR served as the campus focal point for community engagement. CUIR took the lead in calling together university and community representatives to plan grant initiatives, write proposals, coordinate research activities, evaluate program outcomes, and report to research sponsors. Often CUIR brought in other research centers and programs on campus focused on particular issues and expertise, including the Department of Urban Planning (geographic information systems analysis), Center for Economic Development, Center for Urban Community Development, Department of Sociology, and others. In this way, CUIR served as a focal point for campus efforts to connect with community.

Currently, CUIR operates with a staff of one faculty director, twelve professional staff, seven graduate students, and twenty undergraduate researchers and staffers. The Center conducts fifteen to twenty sponsored research contracts at any given time, with projects of small and moderate sizes under contract with local governments and school districts, nonprofit organizations, local foundations, and agencies of state government. For every dollar provided in state funding, CUIR generates two to three dollars in extramural support. In addition to sponsored research projects, CUIR operates two ancillary units totally funded with extramural dollars—one focused on access to college education and the other on supporting the information technology needs of nonprofit organizations. CUIR also sustains an undergraduate research program, hosts an annual urban initiatives conference (community-focused conversation focused on important issues facing the community), publishes a newsletter distributed on campus and in the community (*Research and Opinion*), and conducts research on nonprofit organizations and issues in nonprofit management and governance. (More information on CUIR is available on their web site: http://www4.uwm.edu/cuir/.)

Examples of Research Projects with High Impacts

Engaged research is essentially research with a constituency. Because community partners are at the table when research is conceptualized, there is already a community-identified need for the information or community readiness to use the outcomes in shaping organizational practices, developing a new program, or justifying a initiative for policy changes. Unlike purely academic research, which is designed to inform and shape the body of theory and research within the discipline, engaged research is intended for consumption by a broader audience. Also, given the collaborative nature of engaged research, the action taken as a result of the research may not involve the researcher directly, but rather involve other community leaders, policy makers, or activists who use the research in their work within organizations, work in the community, campaigning for policy change, or challenges to existing policy.

One example of a high-impact research project was a CURL project, completed in cooperation with an Alinsky-style advocacy organization—Organization of the NorthEast (ONE)—and a more traditional comprehensive social service organization—Howard Area Community Center (HACC). The project grew out of a breakfast conversation with the executive directors of the two organizations near one of Loyola's campuses. ONE, a well-established umbrella organization that had a strong track record of preserving affordable housing in communities along Chicago's far northern lakefront, was concerned about the impact of new federal welfare reform legislation on long-term viability of racially, ethnically, and economically diverse communities that had been providing positive opportunities to lower-income residents. At the same time, HACC feared that the new welfare reform legislation could limited resources available to clients using its many programs and ultimately cause them to move out of the community.

Although both organizations were aware of each other's existence, they had never worked together before. HACC did not see its role as an advocacy organization , but the threats posed by federal program changes made the partnership with ONE more attractive. Faculty and staff at CURL had worked with both organizations in the past, so it was the center that provided the link to get the project started.

Over a two-year period, CURL worked with the two organizations on a variety of projects related to affordable housing, economic development, and welfare reform impacts. A series of short research projects focused on key concerns identified by the two organizations. The first project had the most impact of all of the projects completed in this partnership. Alarmed at the potential loss of housing aid and other social service subsidies supporting elderly legal immigrants, CURL researchers sought to document the impact the loss of the program would have on the individuals and the community as a whole. More than a third of the thirty-four thousand legal elderly immigrants in the state of Illinois using this program lived in the three community areas served by ONE and HACC (Center for Urban Research and Learning, Policy Research Action Group, Organization of the NorthEast, & Howard Area Community Center, 1997).

At the suggestion of ONE, research focused on the economic loss to the community in terms of rent subsidies not provided, food stamps not spent at local stores, and other services not purchased locally. For this one program alone, CURL and ONE determined that almost $42 million per year would stop flowing through the local communities. Because both President Clinton and previously President Bush had suggested that churches could pick up some of the slack where welfare reform had cut services and payments, the research team also estimated how much money each of the two hundred religious congregations in the community areas would have to spend each month to cover this one lost program; that figure was $16,000 per month.

The down-to-earth approach in describing the economic impact (largely suggested by the community partners), combined with the fact that statewide immigrant rights groups were already campaigning for state money to cover revenue lost by the federal welfare

329

reform cuts, meant that both the media and state legislators were receptive to issues raised in the report. ONE worked with a publicist who succeeded in getting coverage in both the *Chicago Sun-Times* and *Chicago Tribune.* The report was also covered by Tele-mundo and broadcast in both North and South America. The statewide coalition succeeded in getting some new resources added to the state's funding package to replace those lost at the federal level. CURL did not have a direct role in the media or lobbying efforts. Along with other data, CURL's research was used by community partners and other statewide groups in attracting attention and obtaining the statewide legislative support. (Because the federal government ultimately reinstated some of the support, this state money was moved over to cover more day care support as part of the state welfare support package.)

Another example of high-impact research is a project conducted by the CUIR where the Center was called upon as a research partner by the Milwaukee County Parks Department at a time when the agency was considering closing seven swimming pools because of rising costs and declining usage. After political pushback in local neighborhoods, the County Board of Supervisors halted pool closing plans and commissioned a research study to inform a final decision on shutting down outdoor swimming pools.

Under a contract and through collaboration with the county, CUIR created a multifaceted research design aimed at measuring varied dimensions and perspectives on pool use, community recreation needs, preferences for public services, and quality-of-life needs of neighborhood residents. Data collection efforts and key findings from each effort included the following:

- *Interviews with youth and adult pool users* found that some adults wanted dedicated times to swim laps, teens had little interest in pools (preferring other recreational and social opportunities), and pre-teens enjoyed splashing and playing in pools rather than structured swimming.
- *Interviews with residents living in close proximity to pools slated for closing* found residents to be not very interested in swimming but very interested in more park and green space and places for seniors to gather.
- *Telephone surveys of county residents* documented strong support for and use of public parks and interest in a large water park facility.
- *Examination of existing data* documented the poor quality of outdoor pools, the relatively low (and declining) level of pool attendance, and changing demographics in neighborhoods around pools (declining number of households with children).

Using all of these data, the Parks Department created an innovative plan that called for (1) closing several pools and replacing them with (a) community meeting rooms (created from former administrative offices and bather changing rooms) and (b) wading/splash pools where young children can play; (2) creating one large water park attraction in the county; and (3) enhancing the park facilities where pools were removed to provide more useful gathering places and green space.

Upon receiving the Park Department plan, the Milwaukee County Board of Supervisors applauded both the plan and the research that had been done to inform the plan. One supervisor commented that the county should "make all of our decisions this way, based upon solid research and community feedback." The research expertise of the university, marshaled through collaborative planning with the Parks Department, enabled collection and interpretation of data that informed a creative and community-responsive plan for closing swimming pools and replacing them with other more cost-effective features in local parks.

Conclusions

Just having community and other nonacademic partners involved in conceptualizing—and in some cases other aspects of the research process—represents a significant impact on the research enterprise itself. Although traditional research approaches are effective in building knowledge *within* various academic disciplines, they have marginalized community knowledge. Ignoring community knowledge and input effectively weakens the overall body of knowledge included in the research enterprise. This is analogous to a research vision that is blind in one eye. To produce robust research with high levels of reliability and validity, a *full view* of the world is needed—a full view that includes both university-based and community-based knowledge.

Engaged research should not be the *only* way of collecting data and improving our knowledge base. Rather, engaged research *combined* with traditional approaches will strengthen our understanding of key social problems. More importantly, including community knowledge more systematically in some of our work can enhance our ability to discover solutions that may be sitting right at the doorstep of our universities.

Emerging ERCs have the potential of institutionalizing this university-community partnership by producing a more comprehensive understanding of issues facing our communities. ERCs provide a place where ideas can be exchanged among faculty, students, and community partners on a regular basis. They provide resources in the form of paid staff, faculty fellowships, student fellowships, and community fellowships. ERCs increase the visibility and credibility of this kind of work in university environments where even interdisciplinary efforts within the academy can have a hard time gaining traction.

In times of tightening resources, ERCs are effective tools that universities can use in demonstrating their contributions to the well-being of broader segments of the public, in addition to the important task of educating students. The ability to demonstrate research impacts is of particular importance to public institutions supported by tax dollars and regularly reviewed by state legislatures. ERCs make significant contributions to the public good through their efficient "mining" of *both* university and community knowledge bases. From the point of view of policy makers and taxpayers, indeed from the point of view of citizens, effective use of our creative resources is needed now more than ever.

References

Boyer, E. L. (1990). *Scholarship reconsidered: Priorities of the professoriate.* Princeton, NJ: Princeton University Press.

Bruckhardt, M. J., Holland, B., Percy, S. L., & Zimpher, N. (2004). *Calling the question: Is higher education really ready to commit to community engagement?: A Wingspread statement.* Milwaukee: University of Milwaukee–Wisconsin.

Burawoy, M. (2005). 2004 Presidential Address: For public sociology. *American Sociological Review, 70,* 4–28.

Burawoy, M., Gamson W., Ryan, C., Pfohl, S, Vaughan, D, Derber, C., et al. (2004). Public sociologies: A symposium from Boston College. *Social Problems, 51,* 103–130.

Calhoun, C. (2004). Word from the president: Toward a more public social science. Social Science Research Council. *Items and Issues, 5*(1–2), 12–14.

Center for Cultural Understanding and Research. (2007). *Collaborative research: A practical introduction to participatory action research for communities and scholars.* Chicago: Center for Cultural Understanding and Change, The Field Museum.

Center for Urban Research and Learning, Policy Research Action Group, Organization of the NorthEast, & Howard Area Community Center. (1997). *Unraveling the safety net: 1997 and welfare reform.* Chicago: Loyola University Chicago Center for Urban Research and Learning.

Driscoll, A. (2008, January/February). Carnegie's community engagement classification: Intentions and insights. *Change,* 38–41.

Hawken, P. (2007). *Blessed unrest.* London: Penguin.

Mahoney, E. (2008). Doing research with community partners. *The Engaged Scholar, 3,* 13.

National Institutes of Health. (2008). *Re-engineering the clinical research enterprise: Translational research.* Retrieved December 8, 2008, from http://www.nihroadmap.nih.gov/clinicalresearch/overview-translational.asp.

Nyden, P., Burrows, D., Figert, A., & Shibley, M. (Eds.). (1997). *Building community: Social science in action.* Thousands Oaks, CA: Pine Forge Press [Sage].

Nyden, P., & Wiewel, W. (1991). *Challenging uneven development: An urban agenda for the 1990s.* New Brunswick, NJ: Rutgers University Press.

Nyden, P., & Wiewel, W. (1992). Collaborative research: Harnessing the tensions between researcher and practitioner. *American Sociologist, 23*(4), 43–55.

Peters, S., Jordan, N. R., Adamek, M., & Alter, T. R (Eds.). (2005). *Engaging campus and community: The practice of public scholarship in the state and land grant university system.* Dayton, OH: Charles F. Kettering Foundation.

U.S. Department of Education. (1994). *Urban Community Service Program. Biennial Evaluation Report: Fiscal Years 1993–1994.* Chapter 538. Retrieved December 21, 2008, from http://www.ed.gov/pubs/Biennial/538.html.

PART 4

National Organizational Models

Edited by Lorilee R. Sandmann and Melvin B. Hill, Jr.

National Organizational Models

Lorilee R. Sandmann and Melvin B. Hill, Jr.

Harvard sociologist Daniel Bell points out that "[what is] social today becomes political tomorrow, and economic [in costs and consequences] the day after." For a social and policy issue, the formation of professional and national organizations signals movement from the emergent part of its life cycle to increasing institutionalization and professionalization. Over the past two decades, several "issue groups" or organizations have developed specifically in response to the growth of interest in community-university engagement. These have appeared in addition to a number of existing organizations and disciplinary associations that have begun directly addressing engagement through special sections or task forces.

Besides reflecting the maturation of the community engagement movement, the models in the following chapters also represent important examples of the movement's praxis, that is, its progress from theory to practice. The difficulty of moving from theory to practice has been documented well and repeatedly in every field of endeavor. Finding agreement on what the problem is (defining the problem) as well as how best to address it is difficult, particularly in the highly decentralized field of higher education; hence, the rarity of successful examples of theory in action. But that is what this section provides.

The Models

The six chapters in this section represent a diverse range of approaches and models. All espouse advancement of community-university partnership and the scholarship of engagement, but they vary considerably in many other respects. Organizational age ranges from three years to nearly twenty-five; emphasis includes disciplinary focus and functional focus

335

(service-learning, research, public policy, etc.); structure varies from formal offices and paid staff to being networked, virtual, and volunteer-led; governance is presidential or institutional or individual. It was this very diversity that spawned the Higher Education Network for Community Engagement (HENCE) to provide loose coordination between models. However, these models overlap in some of their national initiatives as well as the types of professional development or member services provided through conferences, information-rich websites, and commissioned studies. They also share an ambitious yet underfunded nature.

Although these models can inform our assessment of the engagement movement and provide best practices, one temptation that must be avoided assiduously is to assume that any of them can be automatically transferred from one environment to another. As robust case studies, these models present useful information on what has worked and what has not in a variety of contexts and settings. The most common denominators may be their driving commitment and intentionality, their passionate start-up leadership, and their timing and creative striving. In addition to the presentation of their various origins, it is their positions in future trends, issues, and challenges that will define the continuing life cycle of the community and civic engagement movement. A brief abstract of each of the models follows.

Robin Goettel and Jamie Haft present Imagining America. This model is a national consortium of colleges and universities committed to public scholarship specifically in the arts, humanities, and design. The authors discuss the organization's history, annual programming, current national initiatives, and growth and organizational challenges over the past ten years. From their comprehensive exploration of how service-learning extends its boundary by emphasizing civic engagement, the authors offer possible work-setting solutions applicable to advanced campus-community partnerships. Imagining America has made significant contributions through several national initiatives: Tenure Team Initiatives (TTI), Publicly Active Graduate Education (PAGE), and Curriculum Project.

In contrast to Imagining America's drawing from a set of disciplines, Campus Compact initially drew from the function of educating students and encouraging faculty in curricular service learning and civic engagement. Dean McGovern and Maureen F. Curley chronicle the evolution of Campus Compact through its nearly twenty-five years from its original emphasis to its current agenda of more broadly fulfilling the civic purposes of higher education through curricular service expressed as academic service-learning, community-based research, and pedagogic civic engagement.

Campus Compact, as the oldest national higher education association devoted solely to campus-based civic engagement, is a coalition of more than 1,100 college and university presidents with a dedicated office employing full-time staff. Because of its longevity, formal staffing, and solid executive membership base, Campus Compact has had a prominent role, in addition to its programming, in advocating public policy and federal funding for civic engagement. When considering future directions, the authors focus on four major trends encouraged by President Obama's signing of the Edward M. Kennedy Serve America Act: a federal commitment to civic engagement demanding more institutional civic engagement work, prompting more engaged work on and by campuses, redefining civic engagement through virtual learning, and finally, supporting continuous research on campus-based civic engagement.

Carol Coletta presents another example of university presidential involvement, CEOs for Cities, a relatively young organization. Founded in response to the changing needs in urban leadership, CEOs for Cities is a national cross-sector network of urban leaders—including university presidents alongside business, city, and nonprofit executives—"dedicated to building and sustaining the next generation of great American cities." Coletta shows how universities have supported these development efforts, giving examples of their contributions to producing talent, retaining talent, and encouraging economic growth. Providing keen insights into the continuing agenda is Michael Porter's (2001) report commissioned by CEOs for Cities, *Leveraging Colleges and Universities for Urban Revitalization: An Action Agenda.* Through its exploration of concepts including "anchor institutions" and civic leadership, CEOs for Cities is raising provocative questions for consideration. For example, with corporate CEOs' tenure getting shorter and more nonprofit leaders becoming the civic leaders, what can civic leadership do and what can it not do?

A model focused specifically on advancing research on service learning and community engagement and supporting the current and emerging researcher is described by Sherril B. Gelmon, the founding chair of the International Association for Research on Service-Learning and Community Engagement (IARSLCE). Providing a dedicated forum for research and researchers, IARSLCE has evolved from an annual gathering to a formal international membership organization that sponsors an annual research conference, publications, a graduate student network, an early career network, communications, and an award for research on service-learning and community engagement domestically and internationally. A recent membership survey suggests future strategies to build organizational sustainability.

Another emergent model, with a mission broader than IASLCE, is the Outreach Scholarship Partnership and Conference featured in the chapter by Karen Bruns. What started in 2001 as three land-grant universities providing a forum for their faculty and staff to share best practices and discuss issues to strengthen their engagement has evolved into a partnership of nine institutions. The National Outreach Scholarship Conference (NOSC) remains the primary venue for the Partnership, uniquely drawing attendees from more than eighty institutions, including all types of higher education institutions and many types of outreach units such as extension, continuing education, public broadcasting, and K–12 partnership offices. In conjunction with the conference, the Partnership has expanded to include an awards program, pre- and postconference special interest group meetings and co-location for others, a preconference workshop for emerging scholars, and a collaboration with the *Journal of Higher Education Outreach and Engagement* to publish an annual special conference issue. The governance of this model has also evolved from a memorandum of understanding to more formal by-laws for the National Outreach Scholarship Conference. Although managed by a Partnership steering committee, the institution hosting the annual NOSC has primary responsibility for that year's activities.

The final model is a type of meta-organization—a virtual network of community-engaged organizations attempting to support and coordinate the work of all other organizations with a community engagement orientation. Authors Lorilee R. Sandmann and David J. Weerts offer the role and work of the HENCE as an organization exploring collaborative strategies to advance the field of higher education and community engagement. Examples of such strategies include coordination of conference calendars to avoid scheduling conflicts and duplication of effort, and coordinating advocacy efforts for enhanced impact and results. The authors also reflect on progress of the HENCE agenda in view of the original declaration developed at its founding at a Wingspread conference in 2006. Finally, they discuss future challenges and opportunities to bring about substantial development of community engagement across diverse engagement-related organizations.

Next Stage of the Issue Life Cycle

We started this introduction to the section of the handbook by placing these national models within an issue's life cycle. The concept, developed in the late 1970s, that social and public issues have a life cycle has grown in acceptance, utility, and complexity. Key to the entire concept of issues tracking and issues management is what William L. Renfro describes in Issues Management in Strategic Planning as the premise that the development of public or social issues can be anticipated by comparison with the behavior of similar issues in the past. The timing of issue cycles varies significantly, but currently all aspects seem to be running faster and faster. The models described in this section have developed relatively rapidly in response to their particular needs, so one can anticipate continued change in the next twenty-five years. What will the models look like in the next handbook? Although the existence of these models indicates that the scholarship of engagement has reached a stage of professionalization and institutionalization, the rate of ongoing change indicates that these models will continue to mature and evolve, with new variations emerging and, perhaps appropriately, some existing ones ending as their need is met or the model becomes less functional.

As residents of Athens, Georgia, we are inspired by the inscription on the base of the statue of Athena poised at the entrance to the Classic Center in downtown Athens. The inscription is of the Athenian Oath, which was taken by the youth of ancient Athens when they reached the age of seventeen. This oath is worth recalling today:

- *We will never bring disgrace on this our City, by an act of dishonesty or cowardice.*
- *We will fight for the ideals and Sacred Things of the City, both alone and with many.*
- *We will revere and obey the City's laws and will do our best to incite a like reverence and respect in those above us who are prone to annul them or set them at naught.*
- *We will strive increasingly to quicken the public's sense of civic duty.*
- *Thus, in all these ways we will transmit this City not only not less, but greater and more beautiful than it was transmitted to us.*

To us, this is a clarion call from the time-honored past for a renewal of our civic commitment, engagement, and responsibility today. The national organizations profiled as models in this section have embraced this responsibility, and they are acting to keep the community engagement movement positioned to continue resolving social and political issues.

Campus Compact—Engaged Scholarship for the Public Good

Dean P. McGovern and Maureen F. Curley

In the mid-1980s, *Time* magazine, reporting on a recently released study of incoming college students, quoted a participant, "I want to go to college to become a doctor ... so I can make some money and then take it easy" (Bowen, 1986). We learned from this study and others like it, from pundits, and from critics that education—and specifically higher education—had become a "troubled institution" (Boyer, 1987).

At the core of the problem, according to certain observers at the time, was that colleges and universities had lost clear direction, purpose, and mission. Students were stricken with an epidemic of careerism, with large numbers attending college only to qualify for better employment or personal gain. Faculty members, driven by the urgency of professional advancement, were shirking their teaching responsibilities to free up time in pursuit of their own selfish, often esoteric activities. Institutions themselves had become fundraising machines, lavishing attention on what they could bring in—money, prestige, and students—at the expense of consideration for what they were meant to produce—namely, well-educated graduates with a sense of right, wrong, and civic responsibility (Bennett, 1984; Boyer, 1987).

Whether one subscribes to such criticism or believes that higher education was unfairly targeted, the result has been a more intense scrutiny of postsecondary education in America. Externally, the general public began closely watching the practices, principles, and modes of operation on college campuses. Internally, administrators and faculty members began to engage in more reflective assessment about the relevance of their work; a refocus on education and scholarship for the public good rather than personal gain; and more holistic outcomes for their graduates.

This scrutiny led to many questions concerning the purpose, direction, and practices of higher education in America. Ezra Bowen (1986), in an article of the same title, asked, "What is college for?" Allan Bloom (1987) charged that higher education failed democracy in his book *The Closing of the American Mind.* In 1987, Charles Sykes argued in his book *Prof Scam: Professors and the Demise of Higher Education* that the mission of higher education had been derailed. Dinesh D'Souza (1992) accused several colleges of squelching free thought in the name of multiculturalism in *Illiberal Education: The Politics of Race and Sex on Campus.* And more recently, Anthony T. Kronman (2007) lamented *Education's End: Why Our Colleges and Universities Have Given Up on the Meaning of Life.*

Serious criticism generally elicits a serious response. It is not surprising that those who work within or care deeply about higher education would want to respond to, if not necessarily refute, the criticism. Arguably, no group is more entrenched, invested, and visible in the work of higher education than college presidents. As spokespersons for their institutions, presidents possess a unique platform from which to drive discussion and change at the local and national level (McGovern, Foster, & Ward, 2002). It stands to reason that in the midst of this round of heavy public critique, a group of college presidents would respond in such an important and profound way.

In 1985, the presidents of Brown, Georgetown, and Stanford Universities teamed with the president of the Education Commission of the States to form Campus Compact. These leaders took the opportunity to unite; not just to respond to the charges, but also to promote the important role of higher education in democratic society (Colby, Beaumont, Ehrlich, & Corngold, 2007). Through investment in the Campus Compact, each encouraged the faculty and students at their institutions to be intentional about fostering civic responsibility in all aspects of college life. To this end, they committed to developing more community service and other civic engagement activities in the student and academic affairs of their campuses. They also enthusiastically encouraged their colleagues across the country, from institutions of all types, to join their efforts.

Campus Compact has since grown to encompass more than a quarter of all higher education institutions in the United States, as well as international members. Its structure, its reach across institutions, and its exclusive focus on higher education's public purposes have made it a recognized leader in engaged campus work. In this chapter, we discuss the evolution of Campus Compact and explicate what we see as the emerging trends for the organization's work in serving this field.

The Evolution of Campus Engagement

As a national organization of college and university presidents, Campus Compact committed itself to renewing the public purposes of higher education by actively and visibly supporting campus-based service and community outreach. These leaders asserted that although students were indeed engaging in some civic activities while in school, students, faculty, and institutions as a whole needed more supportive infrastructure, more encouragement, and more opportunities for these activities, which would lead to more reflective civic engagement and ultimately a better education. With these objectives, Campus Compact set out to realize a greater civic impact for higher education.

Among higher education organizations, Campus Compact's structure is unique. Governance rests with a board of directors who oversee a national office located in Boston, Massachusetts. This board is composed of college and universities presidents as well as nonprofit and corporate leaders who map out strategic directions and positions for higher education within the civic engagement movement. State affiliate offices have emerged across the country as hubs of powerful statewide higher education coalitions. (As of summar 2010, thirty-five state offices had been formally affiliated, with others in development.) Each Campus Compact state affiliate is governed by its own board of directors, and each develops local, state, and regional programming. Many state affiliate offices manage and operate statewide national service initiatives such as AmeriCorps, Learn and Serve, and AmeriCorps*VISTA programs.

Outside higher education, state Compact offices develop strong partnerships with public schools, state commissions on community service, legislators, government agencies, nonprofits, and community organizations. Within higher education, state offices work with disciplinary associations, think tanks, consortia, and research centers, as well as with individuals across functions. State offices regularly collaborate across state lines or across regions of the country to share best practices, design scholarly or practitioner conferences, collect data, and implement multistate programs. Every Compact state office forms strong working relationships with the administration, faculty, staff, students, and community partners of member institutions. These specific constituents receive attention and training to set their goals, design their service programs, and support their institutional service mission. The combination of a state office structure and a nationally guided coalition has given Campus Compact unparalleled breadth of reach and depth of personal relationships within a huge and varied group of institutions.

Since its inception, Campus Compact has been a leader in educating students for citizenship and equipping faculty members with tools to develop, implement, and evaluate rigorous curricular service-learning and civic engagement. The impact of this work has been profound, both on campus and in the community. More than 90 percent of Compact institutions include service or civic engagement in their mission statement. Compact institutions offer, on average, thirty-six service-learning courses and have an average of seventy-seven community partnerships each. Students at Compact institutions contribute a total of $7 billion in service to their communities each year (Campus Compact, 2008).

Trend data show that Campus Compact's work has had a measurable effect on the level of engagement at individual campuses as well as on higher education as a whole. Membership survey data indicate that between 2000 and 2005, the percentage of member campuses that had one or more community partnership increased from 68 percent to a near-universal 98 percent (Campus Compact, 2006). During the same period, the percentage of member institutions offering service-learning courses climbed from 79 percent to 98 percent, and the percentage of member colleges and universities that have an office specifically responsible for the coordination of community work rose from 71 percent to 86 percent. All of these increases occurred during a period of rapid membership growth and a concomitant

341

increase in the number of surveyed campuses, which one might expect would water down these figures.

A key component of Campus Compact's success through the years has been its ability to adapt its strategies to stay on top of the wave of cultural change that occurred in higher education in the waning years of the twentieth century and at the genesis of the twenty-first century. As a diverse organization comprising all institutional types—including two-year, four-year, tribal, historically Black, public, private, community, technical, religiously affiliated, and professional colleges and universities—Campus Compact has worked to stay relevant, useful, and inspirational to a wide variety of constituents. To achieve this goal, the organization has kept a careful eye on the civic and higher education landscapes and adjusted its programs and initiatives according to current needs.

Over time, the campus civic engagement movement has evolved, and Campus Compact has evolved with it. This evolution has yielded increased infrastructure and resources to meet current needs and has pushed the field to advance to the next level. In its early years, Campus Compact focused on getting students involved through volunteerism and community service. It started with a belief that this type of extracurricular service would foster and develop other civic behaviors in students such as voting organizing and engaging in policy discussions at the local, state, national, or international levels (Hollander, 2007). Campus Compact focused its programs and publications to encourage students to give their time to real causes that existed outside of the classroom. Although this strategy produced many unique and varied benefits, such as relevant "real-world" experiences, the service was often bereft of deep learning. Students needed more academic guidance to help them understand the underlying, systemic causes of the disadvantaged conditions they were seeing at soup kitchens, homeless shelters, food banks, housing projects, Indian reservations, domestic abuse centers, and other social service and community arenas. Students were getting firsthand experiences and certainly getting good things done in their communities, but they were not getting the opportunity to formally reflect on what it all meant to them personally and professionally, or what it meant for the society. Ultimately, and most discouraging, their civic behaviors weren't increasing in a significant way. A shift in strategy was necessary. The Compact shifted in two ways: (1) it began to encourage the integration of community service with the academic studies and (2) it began to help member institutions build effective and reciprocal community partnerships (Torres, 2000). Its programs and resources were designed to encourage students to give their time to causes outside of the classroom.

Since that time, the organization's mission has evolved from solely extracurricular community service to the addition of work emphasizing curricular service, including academic service-learning, community-based research, and other forms of civic engagement. In the 1990s, service-learning emerged as an effective pedagogy and a call to action for faculty around the country. Campus Compact, an early voice in the movement to embed community work into the curriculum, created a number of key resources intended to guide individual faculty members (e.g., the seminal *Fundamentals of Service-Learning Course Construction* by Kerrissa Heffernan, 2001), and eventually departments (see Battistoni et al.'s *Engaged Department Toolkit*, 2003).

From the beginning, Campus Compact was unwilling to lay responsibility for students' civic education solely at the doorstep of faculty. The *Presidents' Declaration on the Civic Responsibility of Higher Education* (Campus Compact, 2000) encouraged campuses to explore in greater depth the various ways in which they engage with their communities. Soon after, Campus Compact developed the *Indicators of Engagement,* which served as benchmarks for campuses wishing to advance the public service component of their mission—a road map of sorts for fulfilling higher education's civic responsibility (Hollander, Saltmarsh, & Zlotkowski, 2001).

In recent years, the focus has been not only on using community experience to reinforce academic learning but also on engendering in students the desire and skill to bring about positive social change. With that goal in mind, Campus Compact developed programs and incentives to help students understand the social, economic, and civic factors underlying the problems addressed by their service. Resources for engaged students, as well as the faculty and staff working with them, include *The New Student Politics* by student Sarah Long (2002) and, more recently, *Students as Colleagues: Expanding the Circle of Service-Learning Leadership* (Zlotkowski, Longo, & Williams, 2006), which was co-written by student leaders.

The broad yet resonant notion of civic learning has captured the imagination of recent scholars and practitioners. Again, Campus Compact was an early proponent of this concept, although not necessarily under that name. In addition to the Presidents' Declaration, the widely used *Civic Engagement across the Curriculum* (Battistoni, 2001) addressed notions of civic education across disciplines. More recent initiatives carry on this work, including the History, Civics, and Service project (www.compact.org/history-civics-service/), which drew connections between civic learning and service, as well as ongoing work with Engaged Scholars (www.compact.org/initiatives/civic_engagement/engaged_scholars) who explore multiple aspects of civic understanding.

Emerging Trends

Remaining current and relevant in any field is a continuous and constant task; higher education's civic engagement movement is no exception. In our view, four major trends will help redefine and reshape this movement as the twenty-first century moves past its infancy. First, we see campuses reaching for a new level of engagement with their communities and their constituencies. Recent data from The Center for Information and Research on Civic Learning and Engagement (CIRCLE) reveal that today's traditional-aged college students not only are more civically engaged than those that came before them, but also crave more meaning in their college experience (Cone, Kiesa, & Long, 2007). Many students continue to look for opportunities to connect theory to practice and to relate their "lives of the mind" with their "habits of the heart."

As students seek meaningful service projects and service-learning experiences, colleges and universities will need to respond to the growing demand. They will create new strategies that will move them toward more formalized, regular, and institutional civic engagement work. For example, community service experience will become more expected on college entrance applications. Colleges and universities will change their general education requirements and

343

begin to include some form of civic engagement exercises—service and/or service-learning will increasingly be required for graduation. We will see more faculty members being rewarded for engaged scholarship through revised promotion and tenure structures.

These changes will require some corollary measures to prepare for them. For example, administrators will need to be trained, retrained, and informed about the academic virtues of engaged pedagogy and the accepted techniques and standards of satisfactory work in this area. In addition, incoming faculty members will need to be introduced to engaged scholarship and teaching, including service-learning and community-based scholarship, at the onset of their employment or while in graduate school.

As a result, we believe that service and service-learning activities will break free of their neat and structured server-recipient relationships and their apolitical "do-gooder" themes, and that more faculty and students will view service projects as opportunities to create and foster responsible political action and bring about social justice in neighborhoods, regions, and the world at large. The pedagogy and its projects will be evaluated on the ways in which the service itself improves, expedites, delays, or interferes with social justice. This will require faculty members to work more closely with community partners. Community partners will need to be invited to join as co-educators—including the process of designing and teaching engaged courses and curricula—to ensure a seamless connection between the abstractions and theory of the classroom and the real-world practice of the community.

The second trend we see emerging is that the more engaged campus previously described will change the financial priorities of higher education. Because colleges and universities will invest more in service infrastructure—including campus-based community-service offices, faculty training in engaged scholarship, and graduate-level civic education—we will see a new synthesis in programmatic and resource development strategies. To that end, community initiatives themselves will begin to generate revenue; that is, these projects not only will contribute to educative ends, but they will also contribute to their own institutional sustainability. For example, VISTAs (Volunteers in Service to America) are currently being placed to serve communities from campuses throughout the country. VISTAs serve full-time and have many tasks, but primary among them is to create campus-community collaborations that bring together the resources of the campus, state and local governments, nonprofits, and corporations. Although this type of "cost sharing" for community projects will require campuses to reach out for financial support, it can also save and even create funding. For example, VISTAs may serve in a coordinating role, writing grants, fundraising, and recruiting and training student leaders. In addition, VISTAs and other student alumni form a pool of potential donors who are deeply committed to the service work performed on their campuses and alma maters.

As the engaged work of campuses becomes a more important priority—and consequently reaches greater levels of effectiveness and visibility—these efforts will increasingly become attractive funding options for alumni, friends, and other donors. Alumni magazines have already begun to take note of this opportunity, covering service and civic-engagement initiatives developed by current students as well as alumni. The resources generated through these means will endow campuses with centers of civic engagement, community service, and service-learning. More critical, however, will be developing fundraising strategies around institutional engagement efforts for capital and fundraising campaigns. Institutions will utilize new social networking websites, software, and phone technologies to invite potential benefactors to participate. We are confident, in this landscape, that highlighting campus civic engagement activities will revitalize regular donors and attract new donors, including alumni of these programs, to contribute.

The third trend we see is that campuses will change how they view and talk about civic engagement. Virtual learning through Internet classes and other forms of cyber-education will necessitate changes in how institutions define partnerships, service, and outreach. Faculty, students, and staff will necessarily take more holistic approaches to engagement as they communicate through email, text messaging, Facebook, LinkedIn, Tmtter, Blackboard, MySpace, and other social networking platforms. As mentioned earlier, we predict that community partners will have a more active role in course and curriculum design. Faculty members (as well as students, staff, and administrators) will need to extend explicit invitations to community partners to help meet community needs through joint scholarship and other projects. Community partners, as critical agents in the service and education enterprise, will help assess and define community needs as well as supervise students outside the classroom (Scheibel, Bowley, & Jones, 2005). Colleges and universities will utilize broader, less traditional ways of involving students in civic affairs—for example, encouraging and supporting students to get involved in municipal and state government and issues affecting the towns and cities in which campuses reside. They will utilize their community partnerships to redefine how, with whom, and by whom this engagement occurs.

Finally, the campus-based civic engagement movement will require a continuous stream of definitive research revealing impact, costs, and benefits of this work, which will allow practitioners and administrators to objectively assess the value of projects, techniques, curricular designs, practices, and pedagogies. The energy and vitality of the movement depends on regular injections of widespread data collection, rigorous analysis, and broad dissemination. Young scholars must be mobilized to assess the efficacy of engaged pedagogies and community-service programs. Offices of community involvement and their programs must be evaluated not only by the number of students they engage, but on the basis of the community outcomes they realize. Assessment must therefore include direct input from community partners as well as from the other groups involved (Gelmon, Holland, Driscoll, Spring, & Kerrigan, 2001).

Practitioners and researchers must discover, understand, and demonstrate the true impacts of service and other forms of civic engagement on the students, the faculty, the institution, and the community. That is only part of the equation, however. Advocates must take extreme care to honestly assess the costs and benefits of implementing civic engagement strategies. To gloss over the costs, pitfalls, and challenges of these endeavors will ultimately damage the effort.

Conclusion

To be sure, a college education serves several varied and diverse purposes. To some, the charge of higher education is as succinct as this: to create and disseminate knowledge.

Others see college as a "rite of passage" for young people in the space between high school and their life's calling. We view college as a unique opportunity for personal growth and advancement, but also as an important incubator for the citizens of a vibrant and engaged democracy.

In the preceding pages, we have delineated a brief history of Campus Compact, an organization of college leaders who insist on keeping civic purposes at the forefront of the American postsecondary enterprise. We believe that national organizations like Campus Compact are useful vehicles for addressing future trends. When successful, these organizations are able to remain nimble and responsive to changing environments and provide needed training, data, and support to college faculty, students, and staff. These organizations can keep their collective ear to the ground to stay sensitive to groundswells and trends. They are adept at sharing new information. Campus Compact has successfully built networks and coalitions that have yielded dividends through efficient communication systems, enthusiasm for the work, inclusive strategic planning, and a collection of best practices that serve as a tremendous resource for those seeking to implement change on campus.

We are optimistic about what lies over the horizon as we prepare to move forward in this work. Each of the trends we have identified will require that campuses form and sustain truly reciprocal community partnerships to ensure that students' educational objectives are achieved and community-identified needs are met. These partnerships will ensure that important programs and projects are funded and maintained. It is important to acknowledge that, in many cases, these aspects of campus engagement are being accomplished within the curriculum through new courses and within academic majors in areas such as education, philanthropy, nonprofit management, and social justice. Increasingly, service-learning and civic engagement are being accepted as viable and effective pedagogies throughout the disciplines. As acceptance broadens among various constituencies, the impact on students, on higher education, and on our local and global communities has the great potential to engage and educate new generations of citizens for a changing world.

References

Battistoni, R. M. (2001). *Civic engagement across the curriculum: A resource book for service learning faculty in all disciplines.* Providence, RI: Campus Compact.

Battistoni, R. M., Gelmon, S. B., Saltmarsh, J. A., Wergin, J. F., & Zlotkowski, E. (2003). *The engaged department toolkit.* Providence, RI: Campus Compact.

Bennett, W. J. (1984). *To reclaim a legacy: A report on the humanities in higher education.* Washington, DC: National Endowment for the Humanities.

Bloom, A. (1987). *The closing of the American mind.* New York: Simon & Schuster.

Bowen, E. (1986, November 10). What is college for? *Time.* Available at http://www.time.com/time/magazine/article/0,9171,962830,00.htm.

Boyer, E. L. (1987). *College: The undergraduate experience in America.* New York: Harper & Row.

Campus Compact. (2000). *Presidents' declaration on the civic responsibility of higher education.* Providence, RI: Campus Compact.

Campus Compact. (2006). *5-year impact summary.* Available at www.compact.org/about/statistics/5 year_impact.pdf.

Campus Compact. (2008). *2007 service statistics: Highlights and trends of Campus Compact's annual member survey.* Providence, RI: Campus Compact.

Colby, A. Beaumont, E., Erlich, T., & Corngold, J. (2007). *Educating for democracy: Preparing undergraduates for responsible political engagement.* Carnegie Foundation for the Advancement of Teaching. San Francisco: Jossey-Bass.

Cone, R. E., Kiesa, A., & Long, N. V. (Eds.). (2006). *Raise your voice: A student guide to making positive social change.* Providence, RI: Campus Compact.

D'Souza, D. (1992). *Illiberal education: The politics of race and sex on campus.* New York: Simon & Schuster.

Gelmon, S. B., Holland, B. A., Driscoll, A., Spring, A., & Kerrigan, S. (2001). *Assessing service learning and civic engagement: Principles and techniques.* Providence, RI: Campus Compact.

Heffernan, K. (2001). *Fundamentals of service-learning course construction.* Providence, RI: Campus Compact.

Hollander, E. L. (2007). Foreword. In L. McIlrath & I. MacLabhrainn (Eds.), *Higher education and civic engagement: International perspectives.* Aldershot, UK: Ashgate.

Hollander, E. L., Saltmarsh, J., & Zlotkowski, E. (2001). Indicators of engagement. In L. A. Simon, M. Kenny, K. Brabeck, & R. M. Lerner (Eds.), *Learning to serve: Promoting civil society through service-learning.* Norwell, MA: Kluwer Academic Publishers.

Kronman, A. T. (2007). *Education's end: Why our colleges and universities have given up on the meaning of life.* New Haven, CT: Yale University Press.

Long, S. (2002). *The new student politics: The Wingspread statement on student civic engagement.* Providence, RI: Campus Compact.

McGovern, D., Foster, L., & Ward, K. (2002). College leadership: Learning from experience. *Journal of Leadership Studies, 8*(3), 29–41. Available at http://jlo.sagepub.com/cgi/content/citation/8/3/29.

Saltmarsh, J., Gelmon, S. B., Wergin, J., Zlotkowski, E., & Battistoni, R. M. (2003). *The engaged department toolkit.* Providence, RI: Campus Compact.

Scheibel, J., Bowley, E. M., & Jones, S. (2005). *The promise of partnerships: Tapping into the college as a community asset.* Providence, RI: Campus Compact.

Sykes, C. (1987). *Prof scam: Professors and the demise of higher education.* Washington, DC: Regnery Gateway.

Torres, J. (Ed.). (2000). *Benchmarks for campus-community partnerships.* Providence, RI: Campus Compact.

Zlotkowski, E., Longo, N. V., & Williams, J. R. (Eds.). (2006). *Students as colleagues: Expanding the circle of service-learning leadership.* Providence, RI: Campus Compact.

Small Partnership Leads into National Outreach Scholarship Conference

Karen S. Bruns

In 2001, three land-grant universities formed a partnership "to provide a framework to facilitate communication, cooperation, and mutually beneficial collaborative research and programming." Their shared vision of the program collaborative was to "develop and deliver programs and educational resources that support the development and advancement of the knowledge behind successful outreach initiatives in higher education" (*Memorandum of Understanding*, 2001).

The outreach and engagement leaders who entered into this partnership included Bobby D. Moser, Vice-President Agricultural Administration and University Outreach at The Ohio State University; James H. Ryan, Vice-President Outreach and Cooperative Extension at The Pennsylvania State University; and Kevin Reilly, Chancellor at University of Wisconsin–Extension. These founding members identified as the primary deliverable of the collaboration an annual program that became known as the Outreach Scholarship Conference.

The conference was designed from the beginning to target college and university leaders, outreach practitioners, and faculty and staff who are interested in "engaging" with those outside the academic community (Pennsylvania State University, 1999). This collaborative conference was first held in 2001 and built upon a successful conference that Pennsylvania State University held in 1999.

The conference grew into a national event that supports the advancement of outreach and engagement scholarship. Today, it continues to target faculty members who are interested in connecting their disciplinary expertise with the community through engagement. University leaders, including staff and administrators, are encouraged to come and converse on the issues to expand and strengthen their institutions' engagement. The conference partners have placed additional emphasis on involving students in the

349

dialogue. This includes students who are involved in service-learning courses and graduate students who participate in specific conversations about the scholarship of engagement. Community members are encouraged to attend and participate in the discussion of best practices and how universities and communities can work together to increase university engagement (National Outreach Scholarship Conference Registration Announcement, University of Georgia, personal communication, May 5, 2009). The conference provides a venue for ad hoc committees and communities of learners to gather and advance their discussions.

The conference draws participants from more than eighty institutions annually. The participants are geographically dispersed. At each conference, attendees come from thirty to forty different states, as well as several other countries.

This original partnership has expanded in membership, with the conference rotating between member institutions. Today, the collaborative membership continues to evolve. In 2003, the University of Georgia joined the partnership. Michigan State University, North Carolina State University, and the University of Alabama joined in 2007. In 2008, the University of Kentucky and Purdue University became partners. These initial members have developed a foundation on which the new members who join each year continue to build.

The conference continues to be the primary deliverable of the Outreach Scholarship Partnership. But the partnership has evolved to create a local and national conversation focusing on outreach and engagement. It provides a vehicle for stronger connections between the partner institutions. Sharing of best practices and information related to advancing outreach and engagement has occurred between the partner institutions. Collaborative research concerning university engagement has begun to develop.

The Outreach Scholarship Partnership grew out of common interests and connections of three institutions. It developed into a national presence that lays the foundation for continued growth of the outreach and engagement scholarship discussion. But the road to the transition has taken time and maturing of the partnership.

Returning to Our Roots: The Engaged Institution

In February 1999, the Kellogg Commission on the Future of State and Land-Grant Universities published six reports on the changes occurring in public universities at the time (Association of Public and Land-Grant Universities, n.d.). The commission's report, *Returning to our Roots: The Engaged Institution,* received a great deal of attention from the higher education community. This publication and the work of the commission gave the foundation and context from which the Outreach Scholarship Partnership developed.

The commission's report articulated key factors related to university-community partnerships that provided a foundation for many institutions as they moved engagement forward on their campuses. Its Seven-Part Test helped to define an engaged institution and included principles of (1) responsiveness, (2) respect for partners, (3) academic neutrality, (4) accessibility, (5) integration, (6) coordination, and (7) resource partnerships (National Association of State Universities and Land-Grant Colleges, 2001, p. 16).

This twenty-five-member commission was established in 1996 by the National Association of State Universities and Land-Grant Colleges (today known as APLU, the Association of Public and Land-Grant Universities). Funded by a $1.2 million award by the W. K. Kellogg Foundation, the commission was created "to help define the direction public universities should go in the future and to recommend an action agenda to speed up the process of change" (Association of Public and Land-Grant Universities, n.d.).

1999 Pennsylvania State University Conference—"Best Practices in Outreach and Public Service: The Scholarship of Engagement"

When the Report on the Engaged Institution was published, Pennsylvania State University President Graham Spanier was serving as chair of the commission. He and his colleagues challenged institutions to advance engagement by using five key strategies. These included the need for institutions to (1) transform the thinking about service so that engagement becomes a priority; (2) measure their engagement plans against the seven-part test; (3) encourage interdisciplinary work; (4) develop incentives to engagement for faculty involvement in engagement; and (5) secure stable funding through academic leaders (National Association of State Colleges and Land-Grant Universities, 2001, p.17).

In October of that year, Pennsylvania State University sponsored a conference titled "Best Practices in Outreach and Public Service: The Scholarship of Engagement." The conference responded to the challenge that President Spanier and his colleagues had set for higher education. The general sessions included panel sessions that focused on many of the topics identified by the commission. National leaders spoke to subjects such as creating an outreach culture; recruiting, supporting, and rewarding faculty for outreach scholarship; outreach dissemination as a component of research; and measuring the quality and impact of outreach programs (Pennsylvania State University, 1999.)

The conference drew more than three hundred participants who attended more than seventy sessions (Pennsylvania State University, 2001a). It brought together faculty and staff from institutions beyond Pennsylvania, and connected some of the future partners of the Outreach Scholarship Partnership.

Original Founders

As the Kellogg Commission was doing its work, change was happening on university campuses, including institutions represented by their presidents on the commission and those who would later become a part of the Outreach Scholarship Partnership.

As examples, Pennsylvania State University was looking at the fundamental organizational development issues related to supporting engaged institutions. Ohio State University was building an organizational structure to support university-wide engagement that led to a Vice President position for University Outreach. Wisconsin–Extension was looking at issues of documenting the scholarship of engagement. They were also developing guidelines and developing training materials for their faculty. All of these institutions were taking steps to help create a local culture to implement engagement work, but also building a faculty/staff development model for change that allowed employees to grow in their understanding of engagement.

While this change was occurring locally, it was evident that multi-institutional efforts could help catalyze these changes on both the local and regional/national levels. At the 1999 conference on "Best Practices in Outreach and Public Service," Ohio State University and Pennsylvania State University faculty and staff connected and discussed the possibility of partnering on a future conference to expand the opportunities for faculty. This was followed by a letter from Ohio State expressing interest. In 2000, Ohio State's Bob Moser, Vice President and Chair, President's Council for Outreach/Engagement, and Randy Smith, Vice-Provost, visited Penn State and met with Jim Ryan, Vice President for Outreach and Cooperative Extension, to discuss outreach/engagement. At that time they discussed the Outreach Scholarship partnership and began the initial formation of the group, inviting Kevin Reilly, Chancellor of University of Wisconsin–Extension, to become a partner in forming this new collaboration to advance outreach and engagement scholarship.

Partnership Purpose and Role of the Outreach Scholarship Conferences

According to the 2001 MOU forming the Outreach Scholarship partnership

> the shared vision for the program collaboration is to develop and deliver programs and educational resources that support the development and advancement of the knowledge behind successful outreach initiatives in higher education. The primary deliverable of our collaboration will be an annual conference targeting college and university leaders, outreach practitioners, and faculty and staff interested in "engaging" with those outside the academic community. (Memorandum of Understanding, 2001)

The first Outreach Scholarship Conference was titled "Learning, Discovery, and Engagement" and was held October 14–16, 2001, in State College, Pennsylvania. Vice-President Ryan, Vice-President Moser, and Chancellor Reilly articulated in their announcement their vision for the conference and the impact it would have in higher education institutions:

> The partnership between our three institutions and the conferences that come out of it will help all colleges and universities achieve greater levels of engagement. We are proud to be cosponsors of the conference series that will bring together university leaders and community partners to share and discuss these critical issues. Our goal is to provide practical tools for implementing real change in higher education. (Pennsylvania State University, 2001b)

As stated in the brochure announcing the 2001 conference, the event provided the opportunity to

- Examine best practices
- Offer evidence of the benefits of an outreach culture to the higher education and larger communities
- Establish informal benchmarks in creating an agenda for the engaged university
- Promote closer collaborative linkages between higher education and community leaders
- Provide a forum for exchange of information and open dialogue
- Provide participants with usable tools to implement engagement
- Support the development and advancement of the knowledge base and theory of outreach and engagement. (Pennsylvania State University, 2001b)

Growth of the Partnership

The partnership was barely off the ground when interest developed to include additional institutions in the collaborative. The 2001 conference drew more than 250 participants from institutions throughout the United States. The 2002 conference was hosted by Ohio State and held in Columbus, Ohio. By that time, the conference was already beginning to draw more than four hundred participants from eighty-one institutions in thirty-three states and two countries outside the United States.

University of Georgia Added to the Partnership

At the 2002 conference, the leadership met to discuss inviting an additional institution into the partnership. This discussion was generated because of inquiries received by the planning committee, and a desire to include additional partners, expand opportunities for the constituencies each institution represented, enhance potential markets for the conference, and mitigate risk and expenses incurred by the current partners.

The University of Georgia was identified as a potential partner because of their existing leadership role with the *Journal of Higher Education Outreach and Engagement*. The journal was collaborating with the conference by publishing a special issue focused on the conference. Conference presenters, for both the general and concurrent sessions, were submitting articles for peer review and inclusion in this special issue of the journal.

There was also interest in involving the University of Georgia in the partnership because of the assets they would bring. As stated earlier, the Outreach Scholarship Conference is one deliverable, but the partnership serves other purposes. It is a framework for collaboration between institutions. The University of Georgia had a strong university-wide engagement initiative and strong traditional engagement programs through the Extension system. Their unique approaches to engagement and work across the institution could inform and support the work of the other institutional partners.

The University of Georgia was the first university beyond the Big Ten institutions to join the partnership. The relationship and connections they had with institutions in the southern United States brought new ideas and connections to the conference and to the partnership. This expanded the conversations and networks of both the partnership and the conference.

Partnership Grows to Nine Institutions

By 2007, interest had grown in the conference and the potential for further participation. Several universities began to regularly attend the conference. There was a desire by the original partners to expand the conference partners beyond land-grant institutions. How could the partnership continue to build on the knowledge and participation of colleagues from the southern United States that resulted from the University of Georgia's involvement?

As a result, Michigan State University, North Carolina State University, and the University of Alabama were invited to become members of the partnership. These institutions each brought their own strengths related to engagement. Each had a different organizational structure and focus on how they were advancing outreach and engagement scholarship and

353

community-based partnership within their institutions. The new partners also brought their own set of constituencies that could add to the conversation and best practices and scholarship that could advance the original goals of the partnership—to support the development and advancement of knowledge related to outreach and engagement scholarship.

The partnership began to grow quickly after the addition of those institutions. Purdue University and the University of Kentucky joined the partnership in 2008. Again, these were institutions that had been actively involved in the conference as attendees. They had a strong institutional infrastructure that was supporting university-wide engagement, and they broadened the discussion and dialogue about engagement.

Benefits to Partners from Joining the Partnership

With the maturing of the collaboration, the partnership developed a set of by-laws that guides its work. As articulated in that document, eligible active membership "shall be limited to institutions of higher education that have demonstrated a commitment to engaged scholarship, as evidenced by the Carnegie Foundation's Elective Classification in Community Engagement, or by other demonstrated evidence" (Outreach Scholarship Conference, personal communication, July 25, 2008). Each member institution is required to contribute annual dues that support the work of the partnership and its primary product, the Outreach Scholarship Conference.

As member institutions, the senior leader for engagement/outreach is expected to represent the institution in the partnership and participate in the conference and the other meetings. Each institution must also identify a senior outreach and engagement staff person to serve on the Implementation Committee. This committee meets monthly by teleconference to help plan and implement the goals and objectives of the partnership, including the conference.

The member institutions take turns hosting and planning the Outreach Scholarship Conference. This responsibility takes a two-year commitment of the host institution.

The commitment to the partnership brings benefits to each institution on both a local and a national level. Nationally, their involvement in the conference brings attention to their commitment to outreach and engagement scholarship. It is a venue in which they can showcase best practices from their institutions. The partnership and conference are learning communities in which leaders in the field of higher education engagement share and gain ideas for replication and/or expansion of programming on their own campus.

Hosting the conference is a major commitment of the institution, requiring considerable human and financial resources over a two-year period. This commitment brings with it added local benefits. A broad spectrum of the university community can be engaged in the conference planning process. The institution's engagement work and infrastructure is made more visible locally and nationally. It can serve as a vehicle to elevate the awareness about engagement across all levels of the university and to engage community partners in development and implementation of the learning community.

For the conference hosts, the Outreach Scholarship partners, and the growing community engaged with the conference, there are many benefits to being involved. The conference is a venue for discussion of topics of engagement and scholarship. There are a limited number of conferences that focus on the broad topic of engagement and the many different forms of engagement. This conference draws engagement practitioners from many types of academic organizations (e.g., Extension, continuing education, and public broadcasting) to one location to discuss the work of the engaged institution. It focuses on the broad definition of engagement that includes curricular engagement, community partnerships, and research partnerships and allows for a cross-fertilization of ideas and sharing of knowledge. This makes the conference unique.

There have been concerted efforts to encourage presentations that showcase the scholarship of the best practices of engagement and the growing scholarship in the field of engagement. Presenters are given an opportunity to share their scholarship beyond the conference presentation through a peer-reviewed article in a special issue of the *Journal of Higher Education Outreach and Engagement* devoted to the conference theme.

With this growth in the partnership and the maturation of outreach and engagement scholarship, the conference itself has matured to create an atmosphere for deeper reflection on the scholarship of this work. As stated in the announcement for the 2009 Outreach Scholarship Conference to be held at the University of Georgia:

> The purpose of the 10th National Outreach Scholarship Conference is to provide time and space for a critical examination on the civic purpose of colleges and universities—along with the scholarship that underpins this work—and to strengthen institutional support for engagement and public scholarship. (University of Georgia, 2009)

Thematic Issues Addressed through the Conference

In planning the conference, each partner institution takes the lead in hosting, developing, and implementing the conference. This host university has much latitude and flexibility in deciding and shaping the conference, while learning from the past experiences of conference hosts and the feedback of past participants.

Factors such as institutional strength, issues related to today's engagement, and next steps needed to move engagement forward on their campus may all contribute to the themes and concepts that become the focus of the conference. A local planning committee is identified to give leadership to the conference. The national Implementation Committee, which includes outreach and engagement faculty/staff from each partner institution, provides counsel, support, and assistance in the development and marketing of the conference.

Since 2001, the themes have shown a progression from a general focus on outreach and engagement to more specific themes that focus on current issues.

2001 "Learning, Discovery, and Engagement" (Host, Pennsylvania State University)
2002 "Catalyst for Change" (Host, Ohio State University)
2003 "Excellence through Engagement" (Host, University of Wisconsin–Extension)
2004 "Impact through Engagement—Engaging Communities and Changing Lives" (Host, Pennsylvania State University)
2005 "Transformation through Engagement" (Host, University of Georgia)

2006 "Engagement through the Disciplines" (Host, Ohio State University)

2007 "Access through Engagement" (Host, University of Wisconsin–Extension/ UW Colleges)

2008 "Innovation and Leadership for Engagement" (Host, Pennsylvania State University)

2009 "Pathways of Engagement: Connecting Civic Purpose to Learning and Research— Locally and Globally" (Host University of Georgia)

Participants in the National Outreach Scholarship Conference

The conference is held in late September or early October each year and draws participants from across the country. The higher education participants are as varied as the types of outreach and engagement partnerships represented at the conference. The growth and scope of the conference is reflected in the conference name. In 2009, "National" was added to the Outreach Scholarship name for the conference.

Since its inception, the conference has drawn participants beyond the faculty and staff at the member institutions. Engaged faculty and staff from private to public higher education institutions have attended the conference. They may be working at small private colleges, community colleges, or large research-intensive institutions. The conference attracts individuals who are faculty or staff in outreach units such as Extension, continuing education, public broadcasting, and K–12 partnership offices. It draws individuals who have tenure-track faculty positions in colleges from across the university. Community members are strongly encouraged to attend the conference and are active participants in all aspects of the conference.

Attendance has ranged from 250 to more than 450. Representatives from more than seventy institutions and participants from more than thirty-five states and three countries have attended the conference during a year.

A community of scholars has developed that are regularly attending the conference. Between 7 percent and 11 percent of the participants have attended the conference three years in a row since the 2004 conference. Each year since 2003, 17 percent to 25 percent of the participants have attended the conference the previous year. With this continuity of participants, relationships and networks have developed. It is a place to connect with a cohort of individuals interested in and committed to university-community partnerships.

The conference gives an opportunity for the host institution to provide a leadership role in their state concerning outreach scholarship. It provides a nearby venue for colleagues at other institutions to participant in a national conference with leaders in the field fostering conversation. Since 2002, an average 39 percent of the participants each year have come from the host state. Engaging participants in a local conference opens the door for their participation in future conferences.

Expansion of the National Outreach Scholarship Program

As stated in the original Memorandum of Understanding establishing the partnership, it was designed to "develop and deliver programs and educational resources that support the development and advancement of the knowledge behind successful outreach initiatives in higher education" (Memorandum of Understanding, 2001). The conference continues to be the primary vehicle for the development and advancement of knowledge. It expanded to include an awards program; collaborations to co-locate conferences; pre- and postconference special interest group meetings; and a preconference workshop for emerging scholars.

Award to Showcase Best Practices Added in 2006

At the 2005 Outreach Scholarship Conference at the University of Georgia, discussions began about the concept of an award to recognize outstanding outreach and engagement scholarship. During the same time period, leadership at the National Association of State Universities and Land-Grant Colleges (NASULGC, now known as the Association of Public and Land-Grant Universities, APLU) were having similar conversations. By working together, the two organizations created the concept of an award in which five regional winners would be recognized at the annual Outreach Scholarship Conference. Those five regional winners would then compete for a national award to be presented at the annual NASULGC conference. In 2006, the W. K. Kellogg Foundation committed to supporting the award by the creation of an endowment.

At the 2006 Outreach Scholarship Conference, the establishment of the award was announced. Starting in winter 2007, applications were accepted annually from higher education institutions to compete for the Outreach Scholarship W. K. Kellogg Foundation Engagement Award. From these applications, a national review committee selects regional winners from five regions across the United States.

These regional winners are highlighted at the Outreach Scholarship Conference. Each winning team, including community partners, shares their work during general and concurrent sessions at the annual Outreach Scholarship Conference. The regional winners are reviewed by a team of university presidents who then select the national winner.

All five regional winners are recognized at the opening session of the November annual meeting of the Association of Public and Land-Grant Universities. The national winner is announced and receives the C. Peter Magrath Community Engagement Award at that conference.

In recognition of their work, each regional winner and the national winner receive a cash award that can be used to support the partnership. They also receive financial support to participate in the National Outreach Scholarship Conference.

As a part of the competition requirements, the regional winners prepare a short video that highlights the partnership. These videos provide a case study of best practices and unique engagement partnerships. They are featured at the Outreach Scholarship and APLU conferences; are shared with the W. K. Kellogg Foundation; and are linked on the www.outreachscholarship.org website.

Collaboration in Co-locating Conferences

The Outreach Scholarship Conference has a history of collaborating with organizations that may have similar interests and objectives in advancing university-community partnerships.

To this end, there have been several occasions in which organizations have co-located meetings with the Outreach Scholarship Conference. These conferences have occurred as separate events, but have given an opportunity for expansion of audiences and opportunities for attendees to benefit from participating in both conferences. It has given an opportunity for enriching the conversations at both events.

On several occasions, the public broadcasting leadership at the host university has sponsored meetings of their colleagues to dovetail with the Outreach Scholarship Conference. In 2006, Imagining America hosted their annual conference "Artists and Scholars in Public Life 'Engagement through Place'" in Columbus, Ohio. This conference and the Outreach Scholarship Conference were held in the same location and shared one day of programming.

Pre- and Postconference Special Interest Group Meetings

As the conference continues to grow, it has become a place to meet on other topics. In the early years of the conference, special interest groups may have met for a morning breakfast meeting or on an informal basis. As the conference grew, some of these events have become pre- or postconference meetings.

The meetings of the editorial board of the *Journal of Higher Education Outreach and Engagement* have occurred at the conference. A cohort of colleagues interested in economic development have taken the opportunity to gather at the conference. In 2009, the meeting transitioned into a preconference roundtable on Transformative Regional Engagement.

The conference serves as an opportunity for ideas to be shared and new groups to form. This may be prompted by invitations extended by the host institution or catalyzed by conference participants. As an example, in 2009, the outreach and engagement leaders at the higher education institutions belonging to the Southeastern Conference Academic Consortium were invited to attend the conference and to stay for the first meeting of the universities on outreach and engagement.

Emerging Engagement Scholars Workshop

In 2007, the Emerging Scholars workshop was added as a concurrent offering of the Outreach Scholarship Conference. It provides an opportunity for advanced doctoral students and early-career faculty to engage in intensive discussions and support related to engaged scholarship as a part of their National Outreach Scholarship Conference experience (National Center for the Study of University Engagement, 2009). Led by doctoral students, early-career faculty, and faculty mentors, this workshop broadens the involvement of graduate students and early-career faculty in the conference.

Conclusion

The Outreach Scholarship Conference sprang out of the charge to higher education institutions to examine and advance their engagement with communities. It built on the desire by three universities to give their faculty and staff an environment in which they could broaden their dialogue and understanding of outreach scholarship. It has flourished into a national conference that has become a venue for engaging a broad cross-section of higher education and community partners in a dialogue to advance outreach and engagement scholarship.

Since the foundation laid by Pennsylvania State University with the first conference in 1999, the Outreach Scholarship Conference and the partnership have continued to evolve. It will keep evolving as the scholarship of engagement and university-community partnerships continue to change.

References

Association of Public and Land-Grant Universities. (n.d.). *Kellogg Commission on the Future of State and Land-Grant Universities.* Retrieved May 6, 2009, from http://www.aplu.org/NetCommunity/Page.aspx?pid=305.

Memorandum of Understanding. (2001, July 30). *Outreach Scholarship Conference.*

National Association of State Universities and Land-Grant Colleges. (2001). *Returning to our roots: Executive summaries of the reports of the Kellogg Commission on the Future of State and Land-Grant Universities.* Washington, DC: Author. Retrieved May 6, 2009, from http://www.aplu.org/NetCommunity/Document.Doc?id=187.

National Center for the Study of University Engagement (n.d.). *Emerging Engagement Scholars Workshop.* Retrieved May 7, 2009, from http://ncsue.msu.edu/eesw/default.aspx.

Pennsylvania State University. (1999). *Best practices in outreach and public service: The scholarship of engagement* [Brochure]. University Park, PA: Author.

Pennsylvania State University. (2001a). *Outreach Scholarship 2001 conference information.* Retrieved May 6, 2009, from http://www.outreach.psu.edu/programs/OutreachScholarship2001/attend_toc.html.

Pennsylvania State University. (2001b). *Outreach scholarship 2001: Learning, discovery, and engagement.* [Brochure]. University Park, PA: Author.

University of Georgia. (2009). *Outreach Scholarship 2009 conference information.* Retrieved May 7, 2009, from http://www.georgiacenter.uga.edu/conferences/outreach_conference/index.phtml.

Imagining America: Engaged Scholarship for the Arts, Humanities, and Design

Robin Goettel and Jamie Haft

In 2001, a group of University of Michigan undergraduates spent much of an icy winter well away from the comforts of their Ann Arbor campus. Instead, they were conducting research in senior centers and community centers around the Michigan Central Railroad Station, a key transit point for the Great Migration, in which millions of African Americans moved to the industrial northern states in search of employment and education, and an important landmark in ethnically diverse southwest Detroit. Under the guidance of history faculty and a playwright from Detroit's Matrix Theater, the students conducted oral histories and writing workshops, unveiling the hidden cultural and social life of the railroad station and its environs, and used the results to create a stage presentation entitled *Homelands*. The next year, *Homelands* was performed at the Matrix Theater by local high school students and for local audiences, and formed part of a multiplying group of cultural products, including an exhibit of historic photographs of the station, and a multimedia sourcebook documenting the partnership and providing a template of the project for other groups to use.

This is engaged scholarship in the arts and humanities: created in an equal and sustainable partnership between the university and a community organization, and resulting in new and relevant knowledge both for the academy and for its public, knowledge to be provided directly to the public. As one of Imagining America's early contributors noted:

> The local community must be the microcosm of our pluralistic, inclusive democracy, and the realization of our democratic ideals. Community is, in fact, democracy incarnate, where culture is woven into the fabric of our daily lives, not work as a decoration on its surface, or observed from afar as the province of the privileged few. (Myers, 2001, p. 4)

361

It is to support such engaged cultural work between higher education and community partners that Imagining America: Artists and Scholars in Public Life was founded. Ten years later, Imagining America is a consortium of eighty-five colleges and universities committed to building democratic culture by fostering public scholarship and practice in the arts, humanities, and design. The consortium brings together higher education and community-based artists, scholars, design professionals, and the public to reimagine the possibilities of higher education, with the goal of supporting member institutions as they develop their potential for civic engagement and collective problem solving.

In the following sections, we discuss the founding of Imagining America and the importance of developing a common language and culture; Imagining America's annual programming; current national initiatives; and organizational challenges. Each of these sections is related to Imagining America's overarching goals of constituting public scholarship as an important and legitimate enterprise, encouraging structural changes in higher education to support knowledge creation through civic engagement, and forging comprehensive alliances to build the movement for transforming colleges and universities into centers of democratic renewal. We believe that democracy is dynamic, not fixed, and that a thriving democracy is marked by active, inclusive citizen participation in which individuals act not only in their own self-interest but collectively toward the common good of their community.

History

Imagining America was launched at a 1999 White House Conference initiated by the White House Millennium Council, the University of Michigan, and the Woodrow Wilson National Fellowship Foundation. The conference brought together government officials, scholars, artists, university presidents, foundation executives, and nonprofit leaders to describe, debate, and look for new opportunities for civic engagement in higher education. Participants reached a consensus about what was needed for public scholarship and practice to flourish: a national network, legitimization, and financial support.

After the conference, twenty-one participating college and university presidents agreed to build a national network with the formation of the Presidents Council. This council became the basis for what would become Imagining America's consortium of colleges and universities. (To this day, a college or university president or chancellor must sign the Imagining America membership agreement.)

Confident in the civic engagement leadership of two of its humanities professors, the University of Michigan agreed to be the initial host campus for the consortium. Julie Ellison, who was then working in the University's Office of the Vice President, and David Scobey, who was launching the University's new Arts of Citizenship program, had observed that the arts, humanities, and design were underrepresented in national civic engagement associations. They also saw that there was no analytical framework to aggregate and critically consider the range of endeavors underway. What Ellison called a "language project" to create a common vocabulary and build a discourse around such work became a priority for the new organization.

With support from the Woodrow Wilson National Fellowship Foundation, Imagining America quickly launched its Public Scholarship Grants program, which initially supported thirteen civic engagement projects in the arts, humanities, and design on member campuses. When the projects were completed, Imagining America invited project leaders to come together for a national conference to share and critique their experiences. The conference underscored the need for developing a narrative and accessible language about higher education's history and role in community engagement.

The antecedent for civic engagement work in higher education was service. Increasingly by the 1960s, colleges and universities were incorporating community service into their institutional mission, making it part of the higher education experience, although often as an extracurricular activity. Reflecting an expanding consciousness in the past twenty-five years of the *pedagogical* importance of experiential learning, colleges and universities have integrated service into their curricula. This development from service to service-learning is perhaps best exemplified in the shifting focus of Campus Compact from volunteerism to service-learning during the early 1990s.

Imagining America is among those organizations that have continued to push the boundaries of service-learning by emphasizing civic engagement:

> Engagement goes well beyond extension, conventional outreach, and even most conceptions of public service. Inherited concepts emphasize a one-way process in which the university transfers its expertise to key constituents. Embedded in the engagement ideal is a commitment to sharing and reciprocity. By engagement the Commission envisions partnerships, two-way streets defined by mutual respect among the partners for what each brings to the table. (Kellogg Commission, 1999, p. 13)

Imagining America calls civic engagement work in higher education public scholarship and practice. In the arts, humanities, and design disciplines, engagement is initiated by artists, scholars, design professionals, and citizens and encompasses multiple types of knowledge creation. Such scholarship and practice can take a variety of forms, including work that expands the place of public scholarship in higher education itself by developing new engagement programs, methodologies, and evaluation metrics, as well as artistic, critical, and historical work that contributes to public debates and to understanding pressing social issues. Often, such scholarly and creative work is jointly planned and carried out through campus and community partnerships. The basic unit of such work is more often the project than the course. The final products of this activity also can take a variety of forms, such as books intended for broad audiences, community dialogues, art installations, and collectively conceived performances.

Out of Imagining America's iterative process of defining terms and assessing the public impact of such scholarship and practice, an analytical framework is emerging. As Ellison reflected, "In a nutshell, this common language is the result of the earnest work of translation, listening, and practicing the rare skill of saying what we are *for* as well as what we can *critique,* and the refusal by everybody to dumb everything down. Eventually all of this merges into a common culture, if you're lucky" (Brown, 2002, p. 18). Syracuse University's Chancellor and President Nancy Cantor, a leader in Imagining America's work since its founding,

363

spoke eloquently about public scholarship in a 2008 speech: "We can do really good scholarship, educate our students, and make a difference in the world by … situating our work at the center of the most challenging questions in our disciplines, the most vexing questions of our past, and the urgent issues that will chart the future" (Cantor, 2008, p. 2).

With the energetic leadership of Imagining America's associate director Juliet Feibel, Imagining America's membership has grown to eighty-five institutions. "Despite ever-tightening budgets at both public and private institutions," Feibel says, "this growth indicates that Imagining America is feeding a real intellectual hunger, a desire to unite civic action and scholarly practice. Universities and colleges are looking for ways to grapple with the demand for greater and more sophisticated methods of engagement, and these demands are coming from all sides: from students, faculty, community partners, trustees, and state legislatures" (J. Feibel, personal communication, July 18, 2008).

Annual Programming

Each year an Imagining America member institution hosts the national conference, which emphasizes sense of place. For example, the University of Southern California hosted the 2008 conference in Los Angeles—the most culturally diverse city in the United States—under the banner "Layers of Place, Movements of People: Public Engagement in a Diverse America." To bring conference participants closer to the city's urban realities, the planning committee scheduled one conference day at community organizations. Conference attendees typically include presidents and provosts, deans and chairs, professors, students, artists, and community members; on each individual's conference nametag, no title is listed. A variety of session formats (from panels and workshops to roundtables and poster presentations) help ensure that there is adequate time and space for interaction with peers, and there are special meetings such as that of the National Advisory Board and the Publicly Active Graduate Education (PAGE) Summit. There is also opportunity for various affinity groups to gather—for example, those who wish to network within a specific geographic region, within a discipline, or by professional affiliation (e.g., a meeting of faculty administrators, deans, and chairs).

A spirit of inquiry reverberates in the conference sessions, which go beyond show-and-tell format in an effort to surface and grapple with critical issues. Welcoming critical analysis from all present, participants are not shy about sharing what *didn't* work with their campus-community project. In addition to bringing together a critical mass of scholars and practitioners, the conferences welcome participants from other national civic engagement associations.

By documenting its conferences and the year-round projects of its members, Imagining America is building a body of knowledge about public scholarship and practice. One vehicle for disseminating this knowledge is its series, *Foreseeable Futures*. In *Foreseeable Futures No. 3*, "Transforming America: The University as Public Good," Chancellor Cantor makes a passionate case for the arts as "a context for exchange" and "a medium for participation" in a society where "pervasive and longstanding racial divides persist" (Cantor, 2003). In *Foreseeable Futures No. 4*, "Crossing Figueroa: The Tangled Web of Diversity and Democracy,"

Imagining America's current board chair, George J. Sanchez, describes an alarming contradiction in higher education: while there is widespread growth in university service-learning and community engagement activities, there is also rapid erosion of programmatic support for minority students (Sanchez, 2004). In the 2007 *Foreseeable Futures No. 7,* "Brown University and the Voyage of the Slave Ship *Sally,* 1764–65," James T. Campbell spins the tale of the University's multiyear research project, led by its Steering Committee on Slavery and Justice, to determine how much monetary profit from the slave trade figured in the establishment of Brown, and how now best to compensate for such ill-gotten gains (Campbell, 2007). All of Imagining America's publications, including its semiannual newsletter, are available on its website, www.imaginingamerica.org.

Imagining America also contributes to its host institution, community, and state. At its founding institution, the University of Michigan, the bar for exemplary local work was set high. There, Julie Ellison and David Scobey developed Imagining Michigan, which included an annual meeting of state arts agencies, state humanities councils, and colleges and universities, and the development of an online toolkit to facilitate statewide exchanges. Now, at Syracuse University, Imagining America is helping develop partnerships between campus and community focused on important regional development issues. With the salt industry, Erie Canal, and manufacturing no longer providing robust employment, central New York's economy is struggling, and Syracuse University's public scholarship and community partnerships are pursuing solutions. For example, the Connective Corridor is a mile-and-a-half strip extending from the University through downtown Syracuse and encompassing twenty-five arts and cultural venues. As noted on the Connective Corridor website (Connective Corridor, n.d.), "In the coming months and years, these venues will be stitched together and showcased with new urban landscapes, bike paths, imaginative lighting, public and interactive art, signage, and way finding systems. Participate in the project, and help transform our public places into vibrant social spaces on the Connective Corridor, Syracuse's new urban playground." Imagining America is developing courses and projects to support the Corridor's development. Cantor powerfully articulated the idea of such campus-community partnerships in her vision for Syracuse University as "Scholarship in Action." Her contribution to higher education was recognized nationally in June 2008 when she received the Carnegie Corporation's Academic Leadership Award.

National Initiatives

The goal of the *Tenure Team Initiative* (TTI) is to expand tenure and promotion policies in support of publicly engaged work. The Tenure Team was formed in response to concerns voiced by Imagining America's members and its National Advisory Board about the negative impact of standard tenure and promotion policy on public scholarship and practice. Imagining America's founding director Julie Ellison and its research director Timothy K. Eatman brought together a nineteen-member team, which included higher education presidents, provosts and vice presidents, deans, institute directors, and leaders of higher education associations, as well as senior faculty, artists, and civic professionals knowledgeable about tenure and promotion policy.

365

In October 2005, national TTI co-chairs Nancy Cantor and Steven D. Lavine, President of the California Institute of the Arts, announced the Initiative at the Imagining America national conference at Rutgers University. "We absolutely have to pay attention to the fact that a diverse professoriate and a diverse student body want to be engaged with the broader issues of our communities and publics, locally or around the world," Chancellor Cantor emphatically stated (Imagining America, 2005, p. 1).

The strategy was to create the TTI report and subsequent action steps to help academic and institutional leaders and faculty better understand and make the case for public scholarship and its myriad enactments. Ellison and Eatman began by developing an extensive knowledge base on the topic; creating an online survey, which invited both structured and unstructured responses; and conducting in-depth interviews with team members. After drafting a substantive background study with preliminary recommendations, Ellison and Eatman completed the TTI report, entitled "Scholarship in Public: Knowledge Creation and Tenure Policy in the Engaged University, A Resource on Promotion and Tenure in the Arts, Humanities, and Design," in May 2008. In its Foreword, Cantor and Lavine declare, "To attract and keep a diverse faculty, we need flexible and clear guidelines for recognizing and rewarding public scholarship and artistic production" (Cantor & Lavine, 2008, p. iii).

The report begins by giving examples of commendable public engagement in the arts, humanities, and design. In the arts, for example, the Social and Public Art Resource Center (SPARC) was cited. Judith F. Baca, who founded SPARC in 1976 and is presently a professor at the University of California, Los Angeles, has produced highly participatory, large-scale public art projects, including the Great Wall of Los Angeles, a very long mural that depicts the span of Los Angeles' history. The work of David Scobey at Bates College in Maine furnishes another example of the efficacy of public scholarship. Scobey's collaboration with a local museum and community led to exhibitions telling the story of once-flourishing local mills, thus providing an historical perspective on the current local economy and culture.

Ellison and Eatman organize their recommendations around four continua:

- A continuum of scholarship within which academic public engagement has full and equal standing with other kinds of knowledge making;
- A continuum of scholarly and creative artifacts, noting, for example, that live performances and videos, like self-authored books and essays, document knowledge;
- A continuum of professional pathways for faculty, including the choice to be a civic professional; and
- A continuum of actions for institutional change.

The report includes an informational toolkit for campus action and a chart on Pathways for Public Engagement at Five Career Stages, from deciding to be a public scholar to exercising leadership.

The twelve recommendations in the TTI report are:

- Define public scholarly and creative work;
- Develop policy based on a continuum of scholarship;
- Recognize the excellence of work that connects domains of knowledge;
- Expand what counts;

- Document what counts;
- Present what counts: use portfolios;
- Expand who counts by broadening the community of peer review;
- Support publicly engaged graduate students and junior faculty;
- Build in flexibility at the point of hire;
- Promote public scholars to full professor;
- Organize the department for policy change; and
- Take this report home and use it to start something.

In June 2008, Imagining America held a working conference in New York City with representatives of its own member institutions, members of Campus Compact, and other national leaders in tenure policy for public scholarship. Seventy people attended, identifying and exploring how the TTI report could support graduate students, faculty practicing public scholarship, mid-level academics assessing the work, and upper-level administrators responsible for setting academic policy. At the center of the conversations were questions of how to use the report to promote policy change. As Eatman noted, "What we want to do is make sure there are ways for public scholarship to be evaluated so we can discern what is excellent and what isn't" (June, 2008). Imagining America will continue promoting its tenure recommendations at its own conferences as well as the conferences of other national organizations.

Another major national initiative is the *Publicly Active Graduate Education* (PAGE) program, which supports publicly active graduate students with professional development resources and a social network. As Ellison and Eatman state in the TTI report, "Graduate students are restless. Some are finding dissertation topics and peer mentoring networks that allow them to work out how to integrate engagement into their fields or disciplines" (Ellison & Eatman, 2008, p. 16). PAGE helps graduate students take charge of rethinking the possibilities of their graduate education.

Imagining America annually invites graduate students in the arts, humanities, and design with a demonstrated interest in public engagement to apply to be PAGE Fellows. Since 2004, almost three hundred graduate students have applied for a total of sixty fellowships. At the annual conference, fellows attend a day-long PAGE Summit, which is devoted to building the theoretical and practical language for each fellow to articulate his or her public scholarship. The Summit includes seminar-style discussions of public scholarship readings, in-depth consideration of the theoretical language and practical skills that fellows can take back to their own campuses, and small-group critiques of individual research narratives. Fellows also attend the general conference sessions where they have ample opportunity for discussions with leaders in the field and other students and faculty who are creating and planning publicly active projects and careers, as well as administrators who support public scholarship policy.

Sylvia Gale, PAGE's founding director, notes:

Some fellows come to the conference in the early stages of thinking through the civically engaged manifestations of their research interests. Others arrive having already crafted their own alliances and launched their own programs. Participation in the Imagining America conference has spurred PAGE Fellows to collaborate at other disciplinary conferences, propelled them into new leadership

367

roles on their home campuses, and has helped Fellows to continue strategizing their degrees and advocating for the place of public scholarship within their own departmental and institutional frameworks. (Imagining America, Spring 2007, p. 12)

Current PAGE director Kevin Bott, doctoral candidate at New York University, has launched a new PAGE website as a forum for online resources, sharing, critical discourse, and social networking. He believes the website will help sustain the momentum and enthusiasm graduate students express at Imagining America's national conferences. Bott also hopes to institute a PAGE postdoctoral fellowship to support public scholarship at an Imagining America member institution. As noted in the TTI report,

> The success of PAGE has implications beyond the cultural disciplines. It contains lessons for Preparing Future Faculty (PFF) programs nationwide. PFF programs, as valuable as they are, do not concretely address graduate students' futures as civic professionals or as future faculty in colleges and universities with a strong public mission. Integrating new modules on dimensions of engagement into PFF programs could clarify professional pathways for graduate students and faculty. (Ellison & Eatman, 2008, p. 20)

Imagining America's third major national initiative is *The Curriculum Project*, which enhances curricula for public arts, humanities, and design. The project was conceived in 2007, when three colleagues—artistic director of Appalachia's Roadside Theater Dudley Cocke, then–New York University professor Jan Cohen-Cruz, and consultant Arlene Goldbard—compared notes from their extensive experience with higher education programs for community artists. They recognized a unique moment of opportunity for the field, which they articulated in a white paper entitled "A Call for Excellence in Community Cultural Development Curriculum in Higher Education." The paper highlighted four circumstances that they believed were converging to produce this moment of opportunity: universities across the United States were developing scores of individual courses, certificates, and degree programs in community cultural development; unprecedented numbers of students were matriculating in these programs—creating the circumstances to affect the field by affecting their education; social justice activists were increasingly collaborating with artists and cultural workers to bring cultural awareness into their efforts, understanding that culture is an essential foundation for community development and social change, and at the same time, artists were increasingly seeking intersectional partnerships for their work; and a critical mass of analytic writing and documentation was accruing, bringing new attention to community cultural development theories and practices that had been gathering force over the past four decades.

The shortcomings the co-investigators observed in current public scholarship programs included the imbalance between disciplinary training and community engagement; curriculum gaps, often evidenced in a piecemeal approach; the absence of a larger context of meaning, including recognizing the spiritual and political impulses that often attract students to the work; inequitable campus-community partnerships; the lack of integration between scholarship and practice; the failure to recognize multiple types of knowledge; and an inadequate appreciation for entrepreneurship that effective practice requires (Cocke, Cohen-Cruz, & Goldbard, 2008, pp. 1–3).

Cocke, Cohen-Cruz, and Goldbard proposed to research the current practice and potential for excellence in the education of community artists, and the Nathan Cummings Foundation agreed to support their effort. In June 2007, Cohen-Cruz became director of Imagining America and offered the organization as a home for the project. Three advisors were added to the research team, each with a unique perspective: community organizer Ludovic Blain III; recent graduate of a university program for community artists Jamie Haft; and educator, practitioner, and university vice president for diversity Sonia Bas-Sheva Mañjon. The team's goal was to answer the questions: How are we educating community arts practitioners? How could training in this field be deepened and made more effective?

The first phase of the project focused on research to test the hypothesis that a model curriculum should have a balance of three components: training in both artistic practice and community organizing; community engagement based on reciprocity; and scholarship focused on the field's history and animating ideas. The research included gathering stakeholders' assessment of the state of the field through interviews and surveys and compiling syllabi and course descriptions. In September 2008, the research team published its findings through "The Curriculum Project Report: Culture and Community Development in Higher Education." Written by Arlene Goldbard, the report is framed by the history and terminology of community cultural development, which is described as "a range of initiatives undertaken by artists in collaboration with other community members to express identity, concerns and aspirations through the arts and communications media, while building the capacity for social action and contributing to social change" (Goldbard, 2008, p. 7). The report describes what the research found about the design of an ideal curriculum, the current state of education in the field, the challenges that are producing the gap between the actual and the ideal, and recommendations to close the gap.

The ten recommendations are:

- All parties should recognize that this is a period of action research, marked by experimentation in program design, curriculum, and approach to every element of community cultural development (CCD) education, and should engage in a spirit of true collaboration.
- It is essential that the values shaping grassroots CCD practice inform and influence education in the field.
- Excellence requires a balance of community engagement, training in artistic practice, and scholarship focusing on the field's history and animating ideas, as well as the economic and policy environments for CCD work.
- Vibrant, participatory critical discourse is essential to the success of both higher education and practice in CCD. Higher educational institutions are best positioned to seek support for a sustained, iterative discourse from within their own walls and from resource providers.
- Community cultural development in higher education should have an explicit goal of supporting and developing the field beyond university walls.
- Higher-education programs should develop peer relationships with community-based educational programs for practitioners.

369

- Effective CCD education requires meaningful, equitable, and collaborative relationships between educational institutions and community partners, and developing these relationships requires self-critical awareness from both parties.
- While "champions" may drive new programs as they come into being, it is critical to move toward strengthening programs, so that they don't disappear when their founders move on.
- An overarching aim should be to infuse CCD values across institutions and programs, connecting CCD-focused programs with a matrix of related departments and programs by building relationships with collaborating departments and programs sharing similar values.
- Community cultural development practitioners and educators should collaborate in pursuing emergent opportunities that can benefit both higher education and community-based practitioners. (Goldbard, 2008, p. 4)

By engaging in critical discourse about how community cultural development fits into public scholarship and practice in the arts, humanities, and design, The Curriculum Project deepens Imagining America's effort to define a common language. The report is being used to create more opportunities for exchange around pedagogy, to expand resources for undergraduate education, and to develop more ways for community colleges to benefit from their Imagining America membership. Next steps include translation of the report's findings into pedagogy of the public humanities and design, and web resources to support members' curricular efforts.

To advance and to ground these national initiatives in the realities of its constituents, Imagining America has instituted four to five regional meetings a year. Each meeting typically involves six to ten campuses in geographic proximity to one another, as well as community partners. More information about these three national projects, including project reports for download, can be found on Imagining America's website at www.imaginingamerica.org.

Conclusion

With Imagining America's growth and the increase in visibility and legitimacy for public scholarship, new sets of organizational challenges and opportunities are becoming apparent. The intimacy of the Imagining America national conference has always been one of the features members like most. How will this aspect change as attendance swells? The consortium has traditionally included only institutions of higher education, but although this membership structure aligns with the mission of transforming such institutions, it under-recognizes the institutions' community partners. In 2007, her first year as director of Imagining America, Cohen-Cruz addressed this issue, stating, "An organization committed to campus-community partnerships must find a way to articulate community in its membership" (J. Cohen-Cruz, personal communication, July 15, 2008). In one of her first actions as director, Cohen-Cruz added three community members to the National Advisory Board, each of whom partners with higher education from a community-based perspective, and made it possible for community partners of member institutions to receive *Foreseeable Futures,* newsletters, and correspondences.

Imagining America is attempting to fully involve the diversity of its field, which includes land-grant, comprehensive, and metropolitan colleges and universities; liberal arts and research institutions; public, private, and community colleges; historically Black colleges and universities (HBCUs); tribal colleges; faith-based institutions; and Hispanic-serving institutions. Although Imagining America's mission statement cites design, it is less represented in the membership than the arts and humanities. As a remedy, it is opening its doors to the university members of the recently disbanded CITYbuild, a loose-knit national organization created in response to faculty and students from architecture, design, and urban planning eager to partner with community-based organizations involved in rebuilding New Orleans. Presently, HBCUs, tribal colleges, faith-based institutions, and Hispanic-serving institutions are underrepresented in Imagining America. The consortium's critical discourse will undoubtedly ripen with improved inclusion of such institutions, all of which typically have close relationships with their communities. The spirit of collective achievement, an ethos of "lifting as we climb," is evident throughout the HBCU experience, and sustaining a community's cultural traditions is part of the mission of tribal colleges. And for a number of students, it is faith and spirituality that draw them to service and civic engagement. Addressing these membership gaps will require Imagining America to reflect on the current cost and benefits of membership. Are Imagining America's current services responsive to the interests and orientations of these missing members, or must new benefits and cost structures be created to attract them?

Imagining America serves the important function of a service organization, providing resources to an expanding membership, and it also provides significant leadership to the field of engaged scholarship in higher education. Its principal achievements over the past ten years—coalescing a movement around a common language, building a national membership, fostering a growing body of knowledge and critical discourse, and contributing solutions to the pressing issues of our times—are benefits accrued not only to the membership institutions who have made them possible, but also to scholars, administrators, and students across the nation who learn from and profit by them. At some point, Imagining America will make its second transition to a new host institution within its consortium of colleges and universities. Committed to building democratic culture by fostering public scholarship and practice in the arts, humanities, and design, Imagining America and its members will continue to reimagine the possibilities of higher education, and to work in partnership to make what is imagined a reality.

Authors' Note

Robin Goettel is assistant director and Jamie Haft, program coordinator, of Imagining America. Before coming to the organization, Goettel's involvement in public life included ten years serving on her local school board. Haft is a recent graduate of a publicly engaged arts program. Thanks to director Jan Cohen-Cruz, who gave staff the opportunity to write comprehensively about Imagining America and who, with associate director Juliet Feibel, edited the text. Both Feibel and research director Timothy K. Eatman helped get us started by sharing their Imagining America experience.

References

Brown, D. W. (2002). *New public scholarship in the arts and humanities: An interview with Julie Ellison.* Higher Education Exchange. The Kettering Foundation.

Campbell, J. T. (2007). *Navigating the past: Brown University and the voyage of the slave ship Sally, 1764–65.* Foreseeable Futures No. 7. Syracuse, NY: Imagining America.

Cantor, N. (2003). *Transforming America: The university as public good.* Foreseeable Futures No. 3. Ann Arbor, MI: Imagining America.

Cantor, N. (2008). The two-way street of scholarship in action. Retrieved September 14, 2008, from http://www.syr.edu/chancellor/speeches/2wayst_SIA_University_Address_031808.pdf.

Cantor, N., & Lavine, S. D. (2008). Foreword. In J. Ellison & T. K. Eatman, *Scholarship in public: Knowledge creation and tenure policy in the engaged university.* Syracuse, NY: Imagining America.

Cocke, D., Cohen-Cruz, J., & Goldbard, A. (2007). *A call for excellence in community cultural development curriculum.* Retrieved September 18, 2008, from http://curriculumproject.net/pdfs/CallforExcellence.pdf

Connective Corridor. (n.d.). *Overview.* Retrieved March 13, 2009, from http://connectivecorridor.syr.edu/projectoverview/.

Ellison, J., & Eatman, T. K. (2008). *Scholarship in public: Knowledge creation and tenure policy in the engaged university.* Syracuse, NY: Imagining America.

Goldbard, A. (2006). *New Creative Community: The Art of Cultural Development.* San Francisco, CA: New Village Press.

Goldbard, A. (2008). *The Curriculum Project report: Culture and community development in higher education.* Retrieved September 26, 2008, from http://curriculumproject.net/pdfs/08.CP.report.pdf.

Imagining America. (2005). *Press release.* Retrieved September 16, 2008, from http://www.imaginingamerica.org/IApdfs/05.09.24-TTI.PressRelease.pdf

Imagining America. (2007, Spring). *Newsletter No. 8.* Syracuse, NY: Imagining America.

June, A. W. (2008, June 26). Colleges should change policies to encourage scholarship devoted to the public good, report says. *Chronicle of Higher Education.* Retrieved September 16, 2008, from http://chronicle.com/daily/2008/06/3568n.htm.

Kellogg Commission on the Future of State and Land-Grant Universities. (1999). *Returning to our roots: The engaged institution.* Available at http://www.aplu.org/netcommunity/document.Doc?id=183.

Myers, S. (2001). *The end of the beginning.* Ann Arbor, MI: Imagining America.

Sanchez, G. J. (2004). *Crossing Figueroa: The tangled web of diversity and democracy.* Foreseeable Futures No. 4. Ann Arbor, MI: Imagining America.

CEOs for Cities: Engaged Scholarship for Urban Development

Carol Coletta

CEOs for Cities, a national cross-sector network of urban leaders dedicating to building and sustaining the next generation of great American cities, has always recognized the contribution universities can make to vital urban economies. CEOs for Cities was founded, in part, as a response to the changing needs in urban leadership. Realizing that new partnerships were required for urban success, we were the first (and still the only) organization whose partners work across issues and sectors to develop responses to the opportunities and challenges cities face. Since its inception in 2000, university presidents have sat alongside mayors, corporate leaders, and foundation presidents as partners, recognized equally as urban leaders.

Our Work and the Role of Universities

The University's Role in Producing Talent: The City Dividends

The most significant contribution any university can make to the economic development of its community is, of course, producing more college graduates. In 2008, CEOs for Cities calculated that if the nation could increase college attainment by just one percentage point, the U.S. would realize an additional $124 billion in income.

We call this calculation the Talent Dividend—part of a series of *City Dividends* that were designed to demonstrate to urban leaders the monetary value of making realistic (in fact, meager) improvements in three key action areas: increasing college attainment by one percentage point as outlined above, lowering the number of vehicle miles traveled per person per day by one mile (the Green Dividend), and lowering the number of people living in poverty by one percentage point (the Opportunity Dividend).

373

But we know that Talent is the first among equals and is the dividend that carries the most weight when looking at urban success factors in the knowledge economy. In fact, the only statistic anyone needs to determine the level of a city's success as measured by per capita income is the percentage of its population 25 years and older with a college degree. That generally tells you all you need to know, because every additional percentage point of college attainment represents an additional $736 in per capita income.

One example of the potential for the Talent Dividend in a city comes from Memphis where the one percentage point increase yields an annual Talent Dividend of $1 billion, which is equal in magnitude to the payroll of the largest employer in the city. This one percentage point represents 8,002 additional college graduates. But there are currently more than 124,000 people in Memphis who have completed some college but do not have a degree. This suggests that one strategy the city could focus on to achieve its Talent Dividend would be to focus on moving those with some college to completion.

The University's Role in Retaining Talent

It's not enough, though, to educate college graduates if, upon receiving their degrees, they leave the city. Research shows that colleges and universities can play an important role in talent retention by introducing their students to the city through participation in entertainment and cultural events, volunteering, and internships. The more ties students have to a place, the more likely they are to remain there.

Campus Philly may be the most lauded example of how universities working collaboratively with the economic development organizations, bussinesses, and nonprofits can not only graduate talent, but play a role in keeping them in the city after they graduate. Through its websites, onebigcampus.com and campusphilly.com, Campus Philly works to aid in the recruitment of prospective students to the city, engage students with the civic and cultural life of the city, and keep them in the city by connecting them with business networks and jobs after they graduate.

Our research on the location preferences of the Young and Restless (25- to 34-year-olds with college degrees, who are the most mobile population in the United States) has shown that this age group is 30 percent more likely than other Americans to live close to central cities—that's up from 10 percent in 1980 and 12 percent in 1990, and we suspect that number has grown since 2000. That tells us that these recent graduates will be eying the core city as a place to settle after graduating, and as our research shows, universities are playing an increasingly important role as leaders in urban revitalization. We also know that the universities' roles as engines of economic growth continue to expand.

The University's Role as Economic Engine

In 2001, CEOs for Cities, in cooperation with the Initiative for a Competitive Inner City (ICIC), commissioned Dr. Michael Porter to produce a report on the impact colleges and universities could have on urban economic growth. The insights from the report, *Leveraging Colleges and Universities for Urban Revitalization: An Action Agenda*, were motivating enough to keep the issue on the organization's agenda throughout the decade.

With more than half of the nation's colleges and universities located in central cities and their immediate surroundings, the report called for making it a national priority for bringing college and universities into the fold of inner-city economic revitalization.

The report found that even a dozen years ago, the more than 1,900 urban-core universities spent $136 billion on salaries, goods, and services. That was at the time nine times greater than federal direct spending on urban business and job development. Spending has surely increased since then, and the gap between university spending and federal spending has likely grown wider.

Most of the dollars spent were from nonlocal sources, making colleges and universities a net importer of funds to communities.

Urban colleges and universities are major employers. At the time the report was issued, Porter calculated that they employed two million workers. Contrary to popular assumption, two-thirds of these jobs were nonfaculty administrative and support staff. It is likely that these jobs will increase, because education and knowledge creation is the second fastest-growing industry in the country, with colleges and universities leading the growth.

Colleges and universities are also major landholders. Porter estimated that they held more than $100 billion in land and buildings and spent billions more each year on capital improvements.

These findings make colleges and universities formidable players in urban economies. They attract new funds, employ workers, purchase goods and services, are major landholders, and spend big on capital goods. Their contribution to the local economy is clearly significant.

The question CEOs for Cities and ICIC asked at the time was, can colleges and universities play a more significant role in the revitalization of the inner cities of America through focused strategies?

To accelerate activity and provide a model for planning, Porter developed a strategic framework to define the role of colleges and universities in job and business development. The framework leverages the basic activities of a university in six broad areas: purchasing of goods and services, employment, developing real estate, incubating business, advising business, building networks, and developing workforce.

These six activities are in line with the operating, investing, and learning functions that an academic institution carries out. Purchasing and employment are primarily related to operations. Real estate development and incubating businesses are related to investing. And the roles of advisor/network builder and workforce developer are related to learning.

These functions are part of the institutional fabric of colleges and universities. It was Porter's assertion that in most cases, a slight shift in strategy in each area can have sizable impact on local communities.

Although experience shows that he likely underestimated the task, a number of universities have made remarkable progress.

The University of Pennsylvania is a favorite example. Using an imaginative, multifaceted strategy led by its president and carried out by a network of her academic and business leaders, the university has virtually remade its West Philadelphia neighborhood. The university increased its purchasing the neighborhood, subsidized employee housing there, supported

375

a business improvement district, and started a school nearby. Most significantly, the university turned itself inside out, developing mixed-use spaces at the edge of campus so that the neighborhood flowed seamlessly into the campus. The combined actions of the university have served to transform the neighborhood surrounding it and helped the neighborhood gain its own development momentum.

There are many other examples of universities that, by focusing strategic attention on their immediate neighborhoods, have led significant revitalization and neighborhood improvement.

But as the number of examples grows, the question is being asked: "What's next for anchor institutions?"

Anchor Institutions: An Expanded Definition

One important development in recent years has been to expand the definition of anchor institutions beyond colleges and universities to include hospitals, libraries, performing arts centers and other arts venues, even sports franchises. But some of these may stretch the definition to the breaking point. Libraries, for instance, are generally publicly funded and do not share with universities the need to expand and build regularly. Sports franchises are not necessarily anchored in place, as high-profile moves like the Seattle Sonics' flight to Oklahoma City demonstrate. When the venerable Cleveland Clinic decides to open major operations in Florida and in the Middle East, how much can it be counted on as a local anchor?

It was once assumed that the local bank would always be the local bank—until it wasn't. The same was assumed about the local retailer, the local utility, the local newspaper, and the local TV station—again, until they were bought by corporations headquartered in distant cities and the power of local corporate decision makers disappeared.

So, is it naïve to think that the local university will always be local?

Perhaps one way to answer that question is to lay out the characteristics of anchor institutions that contribute to urban success in meaningful ways.

In May 2007, CEOs for Cities convened urban leaders in San Jose, CA to engage in conversations around strategies for engaging community colleges, parks, libraries, performing arts centers, museums, and hospitals as powerful sources of competitive advantage.

From that meeting, CEOs for Cities produced a briefing paper, "Leveraging Anchor Institutions for Urban Success." Key insights included the following.

Anchor institutions can have impact beyond their walls:
Anchor institutions that think of themselves as institutions whose success depends, in part, on the success of the communities in which they reside (and vice versa) will be in the best position to contribute to urban success.

Anchor institutions can have impact beyond their portfolios:
Anchor institutions should take deep and imaginative inventories of their assets and their needs, then take the broadest possible view of how to act in their own interests and, at the same time, act in the interests of their communities.

Anchor institutions at their best have the opportunity to energize an entire city:
Stimulating new ideas, providing places to meet and share those ideas, gaining acceptance and "pick up" of ideas, and cultivating a culture of risk-taking are critical to innovation. Anchor institutions can play a lead role in providing and encouraging these critical conditions.

Anchor institutions are particularly local institutions:
Anchor institutions will increase their relevance by using resources and leadership to address challenges and opportunities facing their cities. Anchor institutions should be willing to ask where their cities need help and respond imaginatively.

Anchor institutions can be sources of civic leadership:
Whereas many anchor institutions are unusually local, others operate at a global scale, recruiting faculty/employees, guest lecturers and artists, and students/consumers world-wide. Leaders of these anchor institutions can be particularly useful in contributing to the civic dialogue a global perspective on local competitive conditions.

Anchor institutions must move beyond "outreach" to "engagement." That is, anchor institutions cannot simply make their offer and "sell" the community hoping they will buy it. Anchor institutions must engage with the community to shape the offer itself.

As long as anchor institutions are expected to perform only those functions identified by Porter, it may not matter how many locations an anchor institution has, as long as the CEO remains in the community that considers it an anchor. However, to the extent that these functions require CEO attention and presence in the local community, the anchor role is threatened as an institution expands into new geographic markets. And certainly, if the anchor designation presumes that the institution's top executive will perform a local civic leadership role (often being expected to take the place of disappearing corporate leadership), then geographic expansion challenges a leader's ability to focus on just one community. The same proved true with corporate executives as their businesses expanded, merged, and consolidated, leading to decline in local corporate leadership in many communities.

The issue of civic leadership provokes other questions. For instance, what does civic leadership look like when it can't write a check? For that matter, what does civic leadership look like when it is asking for a check?

With CEO tenure getting shorter and with so many mergers and acquisitions—and now bankruptcies—changing the face of business, inevitably the nature of business civic leadership is changing—and not for the better. So, what happens when nonprofit leaders, who generally can't write checks and are generally asking for checks, become the civic leaders? How does that fundamentally change civic leadership? When nonprofit leaders become the civic leaders, what can civic leadership do and what can it not do?

Anchor Institution Transformations: Local Institutions in a Non-local World

Although strong examples of university-community partnerships continue to appear throughout the United States, the movement may be threatened by two developments:

The first is exemplified by the announcement in November 2007 by Northwestern University that it completed a deal to open divisions of its journalism and communications schools in Qatar.

The second is the news that the average tenure for university presidents and chancellors is now down to three to five years.

Universities, in other words, are beginning to sound a lot like corporations. And where once corporations were the source of local community leadership, investment, and distinctiveness, that is rarely the case today. Corporate leaders are too busy competing globally to have much time left for local affairs. And because CEO tenure is short and CEOs are increasingly mobile, there is little local loyalty at a personal level.

Just as a new relationship is being spawned between town and gown, will the movement stall as universities begin experiencing corporate-type pressures?

Anchor Institutions: Can There Be Too Many?

Most communities are happy to have the employment and construction represented by anchor institutions. But can a community have too many anchor institutions? That's a question Providence, Rhode Island has asked. When an increasing amount of land is in the hands of institutions that do not pay property taxes, how is a city supposed to pay its bills? What is a reasonable way for anchor institutions to compensate a government for services rendered? Certainly, many anchor institutions provide services to their campuses and the immediate neighborhood, but so do many neighborhood associations. Yet, homeowners who support their neighborhood associations still pay taxes to support the common good. So what's fair?

This raises the question: How should the contribution of anchor institutions be valued? Should those anchor institutions that bring net new revenue into a community be more highly valued than those that recirculate local dollars? Or, is it more valuable to serve local residents?

Similarly, how should the negative impacts of big anchor institutions be weighed against their positive impacts on their immediate neighborhoods?

The impact of some of the real estate development by anchor institutions is truly impressive, as is the economic development that can result from university research. The benefits to communities are many. And the benefits to anchor institutions can be significant.

Conclusion

I started my consulting firm years ago working with corporations such as Home Depot and Toys R Us on developing what we called their "Strategic Community Investment." Twenty years ago, that meant developing a rationale for how to invest time and money in communities. We worked hard to get big retailers to recognize their obligations to communities where they did business, not just where the home office was located.

Today, corporate social responsibility is defined less by what you give in terms of philanthropic dollars and more by the way you run your business—your hiring and labor practices, your purchasing, your sourcing, and most especially today, your sustainable practices.

The notion of "local" rarely comes up for major corporations because if you operate everywhere, then where is local? (The one exception seems to be food sourcing.) In fact, many companies are now born as global companies. And many companies focus their philanthropy on global concerns. It seems far sexier to tackle global warming in China than in Mountain View, California, or entrepreneurship in India rather than in inner-city Los Angeles.

If we consider the dimensions on which cities must compete in a knowledge economy—talent, connections, distinctiveness, and innovation, with a strong central city as an accelerator of all four dimensions—one important question for anchor institutions is how they can strengthen each of these factors in their local communities.

And if anchor institutions are truly anchored in local communities, it would be exciting and worthwhile to explore how to amplify the value of local (another way of saying the value of distinctiveness) in a globalizing world. Perhaps that is the next frontier of anchor institutions.

If the goal is to accelerate the positive impact anchor institutions have on their communities, perhaps we should be working toward a set of principles—a manifesto of sorts—for anchor institutions that defines an optimum relationship with their local communities, something to strive for. A set of performance standards and designations—think of LEED (Leadership in Energy and Environmental Design)—can be useful in changing behavior.

As CEOs for Cities continues its work exploring the factors that contribute to urban success, it no doubt will include the changing role of universities and other anchor institutions with the times. And although much work has been done to identify and act on the potential of anchor institutions, these questions remain worthy of exploration in future research:

By refocusing on their basic mission, can anchor institutions produce significantly more benefit to their communities?

How will the emergence of anchor institution leaders in civic life change what we should expect from civic leadership? (And what could be accomplished if local anchor institutions worked in collaboration rather than individually, as they are more likely to do?)

Are anchor institutions, in fact, anchored? Or, are they, like corporations, at risk of leaving or lessening their local commitment?

What do anchor institutions owe their communities, particularly in terms of payment for services?

And how should the contribution of anchor institutions be valued?

HENCE: A Federation to Advance Community Engagement across Higher Education

Lorilee R. Sandmann and David J. Weerts

The Higher Education Network for Community Engagement (HENCE) arose from a demonstrated high level of commitment to cooperation across diverse engagement-related organizations in order to encourage the further development and improvement of community engagement. Now a virtual federation of higher education community engagement leadership organizations, HENCE serves as an incubator for collaborative activities to increase impact on the field, reduce duplication, address gaps in activities and resources, advocate for national support for engagement, and promote consistency in practices and policies related to community engagement.

The Community Engagement Movement

America's colleges and universities have a long tradition of connecting their mission of research and teaching to the issues of broader society. As Roper and Hirth (2005) explain, higher education's "third mission" (public service, outreach, and engagement) has evolved with changes in societal needs and expectations of higher education. For example, in the late 1800s, higher education played a vital role in developing the country's agricultural economy through the delivery of short courses, extension programs, and faculty consultation with farmers. Early in the twentieth century, academics became increasingly involved with civic and economic issues by providing expertise to policy makers and business leaders to improve government and industry. And as basic and applied research gained prominence, higher education increased its role in technology transfer—the work of scholars had the effect of facilitating workforce development and growing healthy businesses (Roper & Hirth, 2005).

Through most of the past century, societal benefits from higher education were largely a by-product of traditional forms of teaching and research. That is, academicians historically operated in a dissemination paradigm where scholars transfer or extend knowledge to society through publications, patents, and other dissemination strategies. Because this "expert" model does not reflect reciprocal exchanges with external stakeholders, higher education institutions came to be viewed as "ivory towers" that acted as detached observers of society.

Because of growing concerns that colleges and universities were out of touch, a new discussion emerged in the early 1990s that sought to redefine the relationship between higher education and the communities it serves. During this period a number of leading scholars, national organizations, and nonprofit foundations challenged higher education to redefine its traditional roles and to rethink approaches to scholarly work in ways more directly relevant to communities and societal issues. Fueling these ideas were seminal scholarly works such as *Scholarship Reconsidered* (Boyer, 1990), *Scholarship Assessed* (Glassick, Huber, & Maeroff, 1997), and *Making the Case for Professional Service* (Lynton, 1995), which paved the way for academic work focused on serving broad public interests (Knox, 2001). During this period, leaders called for greater intentionality in the interactions between academic institutions and community interests. Emanating from these discussions was the idea that scholars and communities could "engage" each other in collaborative work that would have mutual benefits.

Against this backdrop, many national associations soon came to define engagement as it applied to the unique characteristics of their member institutions (AASC&U, 2001; CIC, 2005; Kellogg Commission, 1999). One definition created by the Carnegie Foundation for the Advancement of Teaching conceptualizes community engagement as "the collaboration between higher education institutions and their larger communities (local, regional/state, national, global) for the mutually beneficial exchange of knowledge and resources in a context of partnership and reciprocity" (Carnegie, 2008).

Over the past decade, engagement as a mode of scholarly work has grown quickly as academic institutions and communities have begun to document the positive effects of their collaborative work on public issues. Today, more than half of America's community colleges and more than a third of all other colleges and universities are engaging faculty and students in community partnership activities as a valued part of research and teaching activities. Forms of engagement include curricular engagement, with faculty integrating service-learning into their courses and facilitating other community-based learning, and formal and informal campus-community partnerships that involve research, evaluation, program improvement, professional development training, continuing education, and other strategies that strengthen both the institution and the community through joint action.

A number of important external levers have emerged to help facilitate engagement on campuses and across higher education sectors. For example, several systems for classifying and accrediting higher education added measures of community engagement, thus affirming its importance as a contemporary academic priority (e.g., Carnegie, 2008; Higher Learning Commission, 2005). In addition, public policy leaders are aggressively seeking to develop public agendas for higher education (NCPPHE, 2008), ideas that fit squarely with the principles of reciprocity and partnership as articulated in contemporary definitions of engagement.

Creating a Federation for Community Engagement

Because the focus on engagement has grown across institutions of all types, national and regional affiliate organizations supporting this activity have also expanded. For example, some engagement-related organizations have grown out of a full or partial focus on a particular method (service-learning, community partnerships, continuing education, Extension, community-based research, etc.). Others are organized around an institutional type (land grant, community college, urban university, etc.). Some organizations focus on policy and practice issues at the presidential leadership level; others attract scholars/researchers or focus on specific subject areas. Some organizations hold their own annual conferences, publish their own journals or newsletters, commission task forces on special issues, or have created formal membership structures.

All of these organizations seek to provide opportunities and information that will help grow the field of campus-community engagement. However, it became increasingly clear that these organizations often operated so independently of each other that there was little or no collaboration on critical issues or sharing of expertise or limited resources. Recent years have seen growing evidence of duplication, overlap, and areas of unaddressed need, with resultant confusion, wasted effort, and missed opportunities.

When several engagement organization leaders began to explore the need for greater coordination, they approached the Johnson Foundation to assist with convening a national discussion around these ideas. Located in Racine, Wisconsin, the Johnson Foundation has hosted more than a dozen Wingspread Conferences over sixteen years that have informed and energized what has become a national movement in higher education. Declarations, reports, calls to action, strategies for quality improvement, and documentation of principles of best practice were generated by these Wingspread conferences and continue to be a key resource to guide the work of engagement.

In February 2006, Wingspread hosted twenty-eight representatives of formal and informal affiliate organizations so that they might explore cooperative strategies to deepen, consolidate, and advance the field of higher education and community and civic engagement. The purpose of the conference was to plan for the creation of a federation across engagement-related organizations in order to leverage overall capacity through collaboration. Participants coalesced quickly around the idea of a "Higher Education Network for Community Engagement" or HENCE, with the emphasis on the word "network." Thus, a virtual confederation recognizing engagement as a core element of higher education's civic role was born (see Sandmann & Weerts, 2006, for a comprehensive summary of this conference; also see Appendix A at the end of this chapter for a list of founding network organizations).

Since convening in 2006, HENCE has evolved as an affiliate network of organizations that provides access points to other networks and to aspects of the vast audience of engagement

383

researchers, leaders, and practitioners. Today, the organization is pursuing agreed-upon objectives to:

- Create a national network coordinated across leadership organizations
- Develop a coordinated approach to providing resources and data
- Encourage local, state, regional, and national meetings (formal and informal)
- Implement a coordinated agenda for advocacy
- Create an agenda for professional development and recognition.

HENCE is a network of representatives of formal and informal organizations and leaders in the field of community engagement; it is organized as a loose collaborative with shared leadership from a steering committee representing different perspectives. Thus, HENCE is peer led by a steering committee of participant volunteers with rotating terms. Their task is to provide overall coordination of HENCE's workgroups and to track its activities and outcomes. As a virtual organization, its "office" is a website, http://www.henceonline.org, with light infrastructure support from Campus Compact and Michigan State University's Office of University Outreach and Engagement, National Center for the Study of University Engagement.

Holding true to the intention of not adding another membership organization to the mix, there is no membership in HENCE and there are no individual affiliates (people or institutions). Affiliating organizations are represented by one or more persons able to contribute to the workgroups associated with the stated HENCE purposes. New organizations have continued to join the federation since the founding of the network in 2006. There are two types of organizations that affiliate with HENCE:

1. Membership associations that have explicit goals and activities related to the improvement, advancement, dissemination, or recognition of community engagement in higher education; and
2. Networks, funding organizations or agencies, scholarly journals, and technical assistance/training organizations that have a primary focus on the improvement, advancement, dissemination, or recognition of community engagement.

From time to time, HENCE leadership may also decide to invite individuals to participate in specific projects or working groups because of their particular expertise. Applications for membership are reviewed by the HENCE Steering Committee at its regular meetings. Acceptance is based on receiving a majority of votes of the Steering Committee members present. No dues are charged, and all meetings are self-funded or supported by external grants or donations obtained for HENCE activities. Projects or activities that generate costs can be funded by external grants or donations from affiliates or other funding sources.

The Roles of HENCE

Reflecting on the roles of HENCE, one can see that the organization has three important roles: providing coordinative infrastructure for the engagement movement, serving as an incubator for engagement ideas, and symbolizing the systemic institutionalization of the movement. We now elaborate on these three primary roles.

First, HENCE serves an important functional role as a coordinating entity, or clearing-house for engagement-related programs and activities across higher education sectors. Put simply, HENCE is a communication vehicle to connect members on engagement programs or issues of mutual interest. For example, member organizations broadcast their conference schedules through HENCE to encourage attendance from interested parties and prevent overlap of meeting times with other associations. As one leader of HENCE explained during a phone interview, "I enjoy HENCE because it is a nice virtual location in the field, and I get caught up on what other organizations are doing." Another leader explains, "Every aspect of engagement is represented, and so is the potential for all of higher education."

Second, what has evolved from the collaborative synergy is HENCE as an incubator for new ideas in the field. Functioning like economic development incubators on many campuses that provide a fertile environment to spawn and seed new initiatives, HENCE is serving as a start-up site from which initiatives are spun off for development and implementation. For example, the workgroup on research centers, the Emerging Engagement Scholars program, the Engagement Academy for University Leaders, and research on the lives of engaged scholars are four examples of ideas that germinated within HENCE, had development facilitated by HENCE, represent pilots cosponsored by HENCE, and in some cases spun off to single-purposed organizations or stand-alone endeavors. Specifically, HENCE-sponsored gatherings provide a venue to encourage thought and action around engagement both within institutional settings and within the larger fabric of higher education. One member involved with HENCE explained that the organization has shown associations "what is possible" when convening groups of practitioners and scholars around particular issues related to engagement. The success of the Engagement Academy for University Leaders illustrates this point. Convened for the first time in June 2008, the Academy is a professional development seminar aimed at training future and present leaders of engagement. "Just a few people made it happen," explained one HENCE member. "The success of the Academy shows others that haven't been involved or are new that it is possible to do this. You can work across organizations that provide benefit for all institutions. Since we are all representing organizations, we must understand how efforts are going to help our constituencies."

Third, beyond these functional roles, HENCE serves important symbolic purposes. The establishment of HENCE symbolizes widespread commitment to engagement among multiple sectors of higher education. The robust membership of HENCE reflects the diversity of colleges and universities in mission, type, and context. Thus, the existence of HENCE marks community engagement as a legitimate movement in the broad landscape of higher education. In the next section, we provide more details about the work of HENCE and, in particular, specific initiatives under way to facilitate engagement on campuses and across sectors of the higher education community.

The Work of HENCE

Four major themes emerged from the initial Wingspread Conference and follow-up gatherings. These themes of major need frame the HENCE agenda: assessment and documentation; policy, media, and funding; faculty engaged scholarship; and professional development. HENCE participants have formed workgroups around these themes. The following reports their charge and some of their progress to date.

Assessment and documentation.

How do we capture the impact of engagement? How do we communicate it to others? Documenting the quality and impact of engagement is crucial to generating support and ensuring quality. Creating definitions of common measures and creating quality and practical assessment tools is one area that HENCE scholars are addressing as they work toward developing a rubric to guide the development of standard survey instruments that measure impact, institutionalization, and program outcomes in ways that are useful to internal and external audiences.

Policy, media, and funding.

Even as higher education becomes an active contributor to the creation of "public good" through engagement, the sector continues to suffer from negative public stereotypes. A key step that HENCE is pursing is building a cohesive policy agenda around community partnerships and engagement. A grassroots effort at the local level is a logical first step for advocacy, followed by mapping current engagement activities by state and federal legislative districts. Not to be forgotten is that powerful advocacy comes from the compelling stories of students and community partners.

Faculty engaged scholarship.

Sustainability of engagement relies on embedding it in the core of academic values. Although progress on organizational change is noted, HENCE is focused on ways to measure the quality of engaged scholarship and how it contributes to student learning, to fulfilling organizational missions, and to community development. Organizational and cultural values are quite diverse across institutional types and in engagement; there must be a voice for community as well, given its role as a co-generator of knowledge and learning. HENCE is striving to act as a research convener and a clearinghouse to provide information about promising practices in this arena.

Professional development.

HENCE recognizes that community engagement requires new methods and strategies that affect faculty work, institutional leadership, and student experiences. Engagement exists on a foundation of campus-community partnerships that seek to generate mutual benefit through knowledge exchange. This requires training and skill building for campus and community. HENCE participants are working toward research on and career guides for the engaged scholar and a companion piece to help communities work more successfully with colleges and universities. Additionally, HENCE is catalyzing specific professional development offerings, such as Virginia Tech's Engagement Academy for University Leaders, described earlier.

Future Directions for HENCE: Opportunities and Challenges

The prospects for the future of HENCE are bright. First and foremost, the presence of HENCE is a statement of the maturation of the community engagement movement and the demonstrated high level of commitment to cooperation across diverse engagement-related organizations in order to encourage the further development and improvement of community engagement. There continues to be excitement around HENCE, and the early successes stemming from HENCE national dialogues have affirmed its purposes. One member explained, "HENCE has helped its constituent organizations. Now a new group of people are talking about faculty-engaged scholarship and posing questions about roles we can play to advance engaged scholarship." This member elaborated that HENCE could become a "home for good ideas" and that building a track record of successes could position the organization for future funding opportunities. And, as indicated by its roles and by the accomplishment of the workgroups, HENCE is fulfilling its purpose as an entity that is facilitating thinking and acting collaboratively. Workgroups are thinking about their tasks more broadly with multiple perspectives and resources at the table. Although it is fulfilling its purpose to a degree, HENCE has yet to fulfill its promise.

Looking to the future of HENCE, we note a variety of opportunities and challenges that lie ahead for the organization. In the future, HENCE could continue to serve as a convener, broadening the scope of specific initiatives into a larger sphere. This is already happening with various HENCE-affiliated programs. For example, a preconference seminar for graduate students at the National Outreach Scholarship Conference in 2007 was convened by staff from Michigan State University and promoted through the HENCE network. With HENCE as the convening agent, the preconference was broadened beyond a handful of institutions to include a large network of interested associations and their members. Again, the Engagement Academy (EA) for University Leaders is an example of an effort convened by a few but broadened to include many. HENCE provided a forum to advertise EA through its robust network of higher education associations and, as a result, recruited a diverse group of participants for its inaugural seminar.

Important "light" infrastructure has been put in place (e.g., the development of a definition of affiliate status and steering committee rotation processes), but the HENCE virtual organizational model is evolving as operational issues are being addressed. Those issues involve working toward a sustainable model of active institutional involvement for an entity that is committed to peer self-governance and is functioning without staff, budget, or a home organization. The steering committee is to be commended for continuing to advance the organization on a voluntary basis. Work will be done to maximize the web "office" of HENCE. And face-to-face interactions, which occurred through two Wingspread Conferences (the second one framed as "electrifying the network"), have been continued with a meeting hosted by and held in conjunction with the International Association for Research on Service-learning and Community Engagement. Such periodic meetings will be instrumental to continuing the synergistic promise of HENCE.

The primary challenge for HENCE relates to staffing and volunteer support required to sustain the organization into the future. The current leadership is all voluntary. Thus, future

387

successes of the organization depend on the continued availability of these leaders, and ability of the organization to attract new leadership. HENCE was constructed as a network with the idea that support would come from those involved in associations or on campuses, not professional staff. As a result, some of the productivity of HENCE workgroups has been uneven, and largely based on the commitments of volunteer leadership. One leader of HENCE exclaimed, "Someone has to take the ball and run with it," meaning that volunteers must commit themselves to staffing committees and convening monthly calls to forward the work of the organization. She continued, "If we keep depending on people based on the goodness of their heart, everyone will burn out." In order for HENCE to stay vibrant, it must recruit new leaders with fresh ideas.

Another challenge related to staffing is that ongoing projects housed in HENCE need some institutional memory beyond the volunteer who convened the program. Questions such as, "Where is the information stored? Who houses the lists of those involved and minutes of planning meetings? Who is responsible for updating the list?" all emanate from the current loose structure of HENCE, which is heavily volunteer reliant. In short, some structure is needed so that programs can be successfully duplicated from year to year. If additional resources were available, they might be used to host the website, bring members together, and organize conferences, among other things. As this chapter goes to press, discussions about securing funding for HENCE are under way, as funds may be critical to sustaining the organization's vision articulated in 2006 at Wingspread.

From Fulfilling the Purpose to Fulfilling the Promise

HENCE is in its early stages of development and still building. It will face challenges in expanding and sustaining its leadership base to include more executives and policy makers, beyond well-meaning senior faculty or organization administrative staff; having more than one area of emphasis (policy, professional development, research, and resource coordination); searching for a fluid, functional workgroup structure; and securing continued financial commitments and support. Its structure will need to be optimized for it, as a network of higher education institutions, to be flexible and responsive. However, it has the potential to mature into a higher education version of the National Service Learning Partnership, a national network of members dedicated to advancing service-learning as a core part of every young person's life and education (http://www.service-learningpartnership.org/site/PageServer). Despite its early stage development, its emergence is particularly timely as an organization home for a national movement that is accelerating into a bipartisan call for a ServiceNation (http://www.bethechangeinc.org/servicenation/about_us/vision, supported by a Serve America Act, http://s3.amazonaws.com/btcreal/855/Kennedy_Hatch_Serve_America_Act_Summary.pdf). HENCE holds promise as a research and change agenda for higher education to be a vital part of this future. Collaboration across a diverse array of organizations can be prickly. Opportunities for collaboration abound, but honest attention must also be given to the potential for competition and territory, real or perceived (Sandmann, Holland, & Bruns, 2007). HENCE's active presence as cooperative coordinator, incubator, and symbol is attending to and beginning to maximize the collaboration to encourage engagement's quality and impact. Campus-community engagement is here to stay, and yet the nature of the work itself is still being invented and documented. HENCE's purpose and promise is to catalyze new policies and practice and to ensure more efficient opportunities for dissemination, greater visibility, and enhanced policy support for campus-community engagement as a critical strategy for addressing contemporary public issues. These higher education constituencies are learning to work together across their differences in order that higher education, in common, may be successful in recapturing its role and reputation as a crucial source of public good.

References

American Association of State Colleges and Universities (AASC&U). (2002). *Stepping forward as stewards of place: A guide for leading public engagement at state colleges and universities.* Washington, DC: Author.

Boyer, E. L. (1990). *Scholarship reconsidered.* Princeton, NJ: Carnegie Foundation for the Advancement of Teaching.

Carnegie Foundation for the Advancement of Teaching. (2008). *Community engagement elective classification.* Retrieved January 5, 2009, from http://www.carnegiefoundation.org/classifications/index.asp?key=1213.

Committee on Institutional Cooperation (CIC). (2005). *Engaged scholarship: A resource guide* (CIC Reports 800–2000–1242–2005). Champaign, IL: CIC Committee on Engagement. Retrieved January 5, 2009, from http://www.cic.net/Libraries/Technology/Engaged_Scholarship.sflb.ashx.

Glassick, D. C., Huber, M. T., & Maeroff, G. I. (1997). *Scholarship assessed: Evaluation of the professoriate.* San Francisco: Jossey-Bass.

Higher Learning Commission. (2003). *The handbook of accreditation* (3rd ed.). Chicago: North Central Association Higher Learning Commission. Retrieved February 24, 2010, from http://www.ncahigherlearningcommission.org/download/Handbook03.pdf.

Kellogg Commission on the Future of State and Land-Grant Universities. (1999). *Returning to our roots: The engaged institution* [Electronic version]. Washington, DC: National Association of State Universities and Land-Grant Colleges. Retrieved January 5, 2009, from http://www.nasulgc.org/publications/Kellogg/Kellogg1999_Engage.pdf.

Knox, A. B. (2001). Assessing university faculty outreach performance. *College Teaching, 49*(2), 71–74.

Lynton, E. A. (1995). *Making the case for professional service.* Washington, DC: American Association for Higher Education.

National Center for Public Policy in Higher Education (NCPPHE). (2008). *Partnership for public purposes: Engaging higher education in societal challenges of the 21st century* (Special Report by the National Center for Public Policy and Higher Education). San Jose, CA: Author. Retrieved January 5, 2009, from http://www.highereducation.org/reports/wegner/index.shtml.

Roper, C. D., & Hirth, M. A. (2005). A history of change in the third mission of higher education: The evolution of one-way service to interactive engagement. *Journal of Higher Education Outreach and Engagement, 10*(3), 3–21.

Sandmann, L. R., & Weerts, D. J. (2006). *Engagement in higher education: Building a federation for action.* Wingspread Report. Available at http://www.henceonline.org/about/founding_documents.

Sandmann, L. R., Holland, B., & Bruns, K. (2007). Creating a federation to encourage community engagement. *Wingspread Journal, 22–25.*

Appendix A: Founding Organizational Networks

National and Regional Societies and Organizations

American Association of Community Colleges–Service Learning Initiative

American Association of Colleges of Pharmacy

American Association of State Colleges and Universities–American Democracy Project

Association for Community Higher Education Partnerships

Association of American Colleges and Universities

Association of Public and Land-grant Universities-Council on Outreach and Engagement

Carnegie Foundation for the Advancement of Teaching

Campus Compact

Community-Campus Partnerships for Health

Coalition of Urban and Metropolitan Universities

Consortium for the Advancement of Private Higher Education

Corporation for National and Community Service

Extension Committee on Organization and Policy

HBCU Faculty Development Network

Imagining America

International Association for Research on Service-learning and Community Engagement

Kentucky Council on Postsecondary Education

New England Resource Center for Higher Education

The Higher Learning Commission of North Central Association

National and Regional Centers

Clearinghouse/National Review Board for the Scholarship of Engagement

National Center for the Study of University Engagement

National Service Learning Clearinghouse

Scholarly and Professional Journals

Change

Journal of Higher Education Outreach and Engagement

Michigan Journal of Community Service Learning

Urban and Metropolitan Universities

Journal of Extension

College and University Centers

Agape Center for Service Learning, Messiah College

Center for Urban Research and Learning, Loyola University, Chicago

Center for Civic Engagement and Social Responsibility, Tougaloo College

Service Learning Research and Development Center, UC Berkeley

Scholarly Conferences and Meetings

AAC&U conferences

Coalition of Urban and Metropolitan Universities Conference

International Research Conference on Service-learning and Community Engagement

International Service-Learning Research Conference

National Outreach Scholarship Conference

A Catalyst for Research: The International Association for Research on Service-Learning and Community Engagement

Sherril B. Gelmon

As the concept of engagement becomes more widely recognized and accepted within higher education, there is an increasing emphasis on the scholarship of such work. For many years, the venues that offered established and developing scholars an outlet for the dissemination of scholarly work related to engagement were limited. Nor was there a place where graduate students could seek feedback on their work or meet potential mentors. The creation of the International Association for Research on Service-Learning and Community Engagement (IARSLCE) has provided a professional membership association with the sole purpose of promoting research on engagement and related pedagogies and strategies. This chapter describes the background forces driving the establishment of the Association and illustrates how IARSLCE is advancing research on and about engagement.

Background

In 2005, Shelley Billig issued a "Call to Action" for a new international research association on service-learning and community engagement (Billig, 2005). Considerable discussion ensued regarding the need for another association, and the scope and format it would take. Some leaders in the field felt a new association was unnecessary; others observed that there was no one higher education organization that provided a venue primarily for research related to service-learning, community engagement, and related strategies. Billig's call to action was acted upon at the 2005 International Service-Learning Research Conference with an agreement among conference participants to create a new professional membership association, and identification of candidates for board membership. All past chairs of the International Research Conference were invited to join the board, and elections were held for members who would represent perspectives including higher education, K–12, other organizations with similar interests, and international (i.e., non–United States). Elections were held in 2006, and the new board held its first meeting in October 2006 in conjunction with the 2006 International Service-Learning Research Conference in Portland, Oregon.

Terminology

Although there was consensus that a new professional membership association should be established, there was considerable debate among the association founders as to what the organization should be called, given the variations in terminology that are used and had become evident through the submissions to the first five international research conferences. When the international research conference was initiated in 2001, the focus was on service-learning research. Over the next five years an increasing number of submitted and accepted abstracts reflected a research focus that went beyond just service-learning. The most common umbrella terms being used appeared to be civic engagement and community engagement.

Engagement describes collaborations between higher education institutions and their larger communities (local, regional/state, national, global) for the mutually beneficial exchange of knowledge and resources in a context of partnership and reciprocity (Carnegie Foundation, 2006). This definition has gained considerable acceptance because it is the underpinning of the Carnegie Foundation's efforts since 2006 to implement the "Carnegie Elective Classification for Community Engagement" (Carnegie Foundation, 2006).

A more specific term is civic engagement. Robert Putnam, in his book *Bowling Alone*, defined "civic engagement" as the response to the question: "How can I participate effectively in the public life of my community?" (Putnam, 2000). Campus Compact offered its definition as: "Those activities which reinvigorate the public purposes and civic mission of higher education" (Campus Compact, 2000). Rick Battistoni (2002), in his comprehensive review of the literature on civic engagement, has wisely noted that this term is rooted in political science, and that in many other disciplines similar meaning is given to terms such as civic professionalism, social responsibility, connected knowing, and public leadership/scholarship. Similarly, the concept of "civics" may lack meaning outside of the United States.

When considering appropriate terminology across disciplines, as well across national borders where differing sociopolitical orientations may lead to choices of certain language, it became clear among those leading the establishment of the association that it was important to select terminology that crossed disciplines and borders, and that did not create bias toward a certain population group (majority or disenfranchised). Given that much of the scholarly work being presented at the research conference addressed issues of social justice and equity, there was clear sentiment that any name or terminology should not marginalize certain groups; the concept of "civic" engagement in some circles is viewed as linked to citizenship, and the association founders did not want to limit the scope of research only to those with certain legal status.

In seeking acceptable terminology for an association name, there was a strong emphasis on the importance of acknowledging community because most of this research could not be done in the absence of partnerships with communities. "Community involvement" was not felt to be a strong enough descriptor, and there was a strong orientation to using "community engagement" as this term was being adopted in many jurisdictions domestically and internationally. A useful definition of community engagement is: "The application of institutional [academic] resources to address and solve challenges facing communities through collaboration with these communities" (Commission on Community-Engaged Scholarship in the Health Professions, 2005). The breadth of this definition is particularly useful because it includes methods of community service, service-learning, community-based participatory research, training and technical assistance, coalition-building, capacity-building, and economic development.

Some individuals advocated for using Boyer's (1997) terminology of the "scholarship of engagement." Although this language has some cachet, some community advocates have criticized it as being too academically focused, placing the emphasis on the academic study of the process of engagement as compared to scholarly work that addresses the processes and outcomes of engaging with communities on collaborative issue identification and problem solving.

Similarly, the focus of the association was broader than the scholarship of teaching and learning, which Shulman has defined as the "design and investigation of issues in teaching and learning that contribute to thought and practice" (Shulman, 1993). This is clearly an important area of scholarship related to engagement and offers the potential to extend knowledge and advance promising practices related to teaching and learning strategies, yet the practice of community-based learning/teaching is not in itself the scholarship of teaching. To be scholarly requires the accepted methods of inquiry—speculation, focused question, data collection, analysis, synthesis, report, and dissemination (Gelmon, 2007b).

Discussion of these various concepts provided the framework for the newly elected board to come to agreement on an association name and mandate at its first meeting.

Creation of the Association

The first board meeting in October 2006 was an important foundational activity in that three key decisions were made.

1. The name of the Association was agreed upon as the International Association for Research on Service-Learning and Community Engagement (IARSLCE). This name had three key components: (1) it emphasized the international perspective, denoting that the scope of the Association would be broader than just the United States; (2) research was central, and all activities would relate to research (as compared to organizations that emphasize "how-to" trainings, and practice-based delivery); and (3) both the terms "service-learning" and "community engagement" are in the name and reflect the various perspectives that key stakeholders brought to the Association.
2. A mission statement was agreed on: "To promote the development and dissemination of research on service-learning and community engagement internationally and across all levels of the education system" (IARSLCE, 2007). The choice of terminology and language was important in order to be clear that the central purpose of the organization is both

development and *dissemination* of research, and that this research may take place at any level of the education system—K–12, higher education, continuing or vocational education, etc. IARSLCE's view of research is not restricted to any specific part of the educational system, nor does it favor any specific disciplines.

3. The organization would be a membership association with personal memberships only, and no institutional memberships. This would allow individuals to join and participate in the activities of the Association regardless of affiliation or organizational status. This was particularly important given the Association's emphasis on crossing geographic, organizational, and disciplinary boundaries.

The name and mission statement were presented to the participants in the 2006 International Research Conference, and the founding board moved forward to develop bylaws and other founding documents; incorporate as a 501(c)3 nonprofit charitable organization; elect officers; and establish operating principles (Gelmon, 2007a).

Scope of Activities

Within its bylaws, IARSLCE has identified eight primary activities by which it will contribute to advancing the fields of service-learning and community engagement research across the educational spectrum (primary, secondary, postsecondary, and further education):

1. Promoting the exchange of ideas, experiences, data, and research among its members;
2. Disseminating knowledge and research on service-learning and community engagement;
3. Encouraging the continual improvement of the quality and rigor of research in these fields;
4. Providing a forum for the presentation of research findings, ideas, methods, and opinions across educational systems;
5. Facilitating exchange of information and creation of collaborations among scholars and practitioners around the world;
6. Supporting and facilitating the development of new scholars entering the fields of research on service-learning and community engagement;
7. Creating venues for ongoing learning and communication among the members; and
8. Establishing communication strategies that facilitate the dissemination of research beyond the members to other communities of scholars and practitioners.

In addition, IARSLCE may initiate other activities and programs that support the interests of members and advance the fields of service-learning and community engagement. Throughout all of its work, IARSLCE is committed to conducting all activities in a self-supporting, fiscally accountable, and ethical manner. A key discussion early in the development of IARSLCE was whether it was advantageous to link the Association to a host institution or organization. Although there were some potential benefits of security of a stable resource base through such an affiliation, there were many concerns that any "host" might be seen as steering the Association in a specific direction and because of special interests might not enable IARSLCE to fulfill the breadth of the scope of its mission. The lack of such an affiliation might bring some financial risk to the Association, but it was preferable to maintain the autonomy of IARSLCE and its ability to pursue the broad range of activities defined earlier.

Governance

IARSLCE is governed by a twelve- to fifteen-member Board of Directors. All individuals who stand for election to the board must be members of IARSLCE. Board members work in areas related to research in service-learning and community engagement and collectively reflect different settings, disciplines, and constituencies. All are not necessarily researchers them-selves, but are involved in support or promotion of research. The board is composed to have a balance of individuals representing research interests across the educational spectrum. There are designated board seats for two non-U.S. representatives; at least one current grad-uate student; one junior faculty (within first five years of tenure-track appointment); and one representative from another relevant organization. Board terms are for three years, and a board member may stand for election for a second term. Individuals who have served as Board members are listed in table 1, in recognition of their important contributions in estab-lishing IARSLCE.

The board elects its own officers (chair and vice-chair) for one-year terms, once renew-able; the chair is responsible for identifying committee chair and/or member positions for all board members. Committee members establish their committee membership, drawing upon a call to the membership and promotion at the annual conference. At present, the board is supported by eight committees: Conference, Publications, Communications/Out-reach, Awards, Nominating, Membership, Fundraising, and Finance. The GSN and ECN each have a Steering Committee drawn from their membership.

Initiatives of IARSLCE

IARSLCE pursues its objectives through various strategies, programs, and activities that sup-port research and information exchange, member involvement, and dissemination. These include the annual research conference, the *Advances in Service-Learning Research* book series, the Graduate Student Network, the Early Career Network, a website, and research awards. These are described next.

Annual Research Conference

The hosting of an annual research conference actually predates the establishment of IARSLCE. The research conference was launched initially by RMC Research Corporation and the University of California Berkeley, and received support for the first five years from a grant from the W. K. Kellogg Foundation. An initial group of advisors was established to facilitate decision making and advise on directions; the initial focus was on presentation of studies that related to service-learning in K–12 and higher education venues. The early goals of the conference were to provide a place where people could learn about and comment on each other's research, promote research agendas that nurtured more and better research in service-learning, and raise the credibility of the field (Billig, 2005). RMC co-hosted the first

Table 1. IARSLCE Board Members 2006–2009

Board Member Name and Affiliation	Board Term
Jeffrey Anderson, Ph.D., Professor of Education, Seattle University	2007–2009
Shelley Billig, Ph.D., Vice-President, RMC Research	2006–2009
Min Cho, Ph.D., Assistant Professor, Department of Art Education, Virginia Commonwealth University	2006–2008
Nicholas Cutforth, Ph.D., Associate Professor, Curriculum & Instruction, Morgridge College of Education, University of Denver	2008–2011
Jennifer Dorr, Executive Director, Washington Campus Compact; Board Secretary-Treasurer	2006–2008
Janet Eyler, Ph.D., Professor of the Practice of Education, Vanderbilt University	2006–2008
Andrew Furco, Ph.D., Associate Vice President Public Engagement, University of Minnesota	2006–2008
Sherril Gelmon, Dr.P.H., Professor of Public Health, Mark O. Hatfield School of Government, Portland State University; Board Chair 2006–2008	2006–2009
Barbara Holland, Ph.D., Director, National Service-Learning Clearinghouse; Board Vice-Chair 2008–2009	2006–2009
Vincent Ilustre, M.B.A., Executive Director, Center for Public Service, Tulane University; IARSLCE Administrative Director and Secretary-Treasurer	Effective 4/09
Emily Janke, Ph.D., Assistant Director of Service-Learning, University of North Carolina Greensboro	2007–2010
Patricia Paredes, M.A., Executive Director, Texas Campus Compact	2008–2011
Diana Pacheco-Pinzon, Ph.D., Director of Service-Learning, Universidad Marista de Mérida	2008–2011
Gail Robinson, Program Director for Service Learning, American Association of Community Colleges	2007–2009
Cobie Rudd, Ph.D., Chair in Mental Health Nursing and Head of School, School of Nursing, Midwifery and Postgraduate Medicine, Edith Cowan University	2008–2011
John Saltmarsh, Ph.D., Director, New England Resource Center for Higher Education, Graduate College of Education, University of Massachusetts Boston; Board Chair 2008–2009	2006–2009
Robert Shumer, Ph.D., Lecturer, College of Education and Human Development, University of Minnesota; Board Vice-Chair 2006–2008	2006–2009
Trae Stewart, Ph.D., Assistant Professor, University of South Florida	2008–2011
Maria Nieves Tapia, Director, CLAYSS (Centro Latinoamericano de Aprendizaje y Servicio Solidario/Latin American Center for Service-learning)	2006–2008
Nicole Webster, Ph.D., Associate Professor, The Pennsylvania State University	2008–2011
Marshall Welch, Ph.D., Director, Catholic Institute for Lasallian Social Action, St. Mary's College of California	2006–2008

five years of the conference, working with the University of California–Berkeley (2001), Vanderbilt University (2002), the University of Utah (2003), Clemson University (2004), and Michigan State University (2005).

When the Kellogg funding ended, the conference became self-sustaining. At the same time, a shift in the focus of research submitted and accepted for presentation demonstrated the expanding nature of the field beyond service-learning to also include many kinds of research on community engagement. The conference became "The International Research Conference on Service-Learning and Community Engagement" and has been hosted by Portland State University (2006), Florida Campus Compact and a consortium of Florida higher education institutions (2007), and Tulane University (2008). The 2009 conference was the first outside the United States and was held in Ottawa, Canada, with the University of Ottawa as host.

The opportunity to host the conference is available to any institution where a lead faculty or staff person is an IARSLCE member and willing to provide leadership of the conference. Serving as conference host brings the institution high visibility and may help to raise its credibility with respect to support of service-learning and community engagement research. The host institution signs a memorandum of agreement with IARSLCE in which it agrees to designate an experienced individual to serve as program chair for the conference and co-editor of the volume arising from the conference, and to sponsor a President's reception for conference attendees. Most institutions have also found it helpful to designate some administrative or graduate student support to assist the program chair with logistics. The IARSLCE Conference Committee, currently chaired by Gail Robinson, increasingly has continuity of experience from year to year and is able to provide advice and guidance to the program chair.

The conference usually draws 350 to 400 participants and includes researchers, academic administrators, graduate students, practitioners, policy advocates, and funders. Session formats are varied and include substantial opportunities for discussion and debate. Each year, preconference workshops are presented that focus on research development strategies, related to such topics as developing a research agenda, getting one's work published, preparing for tenure and promotion review, and research methodologies.

IARSLCE Publications

A book series, called *Advances in Service-Learning Research*, was established when the conference was initiated. Presenters at the annual conference are invited to submit a full manuscript immediately after the conference, describing their research; selected papers are accepted through a peer-review process and subjected to rigorous editorial review. A new volume is published each year out of the conference and is given to registrants at the next year's conference as part of their registration (as well as being available for regular purchase on an ongoing basis). The series editor is Shelley Billig, and the series is published by Information Age Publishing (www.infoagepub.com). The annual conference program chair is invited to serve as co-editor of the volume arising from their conference and currently works with Barbara Holland and Shelley Billig as the Board Publications Committee Co-Chairs.

From time to time there are calls from the field for the creation of a new peer-reviewed journal, either in hard copy or online. The IARSLCE Board has had extensive discussions about this topic, and although we recognize the need for additional venues for publication of scholarly work related to community engagement, we could only commit to establishing a journal if we were confident that we could produce a quality product—which suggests having the time and resources to adequately support the development, marketing, and production of a journal. For the near future, therefore, IARSLCE will not be establishing a new journal.

Graduate Student Network

In keeping with IARSLCE's commitment to supporting and encouraging graduate students, a Graduate Student Network (GSN) was established in 2007. Emily Janke, who joined the IARSLCE Board as a doctoral student, is the founding chair of the GSN. The GSN hosts a electronic mailing list, encourages discussion and information-sharing among graduate students, convenes an annual session featuring graduate student research at the annual research conference, promotes the graduate student scholarships for the conference, and is responsible for inviting graduate students to the Graduate Student Reception at the annual research conference.

Early Career Network

An Early Career Network (ECN) was established in 2008. Trae Stewart, who sits on the IARSLCE Board as a junior faculty member, is the founding chair of the ECN. The ECN hosts an electronic mailing list, encourages discussion and information-sharing among early career scholars and practitioners, and convenes an annual session featuring early career scholars' research at the annual research conference. The ECN hopes to become a resource both for junior faculty and for practitioners who are early in their careers and wish to learn more about research on engagement. There is also the opportunity for more senior faculty who are new to engaged research to participate in the ECN; demand for such a resource may develop over time.

IARSLCE Communications

An Association website was created very shortly after the organization was established (www. researchslce.org) and serves as one of the major communication vehicles for IARSLCE. Until the establishment of the Association, each conference host had created a new website for the year, which resulted in some fragmentation from year to year. With the creation of a single IARSLCE website, the conference information can always be found in one place (as well as all other IARSLCE information), and this has been an important step in helping to establish the Association's identity. Notices of forthcoming events, award announcements, and other timely information are posted to the website. A members-only page was created where copies of presentations from the annual research conference are posted for members-only access. It is anticipated that selected research papers will soon be made available through the members-only page, including selections from various volumes in the *Advances in Service-Learning* book series (which otherwise are not available via the web).

The Association also maintains a members electronic mailing list and is careful to screen information posted there through a moderator. As with any such list, this is an extremely useful communication vehicle, but IARSLCE needs to be attentive to not overloading its members with unnecessary or duplicative information that may be distributed through other lists.

Recognition of Research Accomplishments

IARSLCE provides support for awards and recognition of scholarly achievements. The Association has established three research awards that recognize and promote distinguished research. It also was the first organization to use the term "Emerging Scholar" to recognize new and developing scholars, and in 2006 first offered designated sessions at the research conference that were selected through peer review and showcased an emerging scholar presenting her or his work and engaging in a public dialogue with a senior scholar who offered critique. The "Emerging Scholar" sessions have continued to be an excellent opportunity to identify and recognize new scholars in the field.

The IARSLCE Distinguished Research Award recognizes outstanding career contributions to scholarly endeavors addressing service-learning and community engagement with particular emphasis on programmatic research. It is designed to recognize research that systematically addresses the exploration and understanding of the field. Nominations are submitted, and a committee consisting of past award recipients evaluates the nominations, taking into account such criteria as quantity and quality of research productivity; impact of research as indicated by products, citations, and utilization; impact on practitioners; record of teaching, mentoring, collaboration, and contributions to the research of others; and leadership. The call for nominations may be found at the IARSLCE website (www.researchslce.org).

Past recipients of the Distinguished Research Award are Andrew Furco, University of California at Berkeley, 2003; Robert Bringle, Indiana University—Purdue University—Indianapolis, 2004; Sherril Gelmon, Portland State University, 2005; Barbara Holland, National Service-Learning Clearinghouse, 2006; Janet Eyler, Vanderbilt University, 2007; and Shelley Billig, RMC Research Corporation, 2008.

The Early Career Research Award was established in 2008 and recognizes outstanding early career contributions to scholarly endeavors addressing service-learning and community engagement. It is designed to encourage research that systematically addresses the exploration and understanding of the field. This award is intended to recognize researchers who have distinguished records of research and scholarly contribution early in their careers. Individuals who have received a terminal degree in their discipline or profession within the past seven years are eligible to apply.

An IARSLCE Board Awards committee evaluates the nominations, taking into account the following criteria: quantity and quality of research productivity; evidence of promising impact on research; impact on practitioners; and plans for continuation of high-quality research that promises to make subsequent contributions to the field. The call for nominations may be found at the IARSLCE website (www.researchslce.org).

The first recipient of the Early Career Research Award was Kerry Ann O'Meara, Associate Professor of Higher Education in the Department of Education Leadership, Higher Education & International Education, College of Education at University of Maryland College Park. Dr. O'Meara is seen as an emerging academic leader and role model for young faculty and graduate students who seek careers of engagement.

The IARSLCE Dissertation Research Award recognizes a dissertation that advances research on service-learning and/or community engagement through rigorous and innovative inquiry. Applicants can be from any academic discipline and must have successfully defended their dissertation during the previous twelve months. Applications are evaluated based on the quality of the research summary and the strength of the dissertation advisor's letter of recommendation. Exemplary dissertations address important questions, develop robust theoretical or conceptual frameworks, demonstrate the use of rigorous data collection and analysis, show compelling conclusions, and expand on the study's results to suggest important implications for theory/research on service-learning and/or community engagement. The call for nominations may be found at the IARSLCE website (www.researchslce.org).

The Dissertation Research Award was also established in 2008. The first co-recipients were Julie Hatcher, Indiana University—Purdue University—Indianapolis, who received her doctorate in Philanthropic Studies from Indiana University, and Emily Janke, University of North Carolina–Greensboro, who received her doctorate in higher education from The Pennsylvania State University. An honorable mention was awarded to Janice McMillan, University of Cape Town (South Africa), who received her doctorate in sociology from the University of Cape Town.

Through these multiple forms of recognition of scholarship, IARSLCE seeks to contribute to advancing research on community engagement, service-learning, and related pedagogies and practices.

Collaboration and Partnerships

Key to the success of all of these activities is IARSLCE's commitment to collaborate with other education and research associations, professional associations, and other associations and networks to support service-learning and community engagement. For example, national Campus Compact has been a sponsor of the research conference almost every year and has helped to promote and disseminate information about IARSLCE activities through its network of state Compacts. The Compact was the sponsor for the 2008 Early Career Research Award. The National Service-Learning Clearinghouse posts information about IARSLCE events on its website. The American Association of Community Colleges and Community-Campus Partnerships for Health have both promoted the Association through member networks and provided support for the annual research conference. Centers such as the Feinstein Institute for Public Service at Providence College, the Edward Ginsberg Center for Community Service and Learning at the University of Michigan, and the Jonathan M. Tisch College of Citizenship and Public Service at Tufts University have helped to support events at the conference. The New England Resource Center for Higher Education has sponsored an annual Graduate Student reception at the conference.

In 2009, the co-host of the international research conference will be the Canadian Alliance for Community Service-Learning (CACSL); the Australian University Community Engagement Alliance (AUCEA) has also been a partner in reciprocal promotion of association events. IARSLCE has been a participant in the Higher Education Network on Community Engagement (HENCE) and provided administrative support to HENCE for much of 2008.

Administrative Operations

The concept of management via an administrative home was selected after review of other associations and their management strategies. In particular, we looked at the recent experiences of the Coalition for Urban and Metropolitan Universities (CUMU), Imagining America, and Community-Campus Partnerships for Health (CCPH). From these experiences, we were able to identify practices that were applicable for a new nonprofit membership association. There are many potential models ranging from highly structured (with staff and substantial financing) to volunteer-driven, and it became clear that we needed to balance some administrative support structure with limited financing for staffing, and thus also needed to rely heavily on volunteers and board leadership.

The initial administrative home was Washington Campus Compact (WACC), housed at Western Washington University in Bellingham, WA. As specified in the bylaws, the senior administrator at WACC (Jennifer Dorr) served as Secretary-Treasurer for IARSLCE. Staffing was provided by existing WACC staff or specially contracted individuals, depending on the work agenda. As of 2009, the Administrative Home is now located at Tulane University, and the Director of the Center for Public Service at Tulane (Vincent Ilustre) now serves as IARSLCE Secretary-Treasurer.

The Association is financed exclusively through conference registration revenue and donations. The initial financial base consisted of revenue generated over the first five years of the conference and from sales of the *Advances in Service-Learning Research* volumes, as well as the net revenue of the 2006 conference. Initial membership in the Association was extended to everyone who attended the 2006 and 2007 research conferences; membership includes a complimentary copy of the newest volume of *Advances in Service-Learning Research* as well as access to a members-only portion of the IARSLCE website. Only members may serve on IARSLCE committees, run for board election, and serve as hosts of the annual research conference. In 2007, a membership fee was established, so that individuals not attending the conference could still become members and receive the benefits of membership. In recognition of the Association's commitment to provide professional development to graduate students, a special graduate student membership category (at a discounted fee) was established. There are plans for a more aggressive membership recruitment campaign in the future; as of early 2009 IARSLCE has approximately six hundred members.

Association leaders seek donations each year to help support the conference and secure sponsorship of special events. As well, sponsorships support scholarships to help graduate students attend the annual research conference, and the research awards.

Strategies for the Future

IARSLCE is still a young organization, formally established in 2007 despite a commitment to the concept of an association since 2004 and the foundations of the research conference since it was first conceptualized in the proposal for Kellogg funding in 2000. Nonetheless, it has articulated a series of strategic directions in order to position itself for the next few years. As in any strategic positioning, plans for the future are based on the best information

403

available; the recent economic downturn may have implications for IARSLCE's actions, but in the short term the intent is to continue with the annual research conference as well as the various networks and awards.

In 2008, IARSLCE conducted its first membership survey to better understand the interests and needs of the membership. The survey included questions about member participation in present and future Association activities conducted to fulfill the IARSLCE mission such as the annual research conference, the *Advances in Service-Learning Research* series, the graduate student network, and other activities. Approximately one-third of the membership responded to the survey. Although a higher response rate would have given a more accurate picture, this first survey provided useful initial information (IARSLCE, 2008a).

Survey respondents indicated that the most important benefits of IARSLCE include learning about new research (90 percent), meeting new scholars in the field (80 percent), networking (74 percent), presenting members' research (63 percent), meeting emerging scholars in the field (61 percent), and providing opportunities for dissemination (59 percent). When asked to rank the importance of current IARSLCE offerings, respondents indicated the following: access to best practices in research (99 percent), opportunity to network with new and existing colleagues (97 percent), offering a place to learn how to do better research on service-learning and community engagement (96 percent), and participating in the annual research conference (96 percent) (IARSLCE, 2008a).

The results of the membership survey helped to guide the IARSLCE Board in articulating its strategic business plan for the current year (IARSLCE, 2008b). Eight strategies were adopted in October 2008:

1. *Information Sharing and Networking:* actions related to the International Research Conference on Service-Learning and Community Engagement for 2009 (Ottawa), 2010 (Indianapolis), and 2011 (RFP to be issued)

2. *Advance Research through Membership and Collaboration:* actions related to membership recruitment and retention, networking, and cross-promotion with relevant special interest groups/organizations domestically and internationally, and development of a research agenda to guide future development of our fields

3. *Support for New and Developing Scholars:* actions related to development and support of the Graduate Student Network and the Early Career Network, opportunities for graduate students and early career scholars to become engaged in IARSLCE activities, and efforts to develop an international peer review board, building on the former National Review Board on Engaged Scholarship

4. *Support for Awards and Recognition:* actions in support of the Distinguished Research, Early Career Research, and Dissertation Research awards, and the Graduate Student Scholarships

5. *Creation and Management of Communication Mechanisms:* actions related to communications and positioning strategies, use of the IARSLCE electronic mailing lists and website, and promotional materials

6. *Dissemination of Findings and Methods:* actions related to *Advances in Service-Learning Research,* posting of research materials to the members-only page of the IARSLCE website, and investigation of other publication and dissemination opportunities

7. *Generate Funding to Support IARSLCE Activities:* actions related to fundraising for the conference, awards, scholarships, and other special projects
8. *Organizational Administrative Effectiveness and Efficiency:* actions related to support IARSLCE as a responsive, timely, effective, and efficient organization, such as creation of the new Administrative Home at Tulane University, Board functions, fiscal accountability, regular bylaws review, and Committee and Board member recruitment.

Conclusion

The International Association for Research on Service-Learning and Community Engagement, (IARSLCE) was founded to create an organization that would have as its sole emphasis the promotion of the development and dissemination of research on service-learning and community engagement internationally and across all levels of the education system. It is certainly not the only organization involved in this work, nor does it aspire to "capture the market," but its intent is to advance this research without any single allegiance to a certain part of the education sector, a specific discipline, or a specific country or region. There is great benefit to future collaborations with others advocating in similar areas by country (e.g., in Australia and in Canada) or by institutional grouping (such as the efforts of both the research and land-grant universities in the United States, although these are both limited to a single country). What sets IARSLCE apart is its ability to cross geographic, political, institutional, and disciplinary boundaries.

Another major area of focus will continue to be the promotion of early-career individuals, whether as graduate students or early-career faculty or research practitioners. These individuals will benefit from a scholarly venue that both welcomes and promotes their work, and where they can identify both mentors and peers as collaborators and advisors on their scholarly efforts. The IARSLCE awards are also an important source of recognition for both developing and established scholars.

There have been calls for an ongoing peer-review resource that could build on the foundational work of the National Review Board on the Scholarship of Engagement, and IARSLCE is currently assessing what role it might play in facilitating such a resource, recognizing what it would take to support this activity and given initiatives such as those of Imagining America and Community-Campus Partnerships for Health. Although some institutions may be unwilling to accept reviews from an outside board, individual faculty have expressed the need for support to make the case for a dossier of engaged scholarship. If the creation (or evolution) of such a board can contribute to IARSLCE's accomplishment of its mission, and the resource demands are feasible, then it is likely that such an activity will be pursued.

IARSLCE recognizes the value of partnerships and continues to devote considerable effort to nurturing existing relationships and establishing new collaborations to pursue mutually beneficial activities. These collaborations may be in the form of knowledge exchange, dissemination, or actual resource support, and the Association remains open to multiple strategies for partnerships in order to best pursue its mission.

As calls for service and engagement in and with communities are issued in many countries across the globe, and there is increasing recognition across higher education that scholarship related to such activities is valid and important, the role of IARSLCE can continue to grow as a venue for the advancement of such scholarship. Many factors may facilitate or discourage these developments, in particular current economic conditions, but this environment may in fact be a positive influence in returning many academics to a community focus—which for scholars can become a focus for scholarly activity and knowledge production. IARSLCE intends to continue to be a major force in advancing research on and about engagement.

References

Billig, S. H. (2005). The International K-H Service-Learning Research Association. In S. Root, J. Callahan, & S. H. Billig (Eds.), *Improving service-learning practice: Research on models to enhance impacts* (pp. 215–224). Greenwich, CT: Information Age.

Battistoni, R. M. (2002). Civic *engagement across the curriculum: A resource book for service learning faculty in all disciplines.* Providence, RI: Campus Compact.

Boyer, E. L. (1997). The scholarship of engagement. *Journal of Public Service and Outreach, 1*(1), 11–20.

Carnegie Foundation. (2006). *Elective classification: Community engagement.* Available at http://www.carnegie foundation.org.

Campus Compact. (2000). *Civic engagement definition.* Available at www.campuscompact.org.

Commission on Community-Engaged Scholarship in the Health Professions. (2005). *Linking scholarship and communities.* Seattle, WA: Community-Campus Partnerships for Health.

Gelmon, S.B. (2007a). The International Association for Research on Service-Learning and Community Engagement. In S. B. Gelmon & S. H. Billig (Eds.), *From passion to objectivity: International and cross-disciplinary perspectives on service-learning research* (pp. 255–257). Charlotte, NC: Information Age.

Gelmon, S. B. (2007b). *A policy agenda for engaged scholarship: innovations, responsibilities, opportunities.* Keynote presentation at the annual conference of the Australian Universities Community Engagement Alliance, Alice Springs, Australia.

International Association for Research on Service-Learning and Community Engagement (IARSLCE). (2007). *Bylaws.* Available at www.researchslce.org.

International Association for Research on Service-Learning and Community Engagement. (2008a). *Report to the membership.* Available at www.researchslce.org.

International Association for Research on Service-Learning and Community Engagement. (2008b). *Strategic business plan 2008–2009.* IARSLCE, internal document.

Putnam, R. D. (2000). *Bowling alone: The collapse and revival of American community.* New York: Simon and Schuster.

Shulman, L. S. (1993, November/December). Teaching as community property: Putting an end to pedagogical solitude. *Change,* 6–7.

PART 5

The Future Landscape

Edited by Theodore R. Alter

The Future Landscape

Theodore R. Alter

L ooking forward, what are the new ideas, what are the new perspectives, what are the new initiatives, that hold promise for positively shaping the future landscape and promise of engaged scholarship and community-university engagement? In this section, several such ideas, perspectives, and initiatives are described and discussed in broad concept and rich detail, provoking thinking, stretching understanding, and illuminating opportunity.

Robert Bringle and Julie Hatcher, both at Indiana University–Purdue University Indianapolis, focus on students and engagement in higher education. They note that engagement with communities adds value to the extent that it enriches student learning and fosters their personal and professional development. Bringle and Hatcher examine trends in student engagement over time through coursework and out of class, and then explore ways to enhance the civic engagement of college students going forward. Jeri Childers and Ted Settle, both from Virginia Tech, detail their experience to date in designing, implementing, and evaluating an initiative for developing highly effective university engagement leaders for the twenty-first century. They tell the story of piloting Virginia Tech's Engagement Academy for University Leaders and outline key lessons learned from this experience that they are using to strengthen their Engagement Academy—lessons valuable to anyone interested in building and sustaining similar initiatives and strengthening academic leadership for engagement in the future.

Angela Allen and Tami Moore, professors at Michigan State University and Oklahoma State University, respectively, address what may be the most important issue for leveraging long-run change in higher education with respect to strengthening community-university partnerships and engaged scholarship. Their focus is on developing emerging engagement scholars who will provide academic and administrative leadership in our institutions of higher education in the future. Allen and Moore discuss the origins, evolution, and early experience with the relatively new and innovative Emerging Engagement Scholars Workshop (EESW). The purpose of the annual EESW is to provide graduate student and early-career scholars substantive opportunity to explore the implications of engagement for their research and teaching, to better understand engaged scholarship and how it might be reflected in and strengthen their work, and to develop and strengthen networks with other emerging and experienced engaged scholars.

Frank Fear, Michigan State, in his chapter titled "Coming to Engagement: Critical Reflection and Transformation," provides an intellectually rich, thought-provoking, moving, and forward- looking contribution to our understanding of engaged scholarship. Professor Fear writes from an autoethnographic perspective, wherein individuals rely on personal experience and deep personal reflection to help illuminate the particular foci of their inquiry. In this chapter, grounded in his experience, Fear reflects critically on engagement practice with the purpose of informing scholarly understanding, which, in turn, can be used to improve the practice of engagement. He makes no claims to truth, necessarily; but he does raise our consciousness and insight into the potentially powerful contributions of engaged scholarship and engagement to personal as well as organizational and community development.

Completing this section on the "future landscape" of engaged scholarship, Professor James Powell at Salford University in the United Kingdom describes experience at his university with what he and his colleagues call "Academic Enterprise" (AE), an approach and mindset that make an imperative of sharing knowledge and expertise between the university and its external stakeholders, business, government, and community, to foster socially inclusive wealth creation. The AE approach encourages and assists faculty and staff to be more enterprising in sharing their individual knowledge and expertise in the context of this shared wealth-creation process. Powell also details a model, based on more than two hundred cases of successful, mutually beneficial community-university engagement, involving four skills critical to enterprising behavior on the part of academic faculty: business acumen, individual performance, social networking intelligence, and foresight enabling skills. Powell shows how this model can be used to strengthen the enterprising behavior of faculty.

Student Engagement Trends over Time

Robert G. Bringle and Julie A. Hatcher

S tudent engagement is an encompassing term that can include a number of dimensions that cut across curricular and co-curricular activities. In higher education, engagement is valued to the extent that it supports student learning and development. This chapter examines patterns of students' engagement in the community that take place through coursework or out-of-class activities. This analysis begins with a brief discussion of engaged learning and definitional issues related to student engagement. Then, an overview of the trends to date is provided; related trends are discussed in other chapters in this handbook (e.g., the chapters by Fretz; Saltmarsh; Ramaley; Vogel, Fichtenberg, & Levin; Stanton & Wagner). The focus then shifts to future work and anticipated areas of growth and research to enhance the civic engagement of college students.

Engaged Learning

Engaged students should learn more, learn more quickly, learn better, and learn with longer lasting results than students who are disengaged (Kuh, 2003; Marchese, 1997; Pascarella & Terenzini, 1991). Being an engaged learner may, in some instances, be an attribute that students bring to a campus. That is, some students are naturally inclined toward learning, intrinsically motivated, find enjoyment across a variety of learning challenges, and demonstrate competence based on their own, independent work. By implication, if students lack this quality of engagement, then its absence is not the educator's fault, nor is it the educator's responsibility to remedy the deficiency. Furthermore, factors outside the purview of the campus (e.g., family experiences, illness, mentoring relationship, travel, work) can contribute or detract from a student's degree of engagement. This can happen unintentionally

411

or when a student's imagination and interests are sparked by a life-changing event. In any case, these events are capricious in their occurrence; therefore, these events cannot be deliberately arranged by the educator.

Alternatively, student engagement may be an attribute of learning environments. As Kuh (2002) notes, what matters most to students achieving learning outcomes is what students do, not who they are. Therefore, promoting student engagement can be, or should be, viewed as a fundamental goal of any educational endeavor, and educators should take seriously their capacity to create, by design, learning environments that engender student engagement across the broadest possible spectrum of students. The challenge, then, for higher education is to understand the nature of student engagement, including those components that are the key determinants of desired outcomes. There is tremendous opportunity for the designers of learning environments (i.e., faculty, professional staff) to create curricula and experiences that enhance the time and energy that students dedicate to their education.

Research demonstrates that high-impact learning opportunities such as learning communities, study abroad, research, capstone courses, first-year seminars, and service-learning classes enhance student engagement and student success (Eyler, Giles, Stenson, & Gray, 2001; Kuh, 2007; Umbach &Wawrzynski, 2005). However, faculty are not the only agents for creating these engaging environments. Hu and Kuh (2003) found that high-quality relationships were positively related to students' motivation and time on task, and they suggest that student affairs professionals have a key role in contributing to the development of those relationships.

Defining Engagement

Engagement is a broad concept and its meaning may be highly dependent upon campus culture. Kuh (2003) defines *student engagement* as "the time and energy students devote to educationally sound activities inside and outside of the classroom, and the policies and practices that institutions use to induce students to take part in these activities" (p. 24). The National Survey of Student Engagement (NSSE) is designed to measure student engagement across this broad domain and focuses on the level of engagement as general student involvement on campus and through classroom activities rather than community engagement per se.

Community engagement, the term used by the Carnegie Foundation for the Advancement of Teaching for its voluntary classification, is defined as "the collaboration between institutions of higher education and their larger communities (local, regional/state, national, global) for the mutually beneficial exchange of knowledge and resources in a context of partnership and reciprocity" (Driscoll, 2008, p. 39). The Carnegie Classification recognizes a campus for curricular engagement, and community partnerships. For our analysis, the use of engagement is more general than the term "student community engagement," which refers to involving students in a variety ways in activities (e.g., attending cultural events, community-based learning, service-learning classes, volunteer activities) in off-campus communities.

"Civic engagement," which is more specific than community engagement, places an added emphasis on the civic aims and civic means of community engagement and includes

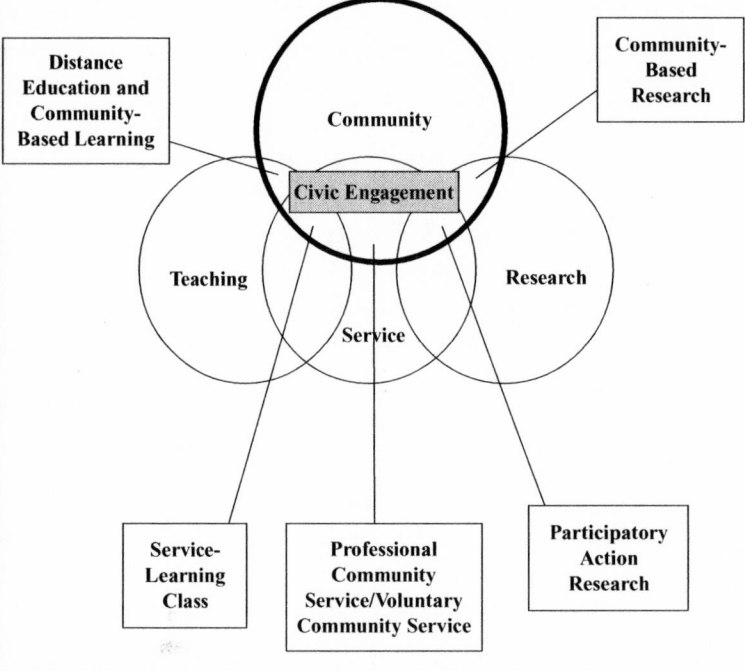

FIGURE 29.1 Faculty and Student Activities in and with the Community

engagement in service, voluntary action, and political activity (Kiesa et al., 2007). Civic engagement focuses on teaching, research, and service (see figure 1) that take place not just *in* the community, but also *with* the community (Bringle, Hatcher, & Clayton, 2006; Bringle, Hatcher, & Holland, 2007). Civic engagement heightens the student's knowledge and understanding of communities, including community organizations and diverse perspectives of residents, so that students develop civic knowledge, skills, dispositions, and habits to work with others in a democratic way toward the common good (Bringle & Steinberg, in press; Hatcher & Steinberg, 2007).

The design of civic engagement activities for students incorporates at least three components: (1) the location of activities in communities; (2) the nature of interactions with community partners and residents that includes mutual goals, reciprocal relationships, and democratic processes; and (3) structured reflection activities and learning goals related to the growth of students, in general, and their civic growth, in particular. The civic engagement of college students can occur through coursework, research, co-curricular activities, or voluntary service activities (Weinberg, 2005). Creating a campus climate to support the civic engagement of students warrants the deliberate, organized, and concerted attention of administrators, faculty, and staff.

Trends to Date in Students' Civic Engagement

There are a number of trends that can be used as indicators of the change in civic engagement among college students. The following areas highlight both co-curricular and curricular engagement.

413

Volunteering and Community Service

Volunteering and community service activities provide a basis for students to develop civic knowledge, skills, and dispositions. Students arrive at college with an increased likelihood that they have been involved in community service (Kiesa et al., 2007). Since 1990, the trend is for a higher percentage of high school seniors and entering college students to report that they have volunteered during the past twelve months, increasing from 67 percent in 1990 to 76 percent in 2001 (Dote, Cramer, Dietz, & Grimm, 2006; Monitoring the Future, 2008; Sax, 2006–7). The most dramatic increases have been for episodic volunteering; the increases are less precipitous for regular volunteering. Furthermore, most of the volunteering is situationally determined (e.g., course requirements, involvement in religious organizations, student groups) rather than it being activities that are generated by the individual (Sax, 2006–7). This increase in participation has been attributed to the increased infrastructure to support voluntary service and service-learning during the 1990s by such organizations as Campus Compact (see chapter ? in this volume), the Corporation for National and Community Service, and the Points of Light Foundation (Kiesa et al., 2007).

Many college campuses have a long tradition of providing opportunities for students to volunteer in communities through student organizations; faith-based activities and organizations; fraternities and sororities; campus-wide events (e.g., Dr. Martin Luther King, Jr. Day-On of Service, Habitat for Humanity building blitz); orientation and welcome week activities; and student government. Some of these opportunities are developed by professional staff, yet a significant portion of them are student-initiated and led (e.g., alternative break trips, service organizations).

However, according to national surveys of college students (Sax, 2006–7), participation in volunteering is greatest during high school, and then drops off during college. In the postcollege years, rates of volunteering increase, but the level never returns to that of students in high school. Those students who volunteered in college are most likely to continue volunteering after college. Sax (2006–7) reports that several types of student involvement during college are related to postcollege volunteering: performing volunteer work; attending religious services; attending racial/cultural awareness workshops; socializing with students of different racial/ethnic groups; talking with faculty outside class; and working full-time. These findings highlight the importance of personal interactions with students, faculty, co-workers, or employers for developing civic consciousness. Astin and Sax (1998; Sax & Astin, 1997) found in a five-year postgraduation follow-up survey that outcomes associated with involvement in community service and service-learning during college include self-reported gains in civic responsibility (e.g., future plans to volunteer, efficacy to change society, commitment to influence social values), academic development (e.g., contact with faculty, aspirations for advanced degree), and life skills (e.g., leadership skills, interpersonal skills, conflict resolution skills) when compared to nonparticipating students and covarying out preexisting differences as first-year students. Nevertheless, these effects wane ten years after graduation (Vogelgesang & Astin, 2005). Thus, colleges are largely ineffective in developing lifelong habits of civic engagement.

Political Participation

Until the last two national elections in 2004 and 2008, there had been consistent and dramatic trends over that past three decades in college students' declining political interests (Sax, 2006–7). College students were routinely described as being more interested in volunteering than voting (Kiesa et al., 2007). Recent data suggest that the gap between volunteering and voting is narrowing (Kiesa et al., 2007).

Several national projects have been implemented over the past decade to increase political interest and participation by college students. In 2002, Campus Compact launched *Raise Your Voice*, a national campaign funded by the Pew Charitable Trusts to increase college student participation in public life. In 2003, the American Association of State Colleges and Universities, in collaboration with the *New York Times*, began the American Democracy Project (ADP), a multicampus initiative focused on higher education's role in preparing the next generation of informed and engaged citizens. Projects through ADP have yielded both curricular and co-curricular changes to promote civic learning outcomes (e.g., Deliberative Polling Project, 7 Revolutions, Stewardship of Public Lands; see www.aascu.org for further information on these programs including information on annual meetings for ADP). In 2003, the Association of American Colleges and Universities established the Center for Liberal Education and Civic Engagement in collaboration with Campus Compact, followed by a number of other programs and grant-funded activities (e.g., Core Commitments, Bringing Theory to Practice, Education and America's Promise). The American Association of Community Colleges has had a long-standing service-learning initiative, which has focused on developing civic learning outcomes. Gottlieb and Robinson (2006) provide a practical guide for community college instructors to enhance civic responsibility through their courses. These initiatives reinforce a firm commitment by higher education to the value of enhancing both curricular and co-curricular programs to increase political involvement of youth.

The Carnegie Foundation for the Advancement of Teaching, in collaboration with the *New York Times*, sponsored the Political Engagement Project to reinforce the importance of curricular strategies to develop civic capacities of undergraduates. This project documents courses, offers web-based resources, and presents case studies (Colby, Beaumont, Ehrlich, & Corngold, 2007; Colby, Ehrlich, Beaumont, & Stephens, 2003) to increase the civic involvement of college students (see http://www.nytimes.com/ref/college/collegespecial10/coll-pep-webresources.html). Each of these programs in higher education complements national initiatives, such as *Rock the Vote*, which is designed to engage and incite young people to register and vote in every election (see http://www.rockthevote.com/about/). As a result, many curricular and co-curricular activities have increased political participation by college students (Kiesa et al., 2007). The most recent research on entering students indicates that 36 percent reported frequently discussing politics in the last year, and this indicates a forty-year high (Pryor et al., 2008).

Despite the promising changes in recent years, a fundamental concern remains about the barriers to youth civic engagement and their lack of interest in formal politics and entering careers in public service. Findings from the 2006 Civic and Political Health of the Nation Survey conducted by CIRCLE, a national study of 386 students from twelve four-year colleges and universities, indicated that although students were more engaged than previous generations, they were more ambivalent about formal politics, and they disliked the polarized debates that shape national politics (Kiesa et al., 2007).

Service-Learning Courses

Although there are many forms of community involvement and civic engagement, service-learning represents the best approach for reaching the central goals of engaging students in ways that contribute to their civic knowledge, skills, and habits (Battistoni, 2002; Billig & Eyler, 2003; Eyler & Giles, 1999; Eyler et al., 2001; Zlotkowski, Longo, & Williams, 2006). As indicated in figure 1, service-learning meets educational goals of instruction as well as providing community service that is of benefit to communities. Accordingly, we limit service-learning to curricular civic engagement by defining it as a "course-based, credit-bearing educational experience in which students (a) participate in an organized service activity that meets identified community needs and (b) reflect on the service activity in such a way as to gain further understanding of course content, a broader appreciation of the discipline, and an enhanced sense of personal values and civic responsibility" (Bringle & Hatcher, 2009, p. 38). In contrast to many other examples of applied learning and community-based instruction (e.g., applied research, cooperative education, field studies, internship), service-learning has as an intentional educational goal the students' civic education and growth. From the point of view of the academy, service-learning involves the faculty, students, and professional staff in educationally meaningful community service. Service-learning also embodies qualities and values to which current models of civic engagement aspire: meeting community and academic goals through reciprocal, democratic partnerships in ways that incorporate all constituencies as co-educators and co-generators of knowledge and that promote the growth and respect of all constituencies.

The values, processes, collaborations, and goals of service-learning courses provide models for other forms of civic engagement focused on research (e.g., participatory action research) and professional service (e.g., collaborative partnerships with the community) (Bringle et al., 2006). Service-learning is one of the fundamental indicators for Carnegie's voluntary classification for community engagement, further evidence of the importance of service-learning in establishing new models for civic engagement in higher education (Driscoll, 2008). An examination of the dossiers from campuses successfully applying for the Carnegie classification demonstrates that institutionalization to support service-learning is still developing, but service-learning is becoming an integral part of academic culture (Bringle & Hatcher, 2009).

Due in large part to the Corporation for National and Community Service and Campus Compact (see the chapter by McGovern and Curley in this volume), the prevalence of service-learning courses has increased dramatically in the past two decades (Campus Compact, 2007). This has occurred for all types of institutions of higher education and across the spectrum of disciplines and professional training programs. An average of thirty-five service-learning courses per campus was reported by Campus Compact's Annual Membership

Survey in 2006, with 20 percent of the campuses reporting fifty or more courses, and this represented 12 percent of the faculty involved in teaching service-learning courses (Campus Compact, 2007).

Emerging Trends in Students' Civic Engagement

This section identifies future trends in students' civic engagement and implications for administrators, faculty, staff, and those who design programs and influence policies in higher education. Each trend has been selected because it holds significant promise for developing the institutional capacity to support student engagement, improving the quality of student growth and learning derived from engagement experiences, shaping public policy, and increasing the number and types of students who have the opportunities to participate in community and civic engagement during their college years.

Bridging Academic Affairs and Student Affairs

There are two primary ways in which campuses involve students in community service: (1) co-curricular service, and (2) curricular-based service-learning. Typically, the former is the purview of student affairs and the latter, academic affairs. This bifurcated division of academic affairs and student affairs is common in higher education and is often accompanied by a corresponding tension concerning roles, goals, methods, respect, and accountability for achieving campus mission (Weinberg, 2005). The gap between these two areas, however, impedes the recognition for the potential of educationally purposeful out-of-class activity (Kuh, Douglass, Lund, & Ramin-Gyurnek, 1994) and disregards the new insights from cognitive sciences that reinforce the value of integrated learning experiences across a variety of contexts (Keeling, 2004). A future trend will be for these two units to work more closely together to align institutional resources in strategic ways to reach student learning outcomes, particularly civic learning outcomes (Hoy & Meisel, 2008).

The increased attention given to college students' civic engagement provides new opportunities for faculty and staff to explore bridging the gap, reduce the tensions, and coordinate programming around common civic goals (Weinberg, 2005). Student affairs staff and programs traditionally focus on leadership development, support student interests, reflect a holistic approach to student growth, promote civic participation, and advocate for values such as democratic participation, justice, diversity, and fairness. Each of these attributes in consistent with civic engagement. Co-curricular service activities have the merits that they invite student-initiated activities, provide excellent opportunities for developing leadership, involve collaboration among students and with community organizations, and accommodate to the students' class schedules. As important as these co-curricular community service activities are, they tend to reach only a small percentage of students on campus and typically have no formal learning objectives that are specified and assessed. Furthermore, co-curricular service activities are seldom represented to external audiences in any formal manner (e.g., a college transcript), they may not take full advantage of faculty input and other educational resources on campus, and they are not well integrated with the academic mission of the institution (Bringle, 1996).

417

This new trend for student affairs to shift the focus from program development to student learning outcomes is evident within the profession. In 2008, the Council for the Advancement of Standards in Higher Education (CAS), which supports professional and program development in student affairs, approved a new set of Learning and Developmental Outcomes for programs and services in higher education (Council for the Advancement of Standards in Higher Education, 2006). Influenced in part by the increased emphasis on assessing student learning outcomes, this set of six domains includes "Humanitarianism and Civic Engagement" and identifies specific learning outcomes (i.e., understanding and appreciation of cultural and human differences; social responsibility; global perspective; sense of civic responsibility) and behaviors (e.g., demonstrates consideration of the welfare of others in decision-making; engages in critical reflection and principled dissent; understands and participates in relevant governance systems; educates and facilitates the civic engagement of others) for each domain (see Council for the Advancement of Standards Learning and Development Outcomes, 2008). In addition, in 2005, CAS developed a set of standards for professionals responsible for service-learning programs, whether located in academic affairs or student affairs.

Weinberg (2005) argues that student affairs can make a fundamental shift in its paradigm, operations, and programs in order for co-curricular programs to be more educationally purposeful (see also Kuh et al., 1994). He traces the development of student affairs over the past forty years and points out that "if the first wave of student affairs work was about control [of student behavior], and the second wave was about services [and programs], the third wave should be about education" (Weinberg, 2005, p. 33). The model he developed at Colgate University incorporates new approaches to organizing residential units, reconceptualizing student organizations as community associations, using community organizing as a means for teaching about democratic processes, increasing faculty involvement in campus life, linking student affairs activities to classes, and encouraging political participation by students (Weinberg, 2005).

Implications. Integrating student affairs and academic affairs around common goals to support student development of civic skills suggests that professional staff must assume a more salient role as educators and requires that the broad learning mission of the institution is well understood by all faculty and staff. This also requires that administrators "hold student affairs staff accountable for articulating the value of life outside the classroom" (Kuh et al., 1994, p. 8) and involve faculty more directly in program development within student affairs. Indiana University–Purdue University Indianapolis created jointly funded shared positions between student affairs and academic affairs to facilitate communication, improve programming, and leverage institutional resources (e.g., student scholarships, student minigrants) to advance civic engagement of students (Hatcher, Bringle, Brown, & Fleischhacker, 2006). Furthermore, advisors, librarians, and student affairs professionals are now part of instructional teams that teach first-year success seminars and Themed Learning Communities. This intentional bridging of student affairs with academic units changes the way that faculty value staff as co-educators. Furthermore, campuses can take an eclectic and comprehensive approach to programming that provides better integration of student affairs and academic affairs in terms of common educational goals that cut across curricular and co-curricular programming. Finally, using Weinberg's (2005) examples, student affairs can reexamine programs to determine how they can be adapted in a manner that is consistent with civic learning outcomes.

Service-Learning and Research

As pedagogy, service-learning provides a rich set of opportunities for educators to explore teaching and learning (Eyler et al., 2001). As a type of high-impact educational practice (Kuh, 2008), service-learning has an additive benefit to student learning, particularly for under-served students. However, as Eyler (2002) has noted, service-learning research "is neither precise nor robust enough to guide decision making about practice" (p. 5).

Empirical research on service-learning is increasing (see Billig & Eyler, 2003). An annual *Title is* International Resarch Conference on Service-Learning and community Engagement provides a showcase for research, as do the associated *Advances in Service-Learning Research* monographs (Billig & Eyler, 2003; Furco & Billig, 2002; Welch & Billig, 2004). The *Michigan Journal of Community Service Learning* publishes both qualitative and quantitative research, and other journals have had special issues focused on service-learning and civic engagement. Research on service-learning is important because of its potential to improve the practice and understanding of service-learning and enhance student learning through engaging pedagogies more generally. Service-learning provides a powerful test bed that is both convenient and appropriate for evaluating theories about teaching in general, campus-community partnerships and how higher education can play an even more significant role in improving the quality of life in communities (Bringle, 2003).

There is increasing evidence that service-learning is effective in helping students develop socially responsive knowledge as well as facilitating learning in the more traditional domains of content and skills, such as the capacity to view phenomena from multiple perspectives and to apply knowledge developed in one setting to other settings (Eyler & Giles, 1999; Eyler et al., 2001). Unfortunately, the large majority of research that has been conducted about service-learning has focused on student outcomes and has largely neglected its influence on faculty, institutions of higher education, communities, and residents (Eyler et al., 2001).

Implications. With an increase in accountability, research on service-learning and civic engagement will be important for the continued support of its institutionalization in higher education. This support will be garnered from executive leaders who control internal resources, and from external constituencies (e.g., granting agencies, foundations) that fund continued growth of service-learning initiatives. Equally important is the support of service-learning by faculty who invest their time in curricular redesign and community partnerships, and by civic leaders and the public who value the active involvement of faculty and students in the community (Sandy & Holland, 2006).

To date, the majority of evidence has been small in scale and only modestly rigorous in design. Further research will need to improve on these examples with longitudinal studies, multicourse studies, multicampus studies, greater control on confounding variables, and more precise and authentic measurement of outcomes (e.g., student learning, retention). In addition, more research must attend to the community outcomes as well as the student

419

and institutional outcomes of well-designed student engagement activities. The increase in scale of research may warrant new networks of researchers, sharing of databases for secondary data analyses, and more concerted activities to gather cross-disciplinary teams to design large-scale studies. This research will have greater impact when data about students' civic engagement can be linked to other institutional data (e.g., NSSE, student satisfaction, institutional research data sets, transcripts, postgraduation employment). In addition, research on students' civic engagement and its outcomes will support institutional accreditation.

International Service-Learning

Study abroad is a form of experiential education, and the Institute for International Education estimates that the rate of increase in study abroad is close to 7.5 percent annually. However, at this rate of annual growth, it is unlikely that the target set by the Commission on the Abraham Lincoln Study Abroad Fellowship Program in 2006 is feasible. The Lincoln Commission set forth the ambitious goal that within a decade there would be one million American students studying abroad each year. In ways similar to establishing the land-grant university and the GI Bill, this national initiative has been described as the next step in the evolution of American higher education (Commission on the Abraham Lincoln Study Abroad Fellowship Program, 2006). The Lincoln Commission, and resulting legislation, has heightened attention to the measures necessary to increase capacity both here and abroad to provide study abroad opportunities for American undergraduates, particularly for underrepresented minorities.

Although study abroad is a powerful pedagogy (Carlson, 1990), it also has shortcomings. Research on study abroad shows that student interactions with resident populations are often limited and students are often disappointed that they did not get to know members of the host culture (Ward, Bochner, & Furnham, 2001). However, when study abroad is integrated with service-learning, there is an additive benefit. International service-learning presents additional ways of interacting with a host culture and developing civic skills in ways that are quite limited in traditional study abroad or domestic service-learning (Plater, Jones, Bringle, & Clayton, 2009). Bringle and Tonkin (2004) note that international service-learning is unique because it adds a significant educational and civic component to traditional study abroad; is located within the cultural context of another country; uses foreign language in an applied setting so that language acquisition is improved; immerses students in cross-cultural community-based experiences; places students in circumstances and roles that may not occur in their roles as students or tourists; and develops a deeper sense of connection and place for students within the host country (Bringle, Tonkin, & Sutton, 2004).

Implications. American higher education realizes that study abroad is a powerful learning experience. Yet, as Green notes, only 1 percent of students study abroad, and rhetorically she asks, "What are we going to do with the other 16,900,000?" (McMurtrie, 2007). In response to the Lincoln Commission, there is an enormous opportunity for higher education to consider how study abroad can be designed to promote student engagement in educationally meaningful ways in general, and, with a service-learning component, civic growth of students.

Campuses have a long history of offering isolated study abroad programs that may incorporate service (Jones & Steinberg, in press), although the typical study abroad experience at a foreign institution for a semester or a year rarely includes service-learning. As study abroad becomes shorter in duration, campuses are exploring additional ways of structuring international study abroad. These can occur during a semester or a year. In addition, hybrid programs that combine study and service in the United States with shorter periods in the foreign country (e.g., during the summer, during spring or fall break) are being developed (Jones & Steinberg, in press).

International service-learning creates extraordinary opportunities for combining two of the most powerful pedagogies in higher education. However, if taken seriously and expanded, it also presents the academy with a host of challenges, such as curriculum and faculty development; student access and support; coordination with a set of international partners (e.g., academic, non-govermental organizations, communities residents); building reciprocal relationships with foreign constituencies; preparation and return of students; and assessing learning outcomes. This requires coordinated activities between offices of international study abroad and service-learning to work together to address these challenges. For example, curriculum development grants, faculty workshops, student orientation sessions (e.g., service-learning, reflection strategies, traditions of service in host country), and strategic partnerships with international universities would all assist the development of international service-learning courses and programs.

Service-Based Scholarships and Federal Work-Study

There exists a significant gap for many students between the price of seeking higher education and their personal or family resources, leading the National Center for Public Policy and Higher Education to predict that higher education will soon be out of reach for many Americans and will thus require increased levels of personal debt (Lewin, 2008). Indeed, the level of debt assumed by college attendees and graduates is putting a disproportionate financial burden on the current generation when compared to all previous cohorts (Draut, 2006). Students now entering higher education report an increased likelihood to work during college, work full-time, base their college choice on financial aid offers, and seek funding sources that will not increase their debt (Pryor et al., 2008). These national trends in financial aid among entering students are occurring at a time when students also report their highest interest in having political conversations and volunteering in the community (Pryor et al., 2008). Considering how existing financial resources can be used to contribute to students' civic engagement warrants systematic attention by executive leaders and professional staff.

Scholarships and federal work-study funds are an important fiscal resource that can be redirected to engage students in the community and at the same time address their need for financial support. Campuses award scholarships that recognize academic achievement and athletic talent as merit. Service, both past performance and future engagement, can also be valued as a form of student merit in designing and awarding campus scholarships (Hatcher et al., 2006). Coupling community service with existing scholarships and financial aid provides a basis for enhancing student civic engagement and gives students the opportunity to

421

give back as an expectation of the scholarship. Honors programs, merit scholars, athletes, and student organizations that receive support could all have that support tied to a service expectation as the result of institutional policy. Service-based scholarships could be directed toward institutional activities (e.g., mentoring other students, assisting with service-learning classes), could support students in leadership roles (e.g., organizing alternative break service trips, campus-wide service events), or could be directed toward community constituencies (e.g., assist community organizations to recruit additional volunteers). Many universities offer service-based scholarships (e.g., Bentley College, College of New Jersey, Drew University, Duke University, Indiana University–Purdue University Indianapolis, Tufts University), and this number will continue to increase as national policy reinforces the tie between financial aid and community service.

Shifting from scholarship awards to service-based scholarship programs is an important strategy to support civic engagement. The Bonner Foundation has developed a national service-based scholarship program on seventy-seven campuses that span institutional type. For the past two decades, the Bonner Scholars program has created a model program to "support students so they can acquire a deep set of commitments, knowledge, and skills that enable them to use their talents effectively to improve the public good" (Hoy & Meisel, 2008, p. 9). Focused on students with financial need, the strengths of this four-year scholarship program include integration of co-curricular and curricular programs; learning outcomes focused on six common commitments; length of the program across a student's four years in college; repeated opportunities for students to have constructive dialogue across differences; and rigorous research, both quantitative and qualitative, to understand student learning outcomes (Hoy & Meisel, 2008; Keen & Hall, 2008, 2009). Students who remain in the program through their senior year report the highest gains, particularly in the area of working across differences with others (Keen & Hall, 2008, 2009).

Federal work-study (FWS) is an existing federal resource designed to support students with financial need and engage them in either on-campus or off-campus employment that results in skills for career preparation. At least 75 percent of the hourly rate for FWS employment is subsidized by federal funds. Most FWS subsidizes employment of students on campus as clerical support in offices and libraries, staff in cafeterias and recreational facilities, and assistants in laboratories and computer centers. This benefit to campuses directly conflicts with institutions more extensively using FWS funds to not only help themselves but also their communities. One of the original statutory purposes of the FWS program was "to encourage students receiving Federal student financial aid assistance to participate in community service activities that will benefit the Nation and engender in the students a sense of social responsibility and commitment to the community" (Bowley, 2007), yet many agree that this is an underdeveloped aspect of FWS. The ExpectMore.gov assessment of FWS by the U.S. Office of Management and Budget declares that the FWS is a "not performing" government program (U.S. Office of Management & Budget, n.d.). In addition to seeking additional information about use of the funds and outcomes, the report recommends a policy change of requiring 20 percent of federal funds to be used for community service placements.

Currently, federal guidelines require that at least 7 percent of FWS funds be allocated to community-based placements, although each campus can decide how to balance the use of FWS within these parameters. Community service FWS is particularly important for civically engaging students from economically disadvantaged backgrounds because of the financial benefit that provides access to "career-fostering internships in the community that are often more readily available to students from affluent families" (Davidson, 2007). The average rate of community placements in 2005–06 was 14.83 percent, according to the U.S. Department of Education. In 1997, the legislation to reauthorize FWS included a new policy to fund children or family literacy programs through the America Reads program with 100 percent of the support provided by federal funds. Subsequently, the America Counts program was implemented and also provides 100 percent funding for college students who tutor math for youth up to grade nine. More recently, the 2008 reauthorization of FWS expanded the capacity for campuses to secure 100 percent funding for students supporting the civic education of others and disaster relief programs (Bowley, 2007).

Implications. All financial aid support for college students is important, particularly when the support is educationally engaging, develops good work habits, and promotes civic skills. The executive leadership of each campus needs to take a careful look at how scholarship and FWS funds could be better utilized to develop reciprocal partnerships with communities and involve college students in educationally meaningful community service. Designing service-based scholarship programs requires a partnership between the offices of financial aid, student affairs, and service-learning. Yet, a well-planned initiative for service-based scholarship programs and FWS bodes well for contributing to institutional priorities such as retention, civic engagement, career preparation, and civic outcomes (Hatcher et al., 2006; Laux, 2007).

Development of Faculty and Professional Staff to Support Civic Engagement

As community engagement and service-learning become increasingly valued in higher education, developing institutional infrastructure to support its growth is crucial (Bringle, Games, & Malloy, 1999; Bringle & Hatcher, 1996; Langseth & Plater, 2004). Attention, therefore, must be given to developing professional staff and faculty who design these civically engaging learning experiences. Most faculty have been trained in traditional and formal pedagogies with heavy reliance on lectures; active learning may have occurred in laboratories, recitations, seminars, and in applied pre-professional activities (e.g., cooperative education, internships). However, most faculty are largely unfamiliar with service-learning as a pedagogy (Abes, Jackson, & Jones, 2002), as they typically have not been students in service-learning courses or learned about the pedagogy in graduate education. In addition to lack of knowledge and concrete experiences, many faculty fail to see how service-learning is relevant to their courses, and they fail to appreciate how community service can enrich the learning of their students (Abes et al., 2002). Additionally, faculty may enter service-learning with a very limited understanding of, or experience with, campus-community partnerships, lacking critical skills necessary to initiate and sustain fruitful relationships with community agencies and service providers. For these reasons, Walshok (1999) contends that campuses must develop new institutional mechanisms,

423

including trained professionals, to facilitate the dialogue and work between faculty and communities.

Implications. Mechanisms need to be developed to respond to the needs of faculty and professional staff who are interested in developing their knowledge and skills to support student civic engagement (Bringle, Hatcher, Jones, & Plater, 2006). In 2004, national Campus Compact began an annual Professional Development Institute for Service and Service-Learning Staff to enhance and develop the knowledge and skills of professional staff who have key responsibilities for service-learning and community service programs. As change agents, staff in these roles may lack support or recognition for their contributions. Campus Compact recognizes that part of institutionalizing service and service-learning is the professional development of staff. The curriculum covers key topics (e.g., institutional strategies for change; campus-community partnerships; assessment and research; faculty development; reflection) for advancing service-learning and civic engagement. Equally valuable, these institutes provide opportunities for professionals to share knowledge across institutions as well as gain a renewed perspective on the unique role that they play in advancing the civic mission of higher education.

Higher education recognizes that more can be done to adequately prepare doctoral students for their future career in the academy (e.g., Boyer, 1994, 1996; Bringle et al., 1999; Calleson, Jordan, & Seifer, 2005; Colby et al., 2003; Harkavy & Puckett, 1994; O'Meara & Rice, 2005). For example, the Carnegie Initiative on the Doctorate seeks to improve the structure of graduate education to include more attention to civic engagement. In addition, disciplinary and professional associations (e.g., history, anthropology, sociology, psychology, health sciences) have heightened the salience of civic engagement as a component of graduate education. The prevalence of Preparing Future Faculty (PFF) programs at more than three hundred universities is evidence of this movement. Each of these initiatives will overcome in future cohorts of new faculty some of the unfamiliarity with service-learning and the lack of understanding of more varied forms of scholarship that we see among current faculty (Abes et al., 2002). Therefore, practitioners in service-learning and civic engagement should work within existing PFF programs to provide training on service-learning, campus-community partnerships, and the scholarship of engagement to support the next generation of faculty.

The Engagement Academy for University Leaders is a week-long summer institute, hosted by Virginia Tech, for those in executive leadership positions who have key responsibilities related to community engagement. The academy is designed to link civic engagement across teaching, research, and service; engage participants in strategic planning at the institutional level; build institutional commitment; and facilitate assessment of its outcomes. For campuses to be able to enhance students' civic engagement, existing infrastructures need to be strengthened or changed and the capacity of campus leaders developed. Whether it is a center for teaching, a center focused on service-learning, or a volunteer and experiential education office, the risk is that traditions are established and there is limited inertia for change. One key component for institutional change are campus executive leaders who can create vision, resources, and reward structures that promote innovative programs that go beyond existing models (Langseth & Plater, 2004; Percy, Zimpher, & Brukardt, 2006).

Conclusion

Trends discussed in this chapter (e.g., voluntary and community service, service-learning classes, political involvement, service-based scholarships, community work-study) provide sufficient evidence that students' civic engagement is a more salient dimension of higher education and student life for today's undergraduates than twenty years ago. Across both curricular and co-curricular domains, new initiatives are enhancing the civic engagement and civic development of students. To support these trends, implications have been identified that will assist in forecasting the changes that are likely to continue over the next decade. Adaptations to these changes on each campus, however, will be unique and highly dependent on campus culture and mission, campus leadership, and resource reallocation. Integrating these trends into the fabric of higher education will require the active and visionary leadership of chief academic officers coupled with creating opportunities for contributions from all constituencies (e.g., students, faculty, community). Unless civic engagement aligns with the academic mission of the institution, there is no clear rationale, particularly in times of decreased state and federal funding for higher education, to maintain civic engagement as a core mission. Academic leadership is critical to shaping students' civic engagement. As Langseth and Plater (2004) note,

> Even though missions change but little over decades or even centuries, there is always opportunity for leaders to give energy, purpose, and optimism to mission in new ways as they adapt colleges and universities to meet changing social, economic, technological, and global conditions. (p. 2)

The success to date in increasing student civic engagement is the result of a number of factors. Associations of higher education, nonprofit organizations, government agencies, and changes in public policy have each supported the growth of programs for students' civic engagement. Furthermore, the process and outcomes for learning from these initiatives is developing a knowledge base that can inform different units of analysis (e.g., individual student, courses, majors, institutions, national initiatives). At the most basic level, the motivation for more deliberate and wide-spread civic engagement of students rests on the desirability of the future activities of those students in communities through their personal and professional lives. For, as Mathews (1995) notes, "Why do we need more than a vocational education? In part, because we live more than a vocational life: we live a larger civic life and we have to be educated for it" (p. 70). Harkavy (1998) broadens that perspective and identifies a set of motives that explicate a basis for why students' civic engagement is an important agenda for higher education. First, he contends that taking civic engagement seriously will improve the core teaching and research activities of faculty. Second, by becoming more civically engaged, institutions of higher education will be modeling a socially responsible behavior for their students that they expect from their students. Finally, civic engagement will serve the self-interests of the academy by garnering recognition from external stakeholders such as funders, government officials, alumni, and community leaders.

425

References

Abes, E. S., Jackson, G., & Jones, S. R. (2002). Factors that motivate and deter faculty use of service-learning. *Michigan Journal of Community Service Learning, 9*(1), 5–17.

Astin, A. W., & Sax, L. J. (1998). How undergraduates are affected by service participation. *Journal of College Student Development, 39,* 251–263.

Battistoni, R. (2002). *Civic engagement across the curriculum: A resource book for service-learning faculty in all disciplines.* Providence, RI: Campus Compact.

Billig, S. H., & Eyler J. (Eds.). (2003). *Deconstructing service-learning: Research exploring context, participation, and impacts.* Greenwich, CT: Information Age.

Bowley, E. (Ed.). (2007). *Earn, learn, and serve: Getting the most from community service federal work study.* Retrieved January 27, 2009, from http://www.compact.org/fws/.

Boyer, E. L. (1994, March 9). Creating the new American college. *Chronicle of Higher Education,* A48.

Boyer, E. L. (1996). The scholarship of engagement. *Journal of Public Service and Outreach, 1*(1), 11–20.

Bringle, R. G. (1996, January). *Partnerships as mission: Implications for work and rewards of institutions, faculty, and students.* Paper presented at the Fourth AAHE Conference on Faculty Roles and Rewards, Atlanta, GA.

Bringle, R. G. (2003). Enhancing theory-based research on service-learning. In S. H. Billig & J. Eyler (Eds.), *Deconstructing service-learning: Research exploring context, participation, and impacts* (pp. 3–21). Greenwich, CT: Information Age.

Bringle, R. G., Games, R., & Malloy, E. A. (1999). *Colleges and universities as citizens.* Needham Heights, MA: Allyn & Bacon.

Bringle, R. G., & Hatcher, J. A. (1995). A service-learning curriculum for faculty. *Michigan Journal of Community Service Learning, 2,* 112–122.

Bringle, R. G., & Hatcher, J. A. (1996). Implementing service learning in higher education. *Journal of Higher Education, 67,* 221–239.

Bringle, R. G., & Hatcher, J. A. (2009). Innovative practices in service-learning and curricular engagement. In L. Sandmann, A. Jaeger, & C. Thornton (Eds.), *New directions in community engagement* (pp. 37–46). San Francisco: Jossey-Bass.

Bringle, R. G., Hatcher, J. A., & Clayton, P. H. (2006). The scholarship of civic engagement: Defining, documenting, and evaluating faculty work. *To Improve the Academy, 25,* 257–279.

Bringle, R. G., Hatcher, J. A., & Holland, B. (2007). Conceptualizing civic engagement: Orchestrating change at a metropolitan university. *Metropolitan Universities, 18*(3), 57–74.

Bringle, R. G., Hatcher, J. A., Jones, S., & Plater, W. M. (2006). Sustaining civic engagement: Faculty development, roles, and rewards. *Metropolitan Universities, 17*(1), 62–74.

Bringle, R. G., & Steinberg, K. (in press). Educating for informed community involvement. *American Journal of Community Psychology.*

Bringle, R. G., & Tonkin, H. (2004). International service-learning: A research agenda. In H. Tonkin, S. J. Deeley, M. Pusch, D. Quiroga, M. J. Siegel, J. Whiteley, et al. (Eds.), *Service-learning across cultures: Promise and achievement* (pp. 365–374). New York: International Partnership for Service-Learning and Leadership.

Bringle, R. G., Tonkin, H., & Sutton, S. (2004, October). *A research agenda for international service-learning.* Paper presented at the Fourth Annual International K-H Service-Learning Research Conference, Greenville, SC.

Calleson, D. C., Jordan, C., & Seifer, S. D. (2005). Community-engaged scholarship: Is faculty work in communities a true academic enterprise? *Academic Medicine, 80*(4), 317–321.

Campus Compact. (2007). *2006 service statistics: Highlights and trends of Campus Compact's annual membership survey.* Providence, RI: Campus Compact. Retrieved February 13, 2009, from http://www.compact.org/about/statistics/2006/service_statistics.pdf.

Carlson, J. S. (1990). *Study abroad: The experience of American undergraduates.* New York: Greenwood.

Colby, A., Beaumont, E., Ehrlich, T., & Corngold, J. (2007). *Educating for democracy: Preparing under-graduates for responsible political engagement.* Stanford, CA: Carnegie Foundation for the Advancement of Teaching.

Colby, A., Ehrlich, T., Beaumont, E., & Stephens, J. (2003). *Educating citizens: Preparing America's undergraduates for lives of moral and civic responsibility.* San Francisco: Jossey-Bass.

Commission on the Abraham Lincoln Study Abroad Fellowship Program. (2006). *Global competence and national needs: One million students study abroad.* Washington, DC: Author.

Council for the Advancement of Standards in Higher Education. (2006). *CAS professional standards for higher education* (6th ed.). Washington, DC: Author.

Council for the Advancement of Standards Learning and Development Outcomes. (2008). *Integrating CAS and learning reconsidered outcomes.* Retrieved February 13, 2009, from http://www.cas.edu/CAS%20Statements/CAS_outcomes_chart.08.pdf.

Davidson, R. (2007). Community service federal work-study: The best-kept secret in higher education? In E. Bowley (Ed.), *Earn, learn, and serve: Getting the most from community service federal work study.* Retrieved January 27, 2009, from http://www.compact.org/ fws/chapters/community_service/.

Dote, L., Cramer, K., Dietz, N., & Grimm, R. (2006, October). *College students helping America.* Retrieved January 27, 2009, from http://eric.ed.gov/ERICDocs/data/ericdocs2sql/content_storage_01/0000019b/80/27/f5/2c.pdf.

Draut, T. (2006). *Strapped: Why America's 20- and 30-somethings can't get ahead.* New York: Doubleday.

Driscoll, A. (2008). Carnegie's community-engagement classification: Intentions and insights. *Change: The Magazine of Higher Learning, 40*(1), 38–41.

Eyler, J. (2002). Stretching to meet the challenge: Improving the quality of research to improve the quality of service-learning. In S. H. Billig, & A. Furco (Eds.), *Service-learning: Through a multidisciplinary lens. Advances in service learning research series* (pp. 3–14). Greenwich, CT: Information Age.

Eyler, J. S., & Giles, D. E., Jr. (1999). *Where's the learning in service-learning?* San Francisco: Jossey-Bass.

Eyler, J. S., Giles, D. E., Jr., Stenson, C. M., & Gray, C. J. (2001). *At a glance: What we know about the effects of service-learning on college students, faculty, institutions and communities, 1993–2000* (3rd ed.). Nashville, TN: Vanderbilt University.

Furco, A., & Billig, S. H. (2002). *Service-learning: The essence of the pedagogy.* Greenwich, CT: Information Age.

Gottlieb, K., & Robinson, G. (2006). *A practical guide for integrating civic responsibility into the curriculum* (2nd ed.). Washington, DC: American Association of Community Colleges.

Harkavy, I. (1998, June). *The institutional service role.* Paper presented at the National Invitational Conference on Higher Education and Civic Responsibility, Tallahassee, FL.

Harkavy, I., & Puckett, J. L. (1994). Lessons from Hull House for the contemporary urban university. *Social Science Review, 68,* 299–321.

Hatcher, J. A., Bringle, R. G., Brown, L. A., & Fleischhacker, D. A. (2006). Supporting student involvement through service-based scholarships. In E. Zlotkowski, N. Longo, & J. Williams (Eds.), *Students as colleagues: Expanding the circle of service-learning leadership* (pp. 35–48). Providence, RI: Campus Compact.

Hatcher, J. A., & Steinberg, K. (2007, October). *Civic-minded graduates: Identifying knowledge, skills, and dispositions to improve assessment and research.* Paper presented at the annual conference of the Association of American Colleges and Universities, Denver, CO.

Hoy, A., & Meisel, W. (2008). *Civic engagement at the center: Building democracy through integrated cocurricular and curricular experiences.* Washington, DC: Association of American Colleges and Universities.

Hu, S., & Kuh, G. D. (2003). Maximizing what students get out of college: Testing a learning productivity model. *Journal of College Student Development, 44*(2), 185–203.

Jones, S. G., & Steinberg, K. A. (in press). An analysis of international service learning design. In R. G. Bringle, J. A. Hatcher, & S. G. Jones (Eds.), *International service learning: Conceptual frameworks and research.* Sterling, VA: Stylus.

Keeling, R. P. (Ed.). (2004). *Learning reconsidered: A campus-wide focus on the student experience.* Washington, DC: The National Association of Student Personnel Administrators; The American College Personnel Association.

Keen, C., & Hall, K. (2008). Post-graduation service and civic outcomes for high financial need students of a multi-campus, co-curricular service-learning college program. *Journal of College & Character, 10*(2), 1–8.

Keen, C., & Hall, K. (2009). Engaging with difference matters: Longitudinal student outcomes of co-curricular service-learning programs. *Journal of Higher Education, 80*(1), 59–79.

Kiesa, A., Orlowski, A., Levine, P., Both, D., Kirby, E., Lopez, M., et al. (2007). *Millennials talk politics: A study of college student political engagement.* Medford, MA: The Center for Information and Research on Civic Learning and Engagement.

Kuh, G. D. (2002, July). *The National Survey of Student Engagement: A tool for strengthening institutional accountability.* Mount Snow, VT: American Association of Higher Education Summer Academy.

Kuh, G. D. (2003). What we're learning about student engagement from NSSE: Benchmarks for effective educational practices. *Change, 35*(2), 24–32.

Kuh, G. D. (2007). What student engagement data tell us about college readiness. *Peer Review, 9*(1), 4–8.

Kuh, G. D. (2008). *High-impact educational practices: What they are, who has access to them, and why they matter.* Washington, DC: Association of American Colleges and Universities.

Kuh, G., Douglass, K., Lund, J., & Ramin-Gyurnek, J. (1994). *Student learning outside the classroom: Transcending artificial boundaries* (ASHE-ERIC Higher Education Report No. 8). Washington, DC: The George Washington School of Education and Human Development.

Langseth, M., & Plater, W. M. (Eds.). (2004). *Public work and the academy: An academic administrator's guide to civic engagement and service-learning.* Bolton, MA: Anker.

Laux, E. (2007). Retention and collaboration: IUPUI's Office of Community Work Study. In E. Bowley (Ed.), *Earn, learn, and serve: Getting the most from community service federal work study.* Retrieved January 27, 2009, from http://www.compact.org/fws/chapters/ models/iupui.

Lewin, T. (2008, December 3). College may become unaffordable for most in U. S. *New York Times.* Retrieved January 27, 2009, from http://www.nytimes.com/2008/12/03/education/ 03college. html.

Marchese, T. J. (1997). The new conversations about learning: Insights from neuroscience and anthro-pology, cognitive studies and work-place studies. In American Association for Higher Education (Ed.), *Assessing impact: Evidence and action* (pp. 79–95). Washington, DC: American Association for Higher Education.

Mathews, D. (1995). The politics of diversity and the politics of difference: Are academics and the pub-lic out of sync? *Higher Education Exchange,* 66–71.

McMurtrie, B. (2007, March 2). The global campus: American colleges connect with the broader world. *Chronicle of Higher Education,* A37.

Monitoring the Future. (2008). *Monitoring the future: A continuing study of American youth.* Retrieved January 27, 2009, from http://www.monitoringthefuture.org/.

O'Meara, K., & Rice, R. E. (Eds.). (2005). *Faculty priorities reconsidered: Rewarding multiple forms of scholarship.* San Francisco: Jossey-Bass.

Pascarella, E. T., & Terenzini, P. T. (1991). *How college affects students: Findings and insights from twenty years of research.* San Francisco: Jossey-Bass.

Percy, L., Zimpher, N., & Brukardt, M. (Eds.). (2006). *Creating a new kind of university. Institutionalizing community-university engagement.* Bolton, MA: Anker.

Plater, W. M., Jones, S. G., Bringle, R. G., & Clayton, P. H. (2009). Educating globally competent citizens through international service learning. In R. Lewin (Ed.), *The handbook of practice and research in study abroad: Higher education and the quest for global citizenship* (pp. 62–74). Florence, KY: Taylor & Francis.

Pryor, J. H., Hurtado, S., DeAngelo, L., Sharkness, J., Romero, L. C., Korn, W. S., et al. (2008). *The Ameri-can freshman: National norms for fall 2008.* Retrieved January 27, 2009, from http://www.gseis.ucla. edu/heri/pr-display.php?prQry=28.

Sandy, M., & Holland, B. (2006). Different worlds and common ground: Community partner perspec-tives on campus-community partnerships. *Michigan Journal of Community Service Learning, 13*(1), 30–43.

Sax, L. (2006–7). *Citizenship and spirituality among college students: What have we learned and where are we headed?* Retrieved February 6, 2009, from http://www.collegevalues.org/ articles. cfm?a=1&id=1023.

Sax, L. J., & Astin, A. W. (1997). The benefits of service: Evidence from undergraduates. *Educational Record, 78*(3–4), 25–32.

Umbach, P. D., & Wawrzynski, M. R. (2005). Faculty do matter: The role of college faculty in student learning and engagement. *Research in Higher Education, 46*(2), 153–184.

U.S. Office of Management and Budget. (n.d.). *ExpectMore.gov website.* Retrieved January 27, 2009, from http://www.whitehouse.gov/omb/expectmore/.

Vogelgesang, L. J., & Astin, A. W. (2005). *Post-college civic engagement among graduates.* Los Angeles: Higher Education Research Institute.

Walshok, M. L. (1999). Strategies for building the infrastructure that supports the engaged campus. In R. G. Bringle, R. Games, & E. A. Malloy (Eds.), *Colleges and universities as citizens* (pp. 74–95). Needham Heights, MA: Allyn & Bacon.

Ward, C., Bochner, S., & Furnham, A. (2001). *The psychology of culture shock.* London: Routledge.

Weinberg, A. S. (2005). Residential education for democracy. *Learning for Democracy, 1*(2), 29–45.

Welch, M., & Billig, S. H. (2004). *New perspectives in service-learning: Research to advance the field.* Greenwich, CT: Information Age.

Zlotkowski, E., Longo, N. V., & Williams, J. R. (Eds.). (2006). *Students as colleagues.* Providence, RI: Campus Compact.

Developing Higher Education Administrators

Jeri L. Childers and Theodore J. Settle

Today, developing and implementing an institutional strategy for engagement is vital for developing the capacity of the university to respond to the needs of its various publics, to educate the whole student, and to realize the potential and promise of its scholars and their impact on society. Core to developing, implementing, and institutionalizing this engagement plan is the development of university leaders for the twenty-first century which necessarily means enhancing the institutional capacity to engage with community partners and to support engaged scholars.

To respond to these challenges, Virginia Tech developed a week-long *Engagement Academy for University Leaders* to help higher education institutions develop partnerships with key external stakeholders in conducting research, teaching, and public service or outreach that will benefit the public and enhance the institution, as well as its faculty, staff, and students. Academy members were selected through a competitive nomination and selection process. The participants learned and applied concepts of engagement and engaged scholarship to develop individualized plans for institutionalizing community engagement within their institutions. This program is supported by a national advisory group, three national associations, a team of national scholars of engagement, a university president serving as a mentor-in-residence, and the recipient of the 2007 C. Peter Magrath W. K. Kellogg Foundation Engagement Award, Virginia Tech. Results of the Academy evaluation (Dubinsky, 2008) indicate that the participants gained a greater understanding of the core competencies of engagement and how to develop and implement institutional plans for engagement.

The Coming of Engagement

Many colleges and universities, including but not limited to land-grant institutions, have a history of being involved with their local communities. For many years this was called public service, and later the term "outreach" came into more general acceptance and use as a way of describing these activities. But, regardless of the language, institutions were extending their resources away from the campus and into the community, generally helping local communities, nonprofit organizations, and companies through various kinds of technical assistance.

In the past decade, along with increasing calls for accountability and decreasing financial support for public higher education, there has been a call for a renewal of recommitment to and strengthening of the purpose of public education institutions to be more engaged with their communities, nonprofit organizations, and companies. This call for engagement implied partnerships with these stakeholders and therefore a two-way interaction. Each partner would invest in a project, and each partner would get a return. For example, the community may provide funds and knowledge of local community networks, and the university may provide intellectual resources and experience through faculty and students to address issues. In return, the community would get solutions to their problems, and the university would have more informed faculty and students, increased research, and increased scholarship emanating from this field-based effort. This call for increased engagement had many and multiple sources. Some of those include the report by the Kellogg Commission on *Returning to Our Roots: The Engaged Institution* (1999). The American Association of State Colleges and Universities followed with *Stepping Forward as Stewards of Place* (2002), and the same year another report followed, *Leveraging Colleges and Universities for Urban Economic Revitalization: An Action Agenda* (2002), a joint venture between the Initiative for a Competitive Inner City and CEOs for Cities that suggested increased connections between reduced state budgets and universities demonstrating value to their stakeholders. Beyond reports and initiatives, engagement is now an accreditation criterion, such as Criterion 5 of the Higher Education Commission of the North Central Association of Schools and Colleges. In 2008, The Carnegie Foundation for the Advancement of Teaching announced the 2008 Community Engagement Classification in which 120 institutions were successfully classified, building on the first classification of this type that was released in 2006.

Many institutions are including engagement in their strategic plans. Some institutions are creating senior level administrative positions with oversight for engagement. Other institutions are figuring out how to best organize for engagement. Some institutions are expanding their engagement activities beyond a strong foundation of service learning. So, as in any new field, engagement is in a state of flux, change, and evolution. Institutions are securing their leaders for this new function from across the institution and developing an institutional capacity.

Given the strategic nature of this capacity building, developing and testing a leadership development model is important. This paper describes the journey that culminated in the *Engagement Academy for University Leaders*, a five-day immersion experience focused on developing and implementing an institutional strategy of engagement.

Historical Perspectives on Program Development

With the increasing attention by institutions to engagement, we began exploring the need for a training model and program to prepare individuals for leadership positions in engagement. Over time, this idea evolved to focusing on preparing individuals for leadership roles in institutions either with or wanting to create a major strategic thrust in engagement. The model chosen implies less a traditional training program and more an organizational development program on leading institutional change. Thus, developing, implementing, and evaluating an institutional strategy for engagement became the driving force behind the development of the Academy model and curriculum.

Phase I: The Early Stage of Program Development

Several factors influenced the development of the Academy model. The National Association of State Universities and Land-Grant Colleges (NASULGC) had been discussing models for leadership development and made recommendations on the future of extension in a report (2002) titled *The Extension System: A Vision for the 21st Century*. Jeri Childers, while at Pennsylvania State University, was the founding chair in 1999 of what became the annual Outreach Scholarship conference that now represents a partnership among numerous institutions to highlight the importance of outreach and the associated role of scholarship. Ted Settle initiated a new Community of Practice on Outreach and Engagement within the University Continuing Education Association. This community was created to respond to the evolving needs of many leaders who had observed their jobs shifting from providing "service" through developing and delivering continuing education programs to "engaging" through multiple products with clients in a partnership mode. Jeri Childers went on to chair this community of practice and lead the establishment of a Promising Practices in Outreach and Engagement Database (Childers, 2007), which collected practices in this emerging area of engagement related to leadership, infrastructure development, and many of the core competencies described elsewhere in this chapter. At the time that Virginia Tech initiated the development of the Academy, no other major association was leading in the development of individuals in the emerging field of engagement, although a niche in the field of engagement, service-learning, had a well-established history of developing leaders.

In this environment, the idea of an educational experience to prepare the next generation of leaders in engagement took root in the Council on Extension, Continuing Education, and Public Service (CECEPS) within the NASULGC. This CECEPS group included several individuals with "engagement" in their job titles. In parallel, representatives from many national organizations involved with engagement met at a Wingspread Conference, and a new organization was formed, the Higher Education Network for Community Engagement or HENCE (Sandmann, 2006). HENCE formed a subcommittee on professional development to explore ways to increase education and training related to the field of engagement. Ted Settle served as its chair.

Phase II: The Middle Stage of Program Development

Over several summer and fall annual meetings of CECEPS, the acceptance of the need, encouragement, and support for the Academy grew steadily. As a reflection of the evolution and acceptance of engagement and the significant shift in people's jobs, CECEPS changed its name to the Council on Engagement and Outreach (CEO) and NASULGC changed its name to the Association for Public and Land-grant Universities.

During this time, the characteristics of the Academy began to take shape. The program should clarify the philosophical and tactical differences among service, outreach, and engagement. It should target senior-level administrators and must be very high quality. It should be highly interactive with an orientation on practice. But, the program should not be designed solely for land-grant universities. In fact, many public and private urban universities and community colleges, usually not NASULGC member institutions, have a long history of civic engagement. This led us to involve two other associations of public universities: the American Association of State Colleges and Universities (AASC&U) and the Coalition of Urban and Metropolitan Universities (CUMU). Altogether, these three professional associations represented 587 public universities.

Several events occurred at Virginia Tech that affected our thinking. The university revised the promotion and tenure guidelines to better support outreach and engagement activities. We experimented with mini-versions of the program on engagement in three graduate courses and with two noncredit continuing education programs. Jeri Childers chaired an annual university-wide conference on outreach which led faculty toward greater understanding and acceptance of "engagement." She also led a campus-wide discussion beginning in 2006 with a preconference workshop on defining engagement, engaged scholarship, and excellence in engagement at the Virginia Tech Outreach NOW Conference and led a task force on student engagement in 2007. Ted Settle led the development of the university's distributed research model that places significant research efforts in communities distant from the main campus.

Phase III: The Final Stage of Program Development

We established a formal management team to develop the Academy, and our intent was to make this venture self-supporting. With institutional funding for a pilot Academy from the Center for Organizational and Technological Advancement (COTA), directed by Jeri Childers, Virginia Tech contracted with an expert to lead the program development of the pilot. Lorilee Sandmann, associate professor at the University of Georgia's Department of Lifelong Education, Administration, and Policy, was hired. COTA served as an appropriate sponsor because its genesis came from a successful, engaged campus-community partnership between Virginia Tech and the City of Roanoke, Virginia, to serve as an executive education and economic development hub for the university.

This program team of three then convened a national program advisory panel with representatives from the major associations and their member institutions. The major outcomes were to focus the Academy on those individuals leading or developing the institutional plan for engagement, identify instructional objectives and possible instruction resources or faculty, and assist with marketing the program to their institutional members. This group finalized the name for the program: *Engagement Academy for University Leaders.*

Phase IV: The Design and Delivery of the Pilot Program

Design Elements

The model for this five-day executive development program integrated several design elements to form a unique and intensive immersion experience across the full range of perspectives on engagement. The objectives of the Academy were to provide a framework for institutional capacity building for engagement, develop the executive's capacity to lead institutional change, and foster cohorts or networks of executives who are prepared to lead institutional change that nurtures the values of engagement, engaged scholarship, and engaged scholars.

A comprehensive model was developed to advance the institutionalization of engagement and engaged scholarship (Sandmann, Saltmarsh, & O'Meara, 2008). The Engagement Academy was based on three assumptions. First, the change process requires institutions to intentionally build a culture of engagement, including an infrastructure to support the development and delivery of programs that provide sustainable results. Building this organizational infrastructure for engagement (Ryan, 1998) requires developing core competencies for engagement among the senior leadership team. Fostering leadership commitment requires the development of a network of leaders within the institution and across institutions who are able to articulate the vision, mission, and strategy of engagement and engaged scholarship. The institutional plan for engagement must link to the overall mission and strategy of the institution. Creating and fostering networks of leaders with these competencies for engagement becomes a major mechanism for organizational change and is a major component of the Academy model.

Second, fostering leaders, leadership commitment, and institutional capacity for engagement and engaged scholarship requires presidents and provosts to create a culture of engagement within institutions that translates into networks of prepared leaders or learning communities (Childers et al., 2002).

Third, successful, thriving, engaged institutions have well-defined engagement strategies and an organizational development plan for engagement that are highly aligned or articulated with the institution's strategic plan. The Academy design encourages participants to develop a customized engagement that builds on an assessment of the history, culture, and mission of their institution. The organizational plan for engagement is based on the unique characteristics of the institution, such as institutional type, mission, history, geographic location, and stage of institutional readiness for engagement. Participants in the Academy conducted preassessment activities involving their president, provost, and executive leadership team to prepare them to develop customized engagement plans to implement on their return. Each plan was to be linked to the level of institutional commitment to engagement, stage of development toward being an engaged institution, engagement infrastructure, and progress in supporting and rewarding engaged scholarship. This design is based on a number of theories of individual and institutional change. Participants in the Academy are asked to explore and compare various theories and types of engagement (civic engagement, democratic engagement, and so on) and types of institutional change (Saltmarsh, Hartley, & Clayton, 2009). Various tools and theories are provided to assess leadership commitment (Holland, 2006) to engagement, and participants explore administrative roles and leadership

435

strategies (Driscoll and Sandmann, 2004) that can be deployed based upon organizational cultures (Kezar, 2001) and institutional readiness for change (Baer, Duin, & Ramaley, 2008). Finally, the Academy model is predicated on the theoretical theory and foundational work of Boyer (1996).

Content and Activities

The content, tools, cases, and activities for the Academy were developed to allow the participants to learn and prepare themselves to share their lessons learned, benchmarking information, and case materials when they returned to their institutions—to create networks or learning communities of engagement champions. Members of the Academy received their preassignments via a members-only website before they arrived on site; used technology to share ideas, peer-coaching, resources, and benchmarking information during the Academy; and were encouraged to maintain their peer relationships after the Academy as a support network or learning community. Formal and informal problem-based activities reinforced the content, strategy, and skill-building process for institutional change. Participants learned how to use the tools and approaches to institutional change through practice, role-play, theater, and daily evaluations and reflection using an online blog.

An important part of the design was to include the role of community partners. The program featured campus-community demonstration projects that were based on the principles of engaged scholarship established by the National Review Board for the Scholarship of Engagement established in 2000. Participants were provided with the definitions and criteria that were used to assess and evaluate engaged scholarship (Driscoll & Sandmann, 2004) and that involved university and community leaders addressing key needs in regions and communities. Administrators reviewed criteria used by scholars related to research goals, the context of theory and practice, research methods, results, communication, and the use of reflective critique within the context of real-world examples of engagement activities. Campus and community partners in Roanoke and Danville, Virginia, assumed the role of Academy faculty and conducted community tours that formed the basis of case studies for Academy members.

Participants received coaching from the mentor-in-residence—a university president who was available the entire week for formal learning and coaching. Participants could request time with this mentor or a variety of coaches with expertise in engaged scholarship, institutional advancement, community relations, organizational change, student engagement, and economic development.

The week's activities required the participants to develop plans for engagement that were refined throughout the week as a result of reflection, peer-to-peer and team feedback, as well as feedback from coaches and the mentor-in-residence. This 360-degree approach, representing the perspectives of multiple levels within institutions from the president to the faculty level, created multiple frames of analysis to represent the variety of stakeholders within institutions.

The content was arranged into modules that were organized around the core competencies of this training model and were developed via a national panel of faculty and validated by a national advisory committee prior to the development of the pilot. Participants were asked to develop competencies in six areas. The competencies were the ability to:

1. Read the institution and community context—assess the institution's engagement quotient, that is, understand the current level of (a) commitment to engagement, (b) existing examples of engagement, and (c) support for engaged scholarship at the institution (Holland, 2006) and align and integrate the appropriate response(s) in the engagement plan;
2. Encourage a variety of institutional and individual leadership responses to the spectrum of change required and to the diverse needs of a variety of stakeholders, that is, customize an organizational development plan for engagement for the institution and a plan to lead the required change strategy (Kezar, 2001; Bolman & Deal, 2003);
3. Lead the development and maintenance of strategic, engagement-related operations (enabling policies, practices, and cultures) and build and maintain networks of change agents (individuals and teams);
4. Develop and articulate the institutional and individual's vision, roles, and responsibilities related to engaged scholarship (Driscoll & Sandmann, 2004; Sandmann, 2008; Sandmann et al., 2008), as well as enhance and maintain leadership commitment to engaged scholarship and the culture that supports engaged scholarship;
5. Lead the resource development (the internal financial commitment and philanthropy) to implement change and to create a sustainable engagement plan; and
6. Lead the development of university-wide programs that have impact, and document and communicate this impact to a variety of internal and external stakeholders.

Early in the development of the model, we struggled to accommodate the participation of institutional teams as well as individual executives. The pilot accommodated both types of participants. In fact, some institutions sent "scouts" to experience the Academy and evaluate its potential for sending others from the institution to future academies, and some institutions did nominate teams even without heavy emphasis on the team component in the marketing materials. The pilot accommodated four teams.

Institutional Leadership Commitment

Leadership commitment is required to foster leaders (Holland, 2006). Thus, we required presidents or provosts to nominate candidates to participate in the Academy. In this nomination process, presidents and provosts were asked to articulate the role of engagement within the institution's overall strategic plan and the role and goal of the candidate or the team after completion of the Academy. In addition, they were involved in the prework, institutional assessments and benchmarking, and plans for engagement and engaged scholarship. The model builds commitment by creating feedback and communication loops with these champions as participants return to their institutions to share what they learned, their plans, and their progress throughout the institutional change process. The model is designed to strengthen this institutional or top-level commitment by involving the champion in the evaluation of the impact of engagement and engaged scholarship as the plan is implemented.

Selection of Participants

Presidents and provosts nominated forty-six candidates for the inaugural Academy. Forty-two candidates applied (twenty-five applicants from NASULGC institutions, thirteen applicants from AASCU institutions, and seven applicants from CUMU institutions). The institutions of twenty-five applicants were members of one of the endorsing associations, those of nine were members of two of the endorsing associations, and one institution was a member of all three associations. Forty candidates were accepted, and thirty-five people attended (13 percent attrition rate). Four institutions sent teams with at least two participants, and thirty institutions were represented in the inaugural Academy. Twenty-two institutions were classified as doctoral-granting and eight were master's colleges and universities. The Academy attracted participants from every region of the country, that is, the West (8), Midwest (4), Northeast (4), and South (14) (Miles, 2008).

The participants were overwhelmingly leaders in academic administration with thirty-one of thirty-five participants in this role. Over half of the participants were deans or higher positions. The participants included two provosts, seven vice provosts/vice presidents/vice chancellors, nine associate vice presidents or deans, 4 associate deans, twelve directors, and seven professors.

Intended Outcome: Development of an Institutional Plan for Engagement

Each participant was asked to develop a customized plans for his/her own institution around strategic themes that have led to the successful implementation of plans for engagement or engaged scholarship at other institutions, that is, build a network of institutional champions within the institution; involve faculty and community partners in identifying priorities in discovery, learning and engagement that are linked to the institution's strategic plan; and utilize these priorities as critical areas for engagement and engaged scholarship (Ramaley, 2007). The model is designed to align or link scholars simultaneously to the overall university strategic plan and to critical local, regional, or global needs. The plan also needed to include strategies to nurture, coordinate, and communicate progress in engagement and engaged scholarship. Finally, the plan needed to demonstrate each of the six competencies.

What Did We Want to Accomplish?

We defined success as the ability to fully enroll a cohort of well-qualified participants, satisfy participant and institutional objectives as well as Academy learning objectives, serve a rich mix of institutions, enroll teams, develop and deliver a high-quality, executive development experience based on a well-researched competency-based model, assemble a team of star faculty, contribute to the scholarship of engagement and the field of higher education, develop a network of leaders of engagement, provide a dialogue that utilizes a world-class venue, provide successful strategies that lead to institutional change, and develop a program worthy of the endorsing organizations and the inspired leadership of leaders in the field who supported the development of this program.

Phase V: The Evaluation of the Pilot Program

Evaluation Process

We employed a team of evaluators for the inaugural Academy that explored major questions about leading engagement that were linked to the underlying assumptions of the model. The answers to these questions provided data for formative and summative evaluations and a basis of engaged scholarship related to leadership for engagement in higher education. Daily, the participants participated in an online evaluation that covered six areas: (1) recruitment, (2) registration and pre-Academy experience (which included information and assignments to prepare them for their on-site experience), (3) classrooms/facilities and co-curricular/extracurricular activities, (4) content, (5) instructional design, media/materials, and learning activities, and (6) Academy faculty.

The participants were also queried daily with reflective and integrative learning questions via an online blog. These questions solicited the perceptions of the participants about the level of engagement of their institutions (measured using frameworks and dimensions provided during the Academy), the approaches to institutional change that might work best within their institutions, the kind of changes, approaches, and resources they personally intended to employ within their roles in the institutions, those enablers that would assist the participants to implement their strategies to institutionalize engagement, and their perceptions of their ability to implement their plan of action. A post-Academy survey was delivered online within one month of the Academy to evaluate their overall experience, and a six-month follow-up survey was conducted. As of publication, evaluators are conducting individual interviews to identify which strategies have been implemented and what progress has been made toward institutional or individual plans.

Participant Feedback

What did we learn from the pilot? The data gathered during the week of the Academy and in the post-Academy survey indicated that the inaugural Engagement Academy for University Leaders was a stunning success. Twenty of the thirty-five participants responded to the post-Academy survey (57 percent response rate). The answers to two key questions point to the Academy's success.

When participants were asked whether or not the Academy fulfilled their expectations and whether or not they would recommend the Academy to a colleague, all twenty respondents answered "yes." These responses can be understood when reviewing the exceptionally positive responses to individual questions in the six areas of evaluation mentioned earlier. That being said, there is always room for improvement. Based on the data gathered, we are planning some changes.

Lesson Learned 1: Recruitment

We will continue to recruit senior-level administrators who are tasked with significant responsibilities for engagement at their institutions and will continue to look for ways to ensure that the Academy participants have significant pre- and post-Academy support from their president or provost. The management team will strongly encourage participants to create with their president or provost a clear vision for engagement at their institution during the pre-planning session, including a well-articulated goal and role for them during the implementation phase on their return.

Part of this recruitment strategy will include planning for leaders at various stages in their career paths, in a variety of functional areas within institutions, with varying levels of experience in their current role or with the field of engagement, and with varying levels of experience or skill in leadership. The management team will develop a process to utilize the endorsing associations, program advisory committee, and Engagement Academy alumni to recruit participants. Over time, the team will expand the recruiting emphasis for participants from a wider range of institutional types in postsecondary education (e.g., private universities and community colleges) and seek endorsement from associations representing these institutions. Another part of the expanded recruitment will include international participants. The team will expand the enrollment goal from thirty-five to forty-five and will use scholarships to increase access for candidates from minority institutions. With the support of the faculty, we established the Judith Ramaley Scholarship Fund to support such efforts. Dr. Ramaley served as our inaugural Mentor-in-Residence and is currently the president of Winona State University, Winona, Minnesota.

When asked during the post-Academy evaluation, 20 percent of the respondents indicated that they wished that they had been part of an institutional team. Therefore, during the pre-Academy stage, teams will be encouraged to attend and place more emphasis on working with the president/provost of institutions to define team goals and roles related to developing and implementing institutional plans for engagement.

Lesson Learned 2: The Registration and Pre-Academy Experience

We will adjust the nomination and application processes to collect additional data to help Academy faculty customize the experience for the participants and facilitate ongoing research on leadership and institutional impact. We will align the pre-Academy assignments with on-site activities to reinforce their connection to the structure of the participants' institutions, the current climate, priorities, level of engagement of the institutions, and the goals of the president/provost related to institutional change and engagement.

Lesson Learned 3: Classrooms/Facilities and Co-curricular/Extracurricular Activities

The majority of the participants were very satisfied with the classrooms and co-curricular/extracurricular activities. The schedule for the week was packed with activities. And, while the participants expressed satisfaction with individual activities, the cumulative effect of the intensive schedule left participants expressing satisfaction and exhaustion simultaneously. The curriculum redesign will seek ways to create an immersion in the world of engagement while effectively linking activities, mentors, and reflection for a more balanced and integrated learning experience.

For example, in the pilot, the participants had planned activities each day from early morning into the evening, which included a ninety-minute bus ride to Danville, Virginia. Although the trip exposed the participants to a nationally recognized, award-winning model of engagement, the travel time for the tour and the activities at the site did not optimize the participants' ability to engage with community leaders and link lessons learned with their current challenges or contexts. One strategy currently being explored is to use the local community of Roanoke as the learning laboratory, selecting particular partnerships or activities that illustrate various forms of engagement or challenges of collaboration. Using this model, Academy faculty could articulate several local examples and encourage individuals or teams to select one or more of them to study during the pre-Academy phase, as well as visiting their case study sites during the Academy to gain further insights. The management team and Academy faculty team agree with the participants that tours, in-the-community case studies, and other ways to engage participants with community leaders and real-world examples of engagement-in-action are very beneficial and introduce a different and effective learning format.

Lesson Learned 4: Content

The Academy faculty identified the need to clarify the instructional objectives as well as to prioritize and tighten the content. In addition, the faculty recommended the creation of affinity groups related to engagement themes, such as student engagement with service-learning, economic development, or institutional advancement.

Lesson Learned 5: Instructional Design, Media/Materials, and Learning Activities

Seventy-five percent of the participants indicated that the institutional assessment and the case statement completed prior to the Academy were valuable or very valuable as currently designed. The design team will realign this activity and will enhance the data collection tools used in the pre-Academy phase to better prepare the faculty for the unique needs of each participant. The faculty intends to use these tools throughout the week as each participant builds his/her customized action plan for engagement. The tools will also enable the participant to prepare an immediate and effective plan to implement on the first morning following the Academy.

We will place more emphasis within each learning module on active learning strategies, linking the content of the module with the particular problems and challenges of the participants or teams, and on peer-to-peer, faculty, or mentor consultative time. We intend to more fully integrate the community voice or community leaders into the faculty team and learning experience.

The current reading materials for the participants were daunting, and we will significantly reduce the overall volume of readings. The faculty will organize the materials and create access to the materials based on the particular situations or contexts the participants are experiencing. This will require the management and instructional teams to "unpack" the materials and collect information during nomination and registration process or the prework stage to interpret their needs. Additionally, the faculty will assign readings each evening to facilitate discussion the next day and to develop common ground around foundational concepts. Instead of providing an oversized notebook filled with worksheets, resources, and readings, we will highlight readings and handouts just in time for instructional activities and make them available in PDF form, on a CD-ROM or a jump drive for use after the Academy.

Although those staging the Academy relied on technology or blogging as the form of daily reflection for the inaugural Academy, several user and logistical issues impacted its overall effectiveness as a tool to facilitate reflection. Therefore, we will continue daily reflections with more time devoted to the daily activities while discontinuing the blog feature for the near term.

Lesson Learned 6: Faculty

The peer consultations, facilitated by the faculty and mentor-in-residence, were among the liveliest and most thought-provoking parts of the week. We will allow more time for these informal and very effective learning experiences. They enabled the participants to receive individualized assistance in building a plan for engagement that matched their institutional and personal leadership needs.

The role of learning integrator was central to the success of the Academy. Through a combination of active listening, personal scholarship and experience, and various assessment techniques, the learning integrator identified the content that was aligned to the competency model, designed the curriculum, assisted in selecting the faculty, and managed the design, development, and delivery of the formal and informal learning activities. On-site the integrator oriented team members, led the faculty team each day, and helped the participants integrate their learning each day. The learning integrator co-designed the evaluation plan for the Academy. The role of the learning integrator was important to the overall success of the Academy and the achievement of learning outcomes for participants.

The star faculty members, all scholars and practitioners in engagement, brought the concept of the Academy to life. The management and instructional teams were diverse, and this Academy will continue to seek faculty representing multiple roles and perspectives within institutions of various types and with a variety of experiences, representing diverse cultures, races, ethnicities, and gender.

Lesson Learned 7: The Overall Experience

Each respondent offered some thoughts on the most beneficial aspects of the Engagement Academy for University Leaders. Here are a few of the responses that exemplify their overall experience:

- "Networking and stopping to think about opportunities was helpful."
- "Immediate access to experts and expert knowledge in the fields of higher education and community engagement in formal and informal conversations ... was invaluable."

- "I developed a better understanding of the integrative nature of community engagement as it relates to teaching, research, and service."
- "The focused and single-topic approach to engagement (was valuable). There were limited distractions, so I was able to really get my head around the concepts and related themes. I found the Academy to be like a language immersion program … It worked for me!"
- "The agenda offered a wide variety of activities and gave us ample time to network with others. The trip to Danville provided a concrete example of engagement. The receptions and joint events also appropriately created engagement."
- "The organizers' flexibility to adapt sessions and group formations according to partici-pants' feedback was appreciated. It allowed for our ideas (and plans) to evolve produc-tively and facilitated intermingling beyond issue areas."
- "Gaining a better overview of what other institutions are trying to do to become engaged, twenty-first century public institutions was very important."

The Academy was well received. The participants enjoyed the experience, and they were exhausted. They found the venue outstanding and the faculty to be an extremely valuable component of their experience. Although the participants, faculty, and the management team had suggestions for improvement, all of the stakeholders would like to see the Acad-emy continue.

Conclusion: Next Steps for the Academy

We have identified two major next steps. First, we intend to evaluate and refine this program and offer it on an annual basis. Second, we are exploring one- or two-day modules on engagement topics such as economic development, institutional advancement, or service-learning that will provide opportunities for in-depth study and networking for leaders in these topical areas of engagement. Given the criticality of engagement as a core competency of institutions and their leaders, it is important to develop training models for institutional executives. These models will necessarily include formal and informal learning activities. Described here is one example of an executive development program that was designed for the unique and evolving needs of university leaders who are creating and possibly imple-menting an institutional strategy for engagement.

Acknowledgment

We would like to acknowledge the editorial review and advice of Lorilee Sandmann, associ-ate professor at the University of Georgia's Department of Lifelong Education, Administra-tion, and Policy in preparation of this article and the important role she played in developing and delivering the first Engagement Academy for University Leaders; Judith Ramaley, President, Winona State University, for her vision and valuable contributions in the role of the Mentor-in-Residence; the editorial review and advice of Jim Dubinsky, associate professor at Virginia Tech's Department of English and the director of the Center for Stu-dent Engagement and Community Partnerships in the preparation of this article and the important role he played in the evaluation process; the ongoing leadership commitment to engagement of our president Charles Steger; our provost Mark McNamee; and the outstanding team in Virginia Tech's Outreach Program Development and the Academy faculty who made the development and delivery of this program possible.

References

American Association of State Colleges and Universities Task Force on Professional Development for Teachers. (2002). *Stepping forward as stewards of place.* Washington, DC: American Association of State Colleges and Universities.

Baer, L. L., Duin, D. H., & Ramaley, J. A. (2008). Smart change. *Planning for Higher Education, 36*(2), 5–16.

Bolman, L., & Deal, T. (2003). Integrating frames for effective practice. In *Reframing Organizations: Artistry, Choice, and Leadership* (3rd ed.). San Francisco: Jossey-Bass.

Boyer, E. L. (1996). The scholarship of engagement. *Journal of Public Service & Outreach, 1,* 11–20.

Childers, J. (2007). *Promising practices in outreach and engagement database.* http://www.opd.vt.edu/promisingpractices. Blacksburg, VA: Virginia Tech.

Childers, J., Martin, M., Dann, M., Dufour, C., Bruns, K., & Wise, G. (2002) Outreach and engagement: Building and sustaining learning communities in higher education. *Journal of Higher Education Outreach and Engagement, 7*(1), 19–27.

Competitive Inner City and CEOs for Cities. (2002). *Leveraging colleges and universities for urban economic revitalization: An action agenda.* Retrieved September 22, 2008, from http://www.edu-impact.com/leveraging-colleges-and-universities-urban-economic-revitalization-action-agenda.

Driscoll, A., & Sandmann, L. (2004). The roles and responsibilities of academic administrators supporting the scholarship of civic engagement. In M. Langseth & W. Plater (Eds.), *Public work and the academy: An academic administrator's guide to civic engagement and service-learning* (pp. 51–68). Bolton, MA: Anker.

Dubinsky, J. (2008). *Engagement academy evaluation.* Unpublished manuscript and related correspondence dated August 8, 2008, Virginia Tech, Blacksburg, VA.

Holland, B. A. (2006). *Levels of commitment to community engagement characterized by key organizational factors evidencing relevance to institutional mission.* Retrieved July 30, 2007, from http://www.henceonline.org/resources/institutional.

Kellogg Commission on the Future of State and Land-Grant Universities. (1999). *Returning to our roots: The engaged institution.* Washington, DC: National Association of State Universities and Land-Grant Colleges.

Kezar, A. (2001). Research-based principles of change. In *Understanding and facilitating organizational change* (pp. 113–123). Washington, DC: ASHE-ERIC.

Miles, T. D. (2008). *Postsecondary U.S. leaders of community engagement.* Unpublished manuscript, University of Georgia, Athens.

National Association of State Universities and Land-Grant Colleges. (2002). *The extension system: A vision for the 21st century.* Retrieved September 26, 2008, from https://www.nasulgc.org/NetCommunity/Document.Doc?id=152.

Ramaley, J. A. (2007). Reflections on the public purposes of higher education. *Wingspread Journal,* 5–10.

Ryan, J. (1998). Creating an outreach culture. *Journal of Public Service and Engagement, 3*(2), 22–34.

Saltmarsh, J., Hartley, M., & Clayton, P. M. (2009). Democratic engagement whitepaper. Boston: New England Resource Center for Higher Education.

Sandmann, L. (2006). Building a higher education network for community engagement. *Journal of Higher Education Outreach and Engagement, 2*(4), 41–54.

Sandmann, L. (2008). Conceptualization of the scholarship of engagement in higher education: A strategic review, 1996–2006. *Journal of Higher Education Outreach and Engagement, 3*(1), 91–104.

Sandmann, L., Saltmarsh, J., & O'Meara, K. A. (2008). An integrated model for advancing the scholarship of engagement: Creating academic homes for the engaged scholar. *Journal of Higher Education Outreach and Engagement, 12*(1), 47–64.

Developing Emerging Engagement Scholars in Higher Education

Angela Allen and Tami L. Moore

A primary purpose of research institutions is to structure educational programs that target contemporary and future needs (Altbach, 1999). Several leading scholars, in their discussions of the faculty role in engagement, have begun to recommend the preparation of graduate students for engagement as a supplement to their disciplinary training (Bloomfield, 2006; Gaff, 2005; O'Meara, 2005; Rice, 2005). Austin and Barnes (2005) specifically discuss how doctoral programs can prepare graduate students for faculty careers with a focus on "the public good" (p. 272). Basing their discussion on a summary of highlights from recent studies regarding graduate education, the authors recommend that doctoral programs should incorporate the following competency areas for graduate students who want to become engaged scholars: developing appreciation of the core purposes and values of higher education institutions; understanding different institutional types and their missions; understanding what public service, outreach, and engagement mean; and developing certain skills specific for success within the academic profession, including research, teaching, teamwork and collaboration, communication, and appreciation for institutional citizenship responsibilities (Austin & Barnes, 2005).

Nelson (2006) also offers suggestions for different disciplinary doctoral programs to use engagement to prepare students for their careers. The author acknowledges that although the focus on research (at the doctoral level, especially) and applied professional program or discipline requirements make it unlikely that the typical model of service-learning will take root in graduate education, developing community-engaged scholars requires collaborative, interdisciplinary research, teaching, learning, and service practices that connect disciplinary and civic knowledge in community problem solving. Sullivan and Rosen (2008) label this approach "pedagogy for practical reason" aimed at deepening students' facility in working

447

at the connection between theory and practice (p. xii). They also acknowledge that this idea runs "against the grain" of traditional approaches in higher education, and few opportunities exist to experience this sort of educational approach.

Austin and Barnes (2005), Nelson (2006), and others clearly value a focus on serving the public good in the preparation of future faculty and higher education administrators. Nelson (2006) and Sullivan and Rosen (2008) demonstrate that new approaches to achieve this goal within traditional curriculum will be established slowly, if at all. In the meantime, it will be important to create other venues for supporting the development of community-engaged scholars. In this chapter, we tell the story of one such program, the Emerging Engagement Scholars Workshop (EESW), a preconference event affiliated with the annual National Outreach Scholarship Conference. In 2009, the workshop enters in its third year. The design and implementation of the event has evolved over time, balanced by the participation of a planning committee including senior scholars, alumni from previous EESW workshops, and other advocates.

Origins and Evolution of the Emerging Engagement Scholars Workshop

In December 2006, the authors proposed a unique professional development and mentoring opportunity for graduate student and nontenured faculty scholar-practitioners in engagement and outreach, to be held at the 2007 National Outreach Scholarship Conference (NOSC). Our proposal for the Emerging Engagement Scholars Workshop was modeled after the American Educational Research Association's (AERA) Division J (Postsecondary Education) annual pre-general conference seminar. The inaugural EESW was co-sponsored by the National Center for the Study of University Engagement at Michigan State University (NCSUE), in partnership with the Higher Education Network for Community Engagement (HENCE). Continuation funding in 2008 and beyond is provided by the NOSC partnership institutions steering committee and NCSUE.

When planning for the 2007 workshop began, we were doctoral students in higher education administration programs, from Michigan State University and Washington State University, respectively. A faculty member introduced us via email in April 2006 for the purpose of collaborating with other scholars on a symposium proposal for the 2006 Association for the Study of Higher Education (ASHE) conference. We shared a common background as former community practitioners who chose to pursue doctoral degrees, in the hopes of connecting our community practitioner experiences with academic research, and increasing the presence of this voice in the scholarly literature. We came together at the 2006 Outreach Scholarship Conference and again at ASHE later that fall. Across these two conferences, we had conversations where we noted the absence of an organized opportunity for graduate student attendees at NOSC to discuss their experiences or scholarly interests. These conversations led to our work, supported by NCSUE and HENCE leaders, to develop a proposal for the workshop, approved by the NOSC Implementation Team in late December 2006. At this point, we convened a twelve-member workshop planning committee. The planning committee for the 2007 Emerging Engagement Scholars Workshop consisted of advanced doctoral students, faculty, representatives of the

National Outreach Scholarship Conference Implementation Team, senior scholars in the field of outreach and engagement, and a scholar-practitioner acting as liaison to NCSUE and HENCE.

After a successful first workshop, the NOSC partnership steering committee accepted a recommendation to formalize the EESW as a permanent feature of the National Outreach Scholarship Conference. The proposal forwarded to the Steering Committee includes a logic model, developed by Lisa Townson of the University of New Hampshire, co-chair of the 2008 Planning Committee, which outlines the goals and desired outcomes for the workshop (see figure 1). The original proposal and this logic model clearly identify goals for the workshop, which in turn informed the structure and evaluation of the program.

Goals of the Emerging Engagement Scholars Workshop

We designed the EESW to be facilitated by an established, national unifying organization similar to AERA. We proposed that participants, targeted as advanced graduate (doctoral-level) students and junior faculty and/or outreach/engagement practitioners, should be able to feed directly from the workshop into the host conference, increasing the collegiality between veteran and emerging outreach and engagement scholars, practitioners, and researchers. The workshop's primary goal in its first year was to facilitate the development of a welcoming mentoring community of scholars and practitioners, based on the common interest of scholarly work. We emphasized the traditional expectation of the academy that these emerging engagement scholars, regardless of career track, would produce scholarship. We wanted to enable participants in the workshop to strengthen their passion for outreach and engagement as well as meet their disciplinary and degree responsibilities through a national community of scholars. In 2008, the goal narrowed in focus slightly, placing greater emphasis on the development of solid research skills for community-university engagement as opposed to programs grounded in extension or outreach models. This approach continues in the planning for 2009 and influences the design for the workshop experience.

Structure of the Emerging Engagement Scholars Workshop

The Emerging Engagement Scholars Workshop is designed to accomplish three things: for early-career scholars, establish a point of easy access to the NOSC and the associated community of outreach and engagement professionals; more importantly, provide mentoring in research and professional development; and build a network of early career professionals committed to strengthening the scholarship related to community-university engagement. These commitments shape the workshop. They run as a connecting set of principles through the application and selection process for participants, workshop curriculum and agenda, the small-group approach to mentoring, and the ongoing evaluation of workshop outcomes.

Participant Demographics and the Application Process

In the 2007 inaugural workshop, twenty-three participants representes sixteen different institutions of higher education. Many of the participants demonstrated a combination of

Inputs	Audience	Outputs — Activities	Outcomes—Impact — Learning Outcomes	Action Outcomes	Impact
Conference space for AM prior to Outreach Scholars Conference—Room for 20 people	Advanced graduate students from any discipline	Pre-readings—(Sandmann, 2006), the program (similar to 2007)	Participants gain an increased awareness of who else in their discipline is working on engaged scholarship	Participants seek out mentors in their discipline	Young professionals and new faculty members successfully incorporate engaged scholarship into their scholarly agendas.
$$ to host a dinner for participants the night before	Junior faculty members from any discipline	Pre-conference workshop (1–3 hours): • What is engaged scholarship? • Current literature/theory on engagement, trends in higher education, toward engaged scholarship • Differences between documenting engaged scholarship and "traditional" research/scholarship	Participants gain knowledge about what engaged scholarship means, how it might be expressed within their discipline, and how to document engaged scholarship activities in the promotion and tenure review process.	Participants include a scholarly component to their engagement/outreach work with community partners	
Website space (through HENCE or other) to post information about the program, nomination, materials, etc.				Participants effectively document their engagement work as scholarly.	
Faculty speakers for panel, and overview. Suggestions: • Lorilee Sandmann—Overview • Senior faculty, administrators, Extension faculty from various institutions and disciplines (i.e. land-grant, community college, urban, etc.)		Panel discussion—Reality—how engaged scholarship is recognized/rewarded, etc. Include tenure track faculty, Extension, community college and department chair/head	Participants have a greater understanding of the potential promotion and tenure implications of spending time in engaged scholarship	Participants determine how much they will be involved in engaged scholarship—pre-tenure.	
		Outreach Scholarship Conference workshops—attending sessions during the conference that focus on community partners.	Participants gain a greater understanding of how to identify community partners for their engaged scholarship	Participants seek out community partners for their engaged scholarship.	Participants involve community partners in a meaningful manner through engaged scholarship.
		OR—this could be an additional 1 hour session as part of the pre-conference.		Participants gain skills in effectively partnering with communities in engaged scholarship projects	
Host website/institution to administer listserv, blog, or wiki		Follow up listserv membership, blog, wiki, or other electronic communication tool		Participants have a greater feeling of community among like-minded faculty in engaged scholarship.	Participants continue connection and communication with others involved in engaged scholarship
		Inclusion of participant list in registration materials		Participants know how to connect with and communicate with other like-minded faculty	

institutional roles in service to the ideals of outreach and engagement in higher education. All participants held dual roles at their institution: graduate student, and administrative professional. The participants represented a diverse range of experiences in integrating scholarly activity across their exposure to outreach and engagement. To illustrate, thirteen of the twenty-three participants in the inaugural workshop were either adjunct or tenure-track faculty, or an executive administrator of outreach or engagement centers, including program coordinators, directors, or lead research associates. One participant served as the executive director of a national association for urban metropolitan universities.

Each cohort has been more diverse than the previous one in terms of institutional type, and disciplinary focus. The 2008 class included a balanced mix of six faculty and eight graduate students, from six institutions across several disciplines, including the arts and humanities, environmental resources, educational administration, nuclear engineering, and sociology. The nineteen members of the 2009 class, selected as this volume goes to press, represent eleven institutions. In addition to disciplines reflected in previous cohorts, the 2009 cohort also has members working in engineering, anthropology, urban planning, and political science. In 2007, most participants came from research and doctoral granting institutions with established commitments to outreach and engagement. Two emerging scholars in the 2008 class represented liberal arts colleges, and one has a faculty appointment at a comprehensive institution; two in the 2009 cohort are employed at minority-serving institutions. Although the majority of the participants represent research universities, EESW participant demographics demonstrate the wide relevance of community engagement beyond the social science disciplines. The 2009 class also reflects the growing interest in engagement outside the United States; three participants represent Canadian universities.

Emerging scholars are chosen through a competitive selection process, with review of the applications conducted by a subcommittee of the workshop's planning committee. The workshop application process attempts to ensure buy-in from the applicant's academic unit by asking their supervisors (graduate mentor, department head, or other administrator) to affirm that should the applicant be chosen to participate in the workshop, their academic unit could continue to support their development through the completion of their graduate programs, or promotion and tenure review.

Several veteran scholars who participated in the planning and sessions of the workshop recommended that strong infrastructure exist within the workshop centered on the research topics, projects, and portfolios of its participants. Since the inaugural workshop, this recommendation has been further developed, as evidenced in the application process. The workshop application packet consists of three documents:

1. The application form: collects applicants' basic demographic information and current status (e.g., graduate student, instructor, outreach/extension coordinator, faculty, or other). Workshop organizers use this information to develop mentoring groups, and where possible, to align the curriculum and structure more closely to participants' professional experiences.

2. Statements of interest/experience: documents the applicant's prior experience and knowledge of the practice and principles of community-university engagement. In 2007,

451

the applicants submitted a 750-word essay describing their disciplinary research interest(s), career plans, experience with engagement, and how attending the workshop would facilitate their professional growth. As the goals of the workshop shifted, placing greater emphasis on scholarship and honing research skills, the requirements for this second piece in the application packet changed as well. In 2008 and beyond, applicants submit a 250-word biographical essay, as well as a proposal of no more than five pages outlining a current or future scholarly project which addresses a community-based issue and includes community partners, or studies engagement in higher education. The outline, following a traditional research proposal format, must address three questions: What do you want to do? How do you plan to do it? and How are community members involved in designing and/or conducting this project?

3. Faculty or supervisor nomination form: provides additional insight on the applicant, and also demonstrates specific knowledge of the applicant's work and the department's interest in supporting scholarly activity in outreach and engagement. To complete the form, the nominator scored the applicant (along a scale of 1 to 3, 3 indicating strongest possession of the quality) in four areas, reflecting the goals of the workshop: involvement or interest in research that contributes to the discipline and that can have an impact on external stakeholders; desire for new learning about outreach scholarship; interest in working across disciplines to explore and learn more about how outreach scholarship might be carried out; and effective communication skills, for disseminating research results to public, academic, and other external audiences.

Workshop Curriculum/Agenda

The workshop was originally intended to span two days, as a preconference workshop. Because of timing and logistics, the agenda and delivery approach has shifted each year. In 2007, the workshop was integrated into the programmatic content of the NOSC general conference. EESW general sessions were then designed to address issues facing emerging scholars in engaged scholarship and the scholarship of engagement. The implementation of this integration model rested on the collaboration and enthusiasm for the workshop by the Outreach Scholarship Conference 2007 logistic and programmatic coordinators, Mary S. Grant and Ann Keim, of University of Wisconsin–Extension.

The 2007 workshop centered on three sessions. Two sessions (one opening the workshop and one closing the workshop) consisted of panels of veteran scholars and community-based practitioners in outreach and engagement. The purpose of the panels was to frame understanding of how outreach and engagement practice has been experienced and developed within and across higher education. The panelists briefly shared their experiences from their positions of influence across their institutions and reputations in outreach and engagement.

Evaluation of the 2007 workshop also identified participants' desire to dedicate more time during the event to discussions of foundational literature that has shaped the field of outreach and engagement in higher education, as well as some model examples of outreach scholarship. In response to this feedback, the 2008 Planning Committee designed two "master class" experiences and distributed a reading list in advance to participants, asking them to prepare these readings as a foundation for the discussions. One class, facilitated by Lorilee Sandmann, introduced the literature and prevailing conceptual models related to community-university engagement. Randy Stoecker introduced topics related to working with or within communities, focusing on power dynamics among partners. Both Sandmann and Stoecker returned for the 2009 workshop.

Participants in 2007 also expressed interest in exploring interest in exploring publication venues for engaged scholarship. The 2008 workshop closed with a panel of journal editors and other representatives discussing the focus, submission guidelines, and review process for the major journals in the field. Journals represented on the panel included the *Journal of Higher Education, Outreach, and Engagement,* the *Journal of Community Engaged Scholarship,* the *Journal of Community Engagement in Higher Education,* the *International Journal of Volunteer Administration,* and *Action Research.* Given the wide interest in this topic, the panel hosted by EESW, will be open to NOSC general conference attendees in 2009.

Small-Group Mentoring

The Emerging Engagement Scholars Workshop connects emerging scholars with veteran mentors in outreach and engagement through small-group mentoring sessions, as an introduction to the conference and to the field of engaged scholarship. Mentoring remains the central focus of the workshop curriculum through 2009. At the first EESW event participants used this time to network, and develop ideas toward integrating outreach and engagement teaching, research, and service in the early career. Initially, workshop organizers created the facilitated dialogue groups based on a synthesis of the applicants' research interests, based on the application essays. The groups coalesced around one of three themes: (1) discipline-based engaged scholarship; (2) scholarship of engagement; and; (3) service-learning and student success. In 2008, small groups were identified based on disciplinary background or research topic, and facilitators wereassigned according to their experience in a particular area.

In the first year, over several conversations, we refined the workshop's definition of "mentor" to mean specifically a visible and active veteran scholar-practitioner who has an established publication record in the scholarship of community engagement, and also in a particular discipline. The mentor would have the singular responsibility of advising the emerging scholars on their scholarly interests during the conference. The individual mentors discuss with the emerging engagement scholars whether or not their relationship could continue beyond the conference. We felt the point of interaction with these mentors would provide emerging scholars with impetus they might need to build stronger relationships across a community of scholars between all of the workshop participants, and those who attended the larger host conference. We aimed the workshop toward the integration of cross-disciplinary scholarly goals as well as their specific disciplinary areas of outreach and engagement. Successful mentoring relationships would provide exemplars for other emergent scholars, thereby creating a snowball effect for recruitment of new participants.

453

Initially, group facilitators were solicited from a larger group identified by the Outreach Scholarship Conference program coordinator of those veteran scholars across outreach and engagement presenting sessions at the general conference who might be interested in serving in such a role. A longer planning timeline in 2008 and 2009 has allowed us to recruit mentors who are recognized for their expertise in the field of community-university engagement, but who are not necessarily presenting at the conference. With the requirement for a research proposal from applicants, the planning committee asked mentors to review and prepare written feedback for each participant in their small group to share during the workshop. The mentor-facilitators were also responsible for leading group discussion of each proposal, allowing all members of the small group to offer suggestions for the further development of each participant's proposed project.

The Emerging Engagement Scholars Workshop reflects intentional planning to realize the founding planning committee's goals for the workshop. By adding the research proposal requirement to the application process, focusing the small group work on these proposals, and offering master classes on the literature and practice of engagement, we have achieved the desired outcomes outlined in the logic model presented in Figure 1, "Outcomes of the Emerging Engagement Scholars Workshop."

Learning Outcomes and Participant Feedback

The primary purpose of the Emerging Engagement Scholars Workshop was initially envisioned as providing mentoring for emerging engagement scholars, while increasing scholarly-based networking experiences for advanced graduate students and early career scholars and practitioners of outreach and engagement. Survey data and participant feedback from the workshop, collected each year, contributes to the ongoing development of the workshop curriculum and pedagogical models, as well as providing data to document the need for and the benefits of an infrastructure for professional development for engagement scholarship.

In 2007, the planning committee conducted a preworkshop survey of the workshop participants (N = 14), as well as a postworkshop evaluation including the original survey's questions as context to their experience of the workshop and postworkshop plans for involvement (N = 15). Prior to the workshop, most participants wanted to learn how to connect community-based research to both their scholarly interests and their professional experience. Specifically, the participants wanted the workshop to help them address the following key topics: how to build an engaged research agenda, integrating scholarly responsibilities with outreach and engagement, building an infrastructure for outreach and engagement in their professional role, building reciprocal and equitable outreach and engagement partnerships with communities, and shaping career as an engaged scholar.

In the postconference evaluation, the 2007 cohort indicated that, as a result of the workshop, they found the following questions answered through their participation: how to build a career as an engaged scholar, how to integrate their scholarly responsibilities with outreach and engagement, and how to build an infrastructure for outreach and engagement in their professional role. Topics suggested by the participants for future workshops explore including opportunities and impacts for university engagement to address broader social issues beyond the program or campus level; balancing professional outreach responsibilities with pursuit of a research agenda, especially for non-tenure-track faculty who are also administrators completing graduate work; and the proactive development of institutional processes and culture change to support engaged scholars.

Moreover, when asked at the evaluation's end what elements of the workshop experience they believed would help them move to the next step in their career as a result of the workshop, the participants found networking with both established and emerging scholars as the most helpful opportunities. Additionally, they emphasized gaining access to more scholarly resources to support their continued professional development in specific areas, including proposing community-based and community-engaged research at small institutions or those institutions that do not have strong commitments to engaged scholarship; designing community-engaged research as multidisciplinary projects; and involving undergraduate students. Participants also asked for examples of application materials or research plans to support their upcoming search for tenure-track faculty or other positions in university engagement initiatives or community-based organizations.

These evaluations suggested that, in 2007, we were successful in providing a workshop experience that met the cohort's stated needs. However, at the recommendation of senior scholars, the workshop planning process shifted in 2008, moving away from meeting the self-identified needs of participants toward the more standardized curriculum discussed earlier, which focuses on foundational scholarship, building research skills, and exploring issues of power in working with or in communities. The 2008 evaluations again confirm the importance and value of the small-group mentoring approach. All respondents agreed or strongly agreed that the discussions helped them look at their own research in a more critical way, and most agreed that the experience broadened their thinking about research methods in engaged scholarship. The small-group mentoring conversations also helped nearly all participants consider ways to more meaningfully include community partners in their research. Participant comments were overwhelmingly positive about the learning facilitated in these small groups as well:

> "Excellent! Most useful part of this entire experience. So great!"

> "This was the best part of the conference, and illustrated the ideals we were here to discuss."

> "Facilitator obviously spent time with my proposal and the written feedback was helpful to take away. Didn't expect others' (peers/facilitator) enthusiasm & interest in my proposal—pleasant!"

The small-group approach is providing workshop participants with what participants call "a very good opportunity" to refine their research, benefiting from the input of established and emerging scholars.

One area where the workshop continues to fall short of its values is in the involvement of community members in the workshop teaching team. In 2007, we offered a closing panel on career paths in community-university engagement. One community representative participated on the panel. She was an effective speaker, and engaging. However, the structure of the panel did not allow for addressing issues inherent in community-university partnerships. In an attempt to address this, the 2008 planning committee added the Engaging with Communities master class and invited a recognized authority on the topic to facilitate the class. The agenda also included an evening presentation on a community-university partnership. EESW participants responded very positively to the master class. All participants responding to the evaluation (n = 12) found the content "very good" or "excellent," and most agreed that the presentation was useful (n = 11). Their comments elaborated on these points:

> "Examples given fascinating [and] pertinent"

> "Group exercise [and] Randy's expertise, model, and examples from real-life experience were very helpful."

> "[Benefited from] very interactive session especially strategy of [identifying] a potential research question and design in small groups."

Despite the high quality of the presentation, 7 of 12 respondents found this presentation of little or no use in their work, and one questioned the relevance of the material to their own research. The specific challenge here is in working with communities with which the workshop planning committee is not familiar. It has proven somewhat difficult to identify community members who are available and willing to participate in the workshop. Those who have participated have typically been fit into a particular slot designed by the workshop organizers, rather than incorporated as teachers. The planning committee remains committed to including community members as workshop faculty. Barriers to be overcome in the process include negotiating the cultural and, sometimes more significantly, resource availability differences between community organizations and universities (Kezar, 2009). Community members do want to be involved in initiatives like the Emerging Engagement Workshop, and we can learn more about realizing this goal from organizations such as Community-Campus Partnerships for Health and the HBCU Faculty Development Network, where community members are regular participants (CCPH, 2007).

We share this element of the planning in this transparent way, because we believe that our experience is representative of the engaged scholar's efforts to work with community members. There is obviously a lot of good will on both sides; still, the relationships require time, commitment, and open communication to develop to their full potential. We continue to work on this element of the workshop and look forward to learning from community members about how we might be better partners in these efforts. We are optimistic about the prospects for further development of the workshop on this and other issues, especially in light of the growing support for, and efforts to build, a coordinated infrastructure supporting professional development of community engaged scholars.

Recalling the recommendations from Austin and Barnes (2005) and Nelson (2006), the EESW planning committee discussed feedback received from participants who do not aspire to be faculty members and want something in the workshop to help them explore other career options. In 2008, the explicit decision was that although there is certainly room to consider non-professoriate-track career development in the large discussion about preparing engaged scholars, this workshop will focus on people who either want to be (and are very close to becoming) or already are faculty members or researchers. Moreover, we need to more actively promote the EESW to those applied professional academic programs such as social work, urban planning, the creative arts and humanities, sociology, and public health. We know that there are other graduate student engagement programs for some of these disciplines through national associations such as Imagining America (creative arts and humanities-focused) and Community-Campus Partnerships for Health (public-health-focused). Since the 2007 EESW, we have disseminated the recruitment announcement through the NOSC membership lists and those of HENCE and NCSUE (which includes contacting executive-level individuals who represent both organizations in HENCE). Yet, we may have to ensure that the individual associations and institutional members are more proactive in additionally disseminating the recruitment announcement.

Sustaining the Emerging Engagement Scholar Workshop

Three themes dominate the service-learning and community-university engagement literature in higher education regarding current and future faculty involvement in community-university engagement: the need to further understand faculty motivations for involvement in community engagement in the context of their traditional academic roles, as well as disciplinary and community perceptions of these efforts (Fear, Rosaen, Bawden, & Foster-Fishman, 2006; O'Meara, 2005; Rice, 2005); the need for more documentation of institutional mechanisms to support faculty involvement in outreach and engagement, especially making outreach and engagement part of the promotion and tenure system (Driscoll, 2000; Gelmon, Holland, Driscoll, Spring, & Kerrigan, 2001; Holland, 1999; O'Meara, 2001, 2002); and the need to understand how junior faculty and undergraduate and graduate students involved in outreach and engagement are socialized about their work within the academy (Austin & Barnes, 2005; Ward, 2003).

The Emerging Engagement Scholars Workshop represents one element of a growing infrastructure of professional development and mentoring programs designed to support faculty as leaders in changing university culture. Advanced graduate students participating in the workshop also benefit from deepening their awareness of and skills in mobilizing key aspects of engaged scholarship. Ward (2003) has argued for reconceptualizing community engagement as an integration of the traditional faculty roles of teaching, research and service, rather than an additional role. The workshop curriculum draws on this idea to model new approaches to faculty work, and in doing so also socializes future faculty to become advocates.

Promising developments such as the annual Engagement Academy hosted by Virginia Tech and faculty development programs such as the University of New Hampshire's Outreach Scholars Academy provide other crucial opportunities for senior administrators and mid-career faculty, respectively. These various programs reflect an intentional commitment on the part of leading institutions and organizations to invest human and fiscal resources in supporting infrastructure building and culture change to realize the promise of policy recommendations encouraging transformation of the perceptions, values, and practices of institutions.

457

References

Altbach, P. (1999). Patterns in higher education development. In P. G. Altbach, R. O. Berdahl, & P. J. Gumport (Eds.). *American higher education in the twenty-first century: Social, political, and economic challenges.* Baltimore: Johns Hopkins University Press.

Austin, A. E., & Barnes, B. J. (2005). Preparing doctoral students for faculty careers that contribute to the public good. In A. J. Kezar, T.C. Chambers, & J. C. Burkhardt (Eds.), *Higher education for the public good: Emerging voices from a national movement.* San Francisco: Jossey-Bass.

Community-Campus Partnerships for Health (CCPH). (2007). *Achieving the promise of authentic community-higher education partnerships: Community partners speak out!* Seattle, WA: Community-Campus Partnerships for Health. Available at http://www.johnsonfdn.org/Publications/ConferenceReports/2007/AuthenticCommunityHigherEd.html.

Driscoll, A. (2000, Fall). Studying faculty and service-learning: Directions for inquiry and development. *Michigan Journal of Community Service Learning, 35–41.*

Fear, F. A., Rosaen, C. L., Bawden, R. J., & Foster-Fishman, P. G. (2006). *Coming to critical engagement: An autoethnographic exploration.* Lanham, MD: University Press of America.

Gaff, J. G. (2005). Preparing future faculty and multiple forms of scholarship. In K. O'Meara K. & R. E. Rice (Eds.), *Faculty priorities reconsidered: Rewarding multiple forms of scholarship.* San Francisco: Jossey-Bass.

Gelmon, S. B., Holland, B. A., Driscoll, A., Spring, A., & Kerrigan, S. (2001). *Assessing service-learning and civic engagement: Principles and techniques.* Providence, RI: Campus Compact.

Holland, B. A. (1999). Factors and strategies that influence faculty involvement in public service. *Journal of Public Service & Outreach, 4*(1), 37–43.

Kezar, A. J. (2009, April). *Culture clashes and their impact on helping low-income students attend college: An examination of partnerships to offer Individual Development Accounts (IDAS).* Paper presented at the annual meeting of the American Educational Research Association, San Diego, CA.

Moore, T. L., & Ward, K. A. (2008). Documenting engagement: Faculty perspectives on self representation for promotion and tenure. *Journal of Higher Education Outreach and Engagement, 12*(4), 5–28.

Nelson, P. D. (2006). *Civic engagement and scholarship: Implications for graduate education in psychology.* Retrieved online February 3, 2006 from http://www.apa.org/ed/slce/altman.html.

O'Meara, K. A. (2001). Assessing and improving outreach through objectives. *Journal of Higher Education Outreach and Engagement, 6*(2), 45–56.

O'Meara, K. A. (2002). *Scholarship unbound: Assessing service as scholarship for promotion and tenure.* New York: Routledge Falmer.

O'Meara, K. (2005). Principles of good practice: Encouraging multiple forms of scholarship in policy and practice. In K. O'Meara K. & R. E. Rice (Eds.), *Faculty priorities reconsidered: Rewarding multiple forms of scholarship.* San Francisco: Jossey-Bass.

Rice, R. E. (2005). The future of the scholarly work of faculty. In K. O'Meara K. & R. E. Rice (Eds.), *Faculty priorities reconsidered: Rewarding multiple forms of scholarship.* San Francisco: Jossey-Bass.

Sullivan, W. M., & Rosen, M. S. (2008). *A new agenda for higher education: Shaping a life of the mind for practice.* San Francisco: Jossey-Bass.

Ward, K. (2003). *Faculty service roles and the scholarship of engagement.* ASHE-ERIC Higher Education Report, Vol. 29, No. 5. San Francisco: Jossey-Bass.

UPBEAT: University Engagement through Virtuous Knowledge Sharing and Academic Staff Development

James A. Powell

O ver the past decade, the University of Salford has responded in a unique way to the national and global challenges it has faced. This reflects the particular academic strength of the staff and the situation in which it found itself in the middle to late 1990s. This strategy, developed in the light of a changing environment, focuses in particular on its development of Academic Enterprise (Æ) as a means of promoting better work not only with industry and commerce, but also with other stakeholders, such as those in civil and voluntary organizations, in the community at large, and not least, within the university itself. This chapter condenses findings relating to the development and formative evaluation of more than two hundred case studies of how universities have successfully built mutually beneficial relationships with their local businesses and communities, giving them the confidence to develop, for themselves, successful social and community enterprises. The result is the UPBEAT matrix, a model for transforming traditional academics into enterprising ones. The UPBEAT approach recognizes four underlying skills that are needed to fertilize a novel academic idea, enabling it to bloom in the knowledge economy: *business acumen* and *individual performance* are two key skills essential in making any social enterprise work effectively and efficiently; *social networking intelligence* and *foresight enabling skills* are also critical to success in today's complex knowledge economy. This chapter demonstrates how the UPBEAT project management matrix helps academics develop and continuously to improve these four skills in parallel. The chapter also briefly illustrates how the tool has been used to achieve success in three quite different social enterprises: Contraception: The Board Game, Community Banks, and Bouncing Higher, a balanced learning approach that helps small businesses become more innovative for wealth creation.

459

Development of Academic Enterprise (Æ)

These are exciting times in higher education as universities work more closely with business and the community to harness the undoubted imagination and reason of formidable academics and combine it with the drive and daring of local entrepreneurs. Local universities in the United Kingdom have always reached out to develop best academic-enterprise practice. In the knowledge economy, academic-enterprise practices may well be the key to future wealth creation and improvement in the quality of all our lives. Salford University recognized the need to undertake this practice and began to prepare itself to virtuously share knowledge with all its partners. This unique form of enterprise developed at Salford University is known as Academic Enterprise (Powell, 2001; Powell, Harloe, & Goldsmith, 2000), and focuses particularly on the development of socially inclusive wealth creation. Academic Enterprise is also an approach to staff development focusing on enabling staff to become more enterprising and thereby to have a greater opportunity to induce cultural change.

In 1998, Burton Clark identified key characteristics that defined the entrepreneurial universities of the day. He focused on those universities that grew, not just in their research and teaching income, but also in working relationships with business and industry. Such universities were characterized by a conscious effort to innovate in how they went about their business and how they positioned themselves to make substantial shifts in organizational character in order to arrive at a more promising position for the future.

In order to bring about the necessary change processes required to embed Æ in the university, it was first necessary to develop an internal vision that could be shared by everybody in the institution. A small Æ core team felt that the real basis for achieving success in the new activity was a strong linkage between the words "academic" and "enterprise" and their joint actions, creating a new phrase (Æ) and activity and suggesting an inseparable interface to guide this new stream of university work. The team wanted academic colleagues to undertake bold new academic pursuits reflecting their clear academic values, knowledge, and capabilities.

The hallmark of Salford University's Æ approach lay in opening up the formidable skills and imagination of its own staff, developed through rigorous evaluation and sound research, undertaken on the basis of the highest academic values, for reasoned specifications for actions in the real world. Academic Enterprise is also about having the daring to work in creative enterprise partnerships to stage-manage novel yet robust ideas, innovations, approaches, and technologies into actual improvements for all partners, and beyond.

The deep partnerships formed with local entrepreneurs became the key focus of everything Salford now does, building on the drive and commercialism of our partners and thereby compleimenting our own capabilities and strengths. Although I believe in the knowledge economy, it is also the case that success will only arise from the right collaborations with those who truly have recognition of the rich systemic and global nature of all future enterprise, partnerships with business, industry, and the community would be those also at the leading edge in terms of practical applications. Together, such partnerships would transfer necessary knowledge and technology between each other for the benefit of the university and its partners, enabling both to flourish. Armed with this image, the Æ team sought to share its vision across the university so that all staff would directly own the Æ vision for themselves. Such ownership was seen as critical in embedding the process of social change more deeply within the institution and ensuring full development of Æ. All too often, new ways of working fail to develop because those involved do not understand their new roles, or find new objectives to be mutually incompatible with their existing ideas, or do not agree with the new vision—or what is even worse, actively disagree with the new vision and continually fight to overturn its implementation.

After almost a decade in full operation, Æ has secured significant changes and many real improvements. Almost 30 percent of our academics are fully enterprising, engaging with business and the community in new and different ways. The university itself has developed improved ways of working with strategic partnerships in industry, commerce, and the public and voluntary sectors. All staff have found that the new Æ way of working leads to real rewards, not only in financial returns or progress in an enterprise itself, but also in their teaching and learning and research. Furthermore, the Æ approach has been seen by our own government ministries, and their funding agencies, as both pioneering and exemplary. Now, Æ is fully integrated into all aspects of University of Salford life.

The Importance of Virtuous Knowledge Sharing and UPBEAT

Key in Æ is the way we share our academic insights with others and thus combine them with the daring insights of our community partners. It is the caring way through which we share knowledge that brings mutual benefits to both sides. Such a concept of virtuous knowledge sharing begins to recognize higher education's obligation to broader society and also acknowledges that knowledge is created in many social and economic practices outside of higher education itself. It also suggests a new paradigm of understanding and action that governments could champion and their policies reflect. Quality engagement with society, the community, and business in general should be the new paradigm, not technology or knowledge transfer. The former implies a genuine interchange, a genuine engagement; the latter implies a one-way movement of knowledge from academe to business and community in general. Considerable evidence now supports the idea that it is through genuine, sustained, and quality engagement with all its external partners that a university makes its own contribution to knowledge production and delivery. It follows from this that the production, transfer, and sharing of knowledge must be seen as iterative rather than linear processes, and that practice and theoretical knowledge are simply subsets of knowledge as a whole. This can be best understood through what I have previously referred to as the model of virtuous knowledge sharing cycle (Powell, Sharp, & Davies, 2003; see figure 32.1).

The starting point for any workable co-creating relationship between a university and an external partner is to identify the strengths that each side brings to the relationship. Traditionally, higher education provides the space and independence to think the unthinkable, to test ideas in a rigorous way, bringing reason to bear, and to turn imagination into a sustainable theory; sometimes this is portrayed by the community as ivory tower thinking. But it also provides the necessary critical distance needed to be foresightful and truth searching. Conversely, time is of the essence in business, industry, and the community; they already have a drive to be daring and need to confirm the possible, rather than agonize over the unlikely, and reject the improbable. Their approach is often characterized as the quick and dirty look. However, both sides now need each other and to work in a transdisciplinary way

461

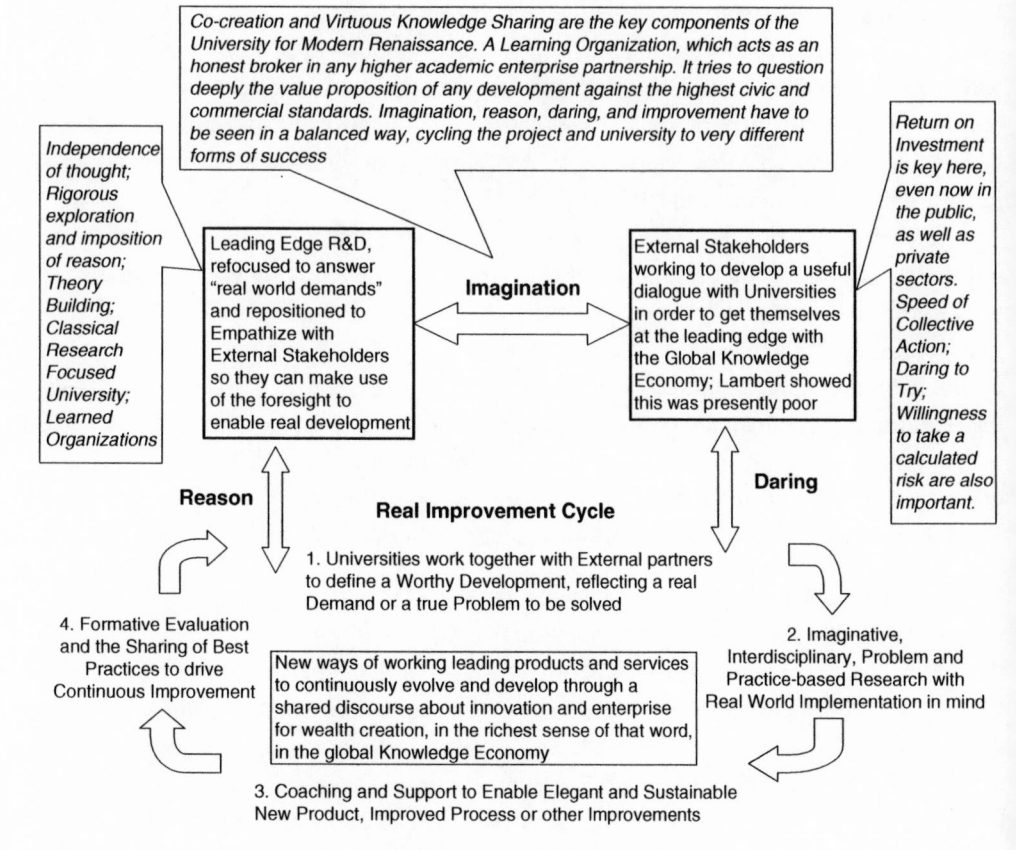

Co-creation and Virtuous Knowledge Sharing are the key components of the University for Modern Renaissance. A Learning Organization, which acts as an honest broker in any higher academic enterprise partnership. It tries to question deeply the value proposition of any development against the highest civic and commercial standards. Imagination, reason, daring, and improvement have to be seen in a balanced way, cycling the project and university to very different forms of success

Independence of thought; Rigorous exploration and imposition of reason; Theory Building; Classical Research Focused University; Learned Organizations

Leading Edge R&D, refocused to answer "real world demands" and repositioned to Empathize with External Stakeholders so they can make use of the foresight to enable real development

Imagination

External Stakeholders working to develop a useful dialogue with Universities in order to get themselves at the leading edge with the Global Knowledge Economy; Lambert showed this was presently poor

Return on Investment is key here, even now in the public, as well as private sectors. Speed of Collective Action; Daring to Try; Willingness to take a calculated risk are also important.

Reason

Daring

Real Improvement Cycle

1. Universities work together with External partners to define a Worthy Development, reflecting a real Demand or a true Problem to be solved

4. Formative Evaluation and the Sharing of Best Practices to drive Continuous Improvement

New ways of working leading products and services to continuously evolve and develop through a shared discourse about innovation and enterprise for wealth creation, in the richest sense of that word, in the global Knowledge Economy

2. Imaginative, Interdisciplinary, Problem and Practice-based Research with Real World Implementation in mind

3. Coaching and Support to Enable Elegant and Sustainable New Product, Improved Process or other Improvements

FIGURE 32.1 Virtuous Knowledge Sharing Cycle (Powell, 2007 Extended)

to develop innovative and cost-effective future enabled technologies, products, and processes that work in complex environments and systems, often influenced by humans who continually change their wants and demands. So, in the global knowledge economy, co-creation is an absolutely necessary process to enable sustainable success.

After having generated a basic process for improving our relationships with business and the community, how did we convince academics to become more enterprising, to engage in Æ? When I started Æ a decade ago, some of my academic colleagues thought I had sold out my intellectual soul to business and commerce. Initially, they were not terribly keen to follow my lead, or to adopt the knowledge-sharing principles I was recommending them to accept as part of the necessary change process. To convince them, I had to create some exemplary major projects in each Faculty (school or department) of the University. So, to get the ball rolling and to make it worthwhile for academics to engage in this new way of working, we sought funding to free up the time of early adopters to get involved in Æ. We then developed a careful reward scheme to attract colleagues into developing their own new academic opportunities beyond the means they were currently employing. I then set about designing and testing a new staff development process that would enable and empower the right kinds of academics to learn how to become more enterprising in the most appropriate ways.

The approach I developed, with four other like-minded universities, was called UPBEAT. UPBEAT stands for University Partnership for Benchmarking Enterprise and Associated Technologies. Our hope was that academics would develop their own more enterprising practices in fast-acting ways. What does the UPBEAT process focus on to improve the capacities of traditional academic who are already excellent teachers and researchers? In short, it attempts to help them understand the importance of four extra human skills that are complementary to their existing roles as academics, but essential for successful development of Æ (see the lower segment of figure 32.2).

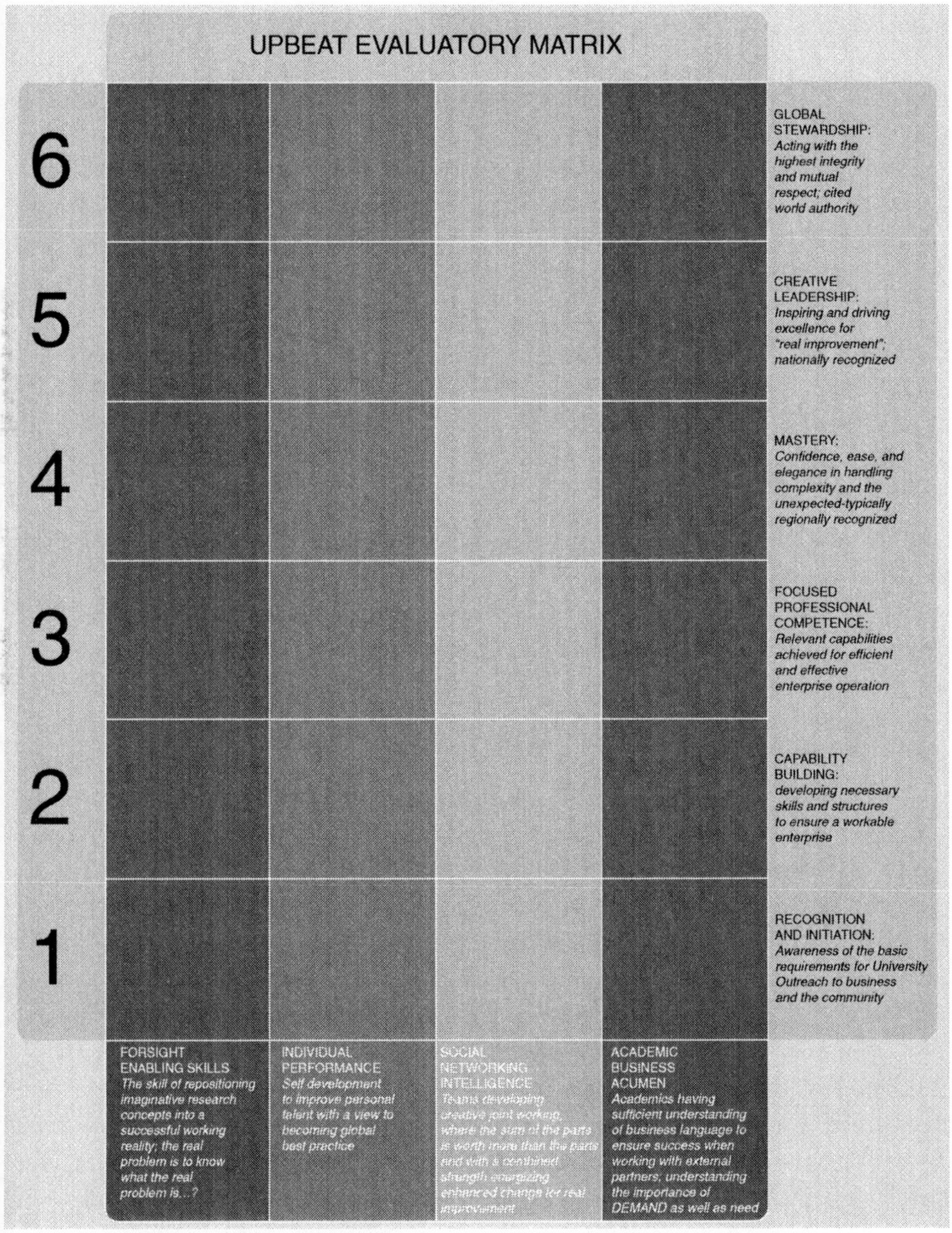

UPBEAT EVALUATORY MATRIX

6 GLOBAL STEWARDSHIP: *Acting with the highest integrity and mutual respect; cited world authority*

5 CREATIVE LEADERSHIP: *Inspiring and driving excellence for "real improvement"; nationally recognized*

4 MASTERY: *Confidence, ease, and elegance in handling complexity and the unexpected-typically regionally recognized*

3 FOCUSED PROFESSIONAL COMPETENCE: *Relevant capabilities achieved for efficient and effective enterprise operation*

2 CAPABILITY BUILDING: *developing necessary skills and structures to ensure a workable enterprise*

1 RECOGNITION AND INITIATION: *Awareness of the basic requirements for University Outreach to business and the community*

FORSIGHT ENABLING SKILLS *The skill of repositioning imaginative research concepts into a successful working reality; the real problem is to know what the real problem is...?*

INDIVIDUAL PERFORMANCE *Self development to improve personal talent with a view to becoming global best practice*

SOCIAL NETWORKING INTELLIGENCE *Teams developing creative joint working, where the sum of the parts is worth more than the parts find with a combined strength energizing enhanced change for real improvement*

ACADEMIC BUSINESS ACUMEN *Academics having sufficient understanding of business language to ensure success when working with external partners; understanding the importance of DEMAND as well as need*

FIGURE 32.2 The UPBEAT Evaluatory Matrix

Whereas academics often develop research ideas that can lead to new products or processes that are meant to satisfy particular human needs or desires, they often do this by undertaking rigorous experimental studies to make sure they fully understand a particular situation or need. They often do not consider how they can turn a theory they have built into useful foresight that will actually enable a real improvement. So, for the development of enterprising academics, the first skill we try to engender, through UPBEAT, is what I call the *foresight enabling skill.* This only requires a small, but hugely important, change in mindset of academics, so they begin to reformulate their often fairly abstract notions with respect to some findings or a theory into something usable that will actually lead to a practical reality or implementation. I have to say, I have found that academics can quickly learn how to turn such conceptual thought into a working reality, when they know what it is they have to explain differently in order to help their external partners understand better the implications of what these partners need to do.

However, it is not sufficient for such academics to know how to express better their scholarly work. Academics also need to get a demand-side view when developing any higher Æ. They need to learn, not to how tell the community what they need to know, but how to have a conversation with the community through which they can properly share knowledge for co-production and co-creation. In particular, they have to learn more than what is needed, but rather, what will be demanded by customers in sufficient numbers so that their enterprise development will eventually become something that will be financially viable. For, in an enterprise context, it is no good to just develop something that is needed, if people won't demand it sufficiently to pay a realistic amount to purchase it. It is my contention that all Æ's have to break even financially, at the very least. Furthermore, academics also need to communicate their ideas in nonjargon language in which any technical information is made truly accessible.

Ideally, academic entrepreneurs should also strive to make a good return on the university investment, in terms of a profit or other relevant reward. I call this skill *academic business acumen,* and such a skill requires enterprising academics to learn sufficient awareness of the demand side, and especially key aspects of business, to have reasoned conversations, and sensitive arguments, with creative partners from business, industry, or the community. Academics need such a skill, not to become business people by themselves, but to be able to incorporate such business thinking into their developing enterprise, to ensure that it eventually becomes a sustainable business.

Knowledge about product design, design for production, and marketing are just three concepts from business academics need to embrace. However, I repeat, the UPBEAT ambition, with respect to academic business acumen, is not to turn academics into business people, only to develop in them a language for meaningful discussion and conversation, so that there can be mutual understanding of each other's position in any joint enterprise.

UPBEAT's third enterprising skill development looks inward to the academics themselves and aims to ensure that they become sufficiently stimulated to want to develop personal individual performance to the highest levels, especially with respect to their particular individual talents. To help drive academic personal performance forward, the university needs to develop an appropriate reward schedule to encourage continuous professional improvement in the academic performance. For most academics, this can often simply be in terms of promotion, on the basis of Æ, up the traditional academic hierarchy. Even then, I believe that academics of the right type, who want to become more enterprising, need to be supported in improving their enterprise by performance and must be willing to work hard to become part of sustainable and creative teams, and ideally also want to eventually lead such teams. I simply call this enterprising academic skills developing strong *individual performance*.

Finally, with respect to developing their enterprising skills, academics also need to develop *social network intelligence,* so they can make the most from their own enterprising capabilities by working in harness with other team members who have complementary skills. For only through proper socialization will the sum of a creative team's parts add innovatively more than the value of the individual parts by themselves. Gone are the days when individuals, no matter how creative they may be, can solve most problems by themselves. Social networking intelligence is initially about collaboration. It grows into creative team work. It then develops into growing interdisciplinary partnerships, and at the highest level it relates to the formation of strategic alliances that drive any innovation on to new heights. It is the binding force that ties all the other skills together.

These four complementary enterprise skills need to be engendered in the traditional academic, to ensure they become usefully enterprising. This model of entrepreneurial staff development is referred to as the Enterprising Academic Model (see figure 2). Having understood the need for the four new skills, it is also important to understand what qualities and levels of these skills need to be developed. It appears that it is the development of qualities and levels of engagement with respect to these skills that is the most generally and important to the progress of almost all forms of academic enterprise.

On the basis of this engagement dimension, it is necessary to create an engagement axis of what can now be seen as an evaluating matrix (see figure 32.2). And this matrix can then be used for any traditional academics who want to continuously improve their own enterprising ability, helping them develop appropriate enterprise skills, gradually, continuously, consistently, and sustainably for the good of any academic enterprise. For any new project the developing academic entrepreneur would have to start by recognizing how, and with whom, they need to engage creatively in order to initiate a sound, yet innovative, enterprise. They would then need to start building necessary enterprise capacity to properly undertake a project from the broad range of perspectives possible to ensure success in the knowledge economy. At engagement level 3 on this axis (figure 2) in the processes of gradually improving a team's creative and systemic development, the immediate enterprise projects starts to be handled competently, so that the team begins to be on top of its immediate job. However, it is not until level 4 that team members have sufficient mastery of their roles that they can properly negotiate an overall solution from a position of strength, where each team member knows when to give and take for the benefit of the overall team performance. At this stage, team members can also think about taking on higher level of even more complex enterprise projects.

The higher engagement levels on this model show the development of the enterprise to be working quite well and is where the team, or at least some of its members, are seen to become creative leaders in their own right. Such leaders often extend the scope of any

465

existing project, spin off new subprojects, or perhaps even start completely new projects. At the top level of engagement, the team or some of its leaders start to act as stewards in a global context, having response from almost everyone, as they become de facto world authorities of their chosen enterprise topic or agenda. So, on the UPBEAT matrix, and for enterprise skill development, there are six levels of engagement, having increasing qualities with respect to engagements within the creative team, between strategic alliances, and increasingly with others in the knowledge economy. Taken together, the development of the four underlying enterprise skills represents, in effect, a balance score card approach to drive forward any enterprising academic development.

In order to help assess a team's enterprising progress, at any given time, the UPBEAT approach provides a set of generic questions to focus an Æ project leader's attention on the next engagement skills that need to be developed. Ideally, all enterprising developments should work to progress the four engagement skills, gradually, measurably, and in parallel. This ensures that increasing the overall performance of the enterprising team really progresses in an optimum way. If the UPBEAT evaluatory matrix is filled in formally, on a regular basis, by the leaders and their teams, they will get an immediate self-evaluation of their progress and a sign of what they next need to do to become even better. This is the best way to quickly improve the quality of a creative team's enterprise engagements, in order that together they will drive real and innovative enterprise progress. The actual performance indicators used to drive such improvements are of necessity individualized to any one innovation project, but the matrix does give a leader, or team members, an early indication of a project situation and its team's progress against other enterprise teams. For these reasons, the team ought to be developing each of the four skills in a balanced and parallel way.

Using the evaluative matrix gives enterprise project leaders a template for staff development and a step-by-step project management guide to any academic enterprise project. It also helps individual academics learn how to improve their own individual enterprising skills, as well as enabling them to recognize what needs to be done to maximize the overall performance of the team. Our evidence on hundreds of cases shows the UPBEAT approach drives improved the enterprise behavior of the academics both quickly and effectively. An UPBEAT analysis can be done quickly and easily, in a fairly comprehensive way, often in less than two or three hours to begin with, and then in a matter of minutes for any upgrade. Then, such an analysis can be used regularly as a project management tool to drive the next stage of improvement of any individual project, and indeed it really does lead to continuous project improvement. The tool can also be used to compare the progress of several projects and to aid enterprise project assessment, development, and management. In order to aid the effectiveness and efficiency of this UPBEATing process, an electronic tool has recently been developed. (A demonstration of this tool can be seen at www.escendency.com—simply hit the UPBEAT demo button at the bottom of the home page for the presentation.) I hope this enabling process will help any university efficiently see the current state of any enterprise project quickly and effectively enable them to evaluate projects against each other and ensure that they develop enterprises conforming to the highest triple-bottom-line (economic, social, and environmental) principles, making them truly fit for purpose in the global knowledge economy.

For Salford University, UPBEAT has become part of a key university goal, as is reflected in its strategic framework. In particular, it is used as the key performance assessment tool helping it measure this primary university goal and thus driving the university to become a world leader in developing successful international partnerships with business and the community. All my studies, including the ones relating to UPBEAT (Powell, 2005, 2007, 2008; Powell et al., 2006), demonstrate that successful higher academic enterprise mainly occurs through co-creation, where new technologies, solutions, products, or services are successfully supplied to satisfy real client/user needs, and then properly applied to meet real business demands. This usually means that the university has to provide a wider range of support and coaching than is conventional, with similar reverse coaching by the eventual end client, sponsor, user, or customer. The key here is deep-level conversations, with active listening and mutual coaching, to ensure a collective understanding to enable real and sustainable change.

Key Indicators of Success

Salford University uses two major indicators to measure the progress of its developing Æs. The first relates to quantitative measures of output, income growth, and gross value added and financial contributions; these are critical for a university wishing to improve the quality and range of its enterprising academic provision, in order to enable it to flourish in a changing world. The second are the qualitative indicators of outcomes, real improvement, and quality of life; these often less tangible indicators normally relate directly to the strategic academic mission and vision of the university, and the detailed objectives developed to show it has achieved success against its own high-level values or goals. An earlier part of this chapter gave an anecdotal feel for some of these impacts, in terms of improved academic interest in, and acceptance of, Æ by staff within the university, and particularly the buzz so far created at Salford University through Æ. These are indeed good qualitative measures of success. However, in this section I also describe some of the other external facing outcomes, specifically measured by us to ascertain progress. I then highlight just three of a myriad of examples of best practice developments to date to give a deeper narrative feel of our many successful projects.

Quantitative Impact: In today's world, it will hardly surprise anyone to learn that finances are a key indicator of overall success. The simple fact is that repositioning the University of Salford as a premier league enterprising university requires considerable investment. In theory, it may be possible to boost investment in new situations where income is declining, but there are not many successful examples of this, at least in the university sector, as far as I am aware. So a primary requirement at the start of Æ was income growth on projects that enabled socially inclusive wealth creation for our partners and ourselves. This latter criterion is a key academic value driver with respect to the university's mission. The institution therefore sought, through Æ, new sources of funding to add to its traditional public resourcing; this in turn would enable me, as the then direct leader of Æ, to have the ability to initiate novel projects as pilots of a change process while appropriately redistributing scarce existing resources to developments more relevant for an enterprising university. I inherited a

467

Table 1. Æ Income/Contribution for the Past Nine Years

Year	1998–99	1999–2000	2000–01	2001–02	2002–03	2003–04	2004–05	2005–06	2006–07	Total
Contribution	Reinvestment	Reinvestment	Reinvestment	£1M	£2M	£1.4M	£1.3M	£1.2M	£6M	£12M
Income (millions to nearest million)	£3M	£5M	£6M	£9M	£16M	£18M	£17M	£17M	£21M	£112M

traditional commercial enterprise function that had lost not only its direction, but even the ability to financially break even, let alone to produce a profit. I soon realized this was because the previous strategy was too commercially focused and did not understand the proper role of a university in reaching out to business and the community. The new strategy saw a dramatic turnaround in this situation as illustrated by the Æ Income/Contribution for the past nine years (see table 1).

Indeed, by way of a fuller example of growth, in the latest year of financial returns the university shows a rise in income from all Æ activities to well over £21 million, with the university's part in developing a purposely designed building to promote innovation with small businesses and the community worth a capital sum of £5 million. The Salford Innovation Forum, as a quality building, developed as a hub to drive improved relations with the citizens of Salford, their small businesses, and the University of Salford and is now regularly used by university staff and their strategic partners as they co-create for mutual benefit.

Furthermore, because Æ was initiated at times of financial stringency in the university, I required all core AE staff to earn 20 percent in excess of their salary so that we could fund necessary revenue costs without needing to call upon the university reserves for extra finances. This amounted to an extra income stream, in those early years of between £300,000 and £500,000, which is not accounted for in table 1. All income surplus to expenditure was reinvested during those early years to keep the division working effectively and until Æ was allowed to use it in more constructive ways to promote university Æ. There are also other value adds to this financial return, and these are shown in table 2.

On a final quick performance indicator note, the national profile of University of Salford's progress in AE has clearly been fully recognized by the Higher Education Funding Council for England. Over the course of three years of development, our allocation from them, known as the Higher Education Innovation Fund (HEIF), will improve from about £650K per annum in the first year to £1.1 million in the second year, £1.5 million in the third year, and 1.8 million in 2009–10. We are now close to being top of the league for enterprise support and will soon be capped for the HEIF allocation; this demonstrates that we are now on a par with some of the best enterprise universities in the United Kingdom. In confirmation of importance of the foregoing returns, an independent financial evaluation of the University of Salford indicates that the university is punching well above its weight with respect to Æ; indeed, their estimate indicates this to be about £5 million above our peer benchmark university group.

Qualitative Impact: At its inception the Æ team set itself some clear targets for qualitative growth, including two major academic enterprise projects per Faculty, and two

468

Table 2. Summarizing Other Value-Added Initiatives Relating to Our Key Performance Measures for a Typical Year

Number of major new Æ projects	20
Number of new spin out/start-up companies initiated and supported	15
Number of students supported under BEST—an enterprise support program	150
Companies under venture development	5
Small business clubs formed	14
New e-learning developments (courses)	10
Number of SMEs assisted through Æ	250
SMEs trading electronically with Æ support	150
Value of new research Activities led by Æ reflected in British Research Selectivity Exercise Returns	£2–3 million
SMEs advised	250
Student placement in business and community	600
New industry networks/clusters formed	20
New products/services to market	35
CPD people training programs	500
Grants and contracts—regeneration activity primarily funded by public agencies	98
Consultancy, products, and services—the provision of expert advice and work involving analysis, measurement, testing, and intellectual input	187
Staff exchanges—staff placements into industry	12
Knowledge Transfer Partnerships—collaboration between a company, a university academic, and a graduate to work on a company project of strategic importance	10

Note: Data only identify partnerships with a financial relationship and exclude non-fee community activity. The definition of partnerships is a sustained and meaningful relationship with an external stakeholder(s) which leads to mutually beneficial outcomes. The financial benchmark is based on a minimum contract value of £2,000.

cross-university projects per annum; all projects were designed and developed to reflect a major ethos and goal of the senior academics leading the different parts of the university. In fact, on average more than twenty new, innovative, and ground, breaking projects have been initiated each year since its inception, with more than 150 examples of good practice.

Before describing three projects in some detail, let me name just a few, to show examples of the range of quality developments so far initiated:

- CONSTRUCT IT won a Queen's Award for the way it has helped the construction industry flourish using academic developments.
- Community Finance Solutions won the Times Higher Education award for Community Enterprise in helping communities develop and manage their own Community Banks; this

team has now increased its interests into the development of develop Community Land Trusts, which will help disadvantaged communities design and run their own affordable housing programs.

- Barbara Hastings-Asatorian was voted one of the top five women innovators for her Contraceptive Board game development (see later detailed example).
- The Salford Film Festival premiered an award-winning Salford short video, and this has led to a resurgence of film making in Salford's New Deal area, with extra finances being made available for community film/video making.
- *Freeflow* is a successful university website that portrays the capabilities of our music students to the world and gets our students jobs on the global stage.
- Our Business Creation Units promote university spin-outs, and also welcome and nurture small businesses spinning in to work with University staff and students for mutual returns.
- Our WISE project helps women entrepreneurs gain confidence to be innovative for their own wealth creation.
- Our links with the Asian Business Federation have led to improved innovation by ethnic minority groups in Manchester City-Region.
- Our Asia Link project has developed productive working links with China, Japan, and Malaysia to promote joint partnerships in the area of Design Management.
- The Salford Community Media Network is a joint project with a small high-tech digital company, the Manchester Community Information Network, aiming to develop local reporters for the broadcast arenas of the British Broadcasting Corporation and Granada.
- Kidscan is a charity set up to enable the development of focused drugs to help children's cancer and has led to two pharmaceutical products in second-stage clinical testing.
- Our Finance section of the University has developed a successful electronic procurement services for higher education.
- The Core team has recently won a major European contract with the Ministries of Education, Industry, and Trade in the Czech Republic to help them develop programs of enterprise and employer-focused education and development that will also help their own universities engage more fully with European businesses and the communities.
- Bouncing Higher is a balanced learning approach that helped 130 small to medium-sized enterprises (SMEs) increase their gross value-added profitability through innovation.

This is an extensive list, and all projects are now developed using the UPBEAT approach as a mechanism to ensure enterprise project management success. Table 2 summarized other value-added initiatives relating to our key performance measures for a typical year. Furthermore, against goal 1 in the strategic framework of the University, we undertook a further twenty-five fully completed UPBEAT analyses during this year, with a further thirty or more presently under analysis. Eight of these are now considered at an international level.

Our university UPBEAT team has further developed its website and is presently producing video vignettes relating to the best British reach-out practices with respect to leadership, governance. and management. (These are available on the UPBEAT web-site–www.upbet.eu.com.) Furthermore, guidance materials and a supporting video have already been produced to accelerate the development of Æ, and they enable more advanced and cost-effective partnering for mutual benefit of ourselves and our partners.

Three examples showing the deeper quality of Salford Æ, presented next, in a narrative form, are brief case studies portraying our success in major new academic enterprise ventures. It is hoped that this will give the reader a better understanding of the depth of our Æ's activities in a contextually rich way.

Contraception—the Board Game

This example of entrepreneurial academics relates to an enterprise development by one of our maternity nurse lecturers, Barbara Hastings-Asatourian. She designed and developed *Contraception, the Board Game* in order to aid young nurse trainees cope better with explaining to other young people how they could avoid unwanted pregnancies. The method of developing this concept was to let the young demonstrate best principles of the safe use of contraception through a simple board game, similar in nature to the game Monopoly, which is played throughout the world. Because some parents had failed to apprise their children of all the implications of unprotected sex, Barbara had developed a game to embed important new attitudes and behaviors with respect to all aspects of contraception in a fun but highly informative way. Thus, previously vulnerable young citizens could learn to act more responsibly.

This development, originally adopted across all Salford Schools, resulted in a significant reduction in local teenage pregnancies. The game has now been used throughout the United Kingdom and in many other English-speaking countries. Originally a game for the use of a few individuals, it has also now been made into a computer game to engage whole classes. It has also been translated into French and Spanish and is being used worldwide. Furthermore, Barbara and her team have recently developed an additional board game based on sociocultural research in Africa. This new game has been developed with particular emphasis on the prevention of acquired immunodeficiency syndrome (AIDS) in South Africa and works well in a totally different cultural context. This game is called *SaferSex*.

Community Finance Solutions and Salford Money Line

After many years working as a housing association professional and Justice of the Peace, Bob Patterson took early retirement to work with Æ staff to develop his idea of community banks. He saw such banks as challenging the mainstream banks and financial institutions and also attacking the stranglehold over the poor held by loan sharks and check-cashing services. After seeing at first hand many cases of poverty and increasing debt, he perceived that there was a need for access to financial services (as basic as a bank account) by an ever-growing excluded group in the poorest and most disadvantaged areas of the UK's cities. This problem is also worldwide.

The Æ funding team helped win the resources necessary to undertake rigorous and ground-breaking research in Salford's Institute of Social Research. Significant sponsorship by the Leverhulme Trust enabled the problem and potential solutions to be properly scoped, and then benchmarked against the world's best practices. Figure 32.3 gives a visual portrayal of the problems that the financially disenfranchised face. What figure 32.3 shows is that,

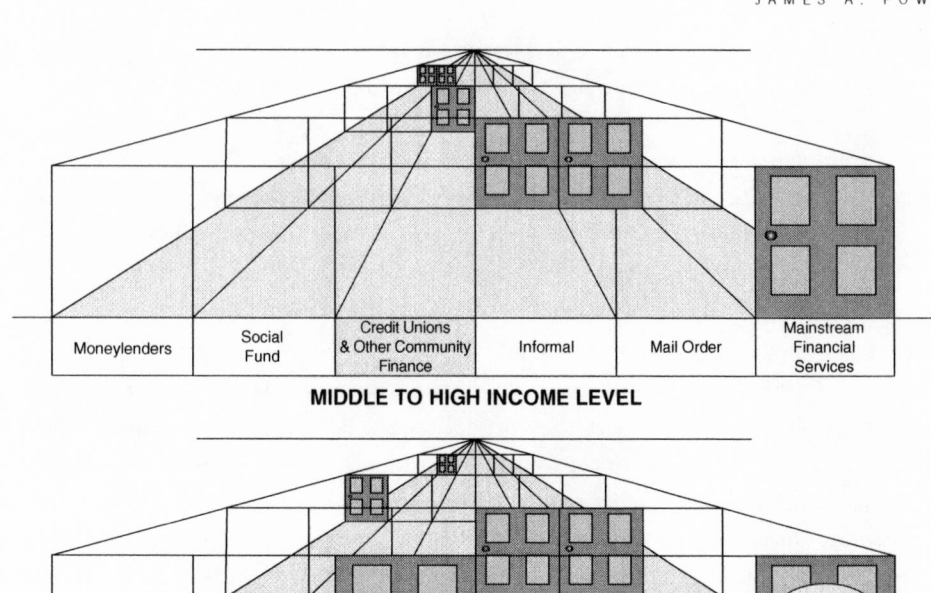

| Moneylenders | Social Fund | Credit Unions & Other Community Finance | Informal | Mail Order | Mainstream Financial Services |

MIDDLE TO HIGH INCOME LEVEL

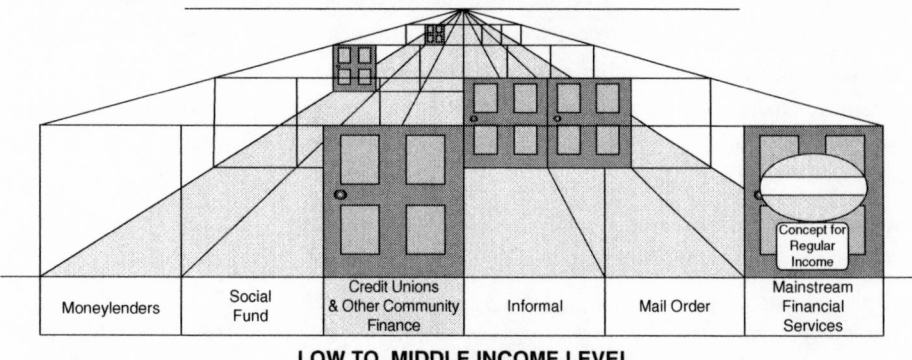

| Moneylenders | Social Fund | Credit Unions & Other Community Finance | Informal | Mail Order | Mainstream Financial Services |

LOW TO MIDDLE INCOME LEVEL

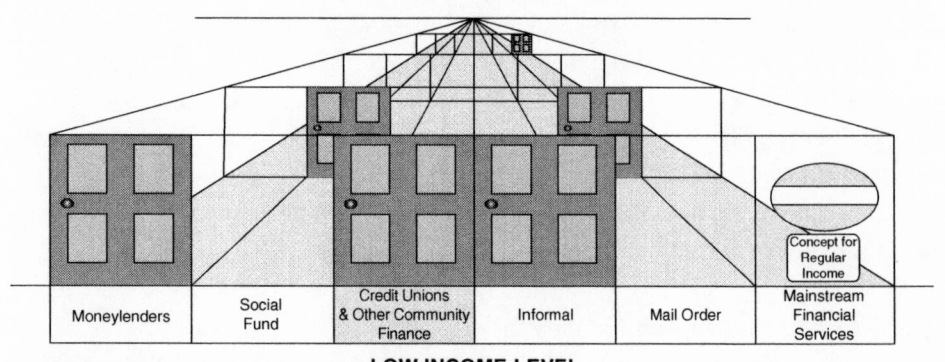

| Moneylenders | Social Fund | Credit Unions & Other Community Finance | Informal | Mail Order | Mainstream Financial Services |

LOW INCOME LEVEL

FIGURE 32.3 A Visual Portrayal of the Problems That the Financially Disenfranchised Face

whereas to most of us the doors are open to mainstream banking and almost any other loan facility, this is not the case for the poor, who often do not have a bank account. In their place, a number of rather seedy alternatives do open up to them, which often forces them further into debt.

This Æ-supported research has led to the setting up of thirteen community banks with collectively more than £20 million on reserve for on-lending. Money Line was launched in December 2000 and now has more than £1.8 million on reserve to help needy individuals and enterprises. This credit risk transfer (CRT) goes beyond the activities of banks and credit unions by supplying credit to those unable to save, owner-occupiers unable to realize their assets, start-up businesses, and other excluded by mainstream financial services.

472

So far, there have been almost £2 million worth of loans made by the thirteen community banks, with a very small number of defaulters to date. The Æ has been central to the development of these and future CRTs by working to facilitate the plans and potential of a number of private, public, and third-sector partners and enabling the contacts to develop in and with the communities that CRTs will serve. Continuous monitoring and formative evaluation by Æ researchers throughout the development are enabling the programs to reach their full potential. Æ evaluators are now undertaking summative evaluation in order to be able to give full recommendations to the British Government as to how it might be able to develop the idea on a national basis with some confidence. Because of the early success of the project, the CRT team is presently working up the next phase of this important community banking. Five city-based and one rural bank are presently being considered.

As well as assisting individuals with low-cost loans to improve lives, the CRTs will be a useful new tool to help various agencies, and ultimately society, to tackle poverty and those who prey on the financially weakest in our town and cities.

Bouncing Higher or Networking North West

Bouncing Higher was a film project at the University of Salford that ran between 2004 and 2007. It was developed to address the issues relating to poor take-up of traditional business support by small to medium-sized enterprises and low levels of engagement of the business community with higher education institutions. Originally funded by the North West Development Agency (NWDA), Network North West was specifically developed to improve innovation, entrepreneurship, enterprise, and wealth creation in the Northwest's SME business community through educational micronetworking, to learn from, and with, others in a similar position in other SMEs using action learning techniques that allow the participants to set the agenda for what they need to learn. At the same time, the project is able to benchmark best practice in this form of business support regionally, nationally, and internationally.

Working with six delivery partner universities across the North West of England, the support was multidisciplinary and multifaceted (including applied research, knowledge transfer, management and professional development, and provision of sector-specific training for employees) and there was potential to deliver support in the form of face-to-face contact or online resources. The project, seen as exemplary by the NWDA, has since delivered support for Manchester Chamber Business Enterprises to a further cohort of SMEs across Greater Manchester and the core process has been adopted as the basis for a second level of intervention for leadership development by the Northern Leadership Academy. It also significantly improved the profitability of the SMEs that took part through the impact of innovative processes and developments enabled by the action learning.

These three examples represent a myriad of Salford's successful higher academic enterprises. They each have enterprising academics in the lead, creative teams that share knowledge with their local business and community partners, and the ability to get academics co-creating with diverse teams of others on worthy projects.

Early Thoughts on a New Model of Universities for Modern Renaissance

From the preceding work, a new model suggested itself to the author for those engaged universities wishing to fully embrace their creative city regions. This has been styled as Universities for Modern Renaissance (UMR) (see table 4). In this context, the following issues were felt to be important as guiding questions in helping us make these thoughts more coherent and concrete, namely:

How can universities best understand that third stream income is more than another source of income and realize the idea of creative outreach to business and community in their city-regions?

Table 4 Early thoughts on the New Model for a Modern Renaissance shown in comparison with the 'Old Renaissance'

Renaissance OLD	Renaissance NEW
University as institution not in the center of the revival	University as institution central actor and initiator of knowledge society activities and structures
Small part of society concerned (but growing, bigger than before, aspiring to grow further)	Large part of society concerned, aspiring to reach as many individuals as possible in the "knowledge society"
Natural sciences not centrally important (decline after early rise in thirteenth century and before rise in early seventeenth century	Natural sciences of central importance and visibility, linked to economic prowess of society
Concepts of Knowledge refers to common canonical body of knowledge, common sources, dream of a commonly held worldview	Diversified sources/labyrinthine source of information, defying possibility of creating common body of knowledge, systematizing knowledge is becoming increasingly difficult, growing specialization creates different knowledge cultures and niches. Nature of systematic understanding is to understand their own position in the system
One religion reviewed, adapted but still upheld as common ultimate reference frame	Many religions and many agnostics. Religious beliefs rigidifying into fundamentalisms or dissolving in their function as common reference frame
Mono	Pluralism, not even trying to systematizing Liberation of knowledge production from institution. Liberating the individual, rebirth in the ownership, live with diversity
Knowledge concentrated	
Individual human as central motor of innovation and heart of creativity	Individual human as central motor of innovation and heart of creativity
Dream of human possibilities being far greater than their realization	Dream of human possibilities being far greater than their realization

(Countinued)

Table 4. (*Countinued*)

Renaissance OLD	Renaissance NEW
Idea of a new relevance of classical knowledge: applying human values and concepts of antiquity to fifteenth/sixteenth century urban society	Idea of new relevance of formal university knowledge?
New thrust of theory into practice, will to link theoretical scholarship with urban (political and economic) practice	New thrust of theory into practice, will to link scientific theories with urban (political and economic) practice
Rise of creative arts	Rise of creative arts?
Rise of engineering, innovation important for urban economic and social welfare	Rise of engineering, innovation important for urban economic and social welfare, proliferation/embedding of engineering know-how in all domains of daily life
New heightened status/ acceptance of scholar or artist (eating at the table of nobility)	New status of knowledge workers (university professors, researchers, experts)

Should some universities also focus in a complementary way on higher academic enterprise, rather than, or as well as, simply being classical or pedagogical universities?

Should universities get away from limiting themselves to the traditional role of pursuing basic research, long-term blue-sky research, teaching, and learning and seek more medium-term relevance to business and society?

Should such universities not show there is complementarity of business relevance and basic research?

An affirmative discussion of these questions led to the formulation of a new model and role for the university. Such a model demands more than opening up universities to the idea of innovation, and contribution to knowledge production and creation of intellectual property. It would call for reaching out to a wider set of actors, with public interest for mutual development of the global knowledge economy for the mutual benefit of all. C^5U is the consortium name of the seven universities involved in the EUA project Creativity in Higher Education. The 5 refers to the five aspects of a creative university: talent and leadership, creative team working, creative relationships and governance, creative communities of practice, and creative city regions. C^5U believes that ideally all enterprising universities that wish to properly engage in the global knowledge economy can help create a modern renaissance for their own city-regions. Such a renaissance best starts within creative cities themselves and can be initiated by the either universities or city region partners, but ideally they should work together in co-production to create solutions that are best fit for purpose in the knowledge economy. Therefore, a major focus of C^5U's work was concerned with seeing if the guiding principles behind Universities for Modern Renaissance could be defined and justified for all those universities that want to have co-creation as a key part of their mission.

However, such a renaissance can only be initiated by a creative university working with its creative communities.

In my view, the University for Modern Renaissance is, and should continue to be, animated by a deep belief that theory can be made relevant for practice and that practice is relevant for theory. Its pursuit of knowledge is thus characterized by combining the reflective distance necessary for finding new paths with a quest to engage in dialogue with the world and to identify and solve its current and future problems through enhanced understanding and systematization. Universities for Modern Renaissance share with the Renaissance itself a belief that human possibilities stretch far beyond their current realization and seeks to explore ways in which human knowledge can help to realize human potential for the good of all. It is thus not just an institution in which reflective scholarship reigns but also a social actor, because it seeks new solutions and practices that compensate for social, political, and economic shortfalls.

Conclusion

The generic model of best practice, namely, virtuous knowledge sharing and the Universities for Modern Renaissance, are not new in the sense that we (the C^{5}U) invented them, but they are important to us because we have tried to reposition relevant other models to make them appropriate for the current context, make them explicit, and explain them in the context of creative universities working creatively with their creative city-regions. We have also based our findings on real-world experience of our universities and others involved in the context of our discussion about creativity. So, for instance, Universities for Modern Renaissance share a core set of values, which inspire and direct their actions. This core is what is new here, and it should determine the characterization of all universities in future. This core also determines a new attitude to the actual types of activities that a given institution of higher education is undertaking. Universities for Modern Renaissance promote a rupture with the prevailing models of higher education. The rupture consists in the explicit, programmatic integration of the pursuit of academic excellence with the engagement with its outside environment. Engagement is not a by-product of real academic work, but it inspires and nurtures all activities of the universities, both traditional on-campus activities and nontraditional activities. In the age of globalization and knowledge society, Universities for Modern Renaissance agree that they need to act differently in order to contribute to and/enable socially inclusive wealth co-creation. Renaissance is justified here because, as for the classical Renaissance, the human being is put in the center of an active and self-liberating approach.

A Final Independent Endorsement of Academic Enterprise

The University of Salford Æ now has a national and international reputation outside the university, with many of its projects being heralded by the Council for Industry and Higher Education, Universities UK, the Higher Education Funding Council of England, and the Lambert Review as being exemplars of best practice. As a major stream of all university activity, Æ is also increasingly being seen to be at the leading edge and a powerful example of its kind by many other universities in the UK, especially by those who are directly aware of its work through UPBEAT. This has been formally endorsed this year, as a result of a major benchmarking exercise undertaken for the Engineering and Physical Science Research Council. In 2007, Lancaster University was commissioned to undertake a series of comparative benchmarks of universities that had adopted open reach-out practices, such as those we have adopted here at University of Salford in Æ. These cases, which included one at Lancaster University, put University of Salford to the top of the list, in terms of good practice. Their review related to the broad range of activities relating to all aspect of Æ, activities that University of Salford is more than happy to have itself judged against, rather than the more conventional one of commercial activity alone. Included in the reference is the study undertaken by Lockett (2007) that clearly spells out what he, and his researchers, felt to be our major strengths, our ability to deliver a broad range of academic enterprises against our core mission. What is particularly heartening to me were the comments made by twenty-five of our own staff when interviewed by Lockett; the staff interviewed came from across all disciplines, from core Æ and in the Faculties, and from academics and support staff. Their positive comments about the powerful embedding of Æ into the Schools and Faculties, together with the recent progress we had clearly made in developing this new University-wide division, were reinforced by other comments made by our external stakeholders; they also waxed lyrical about the innovation, quality, and professionalism of our entire enterprising delivery. This latter study, in its complete form, has been well received by ESRC, who have now commissioned Lancaster University, under the leadership of Professor Mary Rose, to do a fuller study of the most successful universities, leading to a major new book on enterprising university reach-out. This will become a follow up to Burton Clarke's most influential book, on the Enterprise Universities, now almost a decade old.

Looking to the Future

Academic Enterprise is work in progress, so it would be inappropriate to draw any final conclusions. However, looking more broadly forward, the future external development landscape of all university activities will continue to relate more constructively with their local businesses and communities. Such activities must be more responsive and relevant to the needs and demands of clients and end users. They must continue to reflect high academic standards and the findings of rigorous research and scholarship. Finally, because they are to work in the real world, they must either ensure commercial partners keep competitive and flourish financially or truly reflect human aspirations. This university has begun to professionalize all its academic and managerial activities and is learning to become responsive, delivering quickly and effectively and following up consistently. It is now working to ensure that its profile and strengths are visible to all key decision makers, but it never ceases to be on the lookout to spot new and emerging opportunities as they arise.

Our future integrated strategy will be one that shows a true coincidence of purpose and breadth of scope in everything we do. In developing our vision for Æ we are seeking to attract students, partners, collaborators, investors, and employees who wish to participate in,

477

contribute to, and share this vision. The university is also striving to find cost-effective ways of delivering quality products and processes demanded by society. So our goal is to remain at the leading edge in niche markets and deliverables. However, we also must keep our friendly and listening nature, and build on our international partnerships to enable us to achieve more than our resources allow. This is expressed by the clear and simple phrase Enterprising University globally aware for local delivery, or in a more expansive mode, University for Modern Renaissance.

UPBEAT is the University Partnership to Benchmark Enterprise Activities and Technologies project by a consortium of the British Universities of Teesside, Westminster, Leeds Metropolitan, Lancaster, and Salford, with six overseas partner institutions [Twente (Holland), Salamanca (Spain), Deusto (Spain), Hochschule Wismar (Germany), Varna Free (Bulgaria), Budapest Business School (Hungary)] funded by the Council for Industry and Higher Education, Higher Education Funding Council of England, and the Engineering and Physical Sciences Research Council; the consortium seeks to drive improved university reach-out to business and the community or what the consortium prefers to call Higher Academic Enterprise. This chapter is based, in part, on a paper presented at the AUCEA Annual Conference, University of the Sunshine Coast, Queensland, Australia, July 2008.

References

Clark, B. R. (1998). *Creating entrepreneurial universities—Organisational pathways of transformation* (p. 163). Issues in Higher Education. IAU Press/Elsevier.

EUA. (2006), *Creativity in higher education—a Socrates project and briefing note.* Available at http://www.eua.be/eua/jsp/upload/ 2006.

Lockett, N. (2007, October). *Extended knowledge transfer study—Salford University.* Published by Info-Lab 21 for EPSRC. Lancaster University Press.

Powell, J. A. (2001). The noble art of academic enterprise—The Percival Lecture. *Transactions of the Manchester Literary & Philosophical Society.*

Powell, J. A. (2005). *UPBEAT—University Partnership for Benchmarking Enterprise and Associated Technologies.* University of Salford Press.

Powell, J. A. (2007, October). *Creative universities and their creative city regions in industry and higher education* (pp 323–335).

Powell, J. A. (2008, May) An UPBEAT Approach to stimulating enhanced social and community enterprise. In the *Proceedings of the Business University International Forum of Japan,* Niigata.

Powell, J. A., Druzhin, G., Khrykov, Y., Lawrence, K., Matei, L., Ozsoy, A., et al. (2006). *Final report to the EUA in its Socrates funded Creative Education Programme undertaken by the Creative Universities for Creative City-Regions Consortium.* European Universities Association.

Powell, J. A., Harloe, M., & Goldsmith, M. (2000). *Achieving cultural change: Embedding enterprise.* Paper presented at the IMHE Conference "Beyond the Entrepreneurial University," OECD, Paris.

Powell, J. A., Sharp, J., & Davies, J. (2003). Developing entrepreneurs in SMEs. Paper presented at the 13th Annual Small Businesses and Entrepreneurship Development Conference entitled "Research Paradigms in Entrepreneurship and Small Businesses," University of Surrey, Guildford, UK.

Coming to Engagement: Critical Reflection and Transformation

Frank A. Fear

This chapter is an extension of the book *Coming to Critical Engagement* (Fear, Rosaen, Bawden, & Foster-Fishman, 2006), a volume that I co-authored with a multidisciplinary team of Michigan State University (MSU) scholars. Over a period of nearly five years we analyzed our engagement experiences (we had not worked previously on a common project) and considered how our engagement thinking and practices had changed over time. That work set the stage for developing a common frame of reference about engagement: formulating an engagement vocabulary (e.g., engaged learning, a concept to be defined later in this chapter) and articulating a discourse, which we labeled "critical engagement." Critical engagement involves analyzing self, subject, and situation independently and at the intersections. In the book we analyzed *text* ("the work"—service, outreach, and engagement), *subtext* (our evolving selves—from extenders of knowledge to engaged scholars), and *context* (frames of reference associated with our work as engaged scholars—changing circumstances in society, higher education, and our respective disciplines-professions). Through extended dialogue—over time, and about an array of issues—we gained a deeper understanding of how it feels to be engaged, and how (and why) engagement had become an indelible characteristic of our work and identity.

Both contributions—the book and this chapter—are autoethnographic in genre, which is a postmodern form of inquiry (Patton, 2002). In reflexive authoethnography (the intent in this chapter) "authors ... bend back on self and look more deeply at self-other interactions ... [such that] personal experience becomes important primarily in how it illuminates ... [the subject] ... under study" (Ellis & Bochner, 2000, p. 740). In so doing, analysts can expose "a vulnerable self that is moved by and may be moved through, refract, and resist cultural interpretations" (Ellis & Bochner, 2000, p. 739).

Consistent with an autoethnographic style, no truth claims are made in this chapter. Interpretations of two types are made: critical reflection of personally experienced engagement episodes, and observations about engagement experiences, generally. Fundamentally, this chapter represents an expression of engaged scholarship, one dimension of what it means to be a scholar-practitioner. Specifically, it is about reflecting critically on engagement practice for the purpose of informing scholarly understanding. The other dimension of scholarly practice occurs when the outcomes of critical reflection (scholarly understanding) are drawn upon to inform and improve engagement practice. These dimensions are connected dynamically in a never-ending cycle, such that the next step for me (as an engaged scholar, having written this chapter) is to apply this learning in future engagement episodes. There will be extensive applications because engagement is a defining characteristic of my work. It applies—as a stance and practice—in a variety of forms and settings: in project-based university-community partnerships, here and abroad; for student development at the undergraduate and graduate levels; in managing and leading higher education through the administrative function; through faculty leadership and development efforts; and as an engaged citizen in community affairs.

A range of experiences across those domains provides the experiential backdrop for the assumptions, assertions, and conclusions presented in this chapter. The ties that bind are the quest to sharpen my understanding and the desire to share my learning with others, including those who have contributed significantly to my learning.

Engagement as Hospitality

The launch point for this analysis is what can take place when engagement is interpreted as a *response to an invitation*. John B. Bennett (2003) writes expressively about that form of engagement—he refers to it as "hospitable engagement"—with emphasis on "connectivity and imaginative empathy ... and dedication to the needs of the other" (p. 37). Hospitable engagement begins when a person extends to others an invitation to engage. Conversation (and fluid conversation, at that), Bennett asserts, is the bedrock of this form of engagement: there is no master of ceremonies, no keeper of the gate, and no hierarchies or predetermined course of action. What happens among those involved is an emergent property of interaction: a result of being together (face-to-face and through other means)—of exchanging thoughts and feelings, and participating in a give-and-take style.

I have found there to be a "quest for connectedness" in hospitable engagement. For example, a number of my colleagues, friends, and family members are dedicated to voluntary community work. They engage with others in purposeful ways with the intent of serving others through community engagement. They tell me that it gives meaning to their lives and, sometimes, it contributes to a preferred definition of self—a self-interpreted preference, how they want to be known to others. When that happens, engagement becomes an important life feature. That understanding leads me to believe that for some (and certainly for me) engagement is more than a practice routine or an approach to community-based work: it is a way of being in the world, an ethic and an identity, as well as a catalyst for personal and professional growth. The outcome can be transformational. Bennett (2003) elaborates:

480

hospitable engagement can be threatening as well as enriching—challenging our comfortable truths, but also enlarging them and compensating for limitations in our understanding.... A newly, jointly constructed world may then emerge. (p. 48)

There is often a pattern to engagement of this sort: participants come voluntarily; script engagement together in-real time; talk about topics of mutual interest; and create an action plan together. A colleague's experience in a congregational setting is a case in point: through guided facilitation (organized and co-led by her) church members used deliberative dialogue to identify space planning options, evaluate alternatives, and select the optimal option. The experience was democratic and collaborative, that is, engaged.

For me, engagement at its best occurs when people share thoughts and feelings expressively, openly, and respectfully; and they enjoy spending time together and participating in mutual exchange. When that happens there is joy and, because of that, the experience becomes memorable for those involved. In *Coming to Critical Engagement* (Fear et al., 2006), we describe the feeling this way: *"You look forward to (being together), relish being with (each other), and glance fondly back on (the time spent together)"* (p. 297, emphasis added).

Exploring the Felt Experience

This depiction may seem to be an idyllic representation, more hopeful than real. However— and this is one of the messages of this chapter—it does exist. At issue is understanding engagement as felt experience, learning how to stimulate its spread, and making it a more pervasive feature of organizational, civic, and professional life.

From personal experience it seems engagement of this type is more possible when those involved:

- Make a commitment to this way of being together, including investing time in it, and "sticking with it" through stressful times
- View it as an opportunity for learning (about self, other, and the work in which they are involved)
- Believe that important, tangible benefits (personal and otherwise) accrue from its exercise, and
- Conclude that it is worth the investment to engage this way.

Sometimes, this way of being together predates our involvement; others invite us to join them at the table. There are other times when opportunities are made possible through our agency: we initiate things and are hospitable to others. As for outcomes, sometimes this way of being together "works," and the sense of effectiveness begins at (or nearly at) the beginning of an episode. In other instances, it works, but the sense of its value comes only with time. It can also be Sisyphean, those involved trying to make something work, only to have it unravel, and then feeling compelled to start anew. And there is the option of trying but, later, giving up—to disengage. Disengagement happens for any number of reasons, including feeling unwanted; sensing that the time is not right; recognizing personal unwillingness to invest the time, energy, and emotion necessary; and accepting the reality that no matter

481

how hard one tries to make something happen, it is not to be—the situation has been compromised, the relationship(s) broken, and the opportunity lost.

Irrespective of circumstance, *feeling* engaged is the outcome of being in a relationship with others in an effort that has personal meaning, something that is personally worthwhile—"full bodied ... with 'experiential validity and personal valence' (Fear et al., 2006, p. 46). Another way of saying that is to conclude that engagement's value includes, but extends beyond, what can be accomplished by it: there is also engagement's spiritual value. James Moffett (1994, pp. 19–20) addresses the spiritual dimension when he writes:

> Spirit compares to breath, unseen but felt, experienced from moment to moment with every respiration, representing the life force that animates us and the rest of creation, uniting all things within it. *Inspiration is breathing in, aspiration is breathing toward, and conspiring is breathing together.* (emphasis added)

I see *in*spiration (the breathing in) in engagement all the time: somebody, driven by a strong sense of something (be it passion, commitment, or a sense of obligation), makes a public stand or, at the very least, comes forward to exert leadership on behalf of a collective value or goal. Making that declaration draws others to the table, which enables *con*spiration (breathing together). This act of collective intent is expressed (with time and attention) as the desire to achieve specific outcomes that serve the collective interest. Action, when taken, represents *a*spiration (breathing toward), accomplishing something together that improves circumstances. When all of this happens—the outcome of inspiration, conspiration, and aspiration in dynamic interplay—then "leadership for the public good" takes place (Fear et al., 2006, pp. 280–281).

Understanding What It Means to Be and Feel Engaged: A Story

None of what I have just described takes place without feeling emotionally engaged. Consider how this feeling is described by Paulo Coelho in his metaphysical narrative, *The Alchemist* (1988).

Santiago—an Andalusian shepherd boy—travels from his homeland of Spain to the Egyptian desert in search of a treasure he believes is buried in the Pyramids. Along the way, Santiago comes in contact with many people who help him (directly or indirectly) in his quest, including an alchemist. The alchemist offers Santiago this advice: "Remember that wherever your heart is, there you will find your treasure. You've got to find the treasure, so that everything you have learned along the way can make sense" (pp. 116–117). After a seemingly endless journey, Santiago reaches the desert. He believes what the alchemist told him, so he listens closely to what his heart has to say. But he finds that his heart says many things, not just one thing, and he is not sure what that means. Unsettled about a direction or course of action, Santiago presses ahead, hoping that clarity will come. If not, he will not only fail in his quest, he will also be lost in the desert. As he "climbs yet another dune, his heart whispers: *Be aware of the place where you are brought to tears. That's where I am, and that's where your treasure is*" (p. 159, emphasis added).

There is poignant reason for referencing this book and citing the passage from it; and it is all about engagement as interpreted here. The book was read by a group of co-learners in an undergraduate course setting, recommended to those involved (including me) by one of the students, Emily: she had read it with others in high school. The book had meaning to her, speaking to the way that she felt about her family. She thought that reading the book might bring out similar feelings in us, enabling us to connect it to important experiences in our own lives. We agreed to read the book. Afterward, we engaged in robust, emotion-laden discussion. During the discussion I recall one of the students, Rachel, saying that she wanted the passage about tears to be incorporated in her wedding ceremony.

Along with the others in the class, I reflected on the text and what it meant to me in professional terms. I recalled that there were *always* tears associated with my most memorable engagement experiences—sometimes as a response of anticipation, happiness, and joy, and, at other times, as a reaction to anxiety, frustration, and hopelessness. The affirmative emotions were expressions of my passion and commitment—to the people and/or to the "cause"—of feeling exhilarated for being a part, or having been a part, of something important. On the other hand, emotions of anguish came at times when I felt stretched beyond my comfort zone, facing seemingly insurmountable challenges: I did not know what to do, how to respond, or even if I could respond appropriately (Fear, Rosaen, Foster-Fishman, & Bawden, 2001). And there have been times of dismay: with the best intentions and hard work, things did not turn out well—the project or effort failed—leaving me feeling that I had let down others and, with that, that I had let down myself.

The discussion of *The Alchemist* in class came at the time when I was searching for an appropriate way to write the closing pages of *Coming to Critical Engagement*. I thought about the depth of thought and feeling enabled by Emily's hospitality (i.e., offering the book to us); and I reflected on what had transpired through the engaged experience of reading and discussing the book with students. Based on those reflections I decided to include the passage from *The Alchemist* on the second to the last page of the book (Fear et al., 2006, p. 296). Then, on the book's last page, I wrote these words:

Engagement ... is our treasure; it is in our hearts; it helps us make sense of things; and it brings us to tears. But, more than anything else, it fuels passion for our work in ways that Kay Redfield Jamison (2004) describes as *exuberance:* "It spreads upward and outward, like pollen toted by dancing bees, and in this carrying ideas are moved and actions taken" (p. 4). When you are exuberant you are alive, full of energy and hope. (p. 297)

The possibility of Emily's story was enabled by actions taken years earlier—taking the ideas expressed in this chapter (in nascent stage at that time) and creating a learning environment where what happened to Emily, others, and me could become a regular occurrence. It started in the mid-1990s at Michigan State University when I (with others) began exploring what it would be like if we could create an engagement program, primarily for undergraduate students, where students could experience engagement and become proficient at it. After going through the fits and starts of trying to design a learning space and academic program that we had not experienced before, the Bailey Scholars Program emerged (http://www.bsp.msu.edu/). The program is dedicated to whole-person development, organized as a 21-credit undergraduate specialization, and it has been in existence since 1998 (see Fear & Doberneck, 2004).

Students self-select into the program and self-organize their time: each Scholar prepares an individualized learning plan (to guide learning activities and objectives, overall, and to inform 12 credits of elective courses); and all Scholars—including faculty—co-design credit-bearing learning experiences in the form of three 3-credit core courses. The core courses are designed in real time—that is, the syllabus for each course is created anew each time it is offered—by those at the table, together. In Bailey, the faculty members do not teach: they convene learning experiences and participate as co-learners *with* students, such that *all* aspects of course experiences are co-created by participants. Through collaboration, participants decide what to learn; how, when, and where to learn it; and how to assess the quality and impact of learning.

In this learning environment, course participants—such as Emily—are invited to share with others what they want to learn. Emily could have said that she wanted to read a new book—one that she had always wanted to read. Instead, she invited us to read a book that held personal meaning, thinking (and probably hoping) that it might stir similar feelings in us. We accepted her invitation, choosing it from among an array of other options. From that point, what happened was no longer Emily's choice; it was ours.

What takes place in Bailey (as illustrated in Emily's story) is an example of what my colleagues and I describe as *engaged learning*—learning that is simultaneously self-directive and collaborative; deliberative; and situated (Fear, Bawden, Rosaen, & Foster-Fishman, 2002). Looking at engagement that way makes it difficult, if not impossible, to think about this work as the "third leg" of the academic mission, as in "learning, discovery, and *engagement*." Is not learning embedded in engagement? Cannot engagement lead to discovery? With that in mind, my colleagues and I began viewing engagement as an expression that cuts across the academic mission—there are engaged forms of *teaching* (e.g., collaborative learning); engaged forms of *research* (e.g., participatory research); and engaged forms of *service* (e.g., public deliberation). The Bailey program is an example of engagement in teaching and learning, associated specifically with undergraduate education.

The recognition that engagement cuts across the academic mission is a point of departure for sharing another chapter in the Bailey story. Because in the 1990s the Bailey approach was new (to many) and different (to most), we received a number of visitors during the formative years, colleagues wanting to learn more about the program, to see it in action, and to evaluate how things were going. Among them was an Irish colleague, a former employee of *Teagasc,* an organization that is similar (in part) to the U.S. Cooperative Extension Service. Now retired, he was involved actively at the time (and still is) in Irish community development efforts; and he has a passion for connecting higher education with community. At breakfast one day he posed a question: "Have you thought about including a community-based learning program in Bailey? If you do," he continued, "I know a good place to do it."

An initiative was born that day, an initiative known now as "Community Engagement in Rural Ireland" (http://studyabroad.msu.edu/programs/irecommengag.html). Organized in the Bailey style and offered for students as a study abroad program, students work collaboratively with village activists in County Mayo, Ireland (in the Irish West), to design and enact local projects that local people identify as important. Organizing project work is identical to how Bailey students and faculty co-design coursework: those at the table (now including village residents with students) decide what to do; how to do it; who will do it and when; and how it will be done accountably.

The work each year starts in the villages—to determine which projects to undertake and what needs to be done to achieve success. MSU faculty members are involved in that process. Then, there is a matching process, fitting students to local needs/expectations as expressed. Decisions are made jointly (MSU faculty members and village leaders) about general suitability of students (who is admitted into the program) and who among the selected students will work on specific projects and in specific communities. Pre-field orientation and planning take place at that point, designed to enable all involved to make the best use of the time working at the village level.

In May of each year—within days of Spring Semester's end—the students travel to the Irish West. They live and work there for six weeks. It is community engagement, grassroots style: students are collaborators, not interns; students work with volunteers, not professionals; students live one-by-one with local families, not in hotels or together; and it is engaged learning throughout (see Fear, Lillis, & Desmond with Lally & Hartough, 2002).

An indelible memory about this program—and about the emotional dimension of engagement—came at the end of the first year, at a community gathering hall immediately following the final project presentations. I walked outside at the end of the evening to catch a breath of air, not knowing that a student, Megan, had exited the room through another door. Megan was completing a rich experience: she had made many friends and had contributed significantly to local development in the work she had done. There in the dark I found her: body crumpling, sitting on the wooden floor, and crying uncontrollably. Scheduled to leave County Mayo the next day for home, Megan had experienced engagement.

"Be aware of the place where you are brought to tears. That's where I am, and that's where your treasure is." —The Alchemist

Expressiveness in Engagement

The challenge of conveying engagement as a felt, emotional experience—as in the story about Megan—is communicating about it using conventional text presentations, such as the chapter format used here. It is, after all, a lived experience. It would seem that using a more expressive form of communication would better suit (or at least sometimes suit) engagement's visceral quality.

Quite unexpectedly, I came face to face with this issue several years ago. The backdrop: I was invited to make a presentation to a higher education group (in a specific college setting) on principles of transformative change. What began for me as standard preparation—assembling literature, pulling out quotes, organizing citations, and outlining the script—changed dramatically as I stroked the computer keyboard. I was shocked to see what was emerging on the page: rather than conveying my thoughts using conventional academic text, I was expressing my feelings in poetic form. (I had never done that before.) When I finished the task, it was clear that what I had created was *not* an expression about what I *knew about* transformational change from my study *of it*; it was an articulation of how I *felt about* transformational change from my experience *with it*.

485

As I gathered my thoughts to make sense of what had just transpired, it became clear to me that the stimulant was music. Playing in the background that day was the instrumental title cut (with the same title) from Kirk Whalum's jazz album *Unconditional* (2000). There was a section of the song that had special meaning to me. Musically, it made me recall how I *felt* about leading change initiatives in higher education. There was a constant tension, I remembered: on the one hand, of being pulled toward a new reality (with all the excitement that goes along with it) and, on the other hand, of being pulled back to the status quo (with all the safety that goes along with it). If the "pulling toward" won out, I would feel a break-through: it would take me to a new and different level. It was such relief when that happened, I recalled: "Finally! We've made it!"

The song made me remember that feeling and, with it, enabled me to express those feelings in a poem, which I entitled, "Like all the rest" (Fear et al., 2006, pp. 69–70). The poem is intended to speak to the struggle just described: the back and forth, between seeking a new settling place and embracing the status quo. The status quo makes you feel "like all the rest," I thought. But if you want to experience a new reality, then you really have to want it, and want it deeply. It is hard work, frustrating (if not maddening) work—anything but linear with many ups and downs, and with fits and starts. Not many people "get it," I thought; and most tend to come on board and off, often weighing potential benefits in personal terms—deciding whether to "be with you" as opposed to standing on the sideline waiting to see how things turn out. There are those who stand to lose status, prestige, and power—both in influence and position—in the new reality; they will likely fight you each step of the way, sometimes resorting to questionable tactics (the end justifies the means). I would ask myself: "Why bother?" "Is this *really* worth it?" Then, I would fight off those feelings, including the fear of failing, and conclude: "Under no conditions will I accept any outcome *other* than transformation. I will give this my *un*conditional attention, commitment, and persistence."

What irony, I thought, about the source of this understanding. It came quite by accident, stimulated by Whalum's musical composition, a song that just happened to be playing at the time on my system. What emerged serendipitously was how it made me feel about the word "unconditional"—that is, how that word *felt* as personal experience.

On presentation day I came to the meeting with copies of the poem. I began the session by playing Whalum's cut. I asked each participant, in turn, to read a stanza from the poem with the music playing softly in the background. I then asked the group what they thought *and* felt about the poem. At that point—probably no more than twenty minutes into the program—my part was done: "It's now up to you to carry forward with this conversation," I said. The ice was broken when an administrator responded emotionally; it resonated with her. Dialogue ensued. The rest of the day involved reflecting on the campus experience—not just on what had been done, and with what outcome/impact, but how it felt. Engagement enabled a conversation about transformation as felt experience.

Engagement as Significant Relationship

Understanding engagement as a felt, emotional, and expressive phenomenon has motivated me to think more seriously about engagement *as a relationship among significant others.*

Toward that end, in community and organizational settings I often use music—with lyrics selected specifically and carefully—to convey what I perceive to be the underlying emotions of being and feeling engaged. Recently, I have begun adapting lyrics from love songs to establish connecting points between engagement (as discussed in this chapter) and feelings that are commonly associated with intimate relationships. The connection is made more easily than one might think at first blush. Here is how: *love* is often used to express the way we feel about our work and community; *passion* is a common reference to express our level of commitment to causes/efforts (e.g., youth development); *proposals* are frequently prepared to secure funds to make the work possible; *as partners* is how we undertake engagement; and the word "engagement" is used conventionally to convey deep intent—a desire to establish and sustain a special interpersonal relationship.

I have found special meaning in many of the lyrics composed by Marilyn and Alan Bergman. The spousal team has been writing together for more than fifty years and has been honored with nearly twenty Academy Award nominations, with multiple Emmy and Grammy awards, and with three Oscars. I have interpreted lyrics written by them and applied the lyrics to engagement, including passages from the following songs: "So many stars" (1968, Sergio Mendes, composer); "What are you doing the rest of your life?" (1969, Michel Legrand, composer); and "How do you keep the music playing?" (1982, Michel Legrand, composer). Themes in these songs include choice-making, self-awareness, intentionality, and balancing mind, heart, and spirit.

What emerges in these interpretations is this: in engagement as a relationship-among-significant-others people coming together voluntarily. They gather to address an issue or circumstance with personal and shared meaning and work to create something of value. As the work evolves, interpersonal bonds develop. People invariably encounter circumstances that evoke emotions; develop a "we-feeling" and identity in their shared pursuit; and ultimately experience success or failure, together. All of this happens by and through relationship-building—from establishing group norms, to learning how to communicate interpersonally, to managing power and emotional differentials, to handling conflict, among other things—all of the challenges that characterize significant relationships. None of what transpires can be understood completely by describing what people do together *in* engagement. In its complexity, understanding requires learning more about what engagement means, and how it feels, *to* people.

Understanding engagement as a significant relationship is not uncommon, especially in terms of understanding dynamics associated with community-building. Other reference terms to depict this understanding include "a structure of belonging" (Block, 2008); "organic connectedness" (Myers, 2007); and the "pedagogy of hope" (hooks, 2003).

A contributing factor to engagement as relationship-among-significant-others—as with any significant relationship, be it an intimate, friendship, or colleague relationship—is the capacity to communicate authentically: to say what one means and to say it constructively, responsibly, responsively, and meaningfully—and for others to communicate in like manner. The absence of this dynamic inhibits trust-building and represents a stumbling block in engagement. I have experienced that deficiency repeatedly over the years in organizational and community affairs. Given that experience, recently I have begun to address this issue directly with groups, asking questions and stimulating dialogue that otherwise might be reserved for an interpersonal counseling session. Questions include: *"Are you communicating directly?" "Are you able to confront, discuss, and resolve difficult issues?" "Are all voices being heard?" "Can you disagree without being disagreeable?" "Are all the important questions being discussed?"* Answers to these questions represent what it means to engage critically, not just what it means to engage emotionally.

An example of this approach comes from a recent experience associated with a community forum in a small town in another state. The locale is experiencing economic challenges following years of sustained economic success—success resulting from having established a magnetic community image and developing an industry around it. Times have changed and, with it, the need for a reformulated economic approach. Some in the town are outspoken about this need; others are either less sure or reluctant to speak out. There is an undertone in the community, a feeling that some residents are in denial about the situation.

At the forum I made a presentation on the theme of community development as a complex set of relationships among significant others. In that vein, I spoke about quality and depth of communication—being able to talk, deeply and openly, about issues that really matter to people, even if there are disagreements about the nature of issues or how issues should be addressed. I closed my presentation with a request for questions. Silence followed. The lack of response entered the awkward stage—for the forum host and me. As the host got up to thank me, and to bid the audience good night, a hand shot up from the very back of the room. A woman stood up slowly and said: "No, we aren't talking about the things that really matter. Things aren't good here, and they are getting worse."

There was an immediate response to her statement from the other side of the room. The beginning was anything but cordial: accusations were made and demeaning comments followed—of people, circumstances, decisions past, and decisions pending. After a bit of time, pejorative declarations turned to dialogue: people started interacting more respectfully, focusing on important issues, and listening to what each other had to say—about the circumstance they were facing and what to do about it. These were issues that had not been discussed previously, openly, and comprehensively in a diverse, public setting. As the dialogue ensued, I walked from the microphone at the front of the room to a seat on the side of the room and sat down. This was no longer a conversation about me and what I might have to say; it was a conversation meant for those who lived there. After about an hour, with this public talk curtailing, I returned to the microphone and asked what I felt was *the* question: "How are you going to sustain the conversation that began this evening?"

Concluding Observations: Engagement as Transformative Force

Everything that I have addressed in this chapter speaks to the power of engagement—for enabling personal development and for improving organizational and community settings—each significantly. As a felt and emotional experience, engagement can be a portal to personal growth, a means to help individuals mature significantly as human beings—enhancing communicative, empathic, and relational capacity. Engagement can also be a social discipline, a meaningful way for people to relate to one another in organizations and communities—respectfully, responsibly, and authentically. But it would be a mistake to think that engagement will become a transformative force unless actions are exerted mindfully and intentionally to make it happen. The most important thing is to create "engaged spaces"—places in our institutions and associated with civic life—where engagement can flourish. I close the chapter by commenting on three critical ways to create engaged spaces.

First, we need spaces that foster the possibility of being together in the ways described in this chapter. A good example is the work undertaken by the National Issues Forums (NIF) (http://www.nifi.org/), a nonpartisan, nationwide network dedicated to the consideration of public policy issues. The purpose is to help citizens learn how to engage dialogically about major issues facing society (e.g., access to affordable health care). Citizens who participate in NIF forums are introduced to alternative ways of approaching complex, public issues. Forums range from local gatherings, akin to town hall meetings, to study circles that are held in public places or in people's homes. The dialogue is grounded in material presented in "issue guides": each guide includes an overview of an issue and outlines multiple ways of addressing the issue under consideration. Forum participants examine an issue, including evaluating the pros-cons and trade-offs associated with alternative solutions. Through moderated dialogue, citizens are encouraged to arrive at "reasoned public judgment." This approach is influencing work taking place at my institution: in collaboration with the Kettering Foundation (http://www.kettering.org/). The NIF approach is being used to help citizens around Michigan address complex issues in agriculture and natural resources (e.g., what is contributing to the rising cost of food, and what local people can do to cope with rising prices).

Second, we need spaces that enable participants to reflect on their engagement experiences. The stark reality is this: we get so busy "doing engagement" that we often do not take the time to learn from it. The learning I am talking about extends beyond routine (if not required) efforts to evaluate project outcomes and impacts. What I am promoting is taking the time and attention to consider how engagement is influencing our way of thinking, practicing, and (in deeper terms) personhood. The learning is especially rich when there is diversity of participation, including participants with different backgrounds who have worked on different problems and in different settings. The power of diversity is released by focusing collective attention on a common set of thematic issues: what worked and what did not; what choices were made and with what consequences; what experiences were especially instructive; and what has changed (if anything) about how engagement is understood and practiced. These should not be routine, "reporting out" sessions. The sessions should be organized as engagement experiences with participants co-creating their learning agenda—what to learn, how, why, and when.

A community of practice approach, used in our work at Michigan State University, is ideal for achieving this objective (Wenger, McDermott, & Snyder, 2002).

Communities of practice are grounded in the theory of engaged learning. Learning in them is a social act: members learn *with* others (learning generated through dialogue); learn *from* others

489

(gaining insights and practice hints from colleagues); and learn *through* others (imagining what it would be like to adopt others' practices in their work). (Fear et al., 2006, p. xvi)

In the case of Fear et al. (2006), we decided to meet about once a month at the beginning, extending the length between meetings after a period of time. We initiated our learning by sharing and reading literature; writing and sharing case examples of our engagement experiences; and (from that work) identifying core issues and themes to explore, in what (in effect) became a study circle. All of that work set the stage for sharing our learning, first at conferences, and later in the form of articles and book chapters. The learning and sharing culminated in a book project. Taking the time to engage with colleagues in this way prompted us to experience (individually and collectively) a succession of "transformative moments": previously taken-for-granted and prevailing notions about engagement were challenged and changed, replaced by new thoughts and perspectives. None of us is the same from having experienced this time together.

Third, engagement can change the essential nature of what higher education is and does—in the spaces that it enables and the work it does in those spaces—if we allow and nurture those outcomes. The default option (to be avoided, in my opinion) is for engagement to be digested by—to fit—the prevailing institutional frame of reference. In *Challenging Knowledge: The University in the Knowledge Society* (2001), Gerald Delanty labels the prevailing institutional environment *organized modernity*—knowledge generated and controlled by experts for ad hoc purposes. One expression of organized modernity is what Etzkowitz and Leydesdorff (1997) refer to as the "triple helix"—university, industry, and government—three giant monoliths co-evolving in connected fashion with each institution serving the others' needs. It is my contention that outreach, not engagement, is the dominant expression in organized modernity: knowledge generated by experts is brought to bear on issues and problems of interest to end users—with that work often funded by those who seek to benefit from the results.

Outreach is an important—if not critical—university function, but it is not engagement (as this writer sees it), even if done collaboratively and in partnership with end users. Outreach simply does not map well with emergent social realities, including the democratization of knowledge—ways in which knowledge is being created (anywhere, at any time, and from multiple, unrestrictive sources) and (increasingly so) in ways that enable open or near-open access to end users. There is also the matter of contested or disputed science; truth claims generated from science are not always accepted and are becoming (increasingly so) a matter of debate. Given that response, there are instances where is it not sufficient to extend what is discovered through or known from science, especially in areas that pertain to social values and preferences. Instead, there is a need to accommodate multiple (and contrasting) knowledges, each with a distinctive epistemology, ontology, axiology, and methodology.

It is in this regard that engagement is important. Ernest Boyer (1996)—the father of the engagement movement—saw engagement as an opportunity for "the academic and civic cultures ... to ... communicate more continuously ... what ... Geertz describes as the universe of human discourse and enriching the quality of life for all of us" (p. 20). Embracing that vision requires activities that extend beyond the confines of organized modernity. Toward that end, Fear et al. (2006) call for a different university response:

490

Let's call it *discursive post-modernity*. The university will specialize in creating discursive opportunities among various knowledge systems and actors. Rather than seek answers only, universities will encourage people to seek understanding, especially with regard to the most contested, politicized, and problematic matters of the day. This way of thinking, we believe, contextualizes in contemporary reality Boyer's conception of engagement, making it much more than a preference among multiple interpretations of engagement. Instead, it becomes an absolute necessity— a tool for the times. (p. 269)

Discursive postmodernity is the interpretive context for the work described and discussed in this chapter. It has become my discourse of engagement—my preference among others; and it has become my practice field—in the work that I do in the university and in university-community partnerships. In the spaces created through, and enabled by, this discourse of engagement, I am able to be the person and professional I want to be. I feel engaged. I can evaluate the observations made in this chapter as valid, relevant, and meaningful to me and to the work I do. I know what it means to feel engaged and, more so, I know what I mean as a professional for engagement to be a fundamental expression of my personhood.

There are two dimensions in this regard that are most important to me. The first is the way that I seek to engage and the standards by which engagement is evaluated. We describe that in Fear et al. (2006):

Engagement ... abrogates arrogance and stimulates humility. Put bluntly, the things we abhor about elites and elitism—the penchant for exclusivity, dominance, and unilateral exercise of power—are replaced by inclusivity, collaboration, and participation. Simply stated, creating the conditions for critical engagement requires academics to model attributes that endear humans to one another. Anything less jeopardizes the journey to critical engagement, for academics and all others, and mocks the very pillars on which engagement rests. By exhibiting the values of engagement and working with other in like ways, the lived experience of engagement is profoundly democratic, emancipative, and empowering—precisely what engagement in civil society needs to be. (p. 251)

The second dimension is the answer to a pressing question: Engagement for what? Putting the question another way: Why do we engage? These questions provoke me to articulate a stance that befits engagement. My answer: *to lead for the public good.*

Leadership for the public good ... entails the exercise of personal integrity. It requires crossing organizational, political, and ideological boundaries; participating with diverse others on shared initiatives; and committing (in spirit and substance) to actions that embody "the high road." To participate in engagement that way calls for statesperson-like behaviors—seeing the bigger and more complex picture; being trusted as a credible and competent partner; and eschewing intransigence and rejecting narrow mindedness. ...

Leading for the public good, and the statespersonship it connotes, are sorely needed in today's society. Leading for the public good seems to be often trumped by advancing the private good, that is, by-passing the interests of the many and (instead) serving the interests of a few. Engagement ... is an antidote to these tendencies. As a profoundly civilizing enterprise it stands against disturbingly un-civilizing attitudes and behaviors—rampant self-interest, ideological rigidity, unethical comportment, derisiveness, and divisiveness. (Fear et al., 2006, pp. 280–281).

491

In the end, engagement is a compelling force with magnetic attraction. To be engaged. To feel engaged. There is nothing like it.

Acknowledgments

The author thanks those whose insights about engagement contributed to the writing of this chapter: Richard Bawden, David Cooper, Monica Day, Pennie Foster-Fishman, Jan Hartough, Steve Lovejoy, Cheryl Rosaen, and Wynne Wright, all of Michigan State University; Elaine Brown, Michigan Food and Farming Systems; Alice Diebel, C. F. Kettering Foundation; Sandy Hodge, University of Missouri-Columbia; Scott Peters, Cornell University; and William Muse, National Issues Forum Institute.

References

Bennett, J. (2003). *Academic life: Hospitality, ethics, and spirituality.* Bolton MA: Anker.

Block, P. (2008). *Community: The structure of belonging.* San Francisco: Berrett-Koehler.

Boyer, E. (1996). The scholarship of engagement. *Journal of Public Service and Outreach, 1*(1), 11–20.

Coelho, P. (1988). *The alchemist.* San Francisco: HarperSanFrancisco.

Delanty, G. (2001). *Challenging knowledge: The university in the knowledge society.* Buckingham. UK: Open University Press.

Ellis, C., & Bochner, A. (2000). Autoethnography, personal narrative, and reflexivity: Researcher as subject. In N. Denzin & Y. Lincoln (Eds.), *Handbook of qualitative research* (2nd ed.). Thousand Oaks, CA: Sage.

Etzkowitz, H., & Leydesdorff, L. (1997). *Universities in the global economy: A triple helix of university, industry, and government relations.* London: Cassell Academic.

Fear, F., Bawden, R., Rosaen, C., & Foster-Fishman, P. (2002). A model of engaged learning: Frames of reference and scholarly underpinnings. *Journal of Higher Education Outreach and Engagement, 7*(3), 55–68.

Fear, F., & Doberneck, D. (2004). Collegial talk: A powerful tool for change. *About Campus, 9*(1), 11–19.

Fear, F., S. Lillis, S., & Desmond, M., with Lally, M., & Hartough, J. (2002). Beyond convention: An Irish-American collaboration in the West of Ireland. *Ceide: A Review from the Margins, 5*(4), 24–26.

Fear, F., Rosaen, C., Foster-Fishman, P., & Bawden, R. (2001). Outreach as a scholarly expression. *Journal of Higher Education, Outreach, and Engagement, 6*(2), 21–34.

Fear, F., Rosaen, C., Bawden, R., & Foster-Fishman, P. (2006). *Coming to critical engagement: An autoethnographic exploration.* Lanham, MD: University Press of America.

hooks, b. (1994). *Teaching to transgress: Education as the practice of freedom.* New York: Routledge.

Jamison, K. (2004). *Exuberance: The passion for life.* New York: Vintage.

Moffett, J. (1994). *The universal schoolhouse: Spiritual awakening through education.* San Franciso: Jossey-Bass.

Myers, J. (2007). *Organic community: Creating a place where people naturally connect.* North Dartmouth, MA: Baker Books.

Patton, M. (2002). *Qualitative research and evaluation methods* (3rd ed.). Thousand Oaks, CA: Sage.

Wenger, E., McDermott, R., & Snyder, W. (2002). *Cultivating communities of practice.* Boston: Harvard Business School Press.

Contributors

Angela Allen, PhD, Senior Associate, Public Engagement Programs, Public Agenda

Angela Allen provides community technical assistance for Public Agenda's department of Public Engagement programs, including the Center for Advances in Public Engagement (CAPE). Her focus includes capacity-building and cross-sector collaboration strategic planning, pre-community engagement research, and stakeholder engagement work. Angela was an ABD Research Associate at the Charles F. Kettering Foundation in Dayton, Ohio. Angela has a PhD in higher education administration with a specialization in applied developmental science from Michigan State University, a MSW in community organization administration from the University of Michigan-Ann Arbor, and a Bachelor's degree in urban and regional planning from Michigan State University. Dr. Allen's dissertation, "Faculty and Community Collaboration in Sustained Community-Campus Engagement Partnerships," was a case study analysis of nine community-campus partnerships and the collaboration factors that impacted partnership sustainability and the alignment of the academic and civic contexts through partnership knowledge dissemination. In her doctoral program, Dr. Allen spent three years as a graduate assistant with MSU University Outreach and Engagement, co-creating the Emerging Engagement Scholars Workshop of the National Outreach Scholarship, the National Center for the Scholarship of Engagement at MSU, and the Higher Education Network for Community Engagement in 2007. After more than fourteen years of professional experience in community-based program administration in her hometown of Detroit as well as a year as Research Associate at the Charles F. Kettering Foundation, Dr. Allen is establishing an independent consulting practice.

Theodore R. Alter is professor of agricultural, environmental, and regional economics in the Department of Agricultural Economics and Rural Sociology at Penn State University. He served as associate vice-president for outreach, director of Penn State Cooperative Extension, and associate dean in the College of Agricultural Sciences at Penn State from July 1997 through July 2004. His research focuses on the scholarship on engagement in higher education, agricultural economics and agribusiness management, community and rural development, development and public sector economics, and comparative rural development policy.

Burton A. Bargerstock is co-director of the National Collaborative for the Study of University Engagement (NCSUE) and director of Communication and Information Technology for University Outreach and Engagement (UOE). He directs information system development, publications, public/media relations, and event management; and serves on university-wide advisory committees. Since 1994, Bargerstock has participated in a number of institutional research efforts, including the development of the Outreach & Engagement Measurement Instrument (OEMI), which collects data on faculty outreach efforts and activities. Under the aegis of the NCSUE, he leads the OEMI project, heading its implementation at MSU and partnering institutions. Bargerstock also helped shape an ongoing qualitative research project that studies the impact of outreach on scholarship and scholarly lives. Recently, he was involved in the creation and development of MSU Usability/Accessibility Research & Consulting, a University laboratory and technical assistance provider that conducts research on and provides services for the evaluation of human/technology interfaces (e.g., software, websites). He currently serves on the Board of Directors of the University Professional and Continuing Education Association (2010–11), is an associate editor for the Transformations in Higher Education: Scholarship of Engagement book series, is a member of the implementation committee of the National Outreach Scholarship Conference, serves as president of the MSU Chapter of the Honor Society of Phi Kappa Phi, and is an MSU institutional member of EDUCAUSE.

Mary Beckman is Associate Director of Academic Affairs and Research at the University of Notre Dame's Center for Social Concerns, where, among her activities, she created and runs a community-based research program that includes grants to teams of faculty, community collaborators, and students. She is also Concurrent Associate Professor of Economics and Policy Studies and co-directs a Poverty Studies Minor. She received her Ph.D. in economics from the University of Notre Dame in 1986 and was a tenured faculty member at Lafayette College from 1985 to 2001. Her publications can be found in books and journals including *Academic Exchange Quarterly, Journal of Excellence in College Teaching, Journal of Higher Education Outreach and Engagement, Radical Teacher, Review of Radical Political Economics,* and *Women's Studies Quarterly.*

Robert G. Bringle (Ph.D., Social Psychology, University of Massachusetts) is Chancellor's Professor of Psychology and Philanthropic Studies at Indiana University–Purdue University Indianapolis (IUPUI). He has been involved in the development, implementation, and evaluation of educational programs and is widely known for his research on jealousy and close relationships. His work as Executive Director of the IUPUI Center for Service and Learning has resulted in numerous national recognitions for his campus and himself. For his scholarship on service-learning and civic engagement, Dr. Bringle was awarded the Ehrlich Faculty Award for Service Learning and was recognized at the International Service-Learning Research Conference for his outstanding contributions. He was the Volunteer of the Year in

2001 for Boys and Girls Clubs of Indianapolis. The University of the Free State, South Africa, awarded him an honorary doctorate for his scholarly work on civic engagement and service learning.

Karen S. Bruns holds a doctorate degree in human and community resource development from The Ohio Sate University focusing on outreach and engagement in higher education. Her master's degree from The Ohio State University and bachelor's degree from the University of Dayton in Dayton, Ohio, are in human ecology. She has spent her career in higher education focusing on university engagement with communities. The first half of her career was spent building and implementing partnerships in local communities as an Ohio State University Extension educator.

Since 1996, Dr. Bruns has served as leader OSU CARES and Outreach/Engagement at The Ohio State University. In this position, she works with faculty and staff across the university to support and encourage outreach/engagement efforts. Through her OSU CARES responsibilities, she works with OSU Extension to build partnerships between faculty and staff with colleagues in other colleges of the University. As a part of The Ohio State University's Sr. Vice-President for Outreach and Engagement's team, she develops and implements professional development and incentives programs to foster faculty/staff involvement in university/community partnerships. Since its inception, Dr. Bruns has been involved with developing and implementing the National Outreach Scholarship Partnership and Conference. Ohio State University hosted this conference in 2002 and 2006 under the leadership of Dr. Bruns. She has served on the Outreach Scholarship Implementation Committee since it inception.

Cathy Burack is a Senior Fellow for Higher Education at the Center for Youth and Communities (CYC) in the Heller School for Social Policy and Management at Brandeis University. Prior to coming to Brandeis, Cathy was the Associate Director of the New England Resource Center for Higher Education (NERCHE). For the past eighteen years, Cathy has focused on ways faculty, students, and administrators can work together to fulfill the civic missions of their colleges and universities. This focus has been on two interrelated areas: access to higher education, especially by students who are among the first in their families to attend; and the ways in which college and universities engage with their communities. Cathy holds a bachelor's degree in psychology from the University of Rochester, and a doctorate in Administration, Planning, and Social Policy from Harvard University. Cathy's work is undergirded by her core beliefs in the power of reflective practice, collaboration, importance of creating learning organizations, capacity building, and development of communities and the individuals who inhabit them.

Michael Burawoy teaches sociology at the University of California, Berkeley.

Karen McKnight Casey is the director of the Center for Service-Learning and Civic Engagement. Casey facilitates university initiatives that provide academic, curricular and co-curricular, service-based learning and engagement opportunities for MSU students. She works closely with university faculty, administrators, and students to offer opportunities that meet their academic, personal, professional, and civic development goals, while also addressing the expressed needs of community partners. Casey also directs the MSU America Reads/America Counts federal work-study projects. She serves as an adjunct faculty/specialist in the Department of Family and Child Ecology and as a field instructor for the School of Social

Work. She is active on a number of university and community committees and boards, including the board of Michigan Campus Compact. Casey's multiple years of professional experience in higher education and working with community agencies give her unique perceptions and expertise in promoting and implementing service-learning and civic engagement.

Jeri Childers conducts research, publishes, presents, and practices in the area engaging university and community leaders for civic change. Jeri Childers and Ted Settle created *The Engagement Academy for University Leaders* offered by Virginia Tech's **Center** for Organizational and Technological Advancement starting in 2008. This is unique, executive leadership experience designed to build institutional capacity for engagement was built on two decades of research and practice in higher continuing education, campus-community partnerships and institutional engagement. Childers shares innovative ways to engage constituencies and to leverage the intellectual capital and university missions to create positive change within institutions of higher education and communities.

As director of Outreach Program Development at Virginia Tech, Childers leads a team that provides workforce, organizational, and community development solutions locally and globally. She provides leadership for Virginia Tech's engagement activities for the Center for Organizational and Technological Advancement, Continuing and Professional Education, the Center for Student Engagement and Community Partnerships, the Virginia Tech Language and Culture Institute, Upward Bound/Talent Search, Virginia Tech Fine Arts Initiative, *CommunityArtsWork*, and Virginia Tech's programs delivered in the National Capital Region, at the Inn at Virginia Tech and Skelton Conference Center, and at the Hotel Roanoke and Conference Center. Annually, Outreach Program Development offers approximately 450 programs, impacting the lives of more than 35,000 participants.

Childers is an affiliate faculty member in Virginia Tech Higher Education program in the Department of Educational Leadership and Policy Studies and has developed courses related to the engaged university and student engagement in higher education.

Childers has been working in outreach, engagement, and continuing education since 1986. Prior to joining Virginia Tech in 2004, she worked for the Pennsylvanian State University and the University of Missouri-Columbia. Over her 11-year tenure at Penn State, Childers served as the director of Workforce Development, director of Outreach Program Development, and the assistant dean for Continuing and Distance Education in the Smeal College of Business. She also launched the first Outreach Scholarship Conference at Penn State in 1999, serving as the conference chair until 2004. Her research interests include organizational, economic, and community development, continuing professional education, leadership in higher education, and university engagement.

Childers served as guest editor for the *Journal of Higher Education Outreach and Engagement* and is the author of a number of articles on outreach scholarship and engagement, international programs development, and continuing education. She currently serves on the executive committee of the Council on Engagement and Outreach of the Association of Public and Land-Grant Universities, formerly known as the National Association of State Universities and Land-Grant Colleges. She served as the chair of the University Continuing Education Association Outreach and Engagement Community of Practice and is responsible for launching an online database of *Promising Practices in Engagement.* In addition, she serves as a member of the Higher Education Network of Community Engagement and supports the Emerging Scholars Conference, which is held in conjunction with the Outreach Scholarship Conference.

Carol Coletta is president and CEO of CEOs for Cities and host and producer of the nationally syndicated public radio show Smart City. Previously, she served as president of Coletta & Company in Memphis. In addition, she served as executive director of the Mayor's[1] Institute on City Design, a partnership of the National Endowment for the Arts, U.S. Conference of Mayors, and American Architectural Foundation. Carol was a Knight Fellow in Community Building for 2003 at the University of Miami School of Architecture. In 2008, she was named one of the world's fifty most important urban experts by a leading European think tank. Most recently, she was named as one of the top fifty most influential urban thinkers of all time by the readers of PLANetizen.com.

Thomas G. Coon is Director of Michigan State University (MSU) Extension and Professor in the Department of Fisheries and Wildlife at Michigan State University. He is responsible for providing leadership to an organization that has more than 1,200 staff and faculty both on campus and in each of Michigan's eighty-three counties and an annual budget of more than $88 million. MSU Extension provides research-based education programs designed to address community, family, and industry needs in five broad program areas (agriculture, natural resources, families, youth, and community/economic development).

In previous administrative assignments, Dr. Coon has served as Associate Dean for Graduate and International Programs in the College of Agriculture and Natural Resources and as Associate Department Chairperson and Acting Chairperson in the Department of Fisheries and Wildlife at MSU.

Maureen F. Curley is president of Campus Compact, a national coalition of more than 1,100 college and university presidents dedicated to advancing campus-based service, service-learning, and civic engagement. She has more than twenty-five years of experience in the nonprofit sector, concentrating in the areas of aging, community service, and public policy.

Among other leadership positions, Curley has served as Director of Public Policy for the Community Service Society of New York and as Executive Director of the Massachusetts Service Alliance, where she oversaw distribution of $12 million in grants to support AmeriCorps community service-learning and mentoring programs. She also founded the Forum for Women Leaders of Nonprofit Organizations. Most recently, she was the Chief Relationship Officer for Bridgestar, an initiative of The Bridgespan Group, where she developed services to connect executive-level managers with career and board opportunities in the nonprofit sector.

Curley has taught courses on nonprofit and volunteer management at Columbia University, New York University, and UMass-Boston. Currently, she serves on the board of directors of the National Service-Learning Partnership and Friends of the Children—Boston. She also co-chairs Governor Deval Patrick's Commonwealth Corps Commission and is a member of the Board of Governors of Antioch University. Curley holds a B.A. in political science from Emmanuel College and a master's in human services administration from Antioch University, New England.

Diane M. Doberneck, Ph.D., is a research specialist at the National Collaborative for the Study of University Engagement and an adjunct assistant professor in the Liberty Hyde Bailey Scholars Program. Doberneck's research interests include outreach and engagement in promotion and tenure processes; faculty integration of outreach and engagement across their teaching, research, and service responsibilities; faculty pathways to careers as engaged scholars; international community engagement; and effective strategies for teaching and learning community engagement. Informed by this research, Doberneck creates and supports the co-creation of professional development programs on community engagement—including Tools of Engagement (undergraduate students), the Graduate Certificate on Community Engagement (graduate students), the Emerging Engaged Scholars Workshop (graduate students and new/junior faculty), and the Engaged Scholar Speakers Series (faculty, community members). In addition, she coordinates an international collaborative with the Tochar Valley Rural Community Network (Co. Mayo, Ireland) that enhances rural community vitality through community engagement. Together, Tochar Valley community members and MSU students assist communities in developing their own deeper sense of place; individual, organizational, and community capacities; and cultural and natural heritage assets. In 2008, she won MSU's first annual Curricular Service-Learning and Civic Engagement Award in the College of Agriculture and Natural Resources for her international engagement work. Doberneck holds a Ph.D. in organizational and community resource development from Michigan State University.

Frank A. Fear is senior associate dean, College of Agriculture and Natural Resources, Michigan State University. His specialty is engagement practices in organizational and community development. He is co-author of *Coming to Critical Engagement* (University Press of America, 2006). Current interests include strategies for enhancing public deliberation associated with contested issues in agriculture and natural resources. Dr. Fear is a board member of the National Issues Forum, an organization dedicated to encouraging public discourse on matters of societal interest.

Hiram E. Fitzgerald, Ph.D., is associate provost for university outreach and engagement and university distinguished professor of psychology at Michigan State University. He is actively involved with the APLU Council on Engagement and Outreach, the National Outreach Scholarship Conference, and the Higher Education Network for University Engagement. Fitzgerald is a member of the steering committees of the Early Head Start National Research Consortium, and of the American Indian/Alaska Native Head Start Research Center. He is a member of a variety of interdisciplinary research teams focusing on evaluation of community-based prevention programs. His major areas of funded research include the study of infant and family development in community contexts, the impact of fathers on early child development, implementation of systemic models of organizational process and change, the etiology of alcoholism, the digital divide and youth access to technologies, and broad issues related to the scholarship of engagement. From 1992–2008, Fitzgerald served as the executive director of the World Association for Infant Mental Health. Fitzgerald holds a Ph.D. in experimental child psychology (1967) from the University of Denver.

Pennie Foster-Fishman is a professor in the Department of Psychology and a Senior Outreach Fellow in University Outreach and Engagement at Michigan State University. She received her Ph.D. in organizational/community psychology from the University of Illinois at Chicago. Her research interests primarily emphasize systems change, particularly how organizational, interorganizational, community, and statewide systems can improve to better meet the needs of children, youth, and families. Toward this end, she has investigated human service delivery reform, multiple stakeholder collaboration, coalition development, community organizing, comprehensive community initiatives, and resident empowerment as vehicles for systems change. She has also worked with a variety of public sector agencies, not-for-profit organizations, and community and statewide coalitions, aiming to improve their organizational capacity and the efficacy of their programmatic efforts. In all of her efforts, Dr. Foster-Fishman develops a collaborative learning partnership with her community site, incorporating systemic action learning processes to promote transformative change and the production of valued outcomes for the community.

Nancy E. Franklin, Ed.D., is the Director of Strategic Initiatives for Outreach and Cooperative Extension at the Pennsylvania State University and Assistant Director of Outreach for Penn State Institutes Of Energy and the Environment. Her professional focus, as well as her scholarly interest, centers on regional economic and sustainability engagement. Prior to her current role, Nancy served as Virginia Tech's Southside Regional Director of Information Technology and Senior Director of Programs and Planning at the Institute for Advanced Learning and Research in Danville, Virginia, which garnered the 2007 C. Peter Magrath/W. K. Kellogg Foundation National Engagement Award. She holds a doctorate in higher education management from the University of Pennsylvania.

Timothy V. Franklin, Ph.D., is the Director, Office of Economic and Workforce Development at the Pennsylvania State University. His professional focus at Penn State, and previously at Virginia Tech, as well as his scholarly interest, centers on the policies and practices of distributed research innovation, regional stewarding institutions, and transformative regional engagement. At Penn State, he established the Transformative Regional Engagement. Engagement Networks Initiative and has provided leadership to numerous economic engagement efforts. As part of Virginia Tech's "Southside Initiative" from 2001 to 2007, he was founding Executive Director of the Institute for Advanced Learning and Research (IALR). Virginia Tech's Southside Initiative competed with four other finalists at the 2007 Outreach Scholarship Conference and won the national C. Peter Magrath/W. K. Kellogg Foundation Engagement Award at the 2007 NASULGC Conference (now the Association of Public and Land-Grant Universities).

Nicholas Freudenberg is Distinguished Professor of Public Health at Hunter College and the Graduate Center, City University of New York (CUNY) and directs CUNY's doctoral program in public health. For the past twenty-five years, he has worked with and for community organizations, municipal agencies, and others to develop, implement, and evaluate programs and policies to promote health and reduce health inequities in New York City.

Sherril B. Gelmon, Dr. P.H. is Professor of Public Health at Portland State University. Her current research on engagement addresses institutional strategy and establishment of models of faculty roles and recognition for community-engaged scholarship. She was national evaluator for the "Community Engaged Scholarship for Health Collaborative" and is evaluator for "Faculty for the Engaged Campus." She has studied the ten-year impact of Portland State's revised tenure and promotion policies. She was an "Engaged Scholar" with Campus

499

Compact, developing assessment methodologies for service-learning and civic engagement. She was founding Chair of the International Association for Research on Service-Learning and Community Engagement.

Dwight E. Giles, Jr., is Professor of Higher Education Administration and Senior Associate at the New England Resource Center for Higher Education (NERCHE) in the Graduate College of Education, University of Massachusetts, Boston. He has co-authored numerous books and articles on service-learning research including "Where's the Learning in Service-Learning?" with Janet Eyler, and "Service-Learning: A Movement's Pioneers Reflect on its Origins, Practice, and Future" with Tim Stanton and Nadinne Cruz. He is a member of the National Peer Review Board for the Scholarship of Engagement and of the working group for "Creating an Academic Home for the Next Generation of Engaged Scholars." With John Saltmarsh, he is currently conducting a study of reward structures for community engaged scholarship at Carnegie-designated community engaged campuses. He is the co-recipient, with Janet Eyler, of Campus Compact's 2003 Thomas Ehrlich Faculty Service-Learning Award, the 2008 recipient of the National Society for Experiential Education 2008 research award, and the 2009 Distinguished Research Award from the International Association for Research on Service-Learning and Community Engagement.

Robin Goettel is Assistant Director at Imagining America. Goettel joined Syracuse University in 1999. Goettel holds a Bachelor of Professional Studies in Organizational Leadership through SU's University College. Goettel earned her MA from Syracuse University in Higher Education Administration in May 2007. Goettel works closely with Imagining America's Research Director, Timothy Eatman.

Philip A. Greasley is associate provost for university engagement and associate professor of English at the University of Kentucky. He holds the B.A. and M.A. in English from Northwestern University and the Ph.D. from Michigan State. Phil serves on the National Outreach Scholarship Conference Partnership board of directors and the *Journal of Community Engagement and Scholarship* editorial board.

Jamie Haft is Program Coordinator of Imagining America: Artists and Scholars in Public Life. Her responsibilities include organizing local and national programs and contributing to Imagining America's publications. In 2008, Haft was one of three national advisors to *The Curriculum Project Report: Culture and Community Development in Higher Education.* Haft is also a National Organizer for Voices from the Cultural Battlefront: Organizing for Equity, and serves as the editor of its website (www.culturalbattlefront.net). Her article, "Voices from the Battlefront: Achieving Cultural Equity through Critical Analysis," was published in *Community Arts Perspectives: A Publication of the Community Arts Convening and Research Project* (Volume 2, Issue 1, September 2009). Haft graduated in 2007 from New York University's Tisch School of the Arts.

Julie A. Hatcher is Associate Director of the nationally recognized Center for Service and Learning at Indiana University-Purdue University Indianapolis. Her responsibilities include faculty development programs, research projects to assess the outcomes of service learning and civic engagement, and supervising the implementation of a wide range of service-based programs. Her Ph.D. is in Philanthropic Studies and she regularly teaches undergraduate and graduate courses through the School of Liberal Arts. She was awarded the Dissertation

Research Award by the International Association for Research in Service-Learning and Civic Engagement for her dissertation entitled "The Public role of professionals: Developing and evaluating the Civic-Minded Professional scale." Published work and formal presentations have focused on civic engagement and service learning in higher education, international comparative analysis, implications of John Dewey's philosophy for higher education, and reflective practice. She has consulted with numerous campuses on integrating service into academic study, including international projects with faculty from Egypt, Kenya, Macedonia, Mexico, and South Africa.

Melvin B. Hill, Jr. is the Robert G. Stephens, Jr., Senior Fellow in Law and Government Emeritus in the Institute of Higher Education of the University of Georgia, and served as the editor of the *Journal of Higher Education Outreach and Engagement* from 2000 to 2009. From 1983 to 1996, Mr. Hill served as the director of the Carl Vinson Institute of Government of the University of Georgia, overseeing a broad program of instruction, research, and technical assistance for state and local officials, educators, and citizens at large. He is the author of numerous articles and monographs on legal issues relating to the structure and processes of state and local governments in a democratic society. Mr. Hill holds a B.A. degree from Bucknell University, an M.P.A. and a J.D. degree from Cornell University, and is a member of the State Bar of Georgia.

Crystal G. Lunsford is a research associate with the National Collaborative for the Study of University Engagement at Michigan State University. Her current research examines the relationship between faculty scholarship and the public and, in particular, how discipline shapes faculty engagement. She holds a Ph.D. in teaching, curriculum, and educational policy from Michigan State University and a master's degree in sociology and education from Columbia University.

David J. Maurrasse, Ph.D. is the president and founder of Marga Incorporated, a consulting firm providing advice and research to strengthen philanthropy and innovative cross-sector partnerships to address some of today's most pressing social concerns. Often in the role of a *partnership catalyst,* Marga brings expertise, as well as an informed set of eyes, to mutually beneficial multistakeholder partnerships and philanthropic initiatives. Since 2000, he has been on the faculty at Columbia University's School of International and Public Affairs. He is currently an Associate Research Scholar in the School and a Strategic Advisor to the University's Earth Institute Urban Design Lab. Prior to Columbia University, Dr. Maurrasse was an Assistant Professor at Yale University (1995–2000) and a Senior Program Advisor at the Rockefeller Foundation (1998–2000), where he managed a portfolio on community building and an initiative to further higher education/community partnerships.

A leading author, speaker, and researcher on the relationship between major institutions and their surrounding communities, Dr. Maurrasse's publications are all directed toward advancing new thinking about partnerships. *Listening to Harlem: Gentrification, Community and Business* (2006), *A Future for Everyone: Innovative Social Responsibility and Community Partnerships* (2004), and *Beyond the Campus: How Colleges and Universities form Partnerships with Their Communities* (2001) all discuss ways that institutions and businesses have worked with their surrounding communities to pursue common goals. He is a trustee of

501

Bucknell University and the Director of the program on strategic partnerships and innovation at the Earth Institute Columbia University.

Dean P. McGovern is the Executive Director of the Montana Campus Compact, as well as a professor in the College of Education and Human Sciences at The University of Montana-Missoula. Dr. McGovern's work focuses on providing opportunities for faculty, students, staff, and alumni to participate in curricular and extra-curricular civic engagement activities. His scholarship and teaching pertain to creating healthy communities through strong personal responsibly and public policy in education, citizenship, civic and academic leadership, and service-learning. He regularly leads reflective discussions to strengthen campus-community partnerships.

Miles McNall, Ph.D., is the assistant director at the Community Evaluation and Research Collaborative. McNall has extensive experience in the evaluation of health and human service programs. He participated in the evaluation of HIV prevention programs for young men at the University of Minnesota Medical College and oversaw the development of client outcome monitoring systems for agency programs at Catholic Charities of Chicago. At the Hektoen Institute for Medical Research, he evaluated HIV/AIDS care programs and oversaw the agency's quality improvement efforts. Currently, McNall and his colleagues are conducting an evaluation of school-based health centers funded by the Michigan Department of Community Health. McNall holds a Ph.D. in sociology from the University of Minnesota.

Bo Hee Min is a graduate student in sociology at the University of Wisconsin–Madison. Previously, she worked as an information technology researcher in South Korea. Her research interests are in the area of production, modification, and consumption of information technology in various organizational settings, including health informatics, bioinformatics, and business information system.

Meredith Minkler, DrPH, MPH, is Professor and Director of Health and Social Behavior at the School of Public Health, University of California, Berkeley, where she was founding director of the UC Center on Aging. She has more than thirty years' experience teaching, conducting research, and working with underserved communities on community-identified issues through community building, community organizing, and community-based participatory research (CBPR). Her current research and community capacity-building work includes documenting the impacts of CBPR on healthy public policy; empowerment intervention studies with youth and the elderly; an ecological CBPR study of immigrant worker health and safety in Chinatown restaurants; and national studies of health disparities in older Americans. Dr. Minkler is co-author or editor of seven books including the edited volume *Community-based participatory research for health: From Process to Outcomes* (second edition, 2005), and the co-edited book *Community-based participatory research for health: From Process to Outcomes* (with Nina Wallerstein; second edition, 2008).

Tami L. Moore is assistant professor of higher education in the Educational Leadership Program at Oklahoma State University–Tulsa. Her research agenda focuses broadly on the role of higher education institutions in the communities they serve, employing social and critical theory in the reading of community engagement. Her current projects explore issues related to faculty work and community-engaged scholarship, and the relationship between geographic place and community engagement in the United States, the United Kingdom, and Australia. She is founding co-chair of the Emerging Engagement Scholars Workshop at the National Outreach Scholarship Conference, and recipient of the AERA-J Dissertation of the Year Award in 2009.

Paul D. Nelson received his undergraduate education at Princeton University and completed his doctoral studies in psychology at the University of Chicago. Currently retired from full-time employment, though appointed as a Senior Fellow of the Association of American Colleges and Universities, his fifty-year career was equally divided between the United States Navy and the American Psychological Association (APA). In the former, as a commissioned officer, he served as a research psychologist, in research management, and as Director, Navy Medical Service Corps. Following retirement from the Navy, he served the APA in several positions, first as Director, Office of Program Consultation and Accreditation, and then as Director, Office of Graduate and Postgraduate Education, and Deputy Executive Director of the Education Directorate. His research interests of recent years have been focused on issues of quality assessment in higher education.

Philip Nyden is currently Professor of Sociology and Director of the Center for Urban Research and Learning (CURL) at Loyola University Chicago. CURL is a nontraditional research center that involves community partners in all stages of research from conceptualization and research design to data analysis and report dissemination. He has also done extensive research on what produces stable racially, ethnically, and economically diverse communities in the United States. Nyden is currently involved in activist researcher networks linking community-based research across regional and national boundaries. With colleagues at the University of Technology Sydney Shopfront (Australia), he co-edits a new journal, *Gateways: International Journal of Community Research and Engagement.*

Michael J. Offerman served as President of Capella University from 2001 through 2007. During his presidency, Capella University grew from 2,000 students to 22,000 students and developed its award-winning learning outcomes assessment model.

In 2008, he assumed the role of Vice Chairman of Capella Education Company. In this role he works on external university initiatives, including government affairs, regulatory affairs, investor relations, and public relations. He has led a national consumer information and accountability effort for colleges and universities serving adult students at a distance known as Transparency by Design, which publishes the website *College Choices for Adults.* He also publishes the blog *The Other 85%: Working Adults and the New World of Higher Education.*

Penny A. Pasque is Assistant Professor of adult and higher education in the Department of Educational Leadership and Policy Studies and Women's and Gender Studies at the University of Oklahoma. Her research includes strengthening the connections between higher education and society, addressing in/equities in higher education, and qualitative methodologies. She received a Ph.D. from the Center for the Study of Higher and Postsecondary Education at the University of Michigan. Penny has published in the *Journal of College Student Development* and the *Review of Higher Education,* and her latest book, American Higher Education, Leadership, and Policy: Critical Issues and the Public Good is published with Palgrave Macmillan.

Stephen Percy is the Acting Dean of the School of Public Health, Professor of Political Science and Urban Studies, and Director of the Center for Urban Initiatives and Research at

503

the University of Wisconsin–Milwaukee. He has served as the Principal Investigator of grants from the U.S. Department of Education, U.S. Department of Housing and Urban Development, and Fannie Mae Foundation related to university-community partnerships. His interests include public policy and implementation, local government and service delivery, nonprofit governance, disability policy, and creating effective university-community collaboration.

Eur Ing Professor **James A. Powell** OBE DSc is Professor of Academic Enterprise at Salford University, on sabbatical from being Pro Vice Chancellor for Enterprise and Regional Affairs. He coordinated the EUA study "Creative Universities and Their Creative City Regions" and the OECD study of universities in the northeast of England, and is Director of the University Partnership for Benchmarking Enterprise and Associated Technologies and Smart City Futures, which has developed leading edge knowledge of the leadership, governance, and management of best university reach-out to business and the community. His two websites— www.upbeat.eu.com and www.smartcityfutures.co.uk—portray working examples of best academic enterprise practices and short streaming video showing the finest academic entrepreneurial leaders in the world. Recently Powell was appointed by HEFCE as one of the UK Ambassadors for Social Entrepreneurship in Higher Education. He has also been appointed to the Advisory Board of the PASCAL International Observatory for place management, social capital, and learning regions, to lead a new programme encouraging universities that are striving for a modern renaissance.

Jill N. Reich has served as Academic Vice President and Dean of the Faculty at Bates College for the past decade. Her career prior to Bates included serving as Executive Director of the Education Directorate at the American Psychological Association and as a member of the Psychology Department faculty at Loyola University of Chicago where, with colleagues, she began the Center for Children and Families and the Infant Development Project studying the long term effects of prematurity and illness. She received her Ph.D. in experimental psychology with emphasis in cognitive development from Dartmouth College.

Peggy Roberts, M.S.Ed., has worked in the human services field since 1972, highlighted by discharge planning in an Illinois State facility for the mentally ill; family therapist for court-ordered youth and families at risk for child abuse/neglect; foster parent; foster care case manager/program director; and administrator for refugee, homeless, and senior programs for a large nonprofit social services organization. Peggy is currently the Coordinator of Ingham County, Michigan's *Power Of We Consortium*, a "network of networks" committed to improving the intellectual and social development, health, economic, environmental, safety, and community life of its residents.

John Saltmarsh is the Director of the New England Resource Center for Higher Education (NERCHE) at the University of Massachusetts, Boston, as well as a professor in the Higher Education Administration Doctoral Program in the Department of Leadership in Education in the Graduate College of Education. He is the author of numerous book chapters and articles on civic engagement, service-learning, and experiential education, and the co-author of the Democratic Engagement White Paper (NERCHE, 2009) as well as co-editor of the forthcoming book *"To Serve a Larger Purpose:" Engagement for Democracy and the Transformation of Higher Education* (2010). He serves as the chair of the board of the International

Association for Research on Service Learning and Community Engagement (IARSLCE), as well as on the editorial board of the *Michigan Journal of Community Service Learning* and the editorial board of the *Journal of Higher Education Outreach and Engagement*. He is a member of the National Review Board for the Scholarship of Engagement, a National Scholar with Imagining America's Tenure Team Initiative, and a member of the Advisory Committee for the Carnegie Foundation's Community Engagement Classification.

Lorilee R. Sandmann, Ph.D., is professor in the Department of Lifelong Education, Administration, and Policy at the University of Georgia. She has held administrative, faculty, extension and outreach positions at major public research universities. Her research focuses on leadership and organizational change in higher education with special emphasis on the institutionalization of scholarly engagement. As an active scholar, she has presented her work nationally and internationally and has published books, chapters, and more than forty refereed journal articles; her most recent work is a co-edited volume *The First Wave of Carnegie Classified Institutions,* New Directions for Higher Education (No. 147). Dr Sandmann has been inducted into the International Adult and Continuing Education Hall of Fame and serves on the National Advisory Panel for Community Engagement of the Carnegie Foundation for the Advancement of Teaching.

Sarena D. Seifer directs Community-Campus Partnerships for Health, a national non-profit organization dedicated to fostering partnerships between communities and educational institutions that improve health professions education, civic responsibility, and the overall health of communities.

Theodore J. Settle's career covers academia, business, and military. In his current position as Director of the Office of Economic Development, Settle provides leadership to university activities and initiatives that generate economic development throughout Virginia. He serves as the primary access point for business, state and local government agencies, and other potential clients and partners to the university's products and services.

Within Virginia, Settle initiated and led for five years the University-Based Economic Development group, an organization that includes economic development representatives from the public universities, the four major state-level economic development organizations, and a major business publication. The group focuses on integrating public universities and economic development strategies.

Settle has been active in the national engagement conversation for several years. He initiated and served as chair for two years of the Community of Practice on Outreach and Engagement within the University Continuing Education Association. UCEA honored Ted with the creation of an award in his name, "Ted Settle Award for Distinguished Service to the Outreach and Engagement Community of Practice." Within the Association of Public and Land-Grant Universities, he has served as chair of the Council on Engagement and Outreach and currently serves on the Executive Committee of the Commission on Innovation, Competitiveness, and Economic Prosperity. He has been actively involved in the creation of an assessment tool to identify characteristics of an economically engaged university. He initiated and co-led the development of the Engagement Academy for University Leaders, coordinated Virginia Tech's successful application to the Carnegie Foundation for the Advancement of Teaching for their classification of being a 'community engaged' institution, and has been an active partner in Virginia Tech's role with the Institute for Advanced Learning and Research

505

in Danville, Virginia, the recipient of the 2007 C. Peter Magrath W.K. Kellogg Foundation Engagement Award.

Prior to his current position, Settle was Director of Continuing Education at Virginia Tech from 1992–2002, Director of the NCR Management College at NCR Corporation from 1980–1990, and Assistant Director for Academic & Health Affairs at the Illinois Board of Higher Education from 1977–1980. He has delivered in excess of 100 papers, and external presentations and speeches.

Ted earned his B.S. in mathematics from Iowa State University, his M.B.A. from Harvard University, and his Ph.D. in higher education administration from the University of Michigan.

Nicole C. Springer is the Assistant Director with the Center for Service-Learning and Civic Engagement (CSLCE). She began work with the CSLCE as a graduate assistant. Before graduate work at MSU, Springer attended Concordia College, where she worked closely with the Office of Student Leadership and Service and later served with AmeriCorps VISTA in Moorhead, MN. At the CSLCE, Springer is involved in research, outcome evaluation, curriculum development, and other activities related to the scholarship of engagement. She also advises students and assists with faculty consultations related to service and engagement opportunities.

Randy Stoecker is a professor in the Department of Community and Environmental Sociology at the University of Wisconsin, with a joint appointment in the University of Wisconsin–Extension Center for Community and Economic Development. He has a Ph.D. in sociology from the University of Minnesota, and an M.S. in counseling from the University of Wisconsin–Whitewater. He moderates/edits COMM-ORG: The On-Line Conference on Community Organizing and Development (http://comm-org.wisc.edu) and conducts trainings and speaks frequently on community organizing and development, community-based participatory research/evaluation, and community information technology. Randy has written extensively on community organizing and development and community-based research, including the books *Defending Community* (Temple University Press, 1994), *Research Methods for Community Change* (Sage, 2005), the co-authored books *Community-Based Research in Higher Education* (Jossey-Bass, 2003), and *The Unheard Voices: Community Organizations and Service Learning* (Temple University Press, 2009). His complete curriculum vitae is online at http://comm-org.wisc.edu/stoeckerfolio/stoeckvita.htm.

Laurie Van Egeren, Ph.D., is the co-director of the National Collaborative for the Study of University Engagement and director of the Community Evaluation and Research Collaborative. She conducts both program evaluations and community-based research. Van Egeren has led or co-led several statewide evaluations to assess the implementation and outcomes of state-funded programs for children, youth, and families, Van Egeren's research interests focus on contributions of programmatic quality, organizational structure, and community context to differences in child, youth, and family outcomes. She also conducts basic research in co-parenting and family development. She holds a Ph.D. in developmental psychology from Michigan State University.

James C. Votruba is president of Northern Kentucky University (NKU), a sixteen-thousand-student metropolitan campus located in the Greater Cincinnati area. The university is nationally recognized for its community engagement. Prior to NKU, he was Vice Provost for University Outreach and Professor of Higher Education at Michigan State University and Dean of the College of Education and Human Development at Binghamton University. Dr. Votruba has been a long-standing advocate for the public engagement role of colleges and universities.

Erin R. Watson is a Ph.D. student in the ecological-community psychology program at Michigan State University. Her interests center on the implementation and sustainability of systems change efforts, community and coalition capacity, structural oppression and power, and citizen participation within community-based research and action. She has applied her interests to a variety of research areas including comprehensive community initiatives, citizen advisory boards, community organizing, system of care efforts, program evaluation, and community coalitions.

David J. Weerts is assistant professor of higher education in the Department of Educational Policy and Administration at the University of Minnesota. His teaching and scholarly interests include state financing of higher education, university-community engagement, and alumni philanthropy and volunteerism. His research has been published in various scholarly outlets including *The Journal of Higher Education, Research in Higher Education,* and the *Review of Higher Education.* Weerts has eight years of experience in university advancement and has held major gifts officer positions at the University of Wisconsin Foundation and University of Minnesota Foundation. His scholarship has been supported by the Spencer Foundation and the National Forum on Higher Education for the Public Good at the University of Michigan. Weerts holds a Ph.D. in higher education from the University of Wisconsin–Madison.

Craig D. Weidemann leads the largest unified outreach organization in American higher education. Each year, Penn State touches one out of every two households in the Commonwealth, serving more than 95 million participants, viewers, and listeners at more than 125 locations, and from all fifty states and eighty countries through a myriad of outreach programs. Dr. Weidemann has held and currently holds a number of leadership positions including serving on the boards of the University Continuing Education Association, the Commission on Lifelong Learning of the American Council on Education (ACE), the Pennsylvania College of Technology, The Association of Public Land Grant Universities, the Pennsylvania Workforce Investment Board, and the Pennsylvania Chamber of Business and Industry. Dr. Weidemann received his bachelor's degree in psychology from Illinois State University, and his doctorate in educational psychology from the University of Georgia, in Athens.

Index

511

519